LITERACY RESEARCH METHODOLOGIES

Literacy
Research
Methodologies

SECOND EDITION

Edited by

NELL K. DUKE

MARLA H. MALLETTE

THE GUILFORD PRESS

New York   London

© 2011 The Guilford Press
A Division of Guilford Publications, Inc.
72 Spring Street, New York, NY 10012
www.guilford.com

Printed in the United States of America

This book is printed on acid-free paper.

Last digit is print number: 9   8   7   6   5   4   3   2   1

Library of Congress Cataloging-in-Publication Data

Literacy research methodologies / edited by Nell K. Duke, Marla H. Mallette.–
2nd ed.
    p. cm.
    Includes bibliographical references and index.
    ISBN 978-1-60918-162-8 (pbk.) – ISBN 978-1-60918-163-5 (hardcover)
    1. Reading—Research—Methodology.   I. Duke, Nell K.   II. Mallette,
Marla H.
    LB1050.6.L58 2011
    428.407′2—dc22

                                                      2010040306

We dedicate the second edition of this book
to Dr. Michael Pressley. Over his illustrious career,
Dr. Pressley employed and supported a wide range
of research methodologies. In his work he exemplified
the principle that the research question should drive
the choice of research methodology. He strove for rigor,
and demanded it of others, always with the end goal
of improving literacy teaching and learning.
We thank him, and we miss him.

About the Editors

Nell K. Duke, EdD, is Professor of Teacher Education and Educational Psychology, and Codirector of the Literacy Achievement Research Center (*www.msularc.org*) at Michigan State University, East Lansing. Her research focuses on early literacy development, particularly among children living in poverty. Her specific areas of expertise include development of informational literacies in young children, comprehension development and instruction in early schooling, and issues of equity in literacy education. She has used a variety of research methodologies in her own work and teaches courses on research design. Dr. Duke has a strong interest in the preparation of educational researchers and has published and presented on this topic.

Marla H. Mallette, PhD, is Associate Professor of Literacy Education at Southern Illinois University, Carbondale. Her research interests include literacy teacher education, literacy instruction and learning with students of culturally and linguistically diverse backgrounds, and the convergence of early literacy and technology. She is very interested in research methodologies and has used various methodologies in her own work. Dr. Mallette has also published and presented on literacy research methodologies and the preparation of literacy researchers.

Contributors

Diane M. Barone, EdD, is Professor of Educational Specialties at the University of Nevada, Reno. Her research has centered around longitudinal case studies of young children's literacy development. The first of these studies investigated the literacy development of children prenatally exposed to crack cocaine. The second study is nearing completion, as the students she selected to follow in kindergarten are now completing their elementary school experience as sixth graders. This work has focused on the children's literacy development as well as the instruction provided to them in school.

James J. Bason, PhD, is Associate Research Scientist and Director of the Survey Research Center at the University of Georgia, Athens. He is also a fellow at the University's Institute for Behavioral Research. Dr. Bason is the author of several publications based on data collected by the Center in recent years, and is an active member of the American Association for Public Opinion Research, a past president of the Southern Association for Public Opinion Research, and a current executive committee member of the National Network of State Polls. His research interests include survey methodology, elections, and electoral behavior.

James F. Baumann, PhD, holds the Chancellor's Chair for Literacy Education at the University of Missouri–Columbia. His research has addressed classroom reading instruction. Dr. Baumann and his colleagues have conducted mail-survey research exploring teachers' and administrators' perspectives and practices related to elementary reading instruction.

Barbara A. Bradley, PhD, is Associate Professor in the Department of Curriculum and Teaching at the University of Kansas, Lawrence. Her research focuses on early literacy, particularly language development and book sharing with information texts. Dr. Bradley has used a formative experiment approach to investigate language interactions in early childhood classrooms and design research to investigate instructional coaching in middle schools.

Adriana G. Bus, PhD, is Professor of Early Literacy at the Graduate School of Education, Leiden University, The Netherlands. Her research has focused on early reading and writing development. With Marinus van IJzendoorn, Dr. Bus has conducted meta-analyses on book reading, phonemic awareness, and the non-word-reading deficit.

Kristin Conradi, MEd, is a doctoral candidate in Reading Education at the University of Virginia. Her research interests focus on reading attitudes and motivation, urban education, and instructional practices and contexts that work for readers who struggle. She is currently conducting a mixed methods study exploring the interactions between affective dimensions of literacy and resiliency among urban early adolescents.

Anne E. Cunningham, PhD, is Professor of Cognition and Development at the Graduate School of Education, University of California, Berkeley. Known for her research in literacy, she studies the interplay of context and instruction in reading acquisition and development across the lifespan. Dr. Cunningham's research has focused on the cognitive prerequisites for learning to read, such as phonological awareness and orthographic knowledge, as well as the cognitive consequences of reading experience. For her research in this area she has received the International Reading Association's Outstanding Dissertation of the Year and the G. Reid Lyon Award for Research Excellence in Language and Literacy.

Carolyn Denton, PhD, is Associate Professor in the Children's Learning Institute of the Department of Pediatrics at the University of Texas Health Science Center, Houston. Her research is focused on reading interventions, reading difficulties and disabilities, interventions for children with both reading and attention disorders, and the implementation of response-to-intervention models.

Mark Dressman, PhD, is Associate Professor in the Department of Curriculum and Instruction at the University of Illinois at Urbana–Champaign. His recent research focuses on the functions of social theory in literacy research, in particular on an analysis of the multiple theoretical frames currently used to account for the struggles of some adolescent readers.

Nell K. Duke, EdD (see "About the Editors").

Jack M. Fletcher, PhD, is a Hugh Roy and Lillie Cranz Cullen Distinguished Professor of Psychology at the University of Houston. For the past 30 years, Dr. Fletcher, a child neuropsychologist, has conducted research on children with learning and attention disorders and brain injury. He directs a Learning Disability Research Center grant and a program project involving neurobiological factors and learning in spina bifida, both funded by the National Institute of Child Health and Human Development (NICHD). Dr. Fletcher served on the NICHD National Advisory Council, the Rand Reading Study Group, the National Research Council Committee on Scientific Principles in Education Research, and the President's Commission on Excellence in Special Education. He was the recipient of the Samuel T. Orton Award from the International Dyslexia Association in 2003 and a corecipient of the Albert J. Harris Award from the International Reading Association in 2006. He is past president of the International Neuropsychological Society.

Susan Florio-Ruane, EdD, is Professor of Teacher Education at Michigan State University, where she is a past winner of the Distinguished Faculty Award. Her research interests include the preparation of elementary literacy teachers to work in urban classrooms and the social and historical role of culture, literacy, and autobiography in educational research and practice. Dr. Florio-Ruane is co–senior editor of the *Journal of Literacy Research* and also served in a senior editorial role for the

Anthropology and Education Quarterly. Her paper "The Social Organization of Classes and Schools" won the Division K Research in Teacher Education Award of the American Educational Research Association. Dr. Florio-Ruane's book *Teacher Education and the Cultural Imagination* won the National Reading Conference's Outstanding Book Award. She is coeditor of the forthcoming book *Standing for Literacy: Teaching in a Time of Reform.*

Susan R. Goldman, PhD, is Distinguished Professor of Psychology and Education at the University of Illinois at Chicago and Codirector of the Center for the Study of Learning, Instruction, and Teacher Development. Her research focuses on learning and assessment and the analysis of written and oral discourse as a method for investigating them. Dr. Goldman is widely published in discourse, psychology, and education journals and presently heads the Society for Text and Discourse. She has developed and researched several technology-based environments for learning and assessment.

Christine M. Greenhow, EdD, is Assistant Professor in the College of Education and the College of Information Studies at the University of Maryland, College Park. She is also a visiting fellow at the Information Society Project at Yale University and is completing a book on education and social media. Dr. Greenhow's research focuses on learning and literacies in social media contexts from learning sciences and new literacies perspectives. She has developed and researched social networking applications for educational purposes and applies virtual ethnographic methods to studying the literacy practices of adolescent subgroups within and beyond youth-inspired sociotechnical contexts.

Douglas K. Hartman, PhD, is Professor of Literacy and Technology in the College of Education at Michigan State University. He also holds appointments as co–lead editor of the *Journal of Literacy Research,* codirector and principal investigator in the Literacy Achievement Research Center, and research fellow with the Center for Health Intervention and Prevention. Dr. Hartman's research focuses on literacy learning from historical, sociocultural, cognitive, and technological perspectives. He has taught a doctoral seminar on the history of literacy research for 20 years, served as president of the International Reading Association's History of Reading Special Interest Group, and delivered the National Reading Conference's Keynote Research Review on "One Hundred Years of Reading Research—1908–2008."

William A. Henk, EdD, is Professor of Education and Dean of the College of Education at Marquette University. His best-known scholarly work focuses on measuring affective aspects of literacy and includes coauthoring the Reader Self-Perception Scale, the Writer Self-Perception Scale, and a forthcoming reader self-perception instrument for adolescents. Dr. Henk also played a key role in the creation of observation frameworks that assist principals and literacy supervisors in the evaluation and enhancement of reading and writing instruction in classrooms.

Katherine Hilden, PhD, is Assistant Professor in the School of Teacher Education and Leadership at Radford University. Her research interests focus on reading comprehension in the elementary grades. Dr. Hilden is currently exploring whether verbal protocols can be successfully used to measure early elementary students' reading comprehension and, if so, what they tell us about students' comprehension processes.

James V. Hoffman, PhD, is Professor of Language and Literacy Studies at the University of Texas at Austin. His research focuses on teaching and teacher preparation in the area of reading. Dr. Hoffman is former president of the National Reading Conference and former editor of the *Reading Research Quarterly* and the *Yearbook of the National Reading Conference.*

Marla H. Mallette, PhD (see "About the Editors").

Ramón A. Martínez, PhD, is Assistant Professor of Language and Literacy Studies at the University of Texas at Austin. His research explores the everyday literacy practices of bilingual and emergent bilingual Chicana/o and Latina/o students in public schools.

Andrew Maul, PhD, is a postdoctoral researcher in the School of Education at the University of Oslo, Norway, where he both conducts research and teaches courses on educational and psychological testing, research methods, and data analysis. His primary research interests include multidimensional Rasch modeling and validity theory.

Sarah J. McCarthey, PhD, is Professor of Language and Literacy at the University of Illinois at Urbana–Champaign and Associate Head of the University's Curriculum and Instruction Graduate Program. She is also coeditor (with Mark Dressman and Paul Prior) of *Research in the Teaching of English.* Dr. McCarthey's research focuses on the social and cultural contexts of students' literacy learning, in particular students' identities as writers. She has conducted several studies using case study methodology and is interested in the epistemological and theoretical underpinnings of a range of research methodologies.

Michael C. McKenna, PhD, is Thomas G. Jewell Professor in the Department of Curriculum, Instruction and Special Education at the University of Virginia. His research interests include beginning reading, content-area applications, literacy and technology, literacy coaching, and children's attitudes toward reading and writing. Dr. McKenna's research into attitudes led him to coauthor two public-domain instruments featuring the Garfield cartoon character: the Elementary Reading Attitude Survey and the Writing Attitude Survey, both published in *The Reading Teacher.*

Suzanne E. Mol, MSc, is a PhD candidate in the Department of Education and Child Studies at Leiden University, The Netherlands. With Adriana G. Bus, she carries out meta-analyses in the domain of reading and (home) literacy environments.

David L. Molfese, PhD, is a postdoctoral fellow in psychology at the University of Houston. He has a dual background in cognitive science and molecular neuroscience. His research focuses on brain structures and pathways involved in normal language and in learning disabilities. In his research, Dr. Molfese has employed a number of methodologies, including cognitive assessments, event-related potentials, magnetoencephalography, functional magnetic resonance imaging, and molecular-genetic techniques.

M. Kristiina Montero, PhD, is Assistant Professor at Wilfrid Laurier University in Waterloo, Ontario, Canada. Her research focuses on storied understandings of experiences as accessed through oral history research methodologies and narrative approaches to inquiry. Dr. Montero is interested in furthering culturally responsive teaching practices through the study of the development and maintenance of heritage language literacy, teaching and learning in urban contexts, and understanding the educational successes and challenges that students of interrupted formal education and their teachers encounter both in and out of school. Much of her research is conducted within the framework of community-based/engaged scholarship.

Ernest Morrell, PhD, is Associate Professor of Urban Schooling and Associate Director of the Institute for Democracy, Education, and Access at the University of California, Los Angeles. His research focuses on critical pedagogy, adolescent literacy, youth popular culture, and urban education. Dr. Morrell has used critical discourse analysis to make sense of the relationship between urban youth, popular cultural production, and literacy development.

Susan B. Neuman, EdD, is Professor in Educational Studies at the University of Michigan, where she specializes in early literacy development. Previously, she served as the U.S. Assistant Secretary for Elementary and Secondary Education. In this role, Dr. Neuman established the Early Reading First program, developed the Early Childhood Educator Professional Development Program, and was responsible for all activities in Title I of the Elementary and Secondary Act. She has directed the Center for the Improvement of Early Reading Achievement and currently directs the Michigan Research Program on Ready to Learn. Dr. Neuman's research and teaching interests include early childhood policy, curriculum, and early reading instruction, PreK–3, for children who live in poverty.

Anthony J. Onwuegbuzie, PhD, is Professor in the Department of Educational Leadership and Counseling at Sam Houston State University. He teaches doctoral-level courses in qualitative research, quantitative research, and mixed research. Dr. Onwuegbuzie's research areas include disadvantaged and underserved populations such as minorities, juvenile delinquents, and children living in war zones. Additionally, he writes extensively on qualitative, quantitative, and mixed methodological topics. Alongside more than 500 conference/keynote presentations, Dr. Onwuegbuzie has had published more than 230 journal articles, 50 book/encyclopedia chapters, and two books. He also serves as coeditor of the journal *Research in the Schools*.

Andrew C. Papanicolaou, PhD, is Professor and Director of the Division of Clinical Neurosciences, Department of Neurosurgery, University of Texas Health Science Center, Houston. His academic interests center on the development of noninvasive functional brain-imaging procedures for mapping the brain mechanisms mediating sensory, motor, and higher psychological functions, including oral and written language comprehension.

Michael Pressley, PhD, who passed away in May 2006, was University Distinguished Professor at Michigan State University, where he also served as Director of the Doctoral Program in Teacher Education and Director of the Literacy Achievement Research Center. He was an expert on effective elementary literacy instruction, with his research appearing in more than 350 journal articles, chapters, and books. Dr. Pressley served a 6-year term as editor of the *Journal of Educational Psychology*. He was honored with awards from the National Reading Conference, the International Reading Association, and the American Educational Research

Association, among others. Dr. Pressley received the 2004 E. L. Thorndike Award from Division 15 of the American Psychological Association, which is the highest award given for career research accomplishment in educational psychology.

Victoria Purcell-Gates, PhD, is Canada Research Chair in Early Childhood Literacy at the University of British Columbia, Vancouver. Her research has focused on early literacy development, particularly as it interacts with community and home literacy practices. Dr. Purcell-Gates has conducted several ethnographies, one of which—*Other People's Words*—was awarded the 1996 Grawemeyer Award in Education, an international award given in four categories: education, political science, music, and religion.

David Reinking, PhD, is the Eugene T. Moore Professor of Teacher Education at Clemson University. He has been editor and coeditor, respectively, of the *Journal of Literacy Research* and *Reading Research Quarterly*, and he recently served as president of the Literacy Research Association. Dr. Reinking's scholarly interests focus on the relation between technology and literacy. He has conducted design-based research and has written extensively about the use of this approach. He is coauthor (with Barbara Bradley) of the book *On Formative and Design Experiments*.

Misty Sailors, PhD, is Associate Professor of Literacy Education at the University of Texas at San Antonio. The primary investigator of a Teacher Quality Professional Development Reading grant, her research interests focus on comprehension instruction, the professional development of teachers, and the importance of print-rich environments for literacy development. Dr. Sailors has more than 40 publications, including books, research articles, and book chapters. She was recently awarded the prestigious Early Career Award from the National Reading Conference and the Emerging Scholar Award from the American Association of University Women.

Christopher Schatschneider, PhD, is Professor of Psychology at Florida State University and Associate Director of the Florida Center for Reading Research. His research focuses on early reading development and reading disabilities. Dr. Schatschneider is also a trained methodologist who frequently provides assistance to investigators for design and analysis issues that arise when designing experiments and analyzing data from studies of early reading development. He is the editor of *Annals of Dyslexia* and serves on the editorial boards of numerous journals.

Panagiotis G. Simos, PhD, is Associate Professor of Developmental Neuropsychology in the Department of Psychology at the University of Crete, Greece. He has developed and validated special applications of magnetoencephalography for functional brain mapping. Dr. Simos has conducted several studies investigating the brain mechanisms that support language, reading, and memory functions in normally developing children and adults and in special populations such as patients with neurological disorders and learning disabilities.

Norman A. Stahl, PhD, is Professor and Chair of the Department of Literacy Education at Northern Illinois University, DeKalb. Over the years his research has focused on postsecondary reading instruction, with particular interest in the field's history. Dr. Stahl has received honors from the National Association for Developmental Education, the College Reading Association, the College Reading and Learning Association, and the College Literacy and Learning Special Interest

Group of the International Reading Association for his contributions to the field of literacy research and pedagogy. He has served as president of the History of Reading Special Interest Group of the International Reading Association and recently completed his term as president of the National Reading Conference.

Keith E. Stanovich, PhD, is Professsor of Human Development and Applied Psychology at the University of Toronto. For his work on the cognitive effects of reading experience, phonological processing, and models of reading and reading disability, Dr. Stanovich has received the Oscar Causey Award from the National Reading Conference, the Sylvia Scribner Award from the American Educational Research Association, and the Distinguished Scientific Contribution Award from the Society for the Scientific Study of Reading. He received the 2010 Grawemeyer Award in Education.

Marinus H. van IJzendoorn, PhD, is Professor of Child and Family Studies at the Graduate School of Education, Leiden University, The Netherlands. His research focuses on attachment across the lifespan. With Adriana G. Bus, he has been involved in several meta-analyses on topics in emergent literacy.

Frank R. Vellutino, PhD, is Professor of Psychology at the University at Albany, State University of New York, and Director of the University's Child Research and Study Center, a research and student training center. Most of his research has been concerned with reading development, the cognitive underpinnings of reading, and the relationship between reading difficulties, various aspects of language, and other cognitive functions.

Rachelle D. Washington, PhD, is Assistant Professor of Language and Literacy at Clemson University. Her research interests include schooling narratives, using literacy to teach for social justice, and sociocultural aspects of children's literature. Dr. Washington employs narrative research methodology in her research practice and has interests in emerging research methodologies.

Jennifer Wiley, PhD, is Associate Professor of Psychology at the University of Illinois at Chicago. Many of her studies use discourse analysis to gain insight into the cognitive processes and instructional conditions that support effective learning and problem-solving outcomes.

Melissa B. Wilson, PhD, is Lecturer of Early Childhood Studies at the University of the West Indies at Cave Hill, Barbados. Her present research includes using critical content analysis as a way to make sense of how childhood is constructed in children's literature. Dr. Wilson's research interests include comparative childhood studies, Holocaust education, and Buberian analysis of literacy practices.

Preface

This is the second edition of a work originally published in 2004. All of the original chapters of the book have been revised and updated for this edition. In addition, five new chapters have been added, on single-subject experimental design, content analysis, narrative approaches, mixed methods, and methods unique to research in digital contexts. These chapters include both long-standing research traditions and emerging methodologies for literacy research. Together, they add to the riches of research methodologies available to scholars in our field.

This book began with our first conversation, when we, Nell and Marla, were introduced to each other at the National Reading Conference in 1999. We were having dinner with mutual friends when, as aspiring new researchers, we each began to talk about our dissertation research. We found that we shared an interest in the literacy experiences and instruction provided to poor and minority children. However, our research was conducted from very different methodological and epistemological perspectives. Rather than dismissing each other's work on the grounds of lack of commensurability, we listened to one another. We realized that we could gain a deeper understanding of the issues that perplexed us by considering the value of each other's work. We haven't lost sight of the lesson we learned that night, and we hope that the chapters in this volume, taken together, highlight that lesson—many different kinds of literacy research, conducted rigorously, have value; together, they yield greater insights than any one type alone.

Several months later, Nell was at a proposal review session with David Reinking. As a result of conflict of interest, she and David were excused from the review of one of the proposals. As they talked in the hallway, Nell complained to David about what she viewed as the often poor preparation of graduate students to be both producers and consumers of a variety of different kinds of research. Her concerns were based, among other things, on the limited number of hours devoted to research methodologies in doctoral studies contrasted with the plethora of research methodologies being used. David suggested that issue would fit nicely into the "Critical Issues" section of the *Journal of Literacy Research* (*JLR*), of which he was coeditor at the time.

The result was a commentary, "Preparation for New Literacy Researchers in Multi-Epistemological, Multi-Methodological Times" (Duke & Mallette, 2001), that detailed our thinking about this issue. We suggested that, as in many areas of educational research, in recent decades the field of literacy has experienced a diversification of research methodologies (Dunston, Headley, Schenk, Ridgeway, & Gambrell, 1998; Guzzetti, Anders, & Neuman, 1999). Unfortunately, this seems to be resulting in a trend toward fragmentation, a splintering off into subfields. Increasingly, particular literacy conferences are aligned with some methodologies and not others; particular literacy journals publish some methodologies with regularity but not others; researchers using methodologies quite different from one another seem less and less likely to be talking with one another. We argued that literacy researchers need to work actively to reverse this trend, and this work starts with the preparation of new literacy researchers.

There also appeared to us at the time to be a trend away from discussions of methodology in literacy research (we believe now that that trend has been reversing). There seemed to be a great amount of writing and a large number of presentations focused on research methodologies during the period of "qualitative versus quantitative" debates—but since that time they have dwindled. In literacy, the one book specifically designed to provide a comprehensive account of research methodologies (Kamil, Langer, & Shanahan, 1985) is now 25 years old. Yet new methodologies, and new developments in older methodologies, are being created all the time (e.g., Putney, Green, Dixon, & Kelly, 1999). Without dedicating time and resources to understanding methodologies, including new and developing methodologies, there is the danger of misunderstanding and even being ignorant of some forms of research and their potential contributions, which in turn can lead to missed opportunities. It can position literacy researchers to focus more on explaining and defending their methodologies than on discussing the findings they yield.

Some forces are narrowing what even "counts" as "scientific" educational research at precisely the time when the pressure on educational research to yield useful insights and understandings has never been greater (Pressley, Duke, & Boling, 2004). In essence, in some forums, we are being asked to do more with less with respect to the repertoire of accepted or favored research methodologies. Of course, many educational researchers have spoken against this situation and for the value of many forms of research (Shavelson & Towne, 2002). Clearly, it is essential that educational researchers understand the unique contributions as well as limitations of particular forms of research and, just as important, ways in which different forms of research can work together toward useful insights and understandings. For all these reasons, we believed that it was important to bring together a group of scholars well respected for their use of particular research methodologies to create this volume.

We see this volume as a way of beginning where our *JLR* commentary ended. The following concluded that piece:

> Our contention is that the field of literacy needs to emphasize or reemphasize breadth of education, particularly in the area of research method and epistemology. However, this education should reflect the changing times of literacy research. It requires deepening our understanding and appreciation of the diversification of research epistemology and method, as well as providing an historical grounding in how they came to be. (Duke & Mallette, 2001, pp. 357–358)

We hope that this volume will go some way toward building or reinforcing understanding and appreciation of many research methodologies and the contributions they make singly, and together, to knowledge in our field.

REFERENCES

Duke, N. K., & Mallette, M. H. (2001). Preparation for new literacy researchers in multi-epistemological, multi-methodological times. *Journal of Literacy Research, 33,* 345–360.

Dunston, P. J., Headley, K. N., Schenk, R. L., Ridgeway, V. G., & Gambrell, B. (1998). National Reading Conference research reflections: An analysis of 20 years of research. In T. Shanahan & F. V. Rodriguez-Brown (Eds.), *47th Yearbook of the National Reading Conference* (pp. 441–450). Chicago: National Reading Conference.

Guzzetti, B., Anders, P. L., & Neuman, S. (1999). Thirty years of *JRB/JLR:* A retrospective of reading/literacy research. *Journal of Literacy Research, 31,* 67–92.

Kamil, M. L., Langer, J. A., & Shanahan, T. (1985). *Understanding research in reading and writing.* Boston: Allyn & Bacon.

Pressley, M., Duke, N. K., & Boling, E. C. (2004). The educational science and scientifically-based instruction we need: Lessons from reading research and policymaking. *Harvard Educational Review, 74,* 30–61.

Putney, L. G., Green, J. L., Dixon, C. N., & Kelly, G. J. (1999). Evolution of qualitative research methodology: Looking beyond defense to possibilities. *Reading Research Quarterly, 34,* 368–377.

Shavelson, R. J., & Towne, L. (2002). *Scientific research in education.* Washington, DC: National Research Council.

Acknowledgments

We have many people to thank for this book. Most important, we thank the contributors, who have helped make our vision a reality. Their willingness to focus on the core content we requested for chapters, their responsiveness to requests for revision, and the seriousness with which they undertook this task are all deeply appreciated. Still more appreciated are the high standards these scholars have set and met for methodology in their own research. They are truly great assets to our field.

We also thank the larger literacy research community, in particular those who go out of their way to acknowledge the contributions of a range of methodologies to literacy research. Our doctoral students deserve our thanks as well both for reinforcing our belief in the need for this book and for illustrating for us the great promise of the next generation of literacy researchers.

Chris Jennison of The Guilford Press was supportive of this book from the minute we approached him, and Craig Thomas has marshaled us skillfully through the process of developing a second edition. Diane M. Barone, William A. Henk, Don Leu, Ernest Morrell, and Vicki Purcell-Gates also deserve thanks for advice regarding the book's original table of contents and/or other issues that arose in putting the volume together. We are grateful to Marcia Invernizzi, Don Leu, David Reinking, Anthony J. Onwuegbuzie, and others for feedback and suggestions for the second edition.

Finally, we must thank those who have helped us develop as scholars and as people: our mentors and our families. If you're proud of the book, please know that you deserve credit. Where it fails, know that we will keep working to live up to the ideals you set.

Contents

CHAPTER 1

Introduction

Marla H. Mallette
Nell K. Duke

Methodology, as defined in *Webster's New World College Dictionary*, is "the science of method, or orderly arrangement; specifically, the branch of logic concerned with the application of the principles of reasoning to scientific and philosophical inquiry" (Anges, 1999, p. 906). Method, within that, is defined simply as "a way of doing anything" (Anges, 1999, p. 906). In the context of this volume, method is a way of doing literacy research. And our emphasis in this volume is on the plural—methods or methodologies. That is, there are many ways of conducting literacy research.

We initially conceptualized this volume as including an exhaustive account of literacy research methodologies, but realized that it would be impossible to include every methodology and/or variation of methodology used. Thus, we include here only a partial set of literacy research methodologies currently being used in the field. The process of determining which methodologies to include in the first edition began by brainstorming a list. The list was then reviewed by several colleagues, who were asked to add methodologies that were noticeably missing and to reduce redundancy in methodologies already included. For the second edition, we added chapters on long-standing methodologies we regretted not including in the first volume and emerging methodologies coming into their own in literacy research.

Of course, methodologies do not always fall into mutually exclusive categories. Some research can be considered more than one type of research or may combine methodologies in various ways. For example, *Ways with Words* (Heath, 1983) can be considered both an ethnography and a case study and in this book is discussed in both Chapters 2 and 8. Thus, although we have attempted to minimize redundancy in constructing the table of contents and in the editorial process, we have done so with the knowledge that there has been and will continue to be both overlap among and combinations of methodologies used in literacy research.

The chapter authors in this volume have stellar reputations for use of the methodology they write about, with numerous publications of rigorous research using that methodology. Thus, they are well accomplished as literacy researchers rather than solely as methodologists. This results in a volume markedly different from a general methods text. However, the authors often refer readers to these types of texts. We hope readers will take these references seriously. *By no means is the information in these chapters adequate to teach one "how to" conduct particular types of research.* However, we believe the discussions within do provide meaningful information and perspective on each methodology addressed.

The chapters in this book strike a balance between maintaining each author's individual writing style and voice and achieving consistency across them. To achieve this consistency in core content, we asked authors to address the following questions:

1. What is this methodology (including a definition and description of the methodology and, if possible, some key history of the methodology in literacy)?
2. What kinds of questions and claims is this methodology appropriate for?
3. What are standards for quality in this methodology?
4. What is one or more exemplar of this methodology (in literacy), and what makes it so good?

We suggest that readers approach each chapter with these four key questions in mind. We also strongly encourage readers to gather and read the exemplar or exemplars presented for each chapter. A listing of featured exemplars appears in two places: (1) at the end of this chapter, arranged by methodology, and (2) in the Appendix, arranged in alphabetical order.

In addition to the methodology chapters, the volume includes a chapter on the role of theory and epistemology in methodology (Dressman & McCarthey, Chapter 20). We view this as an important part of understanding literacy research. All research, whether explicitly stated or not, is grounded in epistemology, or one's view of what can and cannot be known and how. To understand a research methodology, we must situate the methodology in the epistemological tenets that ground it. The chapter authors also emphasize the need to recognize epistemological strengths and weaknesses of different methodologies. They remind us that just as all methodologies have something to contribute, they also have important limitations.

The final chapter in this volume looks across methodologies. Building on the foundation provided throughout the volume, we identify five core messages about methodology in literacy research:

- Message 1: Many different research methodologies, in fact each research methodology discussed in this book and others, have valuable contributions to make to the study of literacy.
- Message 2: Different types of research are for different types of questions and claims. The match of research methodology to research questions and resulting claims is essential.
- Message 3: There are standards of quality for every type of research. There is better and poorer quality research of every methodology.
- Message 4: Synergy across research methodologies is possible, powerful, and advisable.
- Message 5: We must urgently and actively pursue synergy across research methodologies.

Our discussion of these messages is intended to underscore again the need for all of us to be knowledgeable about and informed by research of a broad range of research methodologies. This book, we hope, provides one tool for doing that.

REFERENCES

Anges, M. (Ed.). (1999). *Webster's new world college dictionary* (4th ed.). New York: Macmillan.

Heath, S. B. (1983). *Ways with words: Language, life, and work in communities and classrooms.* Cambridge, UK: Cambridge University Press.

APPENDIX: LISTING OF FEATURED EXEMPLARS, ARRANGED BY METHODOLOGY

Case Study

Compton-Lilly, C. (2009). The complexities of reading capital in two Puerto Rican families. *Reading Research Quarterly, 42,* 72–98.

Content Analysis

Beach, R., Enciso, P., Harste, J., Jenkins, C., Raina, S. A., Rogers, R., et al. (2009). Exploring the "critical" in critical content analysis of children's literature. In R. T. Jiménez, M. K. Hundley, V. J. Risko, & D. W. Rowe (Eds.), *58th Yearbook of the National Reading Conference* (pp. 129–143). Oak Creek, WI: National Reading Conference.

Hoffman, J. V., Sailors, M., Duffy, G. G., & Beretvas, N. (2004). The effective elementary classroom literacy environment: Examining the validity of the TEX-IN3 observation system. *Journal of Literacy Research, 36,* 303–334.

Marshall, E. (2004). Stripping for the wolf: Rethinking representations of gender in children's literature. *Reading Research Quarterly, 39,* 256–270.

Moss, B. (2008). The information text gap: The mismatch between non-narrative text types in basal readers and 2009 NAEP recommended guidelines. *Journal of Literacy Research, 40*(2), 201–219.

Correlational

A program of research including, among others:

Cunningham, A. E., & Stanovich, K. E. (1997). Early reading acquisition and its relation to reading experience and ability ten years later. *Developmental Psychology, 33*, 934–945.

Digital Contexts

Gillen, J. (2009). Literacy practices in Schome Park: A virtual literacy ethnography. *Journal of Research in Reading, 32*(1), 57–74.

Steinkuehler, C. (2006). Massively multiplayer online video gaming as participation in a discourse. *Mind, Culture and Activity, 13*(1), 38–52.

Steinkuehler, C. (2007). Massively multiplayer online gaming as a constellation of literacy practices. *E-learning, 4*(3), 297–318.

Discourse Analysis: Conversation

Michaels, S. (1981). "Sharing time": Children's narrative styles and differential access to literacy. *Language in Society, 10*, 423–443.

Morrell, E. (2008). *Critical literacy and urban youth: Pedagogies of access, dissent, and liberation.* New York: Routledge.

Discourse Analysis: Written Text

Wolfe, M. B., & Goldman, S. R. (2005). Relationships between adolescents' text processing and reasoning. *Cognition and Instruction, 23*(4), 467–502.

Ethnography

Dyson, A. H. (1999). Coach Bombay's kids learn to write: Children's appropriation of media material for school literacy. *Research in the Teaching of English, 33*, 367–402.

Dyson, A. H. (2003). *The brothers and sisters learn to write: Popular literacies in childhood and school cultures.* New York: Teachers College Press.

Heath, S. B. (1982). What no bedtime story means: Narrative skills at home and school. *Language in Society, 11*, 49–76.

Heath, S. B. (1983). *Ways with words: Language, life, and work in communities and classrooms.* Cambridge, UK: Cambridge University Press.

Purcell-Gates, V. (1993). I ain't never read my *own* words before. *Journal of Reading, 37*, 210–219.

Experimental and Quasi-Experimental

Foorman, B. R., Francis, D. J., Fletcher, J. M., Schatschneider, C., & Mehta, P. (1998). The role of instruction in learning to read: Preventing reading failure in at-risk children. *Journal of Educational Psychology, 90,* 37–55.

Vellutino, F. R., & Scanlon, D. M. (1987). Phonological coding, phonological awareness, and reading ability: Evidence from a longitudinal and experimental study. *Merrill-Palmer Quarterly, 33,* 321–363.

Formative and Design Experiments

Ivey, G., & Broaddus, K. (2007). A formative experiment investigating literacy engagement among adolescent Latina/o students just beginning to read, write, and speak English. *Reading Research Quarterly, 42,* 512–545.

Historical

Monaghan, E. J. (1991). Family literacy in early 18th century Boston: Cotton Mather and his children. *Reading Research Quarterly, 26,* 342–370.

Instrumentation

Henk, W. A., & Melnick, S. A. (1995). The Reader Self-Perception Scale (RSPS): A new tool for measuring how children feel about themselves as readers. *The Reading Teacher, 48,* 470–482.

Meta-Analysis

Bus, A. G., & van IJzendoorn, M. H. (1999). Phonological awareness and early reading: A meta-analysis of experimental training studies. *Journal of Educational Psychology, 91,* 403–414.

Mixed Methods

Benge, C., Onwuegbuzie, A. J., Mallette, M. H., & Burgess, M. L. (2010). Doctoral students' perceptions of barriers to reading empirical literature: A mixed analysis. *International Journal of Doctoral Studies, 5,* 55–77.

Narrative Approaches

Gordon, E., McKibbin, K., Vasudevan, L., & Vinz, R. (2007). Writing out of the unexpected: Narrative inquiry and the weight of small moments. *English Education, 39*(4), 326–351.

Hankins, K. H. (2003). *Teaching through the storm: A journal of hope.* New York: Teachers College Press.

Neuroimaging

Simos, P. G., Fletcher, J. M., Sarkari, S., Billingsley, R. L., Francis, D. J., Castillo, E. M., et al. (2005). Early development of neurophysiological processes involved in normal reading and reading disability. *Neuropsychology, 19*, 787–798.

Single Subject

Mudre, L. H., & McCormick, S. (1989). Effects of meaning-focused cues on under-achieving readers' context use, self-corrections, and literal comprehension. *Reading Research Quarterly, 24*, 89–113.

Neuman, S. B., & Gallagher, P. (1994). Joining together in literacy learning: Teenage mothers and children. *Reading Research Quarterly, 29*, 382–401.

Survey

Baumann, J. F., Hoffman, J. V., Duffy-Hester, A. M., & Ro, J. M. (2000). *The First R* yesterday and today: U.S. elementary reading instruction practices reported by teachers and administrators. *Reading Research Quarterly, 35*, 338–377.

Mesmer, H. A. E. (2006). Beginning reading materials: A national survey of primary teachers' reported uses and beliefs. *Journal of Literacy Research, 38*, 389–425.

Verbal Protocols

Wyatt, D., Pressley, M., El-Dinary, P. B., Stein, S., Evans, P., & Brown, R. (1993). Comprehension strategies, worth and credibility monitoring, and evaluations: Cold and hot cognition when experts read professional articles that are important to them. *Learning and Individual Differences, 5*, 49–72.

CHAPTER 2

Case Study Research

Diane M. Barone

What *can* be done with thousands of children but count them? In mass, children—and the challenges they present—are faceless, nameless, and overwhelming. However, these massive numbers of children are not isolated individuals; they are social participants included, or so we hope, in particular classrooms and schools, in particular institutions and communities.

—DYSON (2008, p. 117)

Dyson (2008) stated the foregoing in her chapter about the importance of case study research to literacy understanding. In earlier work, Dyson (1995) shared that case studies do not offer information about causality regarding teaching practices and learning, for example, but they do provide information on the "dimensions and dynamics of classroom living and learning" (p. 51). Although Dyson is certainly in support of the value of case study research, Yin (1994) noted that social scientists have stereotyped case study as "a weak sibling among social science methods" (p. xiii). Although he began his preface with this statement, his book presented an extended argument as to why this belief was wrong. The lack of status for case study research was particularly evident after World War II, when behaviorist psychology and large experimental studies were seen as the most rigorous form of research (Birnbaum, Emig, & Fisher, 2003). However, this lack of status is no longer documented, and many researchers are using this design because they are dissatisfied with the limited answers they receive by studying percentages or stanines, particularly during the last 30 years (Birnbaum et al., 2003; Dyson, 2008).

Clearly, case study research is supported, maligned, and misunderstood (Merriam, 1988). Although I have touched on its support and criticism, I now consider the misunderstandings attached to it. One misunderstanding centers on seeing case study research as synonymous with single-subject design (Neuman & McCormick, 2000). Although these two are often confused, single-subject design is experimental and considers the relationship between an independent and dependent variable—it is focused on just one individual at a time—and this is where the confusion is centered. A second misunderstanding is that case study research is the same as the cases that are used to help students and teachers understand practice. For example, Shulman, Whittaker, and Lew (2002) presented problem-centered cases on assessment for educators to consider. These cases, although illustrative of dilemmas in practice, are narratives used to explore and reflect on practice, not research studies or reports. Their goal is to allow novices to critically analyze the dimensions built into a case that demonstrate the complexity of teaching, outside the classroom situation.

So what exactly is case study research? Stake (2000), Merriam (1988), and Yin (2009) indicate that this question is not easy to answer. They report that all social scientists and practitioners are engaged in case exploration, sometimes known as casework or case history, in that they observe as a doctor does a patient or a reporter an event. However, case study, as described by Merriam (1988), is a research design that is descriptive and nonexperimental. A critical characteristic of case study research is that it is a study of a bounded system that could be a child, a teacher, or a classroom, for example (Stake, 2000; Yin, 2009). Boundedness is important because it defines what is excluded or included in a study. For example, one first-grade class may be the focus of study by a researcher who is studying a first-year teacher in a high-poverty school. However, the neighboring first-grade class would not be considered for participation because the teacher has taught in the school for several years.

Merriam (1988) further defines four additional characteristics, beyond the issue of boundedness, that are essential when defining this research design: (1) *particularistic*, in that the study is centered on a particular situation, program, event, phenomenon, or person; (2) *descriptive*, in that the researcher gathers rich description of the object of study; (3) *heuristic*, as the study enriches a reader's understanding; and (4) *inductive*, as the data drive the understandings that emerge from the study. In summary, case study is defined as "an intensive, holistic description and analysis of a single entity, phenomenon, or social unit" (Merriam, 1988, p. 16).

Beyond the definition of a case study, Stake (2000) describes three purposes for case study research. The focus of study is not changed based on the purpose of the case. For his first purpose, *intrinsic*, the researcher is seeking a better understanding of a case; that is, he or she is exploring the case because it is interesting, not because it might contribute to theory building. An exemplar of this type of case study within literacy research is the work of Sarroub (2002), who explored the multiple uses of religious and secular text in the school, home, and community of Yemeni high school girls. Her goal was to describe their uses of literacy in multiple settings, not to build a theory around them.

Stake's second purpose of case study is labeled *instrumental*. Here the researcher is looking for insight into an issue. Stake says that in this purpose the case moves to the background of interest because it is being used to understand something else. An exemplar of this type is the work of Rogers (2002). Her focus of study was an African American mother and daughter who lived in poverty and who were able to successfully negotiate the literacy expectations in their home and community, but not in school. Rogers used her study of these two individuals to explain why children from non-mainstream homes may fail to thrive in school.

The last purpose of case study research is *collective case study*, or multiple-case studies, where a researcher investigates numerous cases to study a phenomenon, group, condition, or event. Stake emphasizes that this purpose is a refinement of instrumental case study; the only difference is that the researcher is studying multiple cases. The redundancy of cases is purposeful because the researcher is building a stronger understanding and a more compelling argument for the significance of the work through the use of multiple cases. Exemplars of this purpose include the work of Ladson-Billings (1994), who studied multiple teachers and the way they supported the learning of African American students, and Barone (1999), in her exploration of the literacy development of children who were prenatally exposed to crack cocaine. In both studies, the patterns that were observed occurred across multiple cases and in multiple settings, thus establishing additional credibility for the results.

Wolcott (1994) has criticized the third purpose of case study: collective case study. He compared multiple-case studies with an attempt to replicate quantitative, comparative measures, and he felt that much is lost in the rich detail of the study because it is focused on comparison rather than meticulous description. Miles and Huberman (1994), on the other hand, argue that the results of multiple-case studies are more compelling than those for single-case studies and contribute to literal replication (i.e., prediction of similar results). Thus, clearly, with the multiple-case study design, there are trade-offs that need to be considered. Certainly, as Wolcott warned, there is a loss of detail for each case, but as Miles and Huberman noted, multiple-case studies are often viewed as more compelling than single-case studies.

THE HISTORY OF CASE STUDY RESEARCH IN LITERACY

Case study has a rich history in literacy research. As a way of narrowing this review, I selected case studies that are book length rather than include the numerous case studies published in journals. Lea McGee and I explored book-length cases for a presentation at the National Reading Conference in 2000, and I drew from this exploration for this overview of case study research in literacy. The majority of the studies selected focus on early literacy learning and instruction. This does not suggest that there are not other worthy case studies representing other populations; the narrow selection was meant as a way to bound the studies selected for this chapter.

The data collection for these studies varied from retrospective parent diaries to multiple sources such as observations, interviews, and artifacts. The participants also varied, ranging from many single-participant studies, often the researcher's child or grandchild, to studies of classrooms of students. In the majority of studies reported in this chapter, the researchers had an instrumental focus for their study. In other words, the case participants were selected to gain an understanding of something else, a literacy practice for example.

Earliest Case Studies

White (1956) wrote one of the first book-length case studies that focused on literacy. She was a children's librarian in New Zealand and kept a retrospective parent diary of her daughter Carol's interactions with books from the age of 2 years to 5 years. Within this book, White established the precursors for response to literature research. She described her daughter's life-to-text and text-to-life experiences that were shared through reading. For example, Carol enjoyed books about babies when she had a baby sister. White commented about the significance of her descriptive work:

> We see indeed, a twofold process at work: in some degree Carol's way of life determines the meaning she sees in the stories read to her; yet, on the other hand (and this is perhaps the more obvious), the meaning of things as it has been revealed to her through literature constantly influences the way she interprets the things that happen around her. Seldom, I think, has the interaction of literature and life in these early years been so clearly portrayed. (pp. x–xi)

In 1975, Butler, in *Cushla and Her Books*, studied her granddaughter's interaction with books. Although it shares clear similarities with the work of White, this was a dissertation study conducted under the guidance of Marie Clay, and it focused on a child who was severely handicapped, not a *precocious* child, as White described her daughter. What is particularly amazing is that Butler connected her work to that of Vygotsky (1962) and highlighted the importance of social factors in a child's development. She wrote, "The effects of the particular environment to which the child is exposed—exercise some effect on the rate at which he will pass through all the essential stages, from birth onwards" (p. 90). Her work is certainly one of the first in literacy that recognized the importance of the social environment to a child's literacy development.

These early case studies focused on literature and its importance to young readers. Both researchers engaged in retrospective note-taking following book-reading episodes. They looked closely at how a daughter and granddaughter made connections between books and personal experiences.

And Butler set the groundwork for further exploration of the importance of social settings in the learning of young children.

The 1980s and Case Study Research

From these early beginnings, case studies were established in the literacy community to study the reading of books to young children and their interactions with them. During the 1980s, case study research took on new importance because of the work of Bissex (1980), Calkins (1983), Heath (1983), Cochran-Smith (1984), Baghban (1984), and Taylor and Dorsey-Gaines (1988), among others. These researchers laid the groundwork for research that continues to be explored into the 2000s.

Bissex (1980), in another dissertation study, studied the writing of her son David. Through this work, she helped literacy teachers and researchers understand how David learned to represent words and ideas in print. However, Bissex highlighted additional reasons as to why this study was important. Although her work is not often credited for an understanding of phonemic awareness, she wrote, "The superiority of first graders on segmentation tasks may result from their experience with the printed word" (p. 90). Her observation certainly connects with what is currently known about phonemic awareness (Ehri et al., 2001).

Bissex (1980) also spoke to the importance of case study research: "Case studies widen the parameters within which we view learning to read. They remind us that the methods and time schedules by which these skills are conventionally taught are not necessarily conditions for learning them" (p. 135).

This result, Bissex stated, could only be learned through careful, longitudinal case study research. Moreover, her case study emphasized the dynamic nature of a child's learning about written language. She critiqued the notion of children accumulating discrete bits of information about written language and stated that children "evolve increasingly efficient—that is, comprehensive, informed, and practiced—strategies for understanding the relations between spoken and written language" (1980, p. 194). And although not the remembered focus of her book, Bissex continued in the tradition of White and Butler and shared the connections that David made between reading and writing.

Bissex's work led to numerous studies about invented spelling and error analysis. Most notable are the studies conducted by Henderson (1981) and his students, known as the Virginia studies, and Ehri (1997).

Shortly after Bissex's work, Calkins's (1983) *Lessons from a Child: On Teaching and Learning of Writing* was published. This work centered on the writing process and included consideration of topic choice, routines, revision and editing, and conferencing. Calkins used the case of Susie, a student in a classroom where she observed, to present a vivid image of what revision could be for young students. Her work departed from earlier case studies in two very important ways. Although she studied one child, Susie, this was not Calkins's child or grandchild. In addition, she studied Susie in her school setting and included the importance of her classroom teacher. Whereas Butler talked about the importance of the social environment in the home, Calkins moved this importance to the classroom setting and detailed how one teacher supported the writing development of students, most particularly Susie, in her room.

As did Bissex, Calkins (1983) highlighted the importance of case study research. She wrote:

> My hope is that through closely observing one child's growth in writing, we'll learn to watch for and to respect each child's growth in writing. My hope is that by understanding the pathways one child has taken in learning to write, we may be able to discern and trust the pathways other children will take. Susie is representative of all children in that she, too, is unique. (p. 7)

Calkins continued by saying that "all our students are case studies" (p. 7). Furthermore, she bravely announced that this was "the first study of its kind" (p. 5). This was so because she shared a day-to-day view of how a child experienced writing and revision and, unlike previous work, she did not divide Susie's work into discrete categories or levels. Throughout her book, Calkins used the thoughts of Vygotsky (1962) to explain her results, as did Butler much earlier. She highlighted the idea of instruction preceding development and the idea of the zone of proximal development to shed light on the importance of peer work and teachers conferring with individual students.

Perhaps one of the best known case studies is *Ways with Words: Language, Life, and Work in Communities and Classrooms* by Heath (1983). This work is unique in that it represents a crossover of methodologies: It is also considered ethnography because it was conducted over a period of 10 years and studied the home, the community, and the school. Although I do not spend a lot of time on this study in this chapter, it is essential to include because it identified the importance of family to literacy understandings, in particular the kinds of conversations and stories shared in homes and how they related to children's success in schools.

Heath's work departed from the traditions of earlier case study research in that she studied many children and families who were not considered middle class. She included their community, home, and school experiences and enriched the more limited earlier studies that only considered children in one setting (importantly, Bissex studied her son in school and home settings). As described earlier by Wolcott (1994), the uniqueness of each family or child is secondary to her tripartite comparisons of community, home, and school. However, as evidenced by the continued importance of her work into the 2000s, this limitation did not influence the significance of her work to understandings of literacy as being broader than in-class instruction.

Using a similar design focus, Cochran-Smith (1984) studied all the middle-class children in one preschool classroom to learn about the importance of storybook reading. Her study is considered instrumental, and the students were secondary to the knowledge that Cochran-Smith wanted to acquire about this strategy. In her 18-month-long investigation, she discovered that there were two important rules about the story-reading process: (1) A reader must read differentially depending on the audience, genre, purpose, and setting; and (2) "readers themselves contribute actively to the reading process by bringing their individual knowledge to bear upon texts (hence one book can have many realizations)" (p. 235). Perhaps most surprising to me when reading Cochran-Smith's book were her descriptions of children talking about superheroes such as Batman and Spiderman or the popular culture. Her work predates that of Dyson (1997) by 10 years or more and certainly that of other researchers currently looking at this phenomenon (Alvermann, Huddleston, & Hagood, 2002; Xu, 2002).

Much like White and Butler, Baghban (1984) studied the process of learning to read and write by keeping a diary of her own daughter's development from birth to 3 years of age. Her research was a doctoral study, similar to that done by Bissex. Baghban's work, like that of other researchers, detailed the importance of social aspects in learning to read and write. Beyond this focus, she identified her daughter's connections with environmental print. She described how her daughter, Giti, pointed at the letter *K* in Special K cereal and said "Kmart." Baghban also identified drawing as the fifth language art. She compared writing and drawing by noting that both required motor control, were based on experiences, and moved from more contextualized experiences to decontextualized ones as the symbol systems became internalized.

Perhaps most interesting in this work to the focus of this chapter is Baghban's rationale for using case study. She contended that case study is the best method to use when learning about individuals, and it is particularly effective when studying complex phenomena in real-life situations. Furthermore, to support her use of case study, she noted that in the latest *Annual Summary of Investigations Relating to Reading, July 1, 1979 to June 30, 1980*, Weintraub (1981) claimed that, because there have been so many investigations into single cases, this type of study was "no longer suspect or even unusual" (p. 7). She also extensively discussed the limited generalizability of case study research, but then presented conflicting thoughts by stating, "With a sufficient number of such long-term case studies, generalizations have the opportunity to be validated" (p. 7). It appears that she was arguing that, with many case studies focused on the same topic, generalizations centered on the findings would be appropriate.

The last case study research to be reported that was conducted in the 1980s is that of Taylor and Dorsey-Gaines (1988). They, like Heath, moved to studying low-income families, selecting black, urban families as the focus of their research. Although Heath explored why low-income children had difficulty in school, Taylor and Dorsey-Gaines turned this view inside out in their quest to learn why poor, urban black children were doing well in first grade. They discovered that these children bridged their home literacy to school, their families supported literacy in home and in school, and their families wanted and supported their children in becoming "independent survivors in a sometimes hostile world" (p. 209).

Moreover, while Bissex was merely displeased with much of the schooling her son received, Taylor and Dorsey-Gaines were extremely critical of the instruction they observed:

> Literacy cannot be quantified in numbers, nor is it directly related to the frequency of use. It cannot be taught through a decoding process, nor through a series of disconnected (if well ordered) exercises. We can pull language apart, but we cannot expect children to do the same. Children need to be able to create public and private text worlds with continual opportunities to use their expressive abilities to generate new meanings and maintain personal and shared interpretations of the social, technical, and aesthetic types and uses of literacy. It would be hard to dispute the assertion that, in most of our schools, few such opportunities currently exist. (1988, p. 201)

Their argument continued as they noted that schools did not recognize the lives of students or their complex social and cognitive abilities. Schools preferred to assign exercises and tests that were not relevant to the lives of students and, perhaps more important, were limited to low-level skills. Similar arguments are seen in current research, particularly that of Kris Gutierrez and colleagues (2002).

During the 1980s, case study research became increasingly important to literacy researchers, and, as Baghban wrote, they were "no longer suspect or unusual" (p. 7). These researchers explored writing, invented spelling, storybook reading, successful minority students, and the connections between home and school. They moved from studying their own children to including larger groups of children who were frequently not considered mainstream. And as seen in the work of Bissex and Taylor and Dorsey-Gaines, a critical perspective on schools was evident.

Case Study Research in the 1990s

In the 1990s, case study research extended from its traditions, as seen in the work of Schickendanz, Wolf and Heath, Rowe, Purcell-Gates, Martens, Dyson, Ballenger, and Barone. Their work was similar in some ways as several of these researchers explored the development of their own children (Schickendanz, Wolf and Heath, Martens, and Rowe); however, the research questions became more complex and children representing diverse backgrounds most often became the focus of study. These researchers studied writing, reading and response to literature, and diversity.

Schickendanz (1990) conducted a retrospective study centered on her son, Adam, to learn how children come to understand how words are constructed. In much of her work, you can hear the voice of her son as he explained what he did on assignments and writing that she had saved. Adam's writing understandings began with connections between the physical relationship of things and their representation. Through extended exploration, Adam learned how to use letters to represent sounds in words "making more starts and stops, and then, finally set out a spurt of independent, phonemic-based writing" (p. 31). Schickendanz demonstrated how complicated the process of learning to represent words is when she stated, "I suspect that Adam—and other children—require considerable knowledge about phonemic segmentation and letter–sound correspondences before they can take off on their own and create spelling" (p. 27).

Shickendanz is a careful observer, and her book is filled with fine-grained analyses of her son's writing. And although she has many insights about the development of writing for teachers and researchers, I found one conclusion to be particularly important. She wrote, "Inventive spellers are not taking risks; they think they are spelling words right. The reluctant child knows more and digs in his heels" (p. 104). This finding explains why some children in school refuse to use their best efforts to spell a word; they know it has one single representation and they want to replicate that. They are dissatisfied when their teachers say, "Just write it as best you can."

Continuing in the tradition of studying one's own child, Wolf and Heath (1992) detailed and explained the responses that books brought out in Wolf's two daughters, Lindsey and Ashley. This work is reminiscent of the observations made by White and Butler. Within the two cases, the reader learns about connections from life to literature and literature to life. For example, the girls scrub the floor as the children did in the *Little House* book series, or they explain that they are not the evil stepsister from *Cinderella*. Wolf and Heath highlighted the difference between the act of reading and the experience of reading. In all the examples shared in the book, the reader understands how the girls brought the experiences they read about to create meaning in their own day-to-day experiences. Wolf and Heath wrote about these important experiences: "Literacy is not acquired in a vacuum. Nor does it spring fully formed from our minds, like Athena from the head of Zeus. It is an evolutionary process changing from generation to generation and from life to life" (p. 24).

Within the rich descriptions, Wolf and Heath (1992) noted that Ashley preferred nonfiction text and that, even in this home literacy–rich background, Lindsey had difficulty learning to decode text in first grade. Beyond these discoveries, they detailed how the girls used the rich vocabulary from books. For example, Lindsey asked, "Is a bier like a grave?" after reading *Sleeping Beauty*. This discussion of vocabulary learned in text is similar to the work by Beck (2002), which addresses the importance of vocabulary for reading development and comprehension.

As with other cases already shared, Wolf and Heath (1992) compared the learning that the girls experienced at home and how they had to adapt this learning in school situations. They wrote:

> The comparatively stripped-down life of opportunities for extended discussion, and the emphasis on facts rather than interpretation bear little resemblance to what the girls knew to be reading-to-learn at home. To be successful in school, they would need to adapt their abilities to the tasks of schooling and limit their understandings to finding the prescribed answers to the relatively simple stories of basal readers and other textbooks in the classroom. (p. 191)

Wolf and Heath continued the criticism of schools in that they saw teachers asking low-level, constrained questions that took children away from real experiences with literature.

Moving away from home settings, Rowe (1994) explored the literacy learning of 21 students in a middle-class preschool. Her study is similar to Cochran-Smith's (1984) in that she was more interested in learning about the children's perspectives in general rather than highlighting the children as individuals. Her work saw literacy as something that is "not mastered once and for all time" (p. 3). Rather, this process evolves as a child interprets the semiotic potential within text. Rowe contended that because children's perspectives and knowledge of the social world are different from those of adults, a researcher and teacher must come to understand the child's perspectives of literacy activities.

Her careful analysis is similar to Schickendanz's and she included discourse analysis as well. Through this analysis that occurred while children wrote, Rowe discovered that "literacy activities became embedded in peer culture" (1994, p. 119). Her work is very similar to the research by Dyson (1997) in that she highlighted the importance of peers in literacy development.

In a departure from studying one's own children or children in middle-class preschools, Purcell-Gates (1995) engaged in inquiry centered on Donny and Jenny, a mother and son with Appalachian roots. Unlike Taylor and Dorsey-Gaines (1988), she wanted to understand why this child struggled in school. And unlike earlier work, Purcell-Gates took on a critical stance when she tutored Donny and helped his mother negotiate school.

There were many interesting results to this study. First, Purcell-Gates concluded that phonics instruction needs to be responsive to a child's knowledge. Furthermore, she said, "New skills and strategies are learned mainly through the process of reading itself" (1995, p. 79). Second, although Jenny wanted, and tried, to help Donny with his homework, she was not able to do so. However, the school just saw Donny as lazy because he did not complete his homework. The onus for homework was placed totally on the parent and child. Third, the school used Donny's literacy struggles as further evidence that "Appalachian parents are irresponsible and uncaring about their children's education" (p. 161). Although the deficit view is noted in other works, Purcell-Gates provided careful description in how this view develops when schools do not consider the needs and strengths of the families they serve.

In 1996, Martens engaged in a 3-year case study that centered on her adopted daughter, Sarah. She wanted to discover how a child viewed learning to read and write, an approach used in the work of Schickendanz. Martens's book is filled with carefully described home events that contributed to Sarah's literacy understandings. Although there are numerous examples throughout, Martens highlights the importance of learning to write one's own name and acquiring the alphabetic principle to literacy development. Through these understandings, her daughter could now share her writing with others and they could gain the meaning conveyed in her messages. Sarah's story concludes with her kindergarten year, where her teacher's view of literacy learning and instruction did not match the home experience. Martens offers suggestions for early literacy teachers, encouraging them to observe children and teach based on these observations. What I found interesting in this case is that the mismatch between home and school literacy knowledge is most often noted for children who are from high-poverty backgrounds. In this book, a similar mismatch is observed for a child from a middle-class background, thus making the complexity of teaching literacy to young children even greater.

The next three cases (Dyson, Ballenger, and Barone) move away from consideration of one's own child or only one child. These studies consider high-poverty, language-rich children in the complexity of their classrooms.

Dyson (1997) studied second and third graders over 2 years as part of her research program regarding how children learn to write. In this study, she concentrated on how young children use superhero stories "to feel powerful in a (pretend) danger-filled world" (p. 14). Her book is filled with events where children dealt with issues of power, romance, gender, and race in writing, the theatre enactments of their writing, and their official and unofficial talk.

Dyson's work is powerful in that she argues for parents, teachers, and administrators to be sensitive to the "ideological as well as the social dimensions of literacy" (1997, p. 184). She carefully crafts vignettes so that readers understand the importance of building on and responding to what children know and can do alone and with others. Her work highlights the importance of popular culture to children's personal and academic development.

Ballenger's work (1999) considered young, 3- and 4-year-old, Haitian children. In this study she was both teacher and researcher. She shared that when she first worked with these children she engaged in deficit thinking and considered them to be deficient. Throughout Ballenger's book, she reflected on how she moved from this view to one where she considered each child's strengths. In her study, it was possible to see the tensions of a teacher as she tried to bring her students to middle-class understandings of book reading.

Ballenger's study, unlike Dyson's with a focus on students, was concerned with the teacher's dilemmas in teaching to this group of students.

In much of her study, Ballenger (1999) discussed how she tried to make up for the lack of storybook reading in the home by reading numerous books to her students in the classroom. She shared her frustrations when children considered catalogues to be on par with books. She concluded, "Providing storybook reading experience does not create a child who has a mainstream understanding of books" (p. 78). Rather, "storybook reading was not the same activity in this class as the one described in the literature" (p. 79). Ballenger contended that she had to understand her students' interpretations of book reading, which included not understanding that books represented stories and that they could talk throughout a book reading, before she could let them come to know her understandings. Her work extended that of White, Butler, and Wolf and Heath in that she identified how off-topic comments may, in fact, help children make connections within text and between texts.

Finally, Barone (1999) explored the literacy development of 26 children prenatally exposed to crack cocaine. In her work, she described the children both at home and at school as she tried to understand how each child developed as a reader and writer. Barone's work demonstrated that children with this prenatal history could be successful in learning to read and write in their mainstream classrooms. Her work also highlighted the importance of the teacher in each child's success. Similar to Taylor and Dorsey-Gaines (1988), she found

> Sharp contrasts between the classrooms of the children in schools for middle-class and poor children. I also discovered that children of color who attended middle-class schools could be the victims of discrimination. I found that what I thought were universally endorsed practices for children's literacy development were used infrequently in primary classrooms. I found that parents supported their child's learning but often were distanced from their child's teachers. I found that teachers were often unaware of the home circumstances of the children they taught. (p. 10)

The results of this study, conducted in numerous schools and homes— not just one classroom or home—over 4 years, are reminiscent of many of the case studies already reported. Schools were found to not be particularly supportive of children, especially those from high-poverty backgrounds. The curriculum was often skills based and deficit oriented rather than meaning based and difference oriented. Teachers did not understand the uniqueness of the children they taught, and they taught to the class rather than to individuals. Literacy developed in social contexts where children could talk to each other and the teacher, although these contexts were not always encouraged by teachers. Teachers were critical to each child's literacy learning—they were more important than the curricula they enacted.

Each of the cases shared provides rich descriptions of how children develop into readers and writers, enhancing and deepening our understanding. They also, as seen in the work of Bissex, provide roadmaps for quantitative research that follows. By exploring case studies, a picture of children's learning is shared, as well as the dilemmas of teaching culturally and language-rich children, as particularly seen in the work of Ballenger.

The case studies conducted in the 1990s are more complex than those done earlier. Like earlier studies, they considered writing, reading and response, and reading and writing development. However, they have moved from a consideration of one child, often a family member, to many children in school and home settings. These children most often represent cultures, and have home languages, not considered mainstream. These cases have as their goal an understanding of home literacy practices and school literacy practices so that all children have the opportunity to develop into successful readers and writers.

Case Study Research in the 2000s

Building from the rich case studies of the past, current researchers have embraced the complexity that such designs offer and have created variations as well. It is perhaps surprising that even during a time when experimental studies have been determined to be the gold standard for research design (National Reading Panel, 2000) case study research is flourishing. As exemplars, I chose the work of Dyson, Hicks, Jenkins and Earle, Barone, Compton-Lilly, Lindfors, Ballenger, and Genishi and Dyson. What is unique to many of these studies is their longitudinal focus or their revisiting of previous studies. Additionally, some studies have recaptured previous data and repositioned them to argue against many of today's classroom practices.

Once again, Dyson, in *The Brothers and Sisters Learn to Write* (2003), visits a first-grade classroom to document how children's literacy growth in writing is nonlinear. Given literacy education today, when so many public schools' literacy curricula are organized around pacing guides and daily objectives for all children, Dyson's work is even more critical to consider because she problematizes her results with current literacy expectations. Although the objective to have all children succeed in literacy achievement is a worthy goal, Dyson vividly shows that learning is messy at best and is "not a series of stages nor a set of sequentially learned skills" (p. 11). Similarly, Compton-Lilly, in *Re-Reading Families* (2007), rediscovered the children from her earlier study and conducted a new study when the students were in fourth or fifth grade. She asked her participants to describe their academic experiences since she studied them as first graders. Using their stories, Compton-Lilly shared students' and parents' connections to school, gender considerations, high-stakes testing, and technology. Her study enriches our understanding of literacy learning over time and "how environment and experiences converge in the lives of children over time and space" (p. 111).

Continuing the trend to study children's literacy over time, Barone, in *Narrowing the Literacy Gap* (2006), considered a group of youngsters from kindergarten through sixth grade. The students shed light on the everyday circumstances of literacy learning and instruction in a high-poverty school. Not surprising, the study revealed the importance of trust and respect between teachers and students, the importance of effective and caring teachers who support and expect student learning, and the school's, teachers', and students' beliefs that success is achievable.

While the previous three studies explored the literacy learning of children from highly divergent backgrounds, Hicks (2002) focused on economic diversity only, studying Jake and Laurie, two children from a working-class background attending a middle-class school. Similar to Purcell-Gates (1995) and Martens (1996), Hicks discovered that these children met with great difficulty in their school because, being European American, they were not members of the schools' dominant socioeconomic group.

Shifting to the study of writing once again, Jenkins and Earle (2006) focused their research on nonfiction writing. They selected a third-grade classroom rich in literacy instruction and materials. They discovered "that after two months of varying degrees of exposure to nonfiction literature, only 2 of the 18 third graders chose to experiment with the nonfiction genre" (p. 8). During the third phase of the study, the researchers highlighted the nonfiction writing of two students. Following their showcasing of nonfiction writing, other students explored this genre. This study and the earlier work of Calkins (1983) would be interesting to consider together, as readers compare the writing development of fiction and nonfiction genres.

Finally, the last three studies (Lindfors, Genishi and Dyson, and Ballenger) provide variations of case study research. For example, rather than focusing on a select group of children, Lindfors (2008) chose a setting to form the boundary of her exploration: a classroom for children of abused or abusing parents. Her report shares the reading and responding of children who visited this center from 2001 to 2006. Lindfors used the children's comments and their writing and drawing about books to highlight their language development. She suggested that children need time and places to explore books, teacher modeling of various genres, personal choice in selecting books, and opportunities for response to develop as engaged readers.

Another variation of the more typical case study designs is the work of Genishi and Dyson (2008), who used previous data to argue against current practices in school, especially the one-size-fits-all literacy curriculum. I found it interesting to see how they constructed this argument with snippets of previous case study data to support their view that children need "the time and space to learn about or through language in a way that they choose or that enables them to utilize what they already know" (p. 7). Ballenger (2009), somewhat similar to Genishi and Dyson, used data from her own class and the classes of other teachers in her research group to show how teachers can learn from puzzling moments. For instance, she shared experiences where she was doubtful of how she could support a child's learning. Rather than remaining negative about this circumstance, she turned this moment around, using it as the source for research. Not only did Ballenger share her results, as did the other case studies presented, but she also interspersed her findings with details on how she constructed her case and offered suggestions for other teacher-researchers.

In this section, I have focused on the results of each study rather than the specific details of how the researchers structured their case studies. The exemplar studies were chosen because the researchers engaged in rigorous data collection and analysis that most often included multiple observations, interviews, and artifacts. Rather than repeatedly sharing these details, I chose to highlight the importance of their work to the literacy community. With this foregrounding of results, the importance of case study research to the knowledge base of literacy learning and instruction is clearly documented.

FOR WHAT KINDS OF QUESTIONS AND CLAIMS IS THIS METHODOLOGY APPROPRIATE?

Case study research generally answers one or more questions that begin with *how* or *why* (Yin, 2009). Stake (1995) recommends that the researcher write out 10 to 20 prospective questions and then narrow it down to two or three questions that will guide the data collection and analysis.

Another strategy is to start with one broad question. As the study progresses, other questions emerge that provide more focus. For example, Barone (1999) began her research with one broad question: How do children prenatally exposed to crack cocaine develop as readers and writers? During the second year of her study, she added a second question that included the classroom contexts that were established by teachers. Barone found that just observing children was not sufficient because some teachers did not create learning environments that supported literacy learning. Saying merely that a child did not enhance his or her understandings of literacy during a school year presented a limited view, one that only considered each child and not the classroom context.

McCarthey (1998) used yet another strategy: She started with one question and then used multiple lenses to explore it. With this technique, she found that different interpretations of the data were possible, each enriching the other. For example, if a child was characterized as shy by her teacher, this interpretation of the child's identity was preferred. However, when this child was observed to be the leader in small-group interaction, this identity needed to be reconceptualized. Similarly, Hargreaves, Earl, and Schmidt (2002) studied alternative assessment reform from four perspectives: technological, cultural, political, and postmodern. Thus, they gained a richer understanding of the phenomenon, which could not be garnered from the use of one interpretation.

Although finding the appropriate question for case study is important, it is also necessary to know when to use a case study design. Yin (1994) described a common misconception regarding case study. According to Yin, at one time case studies were only seen as appropriate for exploratory studies. However, today, case studies can be used for description and explanation as well as exploration. Importantly, case studies are most often used when the researcher has no control over the behaviors being studied (e.g., in Dyson's investigation of the writing behaviors of young students). It is misleading to believe, however, that case study can only be used to observe behavior. When a researcher assumes a critical stance, as seen in the work of Ballenger, he or she can use what is discovered during research study to improve the conditions for learning and, therefore, change the environment that is being investigated while the study is occurring.

Once the questions and purpose for the study are established, the researcher needs to select participants, or the unit or units for analysis. Patton (1990) discussed the need for purposeful sampling in case study research. He recommended the selection of "information-rich cases" (p. 169), cases in which the researcher can learn a great deal and thoughtfully answer the question or questions posed. Yin (1994, 2009) described the basic designs or reasons for case study research. These include:

Single-case research
- A critical case to test a theory (single case can be used to determine if the propositions of the theory are correct).
- An extreme or unique case (often used in clinical psychology).
- A representative case that showcases a typical situation.
- A revelatory case that allows for the analysis of a phenomenon previously unavailable to researchers.
- A longitudinal case where a case is studied over time.

Multiple-case research
- Used to predict similar results (literal replication).
- Used to produce contrasting results for predictable reasons (theoretical replication).

Simultaneously with the development of questions, purpose, and sampling, the researcher is expected to create a rigorous design for the case study. This part includes data collection and analysis as well as time in the field.

WHAT ARE STANDARDS FOR QUALITY IN THIS METHODOLOGY?

Yin (1994) described several ways to determine the quality of case study research. First is the use of multiple sources of evidence. These might include multiple observations, interviews, and the collection of artifacts and documents. By using multiple data sources, the researcher can discover "a converging line of inquiry" (p. 92). As a result, the researcher has built a compelling case for his or her results and conclusions. Second, Yin argued for the creation of a chain of evidence: In the case study, the researcher presents his or her evidence in a linear fashion and explains how it contributed to the conclusions reached. In this way, the reader can follow the path of data collection and analysis with the researcher. Third, the case study is reviewed by the key informants before it appears in print. Through this process, the researcher is asking the key informant to correct any misconceptions that may have found their way into the report.

In addition to the strategies noted by Yin, credibility for a case study comes from length of time in the field (Merriam, 1988). Through extended time in the field, the researcher guarantees that what has been witnessed represents a pattern rather than an aberration. Finally, the researcher needs to carefully consider ethical issues. Importantly, any biases that the researcher may personally hold must be identified and reported, along with the precautions taken to keep the bias in check throughout the interpretation of the data. Other ethical issues relevant to case study research include, for example, the researcher's involvement with the persons, issues, or events under study; confidentiality of data; ownership of the data; and problems with the inability to distinguish data from the researcher's interpretations (Merriam, 1988).

WHAT IS ONE OR MORE EXEMPLAR OF THIS METHODOLOGY, AND WHAT MAKES IT SO GOOD?

Although there are many exemplars of this methodology in literacy research, I chose "The Complexities of Reading Capital in Two Puerto Rican Families" by Catherine Compton-Lilly (2009) as a model. In her article, Compton-Lilly demonstrated the qualities essential to exemplary case study research. She shared two of her cases from her larger study focused on defining "students as successful readers in the official context of school and how official embodiments of literacy are reflected within the dialectical relationship that exists between school and local literacy practices" (p. 75). Her work is similar to that of Taylor and Dorsey-Gaines (1988) in that it focused on home and school literacy practices.

Compton-Lilly (2009) used a year-long multiple-case design, with an intrinsic purpose in that she used her 10 parent–child dyads to study the literacy experiences of adults pursuing a GED and their children, in particular their literacy at home and school. Her data collection involved multiple interviews with teachers and staff at the GED center, parents and children, and kindergarten teachers. Compton-Lilly provided tables where she detailed her data collection, in particular her use of interview schedules. Her data-gathering methods were extensive and included not only interviews but also numerous observations at a variety of sites and the research and review of relevant documents, resulting in a rich data set.

As I read and reflected on Compton-Lilly's method section, I realized that it served as a model for others pursuing case study design. Not only did she provide background on the cultural and language practices of Puerto Ricans, but she also situated Puerto Ricans historically in the United States and presented a detailed overview of her case study design and her lens of reading capital (Bourdieu, 1986). Compton-Lilly clearly described her data collection, with all necessary details present, and methodically presented her data analysis journey. Furthermore, she depicted her background as a teacher and researcher and examined the strengths and complications she brought to the study. Finally, she carefully described her research settings.

So why is this study exemplary? First, Compton-Lilly (2009) used multiple sources of data (Yin, 1994, 2009). She conducted many student, parent, and teacher interviews over time. She worked with an insider at the GED center, who introduced her to other teachers and provided necessary information that she could not know as an outsider. Participant data were carefully documented and thoroughly detailed, including each child's literacy development. Compton-Lilly thoughtfully described potential researcher issues, like her role as a teacher/tutor, and how she resolved any problems and conflicts. In her results, she cautiously used her participants' exact words to tell their stories, so that even though she was the writer their stories were carefully represented. Compton-Lilly included tables to help the reader understand how she used the idea of reading capital (Bourdieu, 1986) in complex ways. Finally, she shared how her work departed from the original work of Bourdieu and thus provided new understandings of literacy. In addition, Compton-Lilly did not try to simplify the complexity and contradictions she found in her research. She discovered ways to share this complexity, often through the use of tables, to make her study more compelling in the process. Clearly, Compton-Lilly met the criteria that make for a quality case study.

FINAL WORDS

As was evident in the overviews of case studies presented throughout this chapter, case study research is important to our understanding of literacy. Case studies are complex because they are built around multiple data sources that must be analyzed into themes or patterns. This is no easy task because rigorous case study results in significant amounts of data that are often difficult to reconcile. However, for those who engage in this form of research, the rewards are many. Perhaps most important is that this work is applicable to real life because it relates directly to the reader's experiences, and it facilitates understanding of complex situations, an understanding that cannot be made explicit in most other research designs.

REFERENCES

Alvermann, D., Huddleston, A., & Hagood, M. (2002, December). *What could the WWF and a high school English curriculum possibly have in common?* Paper presented at the annual conference of the National Reading Conference, Miami, FL.

Baghban, M. (1984). *Our daughter learns to read and write: A case study from birth to three.* Newark, DE: International Reading Association.

Ballenger, C. (1999). *Teaching other people's children: Literacy and learning in a bilingual classroom.* New York: Teachers College Press.

Ballenger, C. (2009). *Puzzling moments, teachable moments.* New York: Teachers College Press.

Barone, D. M. (1999). *Resilient children: Stories of poverty, drug exposure, and literacy development.* Newark, DE: International Reading Association.

Barone, D. M. (2006). *Narrowing the literacy gap: What works in high-poverty schools.* New York: Guilford Press.

Beck, I. (2002, August). *Comprehension and vocabulary development in the early grades.* Paper presented at the Institute for Statewide Literacy Initiatives, Harvard Graduate School of Education, Cambridge, MA.

Birnbaum, J., Emig, J., & Fisher, D. (2003). Case studies: Placing literacy phenomena within their actual context. In J. Flood, D. Lapp, J. Squire, & J. Jensen (Eds.), *Handbook of research on teaching the English language arts* (2nd ed., pp. 192–200). Mahwah, NJ: Erlbaum.

Bissex, G. (1980). *Gnyx at Wrk.* Cambridge, MA: Harvard University Press.

Bourdieu, P. (1986). The forms of capital. In J. G. Richardson (Ed.), *Handbook of theory and research for the sociology of education* (pp. 241–258). New York: Greenwood.

Butler, D. (1975). *Cushla and her books.* Boston: Horn Book.

Calkins, L. (1983). *Lessons from a child: On the teaching and learning of writing.* Exeter, NH: Heinemann.

Cochran-Smith, M. (1984). *The making of a reader.* Norwood, NJ: Ablex.

Compton-Lilly, C. (2007). *Re-reading families: The literate lives of urban children—four years later.* New York: Teachers College Press.

Compton-Lilly, C. (2009). The complexities of reading capital in two Puerto Rican families. *Reading Research Quarterly, 42,* 72–98.

Dyson, A. (1995). Children out of bounds: The power of case studies in expanding visions of literacy development. In K. Hinchman, D. Leu, & C. Kinzer (Eds.), *Perspectives on literacy research and practice* (pp. 39–53). Chicago: National Reading Conference.

Dyson, A. (1997). *Writing superheroes: Contemporary childhood, popular culture, and classroom literacy.* New York: Teachers College Press.

Dyson, A. (2003). *The brothers and sisters learn to write: Popular literacies in childhood and school cultures.* New York: Teachers College Press.

Dyson, A. (2008). Children out of bounds: The power of case studies in expanding visions of literacy development. In J. Flood, S. Heath, & D. Lapp (Eds.), *Handbook of research in teaching literacy through the communicative and visual arts* (Vol. II, pp. 109–118). Newark, DE: International Reading Association.

Ehri, L. (1997). Interactions in the development of reading and spelling: Stages, strategies, and exchange of knowledge. In C. Perfetti, L. Rieben, & M. Fayol (Eds.), *Learning to spell: Research, theory, and practice across languages* (pp. 237–269). Mahwah, NJ: Erlbaum.

Ehri, L., Nunes, S., Willows, D., Schuster, B., Yaghoub-Zasdeh, Z., & Shanahan, T. (2001). Phonemic awareness instruction helps children learn to read: Evidence from the National Reading Panel's meta-analysis. *Reading Research Quarterly, 36,* 250–287.

Genishi, C., & Dyson, A. H. (2008). *Children, language, and literacy: Diverse learners in diverse times.* New York: Teachers College Press.

Gutierrez, K. D., Asato, J., Pacheco, M., Moll, L. C., Olson, K., Horng, E. L., et al. (2002). "Sounding American": The consequences of new reforms on English language learners. *Reading Research Quarterly, 37,* 328–347.

Hargreaves, A., Earl, L., & Schmidt, M. (2002). Perspectives on alternative assessment reform. *American Educational Research Journal, 39,* 69–100.

Heath, S. (1983). *Ways with words: Language, life, and work in communities and classrooms.* Cambridge, UK: Cambridge University Press.

Henderson, E. (1981). *Learning to read and spell: The child's knowledge of words.* DeKalb: Northern Illinois University Press.

Hicks, D. (2002). *Reading lives: Working-class children and literacy learning.* New York: Teachers College Press.

Jenkins, C., & Earle, A. (2006). *Once upon a fact: Helping children write nonfiction.* New York: Teachers College Press.

Ladson-Billings, G. (1994). *The dreamkeepers: Successful teachers of African American children.* San Francisco: Jossey-Bass.

Lindfors, J. (2008). *Children's language: Connecting reading, writing, and talk.* New York: Teachers College Press.

Martens, P. (1996). *I already know how to read: A child's view of literacy.* Portsmouth, NH: Heinemann.

McCarthey, S. (1998). Constructing multiple subjectivities in classroom learning contexts. *Research in the Teaching of English, 32,* 126–160.

McGee, L., & Barone, D. (2000, December). *Case studies of young children's literacy learning: Past, present, and future.* Paper presented at the annual meeting of the National Reading Conference, San Antonio, TX.

Merriam, S. B. (1988). *Case study research in education: A qualitative approach.* San Francisco: Jossey-Bass.

Miles, M., & Huberman, A. (1994). *Qualitative data analysis: An expanded sourcebook* (2nd ed.). Newbury Park, CA: Sage.

National Reading Panel. (2000). *Teaching children to read: An evidence-based assessment of the scientific research literature on reading and its implications for reading instruction.* Washington, DC: National Institute of Child Health and Human Development.

Neuman, S., & McCormick, S. (2000). A case for single-subject experiments in literacy research. In M. Kamil, P. Mosenthal, P. D. Pearson, & R. Barr (Eds.), *Handbook of reading research: Volume III* (pp. 181–194). Mahwah, NJ: Erlbaum.

Patton, M. (1990). *Qualitative evaluation and research methods* (2nd ed.). Newbury Park, CA: Sage.

Purcell-Gates, V. (1995). *Other people's words: The cycle of low literacy.* Cambridge, MA: Harvard University Press.

Rogers, R. (2002). Between contexts: A critical discourse analysis of family literacy, discursive practices, and literate subjectivities. *Reading Research Quarterly, 37,* 248–277.

Rowe, D. (1994). *Preschoolers as authors: Literacy learning in the social world of the classroom.* Creskill, NJ: Hampton Press.

Sarroub, L. (2002). In-betweenness: Religion and conflicting visions of literacy. *Reading Research Quarterly, 37,* 130–149.

Schickendanz, J. (1990). *Adam's righting revolutions: One child's literacy development from infancy through grade one.* Portsmouth, NH: Heinemann.

Shulman, J., Whittaker, A., & Lew, M. (2002). *Using assessments to teach for understanding: A casebook for educators.* New York: Teachers College Press.

Stake, R. (1995). *The art of case-study research.* Thousand Oaks, CA: Sage.

Stake, R. (2000). Case studies. In N. Denzin & Y. Lincoln (Eds.), *Handbook of qualitative research* (2nd ed., pp. 435–454). Thousand Oaks, CA: Sage.

Taylor, D., & Dorsey-Gaines, C. (1988). *Growing up literate: Learning from inner-city families.* Portsmouth, NH: Heinemann.

Vygotsky, L. (1962). *Thought and language* (E. Hanfmann & G. Vakar, Trans.). Cambridge, MA: Harvard University Press.

Weintraub, S. (1981). *Annual summary of investigations relating to reading July 1, 1979 to June 30, 1980.* Newark, DE: International Reading Association.

White, D. (1956). *Books before 5.* New York: Oxford University Press.

Wolcott, H. (1994). *Transforming qualitative data.* Thousand Oaks, CA: Sage.

Wolf, S., & Heath, S. (1992). *The braid of literature: Children's worlds of reading.* Cambridge, MA; Harvard University Press.

Xu, S. (2002, December). *Pre-service teachers learn to integrate student popular culture texts into literacy instruction.* Paper presented at the annual conference of the National Reading Conference, Miami, FL.

Yin, R. (1994). *Case-study research: Design and methods* (2nd ed.). Thousand Oaks, CA: Sage.

Yin, R. K. (2009). *Case study research: Design and methods* (4th ed.). Thousand Oaks, CA: Sage.

CHAPTER 3

Content Analysis

THE PAST, PRESENT, AND FUTURE

James V. Hoffman
Melissa B. Wilson
Ramón A. Martínez
Misty Sailors

Jg zpv dbo sfbe uijt, uibol b ufbdifs.
—BOPOZNPVT

In his popular children's book *The Riddle of the Rosetta Stone*, James Cross Giblin (1993) describes the path scholars followed to uncover the mysteries of hieroglyphics using parallel texts in Greek and Egyptian. The essence of content analysis is to be found in this remarkable effort to reconstruct a written (and oral language) that had been lost for centuries. On a much simpler scale, the quote we offer at the start of this chapter can be seen as a similar kind of challenge. Content analysis can lead one to discover both the meaning behind and the patterns used to obscure the meaning of a text like this. More important, in relation to the goals of this chapter, content analysis can reveal the more subtle messages imbedded in a text read by a child in a classroom or by a classroom teacher consulting a manual in preparation for teaching a lesson.

Content analysis has found broad applications in the study of language and literacy, ranging from the analysis of book responses—audio recorded and transcribed as in Sipe (2000)—to the analysis of students' writing, as in Aulls (2003); to the analysis of teachers' role in scaffolding classroom discussion, as in Maloch (2002); to the analysis of the word choice, word repetition, and sentence complexity in beginning reading materials, as described by Hiebert and Martin (2003); and to the analysis of the content of textbooks, as in Beck, McKeown, and Gromoll (1989). The content analysis of discourse, as represented in the first three examples, is addressed in two other chapters in this book. The methods of content analysis that are the focus for this chapter relate to curriculum as in the last two examples, and include the analysis of both learner and teacher texts.

We begin this chapter with a general description of the focus and methods of content analysis, including attention to its historical roots, essential components, and standards for inquiry. We continue with a discussion of the kinds of questions that have been addressed in literacy-related research using this method and present several exemplary studies that reflect the breadth of application of this method to literacy research. In the final section, we call attention to issues and trends for investigators who may be contemplating the use of content analysis in their own literacy research.

DEFINING CONTENT ANALYSIS

Content analysis is a flexible research method for analyzing texts and describing and interpreting the written artifacts of society (White & Marsh, 2006). Babbie (2004) defines content analysis as "the study of recorded human communications, such as books, websites, paintings and laws." Bernard Berelson (1952) defines content analysis as "a research technique for the objective, systematic and quantitative description of manifest content of communications" (p. 15). Neuendorf (2002) offers a six-part definition of content analysis:

> Content analysis is an in depth analysis using quantitative or qualitative techniques of messages using a scientific method (including attention to objectivity-intersubjectivity, a priori design, reliability, validity, generalizability, replicability, and hypothesis testing) and is not limited as to the types of variables that may be measured or the context in which the messages are created or presented.

Content analysis involves the inspection of patterns in written texts, often drawing on combinations of inductive, deductive, and abductive analytical techniques.

White and Marsh (2006) explain "abductive" analysis in terms of the researcher using "rules of inference, to move from the text to the answers to the research questions" (p. 27). The rules of inference in this methodology are of the abductive kind. "Abductive inferences proceed across logically distinct domains, from particulars of one kind, to particulars of another kind" (Krippendorff, 2004, p. 36).

Content analysis has sometimes been challenged for being a positivist methodology, yet there are numerous examples of content analysis that rely on interpretive/qualitative principles (e.g., analysis of transcripts of class-room interactions). "Research using qualitative content analysis focuses on the characteristics of language as communication with attention to the content or contextual meaning of the text" (Hsieh & Shannon, 2005, p. 1278). The goal of this analysis is to provide "knowledge and understanding of the phenomenon under study" (p. 1278). In other words, content analysis is the method of making inferences from texts and making sense of these interpretations in a context surrounding the text.

HISTORICAL BACKGROUND ON CONTENT ANALYSIS

Content analysis has its beginnings in rhetorical analysis from more than 4,000 years ago. Aristotle, in his studies of rhetoric, was concerned with the content of argument when he "put the message content and form at the center of the argument—that we use communication to control our environment, including the actions of others" (Neuendorf, 2002, p. 31). Neuendorf (2002) traces the genesis of content analysis to another source: decryption. According to Neuendorf, the Rosetta Stone discovery in the late 1700s prompted Thomas Young to "translate between the three scripts through a process of quantifying occurrences of signs on the stone and other ancient sources" (p. 31).

Krippendorff (2004) begins his search for the beginnings of content analysis somewhat later. He traces this methodology's start to the 1600s, when theological scholars used content analysis in their dissertations. These scholars, at the Catholic Church's behest, analyzed printed materials for heretical content. The next historical instances of content analysis developed in Sweden during the 18th century, when scholars systematically analyzed a new book of hymns for anti-Christian ideas (Hsieh & Shannon, 2005; Krippendorff, 2004).

Content analysis became more recognized in the early 20th century, when it was used in journalism schools to examine newspapers for "demoralizing, unwholesome, and trivial matters as opposed to worthwhile news items" (Krippendorff, 2004, p. 5). Both Krippendorff (2004) and Neuendorf (2002) acknowledge content analysis's major growth spurt in the United States and western Europe in the 1930s and 1940s. Krippendorff writes about sociologists' extensive use of poling in the 1930s and mass communications scholars' use of the methodology to analyze Nazi propaganda in the 1940s.

After World War II, "the use of content analysis spread to numerous disciplines" (Krippendorff, 2004). Although it was used in the fields of psychology, anthropology, and history, it came to rest primarily in the field of communications, where it is used to analyze mass media. With the advent of more sophisticated electronic hardware and software, much of the "analyzing" is now done on the computer, "with text data coded into explicit categories and then described using statistics" (Hsieh & Shannon, 2005, p. 1278).

Although the tools for content analysis have expanded, with the use of computers in particular, the essential attention to patterns in text has remained the same. The applications of content analysis can be seen across many forms of human activity, from national intelligence (e.g., the analysis of Internet communications that might signal terrorist activity) to business (e.g., analysis of newspaper advertisements to identify buying and selling patterns) to psychology (e.g., patterns of behavior in problem solving) and sociology (e.g., sexist language patterns in public discourse).

ESSENTIAL FEATURES AND STANDARDS FOR CONTENT ANALYSIS IN LITERACY RESEARCH

Content analysis, as a research tool in the context of curriculum materials, typically focuses on the presence of certain words or concepts within the texts or sets of texts. Researchers quantify and analyze the presence, meanings, and relationships of such words and concepts, and then make inferences about the messages within the texts, the writers, the audience, and even the culture and time of which these are a part. Texts can be defined broadly as books, book chapters, essays, interviews, discussions, newspaper headlines and articles, historical documents, speeches, conversations, advertising, theater, informal conversation, or really any occurrence of communicative language (*writing.colostate.edu/guides/research/content/pop2a.cfm*).

Ole Holsti (1969) groups the uses of content analysis into three basic categories: (1) making inferences about the antecedents of a communication (e.g., What messages, themes, belief systems can be inferred from this text?); (2) describing and making inferences about characteristics of a communication (e.g., What is the quality of the communication in this text as measured against some standard?); and (3) making inferences about the effects of a communication (e.g., What impact does a particular text have on patterns of interaction?).

According to Krippendorff (1980, 2004), six questions must be addressed in every content analysis:

1. Which data are analyzed?
2. How are they defined?
3. What is the population from which they are drawn?
4. What is the context relative to which the data are analyzed?
5. What are the boundaries of the analysis?
6. What is the target of the inferences?

Neuendorf (2002) describes a progression, or set of steps, that is typical in any content analysis.

- *Theory/rationale.* The research must identify the focus for the analysis in terms of key variables and a theoretical framework. A hypothesized relationship or set of predictions may be posed. Alternatively, the research may rely on a set of questions that guide the study.
- *Conceptualizing decisions.* The researcher may limit the focus for the content analysis to a particular purpose or set of variables. These decisions are described explicitly and with a rationale.
- *Operationalizing measures.* The researcher defines each variable, construct, or process to be used to guide the analysis of the targeted texts. These definitions must be described in relation to the theoretical framework and explicit enough to guide possible replications.
- *Selecting/identifying a coding scheme.* The coding scheme may be computer based or rely on human analysis. The scheme may be drawn from previous research, adapted from previous research, or constructed for this study.
- *Sampling.* The researcher describes the sampling process used to gather the corpus of text to be analyzed.
- *Training and reliability.* Coders are trained on the process of analysis to levels of agreement. The checks focus on each of the critical variables.
- *Coding.* There must be at least two coders (with at least 10% overlap of material analyzed to check for levels of agreement). Even with computer analysis, there should be spot checking on the reliability of coding.
- *Tabulation and reporting.* The research reports on the analysis procedures, including reliability, leading to the findings.

Of course, these procedures may be modified depending on the content and focus of the study. However, these procedures set a clear standard for researchers who adopt content analysis as their primary method.

QUESTIONS ADDRESSED USING CONTENT METHODS IN LITERACY RESEARCH

Given that content analysis is focused on texts, there might be an expectation for broad application of this methodology in literacy research. But is this true? How often is content analysis used as the primary method of literacy research? What kinds of questions are addressed? Are there particular areas of focus that appear frequently? To explore these questions, we undertook an examination of the research literature that has adopted this methodology. We excluded from our analysis studies that applied methods of discourse analysis, historical analysis, and literature syntheses, focusing exclusively on studies that examined curriculum materials used in instruction. We conducted this search with three goals in mind: to uncover the kinds of questions addressed in literacy research using this methodology; to examine the application of the methodology in recent research in terms of rigor and theoretical frameworks; and to identify a set of studies that might serve as models for inquiry within this methodology.

We set parameters on our examination of the research literature consistent with our questions. Specifically, we limited our inquiry to a particular time period and to a sample of research journals. We chose, as our starting point, Durkin's (1981) investigation of comprehension instruction in the basal teacher guides. There are certainly earlier examples of research in literacy that adopted a content-analysis perspective (e.g., Chall's [1967] analysis of basal materials for code vs. meaning emphasis; Beck and McCaslin's [1978] study of commercial materials to determine how instruction is arranged with respect to decoding; and the many studies of readability from the 1940s through the 1970s). For us, the appeal of Durkin's study as a starting point is threefold: It was one of the first from the Center for the Study of Reading to use content-analysis methods, it was published in the premier reading research journal (*Reading Research Quarterly*), and it was recently complemented by a replication study published in the same journal (Dewitz, Jones, & Leahy, 2009). Following this rationale, we identified our time framework of 1981 to 2009. Second, we limited our examination to studies that have been published in four of the leading literacy-related research journals: *Reading Research Quarterly*, the *Journal of Reading Behavior*, *Research in the Teaching of English*, and the *Yearbook of the National Reading Conference*. This is a limited sampling, and although it would not suffice in a comprehensive review, we were hopeful that it would be appropriate to examine our goal of determining the range of questions being asked through content-analysis methods in literacy research.

In describing the findings from our investigation, we begin with Durkin's (1981) study and Dewitz and colleagues' (2009) follow-up replication study. We then offer a brief "content analysis" of research in literacy that has applied content-analysis methods to curriculum materials, with a focus on the range of questions and topics addressed between 1981 and 2009. Finally, we offer a detailed description of the content-analysis methods used in four studies that seem to represent the breadth of research in literacy.

CONTENT ANALYSIS AND COMPREHENSION INSTRUCTION

Durkin's (1981) research into comprehension instruction was conducted in her association with the Center for the Study of Reading at the University of Illinois at Urbana–Champaign and was featured in two research reports. The first was an observational study investigating the amount and qualities of comprehension instruction in elementary schools with some attention given to content analysis. Durkin first developed an observational tool that was based on her analysis of the research literature on effective practices in the teaching of reading comprehension. She used this tool to observe in classrooms of grades 3–6. Durkin's findings indicated that there was minimal comprehension instruction offered in classrooms. She famously documented, instead, large doses of comprehension "mentioning," the frequent "interrogation" of students with comprehension questions, and the reliance on worksheets to practice comprehension. By the end of this study, Durkin puzzled over the causes for the absence of comprehension instruction in classrooms. She wondered whether it could be the result of the lack of guidance for comprehension instruction in the curriculum guides provided for teachers.

Durkin (1981) followed this line of thinking into her second study of comprehension instruction, this time relying primarily on content-analysis methods. Durkin used the same definition of comprehension instruction from her observational study in the analysis of the basal materials: "A manual suggests that a teacher do or say something that ought to help children acquire the ability to understand, or work out, the meaning of connected text" (p. 518). Durkin articulated specific guidelines for the analysis, including issues of what the coders of the materials would not consider—for example, "Headings for manual segments (e.g., Comprehension Instruction) will not be considered in classifying them" (p. 519)—as well as what would be considered—for example, "Whenever a manual provides comprehension instruction about a topic that was covered earlier but adds something new that is judged to be significant for understanding connected text, it will be called 'elaboration' (not review) and will be counted as an additional instance of comprehension instruction" (p. 520). The features of the content analysis were identified a priori and pilot tested before they were incorporated in the research methods. Further classifications included definitions of terms such as *practice, application,* and *review.*

The procedures followed in the analysis provided for an initial reader coding all of the materials and a second reader analyzing all of the instances identified as comprehension instruction. All disagreements ("very few") were discussed and resolved between the reviewers. In addition, the second reviewer went back to the original materials to check on "missed" instances, and the few that were discovered were resolved through discussion. The entire review process was repeated again by the first reviewer once the initial round of review was completed.

The findings are analyzed and reported by frequency and then broken down by grade level and then by category (e.g., graphic signals, anaphora). These latter categories were not a priori but the result of the content analysis itself. These categories were further divided by the support offered at "less" than the sentence level (20 categories) and "more" than the sentence level (14 categories). Further analysis focused on attention to the qualities of the "discourse" type (e.g., narrative, expository, poetry).

On the basis of this analysis, Durkin concluded that there is far more attention given to application and practice to support instruction than to guidance on explicit instruction. Overall, she struggled with the extreme attention to questions and assessment rather than instruction. In terms of methodology, Durkin (1981) provides a good example of combining a priori and constructed categories based on analysis. She offers substantial detail in coding, although there is far more attention in the technical report than in the journal articles. Although Durkin's research, both the observational and basal-analysis studies, has been critiqued for the a priori definitions used, the studies have stood the test of time within the research community.

Dewitz and colleagues (2009) reported a curriculum analysis of comprehension instruction in basal reader guides (grades 3–5). The study was framed by these questions:

- What skills and strategies are recommended to be taught?
- How are these skills and strategies recommended to be taught?
- What instructional designs do the programs use?
- How do the spacing and timing of comprehension skill and strategy instruction in core programs compare with how these skills were taught in original research studies?

The researchers, for the most part, adopted Durkin's (1981) original definition for comprehension instruction. They "read every lesson" of every program and examined the scope and sequence for each program, looking for alignment between the two. They coded instructional "moves" in terms of what skill was in focus and what the teacher was directed to do. To code lesson elements, Dewitz and colleagues adopted six a priori categories from Durkin (preparation, instruction, application, practice, review, and assessment) and created four more categories as the need for the additional codes was recognized during the coding process. Lessons that were coded as "direct explanation" were further analyzed using Duffy's (1986) criteria (e.g., identification of procedural knowledge, when strategy would be used). Dewitz and colleagues, like Durkin, found little attention to comprehension instruction and few examples of instruction that met Duffy's criteria for explicitness. Furthermore, there was little evidence in their analysis of timing that any attention was given to a "gradual release of responsibility" for the comprehension strategy from the teacher's control to the students.

In terms of method, Dewitz and colleagues (2009) offer remarkably little, if any, information on coding procedures or reliability checks on the coders, although the coding form is included in the appendix of the report. There is no description of the process followed to construct the new categories in the coding system. In fact, there is less explicit attention to the method in the more recent report than in the original by Durkin, and neither Durkin nor Dewitz and colleagues offer any explicit references to the methods used.

CONTENT ANALYSIS OF CURRICULUM MATERIALS

To what degree are these two studies "typical" in terms of focus or methods? To address this question, we—the four authors of the current chapter—conducted a hand search of four literacy research journals (*Reading Research Quarterly, Research on the Teaching of English, Journal of Literacy Research* [formerly *Journal of Reading Behavior*], and the *Yearbook of the National Reading Conference*) from 1981 to 2009 for reports that relied primarily on content analysis. We sought to identify studies that used content analysis of curriculum materials as the primary focus for the research questions and the primary methodology. We excluded studies that relied on discourse analysis, historical analysis, or literature syntheses. We conducted hand searches of each of the volumes from the target journals with these criteria. One coder searched a journal for the articles. A second coder searched a sample of 10% of the journals to check for reliability. Coder agreement on the checks was greater than 80% on the positive hits.

We identified a total of 42 reports that met our criteria for inclusion. These reports were distributed across the four journals as follows: *Journal of Reading Behavior/Journal of Literacy Research,* $N = 11$; *Reading Research Quarterly,* $N = 12$; *Yearbook of the National Reading Conference,* $N = 16$; and *Research in the Teaching of English,* $N = 3$. We applied a constant-comparative method (Glaser & Strauss, 1967) to determine the major focus for the analysis in each of these reports. We identified five major categories:

1. Leveled texts—mostly basal readers (a focus on the features of the text materials read by students, $N = 15$ studies).
2. Instructional (a focus on the materials used by teachers to guide their teaching, $N = 12$ studies).
3. Literature (a focus on the qualities of the literature, $N = 9$).
4. Print environment (a focus on the print qualities in the classroom environment, $N = 4$).
5. Methods textbooks (a focus on the texts used to prepare teachers, $N = 2$).

In some cases, the focus for a particular study spanned across more than one area. However, for the initial presentation of these data, we have classified each study by its major focus. Consistent with our purpose in conducting this review, we further examined each of the studies relative to the kinds of research questions addressed and the methodology.

Leveled Texts

This category represents the largest group of studies in the pool identified. The vast majority of these studies were focused on the analysis of basal readers or content area textbooks and related trends. These are studies that address questions related to the decoding demands and supportive features of the texts used in primary grades and include such traditional constructs as "readability." These are also studies that examine the distribution of different text "types" (e.g., the inclusion of informational texts) and the match between text types represented in the instructional materials compared with the distribution in tests or in standards documents. None of the studies in this category described "content analysis" as their primary method nor were there any citations to indicate the analytical framework being used.

Instructional Studies

This category represents the second largest group of studies in the pool identified. The vast majority of these studies were focused on the analysis of teacher guides in basal readers or content area textbooks. A large number of these reports focused on how, when, and if teachers are guided in the teaching of comprehension (e.g., Are strategies taught explicitly?). As in the previous category, none of the instructional studies described "content analysis" as their primary method nor were there any citations to indicate the analytical framework being used.

Literature Studies

Making up the third largest category, these studies tended to focus on questions related to the literary content of basal readers or children's literature or both. Although there was almost no mention of content analysis as a method, many of the studies were explicit in the ways their analysis drew on sociological or literary theory.

Print Environment Studies

Although this category comprised few studies, the numbers seemed to increase over the period of study. Print environment studies assumed a broader, more inclusive view of the qualities of texts and the functions served in the classroom environment, examining, for example, the range of text types, the particular kinds of texts (e.g., informational), or the medium (e.g., electronic). Some of these studies included an examination of both teacher and students as they engaged with texts in these print environments. There was little mention of content analysis as a method in these studies.

Methods Textbook Studies

Of the two studies represented in this category, one was focused on the attention given to the particular needs of ESL learners in literacy instruction. Interestingly, this study included an examination of journals on this same topic. There was no mention of content analysis as a primary method. The second study focused on references to "literacy" teacher in secondary methods textbooks. This study references content analysis in detail as part of the methods.

CONTENT-ANALYSIS METHODS IN FOUR REPRESENTATIVE STUDIES

Thus far, our findings represent the range of different questions that have adopted a content-analysis perspective. Our next step was to identify examples of studies that reflected a breadth of questions as well as studies that met the standards for procedures and reporting presented by Neuendorf. We identified four studies and describe and highlight features of content analysis within each one in the following sections.

Study 1. The Information Text Gap: The Mismatch between Non-Narrative Text Types in Basal Readers and 2009 NAEP Recommended Guidelines (Moss, 2008)

We chose Moss's (2008) study for several reasons. First, it deals with an area that is receiving prominent attention in current literacy research (i.e., informational texts). Second, it reflects one of the categories we identified as a prominent context for content analysis (i.e., basal reading programs). Third, we believe the methods in this study represent a good application of content-analysis standards.

The Moss study is designed to compare the text genres represented in two recent California-adopted basal readers (grades 1–6). Moss (2008) documents the difficulty children have with comprehending expository passages. She argues that this difficulty may be attributable, in part, to the emphasis on the reading of narrative ("story") texts in the primary grades. Citing Duke (2000), Moss argues that few informational texts are available in the classroom, and that engagement with these kinds of texts is limited for both teachers and students. She cites additional research suggesting that increased attention to informational texts may have benefits. Moss uses the 2009 National Assessment of Educational Progress (NAEP) guidelines (American Institutes for Research, 2005) as the primary referencing point for her investigation. The 2009 NAEP guidelines call for more informational texts in classrooms, recommending that they make up 50% of the classroom library at the fourth-grade level, 55% at the eighth-grade level, and 70% at the 12th-grade level. Moss contextualizes her research in terms of Reading First schools in California, which are limited to the adoption of one of two core (basal) reading programs. Moss argues that for many children this is the only exposure to texts they may receive in the classroom. Thus, she sets out to identify the kinds of text genres included in the student readers of these basal programs as well as the "kinds" of nonfiction texts that are included.

Moss (2008) describes the method of this study as a two-phase descriptive "content analysis." For the first phase, Moss trained two graduate students to classify the selections included in the basal program into one of four genres: narrative fiction, poetry, plays, or nonfiction. These categories were predetermined by Moss using a modification of the classifications used in previous research by Flood and Lapp (1986). For the Moss study, "nonfiction" is "defined as non-narrative texts that included information books, biographies, concept books, information storybooks, or books that combine narrative elements such as characters and plots with informational ones" (p. 208). There was an initial period of training in which the same selections were classified and compared. Then each member of the research team independently classified each of the selections from all grade levels. The interrater reliability was calculated as .94. Discrepancies in coding were discussed and resolved. Pages and percentages of selections were then calculated for each genre.

In the second phase, each nonfiction selection was classified according to one of four categories specified in the 2009 NAEP guidelines: literary nonfiction or one of three types of informational texts—expository texts, argumentation and persuasive texts, or procedural texts and documents. The coding procedure in this second phase was the same as in the first, with an initial coding "together," independent coding (with calculation of reliability), and finally the negotiation of discrepancies. The independent coding agreement in this phase was calculated as .94.

Moss (2008) reports the findings using tables to compare pages and percentages for selections across the genres and then for the types of nonfiction texts. The findings suggest a high percentage of informational texts (i.e., about 40%). In one series there was more of a progression toward larger percentages moving from the primary to the upper grades. In the other series, there was a more abrupt trend, with low levels of nonfiction in the primary grades and high levels in the upper grades. The author argues, using previous research reports, that these numbers represent a substantial increase in attention to informational texts. However, neither series met NAEP guidelines. Moss also identifies, based on her findings, the need to diversify the kinds of nonfiction texts. Classrooms contained little in the way of persuasive and argumentative texts and procedural texts and documents.

Although this study does not make any explicit reference to "content analysis" as a methodology, there is clear attention to each of the steps identified by Neuendorf (2002). The theory and rationale are clearly described with respect to the issues surrounding exposure to informational texts and previous research. The author is careful to identify decisions that were made in a focus on particular variables (e.g., informational texts) and materials (e.g., California basals). Moss (2008) gives clear conceptual and operational definitions for each of the variables, most often linking them to previous research, and likening them to the coding scheme used. The sampling procedures and the training procedures are clearly described, with attention to reliability of coding. Finally, the data are tabulated and reported in a form that directly reflects the movement from coding to analysis.

The author also addresses all six of the questions required by Krippendorff (1980, 2004) for content analysis with respect to the identification and definitions of the data to be analyzed, the population sampled (California basals), the context for the analysis (e.g., importance of informational texts, lack of attention to informational texts, and the policies shaping exposure such as No Child Left Behind). The boundaries are clearly identified (e.g., a focus on the texts read and not on the instructional support in teacher guides), as are the targets of the inferences—researchers and publishers (in particular).

Study 2. Exploring the "Critical" in Critical Content Analysis of Children's Literature (Beach et al., 2009)

We chose to include this study because of its focus on a version of content analysis that is relatively new in literacy research. This study adopts critical content analysis as its framework. Critical content analysis is a "close reading of small amounts of text that are interpreted by the analyst and then contextualized in new narratives; a definition that is a hermeneutic, reader response oriented research stance that can be critical as well. What makes the study 'critical' is not the methodology but the framework used to think within, through, and beyond the text" (Beach et al., 2009, pp. 2–3).

Content analysis is "critical" when the methodology is used to ferret out issues of overt or covert power found in texts. This kind of analysis requires a critical theoretical stance or framework to buttress the analyst's purpose for the study. Examples of critical theoretical stances include feminist studies, queer studies, and childhood studies.

Assumptions about the inherent qualities of texts must be transparent. In order to conduct a critical content analysis on texts, the features of texts must be discussed. The following features are adapted from Krippendorff (2004, pp. 22–25):

1. Texts have no qualities without a reader. The meaning of the text is found in the reading event between the analyst and the text.
2. Texts contain multiple meanings. The meanings found are dependent on the reader's intentions and the context of the study.

3. Meanings found in texts do not need to be shared. It is legitimate if one scholar's reading and interpretation of the same text does not jibe with another scholar's reading and interpretation.
4. The meanings found in texts pertain to other contexts. The analyst uses the meanings from the text to make sense of something outside of the text. Again, the text itself is not the object of study. The object of reading the text is to inform another context.
5. Texts have meanings that speak to particular context. The purpose for the reading influences the meanings found.
6. Content analysts read to draw inferences from texts to be applied to the context of the study. The texts do not speak for themselves in this process but rather speak to or for something else.

This report highlights the reader response and hermeneutic nature of the critical content analysis. Three scholars were asked to analyze the same picture book: *The Day of Ahmed's Secret*, written by Florence Parry Heide and Judith Heide Gilliland and illustrated by Ted Lewin (1990). What makes the analyses different are the various theoretical frameworks used by the analysts. The first analysis, by Vivian Yenika-Agbaw, uses postcolonial theory. Yenika-Agbaw writes that when she comes upon a book that takes place in a foreign culture, she wonders "why the author chose to set the story in a particular region of a country and how much the author knows about that culture" (p. 4). She uses the lens of postcolonial theory because the story takes place in Cairo, Egypt, a place that is, in the Western mind, associated with the mythical "orient." Yenika-Agbaw sees through this lens "stereotypes of exoticism" (p. 4). To counterbalance this reading, she looks for a counter discourse, in this case the child protagonist's sense of agency. By looking at the child character, language use, and the plot, she creates three analytical categories: Ahmed's ownership of space, his ownership of work, and his ownership of personal and cultural identity. Within these categories, Yenika-Agbaw places excerpts from the text that fit. In her discussion, she posits that, despite the cultural stereotypes embedded in the text, her postcolonial reading—her counter discourse—allows her to understand the power dynamics that actually position Ahmed in a role of agency.

Christine Jenkins considers the same text using the Great Books method. She focuses on the "elusive interpretive questions" (p. 9) found in this method. She explains that she attended to parts of the book "where I paused" (p. 10). It is in this pause that Jenkins found anomalies to examine that took the form of questions. She argues that reading this way "is not simply the province of adult scholars, but can and should inform young people's reading experiences" (p. 12). Jenkins sees her focus of this critical content analysis as a jumping-off point for her to "provide readers with multiple opportunities to become critical readers on their own terms" (p. 12).

Rebecca Rogers uses critical discourse theories for her critical content analysis. She decides on this frame because the child protagonist is not in school but works as a butane gas delivery boy. Rogers starts her analysis by investigating butane gas in Cairo at the time the book was published. She finds that butane gas is a major fuel source in Egypt, and the task of making deliveries throughout crowded city streets is dangerous. Rogers sees Ahmed as "literally situated in the economic market, a market that was experiencing severe restructuring" (p. 13). She analyzes the story in terms of "the political-economic backdrop of Egypt during the early 1990s" (p. 13). Through this lens, she is concerned that the policies engineered by the International Monetary Fund (IMF) regarding butane gas hurt poor people like Ahmed. This positioning of the story in global economic terms led Rogers to ask how "Ahmed is positioned to both recognize and naturalize his rightful place in the world" (p. 14). Using textual and visual analyses, Rogers examined the "genre, discourse and style of the book" (p. 14) to understand what choices the writer and illustrator privileged and marginalized. "Unpacking dominant worldviews—in this book, neoliberalism—is an important task in making sure that reading global children's literature offers multi-perspectival learning spaces" (p. 18).

As can be seen, although these were three very different critical content analyses of the same book, their methodology was the same. Each analyst did a "close reading of small amounts of text" from a hermeneutic, reader response-oriented research stance. Each scholar made abductive inferences, took the particulars from one domain, *The Day of Ahmed's Secret*, and applied them to another, in these cases postcolonialism, reader response with children, and neoliberalism. Through these inferences, the researchers illustrated Krippendorff's (2004) qualitative content-analysis text features: The same text was given different meanings through different reading events. The one text contained multiple meanings that were dependent upon the reader's individual intentions and the contexts of the study. The meanings found by the different scholars were all valid; it was/is all right that different scholars found/find different meanings. The meanings found in *The Day of Ahmed's Secret* pertained to particular contexts. The object of reading the text was to inform the other contexts. These content analysts read to draw inferences from texts to be applied to the context of their particular studies. This method is close to content analysis because it seems to satisfy the requirements for qualitative content analysis.

These studies were also informed by critical discourse analysis. All three researchers had a social problem to solve through a text. In the case of Yenika-Agbaw, her concern rested with the social issue of the imbalance of power between the West and its colonized subjects. Jenkins' social problem is the limited opportunities students have to read critically and for themselves. Rogers's issues are with the IMF and the neoliberalization of the third world. The studies all addressed the ideologies surrounding and perpetuating various social problems by attending to power relationships and hierarchies. The three scholars all saw their job as excavating the covert discourses behind the story in order to disrupt the status quo.

Study 3. The Effective Elementary Classroom Literacy Environment: Examining the Validity of the TEX-IN3 Observation System (Hoffman, Sailors, Duffy, & Beretvas, 2004)

We chose the Hoffman and colleagues (2004) study because it deals with an area that is receiving growing attention in the field of literacy research (Hoffman, Maloch, & Sailors, in press). In addition, it reflects one of the categories we identified as a prominent context for content analysis, and we believe its methods represent a good application of the standards for content analysis discussed thus far.

The Hoffman and colleagues (2004) study was designed to validate an instrument that was grounded in a theoretical framework and connected to student achievement. This instrument focused on the assessment of the physical text environment of the classroom, the practices surrounding the use of texts in the classroom environment, and the understanding and valuing of texts in that same environment. By assessing the overall effectiveness of the classroom literacy environment, the instrument can be used to evaluate and support professional development efforts for teachers and can be used for classroom research.

In designing the instrument, Hoffman and his colleagues (2004) drew from the literature that describes literacy as a social practice. Citing the New Literacy Studies Group (Barton, 1994, 2000; Barton & Hamilton, 2000; Barton, Hamilton, & Ivanic, 2000), the research team described literacy as "the way in which members of particular social groups use and value literacy" (Hoffman et al., 2004, p. 309). Furthermore, the intentions, uses, and values of the literacy practices by members of that society "are indicative of the role literacy plays in the lives of those members" (p. 310). To capture the social practices in elementary classrooms, the research team developed the instrument under study across a 2-year period and in various phases. The fully developed instrument comprised three components: text inventory, in-use inventory, and text interviews. The text inventory included 17 different text types, with supporting rubrics that rate text quality based on a 5-point scale). This component yielded individual scores for each of the text types, a holistic score for the text environment, and a holistic rating of the local environment (those texts in the classroom that are written by teachers and students).

The observation-based in-use inventory was designed to capture and record the engagement of the teacher and the children as they used the various texts in the classroom. The inventory includes three types of observations. The first focused on the use of text in a particular subject area; the second captured the use of text among all students in the class; and the third focused carefully on the use of text by three specific students in the class—one on-grade-level reader, one below-grade-level reader, and one above-grade-level reader. Data on the text type in which the three students and teacher engaged and the context of that engagement were also recorded. All data were compiled and used to calculate a Quality Time Engaged (QTE) score, weighting text engagement with text quality.

The text interviews were designed to capture and record the understanding, interpretations, values, and beliefs about the texts in the classroom. The teacher and the three specific children who were the focus of the in-use observations were interviewed. Observers rated the response of the students using a scale ranging from 1 (*low understanding*) to 5 (*high understanding*) and rated the teachers using a similar scale; additionally, teachers were asked to rank the various text types in their classrooms on a scale from 1 (*most valuable*) to 17 (*least valuable*).

Hierarchical linear modeling was used to analyze the data, including the classroom environment data (TEX-IN3) and the student comprehension data collected using the Group Reading Assessment and Diagnostic Evaluation (American Guidance Service, 2001). Findings from these analyses indicated that the holistic and the local text inventories were significant predictors of comprehension scores. The QTE scores that captured the teachers' engagement and the measures averaged across the three representative students were significantly related to adjusted posttest comprehension scores. Likewise, the average students' text understandings and that of the teacher were significant predictors when entered into the analysis equation.

The authors concluded their study by relating their findings to the importance of texts in classrooms and the use of print materials with students, and to the understanding, valuing, and interpretations of texts as critical for student comprehension growth.

Although this study does not make any explicit reference to content analysis as a methodology, there is clear attention to each of the steps identified by Neuendorf (2002). First, the theory and rationale are clearly described with respect to the role of print environments and literacy education. The authors were careful to attend to the sets of variables studied; the sets of rubrics clearly defined each set of operational measures in ways that are replicable. The coding scheme was drawn from previous research (time on task and follow-through studies), and the sampling for the corpus of texts to be studied was clearly described. The training and reliability of data collectors led to an appropriate level of agreement, and the data tabulation and reporting are clear. Finally, the authors of this validation study also addressed all six features presented by Krippendorff (1980, 2004) for content analysis.

Study 4. Stripping for the Wolf: Rethinking Representations of Gender in Children's Literature (Marshall, 2004)

We chose to include this article because it stands as an example of critical qualitative content analysis that reaches outside the traditional communications theory roots of this methodological approach. Drawing on feminist poststructural literary theory, Marshall (2004) seeks to move beyond liberal feminist analyses of children's literature that overemphasize sex-role theory. Although she acknowledges the usefulness and importance of these more traditional feminist approaches to content analysis, she criticizes the way in which they often frame gender as a neutral and static category. Over the past three decades, Marshall notes, feminist critiques of children's literature have focused on the underrepresentation and stereotypical portrayal of girls and women and on how these phenomena might serve to reinforce gender bias. Such a focus, Marshall argues, "sustains a male/female duality" and "relies primarily on white, Western, middle-class, heterosexual notions of femininity" (p. 260). What Marshall proposes instead is a poststructural theoretical framework for analyzing *how* gender is constructed and produced through the content of children's literature. She suggests that this framework extends existing feminist perspectives by allowing for more dynamic theorizations of gender that move beyond sex-role theory to situate the discursive construction of gender within particular cultural and historical contexts.

To illustrate the affordances of poststructural feminist theory, Marshall (2004) analyzes four different variants of the *Little Red Riding Hood* tale—an early oral version and three subsequent written versions. She selects (1) the earliest known oral variant of the tale, "The Story of Grandmother," (2) Charles Perrault's 1697 iteration based on this oral version, (3) *Little Red Cap*, an 1819 adaptation by the Brothers Grimm, and (4) Tina Schart Hyman's 1983 picture book version, *Little Red Riding Hood*, which won the Caldecott Honor. Focusing on the construction of gender and sexuality in each of these versions, Marshall analyzes how the character Little Red Riding Hood is variously represented with respect to issues of femininity, morality, and sexual violation. Although Marshall does not explicitly refer to her approach as content analysis—indeed, she says almost nothing at all about her methods—her approach to analyzing the construction of gender is clearly informed by some of the key principles of qualitative content analysis. In particular, her insistence on situating each version of the *Little Red Riding Hood* tale within its respective historical and cultural context is consistent with Krippendorff's (2004) emphasis on identifying the context relative to which data are analyzed. Marshall explicitly connects each iteration of the tale with the construction of gender and sexuality in its respective historical period, interpreting each in light of its particular context. Moreover, she explicitly discusses how multiple, and sometimes conflicting, interpretations can stem from each version of this story, which is consistent with Krippendorff's discussion of how texts always contain multiple meanings.

Marshall's (2004) poststructural feminist analysis highlights how competing discourses about gender, childhood, and sexuality intersect in children's literature, framing girls as both innocent and vulnerable on the one hand and sexually enticing and in need of moral regulation on the other. As she notes, the four different versions of *Little Red Riding Hood* reflect different historical preoccupations with girls and their sexuality. The earliest oral version, for example, was intended for a multi-aged audience and thus contained explicit references to violence, nudity, and sexual content. Marshall explains that Perrault's version, which is equally explicit, was intended as a cautionary tale and directed specifically toward young girls. She suggests that this adaptation essentially frames Little Red Riding Hood as responsible for her own violation. The Grimms' version, Marshall notes, features the addition of a mother, who warns her daughter not to stray from the path, converting this into a more transparent cautionary tale. Marshall argues that this version also differs from previous versions in that Little Red Riding Hood, although initially eaten by the wolf, emerges unharmed, representing the possibility of rehabilitation. With respect to Hyman's version, Marshall highlights the author's addition of an interior monologue, which serves to characterize Little Red Riding Hood as a rational subject. She further asserts that Hyman goes out of her way to avoid addressing Little Red Riding Hood's sexuality, resulting in a sanitized version of the character that nonetheless reinscribes prescriptive notions of femininity. According to Marshall, despite their differences, all four versions of this tale converge in that they ultimately portray the protagonist as responsible for policing herself and containing her latent sexuality by avoiding certain behaviors. She contends that while more recent iterations of the tale shed some of the explicit violence and sexual content of earlier versions and portray Little Red Riding Hood as more agentive, they reflect a "subtle, yet no less coercive, attempt to contain and regulate the feminine body" (Marshall, 2004, p. 262).

This article is an example of qualitative content analysis in that it is consistent with some of the key principles guiding this methodological approach. Marshall (2004) foregrounds the question, What is the context relative to which the data are analyzed? She makes inferences from four different texts and then makes sense of these interpretations within the cultural and historical contexts surrounding each. This article represents a *critical* approach to content analysis because the author challenges more traditional feminist approaches to content analysis that rely on binary definitions of gender. Marshall seeks to unveil the ways in which dominant constructions of gender are inscribed in children's literature while also allowing for the possibility of multiple meanings and interpretations of the texts in question.

SUMMARY

If you can read this, thank a teacher.
　　　　　—Anonymous

The astute reader of this chapter, applying content-analysis methods, may have already decoded the initial "quote" introducing this chapter. Some of you may have even determined that we simply substituted the next letter in the alphabet to create the coded version—not a very sophisticated scheme but one that can be used to illustrate the value of combining inductive and inductive processes in a content analysis to achieve goals. You may be using a similar process to infer from the body of our chapter the major points we would make regarding content analysis as a research method in literacy. First, the volume of research into curriculum materials using content analysis is severely limited given the important role that curriculum materials play in teaching. Second, many of the studies that have been conducted give limited attention to the methods and standards that have been formulated in content-analysis research. Third, and finally, there are excellent models in place for us to begin to look at content analysis applied within broadening definitions of what "counts" as texts. We hope the future of content analysis in literacy research will continue to grow in directions that reflect the last two points.

REFERENCES

American Guidance Service. (2001). GRADE: Group reading assessment and diagnostic evaluation [Computer software]. New York: Pearson.

American Institutes for Research. (2005). Reading framework for the 2009 National Assessment of Educational Progress: Pre-publication edition. Retrieved November 1, 2005, from *www.nagb.org/what-we-do/reading_fw_06_05_prepub_edition.doc*.

Aulls, M. W. (2003). The influence of a reading and writing curriculum on transfer learning across subjects and grades. *Reading Psychology, 24*(2), 177–215.

Babbie, E. R. (2004). *The practice of social research* (10th ed.). Belmont, CA: Wadsworth.

Barton, D. (1994). *Literacy: An introduction to the ecology of written language.* Oxford, UK: Blackwell.

Barton, D. (2000). Literacy practices. In D. Barton, M. Hamilton, & R. Ivanic (Eds.), *Situated literacies: Reading and writing in context* (pp. 7–15). London: Routledge.

Barton, D., & Hamilton, M. (2000). Literacy practices. In D. Barton, M. Hamilton, & R. Ivanic (Eds.), *Situated literacies: Reading and writing in context* (pp. 167–179). London: Routledge.

Barton, D., Hamilton, M., & Ivanic, R. (Eds.). (2000). *Situated literacies: Reading and writing in context.* London: Routledge.

Beach, R., Enciso, P., Harste, J., Jenkins, C., Raina, S. A., Rogers, R., et al. (2009).

Exploring the "critical" in critical content analysis of children's literature. In R. T. Jiménez, M. K. Hundley, V. J. Risko, & D. W. Rowe (Eds.), *58th Yearbook of the National Reading Conference* (pp. 129–143). Oak Creek, WI: National Reading Conference.

Beck, I. L., & McCaslin, E. S. (1978, March). *An analysis of dimensions that affect the development of code-breaking ability in eight beginning reading programs.* Paper presented at the annual meeting of the American Educational Research Association, Toronto.

Beck, I. L., McKeown, M. G., & Gromoll, E. W. (1989). Learning from social studies texts. *Cognition and Instruction, 6*(2), 99–158.

Berelson, B. (1952). *Content analysis in communication research.* New York: Free Press.

Chall, J. (1967). *Learning to read: The great debate.* New York: McGraw-Hill.

Dewitz, P., Jones, J., & Leahy, S. (2009). Comprehension strategy instruction in core reading programs. *Reading Research Quarterly, 44,* 102–126.

Duffy, G. G., Roehler, L. R., Meloth, M. S., Vavrus, L. G., Book, C., Putnam, J., et al. (1986). The relationship between explicit verbal explanations during reading skill instruction and student awareness and achievement: A study of reading teacher effects. *Reading Research Quarterly, 21*(3), 237–252.

Duke, N. (2000). 3.6 minutes per day: The scarcity of informational texts in first grade. *Reading Research Quarterly, 35,* 202–224.

Durkin, D. (1981). Reading comprehension instruction in five basal reader series. *Reading Research Quarterly, 16*(4), 515–544.

Flood, J., & Lapp, D. (1986). Types of writing in basal readers: The match between texts and tests. *Reading Research Quarterly, 21*(3), 284–297.

Giblin, J. C. (1993). *The riddle of the Rosetta Stone: Key to ancient Egypt.* New York: HarperCollins.

Glaser, B., & Strauss, A. (1967). *The discovery of grounded theory: Strategies for qualitative research.* New York: Aldine.

Heide, F. P., & Gilliland, J. H. (1990). *The day of Ahmed's secret.* New York: HarperCollins.

Hiebert, E. H., & Martin, L. A. (2003). The texts of beginning reading instruction. In S. B. Neuman & D. K. Dickinson (Eds.), *Handbook of early literacy research* (Vol. 1, pp. 361–376). New York: Guilford Press.

Hoffman, J. V., Maloch, B., & Sailors, M. (in press). Researching the teaching of reading through direct observation: Tools, methodologies & guidelines for the future. In M. L. Kamil, P. D. Pearson, E. B. Moje, & P. P. Afflerbach (Eds.), *Handbook of reading research: Volume IV.* New York: Routledge.

Hoffman, J. V., Sailors, M., Duffy, G. G., & Beretvas, N. (2004). The effective elementary classroom literacy environment: Examining the validity of the TEX-IN3 observation system. *Journal of Literacy Research, 36,* 303–334.

Holsti, O. R. (1969). *Content analysis for the social sciences and humanities.* Reading, MA: Addison-Wesley.

Hsieh, H., & Shannon, S. E. (2005). Three approaches to qualitative content analysis. *Qualitative Health Research, 15*(9), 1277–1288.

Krippendorff, K. (1980). *Content analysis: An introduction to its methodology.* Newbury Park, CA: Sage.

Krippendorff, K. (2004). *Content analysis: An introduction to its methodology* (2nd ed.). Thousand Oaks, CA: Sage.

Maloch, B. (2002). Scaffolding student talk: One teacher's role in literature discussion groups. *Reading Research Quarterly, 37,* 94–112.

Marshall, E. (2004). Stripping for the wolf: Rethinking representations of gender in children's literature. *Reading Research Quarterly, 39,* 256–270.

Moss, B. (2008). The information text gap: The mismatch between non-narrative text types in basal readers and 2009 NAEP recommended guidelines. *Journal of Literacy Research, 40*(2), 201–219.

Neuendorf, K. A. (2002). *The content analysis guidebook.* Thousand Oaks, CA: Sage.

Sipe, L. R. (2000). The construction of literary understanding by first and second graders in oral response to picture storybook read-alouds. *Reading Research Quarterly, 35,* 252–275.

White, M. D., & Marsh, E. E. (2006). Content analysis: A flexible methodology. *Library Trends, 55*(1), 22–45.

CHAPTER 4

Of Correlations and Causes

The Use of Multiple Regression Modeling in Literacy Research

Anne E. Cunningham
Keith E. Stanovich
Andrew Maul

Beginning students in the social sciences quickly learn the admonition that "correlation does not imply causation." Ironically, the next lesson they often learn is that in many areas of the social sciences and education all we have are correlational data! Upon deeper investigation, however, students should also discover that there are analytic techniques that can be paired with correlational data that represent a middle ground between unqualified inference and simple association. In this chapter, we illustrate this "middle ground" with a research problem that we have studied in depth implementing primarily correlational techniques: determining the cognitive consequences of reading experience.

THE DILEMMA OF CORRELATIONAL EVIDENCE

Because this discussion simultaneously concerns both study design and analytic method, we must begin with an attempt at disambiguation. The term *correlational* can refer both to a feature of study design (i.e., "correlational data," as distinct from "experimental data") and to a specific analytic technique (most commonly, a Pearson correlation coefficient). The phrase "correlation does not imply causation" reflects the former use of the word *correlation* and thus implies that if one wishes to make an authoritative causal statement, one must look to experimental data.

The power of a true experimental study comes from the integration of three essential elements: comparison, control, and manipulation. Comparison alone is not enough to justify a causal inference. Within an experimental study, a researcher is able to manipulate the hypothetical causal variable while holding other potential factors constant, thus systematically creating levels of variability that can then be compared. Factors not directly under the control of the experimenter can be controlled through randomization. When the elements of control and direct variable manipulation are removed, a researcher's ability to clearly examine the nature of the relationship between certain variables is dramatically limited; yet this is precisely the nature of correlational analyses. Correlational investigations attempt to compare the levels of one variable with those of another without direct manipulation or control.

Because of their lack of control and manipulation, correlational studies limit the conclusions a researcher can draw. Although a researcher would ideally like to proclaim solid causal relationships between variables, this is difficult to do using a correlational design. Going back to our beginning students in the social sciences, we reiterate that the mere existence of a relationship between two variables does not guarantee that changes in one are the cause of changes in another. Here we might consider the well-worn example of the correlation between an increase in ice cream consumption and a rise in drowning deaths during the summer months. The presence of this correlation does not justify a conclusion that eating ice cream causes people to drown.

But what, specifically, about correlational studies is so problematic? Two main potential problems prevent us from drawing causal inferences from correlational evidence. The first is called the "third-variable problem." It occurs when a correlation between two variables arises because both variables are related to some third variable that, to some degree, affects both of the variables in question. This variable may not have been measured or even included in a researcher's overall theory. The correlation between ice cream consumption and drowning deaths is a perfect illustration. Eating ice cream does not cause one to drown, even though an increase in one can be linked to an increase in the other. Instead, both variables are related to a third, confounding variable: heat. As temperatures rise, more people eat ice cream. Likewise, as the temperature rises, more people engage in water sports, thus increasing the incidence of drowning. The variable of heat, therefore, affects both ice cream consumption and drowning rates, which results in a spurious relationship between the latter two variables themselves.

The second problem is called the "directionality problem," or an inability to determine the direction of causality in a relationship between two variables. It creates potential interpretive difficulties because even if two variables do have a direct causal relationship, the direction of that relationship is not indicated by the mere presence of the correlation. In short, a correlation between variables X and Y could arise because changes in X are causing changes in Y or because changes in Y are causing changes in X. The mere presence of a correlation does little to help ascertain which of the two variables may be influencing the other. One example of this problem in education is the positive correlation between reading behaviors and reading ability. Does a student read more because he is a better reader, or has this student become a better reader because he has read more? It is impossible to tell by the mere presence of a correlation.

THE NEED FOR CORRELATIONAL METHODOLOGY

Despite their limitations, correlational studies play an important role in the social sciences and education and are necessary for several reasons. Some variables, such as birth order, sex, and age, are inherently correlational because they cannot be manipulated within the parameters of a study; scientific knowledge concerning them must, therefore, be based on correlational evidence. Other variables, such as human malnutrition or socioeconomic status, simply cannot be manipulated for ethical reasons. Finally, logistical difficulties inherent in carrying out research within classrooms can preclude the use of true experimental designs but leave correlational studies as a viable option.

As with any method, certain preliminary steps are necessary to ensure the quality of the data and the validity of one's analyses. At the highest level, variables considered within a correlational study should be chosen with care. This refers both to variable *selection* and variable *measurement*. With regard to selection, a sound theory that takes alternative explanations into account should be used to determine which variables are of immediate interest. With regard to measurement, especially when "latent" variables (i.e., those that are not directly observable, such as intelligence or motivation) are to be studied, the measures of these variables must be carefully selected or constructed. A researcher must be confident of the reliability and validity of any tests or scales used to measure the constructs of interest if the intention is to make generalizations from data based on those scales, a point we discuss in greater detail later. Also, basic features of study design quality must be verified, such as representativeness, randomness, and sufficient sample size.

Additionally, standard correlational techniques frequently assume that (1) variables in question are related linearly, (2) continuous variables are normally distributed, (3) errors are "homoscedastic," meaning that the model does not make more error at some levels of the outcome variable than at others, and (4) all variables are measured without error. Parametric statistical techniques such as correlations and regressions are generally considered robust to relatively minor departures from these assumptions, and specific corrections exist for more major departures.

Correlational studies also gain power when combined with other types of investigations. Particularly in the domains of classroom and curriculum research, the basis for scientific conclusions generally rests on the convergence of a variety of methodologies, including correlational studies, nonequivalent control group studies, time-series designs, and various other quasi-experimental designs and multivariate correlational designs. All these designs are discussed in this volume, and each have their unique strengths and weaknesses, but together, when the results are amalgamated, they are able to paint a more cohesive picture.

Although limited in their most simple forms, correlational studies can be made more powerful by using statistical techniques that themselves allow for the partial control of third variables, when those variables can be measured (Schneider, Carnoy, Kilpatrick, Schmidt, & Shavelson, 2007). In other words, when it is not possible to *experimentally* control for the influence of all potential confounding variables, it is still sometimes possible to *statistically* control for specific variables when one is aware in advance of particular competing theories regarding the nature of an association, through the use of regression-based statistical modeling techniques. Multiple regression, path analysis, and structural equation modeling all fall into this category. These statistical techniques, in essence, allow the correlation between two variables to be recalculated after the influence of other key variables is removed, or "factored out" or "partialed out." Thus, these types of correlational statistics and designs help to *rule out* certain causal hypotheses, even if they cannot demonstrate the true causal relation definitively. This is often extremely useful in science, both social and physical, because in many cases the leading alternative explanations (potential third variables) are known and can thus be accounted for. Given this background, we illustrate a very typical use of correlational design by discussing our own work examining the cognitive consequences of literacy using multiple regression.

DIFFICULTIES IN INTERPRETING ASSOCIATIONS BETWEEN READING EXPERIENCE AND COGNITIVE OUTCOMES

Many studies in the field of literacy have reported correlations between degrees of engagement in reading activities and various cognitive outcomes. However, such logic, if not supplemented with additional statistical controls, yields data subject to an inordinately large number of alternative explanations. Historical and cross-cultural studies provide some context for understanding this problem.

Consider the international literacy campaigns conducted in nonindustrialized countries during the last three decades and how historians and sociologists used certain cultural correlates of literacy to justify these campaigns. There was, in earlier writings, a tendency to attribute every positive outcome that was historically correlated with the rise of literacy—economic development, for example—to the effects of literacy itself. However, it is now recognized that the potential for spurious correlations in the domain of literacy is quite high. Simply put, high levels of societal literacy are correlated with too many other positive outcomes, and the link between economic development and national levels of literacy has turned out to be much more complex than originally thought (Fuller, Edwards, & Gorman, 1987; Gee, 1988; Graff, 1986; Wagner, 1987). Literacy levels are as much a consequence of economic development as they are its cause. Thus, rather than emphasizing the need for literacy, sociologists may have been equally as justified in campaigning for an increased role of government in promoting factors such as economic development.

The problem at the level of the individual reader is analogous to the problem of comparing the effects of different levels of literacy across different societies; levels of print exposure are correlated with too many other good things. Avid readers tend to be different on a wide variety of cognitive skills, behavioral habits, and background variables than their peers who read less. Attributing any particular outcome to print exposure uniquely is an extremely tenuous inference when based on only the presence of an unpartialed correlation. Early literacy theorists were guilty of possibly "overselling" literacy by attributing to it every positive effect with which it was correlated.

In fact, influential theorists have argued that correlations between literacy experience and cognitive outcomes are largely spurious. One group of theorists in particular has advanced the *environmental opportunity hypothesis*, which can be illustrated by considering vocabulary growth as an example. Although literacy theorists suggested that vocabulary growth was related to literacy experiences, there is considerable evidence that children's vocabulary sizes are correlated with parental education and indicators of environmental quality (Hall, Nagy, & Linn, 1984; Hart & Risley, 1995; Mercy & Steelman, 1982; Wells, 1986). Thus, it has been argued that vocabulary differences are primarily the result of differential opportunities for word learning.

The environmental opportunity hypothesis is countered, however, by theorists who emphasize that differences in vocabulary are caused by variation in the efficiency of the cognitive mechanisms responsible for inducing meaning from context. This stance, labeled the *cognitive efficiency hypothesis*, proposes that superior processing abilities underlie both the cognitive outcomes obtained and the literacy experiences themselves, so that the linkage between the latter two is spurious. Proponents of the cognitive efficiency hypothesis argue that experiential factors are not implicated—or at least are of secondary importance—in explaining vocabulary differences. For example, Sternberg (1985) has argued that simply reading a lot does not guarantee a large vocabulary. What seems to be critical is not sheer amount of experience but rather what one has been able to learn from and do with that experience. According to this view, then, individual differences in knowledge acquisition have priority over individual differences in actual knowledge (p. 307). Jensen (1980) has stated the cognitive efficiency hypothesis in even stronger form:

> Children of high intelligence acquire vocabulary at a faster rate than children of low intelligence, and as adults they have a much larger than average vocabulary, not primarily because they have spent more time in study or have been more exposed to words, but because they are capable of educing more meaning from single encounters with words. . . . The vocabulary test does not discriminate simply between those persons who have and those who have not been exposed to the words in context. . . . The crucial variable in vocabulary size is not exposure per se, but conceptual need and inference of meaning from context. (pp. 146–147)

It is important to recognize that cognitive efficiency explanations of this type are generic and are not necessarily restricted to the domain of vocabulary acquisition. They could, in theory, apply to knowledge acquisition in virtually any domain. Ceci (1996) has discussed how, in an attempt to undermine developmental theories that emphasize the importance of knowledge structures in determining intelligent performance, advocates of the cognitive efficiency hypothesis argue that "intelligent individuals do better on IQ tests because their superior central-processing mechanisms make it easier for them to glean important information and relationships from their environment" (p. 72). The cognitive efficiency hypothesis thus undercuts all developmental theories that emphasize the importance of knowledge structures in determining intelligent performance by potentially trivializing them. According to the cognitive efficiency view, these differences in knowledge bases may affect certain cognitive operations, but the knowledge differences themselves arise merely as epiphenomena of differences in the efficiency of more basic psychological processes. Knowledge differences thus become much less interesting as explanatory mechanisms of developmental differences because they are too proximal a cause.

THE ANALYTIC STRATEGY: MULTIPLE REGRESSION MODELING

As part of a broad-based research program examining the impact of reading experience on cognitive development (e.g., Cunningham & Stanovich,

1997; Stanovich, 1993, 2000), we have tested alternative hypotheses such as the cognitive efficiency hypothesis using multiple regression.

Whereas an ordinary bivariate correlation examines the degree of association between two variables (which can arbitrarily be labeled X and Y), multiple regression allows an investigator to have more than one X (or "predictor") variable simultaneously predicting the Y (or "criterion") variable. Furthermore, this technique effectively holds each X constant while examining the relationship between every other X variable and the Y variable. One or more Xs can thus be added to the model purely for the purpose of holding them constant (variables of this nature are often called "control variables") while examining the relationship between the X variable of primary interest and the criterion variable. Thus, an investigator can assess whether measures of reading experience are associated with criterion variables (such as vocabulary knowledge) even when controlling for cognitive ability measures. (The terms "controlling for," "factoring out," "holding constant," and "partialing out" are essentially synonymous.) In other words, it is possible to statistically address the third-variable problem discussed previously by including the hypothesized third variables as control variables in the multiple regression model.

Furthermore, it is possible to use multiple regression to examine the total amount (in terms of percentage) of variance in the criterion variable that can be explained by all predictor variables in the model (sometimes referred to as the "model R^2," or the "coefficient of determination") and the *unique* variance each particular predictor variable can explain (sometimes referred to as the "semipartial r^2"). In other words, one can ask, How much of the variance in the criterion can be explained by this predictor variable once the contributions of all other variables in the model are partialed out? What is the *unique* explanatory power of reading experience on vocabulary knowledge over and above what can be explained by cognitive ability?

Although the unique contribution of each X variable is directly obtainable from the estimates of a multiple regression model (as the semipartial r^2), another approach, sometimes termed a "hierarchical" approach to model building,[1] is often preferable for conceptual reasons. In this approach, a series of multiple regression models are estimated, and the difference in model R^2 between consecutive models is examined. Each model typically contains all the predictor variables from the previous model and one additional variable. Thus, the difference in model R^2 between two successive models can be directly interpreted as the amount of additional variance in the criterion variable uniquely explained by the predictor variable that has just been added to the model over and above the explanatory power of all other variables in the model. This is mathematically identical to the semi-

---

[1] This use of *hierarchical* is entirely distinct from its use in the term "hierarchical linear modeling," also referred to as multilevel modeling or random effects modeling, which is beyond the scope of this chapter.

partial r^2 described previously and has the conceptual advantage of clearly highlighting the unique contribution of the last variable entered over and above all other variables. This is the approach taken and described in the examples presented in the tables throughout this chapter.

In the examples to be described, we tested the cognitive efficiency hypothesis in just this way. In predicting cognitive outcomes such as vocabulary, we allowed the general cognitive variables or central processing mechanisms described by cognitive efficiency theorists to exert their influence in the explanation of our criterion variable. Once the influence of these variables was accounted for, we were able to examine the unique explanatory power of print exposure. Some of these analyses are quite conservative because we controlled for variables that are likely to be developed by reading itself (e.g., we have partialed out the influence of basic reading skills when, in fact, these skills are likely developed by exposure to print). Nonetheless, the explanatory ambiguities surrounding a variable such as print exposure have led us to continue to structure the analyses in a "worst-case" manner, as far as experience with print is concerned. This allows us to ensure that in our research program we are not "overselling literacy" as previous researchers have argued about the field.

In a study of fourth-, fifth-, and sixth-grade children (Cunningham & Stanovich, 1991), we examined whether print exposure was associated with vocabulary development (and other verbal skills) even when both general and specific (i.e., vocabulary-relevant) abilities were controlled. Variables were selected for analysis in this study based on contemporary theories of reading and vocabulary development. The analyses displayed in Table 4.1 illustrate some of the outcomes of this study. Three different vocabulary measures were used as criterion variables in three separate regression models: a word checklist measure of written vocabulary modeled on the work of Anderson and Freebody (1983; see also White, Slater, & Graves, 1989), a verbal fluency measure where the children had to output as many words as they could that fit into a particular category (e.g., things that are red; see Sincoff & Sternberg, 1987), and a group-administered version of the Peabody Picture Vocabulary Test (PPVT).

Each of these criterion variables were regressed upon print exposure, as measured by the Title Recognition Test (TRT), and a collection of control variables. Recognition tests such as the TRT are a common method for collecting objective information about an individual's exposure to print. The TRT used in this project was modeled after those used in previous research but created specifically for this study. The control variables included in the model were age, scores on Raven's Progressive Matrices as a control for cognitive ability (general processing efficiency), and, as a control for language skills more closely linked to vocabulary acquisition mechanisms, phonological processing ability, as measured by a phonological coding task developed by Olson, Kliegl, Davidson, and Foltz (1985). A variable such as phonological coding skill might mediate a relationship between print expo-

TABLE 4.1. Unique Print Exposure Variance Controlling for Age, Raven Progressive Matrices, and Phonological Coding

Step/variable	R	R^2	R^2 change	F to enter
Word checklist				
1. Age	.103	.011	.011	1.41
2. Raven	.457	.209	.198	32.57**
3. Phonological coding	.610	.372	.163	33.49**
4. Print exposure	.683	.466	.094	22.52**
Verbal fluency				
1. Age	.043	.002	.002	0.24
2. Raven	.231	.053	.051	6.89**
3. Phonological coding	.477	.228	.175	28.47**
4. Print exposure	.582	.339	.111	21.02**
PPVT				
1. Age	.230	.053	.053	7.29**
2. Raven	.393	.154	.101	15.60**
3. Phonological coding	.403	.162	.008	1.21
4. Print exposure	.516	.266	.104	18.19**
Spelling				
1. Age	.179	.032	.032	4.31*
2. Raven	.414	.172	.140	21.95**
3. Phonological coding	.656	.430	.258	58.51**
4. Print exposure	.713	.509	.079	20.42**
General information				
1. Age	.224	.050	.050	6.84**
2. Raven	.362	.131	.081	12.05**
3. Phonological coding	.410	.168	.037	5.68*
4. Print exposure	.492	.242	.074	12.37**

Note. The spanner headings identify the dependent variables in the regression analyses. PPVT, Peabody Picture Vocabulary Test.
*$p < .05$; **$p < .01$.

sure and a variable such as vocabulary size in numerous ways. High levels of decoding skill—certainly a contributor to greater print exposure—might provide relatively complete verbal contexts for the induction of word meanings during reading. Decoding skill might also indirectly reflect differences in short-term phonological storage that are related to vocabulary learning, particularly in the preschool years (Gathercole & Baddeley, 1989, 1993). Thus, print exposure and vocabulary might be spuriously linked via their connection with decoding ability: Good decoders both read avidly and have the best context available for inferring new words. This spurious linkage is controlled by entering phonological coding into the regression model alongside the measure of exposure to print. If print exposure were only an incidental correlate of vocabulary because of its linkage with phonological coding skill, it would not be significantly associated with vocabulary after controlling for phonological coding skill.

The results of the first three analyses displayed in Table 4.1 indicate that, for each of the vocabulary measures, exposure to print accounted for significant variance even after the variance attributable to performance on the Raven Progressive Matrices and the phonological coding measure had been partialed out. The last two regressions indicate that this was also true for two additional criterion variables in the study: spelling ability and performance on the Information subtest of the Wechsler Intelligence Scale for Children (used as a measure of general knowledge). In other words, print exposure uniquely accounted for variance in not only vocabulary, but also spelling ability and general knowledge.

In other studies (Stanovich & Cunningham, 1992, 1993), we focused on whether content knowledge could be linked to print exposure after measures of general processing efficiency and exposure to other media sources had been partialed out, again testing theories that positioned these variables as key factors in the development of content knowledge. One study contained a particularly stringent test of the cognitive efficiency explanation of individual differences in knowledge acquisition. The subjects were 268 college students, and the strong test is displayed in Table 4.2. The criterion variable was a composite index of performance on five general knowledge measures. Four measures of general ability were used in the model as control variables: high school grade point average, performance on the Progressive Raven matrices, performance on an SAT-type mathematics test, and the score on the Nelson–Denny Reading Test.

Regressing general knowledge on this set of tasks surely exhausts any variance in knowledge attributable to general ability, and, as anticipated, general ability does indeed account for a substantial proportion of variance

TABLE 4.2. Hierarchical Regression Analyses Predicting General Knowledge Composite

Step/variable	R	R^2 change	F to enter	Final beta	Final F
1. High school GPA	.372	.139	42.82**	.020	0.32
2. Raven	.447	.061	20.30**	.016	0.20
3. Mathematics test	.542	.094	35.07**	.165	18.19**
4. N-D comprehension	.630	.103	45.11**	.112	9.87**
5. Television composite	.630	.000	0.06	−.039	1.68
6. Print composite	.876	.371	417.63**	.720	417.63**

Note. GPA, grade point average; N-D, Nelson–Denny Reading Test.
*$p < .05$; **$p < .01$.

in the general knowledge composite (multiple $R^2 = .40$). A composite measure of exposure to television was not significantly related to knowledge in this model. However, a composite index of exposure to print was uniquely and significantly associated with the knowledge composite even after controlling for all these variables (uniquely explaining 37.1% of the variance in the composite outcome variable). The results thus indicated that more avid readers in our study—independent of their general abilities (cognitive efficiency) and their television exposure—had more general knowledge.

These results are further corroborated by a longitudinal study conducted by our research group (Cipielewski & Stanovich, 1992), which indicates that exposure to print is related to growth in reading comprehension ability. The regression analyses presented in Table 4.3 display the results of this study, in which growth in reading comprehension ability was tracked by administering the comprehension tests from the Stanford Diagnostic Reading Test and the Iowa Test of Basic Skills (ITBS) to 82 fifth graders who had also taken the ITBS Comprehension subtest in the third grade (as 8- to 9-year-olds).

Fifth-grade scores on both criterion variables were regressed on third-grade reading comprehension and a measure of print exposure. Predicting fifth-grade comprehension using print exposure while controlling for third-grade achievement allows us to interpret any effect of print exposure on the criterion variable as an effect on a student's *growth* in comprehension from third to fifth grade, and thus effectively controls for anything that would equally affect third- and fifth-grade comprehension (such as, to a large extent, background variables such as general cognitive ability and socioeconomic status). In both cases, print exposure significantly predicted variance in fifth-grade reading comprehension ability (uniquely explaining 11% of the variance in the Stanford test and 7.4% of the variance in the ITBS) even after the contribution from third-grade reading comprehension scores had been partialed out. In partialing reading comprehension ability in our studies (across the age range of elementary students to adults), we are

TABLE 4.3. Hierarchical Regressions Predicting Fifth-Grade Reading Ability

Step/variable	R	R^2	R^2 change	F to enter
Fifth-grade Stanford reading comprehension				
1. Iowa comprehension (third)	.645	.416	.416	54.06**
2. Print exposure	.725	.526	.110	17.38**
Fifth-grade Iowa reading comprehension				
1. Iowa comprehension (third)	.545	.297	.297	33.78**
2. Print exposure	.609	.371	.074	9.25**

Note. The spanner headings identify the dependent variables in the regression analyses.
**$p < .01$.

undoubtedly also removing some of the variance in the criterion variable that should rightfully be attributed to print exposure. That print exposure is nonetheless still significantly predictive of reading achievement demonstrates the robustness of our overall finding.

DEVELOPING A LIFETIME READING HABIT: REVERSING THE CRITERION AND PREDICTOR IN REGRESSION ANALYSES

Given that lifelong reading habits are such strong predictors of verbal cognitive growth, what is it that, in turn, predicts these habits? So far the analyses we have described have treated exposure to print as a predictor variable of criterion abilities such as vocabulary and reading comprehension. However, it is generally agreed that comprehension ability and exposure to print are in a reciprocal relationship (Anderson, Wilson, & Fielding, 1988; Stanovich, 1986, 1993, 2000). We controlled for the fact that high comprehension ability leads to high levels of reading experience in a longitudinal study (Cunningham & Stanovich, 1997) in which we attempted to see whether a fast start in the early stages of reading acquisition predicted the tendency to read over and above the overall level of reading skill achieved.

In this study we had available extensive cognitive profiles of a group of children who had been tested as first graders in 1981 (see Stanovich, Cunningham, & Feeman, 1984). About one half of this sample was available 10 years later for testing as 11th graders. At that time, we administered a set of reading comprehension, cognitive ability, vocabulary, and general knowledge tasks as well as several measures of exposure to print. We were thus able to examine which variables in the first grade predicted these cognitive outcomes in the 11th grade.

For this analysis, we estimated a series of regression models (displayed in Table 4.4), each of them regressing exposure to print in the 11th grade on 11th-grade reading comprehension ability (Nelson–Denny performance) and one additional variable. Thus, in each case, we were able to see whether the additional variable in question uniquely predicted 11th-grade print exposure above and beyond its ultimate influence on reading ability. All three measures of first-grade reading ability (Metropolitan Achievement Test, Gates, and Wide Range Achievement Test) predicted significant variance (slightly over 10%) in 11th-grade print exposure even after 11th-grade reading comprehension ability had been partialed out!

Table 4.4 indicates that the two measures of cognitive ability administered in first grade (Raven matrices and PPVT) were not uniquely associated with 11th-grade print exposure when controlling for 11th-grade reading comprehension ability. Finally, third- and fifth-grade measures of reading ability were also associated with 11th-grade print exposure, even more so than the first-grade measures. These analyses demonstrate that an early

TABLE 4.4. Hierarchical Regression Analysis Predicting Exposure to Print in the 11th Grade

Step/variable	R	R^2 change	F to enter	Partial r
Forced entry				
1. Grade 11 N-D comprehension	.604	.364	14.34**	—
2. Grade 1 Metropolitan	.696	.121	5.61*	.435
2. Grade 1 Gates	.681	.100	4.45*	.396
2. Grade 1 WRAT	.686	.106	4.78*	.408
2. Grade 1 Raven	.632	.035	1.39	.234
2. Grade 1 PPVT	.641	.047	1.89	.270
2. Grade 3 Metropolitan	.765	.221	11.09**	.588
2. Grade 5 Metropolitan	.719	.153	6.72*	.484

Note. N-D, Nelson–Denny Reading Test; WRAT, Wide Range Achievement Test; PPVT, Peabody Picture Vocabulary Test.
*$p < .05$; **$p < .01$.

start in reading powerfully predicts long-term literacy experience, and this is true regardless of the reading comprehension level that the individual eventually attains. This is a strong finding because it indicates that, regardless of students' level of reading comprehension in the 11th grade, if they got off to a fast start in reading (as indicated by their first-grade reading ability scores), then they are more likely to engage in more reading activity as adults. Early success at reading acquisition thus could be one of the keys that unlocks a lifetime of reading habits. The subsequent exercise of this habit may serve to further develop reading comprehension ability in an interlocking positive-feedback loop (Juel, 1988; Snow, Barnes, Chandler, Goodman, & Hemphill, 1991; Snow, Burns, & Griffin, 1998; Stanovich, 1986, 1993, 2000).

AN ADDITIONAL NOTE ON THE MEASUREMENT OF VARIABLES

It was mentioned earlier that one of the underlying assumptions of regression is that all variables are measured without error. An astute reader may have noticed that this is almost surely not the case for any of the studies we have presented in this chapter! Specifically, the fact that total scores on tests of latent variables such as cognitive ability were used as variables in the regression models almost surely violates this assumption: Almost no test has a reliability coefficient of 1.00 and an utterly unassailable validity argument.

However, the astute reader will also remember that techniques such as regression are often considered robust to small violations of assumptions. It is very common in most fields (see Peterson, 2009) to estimate regression models such as those we have described in this chapter, using scores from tests as both predictor and outcome variables, and as long as these tests are considered valid and have reasonably high reliability, regression coefficients will not be significantly impacted.

Test *validity* (whether a test measures what it claims to measure; e.g., Kane, 2006) is a topic beyond the boundaries of this chapter, but it should certainly be noted that if a test is invalid as a measure of the construct researchers assume it to be measuring, study results based on that test are themselves potentially invalid. When we report, for instance, a correlation between phonological ability and any other construct, we are assuming that the test being used to represent phonological ability does a good job of capturing this variable. Because of space and focus limitations, we do not report on the extensive background work that went into the preparation and screening of the measures used in the studies we have described; however, in general, it is certainly appropriate to carefully consider whether tests and scales are truly measuring what they claim to measure before accepting the conclusions of any study.

Reliability of measurement (whether a test is consistent and not prone to random error) is also necessary for results to be interpretable. Standards vary between (and within) fields, but a reliability coefficient (estimated, for example, by Cronbach's α) of .80 or above is often considered ideal. If the reliability of a measure is much below this, coefficients from regression analyses may be dramatically attenuated (i.e., made artificially lower). Various methods for disattenuation exist, one of which is structural equation modeling; however, low reliability can also be a sign of low validity, for which there is no statistical correction. Thus, again, ensuring the high quality of measures used in any study is crucial for results to be meaningful and interpretable.

SUMMARY

This chapter represents a selection of our work on the cognitive correlates of exposure to print. In this sampling, we have tried to illustrate how the logic of multiple regression can be used to pare down the number of alternative hypotheses available when a link is found between two variables, such as reading experience and a cognitive outcome variable. For example, in the studies we have reviewed, we have demonstrated that a strong version of the cognitive efficiency account of knowledge acquisition and vocabulary growth is falsified. Variance in print exposure explained a sizable portion of the variance in measures of vocabulary and general knowledge even after variance associated with general cognitive ability was partialed out. Subsequent to the publication of our studies initiating this research, additional researchers have employed similar methodological and statistical techniques to examine the relationship between print exposure and a variety of cognitive outcomes. Convergent with the results described in this chapter, other researchers found print exposure to have unique explanatory power in understanding a variety of individual differences including the oral vocabulary of pre-readers (Frijters, Barron, & Brunello, 2000), the orthographic and morphological learning in adults (Burt, 2006), syllogistic reasoning abilities in adults (Osana, Lacroix, Tucker, Idan, & Jabbour, 2007), and in the vocabulary, reading comprehension, and reading rates of undergraduate students (Martin-Chang & Gould, 2008).

Thus, at least in certain domains, and at least as measured here, individual differences in declarative knowledge bases as well as general problem-solving and reasoning abilities—differences emphasized by many contemporary theories of developmental growth—appear to some extent to be experientially based (Siddiqui, West, & Stanovich, 1998). This does not mean that there might not be some other third variable operating that we have not measured. It does mean, however, that the third variables favored by the cognitive efficiency theorists have been eliminated. Alternative theories with different unmeasured third variables will have to be posited to explain the association between print exposure and cognitive outcomes if the relationship is to be deemed not causal. As the number of such alternative explanations decreases, they become, almost of necessity, less plausible. In many research areas, at some point the alternative explanations become less plausible than the assumption that the original association reflects a causal relationship. In this way, a series of nonexperimental studies using multiple regression (and associated techniques) such as those described here can begin, ever so tentatively, to lead us to a provisional causal inference.

We have illustrated this progression toward a tentative causal inference in this chapter. Researchers and practitioners in the educational community are nearly unanimous in recommending that children be encouraged to spend more time engaged in literacy activities outside school (e.g., Adams, 1990; Anderson, Hiebert, Scott, & Wilkinson, 1985; Cunningham & Stanovich, 2003; Manning & Manning, 1989; Morrow, 2003). From a cultural standpoint, this recommendation is virtually unassailable. What has been less clear, however, is the empirical status of the tacit model of skill acquisition that often underlies the recommendation to increase children's free reading. The tacit model is basically one of accelerating skill development via practice. It is thought that more exposure to print via home reading will lead to further growth in reading comprehension and related cognitive skills. As plausible as this tacit model sounds, until quite recently there was actually very little evidence to support it. Most of the available evidence consisted of simple correlations—for example, research demonstrating that avid readers tend to be good comprehenders (see Guthrie & Greaney, 1996, for a review)—and did not contain any statistical controls of possible third variables. These simple correlations were ambiguous because they were open to the interpretation that better readers simply choose to read more, an interpretation at odds with the tacit model of skill development via practice that underlies efforts to increase children's free reading.

The pattern of regression results in our studies suggests that print exposure does appear to be both a consequence of developed reading ability and a contributor to further growth in that ability and in other verbal skills; thus, these studies bolster the emphasis on reading experience that currently prevails in the reading education community. The results also strengthen the case for advocating a more prominent role for reading activity in general theories of cognitive development (Booth & Hall, 1994; Guthrie, Schafer, & Hutchinson, 1991; Olson, 1994; Stanovich, 1986, 1993, 2000).

There are, in fact, several possible mechanisms by which print exposure could become a mechanism for the growth and preservation of crystallized knowledge. Reading is a very special type of interface with the environment, providing an individual with unique opportunities to acquire declarative knowledge. The world's storehouse of knowledge is readily available for those who read, and much of this information is not usually obtained from other sources. Personal experience provides only narrow knowledge of the world and is often misleadingly unrepresentative. The most commonly used electronic sources of information (television, Internet) lack depth. For example, most theorists agree that a substantial proportion of vocabulary growth during childhood and adulthood occurs indirectly through language exposure (Hart & Risley, 1995; Miller & Gildea, 1987; Nagy & Anderson, 1984; Nagy, Herman, & Anderson, 1985). Obviously, the only opportunities to acquire new words occur when an individual is exposed to a word in written or oral language that is outside the current vocabulary. Work by Hayes (1988; Hayes & Ahrens, 1988; see also Akinnaso, 1982; Biber, 1986; Chafe & Danielewicz, 1987; Corson, 1995) has indicated that moderate- to low-frequency words—precisely those words that differentiate individuals with large and small vocabulary sizes—appear much more often in common reading matter than in common speech.

These relative differences in the statistical distributions of words in print and in oral language have direct implications for vocabulary development. They represent the type of theoretical foundation that, when integrated with evidence that rules out some alternative third variables, can begin to lead a behavioral scientist in the direction of positing a causal hypothesis. Experiments have strong resolving power and correlational studies have weak resolving power when it comes to positing causal paths. However, the weak resolving power of correlational studies can be combined with theory in ways that (much more slowly than true experiments, of course) lead us to some inferences that are at least stronger than those obtainable from simple bivariate correlations. Thus, correlational designs can be viewed as more complex and rich than our beginning students in the social sciences initially conceived them and can provide a relatively powerful alternative for educational and psychological research.

ACKNOWLEDGMENTS

Research discussed in this chapter was supported by grants to Anne Cunningham from the U.S. Department of Education, Institute of Education Sciences (Grant No. R305M05037) and the National Science Foundation (Grant No. 0114854), and to Keith Stanovich from the Social Sciences and Humanities Research Council of Canada and the Canada Research Chairs Program.

REFERENCES

Adams, M. J. (1990). *Beginning to read: Thinking and learning about print.* Cambridge, MA: MIT Press.

Akinnaso, F. N. (1982). On the difference between spoken and written language. *Language and Speech, 25,* 97–125.

Anderson, R. C., & Freebody, P. (1983). Reading comprehension and the assessment and acquisition of word knowledge. In B. Huston (Ed.), *Advances in reading/language research* (Vol. 2, pp. 231–256). Greenwich, CT: JAI Press.

Anderson, R. C., Hiebert, E. H., Scott, J. A., & Wilkinson, I. (1985). *Becoming a nation of readers.* Washington, DC: National Institute of Education.

Anderson, R. C., Wilson, P. T., & Fielding, L. G. (1988). Growth in reading and how children spend their time outside of school. *Reading Research Quarterly, 23,* 285–303.

Biber, D. (1986). Spoken and written textual dimensions in English: Resolving the contradictory findings. *Language, 62,* 384–414.

Booth, J. R., & Hall, W. S. (1994). Role of the cognitive internal state lexicon in reading comprehension. *Journal of Educational Psychology, 86,* 413–422.

Burt, J. (2006). Spelling in adults: The combined influences of language skills and reading experience. *Journal of Psycholinguist Research, 37,* 447–470.

Ceci, S. J. (1996). *On intelligence: A bioecological treatise on intellectual development* (expanded ed.). Cambridge, MA: Harvard University Press.

Chafe, W., & Danielewicz, J. (1987). Properties of spoken and written language. In R. Horowitz & S. J. Samuels (Eds.), *Comprehending oral and written language* (pp. 83–113). San Diego, CA: Academic Press.

Cipielewski, J., & Stanovich, K. E. (1992). Predicting growth in reading ability from children's exposure to print. *Journal of Experimental Child Psychology, 54,* 74–89.

Corson, D. (1995). *Using English words.* Boston: Kluwer Academic.

Cunningham, A. E., & Stanovich, K. E. (1991). Tracking the unique effects of print exposure in children: Associations with vocabulary, general knowledge, and spelling. *Journal of Educational Psychology, 83,* 264–274.

Cunningham, A. E., & Stanovich, K. E. (1997). Early reading acquisition and its relation to reading experience and ability ten years later. *Developmental Psychology, 33,* 934–945.

Cunningham, A. E., & Stanovich, K. E. (2003). Reading matters: How reading engagement influences cognition. In J. Flood, D. Lapp, J. Squire, & J. Jensen (Eds.), *Handbook of research on teaching the English language arts* (Vol. 2, pp. 857–867). Mahwah, NJ: Erlbaum.

Frijters, J. C., Barron, R. W., & Brunello, M. (2000). Direct and mediated influences of home literacy and literacy interest on prereaders' oral vocabulary and early written language skill. *Journal of Educational Psychology, 92*(3), 466–477.

Fuller, B., Edwards, J., & Gorman, K. (1987). Does rising literacy spark economic growth?: Commercial expansion in Mexico. In D. A. Wagner (Ed.), *The future of literacy in a changing world* (pp. 319–340). Oxford, UK: Pergamon.

Gathercole, S. E., & Baddeley, A. D. (1989). Evaluation of the role of phonological STM in the development of vocabulary in children: A longitudinal study. *Journal of Memory and Language, 28*, 200–213.

Gathercole, S. E., & Baddeley, A. D. (1993). *Working memory and language.* Hove, UK: Erlbaum.

Gee, J. P. (1988). The legacies of literacy: From Plato to Freire through Harvey Graff. *Harvard Educational Review, 58*, 195–212.

Graff, H. J. (1986). The legacies of literacy: Continuities and contradictions in western society and culture. In S. de Castell, A. Luke, & K. Egan (Eds.), *Literacy, society, and schooling* (pp. 61–86). Cambridge, UK: Cambridge University Press.

Guthrie, J. T., & Greaney, V. (1996). Literacy acts. In R. Barr, M. L. Kamil, P. B. Mosenthal, & P. D. Pearson (Eds.), *Handbook of reading research: Volume II* (pp. 68–96). New York: Routledge.

Guthrie, J. T., Schafer, W. D., & Hutchinson, S. R. (1991). Relations of document literacy and prose literacy to occupational and societal characteristics of young black and white adults. *Reading Research Quarterly, 26*, 30–48.

Hall, W. S., Nagy, W. E., & Linn, R. (1984). *Spoken words: Effects of situation and social group on oral word usage and frequency.* Hillsdale, NJ: Erlbaum.

Hart, B., & Risley, T. R. (1995). *Meaningful differences in the everyday experiences of young American children.* Baltimore: Brookes.

Hayes, D. P. (1988). Speaking and writing: Distinct patterns of word choice. *Journal of Memory and Language, 27*, 572–585.

Hayes, D. P., & Ahrens, M. (1988). Vocabulary simplification for children: A special case of "motherese"? *Journal of Child Language, 15*, 395–410.

Jensen, A. (1980). *Bias in mental testing.* New York: Free Press.

Juel, C. (1988). Learning to read and write: A longitudinal study of 54 children from first through fourth grades. *Journal of Educational Psychology, 80*, 437–447.

Kane, M. T. (2006). Validation. In R. L. Brennan (Ed.), *Educational measurement* (4th ed., pp. 17–64). Santa Barbara, CA: Greenwood.

Manning, G., & Manning, M. (Eds.). (1989). *Whole language: Beliefs and practices, K–8.* Washington, DC: National Education Association.

Martin-Chang, S. L., & Gould, O. N. (2008). Revisiting print exposure: Exploring differential links to vocabulary, comprehension and reading rate. *Journal of Reading Research, 31*(3), 273–284.

Mercy, J., & Steelman, L. (1982). Familial influence on the intellectual attainment of children. *American Sociological Review, 47*, 532–542.

Miller, G. A., & Gildea, P. M. (1987). How children learn words. *Scientific American, 257*(3), 94–99.

Morrow, L. M. (2003). Motivating lifelong voluntary readers. In J. Flood, D. Lapp, J. Squire, & J. Jensen (Eds.), *Handbook of research on teaching the English language arts* (Vol. 2, pp. 857–867), Mahwah, NJ: Erlbaum.

Nagy, W. E., & Anderson, R. C. (1984). How many words are there in printed school English? *Reading Research Quarterly, 19,* 304–330.

Nagy, W. E., Herman, P. A., & Anderson, R. C. (1985). Learning words from context. *Reading Research Quarterly, 20,* 233–253.

Olson, D. R. (1994). *The world on paper.* Cambridge, UK: Cambridge University Press.

Olson, R., Kliegl, R., Davidson, B., & Foltz, G. (1985). Individual and developmental differences in reading disability. In G. E. MacKinnon & T. Waller (Eds.), *Reading research: Advances in theory and practice* (Vol. 4, pp. 1–64). London: Academic Press.

Osana, H. P., Lacroix, G. L., Tucker, B. J., Idan, E., & Jabbour, G. W. (2007). The impact of print exposure quality and inference construction on syllogistic reasoning. *Journal of Educational Psychology, 99*(4), 888–902.

Peterson, C. (2009). Minimally sufficient research. *Perspectives on Psychological Science, 4,* 7–9.

Schneider, B., Carnoy, M., Kilpatrick, J., Schmidt, W. H., & Shavelson, R. J. (2007). *Estimating causal effects using experimental and observational designs.* Washington, DC: American Educational Research Association.

Siddiqui, S., West, R. F., & Stanovich, K. E. (1998). The influence of print exposure on syllogistic reasoning and knowledge of mental-state verbs. *Scientific Studies of Reading, 2,* 81–96.

Sincoff, J. B., & Sternberg, R. J. (1987). Two faces of verbal ability. *Intelligence, 11,* 263–276.

Snow, C. E., Barnes, W., Chandler, J., Goodman, L., & Hemphill, L. (1991). *Unfulfilled expectations: Home and school influences on literacy.* Cambridge, MA: Harvard University Press.

Snow, C. E., Burns, M. S., & Griffin, P. (Eds.). (1998). *Preventing reading difficulties in young children.* Washington, DC: National Academy Press.

Stanovich, K. E. (1986). Matthew effects in reading: Some consequences of individual differences in the acquisition of literacy. *Reading Research Quarterly, 21,* 360–407.

Stanovich, K. E. (1993). Does reading make you smarter? Literacy and the development of verbal intelligence. In H. Reese (Ed.), *Advances in child development and behavior* (Vol. 24, pp. 133–180). San Diego, CA: Academic Press.

Stanovich, K. E. (2000). *Progress in understanding reading: Scientific foundations and new frontiers.* New York: Guilford Press.

Stanovich, K. E., & Cunningham, A. E. (1992). Studying the consequences of literacy within a literate society: The cognitive correlates of print exposure. *Memory and Cognition, 20,* 51–68.

Stanovich, K. E., & Cunningham, A. E. (1993). Where does knowledge come from?: Specific associations between print exposure and information acquisition. *Journal of Educational Psychology, 85,* 211–229.

Stanovich, K. E., Cunningham, A. E., & Feeman, D. J. (1984). Intelligence, cognitive skills, and early reading progress. *Reading Research Quarterly, 19,* 278–303.

Sternberg, R. J. (1985). *Beyond IQ: A triarchic theory of human intelligence.* Cambridge, UK: Cambridge University Press.

Wagner, D. A. (1987). Literacy futures: Five common problems from industrializing and developing countries. In D. A. Wagner (Ed.), *The future of literacy in a changing world* (pp. 3–16). Oxford, UK: Pergamon.

Wells, G. (1986). *The meaning makers.* Portsmouth, NH: Heinemann.

White, T. G., Slater, W. H., & Graves, M. F. (1989). Yes/no method of vocabulary assessment: Valid for whom and useful for what? In S. McCormick & J. Zutell (Eds.), *Cognitive and social perspectives for literacy research and instruction: 38th Yearbook of the National Reading Conference* (pp. 391–397). Chicago: National Reading Conference.

CHAPTER 5

Research Methods Unique to Digital Contexts

AN INTRODUCTION TO VIRTUAL ETHNOGRAPHY

Christine M. Greenhow

INTERNET TRENDS SHAPING LITERACIES, LITERACY RESEARCH METHODS, AND CONCEPTIONS OF SCHOLARSHIP

The average young American (ages 8–18) now spends practically every waking minute—except for the time in school—using a smartphone, computer, or other electronic devices. . . . Young people spend more than 7.5 hours per day with media.
　　　　　　　　　　　　　　　　　　　　—LEWIN (2010)

We live in an age where online social networking is the dominant out-of-school, leisure time computer-using activity among young Americans (Rideout, Foehr, & Roberts, 2010). The proliferation of the Internet and its emerging forms of social media are shaping how people learn, work, play, communicate, share information, and spend their time and money. Human desires and changing practices, in turn, are shaping the cultural, social, and technological landscape. Indeed, the 21st century is witnessing a *renaissance*, where young people especially are creating more, sharing more, and advocating and communicating more in their online everyday lives (Bull et al., 2008); they are pooling their time, effort, and knowledge into the publishing of potentially beneficial and revolutionary online resources (e.g., Wikipedia), with tremendous consequences for education and literacy education (Greenhow, 2008, in press).

　　Not surprisingly, sectors outside education are considering how to harness this *cognitive surplus* (Shirky, 2008) to advantage on national and global scales. Businesses are tapping their employees' "social connections, institutional memories and special skills—knowledge that large, geographically dispersed companies often have a difficult time obtaining," using social networking software to connect employees into a single private Web forum (Gratton, 2007; Stone, 2008, p. C2). News media are increasingly incorporating viewer participation in the form of online comments and testimonials, independently produced videos, and citizen-journalist blog entries to enhance the truth and spread of centrally produced stories such as CNN's documentary *Black in America* (Nelson, 2008). And, of course, evident in the 2008 presidential election campaign was a new style of "Netroots" politics: "open-sourced and inclusive, multi-racial and multi-cultural" where potential voters didn't just consume campaign propaganda but helped to write and disseminate it via online meet-ups, blogs, videos, and social networks (Sheehy, 2008, p. 79).

The convergence of economic, social, and technological trends, as these examples suggest, warrants a re-envisioning of both the goals and the means of production. In literacy education, this will require substantial inquiry and understanding of how new technological affordances and students' uses and needs reshape traditional literacy education agendas, pedagogies, and the content that gets taught. This reimagining is already underway within organizations such as the National Council of Teachers of English (NCTE) and International Reading Association (IRA). These organizations have observed that "new global employees engage with a technology-driven, diverse, and quickly changing 'flat world'" to question traditional learning objectives and consider new desired competencies (IRA, 2009; National Center on Education and the Economy, 2006; NCTE, 2008). They have noted among students a decline in reading novels for pleasure and an increase in out-of-school online reading and writing through fan fiction (e.g., *www.fanfiction.net*) and social network sites (National Endowment for the Arts, 2007). They are tackling questions that open up conceptualizations of "literacy" and possibilities for research. For example, what does it mean to *read* in the digital age? To what extent does online reading build on traditional reading skills? What new reading skills are required for navigating the Web and synthesizing information that comes in many different forms? (See NCTE, 2007; Rich, 2008.)

Changing Conception of "Literacies"

Situated in this context, contemporary scholars working under the umbrellas of either New Literacy Studies (e.g., Gee, 1996; Heath, 1983) or New Literacies (e.g., Coiro, Knobel, Lankshear, & Leu, 2008; Lankshear & Knobel, 2006) espouse definitions of literacy that extend traditional notions of print-based reading and writing to involve people in potentially novel ways of producing, distributing, and responding to texts; these "new literacy practices" or "new literacies" are seen as synergistic with digital technologies, the blends of semiotic resources with which they are associated, and the methodologies with which these are studied:

> New technologies such as blogs, wikis, massively multiplayer online games, social networking technologies and video- and music-dissemination technologies have rapidly spread, by means of the Internet, each with additional, new literacy forms and functions that are reshaped by social practices . . . literacy has now come to mean a rapid and continuous process of change in ways in which we read, write, view, listen, compose, and communicate information. (Coiro et al., 2008, p. 5)

Four important elements characterize the conceptualization of new literacies and, therefore, are important to conceptualizing research methods in digital contexts: (1) New literacies necessarily include new skills, strategies, dispositions, and social practices required by the Internet and new information and communication technologies; (2) the development of new literacies is viewed as essential to full civic, economic, and personal participation in a world community; (3) new literacies are dynamic and situationally specific; and (4) new literacies are multiple and multimodal and are best investigated from multidisciplinary perspectives (Coiro et al., 2008).

Thus, literacies change because the technologies available are constantly changing. Within changing contexts, meanings are negotiated, shifting from space to space, person to person, moment to moment. The emphasis is on understanding the situated nature of literacy practices and how membership in a particular social group is signaled (through words, actions, values, and beliefs) (Gee, 1996). The writer of multimodal texts is, in essence, a designer "assembling according to one's designs" (Kress, 2003, p. 6), which allows meaning to be distributed across different modes; multimodal texts can also be interactive, with users able to "write back," further blurring the lines between authorship, readership, and production and consumption and requiring new skills, sensibilities, social practices, and roles for researchers.

Changing Conceptions of Literacy Research and Scholarship

What constitutes literacy research methodologies where data are continuously updating and can be collected around the clock, across the globe, and without the costs (time, transcription errors) associated with more traditional methods of research? As literacy researchers, we need new competencies for conducting research in collaborative digital contexts; in developing these, we may find ourselves shifting not only in our notions of "literacy" and "method" but also in our fundamental ideas of scholarship and sense of our own identities. For instance, *social scholarship*, a practice being debated within library sciences, education, communications, and other disciplines (Cohen, 2007; Taraborelli, 2008), applies Web 2.0 capabilities to change the ways in which academic writing is accomplished within social networks. It connects traditional, formal scholarship practices such as writing a research article with more informal, social Web-based practices, such as posting unfinished writing in an online collaborative space and inviting readers to comment or even contribute (e.g., see *schoolcomputing.wikia. com/wiki/Why_We_Like_Diigo*). Using social media tools such as CiteU-Like, Delicious, Diigo, and others, researchers can compile, annotate, recommend, and share resources (e.g., websites, journal articles, books, and contacts) and usher in new scholarly reading and writing practices.

These prior examples suggest that as literacies evolve across a dynamic sociotechnical landscape, our scholarly practices and corresponding methods for literacy research also need to evolve in order to adequately capture, describe, and interpret (Greenhow, 2009; Greenhow, Robelia, & Hughes, 2009). What kinds of methods are needed? How are these unique to digital contexts? In this chapter, I focus on *virtual ethnography* as an evolving method uniquely suited to emerging and experienced scholars interested in researching and cultivating new literacies in digital contexts. The sections that follow define virtual ethnography, locating it within prominent definitions of ethnography and the discourse surrounding the Internet's impact on identity, society, and culture that "bring into sharp relief assumed and invisible epistemologies and practices of inquiry" (Baym & Markham, 2009, p. vii). Next, I discuss questions and claims particularly suited to the application of virtual ethnographic methods in literacy research before turning to a discussion of methodological quality and rigor. The chapter concludes with examples of virtual ethnography for new and seasoned researchers seeking to adapt and apply this approach.

AN INTRODUCTION TO VIRTUAL ETHNOGRAPHY

Understanding the boringness and routineness of everyday Internet research is captivating and important work. One of the reasons for its importance is that research into digital literacies will, one hopes, yield richer understandings of nondigital literacies as well. One of our current limitations in achieving this kind of cross-fertilization of theory building is to confront . . . some of the haunting dichotomies: computer-mediated versus face-to-face, online versus offline, virtual versus real, and in the new literacy studies, in school versus out of school. How do we work toward building knowledge that might take Internet practice out of the exotic and assert their everydayness and their qualities of the *quotidian*?
—LEANDER (2008, p. 33)

If beginning ethnographers, writing in the late 19th and early 20th centuries and sprung from Western traditions, were drawn to exploring the "exotic otherness" of non-Western societies, today studying the "boringness" of one's own culture, and of oneself as part of that culture, especially in the presence of rapid technological change, is necessary, important, and, it is hoped, captivating work for literacy researchers (Patton, 2002, p. 84).

Virtual ethnography provides a particularly powerful tool in this regard. To introduce it, I first briefly review basic tenets of ethnography. Victoria Purcell-Gates's definition of *ethnography* in this volume (see Chapter 8) is especially useful:

> Literacy researchers who operate out of a theoretical frame that views literacy as cultural practice are particularly drawn to *ethnography* as a methodological tool . . . ethnography is grounded in theories of culture and allows researchers to view literacy development, instruction, learning, and practice as they occur naturally in sociocultural contexts . . . to explore and come to understand phenomena about which little is known . . . ethnographic consumers can . . . use [these ethnographic findings] to enhance their own understandings of similar actors and contexts. (p. 135)

Similarly, Patton (2002) defines ethnography as the study of *culture*, or the collective set of patterns and beliefs that constitute standards for decision making and action. As cited in Purcell-Gates (2004), LeCompte and Schensul (1999) assert, "Ethnography generates or builds theories of culture—or explanations of how people think, believe, and behave—that are situated in local time and space" (p. 8). Thus, appropriate questions for ethnographic research are: What is the culture of this group? What is happening, why, how, and what does it look like? What does this mean to the different actors who make up the situation? What are the layers of context surrounding this phenomenon? How does my own experience of this culture connect with or offer insights (Anderson-Levitt, 2006; Patton, 2002; Purcell-Gates, 2004)?

Traditionally, ethnographers have used methods of *participant observation*, which typically entails intensive fieldwork in which the investigator is immersed in the culture under study (Patton, 2002; Purcell-Gates, 2004, Chapter 8, this volume); however, there is considerable variation in how this is interpreted and carried out in practice (Atkinson & Hammersley, 1994), and notions of "participation" and "field" have been problematized with the emergence of the Internet and digital contexts for research. For instance, how much the researcher is known by those studied (e.g., by all, only some, or no subjects in the case of a "lurker") and how much the researcher participates and adopts the orientation of insider or outsider will vary considerably.

Thus, arising from the ethnographic tradition, virtual ethnography, or cyber-ethnography, is an interpretive method for studying the dynamic culture of online communities or virtual worlds (Hine, 2000; Ruhleder, 2000). Its relevance for the field of literacy research can be traced to its roots in the 1990s, with the increasing mainstream adoption of the Internet; researchers within computer-mediated communication, science, and technology circles and other fields sought to understand the internet as a tool, as a place where one could shape relationships, identities, and so on apart from the material world, and eventually as a way of being (Jones, 1995, 1997; Markham, 1998). Working from a variety of disciplinary traditions, virtual ethnographers have examined human relationships in cyberspace (Carter, 2005), social relations (Hine, 2000), and identity (Thomas, 2007; Turkle, 1995). For a more complete historical overview, see Christine Hine's *Virtual Ethnography* (2000), which presents the schools of thought and issues that are foundational to the development of this method.

Moreover, virtual ethnography, like ethnography generally, relies on mixed methods approaches (see Onwuegbuzie & Mallette, Chapter 14, this volume). It may combine more commonly known qualitative procedures for studying literacy, such as interviews, observations, think-alouds, focus groups, and document analysis, with qualitative and quantitative procedures appropriate to studying subjects within online contexts. For example, procedures important for documenting and capturing communication, online reading comprehension, and interactions within digital contexts include screenshot captures, monitoring of screen moves, eye tracking, recording of Internet usage statistics (e.g., Facebook or Google analytics), online interviews, online focus groups, archived transcripts of online speech, and social network analysis. These may all be used by literacy researchers applying virtual ethnography to explore World of Warcraft (Steinkuehler, 2006) or Schome Park (Gillen, 2009) or Facebook (Greenhow & Robelia, 2009a, 2009b) as both sites of literacy practices and new literacies themselves.

That said, Leander's quotation introducing this section of the chapter is cautionary; the "dichotomies" between computer mediated and face to face, real and virtual, online and offline, and in school and out of school are categorical conveniences at best and harmful limitations to research at worst. The characteristics that distinguish ethnographies from other methodologies (e.g., ethnography is carried out in naturalistic settings rather than a laboratory, involves intimate face-to-face interactions with participants, presents an accurate reflection of participants' perspectives and behaviors, and uses inductive, interactive, and recursive data-collection and analytic strategies to build local and cultural theories) (LeCompte & Schensul, 1999, p. 9) must necessarily be renegotiated in conducting the virtual literacy ethnography (Gillen, 2009). For instance, bounding the research context to the online community despatializes notions of community, focusing on cultural processes rather than physical space; however, this can also unduly minimize connections with offline life when, in fact, our everyday literacies integrate online–offline seamlessly. Taking a connective approach to virtual ethnography (Hine, 2000; Leander, 2008) allows one to conceptualize the space for research as "the space of flows" (e.g., flows of people, information) organized around connection rather than location. This is important because it enables meaningful exploration of the online–offline (e.g., What does the traversal of space [or not] mean to the participants, and what does it accomplish?) rather than assuming a priori the online–offline boundary. Similarly, applied to the study of literacy, the connective approach to virtual ethnography is important because it "works the tension" between treating digital literacy practices as fascinating, worthy of study, and unique and, on the other hand, "as flowing within and interconnected to streams of other literacy practices, material culture, traditional media, movements of people, identity practices, and social construction of technologies" (Leander, 2008, p. 34). Virtual ethnographic methods attend to the layers of context and their interrelationships surrounding literacy practices (see Purcell-Gates, Chapter 8, this volume).

QUESTIONS PARTICULARLY SUITED TO VIRTUAL ETHNOGRAPHY

"Ethnographic" characterises a certain commonality of interest in capturing the manifold dimensions of (new) literacy practices . . . for those who practise virtual ethnography with particular attention to literacy practices . . . there is an opening then to . . . applying diverse interpretive methods and reflexive understandings to the meaning-making practices of a virtual community, particularly attending to the practices of authoring and reading written, multi-modal texts.
—GILLEN (2009, pp. 66–67)

Virtual ethnography is a methodology particularly well suited to researching literacy—as tool, place, and way of being (Steinkuehler, Black, & Clinton, 2005). With the rapid pace of social, economic, and technological change, literacy and being literate are in a constant state of flux. Virtual ethnography offers a framework for systematic inquiry into literacy phenomena that are continuously changing or about which little is known. By no means exhaustive, some questions appropriate for literacy research applying virtual ethnographic methods are as follows:

- What literacy practices (e.g., forms and functions) are happening here, why, how, and what are their essential characteristics?
- How do people understand or make sense of their experiences? What role or significance do these practices play in their lives?
- What roles do different languages, script systems, images, music, or other forms of communication play?
- How do language and modes of participation develop over time?
- How are digital literacy practices used to perform identity and social networks?
- Are online literacy practices experienced as different from offline/school-based/etc., and if so, how?
- How does my own experience of this connect with or offer insights?

Virtual ethnography is a promising approach to studying (new) literacies in everyday life. It acknowledges and seeks to delineate complex literacy phenomena in digital contexts and beyond. Moreover, it can serve as a useful precursor to more focused inquiry and to other methodologies such as formative and design experiments (Reinking & Bradley, 2004).

ISSUES AND STANDARDS FOR QUALITY IN VIRTUAL ETHNOGRAPHY

Numerous scholars have debated the topic of quality in educational research. For instance, Freeman, deMarrais, Preissle, Roulston, and St. Pierre (2007), writing in *Educational Researcher*, argued for steps to ensuring quality of evidence in qualitative research; they called for more thorough description of research designs and methods, including greater transparency in how researchers access and enter the research setting and in how they select, collect, and analyze data. In writing up results, researchers should adequately demonstrate the relationship between claims and data and render a thoughtful consideration, or balancing, of the relative strengths and limitations of their methodological decisions and interpretations. Novice literacy scholars especially will benefit from reviewing these and similar guidelines for ensuring quality in the research process.

Beyond these general guidelines, Purcell-Gates (2004, Chapter 8, this volume) articulates well the competencies needed for conducting ethnographic research. These include the ability to shape theory; sharp observational skills; the ability to understand the perspective of others, to write engagingly and vividly, and to think generatively and analytically; and strict adherence to rules for rigorous data collection, data management, and data analysis.

Principles of Virtual Ethnography

Considering the conduct of virtual ethnography, Hine (2000) presented six principles that are useful for conceptualizing this method and adapting it to one's research goals in ways that are reflexive and rigorous.

- Virtual ethnography is used to render the use of the Internet, and its new technologies, as problematic: the status of these technologies as literacy forms and functions, as ways of communicating, as sites of literacy practices, is determined (rather than predefined) by the ways in which they are used, interpreted, and reinterpreted.
- Interactive media such as the Internet can be understood as both culture and cultural artifact. Privileging one or the other perspective leads to an impoverished view.

- The concept of the field site is questioned. Concentrate on flow and connectivity rather than location and boundary as an organizing principle for inquiry.
- Boundaries are not assumed a priori but rather interrogated through the course of study.
- Immersion in the setting is only partially achieved. Engagement with mediated contexts fits in with other interactions and activities of both the ethnographer and the subjects.
- Technology enables relationships, including researcher–subject relationships, to be intermittent or sustained across temporal and spatial divides. All forms of interaction, not just face to face, are ethnographically valid. Thus, the intimate, face-to-face interaction with participants often assumed in ethnographic research is problematized, indeed often not possible in virtual ethnography.

Applying virtual ethnography successfully is labor intensive. To do it well requires inductive, interactive, and recursive data collection and analysis. Understanding of language and literacy in situ warrants the researcher's role as participant-observer, but this can mean that the researcher is contributing to the construction of text and literacy practices "in the field." Performing rigorous virtual ethnography requires constant reflection and sensitivity to one's role in the culture under study and in the construction of cultural artifacts.

Methodological and Ethical Issues in Internet Research

I now briefly highlight some of the issues in conducting virtual ethnography, as a form of Internet research, that are worth considering at the outset. (For a more complete discussion, see Baym & Markham, 2009.) Indeed, the Internet and the rise of social media to mainstream prominence (2003–present) has helped bring about four major transformations that affect the choice of research foci, engagement with research fields, and design and conduct of qualitative inquiry: "(1) media convergence, (2) mediated identities, (3) redefinitions of social boundaries, and (4) the transcendence of geographical boundaries" (Baym & Markham, 2009, p. x).

These trends make virtual ethnography an especially apt and important tool for the literacy researcher's tool kit but also raise implementation issues. First, media convergence, evident in the collision of face-to-face conversation, telephones, radio, television, and film into single, handheld mobile devices, challenges traditional distinctions between reading and writing, speaking and listening, and digital and nondigital communication that have partially ordered the focus and site of literacy research. Second, the mediation of identities, distributed and produced through multiple media, makes understanding one's subjects—their perspectives and self-expressions—an increasingly complex task. "When conceptualizing, defining, protecting, interviewing, or observing the subject of inquiry, tradition dictates that the research participants have demographically verifiable characteristics" (Baym & Markham, 2009, p. x). Discerning the truth or reliability of subjects is problematic in studying online–offline communities where identity construction and playing with identity are central features. Third, the shifting nature of public and private, highlighted by newer Web technologies and social media, challenges the researcher's ability to formulate clear boundaries for the research field, engagement "in the field," and ability to obtain informed consent. For instance, in online social network sites, it may be impossible to obtain informed consent from all the individuals who are writing, reading, chatting online, and invited into the site, impacting the dynamic content under study. Fourth, in today's digitally mediated world, people can communicate and interact presumably anytime anywhere without necessarily occupying the same geographical and/or temporal space. Researchers cannot always simply bind the study to a physically grounded site or, in the case of literacy research, to face-to-face conversation or the printed page. Limiting the study of literacies to digital contexts and the study of "place" fails to represent adequately its "cultural complexity" (Hine, Kendall, & Boyd, 2009, p. 10).

Just as the Internet can be understood as both a way of conducting social interactions (culture) and a product of those interactions (cultural artifact) (Hine 2000), so too can virtual ethnography be viewed as both a method and a product. When considering rigor in virtual ethnography, therefore, consider how credible and transferable the researcher's presentation of the ethnography seems as well as its apparent utility for an audience, such as the participants in the online community being researched, others interested in the phenomena, and researchers adapting the methods (Hine, 2000). As mentioned, one can judge the credibility of a virtual ethnographic work by looking at how well (or not) the researcher has described the details of the ethnographic process, maintained a critical stance on his or her own work, and returned to the field for feedback and analysis. For instance, has the researcher sufficiently described how access and entry into the field of study was negotiated, including a critical examination of his or her role as participant/observer online and offline? Has the researcher demonstrated critical thinking in the formulation of boundaries for the research field and engagement in the field, resisting simple dichotomies and predefined limits? Was the field of study and relevant background context (e.g., history, culture, technical architecture) sufficiently described so that readers can situate themselves within it? This scene setting will often involve visual images of the online community and possibly hyperlinks, embedded videos, or other multimedia with which readers can interact if the ethnography is published online. One can judge how well the virtual ethnography transfers to or seems similar enough to other cases to illuminate them by examining how clearly the methods of data collection, data management, and analyses were described and interrogated. For instance, did the researcher not only describe his or her data collection and analysis procedures but also demonstrate a healthy skepticism toward methodological decisions, underlying assumptions, and interpretations? Was the digital context sufficiently and effectively mined for data and, where multiple forms of online data are available and continuously updating, how well did the researcher justify the choice of data sources? Did the researcher return results to the field of study, such as an online community, and describe how emerging ideas were tested and alternatives explored? Does the virtual ethnography appear to be an authentic account, and does it present insights that seem useful to those studied and to the world at large? By no means exhaustive, and not always applicable (e.g., returning results to an online community composed of young children would likely be inappropriate), these are just some of the marks of quality in virtual ethnography.

EXEMPLARS OF VIRTUAL ETHNOGRAPHY

Examples of virtual ethnography in literacy studies are gaining in popularity. A persistent theme in this chapter, however, is to resist oversimplified demarcations and superficial boundaries in favor of a more open and integrative approach. Literacy researchers who seek to use ethnographic methods will gain from recognizing and collaborating with relevant research and theory occurring outside of language and literacy departments in the fields of communication (Holloway & Valentine, 2001), science and technology studies (Hine, 2000), cultural studies (Wilson, 2006), and information sciences (Ito et al., 2009), to name a few.

Next, I describe three recent or current ethnographic projects in language and literacy that apply virtual ethnographic methods. I chose two published studies to serve as exemplars because (1) the work was published recently in a well-regarded literacy journal; (2) the researchers demonstrated many of the elements of quality in virtual ethnographic research described previously; and/or (3) the ethnographic findings are recognized as significant to the field of literacy, digital media, and learning. Interestingly, a search of the contents of three prominent literacy journals (2003–2009): *Reading Research Quarterly, Journal of Adult and Adolescent Literacy*, and *Journal of Research in Reading* revealed only a handful of articles (*n* = 8) employing virtual ethnography or some variation thereof (e.g., Black, 2005; Chandler-Olcott & Mahar, 2003; Gillen, 2009; Jacobs, 2004; Leander, 2003; Luke, 2003; Moje et al., 2004; Wade & Fauske, 2004). Although virtual ethnography as a research method has existed for more than a decade, its use in literacy studies is nascent and evolving. The two published studies I have selected are notable for their exploration of literacy practices and youth-initiated, emerging digital contexts (i.e., massively multiplayer online game worlds [Steinkuehler, 2006, 2007] and a three-dimensional virtual world [Gillen, 2009]). Furthermore, both studies embrace a connective approach, resisting simple dichotomies between online and offline or in-school and out-of-school practices in favor of the relationships and understandings across settings and media. Finally, I reflect upon my own work in studying the literacy practices of low-income, urban high school students and college students in naturally occurring online social network sites and a social networking application, respectively. For additional examples of virtual ethnography in literacy studies, see Lam's (2004) examination of digital literacy practices among immigrant youth in the United States and Leander and McKim's (2003) tracing of adolescent practices across online and offline spaces.

Steinkuehler (2006, 2007) applied virtual ethnographic techniques and Hutchins's (1995) notions of cognitive ethnography in her 2-year study of a massively multiplayer online game: Lineage. She sought to understand the literacy practices that constitute young people's game play *within* the game (e.g., transcripts of online social interaction, in-game letters) and *beyond* the game (e.g., online game forums, created fan sites, and fan fiction). Her agenda was to argue against popular contempt for video games as replacing literacy activities. She suggests instead that a more accurate, evidence-based, and generative framing for educators and literacy researchers is found by viewing game play as a "constellation" of literacy activities. She draws on Gee's (1996) notions of discourses to illuminate the complexities and manifold dimensions of gamers' literacy practices.

Julia Gillen (2009) also applies techniques of virtual ethnography to examine the multidimensional literacy practices of teenagers in Schome Park, an out-of-school project involving use of a (teen) Second Life three-dimensional virtual world. Like Steinkuehler, Gillen takes a longitudinal approach (15 months) to analyzing the meaning-making practices of the virtual community. Specifically, she attends to the practices of authoring and reading written, multimodal texts and analyzes data from three main communicative channels: chat logs, wiki postings (including images captured in-world to record events); forum postings, in-world sensor measurements (of how many people are in-world and where every minute), and field notes. Like Steinkuehler (2006, 2007), her agenda is to argue for a more fruitful framing of adolescent literacy practices within and beyond popular culture–inspired spaces and against "overly dichotomised boundaries between new literacies and those more established" (Gillen, 2009, p. 67).

Both Gillen (2009) and Steinkuehler (2006, 2007) demonstrate an adaptive approach to applying virtual ethnographic techniques. In both cases, the authors must synthesize theory and methods to cultivate a research design that works for their specific questions and purposes. As Hine (2000) and others have mentioned, there is no precise formula for the virtual ethnographer to follow, only detailed accounts of the journeys others have taken, the methodological decisions they have made, and the implementation issues and outcomes.

Finally, I conclude with a few reflections from my own work in taking a virtual ethnographic stance to understanding the literacy practices of different adolescent subgroups within and beyond online social networking sites (e.g., MySpace) (Greenhow & Robelia, 2009a, 2009b; Greenhow, Walker, & Kim, 2009) and an open-source social networking application, designed and implemented within Facebook, for environmental education purposes (Greenhow, 2010, in press). In both projects, the goals were to examine what was happening from the participants' perspective. To do so required negotiating the boundaries of participant-observer. For instance, to begin to identify students' perspectives, it was necessary to learn the sociotechnical features being used and, especially, how to manipulate default settings and code (e.g., "pimp my profile") as the subjects did. Gaining access to the dynamically updating social network site pages meant requesting "friend" status from our subjects and documenting complex series of decisions with respect to what we regarded as "public" versus "private" or "semiprivate" but usable under the informed consent process. In addition, strict adherence to rules for rigorous data collection, data management, and data analysis, as Purcell-Gates (2004) argues for in ethnographic research, became challenging in practice, as online comments, votes, chat transcripts, uploaded song lyrics, tagged images, and background layouts and graphics seemingly transform minute by minute. Capturing, charting, and interpreting the nature and development of literacy practices as they are occurring forces one to come face to face with his or her own time- and data-management limitations and life beyond the network. This is the cost of performing virtual ethnography. The benefits are a more nuanced view of established literacy practices and those on the horizon, greater cross-fertilization with other fields, advancement of methods well suited to digital contexts, and a sense of ourselves as literacy scholars who are conversant in changing times.

REFERENCES

Anderson-Levitt, K. (2006). Ethnography. In J. Green, G. Camilli, & P. Elmore (Eds.), *Handbook of complementary methods in education research* (pp. 279–295). Mahwah, NJ: Erlbaum.

Atkinson, P., & Hammersley, M. (1994). Ethnography and participant observation. In N. K. Denzin & Y. S. Lincoln (Eds.), *Handbook of qualitative research* (pp. 248–261). Thousand Oaks, CA: Sage.

Baym, N. K., & Markham, A. N. (2009). Introduction: Making smart choices on shifting ground. In A. N. Markham & N. K. Baym (Eds.), *Internet inquiry: Conversations about method* (pp. vii–xix). London: Sage.

Black, R. (2005). Access and affiliation: The literacy and composition practices of English-language learners in an online fanfiction community. *Journal of Adolescent and Adult Literacy, 49*(2), 118–128.

Bull, G., Thompson, A., Searson, M., Garofalo, J., Park, J., Young, C., et al. (2008). Connecting informal and formal learning: Experiences in the age of participatory media. *Contemporary Issues in Technology and Teacher Education, 8*(2). Retrieved July 1, 2008, from *citejournal.org/vol8/iss2/editorial/article1.cfm*

Carter, D. (2005). Living in virtual communities: An ethnography of human relationships in cyberspace. *Information, Communication and Society, 8*(2), 148–167.

Chandler-Olcott, K., & Mahar, D. (2003). "Tech-savviness" meets multiliteracies: Exploring adolescent girls' technology-mediated literacy practices. *Reading Research Quarterly, 38*, 356–385.

Cohen, L. (2007, April 5). Social scholarship on the rise. Retrieved October 7, 2008, from *liblogs.albany.edu/library20/2007/04/social_scholarship_on_the_rise.html*.

Coiro, J., Knobel, M., Lankshear, C., & Leu, D. J. (2008). Central issues in new literacies and new literacies research. In J. Coiro, M. Knobel, C. Lankshear, & D. J. Leu (Eds.), *Handbook of research on new literacies* (pp. 1–21). Mahwah, NJ: Erlbaum.

Freeman, M., deMarrais, K., Preissle, J., Roulston, K., & St. Pierre, E. A. (2007). Standards of evidence in qualitative research: An incitement to discourse. *Educational Researcher, 36*(1), 25–32.

Gee, J. P. (1996). *Social linguistics and literacies: Ideology in discourses* (2nd ed.). London: Taylor & Francis.

Gillen, J. (2009). Literacy practices in Schome Park: A virtual literacy ethnography. *Journal of Research in Reading, 32*(1), 57–74.

Gratton, L. (2007). *Hot spots: Why some teams, workplaces, and organizations buzz with energy—and others don't.* San Francisco: Berrett-Koehler.

Greenhow, C. (2008). Connecting formal and informal learning experiences in the age of participatory media: Commentary on Bull et al. (2008). *Contemporary Issues in Technology and Teacher Education, 8*(3). Retrieved June 1, 2009, from *www.citejournal.org/vol8/iss3/editorial/article1.cfm*.

Greenhow, C. (2009). Social scholarship: Applying social networking technologies to research practices. *Knowledge Quest, 37*(4), 43–47.

Greenhow, C. (2010, April). *Literacies and community formation in social network sites: Understanding a complex ecology.* Paper presented at the annual meeting of the American Educational Research Association, Denver, CO.

Greenhow, C. (in press). Youth as cultural producers in a niche social network site. *New Directions in Youth Development.*

Greenhow, C., & Robelia, E. (2009a). Informal learning and identity formation in online social networks. *Learning, Media and Technology, 34*(2), 119–140.

Greenhow, C., & Robelia, E. (2009b). Old communication, new literacies: Social network sites as social learning resources. *Journal of Computer-Mediated Communication, 14*, 1130–1161.

Greenhow, C., Robelia, E., & Hughes, J. (2009). Web 2.0 and classroom research: What path should we take now? *Educational Researcher, 38*(4), 246–259.

Greenhow, C., Walker, J. D., & Kim, S. (2009). Millennial learners and net-savvy teens? Examining Internet use among low-income students. *Journal of Computing in Teacher Education, 26*(2), 63–69.

Heath, S. B. (1983). *Ways with words.* London: Cambridge University Press.

Hine, C. (2000). *Virtual ethnography.* London: Sage.

Hine, C. (Ed.). (2005). *Virtual methods: Issues in social research on the Internet.* New York: Berg.

Hine, C., Kendall, L., & Boyd, D. (2009). How can qualitative Internet researchers define the boundaries of their projects? In A. N. Markham & N. K. Baym (Eds.), *Internet inquiry: Conversations about method* (pp. 1–26). Los Angeles: Sage.

Holloway, S. L., & Valentine, G. (2001). "It's only as stupid as you are": Children and adults' negotiation of ICT competence at home and at school. *Social and Cultural Geography, 22,* 25–42.

Hutchins, E. (1995). *Cognition in the wild.* Cambridge, MA: MIT Press.

International Reading Association. (2009). New literacies and 21st century technologies: A position statement of the International Reading Association. Newark, DE: Author. Retrieved from *www.reading.org/Libraries/Position_Statements_and_Resolutions/ps1067_NewLiteracies21stCentury.sflb.ashx.*

Ito, M., Baumer, S., Bittanti, M., Boyd, D., Cody, R., Herr-Stephenson, B., et al. (2009). *Hanging out, messing around, and geeking out: Kids living and learning with new media.* Chicago: MacArthur Foundation Series on Digital Media and Learning.

Jacobs, G. E. (2004). Complicating contexts: Issues of methodology in researching language and literacies of instant messaging. *Reading Research Quarterly, 39*(4), 394–406.

Jones, S. G. (1995). *Cybersociety: Computer-mediated communication and community.* Thousand Oaks, CA: Sage.

Jones, S. G. (1997). *Virtual culture: Internet and communication in cybersociety.* London: Sage.

Kress, G. (2003). *Literacy in the new media age.* New York: Routledge.

Lam, W. S. E. (2004). Second language socialization in a bilingual chat room. *Language Learning and Technology, 8*(3), 44–65.

Lankshear, C., & Knobel, M. (2006). *New literacies: Everyday practices and classroom learning* (2nd ed.). Maidenhead, UK: Open University Press.

Leander, K. M. (2003). Writing travelers' tales on new literacyscapes. *Reading Research Quarterly, 38,* 392–397.

Leander, K. M. (2008). Toward a connective ethnography of online/offline literacy networks. In J. Coiro, M. Knobel, C. Lankshear, & D. J. Leu (Eds.), *Handbook of research on new literacies* (pp. 33–65). Mahwah, NJ: Erlbaum.

Leander, K. M., & McKim, K. K. (2003). Tracing the everyday "sitings" of adolescents on the Internet: A strategic adaptation of ethnography across online and offline spaces. *Education, Communication, and Information, 3*(2), 211–240.

LeCompte, M. D., & Schensul, J. J. (1999). *Designing and conducting ethnographic research.* Walnut Creek, CA: AltaMira Press.

Lewin, T. (2010, January 20). If your kids are awake, then they're probably online. *New York Times.* Retrieved June 5, 2010, from *www.nytimes.com.*

Luke, A. (2003). Literacy and the other: A sociological approach to literacy research and policy in multilingual societies. *Reading Research Quarterly, 38*(1), 132–141.

Markham, A. (1998). *Life online: Researching real experience in virtual space.* Walnut Creek, CA: AltaMira Press.

Moje, E. B., Ciechanowski, K. M., Kramer, K., Ellis, L., Carillo, R., & Tehani, C. (2004). Working toward Third Space in content area literacy: An examination of everyday funds of knowledge and discourse. *Reading Research Quarterly, 39*(1), 38–70.

National Center on Education and the Economy. (2006). *Tough choices, tough times: The report of the New Commission on the Skills of the American Workforce.* New York: Jossey-Bass.

National Council of Teachers of English. (2005). Position statement on multimodal literacies. Retrieved July 28, 2008, from *www.ncte.org/positions/statements/multimodalliteracies.*

National Council of Teachers of English. (2008). 21st century literacies: A policy research brief produced by the National Council of Teachers of English. Retrieved July 28, 2008, from *www.ncte.org/library/NCTEFiles/Resources/Positions/Chron1107ResearchBrief.pdf.*

National Endowment for the Arts. (2007, November). *To read or not to read: A question of national consequence* (Research Report No. 47). Retrieved July 28, 2008, from *www.nea.gov/research/ToRead.pdf.*

Nelson, M. (Executive Producer). (2008, July 23). *CNN presents black in America: The black woman & family* [Television broadcast]. New York: Turner Broadcasting Service. Retrieved March 23, 2010, from *www.cnn.com/SPECIALS/2008/black.in.america/.*

Patton, M. Q. (Ed.). (2002). *Qualitative research and evaluation methods* (3rd ed.). London: Sage.

Purcell-Gates, V. (2004). Ethnographic research. In N. K. Duke & M. H. Mallette (Eds.), *Literacy research methodologies* (pp. 92–113). New York: Guilford Press.

Reinking, D., & Bradley, B. A. (2004). Connecting research and practice using formative and design experiments. In N. K. Duke & M. H. Mallette (Eds.), *Literacy research methodologies* (pp. 149–169). New York: Guilford Press.

Rich, M. (2008, July 27). Literacy debate: Online, R U really reading? *New York Times,* pp. 1, 14–15.

Rideout, V. J., Foehr, U. G., & Roberts, D. F. (2010, January 20). *Generation M²: Media in the lives of 8- to 18-year-olds* (Report No. 8010). Menlo Park, CA: Kaiser Family Foundation.

Ruhleder, K. (2000). The virtual ethnographer: Fieldwork in distributed electronic environments. *Field Methods, 12*(1), 3–17.

Sheehy, G. (2008, August). Campaign Hillary: Behind closed doors. *Vanity Fair,* pp. 79–86.

Shirky, C. (2008, April 23). Clay Shirky keynote at Web 2.0 Expo [Video file]. Retrieved June 1, 2009, from *video.google.com/videoplay?docid=-2708219489770693816#.*

Steinkuehler, C. (2006). Massively multiplayer online video gaming as participation in a discourse. *Mind, Culture and Activity, 13*(1), 38–52.

Steinkuehler, C. (2007). Massively multiplayer online gaming as a constellation of literacy practices. *E-learning, 4*(3), 297–318.

Steinkuehler, C. A., Black, R., & Clinton, K. A. (2005). Researching literacy as tool, place, and way of being. *Reading Research Quarterly, 40*(1), 95–100.

Stone, B. (2008, June 18). At social site only the businesslike need apply. *New York Times*, pp. C1–C2.

Taraborelli, D. (2008, May). Soft peer review. Social software and distributed scientific evaluation. In *Proceedings of the 8th International Conference on the Design of Cooperative Systems*. Retrieved October 3, 2008, from *coop. wineme.fb5.uni-siegen.de/?id=coop2008*.

Thomas, A. (2007). *Youth online: Identity and literacy in the digital age*. New York: Peter Lang.

Turkle, S. (1995). *Life on the screen: Identity in the age of the Internet*. London: Weidenfeld & Nicolson.

Wade, S. E., & Fauske, J. R. (2004). Dialogue online: Prospective teachers discourse strategies in computer-mediated discussions. *Reading Research Quarterly, 39*, 134–160.

Wilson, B. (2006). *Fight, flight, or chill: Subcultures, youth, and rave into 21st century*. Montreal: McGill-Queen's University Press.

CHAPTER 6

Discourse Analysis
Conversation

Susan Florio-Ruane
Ernest Morrell

In this chapter we discuss research on oral discourse in education. While in ordinary life and language we use the term *discourse* in nontechnical ways to refer to discussion or conversation or formal talk (e.g., speeches), it is also a technical term in research referring to oral or written communication in units longer than the sentence. When we speak of oral discourse, we are referring to spoken exchanges between or among participants in particular activities, social contexts, and cultural settings. These exchanges have theoretical significance in that they reveal human beings creating and negotiating social identity and meaning in their talk (Hymes, 1974). Talk is deeply woven into the social fabric of any community or culture. It is a primary source of information about that community and also a means by which the community's cultural beliefs and practices are shared, passed on, and changed. Closely tied to both cultural transmission and transformation, the study of oral discourse in educational settings has been a mainstay of research on teaching and learning for the past half-century both in the United States and abroad.

Ours is not a "how-to" chapter. There is already a considerable body of published information on ways to record and analyze oral discourse, much of it relevant to the classroom. There are also reviews of research containing exemplary studies of classroom discourse (e.g., Cazden, 1988). Yet it remains important for students of educational research to ask, "What is oral discourse, and why study it in research on education in general and literacy education in particular?" There are numerous answers to this question, many of them emanating from practical concerns of curriculum, instruction, classroom management, assessment, and educational policy. However, underlying these are fundamental questions about the role of oral discourse in the social construction of knowledge, power, and identity in classrooms, schools, and elsewhere in society. Our chapter looks at both kinds of questions and, importantly, at their intersection in both educational practice and research.

BACKGROUND OF RESEARCH ON ORAL DISCOURSE IN EDUCATION

There is considerable interest in discourse analysis among educational researchers in Europe, Australia, and the United States. Interdisciplinary fields such as sociolinguistics emerged in the last half of the 20th century, along with technologies making it easy to record speech in real time and in naturalistic settings for closer analysis, to review collaboratively with participants, and to sample discourse in multiple ways, both across numerous reproducible speech-related units of activity and in triangulation with data collected within an activity context or social setting by other means (e.g., field notes, interviews, work products).

Researchers study oral language in relationship to linguistic and social differences in communication among members of diverse cultural groups. They also study oral communication in relation to multiple, diverse forms of text-based knowledge, or literacies, within and among communities (e.g., reading, writing, visual literacy). Moreover, in contemporary life, conversation and literacy are not only local but also global phenomena in which people come together rapidly and across time and distance by means of electronic media (e.g., in talk, print, audiovisual media, and cyber communication). Contemporary educational researchers thus add to their prior interests the study of the power of language in immediate (if not necessarily face-to-face) contact and interaction to organize activities and practices of communities rapidly as they shape social relations and develop knowledge and identity.

Just as 20th-century advances in video- and audio-recording technology made capturing sequences of oral discourse in naturalistic settings feasible, it also made oral language a wider reaching, more powerful social, educational, and political tool. In our time, digital technology makes it possible to manipulate discourse sequences so that they can be studied, in hypermedia, in a variety of revealing ways: synchronically, diachronically, comparatively, and in conjunction with other forms of textual information relevant to the talk and context under study. Thus, we are able to examine oral discourse in multiple, layered situational contexts and begin to understand learning and practice within complex, indeterminate domains such as teaching (Au, Raphael, Florio-Ruane, & Spiro, 2000; Spiro, Feltovich, Jacobson, & Coulson, 1990). This move from certainty to uncertainty raises the possibility that everyday practices can be analyzed, taught, and learned critically (Britzman, 2002).

DISCOURSE AS INSTRUCTIONAL CONVERSATION

Notwithstanding the swiftly changing landscape of research on oral discourse, a primary site for such research remains the classroom. The first collection of classroom studies of oral communication in education, *Functions of Language in the Classroom* (Cazden, John, & Hymes, 1972), illustrated the breadth and depth of this study for understanding such important issues as differential treatment and access to knowledge in linguistically diverse classrooms, the role of culture in communication style both in and out of school, and the possibilities of literacy instruction enhanced by awareness of and adaptation to the varied prior knowledge that students and teachers brought to text-based conversations in the classroom (Heath, 1983).

Classrooms are language-rich environments, and much of that language takes the form of talk about texts, knowledge, and ideas. In cross-cultural research on thinking, for example, Cole (1996) and his associates found that the chief way in which people who experienced formal schooling differ from those who did not is in their fluency manipulating concepts in and through language, both written and oral. One way to study educational discourse within school settings is by analyzing the classroom's instructional conversations: their nature, content, and purposes. For literacy researchers, the study of oral discourse is further specified as analysis of talk within what Heath (1983) called "literacy events," those situations and activities in which written text and literate practices are central to classroom talk and activity.

A related way to think about discourse is as what linguist James Gee (1996) calls a social linguistic "identity kit." Viewed this way, discourse includes, but is not limited to, conversation. Although it includes language, discourse is social as well as linguistic. It is a way of behaving and making sense, and includes language code (as well as dialect or speech style) as well as the social norms, values, and practice within shared activity systems. The classroom offers learners one of their first opportunities to learn a "secondary discourse" as they venture out from the primary discourse into which they have been socialized by the family. In school, language and literacy learning are part of a secondary discourse, and students assume a new identity as learners in a community in which text will be central and talk will serve instructional, curricular, and assessment purposes.

Conversation is essential to learning and sustaining participation in a discourse, but that discourse is not neutral. It is a system of sociolinguistic identification partly created by teachers and students anew in their day-to-day interactions and partly constrained by social, historical, cultural, and political forces and factors. It is by a process of reflexivity, or the mutual construction of conversation and culture, that shared meaning is possible. A significant factor in the development of identity and literacy, which is both limiting and enabling of learning and learners' futures, it is important to study the structure of educational discourse closely and critically.

In a comprehensive review of language in relation to social theory, Erickson (2004) describes the power of this structuralist view of the relation between language and society and its dominance in the theoretical framing of research, its assumptions, questions, and analytic methods, for much of the mid- and late-20th century. Subsequently, however, as theorists such as Erickson (2004) and Giddens (1979) have noted, research interest in oral discourse, and with it the making of local meaning in practice, is central to the process of incremental change within societies and their institutions. Additionally, they acknowledge human agency operant within local context and activities as well as within the wider structuring forces of social history. This view is considered to be one of rule-governed activity in context, rather than action predetermined by externally imposed structure. When talk is meaningfully situated within activity settings such as classrooms, it has its own local agency (e.g., teachers enable children to learn to read independently). Gradually, this agentive local work can impact social history and, at the same time, be conducted within social historical boundaries (e.g., a state or a nation's policies regarding reading curriculum). Giddin's (1984) calls this process, "structuration."

Both constancy and change are important to researchers who study the oral discourse of teaching and learning. It is difficult to write about analysis of discourse as educational talk without addressing three key features of conversation as a cultural activity: (1) It is jointly constructed by participants in connected oral text; (2) it is a medium for the negotiation of meaning by speakers within particular social contexts; and (3) it is rule-governed in order to be held in common with others, but it is also creative, with improvisation necessary as conversation moves from turn to turn, topic to topic, speaker to speaker.

ORAL DISCOURSE AND EDUCATION

Oral language plays an important role in schooling. We explicitly use talk in our teaching when, for example, we explain a concept or assess students by listening as they answer questions about what they have learned. However, the educational importance of talk extends far beyond these uses. It also can bring diverse people together and foster the learning of others' language codes and literate practices. To master the oral and written language systems is to be able to wield the power of language as a tool for communication, self-expression, creativity, and thinking.

If talk is to be a key tool for teaching and learning the literacy curriculum, and teachers must plan for and enact it with youngsters in thoughtful ways, then classroom talk is clearly an area deserving of considerable educational research. Yet talk as an aspect of teaching—a part of tacit, local knowledge—is often the component most taken for granted. There are a variety of approaches to the study of ordinary language, or conversation, in educational research, and these methods are linked to researchers' theories, interests, and questions (Schiffrin, 1994). Yet, although they vary, these approaches are loosely associated and often referenced by the term *analysis of discourse*. Scholars use the term *discourse* when referring to oral as well as and written language (both are also referred to as "text") and to both the process of talk and its functions in social life (see Goldman & Wiley, Chapter 7, this volume).

Once we move beyond the sentence, it is difficult to understand how talk works as "text." Understanding text—discourse—involves far more than vocabulary and grammar. It involves an understanding of culture and social life. This is as true for the young child entering her first classroom as it is for the traveler who, armed with grammatical knowledge of a language, finds himself lost in the sea of its use by native speakers. Educators and researchers are interested in how people acquire, learn, and practice discourse as they learn to reason, to participate in a variety of activities, and as they attain mature and metacognitive awareness of discourse strategies. Participation in discourse involves a network of knowledge, including the following:

- Understanding and using a spoken language system and a repertoire of accompanying paralinguistic and nonverbal behaviors.
- Knowing (explicitly/tacitly) social contexts, roles, and activities within which conversations occur.
- Producing as well as interpreting appropriately conversational behaviors.
- Managing conversation's ensemble, improvisational, and negotiated qualities.

The study of conversational discourse has roots in several fields, including anthropology, linguistics, sociology, cultural studies, child development, and critical theory. Discourse has been analyzed for purposes of understanding how children learn to speak, the process of language acquisition across diverse languages and culture, and the ways people "do things with words" to, with, and in response to one another. Obviously, education in general (and literacy education in particular) is an area in which oral discourse is of central importance in part because words saturate the learning environment, much learning involves learning new discourses, much learning occurs in the medium of conversation, and language is a means for creating, sustaining, and transforming social systems. Given that, in schools, social forces operate in ways that affect access to knowledge, the study of oral discourse within the conversations of the classroom is one primary way to witness those forces in participants' talk and activity. Understanding the dynamics of educational conversation opens possibilities for researchers learning about teaching, learning, and educational reform.

There are many kinds of discourse analysis, some of which might be called critical discourse analysis, some that resemble sociolinguistic study, some using narrative analysis to inform the study of conversation, and many that innovate in ways using theory and method drawn from ethnography and sociolinguistics. Examples of these approaches might be critical discourse analyses such as those collected in Barton and Hamilton's *Local Literacies* (1998), sociolinguistic analyses such as those by Michaels (1981; detailed later), studies of teachers' literary and autobiographical talk about culture and text (Florio-Ruane with deTar, 2001), and studies of reading instruction among Hawaiian youngsters conducted by Kathryn Au (1980) and reviewed in detail by Florio-Ruane and McVee (2000). Although the length and purpose of this chapter preclude detailed review of all of these, later in the chapter we briefly examine several exemplars of research illustrating different approaches to analysis of discourse in literacy education.

DOING THINGS WITH WORDS

The analysis of oral discourse within classrooms, families, and other social groups and settings came into its own in the United States in the mid-20th century, when both funds and public concerns converged on problems of inequality, especially unequal access to learning in school. At the same time, researchers were questioning not only how people acquire language but how they acquire social competence—or the ability to use language to communicate. There was burgeoning interest in language variation of all kinds and in the tremendous amount of experience and local knowledge encapsulated in even the simplest slice of discourse. Finally, researchers were raising learning questions of another sort: How, out of the language we exchange, are we creating, sustaining, and possibly reinventing social relationships?

Embedded in each act of communication is not only referential information but a large store of situational knowledge. As we grow and learn we become more able to make sense of our language and culture. These work together to express shared norms, or rules for treating one another in particular ways; convey shared values about what is important (what and who deserves our respect); determine our sense of etiquette; and teach us biases and prejudices. Thus culture and communication are learned and conducted in ways that are both enabling and limiting. In the past three decades, critical linguists have focused on these dimensions of conversation and culture. They are interested in the roles that language and culture can play not only to limit and separate but also to transform and enable democratic education in a diverse society.

AN EXAMPLE OF DISCOURSE ANALYSIS IN EDUCATION BY MICHAELS (1981)

From the outset, the application of the study of discourse to teaching and learning was colored by concerns about and interest in social norms. By studying discourse, we could obtain insight into what people believe and how they negotiate, construct, and reconstruct their beliefs. This is at the core of examining differential treatment and access to knowledge, and it is also potentially at the core of social change. One exemplar illustrating this convergence is Sarah Michaels's (1981) sociolinguistic research on oral language in a literacy-related conversation in a diverse primary classroom.

In Michaels's pioneering research, close study of the conversation of teacher and students in a primary classroom's "sharing time" uncovered some troubling patterns. The teacher's schema for an appropriate oral sharing was brief and topic centered: a spoken paragraph. Some children, mainly from middle-class backgrounds and European American speech communities, knew that this was the appropriate way to share in school, even without having to be told by the teacher. They were making manifest in their talk not only the information they had to share but also a great deal about their social standing.

Students who did not already know or who for other reasons did not produce the school-appropriate sharing talk tended to tell longer, more complex, and thematically linked stories. These would be appropriate in nonschool contexts and perhaps in particular speech communities. However, in this context, they were inappropriate. The teacher did not explicitly address their structure with an explanation of rules for talk, but she did offer them different kinds of responses, less topically relevant and more related to the structure of their narratives. The public, evaluative nature of this kind of classroom conversation produces not only differential access to knowledge but also different available personae to participants. The less school-appropriate narratives were offered most often by lower income students of color. These narratives might well be assessed as showing lack of readiness for school literacy work, especially writing, as well as less mature participation.

Because talk is permeable and improvised and is related to the shifting landscape of identity and activity, participants have options in how they will participate—and some of these options are influenced by their involvement in discourse communities, including families, ethnic communities, gendered groups, and occupations. Idealized views of conversation, particularly when applied to communication in educational activities, are limited because they imply a closed system with few options: initiation, reply, evaluation.

Cazden (1988) notes that, although this system may well be the "default" mode in European American education, it is not universal and, moreover, can be altered by explicit effort. Burbules (1993) offers two ways of thinking about such alteration in democratic classrooms: (1) that within even a single conversation participants may apply diverse conversational "genres" to accomplish the work of reasoning and (2) that these genres reflect shifting perspectives on "who we are and what we are doing." In some cases, consensus is the aim, in others divergence of thinking.

Of research findings such as those of Michaels, Gee (1996, 2008) (who has contributed additional analyses of Michaels's data in his own writing about social linguistics) argues that the subtle yet powerful dynamics of sharing time—both as a social event and as an oral preparation for topic-centered writing—illustrates the power of our words to shape both learning and social identity and the ways that, tacitly, the wider social context of teacher–student interaction, even in an activity as simple as sharing time, can make a vast difference in students' public identities, opportunities to learn, and recapitulation of social inequality based on race. Vivian Paley, in her book *White Teacher* (2000), analyzed her own practice and made similar findings. Describing the problem she discovered as hers, not that of her pupils, Paley recounted her efforts to come to terms with her own biases and to pay close attention to talk and learning in her classroom as part of her responsibility as an educator. In that vein, Gee (2008) urges us to analyze classroom talk to understand this problem better. Furthermore, Gee strongly advises that when we recognize a situation in education in our society in which members of a community are harmed or disadvantaged by dominant discourse practices, we have a moral and ethical responsibility to engage in critical discourse analysis to identify the sources of inequality and to implement reform of practice to redress it. Critical discourse analysis is a genre of discourse research with these explicit purposes and commitments and is described and exemplified in greater detail later.

Critical discourse analysis is a prominent approach to analysis of oral and written text focused on the power exercised in and expressed by social linguistic activity. It contrasts with the previously described analysis of oral discourse in the explicitness of its focus, its wider theoretical underpinnings, and its subsequent openness to more varied data sources and analytic techniques than discourse analysis rooted in ethnography and sociolinguistics. Although these approaches differ, both are widely used in contemporary educational and literacy research, and they share an abiding concern for the relationship between language and society.

In addition to the identification of sources of inequality and the reform of discourse practices to redress it advanced by Gee (2008), other concerns of critical discourse analysts have included an interrogation of the politics of representation and exclusion in the popular media. Fairclough (1989, 1995), for example, examines the media depictions of the actions of prominent politicians such as Ronald Reagan and Margaret Thatcher. Kress (2003) discusses the relationship between the proliferation of new media literacies and the confluence of spoken language and textuality in developing a Foucault-inspired framework of discourse analysis that could be applied to a conversation among peers or an examination of the nightly news. According to Kress, no text, whether conversational or new media, escapes the shaping influence of discourse (2003, p. 47). Douglas Kellner (1995) examines how media discourses socialize and define identities in ways that both reproduce and resist existing power relations. Kellner's work critically examines the functions and usage of spoken language in films, youth music, and television news and entertainment. His work is not only descriptive but also prescriptive in articulating a method to be used by discerning citizens to make sense of their positioning vis-à-vis dominant media discourses.

CRITICAL DISCOURSE ANALYSIS: AN EXAMINATION OF LANGUAGE AND POWER

Critical scholars of discourse wish to analyze texts and conversations in the contexts of social reproduction, knowledge construction, agency, and, ultimately, critical language awareness (Alim, 2005) and social transformation. Because they argue that language is a central vehicle in the process whereby people are constituted as individuals and as social subjects, and because language and ideology are closely imbricated, careful systematic analysis of the language of texts, critical discourse analysis can expose some of the workings of texts and, by extension, the way that language either bestows or withholds power within current social structures. Those from linguistics, education, cultural studies, and other disciplines who use the tools of critical discourse analysis are attempting to integrate poststructuralist questions of power, truth, and knowledge within their linguistic analytical methods (Mills, 1997). Their definition of discourse draws heavily upon the work of French philosopher and social theorist Michel Foucault (1926–1984), although they provide a substantial modification of the term because they are concerned with a more ground-level approach to language than Foucault; they thus provide more working models and concrete examples of how texts and conversations work to create inequalities of power and are more concerned with the mechanics of discursive functioning.

THE CONSTRUCTION OF KNOWLEDGE IN DISCOURSE

Foucault (1969/2002) believed that one of the most productive ways of thinking about discourse is not as a group of signs or a stretch of text but rather as "practices that systematically form the objects of which they speak" (p. 54). In this sense, discourse is something that produces something else rather than something that exists in and of itself and that can be analyzed in isolation. Foucault (1981) also believed that each society has its regime of truth, its general politics of truth: that is, the types of discourse it harbors and causes to function as true. Truth, therefore, is something that societies have to work to produce rather than something that appears in a transcendental way. Foucault's philosophical project explored the ways that societies have historically worked to construct truth, and this work led him to understand the importance of discourse in this process.

Whereas a nutritionist might argue that "You are what you eat," Foucault would argue that we are who we have been codified to be through discourse—not as catchy as the medical maxim, but you get the picture. Historically, an example of this is the discourse of race. Although people understood themselves to be different from one another, and various explanations had emerged throughout history for determining which groups were superior to others, there was nothing that approximated the tenor or the absolute certainty of human distinction based on race until it became necessary, at the height of colonialism, to distinguish European colonizers from the brown and black bodies they intended to displace and enslave. The concept of race, then, was born of necessity, and the discourse of race made true what was, in actuality, a social construction of difference. Today it is difficult to see people outside of their racial group, and race has led to a great amount of violence and repression over the past 400 years. As Foucault-inspired discourse analysts, we might trace the development of the discourse of race and show how the racial hierarchy has become ingrained in social thought through its existence in social texts and social language.

Discourses do not exist in a vacuum but are in constant conflict with other discourses and other social practices that inform them over questions of truth and authority. Foucault was not interested in which discourse is a true or accurate representation of the real; rather, he was concerned with the mechanics whereby one becomes produced as the dominant discourse. Foucault argued for the imbrication of power with knowledge, so that all of the knowledge that exists is the result or the effect of power struggles. Most theorists of power have seen individuals as either benefiting from or oppressed by existing power relations, but Foucault saw them as the effects or instances of power relations. This is why Foucault's archaeological analysis of discourse is so important: He was not interested in simply analyzing the discourses that circulate in our society; his work challenges us to see the arbitrariness of this range of discourses and the strangeness of those discourses in spite of their familiarity. He also charted the development of certain discursive practices, so that we can see that, rather than being permanent as their familiarity would suggest, discourses are constantly changing, and their origins can be traced to certain key shifts in history.

TALK AND PERSPECTIVE

More recent work in critical discourse analysis has shown that utterances do not simply mean one thing and that they cannot be interpreted from the standpoint of the speaker or hearer alone. Fairclough (1995) assumes that each of the participants will view the functioning of utterances from a standpoint made up of different personal interests and preoccupations—

and the analyst must thus be careful not to elide his or her position of analysis in favor of that of a participant. Critical linguists have, therefore, been concerned with inflecting Foucault's analysis of discourse with a political concern for the effects of discourse, for example, the way that people are positioned into roles through discursive structures, the way that certain people's knowledge is disqualified or not taken seriously in contrast to authorized knowledge, and so on. It is the shift away from mere description to a more analytical and critical perspective that is a significant reinterpretation of Foucault's work through the matrix of linguistics' concern for replicable, verifiable analyses.

Foucault is so important to critical linguistics because of his emphasis on the major role of discourse in the constitution of social subjects. Fairclough argues that Foucault's work on discourse can be usefully drawn on by scholars interested in the critical analysis of discourse for two main insights: (1) the constitutive nature of discourse—discourse constitutes the social, including "objects" and social subjects, and (2) the primacy of interdiscursivity and intertextuality—and discursive practice is defined by its relations with others and draws upon others in complex ways. A concern for the relation between the individual interaction and the wider discursive and social structure makes for not only a form of analysis that is more complex and more finely nuanced but also an analysis that is self-critical in terms of its own claims to "truth" and is aware of the dangers of naively ascribing meaning to texts. It is this type of fusion of larger social questions with smaller scale analytical questions that holds the greatest potential for future work in this field.

Michel Pecheux (1982) views a discourse as language use that may be identified by the institutions to which it relates and by the positions from which it comes and which it marks out for the speaker. The position does not exist by itself, however. Indeed, it may be understood as a standpoint taken up by the discourse through its relation to another, ultimately an opposing discourse. Most critical approaches consider discourses to be principally organized around practices of exclusion. Pecheux's work on discourse is important in that he sets out to analyze the meanings of words and their relations to larger structures without assuming that words and sentences had a meaning in themselves. It is also significant in that he stresses more than Foucault the conflictual nature of discourse: That is, it is always in dialogue and conflict with other positions. He stresses that ideological struggle is the essence of discourse structure.

Pecheux is concerned that, for example, people who are not privileged within a class system, through lack of access to education, knowledge, and familiarity with information networks and capital, are similarly prevented from having easy access to discourses. Discourses structure both our sense of reality and our notion of our own identity. For Pecheux in particular, discourses do not exist in isolation but are the object and site of struggle. Discourses are thus not fixed but are the site of constant contestation of meaning.

Feminist and postcolonial scholars have drawn upon the French discourse analyses of Foucault and Pecheux to overtly political ends. Feminists, for instance, have used discourse analysis to move away from conceptions of women as victims of male domination to examine the ways in which power manifests itself and is resisted in everyday life (Mills, 1997). Postcolonial theorists are able to use discourse analysis to map historical, cultural, and political shifts in relations between subaltern cultures and the West through examination of discursive representations (Loomba, 2001). Similar to the feminists, postcolonial theorists also resist simple characterizations between dominant and subordinate groups and have used discourse analysis not only to characterize contemporary relations but to challenge problematic and disempowering historical narratives.

Of particular note is the way that educational scholars have begun to use critical discourse analysis as a way to understand not only how language codifies power in a descriptive sense but also how social actors who have been historically marginalized can intentionally use language to speak back to power and change their relationship to existing structures of power. One such example is the work of H. Samy Alim, who, in *Roc the Mic Right: The Language of Hip Hop Culture* (2006), shows the sophisticated use of language by participants in hip hop communities. Their counterlanguage becomes a site of cultural production and resistance to dominant systems that have generally disregarded both their reality and their modes of representing their reality. Maisha Fisher (2007) profiles a literacy classroom in the Bronx where youth use spoken-word poetry to critique dominant knowledge systems and to redefine themselves as empowered and agentive. This process proved transformative for the students involved, and it also created a counterdiscourse in the classroom, the school, and the community. Kirkland (2008) encourages us as educators to reconsider the discourse production of youth as we develop curricula and pedagogies in language classrooms.

This fundamental shift in critical discourse analysis holds tremendous implications for our field. For one, it moves beyond some assumptions in earlier work about subjects as relatively passive and unconscious participants in discourse. It also opens up space to think about discourse as something that can be exposed, and hence attacked. Finally, it opens up the door for the question of pedagogy. That is, there can be a role for critical educators in helping historically marginalized youth to understand how discourse works and to create their own empowered conversations as intentioned and intellectual producers of discourse.

AN EXAMPLE OF CRITICAL DISCOURSE IN EDUCATION BY MORRELL (2008)

On example of research in literacy education approaching discourse in terms of institutionalized power, inequality, and historical narrative is

Morrell's examination of the discursive production of city youth who, as apprenticing critical sociologists, investigate and intervene in oppressive conditions in their schools and communities. Morrell investigated the relationships between youth's development as action researchers, their literacy production that accompanied their action research, and the changing relationships with educators, community members, and power brokers that becoming experts in the sociology of education afforded them. Each of these outcomes has some relation to this reconsideration of critical discourse analysis. In their rereading of their own lived experiences in schools, students developed a critical language awareness (Fairclough, 1995) of the way that discourses about inequity and achievement had framed their own educational experiences. As critical researchers, they became architects of their own critical discourse as they reframed "problems" in urban education and even offered solutions to these seemingly intractable conditions. It is the area of changing relationships that we want to highlight. In their conversations with leaders and community members, where they present their research and offer solutions, the students are creating their own empowered discourse in their position as experts and intellectuals. They have control over the conversation about urban educational reform that takes aim at institutional discourses and practices, not at youth, who have frequently been the targets of misguided educational reform.

In his research on critical discourse and literacy education in urban high schools, Morrell (2008) has worked at the borders of discourse communities. He tapped students' expertise in one discourse (that of popular culture and students' ownership over their own lived experiences) not only to master academic literacies but to enter even more explicitly powerful discourse of political and social activism in one's community. In building upon the literacy and learning theories of Paulo Freire (1970) and John Dewey (1915), Morrell found that situating academic dialogue in the context of students' real lived experiences in schools and communities becomes a useful context for developing academic skills, critical consciousness, civic agency, and collaborative actions for change.

Morrell's work is also built upon the ethnographic and sociolinguistic research of Moll, Amanti, Neff, and Gonzalez (1992), who prepared teachers to become ethnographers in the home communities of their students and learn about the "funds of knowledge" within those communities that might be brought into the classroom to embody the school curriculum in the knowledge and practice of important adults in the child's life and first language. Similarly, Gutierrez (2008), in her advocacy for sociocritical literacies, identified by means of discourse analysis in bilingual classrooms, those activity settings in which students are able to bridge home and school and often transcend the norms of either community to forge a powerful linguistic and educational synthesis. Gutierrez called these "third spaces," and advances both research and recommendations for practice based on her research among youngsters for whom English is a second language.

In all three of these examples, researchers tackle not only discourse analysis in ethnographic perspective but the move toward innovation and intervention as they attempt (or encourage and study) innovative practices that seem to break the frame of our taken-for-granted assumptions about how language and literacy are constituted within the established institution of U.S. public schooling. Each study also exemplifies the ways that the researchers followed rigors of analysis of discourse in its social and cultural context as part of developing, implementing, and studying innovative curriculum and instruction within the institution of schooling.

To work at this level of depth and sensitivity, researchers must take pains to collect data among speakers engaged in authentic activities (as well as or in addition to other kinds of data based on surveys or tests or analysis of artifacts). They must look at social, political, and historical contexts as frames for interpretation. They must sample extensively from the speech data available within a particular discourse community or speech event and report analyses both descriptively and analytically, giving evidentiary warrant for the interpretation/description as they have written it and considering both alternate readings of the same data and disconfirming examples. Florio-Ruane (1987, p. 195) identified the following maxims as important components when conducting or assessing research on classroom discourse:

- Go to the people.
- Pay attention to what is said and done.
- Plan your recording carefully.
- Proceed inductively.
- Be alert to interpretation.
- Find locally meaningful units of analysis.
- Balance explanation with narration and verbatim examples.
- Look for disconfirming evidence and discrepant cases.
- Think about your informants.

We judge the adequacy of research on oral discourse by its closeness to speakers, their speech, and the cultural contexts of their social and linguistic activities. Research of this kind is concerned not only with identification of local meaning in speakers' terms but also with its power. Having done this, many researchers move from descriptive, analytical, and critical studies to innovations aimed at educational improvement.

TALK, POWER, AND INSTITUTIONAL CHANGE

We judge analysis of discourse (defined both as extended sequences of talk and as the social process of identification by means of talk) by its closeness to speakers and speech—by its concern for identification of local meaning in speakers' terms and also by its power to see the multiple form–function relationships possible in a language system and the ways that disambiguation of those relationships depends on cultural knowledge, especially that knowledge acquired in use and by participation. Ultimately, we value a study of oral discourse in terms of its pertinence to the educational questions asked. It is especially useful in addressing the following sorts of question in education: What is happening, specifically, in the social action that takes place in this particular setting? What do these actions mean to the actors involved in them at the moment they are taking place? How are the happenings organized in patterns of social organization and learned cultural principles for the conduct of everyday life—how, in other words, are people in the immediate setting present to each other as environments for one another's meaningful actions? How is what is happening in this setting as a whole (i.e., the classroom) related to happenings at other system levels outside and inside the setting? How do the ways that everyday life is organized in this setting compare with other ways of organizing social life in a wide range of settings and at other times (Erickson, 1986, p. 121)?

From these examples and rigors, it should be evident that the study of discourse in education is not a static, decontextualized process. It is a study of people actively engaged in communicating information and negotiating roles, statuses, and identities. This line of inquiry leads to an examination of the social organization of inequality, the ways language is used to sustain particular norms, and the ways metalinguistic awareness can foster critique and reasoning about complexity. Finally, the approach to research is useful for studying—and designing and assessing—transformative discourse situations and practices generative of new possibilities for thought, action, and identification. For these reasons, it is an important tool for research on learning education.

REFERENCES

Alim, H. S. (2005). Critical language awareness in the United States: Revisiting issues and revising pedagogies in a resegregated society. *Educational Researcher, 34*(7), 24–31.

Alim, H. S. (2006). *Roc the mic right: The language of hip hop culture.* New York: Routledge.

Au, K. H. (1980). Participation structures in a reading lesson with Hawaiian children: Analysis of a culturally appropriate instructional event. *Anthropology and Education Quarterly, 11*(2), 91–115.

Au, K. H., Raphael, T. E., Florio-Ruane, S., & Spiro, R. (2000, March). *Seeing worlds in grains of sand: Cases, complexity, and cognitive flexibility in the Teachers' Learning Collaborative.* Paper presented at the annual meeting of the National Reading Conference, Scottsdale, AZ.

Britzman, D. (2002). *Practice makes practice* (rev. ed.). New York: Teachers College Press.

Burbules, N. C. (1993). *Dialogue in teaching: Theory and practice.* New York: Teachers College Press.

Cazden, C. B. (1988). *Classroom discourse: The language of teaching and learning.* Portsmouth, NH: Heinemann.

Cazden, C. B., John, V. P., & Hymes, D. (1972). *Functions of language in the classroom.* New York: Teachers College Press.

Cole, M. (1996). *Cultural psychology: A once and future discipline.* Cambridge, MA: Harvard University Press.

Dewey, J. (1915). *The school and society/the child and the curriculum.* Chicago: University of Chicago Press.

Erickson, F. (1986). Qualitative methods in research on teaching. In M. C. Wittrock (Ed.), *Handbook of research on teaching* (3rd ed., pp. 119–161). New York: Macmillan.

Erickson, F. (2004). *Talk and social theory: Ecologies of speaking and listening in everyday life.* Cambridge, UK: Polity Press.

Fairclough, N. (1989). *Language and power.* London: Longman.

Fairclough, N. (1995). *Critical discourse analysis: The critical study of language.* London: Longman.

Fisher, M. (2007). *Writing in rhythm: Spoken word poetry in urban classrooms.* New York: Teachers College Press.

Florio-Ruane, S. (1987). Sociolinguistics for educational researchers. *American Educational Research Journal, 24*(2), 185–197.

Florio-Ruane, S., & deTar, J. (2001). *Teacher education and the cultural imagination: Autobiography, conversation, and narrative.* Mahwah, NJ: Erlbaum.

Florio-Ruane, S., & McVee, M. (2000). Ethnographic approaches to literacy research. In M. Kamil, P. D. Pearson, & R. Barr (Eds.), *Handbook of reading research: Volume III* (pp. 153–162). Mahwah, NJ: Erlbaum.

Foucault, M. (1981). The order of discourse. In R. Young (Ed.), *Untying the text: A poststructuralist reader* (pp. 48–78). Boston: Routledge & Kegan Paul.

Foucault, M. (2002). *The archaeology of knowledge.* New York: Routledge. (Original work published 1969)

Freire, P. (1970). *Pedagogy of the oppressed.* New York: Continuum.

Gee, J. P. (1996). *Social linguistics and literacies: Ideology in discourses* (2nd ed.). London: Routledge.

Gee, J. P. (2008). *Social linguistics and literacies: Ideology in discourses* (3rd ed.). London: Routledge.

Giddens, A. (1979). *Central problems in social theory.* Berkeley: University of California Press.

Giddens, A. (1984). *The constitution of society: Outline of the theory of structuration.* Berkeley: University of California Press.

Gutierrez, K. (2008). Developing a sociocritical literacy in the third space. *Reading Research Quarterly, 43*(2), 148–164.

Heath, S. B. (1983). *Ways with words: Language, life, and work in communities and classrooms.* Cambridge, UK: Cambridge University Press.

Hymes, D. (1974). *Foundations in sociolinguistics: An ethnographic approach.* Philadelphia: University of Pennsylvania Press.

Kellner, D. (1995). *Media culture: Cultural studies, identity and politics, between the modern and the postmodern.* New York: Routledge.

Kirkland, D. (2008). The rose that grew from concrete: Postmodern blackness and new English education. *English Journal, 97*(5), 69–75.

Kress, G. (2003). *Literacy in the new media age.* London: Routledge.

Loomba, A. (2001). *Colonialism/postcolonialism: The new critical idiom.* London: Routledge.

Michaels, S. (1981). "Sharing time": Children's narrative styles and differential access to literacy. *Language in Society, 10,* 423–443.

Mills, S. (1997). *Discourse: The new critical idiom.* London: Routledge.

Moll, L. C., Amanti, C., Neff, D., & Gonzalez, N. (1992). Funds of knowledge for teaching: Using a qualitative approach to connect homes and classrooms. *Theory into Practice, 31*(2), 132–141.

Morrell, E. (2008). *Critical literacy and urban youth: Pedagogies of access, dissent, and liberation.* New York: Routledge.

Paley, V. G. (2000). *White teacher* (2nd ed.). Cambridge, MA: Harvard University Press.

Pecheux, M. (1982). *Language, semantics, and ideology.* New York: Macmillan.

Schiffrin, D. (1994). *Approaches to discourse.* London: Blackwell.

Spiro, R. J., Feltovich, P. J., Jacobson, M. L., & Coulson, R. L. (1990). Cognitive flexibility, constructivism, and hypertext: Theory and technology for the nonlinear and multidimensional traversal of complex subject matter. In D. Nix & R. J. Spiro (Eds.), *Cognition, education, and multimedia: Exploring ideas in high technology* (pp. 163–205). Hillsdale, NJ: Erlbaum.

CHAPTER 7

Discourse Analysis

WRITTEN TEXT

Susan R. Goldman
Jennifer Wiley

Written text can be approached from a variety of disciplinary perspectives and purposes. In the context of this volume, we approach discourse analysis of written text by asking why written texts are of concern to literacy researchers, why they need to be analyzed, and how the texts and their analyses inform theoretical and empirical research in literacy. Written texts are of concern to literacy researchers because the ability to read and understand them is definitional to literacy, at least in Western culture. But *written text* is far from monolithic. There are any number of written text genres, differentiated by their purpose or function as well as their structure or form (e.g., narrative, poetic, persuasive, informative). And within a genre texts vary in both their form and their content. A primary goal of the analysis of written text is to describe structure and content. It is important to do so because well-established empirical findings indicate that structure and content affect how readers read, understand, remember, and learn from written texts (Goldman, 1997; Goldman & Rakestraw, 2000; Hiebert, Englert, & Brennan, 1983; Lorch, 1989). The discourse analysis of written text provides a method for systematically describing texts that students read as well as those they write.

To get a sense of what we might want our analysis of written text to capture, read over the following example texts 1 and 2. They each deal with the topic of river ecosystems and were written to introduce young adolescents (11- to 13-year-olds) to the ideas of interdependence and environmental pollution. As you read them, think about how you might describe their characteristics, their similarities, and their differences. (Do this now before reading on in the chapter.)

TEXT 1: THE TUPELO RIVER MYSTERY

In the spring of 1999, a new nuclear power plant in the town of Bregsville went into operation. Local citizens and environmentalists were concerned because the power plant was located along a branch of the Tupelo River. They knew that a river is a very fragile **ecosystem**. The word *ecosystem* connects the idea of *eco*, which means a habitat or environment, with that of *system*, which means a set of relationships. Environmentalists were worried that the nuclear power plant would upset the balance of relationships among everything in the Tupelo River ecosystem.

There are many parts of the Tupelo River's ecosystem. Some are organisms such as fish, insects, animals, and plants. They live in and around the river. River systems also contain nonliving things such as water, the rocks on the bottom, and the mud on the banks of the river. The most important concept about any ecosystem, including the Tupelo River's, is that everything depends on everything else. A change in one part of the ecosystem could introduce changes in all parts of the ecosystem. There was concern that the operation of the nuclear power plant would introduce changes.

TEXT 2: ECOSYSTEMS

Any group of living and nonliving things interacting with each other can be considered as an ecosystem. Within each ecosystem, there are habitats that may vary in size. A habitat is the place where a population lives. A population is a group of living organisms of the same kind living in the same place at the same time. All of the populations interact and form a community. The community of living things interacts with the nonliving world around it to form the ecosystem. The living members of a river's system are the plants and animals that live around and within the river—and they are all connected to each other in what is called a food web.

Anything that is added to the water of our aquatic ecosystems that is not a normal part of the systems, and that should not be there, is a type of water pollution. There are many sources of water pollution. Some types of pollution can be traced directly to a particular spot, such as a factory or industrial plant. These sources of water pollution are easier to control because the actual point where the pollution is being added to the water can be identified.

Here are some of the things you might have come up with to describe the characteristics and the differences.

1. Text 1 is a story about a town; text 2 is more straight "content."
2. They both define ecosystem but they do it differently.
3. They are both about the same length and have the same number of paragraphs.
4. Text 2 talks about water pollution in general; text 1 talks about the impact of the nuclear power plant but doesn't say it is a potential source of pollution.
5. Text 2 talks about the food web, but text 1 just says that things in an ecosystem depend on each other.

We suspect that as you engaged in the analysis and comparison process, you were unsure of precisely how to describe what you were noticing. Discourse analysis provides a means to engage more systematically in the descriptive analysis and comparison of written texts. The particular perspective we take in this chapter assumes that discourse analysis is informed by knowledge of the content domains that the text is about. In other words, the method is not "content free."

WHAT IS THE METHOD?

Discourse analysis of written text is a method for describing the ideas and the relations among the ideas that are present in a text. The method draws on work in a variety of disciplines, including rhetoric, text linguistics, and psychology. These disciplines provide ways to describe and analyze how the structure and content of the text encodes ideas and the relations among the ideas. In describing these relations, it is important to initially define the genre to which the text belongs because structures differ across genre. For example, narrative stories differ from persuasive essays; news articles have a different form than editorials; and fiction texts have different structures than nonfiction. Differences in structure imply different relations among the ideas in the texts, especially at the global level. With respect to the differences between the example texts 1 and 2, the first difference we listed reflects just such genre differences.

The global level of relations is often referred to as the rhetorical structure of the text. Different rhetorical structures are appropriate for different genres. For example, the rhetorical structure of many stories involves the occurrence of a problem that protagonists attempt to resolve and, in "happy ending" stories, are successful at resolving. The story typically consists of a series of episodes that are causally related. A common form of episode relations occurs when there are a number of preconditions that must be met in order to resolve the overall problem. In other narrative rhetorical structures, the interepisode relations may be temporal, with one episode succeeding another but with goals that are not particularly related. (For further information about narrative structure, refer to Bamberg, 1997; Bloome, 2003; Mandler & Johnson, 1977; McCabe, 1997; Stein & Albro, 1997; Stein & Glenn, 1979; Trabasso & van den Broek, 1985.)

The global structure of nonfiction texts contrasts with those of fictional texts, and there is less agreement about the rhetorical structures that apply. Meyer (1985) proposed a set of five "top-level" rhetorical structures in an attempt to systematize the structure of the major genre of expository texts: collection or list, description, causal, comparative, and problem/solution (see also Weaver & Kintsch, 1991). These rhetorical structures may be signaled by particular words or phrases but do not have to be. Example text

2 is a description. Example text 1 is a bit more complicated, but we think it may be best described as a nonfiction narrative perhaps similar to a feature article in a news magazine or newspaper.

The analysis of written text is also concerned with understanding the local relations among the ideas conveyed in a text (i.e., relations among information in sentences occurring relatively close together in the text). It is precisely the relations among ideas that define the coherence of the text and make it more than the sum of its parts. Indeed, Sanders, Spooren, and Noordman (1992) defined coherence relations as the "aspect of meaning of two or more discourse segments that cannot be described in terms of the meaning of the segments in isolation. In other words, it is because of this coherence relation that the meaning of two discourse segments is more than the sum of its parts" (p. 2). There are a number of ways coherence relations are established. Halliday and Hasan (1976) identified four primary logical connector relations: temporal, as in an ordered sequence of events (e.g., the steps in a mathematical proof); additive, as in elaborations of an idea (e.g., main idea followed by details); causal, as in antecedent and consequent events; and adversative, as in the juxtaposition of contradictory information.

A number of discourse markers (also called linguistic cues) are relevant to understanding local relations among ideas. A specific class of discourse markers, called connectives, express, signal, or cue the underlying conceptual coherence relations. Examples of connectives are *because, furthermore*, and *however*. Other kinds of signaling devices (Lorch, 1989) signal the relationships of sentences to paragraphs and of paragraphs to one another and to the overall theme of the text.

Lorch (1989) distinguished signaling devices from those aspects of a text that communicate the semantic content: Signals *emphasize* particular aspects of content or structure, but they do not add content (Lorch, 1989). Signaling devices help readers pick out what to selectively attend to and how to differentiate the importance of different information in the text (Goldman & Durán, 1988; Goldman & Saul, 1990; Guthrie, 1988; Lorch & Chen, 1986; Lorch & Lorch, 1996). Lorch identified a variety of signaling devices used in expository prose, including titles, headings, and subheadings; repetition of content to emphasize, preview, or summarize; function indicators (pointer words such as *thus*, pointer phrases such as *in summary*, pointer sentences such as *let me summarize what has been said*); relevance indicators (*let me stress that*); enumeration devices; and typographical cues (underlining, boldface, and spatial layout such as indenting and centering).

A large body of empirical research indicates that some genres and content structures are more difficult for readers to understand than others. For example, knowledge of narrative structure generally appears earlier than knowledge of expository structure (Crowhurst, 1990; Englehard, Gordon,

& Gabrielson, 1992; Grabe, 2002; Langer, 1986; Scott & Windsor, 2000; Tolchinsky, Johansson, & Zamora, 2002). Of course, this may be a result of typical instructional practices of concentrating on narrative text in primary grades and not introducing expository forms until later (Duke, 2000; Pappas, 1993). When readers have knowledge of informational content structures and use that information to guide their processing of text, their understanding and memory are better than in the absence of such knowledge (Carrell, 1992; Englert & Hiebert, 1984; Garner et al., 1986; McGee, 1982; Meyer, Brandt, & Bluth, 1980; Taylor & Beach, 1984; Taylor & Samuels, 1983). Although literacy researchers have always been aware of genre, content, and structure differences among texts, historically there was far less recognition of the role that such differences might play in outcomes for readers and the implications for literacy education. This is no longer the case. Thus, it is critical for literacy educators to describe and understand the content and structure of written texts, the demands they place on readers, and the relationship between written texts students read and those they write.

THE ANALYSIS OF WRITTEN TEXT

The goal of analyzing written text is to arrive at systematic descriptions that provide a basis for comparing written texts with one another. But what kind of description? There are a number of issues to consider in answering this question, the most important of which is what questions the researcher wishes to address with the analysis. If, for example, interest is in how much of the text a student remembers exactly as it was presented, counting the number of words that can be reproduced in correct order and position might be all that is necessary. Of course, even word counting can become more complex (e.g., if location in the text—beginning, middle, end—was important). Indeed, early work on memory for written text used the word-counting method (Clark, 1940, cited in Carroll, 1972; Gomulicki, 1956; King, 1960, 1961, cited in Carroll, 1972). Word counting might also be useful if interest is in a simple measure of fluency of producing written text.

A fairly common reason for wanting a systematic description of written text is to determine the reading difficulty of a passage, referred to as passage *readability*. Traditional readability formulas such as the Flesch Reading Ease index make extensive use of word complexity (assessed via number of syllables), number of sentences, and number of sentences per 100 words (see Klare, 1974–1975, for review). However, readability formulas do not correspond well with how easy the text makes it to understand the concepts and ideas. One reason for this is that making explicit the local relation between ideas sometimes results in longer sentences. Consider the contrast between examples 1 and 1a:

1. Torrential rains fell on Saturday. The road collapsed.
1a. The road collapsed because of the torrential rains that fell on Saturday.

Even though example 1a is a longer sentence, readers find it easier to understand the causal connection than in example 1 (Pearson, 1974–1975).

Traditional readability formulas also fail to consider the familiarity of the concepts in the passage. More recently, the Lexile has been used to assess readability (Stenner & Wright, 2002). The Lexile determines readability using sentence length and word frequency. Word frequency is a rough index of concept familiarity and is being widely used. (For additional information, see *www.lexile.com*.) In addition to underestimating the impact of readers' knowledge of the passage topic, readability formulas do not take into account the text as a whole. That is, texts have global structure that transcends the individual words and sentences. It is perfectly obvious, for example, that the meaning of a text is entirely different when we reorder the sentences.

To illustrate the limitations of text descriptions that are based only on readability formulas, we need only refer back to the example texts 1 and 2. A number of the differences we noted would have been masked if all we had done was look at word counts and readability indices. Comparing example texts 1 and 2, the relevant data are, respectively, 190 versus 201 words; 12 versus 11 sentences; 15.8 versus 18.2 words per sentence; 6 versus 5.5 sentences per paragraph; 47.3 versus 58 for the Flesch Reading Ease; 10.5 versus 9.6 for the Flesch-Kincaid grade level; and 970 versus 1030 for the Lexile measure. On the basis of these data the two texts are hard to distinguish. Thus, readability formulas provide only a rough descriptive and comparative index and miss many of the important characteristics of texts.

Typically, it is the ideas in text and their interrelations that are of interest to the literacy researcher. Some ideas can be conveyed in a word or two; others require several sentences and paragraphs. How then do we systematically describe the ideational content and structure of written text?

The most commonly accepted unit of analysis among literacy researchers is some form of the proposition, a construct that appeared in the work of a number of linguists, psychologists, and computer scientists during the 1970s (e.g., Anderson, 1976; Fillmore, 1968; Frederiksen, 1975; Kieras, 1981; Kintsch, 1974; Kintsch & van Dijk, 1978; Meyer, 1975; Schank, 1972; van Dijk, 1972). A widely used formulation, and the one we favor, is that of Kintsch and van Dijk (1978). Specifically, van Dijk and Kintsch (1983) defined the proposition as a theoretical unit that corresponds roughly to the meaning of a clause. A whole text is represented by organizing the set of propositions derived from the clauses and sentences in the text. Different forms of organizing the propositions include hierarchical lists, semantic networks, and procedural networks. The proposition itself consists of the simple concepts or *atomic propositions* and the *propositional scheme* (or complex proposition) into which the atomic propositions are arranged. The propositional scheme consists of a *predicate* and one or more *arguments*. Predicates are main verbs of clauses or connectives between clauses. Arguments have functional roles with respect to the predicate (e.g., agent, patient, and object location) or can be embedded propositional schemes. A proposition refers to a state, an event, or an action. The psychological plausibility of clause-level propositional schemes has been demonstrated in a variety of research studies, although we do not review them here (Anderson & Bower, 1973; Graesser, 1981; Kintsch & Keenan, 1973; Ratcliff & McKoon, 1978).

In Figure 7.1, we present a schematic of the propositional scheme for the first sentence in example text 1: *In the spring of 1999, a new nuclear power plant in the town of Bregsville went into operation.* To generate the propositional representation shown in Figure 7.1, we analyze its elements and decide whether it is an event or a state. As shown in Figure 7.1, the decision we reach is that it is an EVENT. The decision is based on our understanding that the words *went into operation* mark a change in state of some entity, in this case *a new nuclear power plant*. Because it is an inanimate entity, we refer to the plant as an Object. We also know that events occur in time and space, and indeed the first sentence provides us with this information. Time and place are indicators of the circumstances of the event. The structure of the propositional scheme conveys these relations. But the schematic in Figure 7.1 does not accurately reflect the *atomic level* of analysis. The atomic level, resulting from further analysis of the phrases in the schematic, is shown in the lower portion of Figure 7.1. The atomic level can be considered the basic, core level of meaning, and although it may be useful from linguistic or philosophical perspectives to capture this level, it is often too detailed for purposes of looking at understanding and learning. For our purposes, we typically represent propositions at the more molar level shown in Figure 7.1.

Figure 7.2 shows the same sentence represented as a semantic network. We have left the links unlabeled, but they could be labeled with object, time, and location.

Although it is useful for didactic purposes to work out several sentences at the level of detail shown in Figure 7.1, it is often impractical to draw such structures for every sentence in a written text. The typical way in which we create the propositions of a text is in a list format as shown here.

    i. Went into operation (OBJECT: new nuclear power plant, TIME: ii, PLACE: iii)
   ii. In the spring of 1999
  iii. In the town of Bregsville

We refer to the proposition labeled *i* as the predicate proposition; *ii* and *iii* specify the time and place of the main action. We use indentation to show

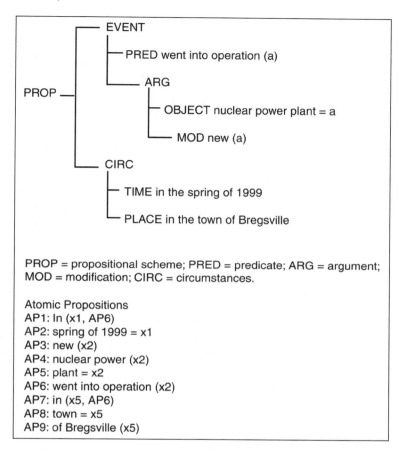

PROP = propositional scheme; PRED = predicate; ARG = argument; MOD = modification; CIRC = circumstances.

Atomic Propositions
AP1: In (x1, AP6)
AP2: spring of 1999 = x1
AP3: new (x2)
AP4: nuclear power (x2)
AP5: plant = x2
AP6: went into operation (x2)
AP7: in (x5, AP6)
AP8: town = x5
AP9: of Bregsville (x5)

FIGURE 7.1. Propositional scheme representation for the sentence *In the Spring of 1999, a new nuclear power plant in the town of Bregsville went into operation.*

that propositions *ii* and *iii* are subordinate to the predicate proposition. Depending on the discourse analyst, there might be additional propositions reflecting the adjectival modifiers of *plant*—for example, *iv.* TYPEOF plant: nuclear power; *v.* MOD plant: new. These would also be indented to show that they are subordinate to the main action. The level of detail needed in the proposition specification depends on the questions the researcher is addressing. The next sentence in the paragraph would be similarly represented, as shown in Figure 7.3. In sentence 2 there are two clauses that are causally related, shown in the figure as a BECAUSE node (shaded and rectangular). The argument *power plant* is common to sentences 1 and 2; this overlap is shown in Figure 7.3 by having the node, shaded for emphasis, linked to the predicate of each sentence. Similarly, sentences 2 and 3 share an argument (*local citizens and environmentalists*). Understanding

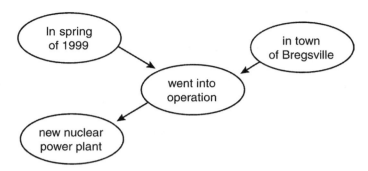

FIGURE 7.2. Semantic network representation of the propositional scheme for the sentence *In the Spring of 1999, a new nuclear power plant in the town of Bregsville went into operation.*

this connection requires the resolution of the referent for the pronoun *they* in sentence 3. Note that showing node overlap in the list format can get messy, but arrows are often used to show which cross-sentence overlaps exist. Illustrations of this can be found in a number of published papers (e.g., Goldman, Varma, & Coté, 1996; Goldman, Varma, Sharp, & the Cognition and Technology Group at Vanderbilt, 1999; Goldman & Varnhagen, 1986; Trabasso & van den Broek, 1985).

If we carried out the process demonstrated in Figures 7.2 and 7.3 for the remainder of the sentences in the paragraph and passage, the result would be an organized network or list of propositions connected on the basis of the meaning relations among the ideas. Organizing the individual clauses into a network or list depends on the semantic relationships among the ideas, often producing a hierarchically organized structure of super- and subordinated ideas. The title and first several sentences usually establish concepts that are subsequently repeated throughout the passage as more information about them is provided. Subsequent incoming information "attaches" to these concepts, creating the subordinate or supporting relation, as illustrated in Figures 7.1, 7.2, and 7.3. Sentences that have many subsequent sentences connected to them take on more superordinate, thematic status in the passage (e.g., Goldman et al., 1996; Kintsch & van Dijk, 1978; Meyer, 1975).

Texts in which the individual clauses are explicitly connected have high cohesiveness (Halliday & Hasan, 1976). Example 1a, previously discussed, is a highly *cohesive* sentence. *Coherence* is reflected in the connectedness among propositions in readers' representations. In example 1, readers might infer the causal relation that is explicit in example 1a, in which case the representation would be similarly coherent for examples 1 and 1a. Similarly, in Figure 7.3, we noted that the reader needs to make an anaphoric refer-

Identification of the clauses in the first two sentences
1. In the spring of 1999, a new nuclear power plant in the town of Bregsville went into operation.
2.1 Local citizens and environmentalists were concerned
2.2 because
2.3 the power plant was located along a branch of the Tupelo River.
3.1 They knew 3.2
3.2 that a river is a very fragile ecosystem.

Shorthand of the Propositional Schemes in the first three sentences.
    1.1. went into operation (OBJECT: new nuclear power plant, TIME: 1.2, PLACE: 1.3)
        1.2. in the spring of 1999
        1.3 in the town of Bregsville
    2.1 were concerned (AGENTS: local citizens and environmentalists)
    2.2 because (2.1, 2.3)
    2.3 was located (OBJECT: power plant, LOC: 2.4)
        2.4 LOC: 2.3, along a branch of the Tupelo River
    3.1 They knew 3.1
    3.2 is (OBJECT: river, OBJECT: ecosystem)
        3.3 very fragile (ecosystem)

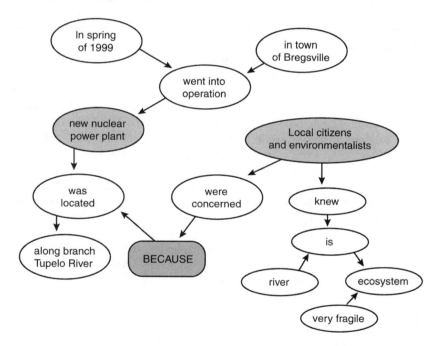

FIGURE 7.3. Construction of the representation of the initial part of text 1.

ence to resolve the referent for the pronoun *they* in sentence 3. If readers do not make that connection, they might make one between *Tupelo River* in sentence 2 and *river* in sentence 3, an inference based on the specific river being an instance or example of the general class of rivers. If readers failed to make either the anaphoric or the general-to-specific inference, the two sentences would be unconnected and a gap in local coherence would exist. Lack of coherence in readers' representations of text make it difficult to understand the meaning of the text as a whole; information remains in bits and pieces, so to speak.

To foster the development of coherent representations, texts often supply cues (cohesive devices). This should make it easier to establish coherence but only for those readers who understand how to interpret the cues (Goldman & Rakestraw, 2000). Texts that have few cohesive devices require that readers work to fill in the gaps among ideas. Doing so frequently requires that readers have requisite prior knowledge of the content domain or knowledge of the genre of the text. If they do not and the text has few cohesive devices, understanding is often not very good. As might be expected, comprehension by readers who know little about the topic of a text is aided by cohesive text. However, researchers have found that readers who have high content knowledge achieve deeper understanding of a text in which the cohesion is not obvious compared with those in which cohesion is explicit (Kintsch, 1990; Loxterman, Beck, & McKeown, 1994; McNamara, Kintsch, Butler-Songer, & Kintsch, 1996; Voss & Silfies, 1996). Discourse analysis permits researchers to compare texts in terms of propositional structure and the ease with which connections across propositions, hence coherence, can be achieved.

The interaction with prior knowledge notwithstanding, text cohesion is an important predictor of text difficulty that is not taken into account by traditional readability indices even when augmented by word frequency measures as in the Lexile method. In response to the need to develop indices of text cohesion, Graesser, McNamara, Louwerse, and Cai (2004) have developed a computational approach called Coh-Metrix. Coh-Metrix calculates indices of predictors of text difficulty at the surface, propositional, representational, and genre/rhetorical levels (Graesser & McNamara, in press). Indices that have been found to distinguish between high- and low-cohesion texts include coreferential noun overlap, sentence-to-sentence meaning overlap, and causal explicitness (McNamara, Louwerse, McCarthy, & Graesser, 2010). In the same study, McNamara and colleagues (2010) reported that surface code indices by themselves did not reliably discriminate between high- and low-cohesion texts. The research around the development of Coh-Metrix empirically demonstrates the need to take into account multiple levels of discourse in determining text difficulty. There is a public version of the Coh-Metrix tool (*cohmetrix.memphis.edu*, version 2) that we encourage interested readers to explore.

The Role of Prior Knowledge

Why should it be the case that readers with high knowledge of the topic achieve deeper understanding when they have to create coherence? Answering this question involves expanding our discussion of text representation to include an interpretive level. Researchers in the early 1980s recognized a distinction between creating a representation of the text itself and integrating the information in the text with prior knowledge, thereby constructing a representation of the situation described by the text. The representation of the text itself, labeled the *textbase*, is what we have been constructing thus far (see Figure 7.3). The representation of the situation is referred to as a *mental model* (Johnson-Laird, 1983) or *situation model* (van Dijk & Kintsch, 1983) and reflects readers' interpretations of the meaning of the text (Perfetti, 1989), constructed by integrating prior knowledge with the ideas in the textbase. Interpretations come about through elaborative, explanatory, and evaluative processes. To conclude that learning has occurred, evidence of a situation model representation is needed (Kintsch et al., 1993; McNamara et al., 1996). Assessment of learning thus involves going beyond reproductive or recognition memory; readers need to demonstrate that they have formed a coherent model of the situation described in the text. This can be demonstrated in a variety of ways, such as by applying the information to a new situation (Wiley & Voss, 1999), verifying inferences that go beyond the information presented in the text (Wiley et al., 2009), providing verbal explanations or drawings that illustrate how something works (e.g., Chi, De Leeuw, Chiu, & Lavancher, 1994), or successfully carrying out a procedure (Mills, Diehl, Birkmire, & Mou, 1995).

Discourse Analysis of Texts Produced by Readers and Learners

Written discourse is not only a medium of information presentation. It is also a window into the mental model of the learner. Frequently, readers and learners are asked to produce text, sometimes to demonstrate what they have learned from reading a particular textbook selection, passage, or set of passages. These learner-produced texts can be analyzed and compared with what learners read or were presumed to have read. Other times learners produce written discourse "spontaneously" and in the absence of some just read "stimulus" material. In these situations, the written discourse communicates writers' content knowledge, beliefs, feelings, and command of the language. In the discussion that follows, we focus on learner-produced writing in the context of presented texts and only briefly discuss spontaneous writing.

Writing in Response to Presented Text

When learners produce essay responses to open-ended questions, their writing samples can be analyzed with respect to "how close" they are to the presented text and how much they go beyond what was "in" the text through inferences and elaborations. We can look for evidence of coherence in the mental model and of appropriate integration of new and prior knowledge, both important benchmarks of understanding (Coté & Goldman, 1999; Coté, Goldman, & Saul, 1998). As such, they act as a window into the internal representations that readers have constructed. By comparing texts learners write with those they have read, it is possible to characterize comprehension and understanding. For example, we might want to know the degree to which they have accurately understood the meaning of the text or how they have interpreted the information, as reflected in elaborations and explanations. To facilitate such analyses, we want to conduct discourse analyses of the written texts produced by readers and learners and do so in a form that is compatible with the representation of the material that they read and from which they learn.

Responses to Specific Prompts and Questions

Consider the three student-produced written texts provided in Table 7.1. These are the responses of three seventh-grade students who had read "The Tupelo River Mystery" text in its entirety. They were asked to respond to the specific probe item, "Explain the idea of an ecosystem." The researchers (Goldman et al., 2003; Oney et al., 2003) used this type of probe because they were interested in what students had understood about ecosystems. They were not interested in learners' memory for the story per se, so rather than asking for recall of what they remembered from "The Tupelo River Mystery," the researchers gave students a targeted prompt.

To understand the students' writing samples, it is important to know the gist of "The Tupelo River Mystery" beyond the two paragraphs in the example at the beginning of the paper. (Full text is available at *litd.psch. uic.edu/docs/river_7th.doc*.) Briefly, scientists decided to monitor the river to see whether any changes in the ecosystem occurred. Over a 10-month period they found that the mayfly population had declined by over 70% and the rainbow darter by 50%, but the Elodea plant population had increased by 20%. This was explained in terms of a food chain in which the mayflies were central, serving as food for the darter and eating the Elodea. The cause of the food chain disruption was a 5-degree increase in the river temperature, resulting in less dissolved oxygen and the negative impact on the mayfly population. The scientists traced the rise in temperature to thermal pollution from the nuclear power plant.

We noticed several things about the seventh graders' responses. (Before reading on, you might want to take the researcher's role and read over the responses, thinking about similarities and differences among them and between each and the passage.) First, the responses differ in length; however, longer is not necessarily better. Student 3 has the shortest response but perhaps the best explanation of an ecosystem. Student 2 likens an eco-

TABLE 7.1. Three Seventh-Grade Students' Responses to the Prompt "Explain the Idea of an Ecosystem" Based on "The Tupelo River Mystery" Passage

Student 1

An ecosystem is kind of like a cycle. A cycle that depends on its self. For example the insects that live in the water play in an important in the cycle. The insects eat a certain plant which helps the water in certain ways. Also the insect is a major food source for a certain species of fish. This insect does a very important part in keeping this ecosystem [flawless?]. If you remove this insect there will eventually be no fish and a huge surplus of plants. This is what I believe an ecosystem is.

Student 2

The ecosystem is like a chain that connects different species together and the different animals depend on each other and if one species becomes endangered then that mess the whole system up and the other animals won't be able to live right. When pollution is occurred it can kill off lots of animals and destroy the whole ecosystem. An ecosystem is also similar to a food chain because if one species die or if a certain type of plant isn't growing any more then it will knock off the whole system. If an animal kills another species than that also will affect the ecosystem as well. Also if one animal dies then the other animal won't be able to eat and then the next animal will die off and then the whole system will be gone.

Student 3

An ecosystem is the relationship among the things in an environment. In an ecosystem, everything is related to one another. If one thing is removed, many other things are effected. In the story, the water temperature increased and it caused Mayflies to die. Fishes that feed on Mayflies began to die too. In contrast, the plants the Mayflies ate increased in number. That's an example of a food chain in the ecosystem.

system to the food chain and includes a number of specifics about how the death of one animal or plant will affect what happens to others. Student 2 seems to have accurate details but lacks the more interpretive understanding that student 3 seems to have achieved. Finally, student 1 seems to have bits and pieces of what the text contained, but they are not connected in ways that show the interrelationships. If we were to paraphrase student 1's response, it might go something like the following: "An ecosystem is a cycle in which insects are important. They eat plants and are a food source for certain fish." The more general notion of an ecosystem is missing. This contrasts dramatically with student 3, who uses the specifics in the story to exemplify the general principles of an ecosystem.

If we want our analyses of these data to be capable of revealing the differences among these three kinds of responses, how are we to accomplish this? We need to specify the conceptual elements of an ecosystem as they are communicated in the text and look for correspondences in the students' responses. We start by dividing the responses into clauses, just as we did the text, and ask whether these clauses are meaning preserving of propositions from the passage. We also look at how the relations among the concepts are expressed and whether they are organized in a way that conveys a coherent situation or mental model of an ecosystem. This is the advantage of student 3's response over those of the other two. Student 3 has inferred a set of core principles about ecosystems based on the information in the text ("An ecosystem is a relational environmental system. In an ecosystem, everything is related to one another. If one thing is removed, other things are effected."). These principles are then exemplified with the specific species and causal chain (water temperature increase → decrease in mayfly → decrease in fish and increase in plant) that is described for the Tupelo River ecosystem. Student 3 seems to have used information from throughout the whole text in developing a mental model. In contrast, student 1 appears to be largely focused on the information contained in the two paragraphs in the text about the food chain. Like student 1, student 2 seems to draw on these paragraphs but the response is less tied to the specifics of insects and fish, suggesting more integration with prior knowledge of endangerment and interdependence in an ecosystem. These ideas are similar to the principles student 3 expresses, yet student 2 does not abstract them beyond specific animals. We might conclude that student 2 has a more concrete or specific situation model than student 3.

Specific prompts such as the one illustrated for "The Tupelo River Mystery" and other kinds of open-ended questions are one way to elicit information from learners and are quite similar to the kinds of questions teachers might pose to students on end-of-unit classroom tests for purposes of assessing learning. The recall task is another method that researchers commonly use to elicit text from students.

Writing in Response to Presented Text: Recall

The recall (or retell) task asks students to write down (or say) what they remember from the text they have heard or read. This task is quite commonly used with many text genres. Here we focus on recall of an informational passage on metabolism typical of those used by many researchers. In research with passages of this genre, subjects typically recall about 25 to 40% of the predicate propositions from the textbase. In crediting students with recalling propositions, researchers need to decide whether to adopt stringent or looser criteria. Using stringent criteria means that for credit to be given the students' wording must be very close to the passage wording. More commonly, looser criteria are used so that credit for inclusion of a proposition is based on comparability of meaning across the passage and students' productions. Comparability of meaning is usually based on the core idea of the predicate proposition.

The "Metabolism" passage shown in Table 7.2 has been used in research with children ranging in age from 8 to 12 years (Coté et al., 1998; Coté & Goldman, 1999). The "Metabolism" passage, along with several others that were used in the same experiment, was written to begin in the style of a feature article in a newsmagazine and to conform to a specific content structure (Coté et al., 1998; Coté & Goldman, 1999). For example, in the "Metabolism" passage, the first paragraph reported a new scientific invention, which we hoped would provide students with a reason for wanting to learn more about metabolism. From there, the passage structure is typical of the informational text genre. The second paragraph provided definitional information on metabolism; the next four paragraphs provided information on "four factors that affect metabolic rate." The final paragraph related back to the first, stating how the new invention would measure metabolism. For the most part, each sentence contained one predicate proposition, and in cases where there were two clauses in a sentence, we focused on the predicate that introduced new information. (For example, in sentence 4, *Different people have different metabolic rates that indicate how easily they can produce energy*, the new information and the main predicate we focused on was the underlined portion because the information in the second clause had already been given in the passage.)

Also in Table 7.2 are two examples that are representative of recall protocols obtained when students read the passage and were subsequently asked to recall "everything you remember." Several differences between the two recalls and between the recalls and the passage are evident. First, both recalls leave out much of the information in the passage. Student 1 wrote everything in a single paragraph, and student 2 created a list, using up and down arrows, which we assumed meant *increase* and *decrease*, respectively. What about content? Both students have changed much of the wording from the exact wording of the passage. This is fairly typical, and researchers often adopt the *meaning-preserving* criterion: Does the statement in the recall capture the meaning that was in the passage? If so, the student is credited with having remembered the information. By the *meaning-preserving* criterion, each student would be credited with remembering the four factors. In addition, student 1 included information from the passage to convey the impact the factor has on metabolism. In contrast, student 2 just indicated the relationship. Notice, however, that the way student 1 expressed these relationships is not identical to the propositions in the text. To take just one example, the passage stated:

> *For example, <u>some foods are hard to digest</u>, such as complex carbohydrates like rice. The body has to work harder to get energy from rice. If a person ate a steady diet of rice, the result would be a higher metabolic rate.*

Student 1 wrote:

> *Rice is hard to digest, so the metabolism would be high for someone on an all-rice diet.*

TABLE 7.2. Metabolism Passage and Recalls by Undergraduates

Metabolism

Customers in many pharmacies may soon be seeing the latest in new devices for the health conscious. A sports physiologist is developing the metabometer, a device that he hopes will measure the human body's ability to produce energy efficiently.

The rate at which the body produces energy is called metabolism. Different people have different metabolic rates that indicate how easily they can produce energy. The same person may have different metabolic rates, depending on the circumstances. Different species of animals also have different metabolic rates.

There are several factors that affect metabolic rate. One factor is the type of food a person or animal eats. For example, some foods are hard to digest, such as complex carbohydrates like rice. The body has to work harder to get energy from rice. If a person ate a steady diet of rice, the result would be a higher metabolic rate.

Another factor affecting metabolism is the climate of the environment. Temperature may cause the metabolism to change. People and animals that live in cold environments need to produce more energy in order to keep warm. Most animals that live in polar regions have high metabolisms. If people move from a warm to a cold climate, their metabolic rates will increase.

Metabolic rate also differs depending on activity level. Changing the level of activity may cause the body to change its metabolism because different activities require different amounts of energy. For example, basketball players use more energy than golfers so their metabolic rates are generally higher.

To some degree, metabolic rate is influenced by genetic inheritance. Children of parents who have high metabolic rates tend to have high metabolic rates also. This is because the body chemistry of the children is a combination of the body chemistry of the parents.

Metabolism is regulated by hormones produced by the thyroid gland, a tiny gland located at the base of the neck. These hormones regulate the behavior of all the cells in the body so that enough energy is produced. The metabometer will work by measuring hormone levels in the blood.

Student 1

A sports physiologist is trying to measure the metabolic rate by creating the metabolar. Metabolism is affected by many things. It depends on what someone eats. Rice is hard to digest, so the metabolism would be high for someone on an all-rice diet. Climate accounts for metabolism. People in colder climates have higher metabolic rates than people in warm climates. Genetics is responsible for metabolism too. If a child's parents both have high metabolic rates, the child will have a high metabolic rate too. Activity changes the metabolism. A golfer will have a lower metabolic rate than a basketball player because Golf does not require as much energy as Basketball.

Student 2

Metabolism: Deals w/ability of body to produce energy
Influenced by 4 things:

1. Diet: harder food to digest = ?? metabolism
2. Climate: ?? temperature = ?? metabolism
3. Physical activity: ? activity = ?? metabolism
4. Genetic: hormone released from thyroid, located at bottom of neck ?

The new "metabometer" measures the hormones being released.

Student 1 received credit for remembering the underlined portions of the passage. Student 2 received credit for the same underlined information even though *rice* was not mentioned. Although other researchers might argue with this scoring decision, the important point is that such decisions need to be made on a principled and reliable basis. To achieve this, we have found it not only useful but necessary to keep a log of coding decisions so that inter- and intrarater reliability can be achieved.

In general, the task of deciding on *meaning preserving* is nontrivial because of the variability in how people recall information they have read, even when they are accurate. As these two student examples illustrate, people combine multiple sentences and produce summary statements; they combine ideas from parts of different sentences; they make accurate as well as inaccurate inferences; and they express what they remember in different structural forms. To the degree that learners combine information and add information that goes beyond what is present in the text, we would credit their recall as reflecting situation-model-level understanding. (For a more detailed discussion, see Coté et al., 1998; Kintsch, 1994, 1998; McNamara & Kintsch, 1996; van Dijk & Kintsch, 1983; van Oostendorp & Goldman, 1999.)

In the analysis of the responses to "The Tupelo River Mystery" and "Metabolism" texts, we have attempted to model the kind of thinking that researchers need to do when they are attempting to understand what students have learned from reading a passage or set of passages on specific topics. You might have noticed that this thinking depends on understanding the conceptual domain as well as how that information is encapsulated in the specific passage. If one goal of reading informational text is to enable learners to acquire conceptual knowledge, the content and structure of that conceptual domain must be part of the discourse analysis of written text. This is as true for the analysis of passages and what they afford in the way of opportunities to learn concepts and relations in a particular domain as it is for understanding the situation models that are suggested by what learners write about these topics after reading.

Spontaneous Production of Written Discourse

The analysis of written text is often useful for assessing learners' prior knowledge, beliefs, feelings, and facility with the writing process. As indicated previously in our discussion, prior knowledge has a powerful impact on the way learners process, understand, and write about what they read. For informational text it is important to have a model of the conceptual domain in order to analyze both informational passages learners are provided with and what they learn as manifest in their written work. It is also possible to analyze essays that learners produce prior to any instruction in a topic area. These can be analyzed with respect to a conceptual model of the domain to estimate the contents and organization of learners' preinstruction grasp of the domain. This information can be used in several ways, two of which are extremely important from the standpoint of literacy and instruction: as baseline assessments of domain understanding that can be compared with understanding at a later time and to select materials that are optimally suited to learners' incoming knowledge level. (See Wolfe et al., 1998, for an alternative method for matching texts to readers.)

Written productions can also be quite informative with respect to children's cognitive and social development. Both content knowledge and knowledge of linguistic conventions, especially genre, are evident in children's writing. For example, in a study by Chapman (1994, 1995), first graders' productions during writer's workshop were analyzed in terms of what genres they represented. Chapman noted that over the course of the year children's writing became increasingly differentiated in terms of genre. Dyson (1997, 2003) examined the ways in which children construct their roles and relationships in text. In work with children in urban neighborhoods, she documented both challenges to and adoption of gendered and cultural stereotypes (Dyson, 2003). From an instructional perspective, reader response logs are frequently advocated as a means by which children can develop engagement and enjoyment in text as well as comprehension and reflective processes (Barr, Blachowicz, Katz, Kaufman, & Wogman-Sadow, 2001).

Subjective but Scientifically Sound

Discourse analysis of written text is a necessarily subjective activity. Subjectivity does not, however, mean idiosyncratic or arbitrary. Scientifically sound discourse analysis follows principles and processes that ensure the rigor and reliability of the endeavor. For example, discourse analysis needs to follow the standard procedures for developing coding schemes that can be used reliably by multiple coders (e.g., Strauss, 1987; Strauss & Corbin, 1998). These processes bring a greater degree of objectivity to the analysis. As mentioned previously, logs of decisions or difficult cases can help a rater maintain consistency across samples. In addition, it is standard practice to include some measure of interrater reliability. Reliability measures may be reported as simple correlations between raters, or when there is a finite set of possible observations and one can compute both hits and misses in the coding of observations, Cohen's (1960) kappa may be used. The purpose of having a second person code the data is to ensure that codes are applied in a principled manner. If two people can concur in their use of a coding scheme, it seems more likely that the coding scheme represents an objective set of criteria for differentiating among examples, and that differences in coding are meaningful and not just arbitrary or subjective judgments. With such evidence of reliability, discourse analysis can fulfill its promise as a tool for description and distillation of important similarities and differences in written texts.

AN EXEMPLAR OF THE ANALYSIS OF WRITTEN DISCOURSE

In this section, we provide an exemplar study that has leveraged discourse analysis methodology in order to better understand how students process and learn from written text. Using this particular study (Wolfe & Goldman, 2005), we highlight four ways in which discourse analysis was used to support the exploration of how students learn from a set of two historical documents. Specifically, discourse analysis was used to:

1. Inform the design of the texts that students were given to read and to describe, characterize, and quantify.
2. Analyze performance on open-ended prior knowledge assessments.
3. Document-processing strategies during the reading of the texts.
4. Analyze the reasoning in student explanations generated after reading.

A final affordance was the ability to examine relationships among the measures, particularly through correlations of measures derived from the discourse analysis of comments made during reading the written texts and the measures derived from the discourse analysis of explanations that students generated after reading the texts.

In this exemplar, Wolfe and Goldman (2005) were interested in adolescents' processing of information from multiple texts, reasoning about that information, and the relation between processing and reasoning. The texts represented two parallel accounts of a historical event, the Fall of Rome. Students first completed a prior knowledge assessment and then read the two texts, one after the other. Students thought out loud as they read each text. After reading the texts, students provided their own explanation for why Rome fell. The participants were sixth-grade students who had completed a 6- to 8-week unit on the Roman Empire approximately 2 months prior to the study. The materials consisted of two "historical documents" that were written by the researchers, a map of the Roman Empire (taken from the students' textbook) with an accompanying time line of major events in the rise and fall of the Empire, and a list of facts that were "additional" to the information in the other materials.

Design of Written Texts

The first instance in which discourse analysis was used in this study was in the design of the two texts. These texts were written to appear as if they were historical interpretations developed by two different historians. Each provided a different perspective on why the Roman Empire could not defend itself during the Barbarian invasion of 476 A.D.: hedonism (instantiated in terms of laziness) or the sheer size of the empire and its implications for defensibility. The texts were constructed to be structurally isomorphic, to agree on some information, including the Barbarian invasion, but to disagree as to the underlying cause of why the empire could not defend itself. Each text began with an explicit statement of disagreement with the theory presented in the other text. This was followed by a sentence indicating that the author had collected evidence to support his or her theory, followed by an explicit statement of his or her theory. Each text then developed a causal sequence of events that led to a conclusion: (1) the Roman Empire consisted of lazy citizens who could not effectively defend themselves, or (2) the Roman armies were too spread out to be able to defend against an attack on Rome. Each text cited a primary source in support of its argument (a painting or a diary). The last two sentences of each text stated that the Barbarians attacked and defeated the Roman Empire and reiterated the specific theory about the cause of the defeat. In addition to this attention to content and structure, the texts were also of comparable length and readability. The "lazy citizens" text was 12 sentences long, contained 209 words, and had a Flesch-Kincaid grade-level score of 5.1. The "empire size" text was 15 sentences long, contained 203 words, and had a Flesch-Kincaid grade-level score of 5.5.

Open-Ended Prior Knowledge Assessments

Before reading the texts, students were asked what they remembered about the Roman Empire and why it fell. The second instance of discourse analysis in this study was to characterize and quantify these open-ended responses. This prior knowledge assessment was scored as the number of correct clauses provided about the Roman Empire. One point was given for each correct clause, and one-half point was given for the mention of a name or city without further information. Some example comments are as follows: "They copied their agriculture from the Greeks," "If you were a woman you have very few rights," and "They would watch chariot racing in the Coliseum." Except for one student who was scored more than 3 standard deviations above the mean, most students were able to generate about four correct ideas about the Roman Empire.

Document-Processing Strategies

The third instance in which discourse analysis was used was in the coding of the think-aloud protocols as students read the two written texts. As a first step, the transcriptions of the think-alouds were divided into comments. A comment is the speech burst following the reading of a text sentence and corresponds to the coarse grain size used by Chi and colleagues (1994) in coding verbal protocols. Each comment was further parsed into events following procedures used by Coté and colleagues (1998) and corresponding to Chi and colleagues' use of the idea unit. Events reflect different kinds of processing or ways of thinking about the text. For example, one student said, "I guess he disagrees with the other person because she thought that the army was too spread out. So he doesn't think they covered too much territory." This comment contains two events. The first event (first sentence) connects the content of this sentence to the other text and the other historian's position. The second event (second sentence) is a paraphrase of the content of the sentence that was just read. Think-aloud data for all participants were coded by two independent coders, with disagreements resolved through discussion. Interrater agreement on number of events was 90%.

Next, these think-aloud events were classified into one of five categories reflecting different kinds of processing of, or thinking about, the text: paraphrases (repeating gist), evaluations (positive or negative comments about the texts), comprehension problems (i.e., difficulty resolving pronoun references), comprehension successes (commenting when things make sense), and elaborations (adding meaning). These categories were based on prior research (Coté et al., 1998) but adapted to accommodate the multiple-text aspect of this task. Two independent raters agreed on the classification of 92% of the think-aloud events. Disagreements were again resolved in discussion.

Elaborations constituted the majority of the events (58%). Paraphrase events (22%) and evaluative events (13%) were also present. There were few comprehension monitoring comments of either kind (3% each).

Because elaborations were the most frequent category of comments, two additional codes were developed in terms of (1) the source of the additional information and (2) the kind of processing involved. To determine the source of the information contained in elaborations, discourse analysis was used to identify overlap of information in comments with information from earlier in the text (same text); information from the other text, the map, or the time line (previous text); or information from a previous think-aloud comment. If there was no match with one of these sources, the information was attributed to prior knowledge. Almost half of the information used in elaborations was from prior knowledge (49%). However, the prior knowledge was overwhelmingly general world knowledge or personal experiences, not knowledge of the topic. The other sources of elaborations were distributed about equally across information from the same text (16%), the other text (18%), or a prior think-aloud comment (17%). What is of significance in this pattern is that 34% of the elaborations involved connections between the focal sentence and information that was directly traceable to other text materials that were processed during the session, suggesting that students were attempting to compare and contrast across sentences.

The way that students made use of information in their elaborations was also coded. The three types of elaborative processing that encompassed almost all of the comments were self-explanation, surface text connection, and irrelevant associations. Elaborations were divided about equally between associating (45%) and self-explaining (41%). Associative processing refers to connections that were not relevant to constructing a coherent understanding of the text (e.g., "My aunt visited Rome last year"). On the other hand, self-explanations involve meaningful integration of text content with prior knowledge or generation of a connection between text information that was not explicitly stated in the text. An example comment in this category is, "So they were afraid that something would happen because it was so far away or something." This is a causal self-explanation because it adds a causal connection between a sentence from the text ("It was so far away") and an emotional state (being afraid), presumably based on prior knowledge of circumstances that generate fear. Thus, the elaboration used prior knowledge to make a causal inference. Only 12% of comments represented surface text connections in which the reader related one sentence to another sentence on the basis of surface features ("That talked about distance too"). Interrater agreement on coding of the elaboration events was 86%.

The relation between these two coding schemes was also informative because students used the different sources of information in different kinds of processing activities. This point is important because certain types of processing are more likely to contribute to the formation of coherent representations of the texts. For example, although students used prior knowledge in about half of the elaboration events, 70% of these were irrelevant associations, which may not contribute to understanding. Only 23% of the instances of prior knowledge use were in the context of causal self-explanations, a kind of processing that is more likely to contribute to building a coherent representation of the texts.

Explanations for the Fall of Rome

A fourth way that discourse analysis was used in this study was to code the open-ended explanations that students generated after reading. These explanations were coded along three dimensions: number of causes generated, complexity of reasoning, and integration of causes. The first coding dimension was a count of the number of causes included in the final explanation. These could be one or both of the causes from the texts (laziness of citizens or large size of empire) or causes taken from the additional information that was provided or generated from prior knowledge (e.g., "The Barbarians were too strong"). Beyond this simple count, the complexity dimension attempted to capture the variation in how students talked about the causes they listed. Some participants listed a cause or causes and wrote nothing else about them (these responses received no points for complexity). Other students provided additional information. Additional information that elaborated on the causes but did not explain why they were being mentioned received 1 point for complexity. Responses that explained why causes were being stated received 2 points for complexity. A final dimension of the coding focused on whether students related causes to each other. When participants' responses integrated multiple causes by explaining the relation between (or among) the causes they had stated, they received an additional point. The points on these three dimensions were summed to give a score reflecting the level of reasoning demonstrated in these explanations. Ten of the explanations were coded by two raters, and agreement was 90% or better on each of the three dimensions. Differences were resolved through discussion. The remaining explanations were then coded by one of the raters. This analysis resulted in a mean reasoning score of 2.77, a mean number of causes of 1.48, and a mean complexity score of 1.18, indicating that students tended to do a little more than simply list the causes. However, only five students brought the alternative accounts together, explaining how the two causes from the texts combined to create the Fall of Rome.

Relations between Document-Processing Strategies and Explanation Coding

A final question of interest for this study was whether and how processing of the historical documents was related to the level of understanding that students achieved about the Fall of Rome. To address this question, the measures derived from the document-processing analyses were correlated with the reasoning scores. One main finding was that causal self-explanation during reading was related to better reasoning scores. A subsequent regression showed that causal self-explanations involving either prior knowledge or information from the other text were significant predictors of reasoning scores. Interestingly, noticing surface connections within the same text was also related to the reasoning score and contributed to the best fitting regression model. These surface connections may offer complementary mechanisms for constructing coherent representations. Furthermore, given the low correlation between prior knowledge self-explanations and surface connections, the data suggest that these alternative mechanisms are being used by different students. Finally, it is interesting to note that associative reasoning events (in which students made connections to irrelevant prior knowledge) were not predictive of reasoning scores. In other words, the discourse coding revealed specificity in the kinds of processing that benefited understanding of the topic.

Summary of Findings and Role of Discourse Analysis

The main goal of this exemplar study was to explore adolescents' processing of information from multiple texts, reasoning about that information, and the relation between processing and reasoning. To achieve this goal, discourse analysis was pivotal in at least four areas of the methodology. First, it was used to create a set of reading materials with similarity on a number of critical dimensions. Second, it was used to evaluate open-ended responses to a prior knowledge assessment. This was important to provide a baseline of student understanding before the reading activity. Third, it was used to classify and quantify the document-processing strategies that were used by students, including determining the source of information that was mentioned from either of the texts or the prior discourse and the way it was used. Fourth, it was used to classify and quantify the quality of students' final understanding of what caused the fall of the Roman Empire. It is perhaps these last two instances that best illustrate the power of discourse analysis and how it can inform our understanding of the relation between reading and learning processes. Importantly, this study was able to demonstrate that not all kinds of comments or "elaborative" processing lead to better understanding. Consistent with previous research using the think-aloud method (e.g., Chi et al., 1994; Coté & Goldman, 1999; Coté et al., 1998), self-explanation during reading was related to better reasoning on the postreading assessments. However, this study offers two additional insights. First, when students are learning from multiple sources, making connections across those sources can lead to better reasoning (see also Britt & Aglinskas, 2002; Wiley & Voss, 1999; Wiley et al., 2009). Second, for some students, making connections across sentences by using surface features may be an important route to bootstrapping comprehension. In summary, discourse analysis allowed for a fine-grained exploration of exactly which kinds of processing during reading led to better understanding. The coding involved in this exploration took into account the content structure and function of the information within a single text and across multiple texts (see also Wiley et al., 2009).

CONCLUDING COMMENTS

The approach to analysis that we have illustrated here provides a more complex picture of written discourse and students' understanding of it than is provided by a typical "right-answer" approach to scoring students' responses. Although more complex, the approach conveys information about specific concepts and ideas that students understand and how deeply they understand them. It also conveys information about how students' thinking differs from the information conveyed in the text, their misconceptions, and gaps in their understanding. As such, discourse-analytic approaches provide information that could guide instructional decision making in the classroom in ways that points on a multiple-choice or short-answer test cannot. In the future, we hope that the discourse-analytic approach will be more tractable for teachers to use in classroom instruction and assessment. Some research efforts are under way that are attempting to address this challenge through the use of various computational technologies (e.g., Foltz, Laham, & Landauer, 1999; Golden et al., 2003; Goldman, Golden, & van den Broek, 2007; Kintsch, Steinhart, Stahl, & LSA Research Group,

2000; Lawless, Goldman, Gomez, Manning, & Braasch, in press; McNamara, Graesser, & Louwerse, in press; Wolfe et al., 1998).

In closing, we wish to stress that researchers undertaking discourse analysis of written texts need to understand that it is an iterative process. It is driven by both theoretical and conceptual orientations and by the contents of the written discourse. In other words, even when researchers collect data with a priori ideas about the features or relationships that might be important, these ideas change as researchers engage in careful, scientific analysis of the written text that people produce. Discourse analysis is a process that successively approximates ways to adequately capture systematicity and variance across written texts and draw inferences about knowledge and learning.

ACKNOWLEDGMENTS

The development and research on the ecosystem materials was supported by a grant from the National Science Foundation (No. RECOI13669) to Susan R. Goldman, although no official endorsement by the Foundation should be inferred.

REFERENCES

Anderson, J. R. (1976). *Language, memory, and thought.* Hillsdale, NJ: Erlbaum.

Anderson, J. R., & Bower, G. (1973). *Human associative memory.* Washington, DC: Winston.

Bamberg, M. A. (1997). A constructivist approach to narrative development. In M. Bamberg (Ed.), *Narrative development: Six approaches* (pp. 89–132). Mahwah, NJ: Erlbaum.

Barr, R., Blachowicz, C. L. Z., Katz, C., Kaufman, B., & Wogman-Sadow, M. (2001). *Reading diagnosis for teachers: An instructional approach* (4th ed.). New York: Pearson Allyn & Bacon.

Bloome, D. M. (2003). Narrative discourse. In A. C. Graesser, M. A. Gernsbacher, & S. R. Goldman (Eds.), *Handbook of discourse processes* (pp. 287–320). Mahwah, NJ: Erlbaum.

Britt, M. A., & Aglinskas, C. (2002). Improving students' ability to identify and use source information. *Cognition and Instruction, 20,* 485–522.

Carrell, P. L. (1992). Awareness of text structure: Effects on recall. *Language Learning, 42,* 1–20.

Carroll, J. B. (1972). Defining language comprehension: Some speculations. In J. B. Carroll & R. O. Freedle (Eds.), *Language comprehension and the acquisition of knowledge* (pp. 1–30). Washington, DC: Winston.

Chapman, M. L. (1994). The emergence of genres: Some findings from an examination of first-grade writing. *Written Communication, 11*(3), 348–380.

Chapman, M. L. (1995). The sociocognitive construction of written genres in first grade. *Research in the Teaching of English, 29*(2), 164–192.

Chi, M. T. H., De Leeuw, N., Chiu, M., & Lavancher, C. (1994). Eliciting self-explanations improves understanding. *Cognitive Science, 18,* 439–477.

Cohen, J. A. (1960). A coefficient of agreement for nominal scales. *Educational Psychology Measurement, 20,* 37–46.

Coté, N., & Goldman, S. R. (1999). Building representations of informational text: Evidence from children's think-aloud protocols. In H. Van Oostendorp & S. R. Goldman (Eds.), *The construction of mental representations during reading* (pp. 169–193). Mahwah, NJ: Erlbaum.

Coté, N., Goldman, S. R., & Saul, E. U. (1998). Students making sense of informational text: Relations between processing and representation. *Discourse Processes, 25,* 1–53.

Crowhurst, M. (1990). The development of persuasive/argumentative writing. In R. Beauch & S. Hynds (Eds.), *Developing discourse practices in adolescence and adulthood* (pp. 200–223). Norwood, NJ: Ablex.

Duke, N. (2000). 3.6 minutes per day: The scarcity of informational texts in first grade. *Reading Research Quarterly, 35,* 202–224.

Dyson, A. H. (1997). *Writing superheroes.* New York: Teachers College Press.

Dyson, A. H. (2003). *The brothers and sisters learn to write: Popular literacies in childhood and school cultures.* New York: Teachers College Press.

Englehard, G., Gordon, B., & Gabrielson, S. (1992). The influence of mode of discourse, experiential demand, and gender on the quality of student writing. *Research in the Teaching of English, 26,* 315–336.

Englert, C. S., & Hiebert, E. H. (1984). Children's developing awareness of text structure in expository materials. *Journal of Educational Psychology, 76,* 65–74.

Fillmore, C. J. (1968). The case for case. In E. Bach & R. T. Harms (Eds.), *Universals of linguistic theory* (pp. 1–88). New York: Holt, Rinehart & Winston.

Foltz, P. W., Laham, D., & Landauer, T. K. (1999). The Intelligent Essay Assessor: Applications to educational technology. *Interactive Multimedia Electronic Journal of Computer-Enhanced Learning, 1*(2). Retrieved January 10, 2003, from *imej.wfu.edu/articles/1999/2/04/index.asp.*

Frederiksen, C. H. (1975). Representing logical and semantic structure of knowledge acquired from discourse. *Cognitive Psychology, 7,* 371–458.

Garner, R., Alexander, P., Slater, W., Hare, V. C., Smith, T., & Reis, R. (1986). Children's knowledge of structural properties of expository text. *Journal of Educational Psychology, 78,* 411–416.

Golden, R. M., Goldman, S. R., Thomas, C., Oney, B., Macleod, S., & Lauterbach, M. (2003, June). *Modeling text understanding: Applications for diagnostic assessment of reading.* Paper presented at the International Conference on Higher Level Language Processes in the Brain: Inference and Comprehension Processes, Hanse Institute for Advanced Study, Delmenhorst, Germany.

Goldman, S. R. (1997). Learning from text: Reflections on the past and suggestions for the future. *Discourse Processes, 23,* 357–398.

Goldman, S. R., & Durán, R. P. (1988). Answering questions from oceanography texts: Learner, task and text characteristics. *Discourse Processes, 11,* 373–412.

Goldman, S. R., Golden, R. M., Thomas, C., Oney, B., Macleod, S., & Lauterbach, M. (2003, June). *Applications of text processing models to diagnostic assessment of reading.* Paper presented at the 13th annual meeting of the Society for Text and Discourse, Madrid, Spain.

Goldman, S. R., Golden, R. M., & van den Broek, P. (2007). Why are computational models of text comprehension useful? In F. Schmalhofer & C. A. Perfetti (Eds.), *Higher level language processes in the brain: Inference and comprehension processes* (pp. 27–51). Mahwah, NJ: Erlbaum.

Goldman, S. R., & Rakestraw, J. (2000). Structural aspects of constructing meaning from text. In M. L. Kamil, P. B. Mosenthal, P. D. Pearson, & R Barr (Eds.), *Handbook of reading research: Volume III* (pp. 311–335). Mahwah, NJ: Erlbaum.

Goldman, S. R., & Saul, E. U. (1990). Flexibility in text processing: A strategy competition model. *Learning and Individual Differences, 2,* 181–219.

Goldman, S. R., Varma, S., & Coté, N. (1996). Extending capacity-constrained construction integration: Toward "smarter" and flexible models of text comprehension. In B. K. Britton & A. C. Graesser (Eds.), *Models of understanding text* (pp. 73–114). Mahwah, NJ: Erlbaum.

Goldman, S. R., Varma, K. O., Sharp, D., & Cognition and Technology Group at Vanderbilt. (1999). Children's understanding of complex stories: Issues of representation and assessment. In S. R. Goldman, A. C. Graesser, & P. van den Broek (Eds.), *Narrative comprehension, causality, and coherence: Essays in honor of Tom Trabasso* (pp. 135–160). Mahwah, NJ: Erlbaum.

Goldman, S. R., & Varnhagen, C. K. (1986). Memory for embedded and sequential story structures. *Journal of Memory and Language, 25,* 401–418.

Gomulicki, B. R. (1956). Recall as an abstractive process. *Acta Psychologica, 12,* 77–94.

Grabe, W. (2002). Narratives and expository macro-genres. In A. M. Johns (Ed.), *Genre in the classroom: Multiple perspectives* (pp. 249–267). Mahwah, NJ: Erlbaum.

Graesser, A. C. (1981). *Prose comprehension beyond the word.* New York: Springer Verlag.

Graesser, A. C., & McNamara, D. S. (in press). Computational analyses of multilevel discourse comprehension. *Topics in Cognitive Science.*

Graesser, A. C., McNamara, D. S., Louwerse, M., & Cai, Z. (2004). Coh-Metrix: Analysis of text on cohesion and language. *Behavioral Research Methods, Instruments, and Computers, 36,* 193–202.

Guthrie, J. T. (1988). Locating information in documents: Examination of a cognitive model. *Reading Research Quarterly, 23,* 178–199.

Halliday, M. A. K., & Hasan, R. (1976). *Cohesion in English.* London: Longman.

Hiebert, E. H., Englert, C. S., & Brennan, S. (1983). Awareness of text structure in recognition and production of expository discourse. *Journal of Reading Behavior, 15,* 63–79.

Johnson-Laird, P. N. (1983). *Mental models.* Cambridge, MA: Harvard University Press.

Kieras, D. E. (1981). Component processes in the comprehension of simple prose. *Journal of Verbal Learning and Verbal Behavior, 20,* 1–20.

Kintsch, E. (1990). Macroprocesses and microprocesses in the development of summarization skill. *Cognition and Instruction, 7,* 161–195.

Kintsch, E., Steinhart, D., Stahl, G., & LSA Research Group. (2000). Developing summarization skills through the use of LSA-based feedback. *Interactive Learning Environments, 8,* 87–109.

Kintsch, W. (1974). *The representation of meaning in memory.* Hillsdale, NJ: Erlbaum.

Kintsch, W. (1994). Text comprehension, memory, and learning. *American Psychologist, 49, 294–303.*

Kintsch, W. (1998). *Comprehension: A paradigm for cognition.* New York: Cambridge University Press.

Kintsch, W., Britton, B. K., Fletcher, C. R., Kintsch, E., Mannes, S. M., & Nathan, M. J. (1993). A comprehension-based approach to learning and understanding. In D. L. Medin (Ed.), *The psychology of learning and motivation: Advances in research and theory* (Vol. 30, pp. 165–214). New York: Academic Press.

Kintsch, W., & Keenan, J. (1973). Reading rate and retention as a function of the number of propositions in the base structure of sentences. *Cognitive Psychology, 5, 257–274.*

Kintsch, W., & van Dijk, T. A. (1978). Towards a model of text comprehension and production. *Psychological Review, 85, 363–394.*

Klare, G. R. (1974–1975). Assessing readability. *Reading Research Quarterly, 1, 63–102.*

Langer, J. A. (1986). *Children reading and writing: Structures and strategies.* Norwood, NJ: Ablex.

Lawless, K. A., Goldman, S. R., Gomez, K., Manning, F., & Braasch, J. (in press). Assessing multiple source comprehension through evidence centered design. In J. P. Sabatini & E. R. Albro (Eds.), *Assessing reading in the 21st century: Aligning and applying advances in the reading and measurement sciences.* Lanham, MD: Rowman & Littlefield.

Lorch, R. F., Jr. (1989). Text signaling devices and their effects on reading and memory processes. *Educational Psychology Review, 1, 209–234.*

Lorch, R. F., Jr., & Chen, A. H. (1986). Effects of number signals on reading and recall. *Journal of Educational Psychology, 78, 263–270.*

Lorch, R. F., Jr., & Lorch, E. P. (1996). Effects of organizational signals on free recall of expository texts. *Journal of Educational Psychology, 88, 38–48.*

Loxterman, J. A., Beck, I. L., & McKeown, M. G. (1994). The effects of thinking aloud during reading on students' comprehension of more or less coherent text. *Reading Research Quarterly, 29, 353–367.*

Mandler, J. M., & Johnson, N. S. (1977). Remembrance of things parsed: Story structure and recall. *Cognitive Psychology, 9, 111–151.*

McCabe, A. (1997). Developmental and cross-cultural aspects of children's narration. In M. Bamberg (Ed.), *Narrative development: Six approaches* (pp. 137–174). Mahwah, NJ: Erlbaum.

McGee, L. M. (1982). Awareness of text structure: Effects on recall of expository text. *Reading Research Quarterly, 17, 581–590.*

McNamara, D. S., Graesser, A. C., & Louwerse, M. (in press). Sources of text difficulty: Across the ages and genres. In J. P. Sabatini & E. R. Albro (Eds.), *Assessing reading in the 21st century: Aligning and applying advances in the reading and measurement sciences.* Lanham, MD: Rowman & Littlefield.

McNamara, D. S., Kintsch, E., Butler-Songer, N., & Kintsch, W. (1996). Are good texts always better?: Interactions of text coherence, background knowledge, and levels of understanding in learning from text. *Cognition and Instruction, 14, 1–43.*

McNamara, D. S., & Kintsch, W. (1996). Learning from texts: Effects of prior knowledge and text coherence. *Discourse Processes, 22, 247–288.*

McNamara, D. S., Louwerse, M., McCarthy, P. M., & Graesser, A. C. (2010). Coh-Metrix: Capturing linguistic features of cohesion. *Discourse Processes, 47*, 292–330.

Meyer, B. J. F. (1975). *The organization of prose and its effects on memory.* Amsterdam: North-Holland.

Meyer, B. J. F. (1985). Prose analysis: Purposes, procedures, and problems. In B. K. Britton & J. Black (Eds.), *Analyzing and understanding expository text* (pp. 11–64, 269–304). Hillsdale, NJ: Erlbaum.

Meyer, B. J. F., Brandt, D. M., & Bluth, G. J. (1980). Use of top level structure in text: Key for reading comprehension of ninth grade students. *Reading Research Quarterly, 16*, 72–103.

Mills, C. B., Diehl, V. A., Birkmire, D. P., & Mou, L. (1995). Reading procedural texts: Effects of purpose for reading and predictions of reading comprehension models. *Discourse Processes, 20*, 79–107.

Oney, B., Goldman, S. R., Lauterbach, M., Braasch, J., Kusumgar, R., Brodowinska, K., et al. (2003, April). *Assessing complex comprehension through computer based and paper and pencil testing.* Paper presented at the annual meeting of the American Educational Research Association, Chicago.

Pappas, C. C. (1993). Is narrative primary?: Some insights from kindergarteners' pretend readings of stories and information books. *Journal of Reading Behavior, 25*, 97–129.

Pearson, P. D. (1974–1975). The effects of grammatical complexity on children's comprehension, recall and conception of semantic relations. *Reading Research Quarterly, 10*, 155–192.

Perfetti, C. A. (1989). There are generalized abilities and one of them is reading. In L. B. Resnick (Ed.), *Knowing, learning, and instruction: Essays in honor of Robert Glaser* (pp. 307–333). Hillsdale, NJ: Erlbaum.

Ratcliff, R., & McKoon, G. (1978). Priming in item recognition: Evidence for the propositional structure of sentences. *Journal of Verbal Learning and Verbal Behavior, 17*, 403–417.

Sanders, T. J., Spooren, W. P. M., & Noordman, L. G. M. (1992). Toward a taxonomy of coherence relations. *Discourse Processes, 15*, 1–35.

Schank, R. C. (1972). Conceptual dependency: A theory of natural language understanding. *Cognitive Psychology, 3*(4), 552–631.

Scott, C., & Windsor, J. (2000). General language performance measures in spoken and written narrative and expository discourse of school-age children with language learning disabilities. *Journal of Speech, Language, and Hearing Research, 43*, 324–339.

Stein, N. L., & Albro, E. R. (1997). Building complexity and coherence: Children's use of goal-structured knowledge in telling stories. In M. Bamberg (Ed.), *Narrative development: Six approaches* (pp. 5–44). Mahwah, NJ: Erlbaum.

Stein, N. L., & Glenn, C. (1979). An analysis of story comprehension in elementary school children. In R. Freedle (Ed.), *New directions in discourse processing* (Vol. 2, pp. 53–120). Norwood, NJ: Ablex.

Stenner, A. J., & Wright, B. D. (2002). *Readability, reading ability, and comprehension.* Paper presented at the Association of Test Publishers Hall of Fame Induction for Benjamin D. Wright, San Diego, CA.

Strauss, A. (1987). *Qualitative analysis for social scientists.* Cambridge, UK: Cambridge University Press.

Strauss, A., & Corbin, J. (1998). *Basics of qualitative research techniques and procedures for developing grounded theory* (2nd ed.). London: Sage.

Taylor, B. M., & Beach, R. W. (1984). The effects of text structure instruction on middle grade student comprehension and production of expository text. *Reading Research Quarterly, 19,* 134–146.

Taylor, B. M., & Samuels, S. J. (1983). Children's use of text structure in the recall of expository material. *American Educational Research Journal, 40,* 517–528.

Tolchinsky, L., Johansson, V., & Zamora, A. (2002). Text openings and closings: Textual autonomy and differentiation. *Written Language and Literacy, 5,* 219–254.

Trabasso, T., & van den Broek, P. (1985). Causal thinking and the representation of narrative events. *Journal of Memory and Language, 24,* 612–630.

van Dijk, T. A. (1972). *Some aspects of text grammars.* The Hague, The Netherlands: Mouton.

van Dijk, T. A., & Kintsch, W. (1983). *Strategies of discourse comprehension.* New York: Academic Press.

van Oostendorp, H., & Goldman, S. R. (Eds.). (1999). *The construction of mental representations during reading.* Mahwah, NJ: Erlbaum.

Voss, J. F., & Silfies, L. N. (1996). Learning from history text: The interaction of knowledge and comprehension skill with text structure. *Cognition and Instruction, 14,* 45–68.

Weaver, C. A., III, & Kintsch, W. (1991). Expository text. In R. Barr, M. L. Kamil, P. Mosenthal, & P. D. Pearson (Eds.), *Handbook of reading research: Volume II* (pp. 230–243). New York: Longman.

Wiley, J., Goldman, S. R., Graesser, A. C., Sanchez, C. A., Ash, I., & Hemmerich, J. (2009). Source evaluation, comprehension, and learning in Internet science inquiry tasks. *American Educational Research Journal, 46,* 1060–1106.

Wiley, J., & Voss, J. F. (1999[0]). Constructing arguments from multiple sources: Tasks that promote understanding and not just memory for text. *Journal of Educational Psychology, 91,* 1–11.

Wolfe, M. B., & Goldman, S. R. (2005). Relationships between adolescents' text processing and reasoning. *Cognition and Instruction, 23*(4), 467–502.

Wolfe, M. B., Schreiner, M. E., Rehder, B., Laham, D., Foltz, P. W., Kintsch, W., et al. (1998). Learning from text: Matching readers and texts by latent semantic analysis. *Discourse Processes, 25,* 309–336.

CHAPTER 8

Ethnographic Research

Victoria Purcell-Gates

Literacy researchers who operate out of a theoretical frame that views literacy as cultural practice are particularly drawn to *ethnography* as a methodological tool. This is because ethnography is grounded in theories of culture and allows researchers to view literacy development, instruction, learning, and practice as they occur naturally in sociocultural contexts.

Ethnography contributes to the quilt of research methodologies in that it allows literacy researchers to explore and come to understand phenomena about which little is known. As such, it provides those researchers who are so inclined a method for exploring and making sense of their data that is scientific and trustworthy. If done appropriately, the results, or outcomes, of ethnographies provide critical understandings of language and literacy in situ. They offer hitherto unknown maps and perspectives on literacy learning and development, without which teachers and researchers would be operating more or less blindly, in the dark, as they plan for and implement instructional strategies that "should" work according to other research paradigms.

Ethnographies provide the landscapes and the details of worlds. They aim to discover, understand, and describe human behavior holistically, as it occurs naturally within social and cultural contexts. In so doing, ethnographers can look for patterns and themes that ethnographic consumers can take away and use to enhance their own understandings of similar actors and contexts.

Although much, but not all, of the data collected by ethnographers is *qualitative*, ethnography is distinguishable within the category of qualitative research in that it is rooted in the concept of culture. This is not true of all qualitative research. As LeCompte and Schensul (1999b) emphasize, "Ethnography generates or builds theories of cultures—or explanations of

135

how people think, believe, and behave—that are situated in local time and space" (p. 8).

LeCompte and Schensul (1999b) list seven characteristics of ethnography that are useful when conceptualizing this methodology and differentiating it from others:

- It is carried out in a natural setting, not in a laboratory.
- It involves intimate, face-to-face interaction with participants.
- It presents an accurate reflection of participants' perspectives and behaviors.
- It uses inductive, interactive, and recursive data collection and analytic strategies to build local cultural theories.
- It uses multiple data sources, including both quantitative and qualitative data.
- It frames all human behavior and beliefs within a sociopolitical and historical context.
- It uses the concept of culture as a lens through which to interpret results.

Our understandings of literacy and literacy learning have been enhanced and advanced by an array of ethnographies over the years. In the following sections, I draw on several of these to illustrate methodological points. I used several criteria for the ethnographies I have chosen for illustrative purposes: (1) The study has won awards; (2) the author is particularly well known for methodological rigor; (3) the ethnographic findings are recognized as being of high significance to the field of literacy; or (4) I am particularly familiar with the work because it is my own and I can "think aloud" about research decision making in ways I could not do with the work of others.

QUESTIONS PARTICULARLY SUITED TO ETHNOGRAPHIC INQUIRY

As is true for other research methodologies, ethnography follows from particular types of research questions or, more appropriately for ethnography, research foci. Because ethnography seeks to *explain, describe,* and *provide insight* into human behavior in context, it is appropriate for questions that ask *why, how, what is happening,* and *what does it look like.* It is *not* appropriate for inquiries that seek to isolate factors for causal implication (experimental/quasi-experimental). Nor is it appropriate for studies that seek to describe, count, or index items, groups, or events that are identified as of interest prior to the research (descriptive), although descriptive data may be incorporated within an ethnography.

Ethnography is not for researchers who already know what they are seeking or for those who have strong hypotheses to test. Rather, it is for those researchers who are truly wondering, seeking, curious about some aspect of literacy as it occurs naturally in sociocultural contexts. These contexts can be schools, classrooms, homes, communities, workplaces— any naturally occurring context for literacy use. Theoretically, even the context of a scientific laboratory is considered to be sociocultural, and ethnographic inquiry would be appropriate given the research focus of coming to understand and describe literacy use as it occurs and is practiced within the culture of a scientific lab. In her award-winning ethnography (the Edward B. Fry Book Award, presented at the 2002 annual meeting of the National Reading Conference in Miami, Florida), *Literacy Practices as Social Acts: Power, Status, and Cultural Norms in the Classroom* (2001), Cynthia Lewis states as her research focus or goal: "*To understand* the ways that the literacy culture of a classroom is created within the interwoven social contexts of classroom and community" (p. xi, emphasis added). She elaborates by describing her focus on response to literature as it occurs in peer groups and by including issues of power and status in her lens.

Anne Haas Dyson, in her book, *The Brothers and Sisters Learn to Write: Popular Literacies in Childhood and School Cultures* (2003), proposes similar research actions in her description of her "broad research aims . . . *to document* the cultural landscape . . . *to analyze how* . . . ; *to trace changes* in how . . . ; to examine the consequences of . . ." (p. 25, emphasis added).

Shirley Brice Heath, in her landmark ethnography that has been so influential in the literacy field, *Ways with Words: Language, Life, and Work in Communities and Classrooms* (1983), describes her research focus as follows: to explore answers to the questions of "*why* students and teachers often could not understand each other, *why* questions were sometimes not answered, and *why* habitual ways of talking and listening did not always seem to work" (p. 2) in communication attempts among three different cultural groups in the Piedmont region of the Carolinas. Related to these goals was the research focus on the need to fully *describe*:

> The primary face-to-face interactions of children from community cultures other than [the] mainstream one. The ways of living, eating, sleeping, worshiping, using space, and filling time which surrounded these language learners would have to be accounted for as part of the milieu in which the processes of language learning took place. (p. 3)

In summary, ethnographic design calls for research questions, or research foci, that seek to situate the researcher into a cultural landscape for the purpose of exploration and discovery of answers to questions like *why, what is happening, what does it look like, how does it work*, and so on.

It is important to note that ethnographic questions do not emerge spontaneously or serendipitously. Rather, as for other types of research, they need to surface within a theoretical framework and to relate to issues recognized by others as significant and interesting. Schensul, Schensul, and LeCompte (1999) also stress that it is important to build the research focus and theoretical models in conjunction with the local population with which the research is going to be conducted. This involves learning as much as possible about this population at this early stage through study and interactions with members of the group.

Because of space constraints, it is impossible to represent the broad range of different types of ethnography that are available to literacy researchers in this chapter. The reader is strongly encouraged to consult other sources that address this research methodology more fully and with more detail. Sources that have been especially helpful for me include Schensul and LeCompte (1999), Goetz and LeCompte (1984), and Miles and Huberman (1994).

ETHNOGRAPHIC LENSES REPRESENTED IN LITERACY RESEARCH

Not all literacy ethnographies result from research conducted within the same epistemological paradigm. Many of them incorporate a phenomenological or interpretive stance. Others, though, represent more of an ecological perspective. Finally, critical research and network research are also represented in the literacy world. Although each of these approaches exists more or less independently of the others, readers may encounter literacy ethnographies that include a synthesis of two or more. This is a reflection of the important-to-understand fact that ethnography, as a method, can be approached and conducted in many different ways, making it difficult to describe technically. Next, I provide brief descriptions of each of the approaches. I am indebted to LeCompte and Schensul (1999b) for these categorical distinctions.

Phenomenological Approach

The researcher taking primarily an interpretive or phenomenological approach is concerned with coming to understand the world from the participants' perspectives. This lens assumes that knowledge, beliefs, and values are socially constructed through social interaction and thus are constantly changing and evolving. To understand participants' perspectives, the researcher must live in their world as a participant, interacting with group members, observing, and interviewing. My study of the urban Appalachian family (honored with the Grawemeyer Award in Education in 1996) in which no one could read or write (Purcell-Gates, 1995) reflects this perspective. My goal was to understand how a young child from this family takes and does not take from traditional literacy instruction in school and how this helps to explain his successes and his struggles in learning to read and write. In the process of this study, I worked as his tutor as well as an occasional tutor for his mother. This was my way of entering and partici- pating in the family and ultimately the community as I complemented the tutoring with participation in daily routines, meals, and informal conver- sational interviews.

Ecological Approach

The researcher from the ecological perspective studies the ways that indi- viduals and groups are defined by social structures at different levels of influence (LeCompte & Schensul, 1999b). These are structures such as family, peers, school, work, community, and society. Whereas the inter- pretive researcher strives to participate in the community of interest, the ecologically framed researcher remains more detached and objective. His or her goal is to observe behavior and elicit participant perspectives so that the analysis of systemic structures and meanings can proceed. Barton and Hamilton's (1998) ethnography of reading and writing in a Lancaster, Eng- land, neighborhood reflects an ecological frame in that it documents the many different ways that people in that community use literacy and how those literacy practices are shaped and interact with such social factors as role, domain, institutions, power relationships, and historical contexts.

Critical Approach

The researcher who takes a critical stance views the world through a lens that forefronts inequality, oppression, and marginalization resulting from unequal power relationships. This research is focused on uncovering and describing these inequalities and oppressive sociopolitical structures with the goal of bringing about change. Within this, the researcher and the researched inform each other and work together for empowerment and ultimate resolution of the unequal power relationships. The researcher is very much involved in the lives of the participants and works with them to understand power and oppression. As such, this research approach can be described as activistic as well as educative. Ellen Cushman's (1998) eth- nography of the ways in which inner-city women used literate strategies to empower themselves within oppressive systems is a classic example.

Network Approach

Literacy can also be studied as it is influenced by and occurs within social networks in specific cultural domains. This is a relatively new research approach to literacy researchers. Sociologists, however, have employed this lens for a number of years, and analytic frames for social network data have been developed and used for a wide variety of research questions. Wasserman and Faust, authors of *Social Network Analysis: Methods and*

Applications (1994), state that "the network perspective allows new leverage for answering standard social and behavioral science research questions by giving precise formal definition to aspects of the political, economic, or social structural environment" (p. 3). Deborah Brandt's *Literacy in American Lives* (2001) reflects a type of social network approach. This historical study documents how families pass on literacy to their children within times of social and technological change as well as the social impact on literacy skills of adults.

ESSENTIAL ELEMENTS OF ETHNOGRAPHIES

Clearly, there are many different lens that researchers can use to approach ethnographic research. Also, there is no one way to conduct an ethnography within any one of these lens. However, there are generally agreed-upon elements to ethnographic research that researchers must consider to ensure rigor, validity, and reliability of their data, data analysis, and final conclusions and interpretations. I list these later. First, however, I provide a brief discussion of the constructs of validity and reliability as they apply to ethnographic research because they do not hold the same meanings, nor are they arrived at in the same ways, as for experimental research.

Validity

Validity in ethnographic research refers to the degree to which one's data and interpretation correspond to the "way it is" within the phenomenon being investigated. Granted, this is a very fuzzy concept, but ethnographers have procedures for approaching it to guarantee rigor. One procedure that is absolutely required to ensure validity is *triangulation*—the gathering of data from different sources to confirm the validity of data. For example, if one is documenting through observation that a participant in a book club discussion group feels disempowered by the group, one would want to cross-check that with, perhaps, interviews with the participant and examples of her journal writing that would relate to this observation. In my book *Other People's Words* (Purcell-Gates, 1995), I concluded that Jenny, the nonliterate urban Appalachian mother whose son I was tutoring, could not penetrate the world of print partly because the structure and vocabulary of written language were so unfamiliar, and thus nonfunctional, for her. This conclusion was based on several sources of data: (1) my documentation that, while she was young, no one in her family read or wrote in ways that were visible to her; (2) many statements from her to the effect that the way she talked was not the way the books "talked"; and (3) discourse analysis of a taped session with her in which I helped her to read and answer a printed parent survey from the school; and (4) her report of difficulty with vocabulary in church material and my own observations as she tried to read this and other texts.

Reliability

The construct of reliability in ethnographic research is closely related to that of validity. If instruments are being used in the study, they, of course, should have demonstrated reliability, both internal and external. However, observational data also need to be considered reliable. One of the more trusted ways to achieve this reliability is to build in the factor of time when designing a study. To ensure that behaviors coalesce to constitute patterns, the research needs to continue over a long enough period. This allows one to watch for recurrence, to observe similar behaviors in different contexts, and to enable the revelation of behaviors, thoughts, and feelings that may have been repressed because of the presence of the researcher. One of the things to guard against is the phenomenon of seeing only what the researcher expects to see and perhaps wants to see. Building in enough time in the cultural context of interest will allow the researcher to stop seeing the world only through his or her own eyes and begin to see it also through those of the participants. Procedures for ensuring validity and reliability are built into all aspects of the ethnographic research process, as becomes clear as I discuss field entry, data collection, data analysis, and informant checks.

Field Entry

Entering the field involves the researcher forming the types of relationships that allow for the learning that needs to take place during the course of the study. It involves learning the language, the social customs, and the patterns of behavior that exist in a setting that is new in many respects to the researcher. Field entry depends on building rapport with the participants, and this is dependent on trust and reciprocity. Most ethnographers find some way to "give back" to the communities they study. This may be in the form of contributing expertise to community problems, materials for community use, or simply time, helping out with chores or errands as needed. These types of activities also contribute to the process of becoming a participant in the community of study and help to develop reciprocity. Occasionally, some ethnographers may pay informants for their time. Field entry always involves some type of initial approach or cover story. For the researcher, this is often an uncomfortable aspect of the ethnographic research process. Schensul and colleagues (1999) make the point, however, that few people in the research setting pay attention to the initial explanation of the project or study. Rather, "rapport ultimately rests on the connections through which ethnographers have been introduced to the community setting, how comfortable researchers are with the people in the field, how well they maintain confidentiality, and how fast they learn local customs and norms" (p. 75).

While much literacy ethnography takes place in classrooms, it is important for researchers to realize that although they may have been students and teachers themselves, it does not obviate the need to view each new classroom as a new and unfamiliar community. Care must be taken to develop trusting relationships and rapport with classroom members. Time must be devoted to coming to see the world of the classroom through *these* participants' eyes, guarding against assuming realities that come from the researcher's past experiences. Dyson, who has conducted many in-depth ethnographies of children learning in classrooms (1989, 1993, 1997, 2003), reports that she always devotes many days and weeks to just sitting in a new classroom and observing before she knows what she is seeing well enough to begin to call them data.

SAMPLING

There are as many different ways to approach selecting who to research as there are types of ethnographies. Schensul and colleagues (1999) list and describe up to 14 different approaches to sampling for ethnographic research, ranging from extreme case selection to random selection. (Note that the topic of ethnographic research is much broader and inclusive than I am able to attend to in this chapter. Many good sources are available for students of ethnography, and those who wish to explore the topic beyond this introductory treatment of ethnographic literacy research are urged to consult them.)

The type of study and the goals of the study determine the selection procedure. The type of sample, furthermore, determines the degree to which the findings can be generalized.

Ethnographies of literacy have for the most part involved sampling that could be described as "convenience samples that fit the research focus or question." For example, the classroom in which Lewis (2001) conducted her study of the social dynamics of peer response was selected because (1) the teacher was known for valuing and teaching for peer response to literature; and (2) the teacher and the school were available to Lewis in terms of both proximity and willingness to participate in research. However, within the classroom, Lewis reports that she chose five focal children who were representative of the population of the classroom and who would provide contrasting characteristics. Thus, Lewis was attending to *representation* to expand the generalizability of her findings and to *contrast* in order to achieve the variation needed for increased validity. This could be labeled both *representative sampling* and *contrastive sampling*.

Dyson, on the other hand, samples primarily to find situations where she can examine her construct of interest: how young children construct their understandings of symbolic communication, including learning to write. She, therefore, purposively seeks teachers whose instruction is "open" enough to allow children's own constructions of their understandings to surface in an accepting environment. Within such classrooms, she seeks child informants who not only take advantage of such an instructional context by visibly producing their evolving constructions of writing but also are open and relaxed enough with her to talk about their work and to answer her questions about what they are doing. This type of sampling is sometimes referred to as *purposive sampling*.

In my own work (Purcell-Gates, 1995), I selected Donny and his mother, Jenny, to study because I was interested in how the literacy that young children learn in their homes before school helps them learn to read and write in school. Jenny conveniently presented herself to me as a non-reader and wanted her son, Donny, to be tutored in the literacy center that I directed. Perhaps this is an instance of what can be termed *providential sampling*!

Other literacy researchers select whole communities as their sample, depending on their research focus. David Barton and Mary Hamilton (1998), for example, selected the Lancaster, England, community to study "local literacies" because it was representative of working-class communities and it was close in proxity to the university where they both worked.

Generalizing from Ethnographic Research

Ethnographic research is not designed or intended to provide statistical generalizability of results. However, the degree to which readers of such research can generalize the findings depends on the type of sampling (e.g., representative sampling affords a different level of generalizability than does convenience/purposive), context, and characteristics of the participants. Readers are usually advised to consider the degree to which these factors are similar to or different from their own situations when considering issues of generalizability. Always, however, the ethnographic researcher provides insights into issues of concern that others can take away and ponder, applying them as seems appropriate to their own situations.

ETHNOGRAPHIC DATA COLLECTION

Participant Observation

Traditionally, the ethnographic researcher collects data as a participant-observer in the community of study. The relationship between *participant* and *observer* is often described as a continuum, with the researcher, depending on the design of the study and on the community being studied, locating him- or herself at varying points along this continuum. For studies that call for, and communities that allow, full participation, the researcher finds ways to immerse him- or herself in the community. Again, the researcher must take care to learn the language, language patterns, social customs, and behaviors quickly in order to become as unobtrusive a presence as possible. At the same time, the researcher needs to ensure that he or she has a regular time to withdraw from participation in order to write up notes on what he or she has been observing.

For researchers studying in settings that are very different from their own, participation to the fullest extent possible is often the best way to begin to see and understand a different cultural context. My coresearcher and coauthor of *Now We Read, We See, We Speak* (2000), Robin Waterman, followed this immersion approach in our study of literacy development in a women's literacy class in rural El Salvador. Our purpose with the study was to explore how learners developed their reading and writing abilities within a class framed by the pedagogy of Paolo Freire (1993). Robin lived in the community (she spoke fluent Spanish) in a mud-walled hut like the other community members. She shared in community events, attending religious services and *asambleas*; she bathed and washed her clothes in the river with the other women; she took her water from the same pipe; and she carried her food and other market sundries as she traveled on foot from the bus stop on the paved highway to the community, a 1-hour trip. Her role in the rural district was to train adult literacy teachers, and within the village she taught the class herself while apprenticing a local teacher. Almost every afternoon or evening, she would write up her notes for the research study, sending them to me by courier about every 2 weeks.

Classroom ethnography, on the other hand, often positions the researcher closer to the observer end of the continuum. The ethnographer in classrooms is often interested in such things as teacher–student transactions, learner beliefs and interpretations, peer-group response, the ways that teachers use texts with different students, and so on. While acknowledging their own influence on these different aspects of classroom life, classroom ethnographers strive to understand phenomena as they happen naturally. This compels many of them to adopt more of an observer position and work to make themselves as unobtrusive as they can to the ordinary life of the classroom. Several common techniques are employed to achieve this goal: Being present over long periods so that participants begin to ignore them, and adopting a nonparticipatory stance in the life of the class. Let's look at the Lewis and Dyson studies as examples.

Lewis (2001), in her study of peer-group response to literature in a middle school classroom, wished to avoid influencing the instruction by assuming any authoritative role as a teacher. She was also worried that assuming a "teacher" status would make the students more guarded in sharing their beliefs with her. On the other hand, she did not want to influence the nature of the student response by participating as a member of the response groups. She did not want them to exclude her either. Thus, she chose to take a friendly observer stance, describing this by quoting Bogdan and Biklen (1992): "Given the challenge of researching children, the best option may be to establish oneself, not as an authority figure, and not as a peer, but as a "quasi-friend" or "tolerated insider in children's society" (p. 88).

Dyson takes a similar stance with very young children. In *The Brothers and Sisters Learn to Write* (2003), Dyson describes how she positioned herself in the classroom so as to be unobtrusive and yet interested in what the children were doing and in what they could tell her about themselves:

> I made no effort to become one of the gang. I was "busy" with writing in my notebook, I was "interested" in "children," and I wouldn't "tell on them." So, as Rita taught a lesson, circulated among the children, or modeled working on her product, I sat, pen in hand, legal pad on lap, watching and writing without looking at the pad (a feat that never fails to impress first graders). (p. 21)

Lewis conducted her research over the course of a full school year, as did Dyson. Lewis began the year with daily, full-day observations, cutting back to three times a week for the rest of the year during the literature class. Dyson observed the children 4–6 hours a week for the year during their language arts period. She also followed them out to the playground during recess and occasionally stayed all day.

Beginning Observation

As stated, ethnographic observation needs a length of time before researchers can be reasonably sure that what they are observing is "natural" and before they can begin to ascribe meaning to it from the participants' perspectives. This means that there is always a period at the start of observation that must be devoted to orienting. Detailed, descriptive notes can be taken at this time to document what the researcher is seeing during these early days. This documenting activity is often referred to as "Census, Map, and Calendar": The researcher notes who the participants are/who is "there," details of the setting (e.g., for classrooms, the arrangement of desks, blackboards, bookshelves), and the events and event sequences. Diagrams can be drawn; the day's and class activities can be noted; the names and descriptions of students, teachers, aides, and so on can be noted.

The Census, Map, and Calendar procedure will ground the observations to follow and make it easier to take field notes by providing the researcher with a shorthand way of documenting the context for the observations. For example, once the routine of Daily Morning Message is established through observation, the researcher need not document the routine and players each time something is observed during this activity. He or she can simply note for context "DMM," for example. Of course, any alteration in the routine would need to be documented and noted.

Field Notes

The writing of field notes is the backbone of ethnographic data collection. In the field notes, researchers record what they are observing. There are many different forms for recording field notes, and most have some way of recording on each page the following: (1) date; (2) time; (3) setting; (4) observer; (5) what was observed; and (6) researcher's comments.

Good field note procedure requires that behaviors be noted as they happen and are observed, without the researcher's interpretation of them. For example, if the researcher is noting that William is sitting at his desk, squirming, yawning, and glancing around the room, these behaviors should be noted as such. It is inappropriate, and a threat to the validity of the data, to record these behaviors as "William is restless and bored and not paying attention." The researcher's interpretation of the behaviors should be recorded, if needed, in the section of the field note form set aside for such comments.

Many literacy researchers supplement field notes with audiotaping. Audiotapes provide backup for researchers who may not be able to capture in field notes complex, fast-moving events such as classroom teaching, peer-group work, or play. They are also a source of language and exact quotes to be used in the final written report of the study. Some literacy ethnographers also incorporate videotaping into their data collection procedures. Videotapes serve many of the same purposes for the ethnographer as audiotapes. They provided the additional benefit of capturing interaction visually, complete with body language and paralinguistic behaviors.

Interviews

Interviews are almost always a part of ethnographic data collection. They allow the researcher to elicit insider information from informants and to explore topics in greater detail. Interviews can be informal, off-the-cuff question–answer events or more structured and carefully planned.

Many questions for informal interviews occur to the researcher during early stages of data analysis as he or she reads over field notes and looks for patterns and demonstrations of local meaning. When the next available opportunity arises to ask a participant about the meanings of a term or about the history of an event, the researcher is prepared.

More formal, semistructured interviews are often used later in the data analysis to further clarify and/or triangulate interpretations. The content of the preformulated questions can come from both the goals and focus of the study and the conclusions or interpretations of the researcher. Some general considerations to keep in mind when constructing semistructured interview protocols include the following:

- Avoid asking questions that elicit a "yes" or "no" answer. Instead, begin questions with open-ended phrases such as "Tell me about . . . ," "If I asked you what X means, what would you say?," or "Why do you think . . . ?"
- Be sure to use language that is familiar and comfortable to your informant.
- Include possible probes with questions to allow you to follow up on answers to achieve more information; for example, "Tell me more . . ." or "That's fascinating! What about. . . ?"

- Ask less sensitive or threatening questions early in the interview and save the more threatening ones for the end. Remember the cultural context of your community when deciding the subjects that are more or less threatening.
- During any interviewing process, strive to maintain the rapport and reciprocity you have developed with your informants and within the community. This may mean volunteering and sharing information about yourself as your informant answers your questions. It also often happens, if the atmosphere is relaxed enough, that the informant will ask his or her own questions of you, in turn, as the interview proceeds.

Readers are referred to the following for more detail regarding ethnographic interviewing: Babbie (1995), Fink (1995), Levy and Holland (1998), Schensul and colleagues (1999), and Sudman and Bradburn (1982).

Artifact and Archival Data

The final type of data I describe, and a type that is used often by ethnographic researchers of literacy, is artifacts and archival data. *Artifacts* for literacy researchers usually mean physical evidence of literacy instruction, learning, or practice. Examples include copies of worksheets, writing samples, book reports, test results, drawings, newspapers, and public notices. Artifacts are sought by literacy ethnographers to triangulate observation data and to document literacy learning and practice much as a portfolio would.

Archival data are defined by Schensul and colleagues (1999) as "materials originally collected for bureaucratic or administrative purposes that are transformed into data for research purposes" (p. 202). Examples include census data, demographic data, surveys, and records of governmental expenditures. These data are used by ethnographers to build context for their studies and contribute valuable information to be used in the analysis of the observational and interview data. For *Now We Read, We See, We Speak* (2000), Waterman and I used archival data to construct the historical context of the civil war in El Salvador, the literacy rates as they evolved over time, and the current context of the Peace Accords and their impact on the lives of the participants.

DATA ANALYSIS

Analysis of ethnographic data begins in the field and continues past the time the researcher has left it. LeCompte and Schensul (1999a, p. 3) quote Patton (1987) on the results of analysis:

- It brings order to the piles of data the ethnographer has accumulated.
- It turns the big piles of raw data into smaller piles of crunched or summarized data.
- It permits the ethnographer to discover patterns and themes in the data and to link them with other patterns and themes.

Intersubjectivity

An important distinction needs to be drawn about a fundamental difference between analysis of ethnographic data and that of causal, correlational, and descriptive data. This lies in the epistemological lens used by ethnographers. Ethnographers admit to, and use, the fact that research data and analysis is always affected by the researcher. Regarding study design and data collection, Dobbert (1982) explains it this way:

> All scientific information is filtered; first, through the scientist's cognitive model; second, by any collecting instruments; and third, through the sense modalities of the recording scientist. The presence of this filtering process is not a weakness in scientific procedure. If human beings did not design research and filter data through their natural modes of perception, the results would be both useless and meaningless. (p. 6)

Data analysis in ethnography is also considered interpretive, filtered through the researcher's culturally learned frames for interpretation. Several procedures are used to ensure that inappropriate conclusions are not drawn from this perspective. The first is the search for disconfirming evidence. This procedure is intended to prevent the researcher from accepting early, or sometimes favorite, interpretations that arise from the data analysis without double-checking that evidence may exist to disconfirm these perhaps biased findings. The search for negative evidence also allows the researcher to discover nuances and variation in the data that may lead to the discovery of new patterns and categories of interest.

Another procedure that ensures greater validity of the data analysis and interpretation is that of informant checking. For this, the researcher shares his or her evolving interpretations of the data with study participants to gain their perspective. Through this process, the researcher can often gain new insights into local meanings from the participants and community members. These may deepen the final analysis as well as guard against overenthusiasm about the researcher's favorite interpretations.

Finally, to ensure that readers of ethnographies do not inappropriately interpret the researcher's interpretation, the authors of these studies need to engage in what has been termed *location*: Authors include in the write-up a section in which they share "the basis of one's subjectivity in approaching [the] research problem; i.e., making clear one's theoretical, methodological, and personal preferences and biases to the extent that they may affect research processes and outcomes" (Dobbert, 1982, p. 6). These authors also often illuminate these preferences and biases with short histories of their lives as they relate to the research and research focus. Following are a few statements of location from different ethnographies:

> I am a middle-aged White woman and I study in local schools, in which the social category of race, and its links to socioeconomic class, is consistently enacted. (Dyson, 2003, p. 20)

> My own assumptions as a researcher include a belief that context is dynamic, shifting, and manifold. Although the site for this study lacked diversity as it is often defined (i.e., ethnic or racial diversity), my goal has been to examine this context in ways that reveal its complexity and reconsider the meaning of diversity. (Lewis, 2001, p. 183)

> One of my first decisions was, for ethical reasons, to place my role of teacher above that of researcher. . . . This sometimes meant that I did not gather information that would inform the research at all or at the appropriate time if I felt that the act of obtaining the data would hinder Jenny's or Donny's progress. (Purcell-Gates, 1995, p. 203)

In the Field

Analysis of the data begins in the field as the researcher *cooks his or her field notes* (i.e., the process of going through the handwritten notes from the field, cleaning them up, clarifying, perhaps synthesizing audiotaped data, and entering them into a database, or rendering them in a typed or word-processed form), organizes the artifacts, and transcribes audiotapes and/or videotapes. It is imperative that the researcher begin this type of work early and stay on top of it to avoid drowning in a sea of data. I learned early in my career to organize and type my field notes for the day before I allowed myself to go to sleep. The few times this discipline wavered, I regretted it for months as I sought to catch up. In addition to avoiding feeling overwhelmed, cooking notes and organizing data on a continuous basis allow the researcher to identify emerging patterns and areas of interest in a timely fashion. This enables the creation of new data collection procedures to investigate these insights. This is the recursive nature of ethnographic data collection and analysis.

Coding

Coding, or categorizing, the data to reduce them to manageable form follows the initial cleaning up. Early coding begins while the researcher is in the field but not until the research has reached the point where patterns are beginning to emerge and researcher enculturation is well on its way.

Coding is done both inductively and deductively as the researcher, focusing on the research area of interest, categorizes events, behaviors, indications of beliefs, and so on. Inductive, or bottom-up, coding involves some form of organizing events, players, settings, and so on that are present in the data. Deductive codes for the data for *Other People's Words* (Purcell-Gates, 1995) marked categories such as "writing attempts," "reading attempts," "reading refusals," "notes from teacher," and "using signs to navigate space." As analysis proceeded, these deductive codes became more differentiated but still marked categories of interest to the research focus that existed in the data.

Deductive coding categorizes and patterns events, actions, beliefs, and so on from domains of interest or theories held by the researcher. Often these are built in to the research questions or focus. For example, inductive codes for *Other People's Words* included "experience with print in names," "evidence of lack of knowledge of semiotic role of print," and "attribution of failure to spoken dialect."

As coding proceeds, both top-down and bottom-up, the researcher recursively checks and rechecks all data, moving toward more refined and nuanced insights regarding the research focus and toward grounded theory, which is based on specific observations that provide the basis for generalization. The researcher is well served to keep notebooks for (1) codes and their meanings; (2) coding decisions, including the date each was made and the data one was analyzing when the decision was made; and (3) evolving hypotheses or thoughts about the progress of the analysis.

Interpretation

While even the coding process is inevitably interpretive, most ethnographers identify the separate analytic phase of interpretation. This is the final phase where the researcher arrives at, and presents in written form, the meaning of the results of the analysis. The interpretation goes beyond description of a phenomenon. It imposes meaning to categories and patterns of behaviors, values, and beliefs. It puts the pieces of the puzzle together to create a whole. It answers the questions: What's going on here? Why does what happens here happen here? What are insights we can take away from this?

Interpretation of ethnographic results requires going beyond the data in a principled way in order to ascribe meaning to them. It involves speculating and drawing implications. It is helpful, always, to return to the original, or evolved, research questions to focus the interpretation. Reviewing the theoretical and research literature around the issue at hand helps to place the results and the interpretation in the scientific field and clarify them for the reader. One way to think about interpretation of ethnographic results is "this is what we can learn from this study, and I can support this with concrete, specific examples."

WRITING UP ETHNOGRAPHIC RESULTS

Ethnographies, at least in the field of literacy, often are published in book form rather than as articles, although the latter certainly do appear. Authors may choose to present their studies in books because the complexity of results from ethnographic research is difficult to compress into research article form.

The final presentation of the results of an ethnography is often referred to as the "telling of a story," in which the researcher pulls together the pieces of the study and results into a meaningful whole—the interpretation. Thus, key elements of the final report are usually organized around the elements of the interpretation. This differs somewhat from other empirical research write-ups for which the data collection, analysis, results, and discussion are presented separately and in assumed temporal order. The ethnographic write-up, on the other hand, uses the interpretation as the organizing frame.

Another distinguishing aspect of the final presentation of ethnography is the amount of space given to descriptions of context. This, of course, reflects the underlying epistemology of ethnography that behaviors, values, and beliefs can never be viewed or analyzed outside sociocultural contexts. Usually, several chapters of book-length ethnographies are devoted to establishing the historical, geographical, and social contexts of the communities of interest.

Finally, readers of ethnographies should be able to find chapters related to the issue under consideration with the appropriate relevant literature cited and discussed. They should also find chapters or sections (often appendices) devoted to a description of the methodology and the location of the author(s).

Smaller Than a Book

Ethnographies can be written up as articles or book chapters (e.g., in an edited book). Readers should be aware, however, that these smaller-than-a-book texts relate to entire studies differently. One version of the ethnographic article or chapter presents as an excerpt from a larger study that is, or will be, published as a book. Excerpts such as this may be a close version of a chapter in the book such as my article "I Ain't Never Read My *Own* Words Before" (Purcell-Gates, 1993) or as rewritten to present a topic or theme that emerged in the larger study. Heath's "What No Bedtime Story Means: Narrative Skills at Home and School" (1982) is a representation of an important finding from her larger study presented in book form, *Ways with Words* (1983). Dyson's (1999) "Coach Bombay's Kids Learn to Write: Children's Appropriation of Media Material for School Literacy" is another example of this type of article, relating to her book *The Brothers and Sisters Learn to Write* (2003).

While relating to their larger studies in slightly different ways, all of the examples of articles just mentioned are broadly considered to be of high quality because of the following characteristics: (1) They provide an abbreviated description of the focus of the larger studies from which they came; (2) they provide enough detail of the contexts for the larger study that readers can use to situate themselves within them; and (3) they describe how the authors came to select the particular focus for the article and describe in appropriate detail and clarity how the data that were used for the analyses presented in the chapter were analyzed. Finally, the results of the analyses are presented in ways that allow the chapters to both stand on their own as a mini-study, or a study within a study, while still linking to the larger ethnography of which they are essential pieces.

Readers may also find smaller-than-a-book ethnographies written in full within edited books of ethnographies around a central theme. Sometimes these types of ethnographies are referred to as "mini-ethnographies" or as ethnographic case studies. Two examples of this type of presentation of shorter ethnographic texts are (1) Brian Street's (2001) edited book *Literacy and Development: Ethnographic Perspectives* and my edited book, *Cultural Practices of Literacy: Case Studies of Language, Literacy, Social Practice, and Power* (2007).

STANDARDS FOR QUALITY

Ethnography is arguably one of the most labor-intensive and cognitively challenging types of research to carry out. High-quality ethnography demands the following:

- A deep understanding of, and the ability to shape, theory.
- Sharp and insightful observational skills.
- The ability to decenter to the degree needed to identify and come to understand the perspectives of others.
- Strict adherence to rules for valid and rigorous data collection, data management, and data analysis.
- The ability to think generatively as well as analytically.
- The ability to write engagingly and vividly so that readers can see and grasp the meanings that the ethnographer has discovered or interpreted.

The "story" that emerges at the end of the research process is not only a story, to be read and enjoyed and then discarded. Rather, it is a bringing together again into a whole that which the researcher has taken apart, struggled over in the search for meaning, double- and triple-checked for bias, and worked to discover the threads of meaning that can be pulled together to inform theory and future research.

Each of the exemplars used in this chapter to illustrate and illuminate methods that help to guarantee high-quality ethnography meets these demands. They have either won national or international awards as exemplars of research or were written by authors who have won such awards in the past. Readers are referred to these texts, and particularly to their methodology sections, for examples of ethnographic methodology that is publicly held up as exemplary.

REFERENCES

Babbie, E. (1995). *The practice of social research* (7th ed.). Belmont, CA: Wadsworth.

Barton, D., & Hamilton, M. (1998). *Local literacies: Reading and writing in one community.* New York: Routledge.

Bogdan, R. C., & Biklen, S. K. (1992). *Qualitative research for education: An introduction to theory and methods* (2nd ed.). Boston: Allyn & Bacon.

Brandt, D. (2001). *Literacy in American lives.* Cambridge, UK: Cambridge University Press.

Cushman, E. (1998). *The struggle and the tools: Oral and literate strategies in an inner city community.* New York: State University of New York Press.

Dobbert, M. L. (1982). *Ethnographic research.* New York: Praeger.

Dyson, A. H. (1989). *Multiple worlds of child writers: Friends learning to write.* New York: Teachers College Press.

Dyson, A. H. (1993). *Social words of children learning to write in an urban primary school.* New York: Teachers College Press.

Dyson, A. H. (1997). *Writing superheroes: Contemporary childhood, popular culture, and classroom literacy.* New York: Teachers College Press.

Dyson, A. H. (1999). Coach Bombay's kids learn to write: Children's appropriation of media material for school literacy. *Research in the Teaching of English, 33,* 367–402.

Dyson, A. H. (2003). *The brothers and sisters learn to write: Popular literacies in childhood and school cultures.* New York: Teachers College Press.

Fink, A. (1995). *How to ask survey questions.* Thousand Oaks, CA: Sage.

Freire, P. (1993). *Pedagogy of the oppressed* (20th anniversary ed.). New York: Continuum.

Goetz, J. P., & LeCompte, M. D. (1984). *Ethnography and qualitative design in educational research.* Orlando, FL: Academic Press.

Heath, S. B. (1982). What no bedtime story means: Narrative skills at home and school. *Language in Society, 11,* 49–76.

Heath, S. B. (1983). *Ways with words: Language, life, and work in communities and classrooms.* Cambridge, UK: Cambridge University Press.

LeCompte, M. D., & Schensul, J. J. (1999a). *Analyzing & interpreting ethnographic data.* Walnut Creek, CA: AltaMira Press.

LeCompte, M. D., & Schensul, J. J. (1999b). *Designing & conducting ethnographic research.* Walnut Creek, CA: AltaMira Press.

Levy, R. I., & Holland, D. W. (1998). Person-centered interviews. In H. R. Bernard

(Ed.), *Handbook of methods in cultural anthropology* (pp. 333–364). Walnut Creek, CA: AltaMira Press.

Lewis, C. (2001). *Literacy practices as social acts: Power, status, and cultural norms in the classroom.* Mahwah, NJ: Erlbaum.

Miles, M. B., & Huberman, M. (1994). *Qualitative data analysis: An expanded sourcebook* (2nd ed.). London: Sage.

Patton, M. Q. (1987). *Qualitative evaluation methods.* Newbury Park, CA: Sage.

Purcell-Gates, V. (1993). I ain't never read my *own* words before. *Journal of Reading, 37,* 210–219.

Purcell-Gates, V. (1995). *Other people's words: The cycle of low literacy.* Cambridge, MA: Harvard University Press.

Purcell-Gates, V. (Ed.). (2007). *Cultural practices of literacy: Case studies of language, literacy, social practice, and power.* Mahwah, NJ: Erlbaum.

Purcell-Gates, V., & Waterman, R. (2000). *Now we read, we see, we speak: Portrait of literacy development in an adult Freirean-based class.* Mahwah, NJ: Erlbaum.

Schensul, J. J., & LeCompte, M. D. (1999). *Ethnographic toolkit.* Walnut Creek, CA: AltaMira Press.

Schensul, S. L., Schensul, J. J., & LeCompte, M. D. (1999). *Essential ethnographic methods.* Walnut Creek, CA: AltaMira Press.

Street, B. (2001). *Literacy and development: Ethnographic perspectives.* London: Routledge.

Sudman, S., & Bradburn, N. M. (1982). *Asking questions.* San Francisco: Jossey-Bass.

Wasserman, S., & Faust, K. (1994). *Social network analysis: Methods and applications.* Cambridge, UK: Cambridge University Press.

CHAPTER 9

Experimental and
Quasi-Experimental Design

Frank R. Vellutino
Christopher Schatschneider

According to many historians and philosophers, the experimental approach to scientific inquiry dates back to at least the 16th and 17th centuries and was ushered in with the seminal experiments of such notable students of nature as Galileo, da Vinci, Gilbert, and Copernicus (Drake, 1981). The work done by these and other experimenters in the natural sciences during this period represented a distinct departure from the approach used by philosophers in the Aristotelian tradition, whose writings and teachings about natural phenomena were based largely on inductive reasoning and intuition rather than systematic observation and empirical evidence. This work broke with tradition in three ways. First, scientific inquiry during the 16th and 17th centuries increasingly questioned rather than supported explanations of natural phenomena based on dogma. Second, passive observations of nature were increasingly accompanied by deliberate attempts to manipulate entities and elements in the physical world so as to produce changes that might provide useful information about cause–effect relationships. Third, experimenters during this period became increasingly appreciative of the need to take into account and possibly control extraneous influences that might compromise the investigator's objectivity, or constrain, in unintended ways, observations and interpretations of causal relationships. As a consequence, relevant procedures to accomplish these objectives were developed and implemented with positive effects in given areas of inquiry, and controlled experimentation became firmly entrenched in disciplines that adopted the experimental method, especially in natural sciences such as astronomy, chemistry, and physics.

However, it soon became evident that controlled experimentation was more easily accomplished in laboratory sciences such as physics and chemistry than in field-based sciences such as public health, sociology, economics, psychology, and education. As researchers in these fields began employing the experimental method to study causal relationships, they increasingly discovered sources of bias that called for different methods of controlling extraneous influences that might compromise the integrity of their experiments. As a result, new methods of controlling extraneous influences were developed, such as random assignment to treatments (Fisher, 1925, 1935), the use of control groups, pre- and postexperimental assessment, and statistical control. In the related disciplines of psychology and education, much has been learned about research methodology in terms of the constraints imposed on the investigator by the research questions typically addressed in these fields, relative to the populations, experimental designs, technologies, and resources available to address those questions practically and meaningfully. Much of this work has been done by pioneers such as Lee Cronbach, Donald Campbell, Julian Stanley, and Thomas Cook, whose influential ideas have been summarized and significantly expanded in an excellent text concerned with generalized causal inference (Shadish, Cook, & Campbell, 2002). We have drawn generously from this text in preparing this chapter and acknowledge its influence on our thinking (see also Campbell & Stanley, 1963).

In the sections that ensue, we discuss methodologies for establishing causal relationships, focusing on two experimental approaches that have been used for this purpose: experimental and quasi-experimental research designs. We first discuss the experimental method in general terms, in the interest of providing some basic understanding of key concepts that define this approach to scientific inquiry. We then discuss the concept of validity in experimentation and describe different types of validity that must be considered in establishing and generalizing causal relationships. We then discuss experimental and quasi-experimental designs and provide examples of these designs that have been used in literacy research. We should point out, however, that because of space constraints our treatment of these topics must necessarily be limited, both in scope and depth. However, it is hoped that we provide the reader with enough incentive to explore these and related topics more comprehensively.

THE EXPERIMENTAL METHOD: SOME BASIC CONCEPTS AND DISTINCTIONS

Counterfactual Inference

For the purposes of this chapter, an experiment can be defined as a deliberate attempt to administer a treatment in order to observe the effects of that treatment. To be able to infer whether an experimental treatment has any effect(s), it is crucial that we have some knowledge of what would have happened if the treatment had not been administered. Inferring treatment effects by comparing them with what would have happened if the treatment had not been administered is called *counterfactual inferencing* (Shadish et al., 2002). The idea of counterfactual inferencing was first explicitly stated by Hume (1748/1999) and expounded upon by Mill (1843/1987) and, more recently, Lewis (1973). The main idea of counterfactual inferencing is that we can only know if event *C* caused event *E* if it were the case that if *C* had not occurred *E* would not have occurred.

Obtaining appropriate counterfactual information is difficult. In practice, once a treatment is delivered, it cannot be undelivered. In most (if not all) cases, it is impossible to know exactly what would have occurred had the treatment not been delivered. The main goal of experimental and quasi-experimental design is to create hypothetical counterfactuals (Dawes, 1994) that approximate, as closely as possible, what would have happened if the treatment had not been administered. How this approximation is obtained is the main distinction between experimental and quasi-experimental designs. Experimental designs employ random assignment of units to conditions as the methodology for generating hypothetical counterfactuals. That is, some units (e.g., children or classes) are assigned at random (using tables of random numbers, found in most statistics texts or software) to receive the treatment and some are not. We then infer that what happened to units that did not receive the treatment—the control group—reflects what would have happened to the other group of units had they not received the treatment. Quasi-experimental designs do not randomly assign units to conditions. Rather, they compare groups that already exist (e.g., children in one school with children in another school) using various types of design and/or statistical controls to try to ensure that those groups are as comparable as possible in every respect except for receiving the experimental treatment(s). Here again, we infer that what happened to the units that did not receive the treatment—the comparison group—reflects what would have happened to the other group(s) had they not received the treatment.

Experimental Causes and Experimental Effects

The purpose of conducting an experiment is to determine whether or not a given treatment caused a given effect. Shadish and colleagues (2002) suggest that experiments are well suited to studying *cause* and *effect* relationships because they (1) ensure that a presumed cause is deliberately manipulated and thereby precedes the observed effect; (2) incorporate procedures that help determine whether the cause is related to the effect; and (3) incorporate procedures to minimize and/or assess the influence of extraneous factors that could produce the effect presumed to be attributed to the cause. In contrast, nonexperimental, correlational studies are not as well suited to studying causal relationships because, although they may allow one to determine whether two variables are related to each other, they cannot establish which of the two is the cause and which is the effect, and they cannot rule out alternative explanations for observed relationships, often called *confounds*.

The experimental paradigm can be conceptualized as having two parts: experimental causes (treatments) and experimental effects. In the study of literacy development, a treatment might consist of an instructional program designed to facilitate acquisition of reading and writing skills, implemented either with individual children or with entire classrooms of children. However, for the sake of illustration, let us suppose that the treatment consists of a remedial intervention program designed to improve reading skills in struggling readers (e.g., daily one-to-one tutoring using a theoretically motivated approach to intervention). Outcome measures to assess the effects of the intervention might include tests evaluating word-level skills such as phonological awareness, phonological decoding, and word identification; tests evaluating reading comprehension; or different combinations of these measures. The investigator is, of course, interested in determining whether the intervention, as the putative cause, had any effect on the children's reading skills, as assessed by the outcome measures. Yet establishing cause–effect relationships in any given experiment turns out to be a complicated undertaking. Consider the concept *experimental cause* in this context. It might be inferred that any positive change on a reading outcome measure used to assess the effect of the intervention was due to the particular type of intervention administered in the study. However, this inference may or may not be warranted. For example, positive change on the outcome measure could have been due to the fact that the children who received the intervention were also receiving classroom instruction that would have produced such change, even in the absence of the intervention. Or the change could have been produced simply by the fact that the children were receiving daily one-to-one tutoring (perhaps any kind of tutoring could have produced the effect) or even by the fact that some of the worst readers dropped out of the study, thereby increasing the probability that the remaining children would show gains on postintervention outcome measures. In short, there are many possible causes of a given effect. Thus, to the extent possible, the investigator must endeavor to control for and/or evaluate factors that could influence results on an outcome measure other than the treatment under study.

Consider now the concept *experimental effect*. Shadish and colleagues (2002) define an effect produced by an experimental treatment as a hypothetical difference between what did happen when individuals received a treatment and what would have happened if the same individuals had not received the treatment. This entails a comparison of the treatment group with the hypothetical counterfactual. To correctly estimate a treatment effect, two things are essential: (1) One must have a reasonable and defensible hypothetical counterfactual that is as similar as possible to the treatment group; and (2) one must be able to compare this group with the group that received treatment. For example, in the case of the intervention study example given previously, the investigator could randomly assign struggling readers to intervention and nonintervention (control) groups, take steps to ensure the fidelity of the intervention program, control and/or assess extraneous factors that could produce the desired outcome, and compare the performance of the two groups on appropriate postintervention outcome measures. If random assignment to treatment and control groups is not possible, then other procedures could be employed to help the investigator establish cause–effect relationships, some of which we discuss later. In either case, the use of a control group provides a basis for making a claim for the existence of a treatment effect because it allows the investigator to approximate the magnitude and direction of change on the outcome measure(s) in the children who received the intervention under (the hypothetical) conditions where the same children had not received the intervention. Thus, as pointed out by Shadish and colleagues, "two central tasks in experimental design are creating a high-quality but necessarily imperfect source of counterfactual inference and understanding how this source differs from the treatment condition" (p. 6).

THE CONCEPT OF VALIDITY IN EXPERIMENTATION

In the present context, the term *validity* can be defined as "the approximate truth of an inference" about given aspects of an experiment (Shadish et al., 2002, p. 34). When discussing causal relationships between treatment and outcome measures, the term *validity* refers to inferences about whether a given treatment actually produced an observed effect. When discussing results associated with experimental treatments, the term *validity* refers to inferences about causal relationships based on the statistical analyses used to evaluate the size and direction of treatment effects. When discussing the operations involved in implementing an experiment, the term *validity* refers to inferences about whether the particular units (e.g., individuals, classrooms), treatments, assessment instruments, and settings used in the experiment are representative examples of the higher order constructs defining these operations. When discussing generalization of experimental outcomes, the term *validity* refers to inferences about whether specific cause–effect relationships can be observed across variations in units, treatments, outcome measures, and settings. These different types of inferences correspond, respectively, with what Shadish and colleagues (2002) call *internal validity, statistical conclusion validity, construct validity,* and *external validity.* We briefly describe each in the sections that follow.

Internal Validity

The validity of inferences about cause–effect relationships is dependent on the degree to which the researcher demonstrates that (1) a treatment preceded an observed effect, (2) the treatment is related to the effect, and (3) there are no other plausible explanations for the effect. The first of these criteria is guaranteed by experiments because they require that treatments be implemented before the effects of the treatments are measured. The second criterion is dependent on the degree to which the statistical procedures used for data analysis are able to detect treatment effects (discussed later), and the third depends on the degree to which the investigator takes into account plausible threats to internal validity—that is, circumstances that may compromise the accuracy of inferences about causal relationships. Examples of common threats to internal validity discussed by Shadish and colleagues (2002) include *selection bias, history, regression to the mean, attrition, testing*, and *instrumentation*.

Selection bias occurs when individuals assigned to given treatments happen to be different at the outset of the experiment in ways that might erroneously be attributed to the treatment, for example, having different levels of ability in word recognition prior to being assigned to experimental conditions that are hypothesized to have differential effects on outcome measures of word recognition. *History* refers to differential experiences of individuals in comparison groups that might affect experimental outcomes, for example, having treatment and control groups (inadvertently) come from classrooms characterized by strong and weak literacy instruction, respectively. *Regression to the mean* refers to the tendency of individuals with extreme scores on one assessment to obtain scores that are closer to the population mean on a subsequent assessment. So whereas individuals with high scores on a pretreatment assessment will tend to have lower scores on a posttreatment assessment, individuals with low scores on the pretreatment assessment will tend to have higher scores on the posttreatment assessment, even in the absence of treatment effects. Such propensities could present a spurious account of any bonafide treatment effects that might have been observed. *Attrition* refers to unanticipated reduction in the number of participants completing the experiment. If those who drop out of the experiment differ in important ways from those who completed the experiment (e.g., they may be the worst readers), then the accuracy of causal inferences may be compromised.

Finally, *testing* threats to internal validity occur when taking a test creates practice effects or other reactive biases that could be mistaken for treatment effects. *Instrumentation* threats occur when the scaling properties of an assessment instrument change over time in ways that could influence test scores. For example, scoring 1 year below grade level in second grade does not imply the same degree of reading skills deficiency as scoring 1 year below grade level in seventh grade.

Statistical Conclusion Validity

Statistical conclusion validity is concerned with two major dimensions of causal inference: (1) the degree to which the cause is related to the observed effect and (2) the magnitude and direction of the effect. In regard to the first, the investigator might erroneously conclude from the use of faulty statistical procedures that the cause is related to the effect (*type I error*), or he or she might erroneously conclude that the cause is unrelated to the effect (*type II error*). In regard to the second, it is possible to either overestimate or underestimate both the magnitude of an effect and the degree of confidence in the effect. Therefore, the quality of causal inferences is directly dependent on the use of appropriate statistical procedures that take into account the unique sampling and measurement problems associated with an experiment.

Examples of the most common threats to statistical conclusion validity include *low power, violation of assumptions of statistical tests, unreliability of measurement, restriction of range,* and *fidelity of treatment problems. Low power* is the inability of an outcome measure to detect an experimental effect and is caused by small sample sizes, unreliability of measurement, range restriction, and diffusion of treatment(s), among other circumstances. *Violation of statistical assumptions* refers to the failure to take into account theoretical assumptions associated with given statistical tests (e.g., assumptions about population distributions, freedom from sampling biases, independence of measurement, equivalent variability in the treatment and comparison groups). A typical consequence of such violation is to underestimate error of measurement while overestimating treatment effects. *Unreliability of measurement* refers to erroneous estimation of causal relationships owing to low reliability in one or more of the measuring instruments evaluating these relationships. *Restriction of range* refers to low variability in test scores manifested either in *ceiling effects* (too many high scores) or in *floor effects* (too many low scores). Range restriction increases the probability that treatment effects will not be detected and can occur, either because treatments being compared are highly similar or because measuring instruments do not adequately sample the full range of abilities being evaluated in an experiment.

Construct Validity

Constructs are category labels for theoretical entities. In experimental research, constructs refer to the sampling components of an experiment (i.e., units, treatments, assessment instruments, and settings). Construct inferences are judgments about the degree to which a sampling component is a representative example of the construct it instantiates. In literacy research, a *unit* may consist of individuals or aggregates of individuals such as classrooms or schools. Construct inferences about units are concerned with whether a particular type of unit is representative of the population from which the experimental sample was drawn. For example, the construct label *struggling readers* may be overinclusive and inaccurately represent the population, if the sample included second-language learners or participants coming from classrooms servicing emotionally handicapped children. In contrast, there is less ambiguity about construct labels such as *males or females*. Similarly, a treatment in a literacy experiment may be a certain type of reading instruction that the investigator calls *comprehension strategy instruction*, and the question that needs to be addressed, in drawing conclusions about results generated by the experiment, is whether or not the instruction employed in the experiment is a representative example of comprehension strategy instruction as it has been defined in literacy research. Inferences as to the construct validity of assessment instruments used as outcome measures are concerned with the question of whether such instruments are valid measures of change in capabilities hypothesized to be causally related to an experimental treatment. For example, a test of word-recognition skills as a measure of the theoretical construct called *reading ability* would have inadequate construct validity, if this test were used as a proxy measure of reading comprehension ability.

Finally, inferences as to the construct validity of the settings in which an experiment is carried out are concerned with the question of whether these settings are representative examples of the population of settings to which the investigator wishes to generalize results from the experiment. Consider, for example, the construct *second-grade classrooms in public schools located in densely populated, urban areas*. If even a small number of children in the sample came from schools located in suburban and/or rural areas, then the research sample would not adequately represent children being educated in the settings of special interest to the investigator, and the construct validity of both the participants in the experiment and the experimental settings could be questioned.

Perhaps the most common threat to construct validity is the failure to fully explicate and define a given construct. All the examples given earlier, to some extent, have this problem in common. For example, the category label *struggling readers from disadvantaged backgrounds* implies a set of descriptors defining children from a population that is different, in many important ways, from the population of children defined by the set of descriptors implied in the category label *struggling readers from advantaged backgrounds*, in terms of factors that might differentially influence response to experimental treatments in these two groups (e.g., knowledge of print concepts, vocabulary knowledge, phonological awareness). Such distinctions are not adequately reflected in the more general category label *struggling readers* exemplified previously. Thus, in describing the research sample being studied, the experimenter must take pains to use descriptors and category labels that clearly define the population from which the sample was drawn and that distinguish it from other populations, to ensure that causal inferences about treatment effects observed in this sample are valid and that such effects are generalized only to individuals in the population represented by the sample.

Another common threat to construct validity is confounding of constructs. A good illustration of such confounding is provided by the construct labeled *second-grade classrooms in public schools located in densely populated, urban areas*, which we discussed earlier. It is worth reiterating in this context that including even a small number of children from second-grade classrooms located in rural areas in the sample defined by this construct confounds the construct with one that might be labeled *second-grade classrooms located in sparsely populated, rural areas* and thereby limits the experimenter's ability to generalize research findings to the populations represented by either construct.

Using only one implementation of a given construct is yet another common threat to construct validity (called *mono-operation bias* by Shadish et al., 2002)—for example, using only word-level intervention to improve reading comprehension skills or only a single measure of reading comprehension to evaluate the effects of word-level intervention on growth in reading comprehension. A similar threat is *mono-method bias*, or the use of a single method of operationalizing a given construct—for example, using only the *cloze method* of evaluating reading comprehension. One other threat to construct validity in experimentation worth mentioning is *treatment diffusion*. This type of threat is handily exemplified in a situation in which the effects of an experimental classroom reading program are distilled when teachers in control classrooms advertently or inadvertently import and implement materials and/or procedures implemented by teachers in experimental classrooms. There are other threats to construct validity discussed by Shadish and colleagues (2002) that are not discussed here, and the reader who is interested in a more comprehensive treatment of this topic is well advised to consult that text.

External Validity

As we indicated in an earlier section, external validity is concerned with inferences about the degree to which experimental effects can be generalized across variations in units, treatments, assessment instruments, and settings. In the rare instances in which random sampling of given study operations employed in an experiment is possible, there is some degree of certainty that treatment effects obtained with the particular study operations can be generalized to the larger populations from which they were drawn—for example, to children having demographic characteristics similar to those who participated in the experiment (units); to reading intervention activities comparable to but different from those used as the treatment(s) in the experiment (treatments); to word-recognition and/or reading comprehension measures comparable to but different from those used to evaluate treatment effects (assessment instruments); and to schools having demographic characteristics similar to those participating in the experiment (settings). However, under the more common circumstance where random sampling from given populations is not possible, the investigator must either provide documentation that the research sample consists of representative exemplars from those populations or make it clear, in reporting research findings, that experimental results may not readily be generalized to the populations because there is no certainty that research samples were drawn from the populations. For example, if the researcher uses an experimental test of reading comprehension to evaluate the effects of a reading intervention program, he or she might justify the use of the test for this purpose by demonstrating that the operations used to evaluate reading comprehension are essentially the same as those used in existing, well-established comprehension tests (content validity); that these operations are theoretically well grounded (construct validity); and that correlations between performance on the experimental reading comprehension test and performance on existing, well-established tests of skills that underlie reading comprehension (e.g., word recognition and language comprehension) are comparable to correlations between such tests and existing tests of reading comprehension (empirical validity). Without such documentation, the investigator is obliged to limit generalizations about experimental effects to results produced by the experimental test.

Similarly, it is often the case that researchers wish to generalize from an experimental sample drawn from a well-defined population to broader or different populations, for example, from children being educated in suburban schools to children being educated in inner-city schools or from implementation of a particular type of reading intervention program outside the classroom to implementation of essentially the same program in the classroom. The investigator may even wish to generalize experimental effects more narrowly, for example, from the children in the research sample, who, by virtue of sampling criteria, did not have general language impediments to children who do have general language impediments. The external validity question raised in each of these instances is whether experimental effects observed with given units, treatments, assessment instruments, and settings employed in an experiment will generalize in the various ways exemplified (among others of interest). It will suffice to reiterate that without evidence that results can be generalized to populations other than the one from which the research sample was drawn, the investigator is constrained to generalize experimental effects to the intended population and must conduct additional research to address the question of whether such effects can be generalized to other populations.

All of the foregoing examples illustrate variations in sampling particulars that were not included in a given experiment, but the external validity question also arises in the case of some that may have been included in the experiment. For example, more fine-grained analyses of results from a reading intervention study may show that children with at least average-level language abilities were more responsive to reading intervention than children with below-average language abilities. Or such analyses may show that change on outcome measures was greater with reading intervention *A* than with reading intervention *B* or that intervention effects were more strongly observed on outcome measure *A* than on outcome measure *B*. Such circumstances call for qualification of experimental results in any forum or document where statements about the degree to which these results will generalize to target populations are presented to the research community.

Inherent in the examples given previously are common threats to external validity. One of the most common is that effects obtained with one type of unit (e.g., persons, schools) may not be obtained with different types of units. For example, intervention in small groups might be more effective with moderately impaired readers having at least average language abilities than with severely impaired readers having below-average language abilities, who may require more individualized and more intensive intervention. The latter example underscores a related threat to external validity, specifically that an effect obtained with one variation in treatment (e.g., one-to-one tutoring) may not be obtained with another variation in treatment (e.g., small-group instruction). Another such threat is that an experimental effect observed with one type of outcome measure may not be observed with different outcome measures. For example, instruction to improve alphabetic coding skills may have a salutary effect on measures of word-recognition and phonological decoding skills but not on measures of reading comprehension skills. Still another threat to external validity is one where an effect observed in one kind of setting may not be observed in a different kind of setting, as exemplified in the question of whether significant progress made by struggling readers in a reading intervention experiment involving one-to-one daily tutoring implemented by experimental personnel outside the classroom would have been observed if the same type of intervention was implemented by the same experimental personnel in the children's classrooms, given the different types of potentially influential environments provided by the two venues.

Finally, in instances in which the investigator has clearly delineated populations of units, treatments, assessment instruments, or settings from which to obtain experimental samples, and can sample from each of these populations with known probability, *random sampling* from these populations, when feasible, is highly desirable. Random sampling from a population entails sampling in a way that ensures that given members of that population can be selected with equal probability, for example, by using tables of random numbers (provided by most statistical texts). When attrition is low, random sampling allows the investigator to generalize causal inferences to the population from which a given sample was drawn, within the limits of sampling error. However, because of practical and logistical problems, especially in terms of such barriers as theoretically constrained choice of treatments and/or availability of appropriate assessment instruments or settings, random sampling is not often feasible in field research and is much less frequently used in such research than what has been called *purposive sampling* (Shadish et al., 2002), that is, nonrandom, deliberate sampling from specific populations of interest. Purposive sampling of diverse exemplars, such as members of different ethnic groups and/or different genders, may enhance external validity by allowing the investigator to assess the degree to which causal inferences can be generalized across these diverse populations. Similarly, purposive sampling of typical exemplars, such as poor versus normal readers, domain-specific assessment instruments with well-known statistical properties, or different settings with demographic properties of special interest (e.g., urban vs. suburban schools), may enhance external validity by allowing the investigator to assess the degree to which different units, instruments, or settings produce essentially the same pattern of results under given experimental circumstances. And, of course, purposive rather than random sampling is necessary when the investigator wishes to generalize experimental results to and compare specific populations of interest that are not represented in sufficient numbers in available populations to allow random sampling from those populations, for example, impaired readers equated with younger, normally developing readers on measures of word recognition and spelling ability.

However, in view of the limited applicability of generalizations from single experiments, the external validity of given causal inferences will probably depend, in the long run, on programmatic research, across many research settings, that produces reliable results over wide variations in units, treatments, assessment instruments, and settings.

Interrelationships among Different Types of Validity

It may be useful to point out that although we discussed the different types of validity separately, some degree of reflection will make it clear that they are functionally interdependent. For example, inferences about causal relationships (internal validity) are dependent, in large measure, on the nature and quality of the statistical analyses documenting the relationship between a hypothesized cause and an observed effect (statistical conclusion validity). Similarly, the nature and quality of statistical analyses performed for purposes of documenting cause–effect relationships and the quality of causal inferences based on those analyses depend significantly on theoretically grounded explication and generalization of the construct inferences associated with the units, treatments, assessment instruments, and settings employed in an experiment (construct validity). And the quality of the target generalizations presented in forums and documents reporting results of an experiment, regarding units, treatments, assessment instruments, and settings employed in the experiment (external validity), depend significantly on the quality of inferences about causal relationships, the quality of statistical analyses leading to those inferences, and the quality of the theoretical constructs underlying the operations that define the experiment.

Before leaving the topic of validity, it might be worthwhile to note that no design perfectly controls all threats to validity. All have potential weaknesses and flaws. Oftentimes strengthening a design against a particular threat to validity may increase the threats to other types of validity. For example, trying to control many aspects of a study to increase its internal validity may have the consequence of decreasing its external validity. That is, as we incorporate more controls in an experimental design, we increase the likelihood of introducing artificial elements that would not generalize to the target population. This is not an argument for less controlled studies, but the researcher is urged to be mindful of all the threats to validity in order to make sound judgments about experimental design.

EXPERIMENTAL AND QUASI-EXPERIMENTAL DESIGNS

As we indicated earlier, the central distinction between experimental and quasi-experimental designs is how the units being observed are assigned to conditions. Experimental designs assign units (e.g., persons, classrooms, schools) to experimental conditions (e.g., treatment or control groups) via random assignment. Random assignment ensures that every unit has the same probability of being assigned to given conditions because assignment to each condition is based purely on chance. Thus, in an experiment with only two conditions, random assignment to each could be accomplished by repeated tossing of a (fair) coin, which has a 50% chance of coming up heads or tails on each toss. Units designated as "heads" would then be assigned to one experimental condition whenever heads came up on given tosses, and units designated as "tails" would be assigned to the other condition whenever tails came up. In a randomized experiment with six conditions, there is a 16.7% chance that a given unit will be assigned to one of the six conditions, and random assignment could be accomplished by repeated rolling of a (fair) die that has the numbers 1 through 6 on its sides. In most cases, however, investigators tend to use more formal methods of random assignment such as tables of random numbers, but these simple examples should serve to illustrate the concept of randomization (see Shadish et al., 2002, for other examples).

There are several advantages in using random assignment to experimental conditions when this procedure is feasible. If implemented correctly, it creates two or more experimental groups that will be similar to each other on relevant variables (on average) before any treatment is administered, barring pretreatment differences among given groups that may occur by chance, which become increasingly less probable as sample sizes increase. As a result, any observed differences between (or among) groups on outcome measures are likely to be due to the experimental treatments rather than to group differences that existed before the experiment was initiated. Additionally, because randomization is used to assign units to conditions, the process of selection is known and the possibility of selection bias, which plagues all quasi-experiments, is minimized. Randomization also makes alternative explanations of treatment effects that constitute threats to internal validity less plausible by distributing these threats randomly over experimental conditions. This means that extraneous factors that could influence performance on outcome measures should occur with equal probability among experimental groups, thereby increasing the probability that the only systematic differences that occur between and among groups should be due to experimental treatments. Finally, randomized designs also provide the best chance of creating adequate hypothetical counterfactuals that are so important in estimating treatment effects.

Note also that Shadish and colleagues (2002) describe several procedures that can be used to improve the random assignment process for purposes of improving experimental control, increasing power, assessing specific experimental effects (e.g., interaction effects), and/or dealing with practical problems that may arise in addressing certain types of research questions (e.g., proportional imbalance in number of units in conditions, small number of units available at a given point in time, ethical objections to depriving control group units of treatment). Two of the procedures discussed that have often been used in literacy research are "matching" and "stratifying." Despite the merits of random assignment in equating treatment and control groups on variables that may influence results on outcome measures, there is always the possibility that simple random assignment will, nevertheless, fail to equate these groups on one or another of these variables. As Abelson (1995) states, "Chance is lumpy." In an effort to minimize the chance of unhappy randomization (Kenny, 1975), the investigator can equate units (i.e., individuals, classrooms, schools) on relevant variables before randomly assigning them to treatment and control groups. Matching and stratifying are often used to achieve this objective. Both involve a priori matching of units before these units are randomly assigned to conditions being compared; both can be used to help in controlling the proportion of units assigned to given conditions; both greatly increase the probability that conditions have similar pretest means and variances on outcome measures used to assess treatment effects of interest; and both may increase the power of the experimental design to detect such effects by equating units, a priori, on variables that may influence results on outcome measures.

However, whereas matching produces a number of matched units that, in the aggregate, equals the number of conditions to be compared, stratifying produces matched units within given strata and, therefore, produces a number of matched groups that is greater than the number of conditions. For example, to match on reading ability in a two-group intervention experiment, the two participants with the highest scores on a test of a relevant reading skill (e.g., word identification) would form a pair and one member of the pair would be randomly assigned to the treatment condition and the other to the control condition. This procedure would be systematically repeated through the pair with the lowest reading scores and should produce treatment and control groups that are equated on the pretreatment measure of reading skill. Units can be matched on any of a variety of other relevant factors (e.g., grade level, risk status, socioeconomic level), depending on the nature and purpose of the experiment.

Similarly, a stratification procedure may be required when the investigator is interested in assessing interactions between treatments and factors at given strata. For example, the investigator may be interested in assessing the hypothesized interaction of a given treatment with reading ability and grade level. An example of such an experiment is given later (see Shadish et al., 2002, for a more detailed discussion of the use of matching and stratifying in randomized-trials designs).

Despite the merits of the randomization procedure used in experimental designs, as discussed previously, random assignment of units to conditions is oftentimes impossible or prohibitive. But just because some situations are not conducive to random assignment and experimentation does not mean that we are left without recourse. Studies can be designed to investigate cause and effect that do not employ random assignment. These types of studies make use of what have come to be called quasi-experimental designs (Campbell & Stanley, 1963). These designs are similar to experimental designs in every respect except one: The assignment of units to conditions is not random because random assignment is precluded by practical problems. For example, in literacy research, it is sometimes not possible to randomly assign schools or classrooms to receive a particular kind of curriculum or intervention. Most school administrators have definite ideas about which programs are better than others, and it may not be possible, in given instances, to convince them to agree to implement a different literacy program. If the design also calls for randomization of interventions within schools, it is also sometimes difficult to persuade teachers to comply with the dictates of the randomization procedure (especially when they have been designated to be in the control group). Oftentimes, these limitations will compel a researcher to employ a quasi-experimental design, where groups are assigned nonrandomly. In such cases, the groups may be assigned by an administrator or perhaps via a joint decision of the researcher and a school official.

Yet quasi-experimental designs do not have the advantages that come with random assignment. In instances where random assignment is not employed, the adequacy of the hypothetical counterfactual is called into question. Without random assignment, we have no way of distributing potential confounds equally across all groups. For example, suppose that those administrators inclined toward one intervention over another assign more effective teachers to that condition, and the overall effectiveness of those teachers causes differences in student growth. How do we know that observed differences are the result of the intervention or the result of the influence of the administrator? In addition, without an adequate counter-factual, any attempt to estimate treatment effects could be confounded with other causes that were not evenly distributed among the preexisting groups. Nevertheless, when random assignment to experimental conditions is not feasible, important information can still be obtained regarding potential causal effects, as we suggested earlier. While (randomized) experiments rely on random assignment to make other explanations for treatment effects implausible, Shadish and colleagues (2002) argue that researchers can use other techniques to make the same case. Specifically, they cite three related principles to follow in an attempt to make other plausible explanations of treatment effects implausible: (1) *identification and evaluation of plausible threats to internal validity*, (2) *primacy of control by design*, and (3) *coherent pattern matching*.

Identification and Evaluation of Plausible Threats to Internal Validity

What would make the groups different at the outset or during treatment, and would this difference affect the estimation of a treatment effect? These are the questions that need to be asked when assessing potential threats to internal validity. One major problem could occur if treatment and control groups differ on variables thought to affect treatment. This would be a form of *selection bias*. Another problem could occur if the groups were treated differently during implementation of the treatment and this difference was not a part of the treatment. An example of this circumstance is where one group of schools agrees to implement a particular treatment program and another group of schools agrees to act as a control, and some of the treatment schools decide to implement a pull-out tutoring program outside the scope of the research project. This would mean that any differences found in comparisons of treatment and control schools are potentially confounded with the effects of the pull-out tutoring program, which was not included in the original treatment protocol. This is an example of a *history* effect.

Another potential threat to validity can occur when the groups are differentially identified based on their performance on preselected variables. For example, one technique employed in literacy research is the "matched reading level" design (Backman, Mamen, & Ferguson, 1984; Bryant & Goswami, 1986; Vellutino & Scanlon, 1989). This design entails matching children who have reading problems with younger children who are reading at the same overall skill level but are developing normally in relation to their peers. In this case, the older group of children, who, in relation to their peers, are at the lower end of the reading ability distribution, may show an increased *regression to the mean* in comparison to the group of younger children, who were selected to be in the average range of their reading ability distribution. This effect can be substantially reduced by using multiple measures at multiple time points in order to place children into groups.

Primacy of Control by Design

Once threats to validity have been identified, attempts to minimize their effects can be implemented. Shadish and colleagues (2002) suggest ways in which threats to internal validity can be minimized by adding design controls, such as administering more measurements at pretest and employing additional control groups. The overall goal is to prevent the confounding of treatment effects with other effects while investigating whether given confounds could plausibly influence the treatment effects. These confounds are best controlled by adding design elements that address the particular threats to validity. For example, adding multiple control groups would have the benefit of increasing the chance that one of them would be suitable as a hypothetical counterfactual. Actively controlling what happens to the control group can also help reduce threats to validity. Adding multiple pretests would help identify preexisting differences among the groups and would also reduce the chances of a regression to the mean effect being confounded with a treatment effect. That is, children shown to be consistently below average on an ability using multiple measures of that ability administered over time will manifest less regression to the mean than children identified as below average using only one measure at one time point.

The alternative to using design elements to control for these threats is to use statistical controls to try to remove potential confounding influences on the treatment effects through statistical adjustments. The main tool in this strategy is the use of covariates to control for preexisting differences among the groups that may relate to treatment outcome. The thinking behind this strategy is that groups can be made to be equivalent statistically at baseline on variables thought to affect treatment. Groups are made to be statistically equivalent by adding or subtracting a statistically determined value to everyone's predicted score on the dependent variable. For example, the researcher may discover that his or her treatment groups differed significantly on an important pretest measure and may use that measure to statistically control for pretest differences.

Statistical control of confounds is seen as an inferior method of controlling for threats to validity compared with the use of design elements. It is impossible to statistically control for all the potential ways that groups can differ on variables that relate to outcome, often called the *hidden bias* (Shadish et al., 2002). Unmeasured variables cannot be controlled statistically. This is the main reason why experimental designs hold the advantage over quasi-experimental designs. While unmeasured effects cannot be controlled, they can be randomly distributed across the groups when assignment to experimental conditions is randomized. Also statistical controls are often employed incorrectly. One assumption of using statistical controls is that the variable being covaried has an equal (and linear) relationship with the dependent variable across all levels of other independent variables. That is, one of the assumptions of using a covariate (such as in an analysis of covariance) is that it does not interact with other variables. Another is that it does not have a curvilinear relationship with the dependent variable. If either of these assumptions were violated, it would render the statistical adjustments invalid. There are, of course, a number of ways to adjust an analysis to reflect these situations, but it is all too common to leave these potential violations unexplored. This is not to say that there is no place for statistical controls. However, these controls should be used *after* design controls have already been employed to control for minimal differences that may remain, and they should be used as a "method of last resort." Winship and Morgan (1999) provide an excellent review of the use of statistical controls in experimental design.

Coherent Pattern Matching

This principle involves making a complex prediction about a particular causal hypothesis that would leave few viable alternative explanations. The logic behind coherent pattern matching is that the more complex the prediction, the less likely it is that a given alternative could generate the same results. One example of this principle in literacy research is a study evaluating a reading curriculum designed to increase reading achievement that emphasized working on phonological awareness and decoding skills but not on reading fluency or comprehension skills. In this instance, the experimenter could assess the efficacy of the curriculum by investigating whether increases in reading achievement were related to greater gains in phonological awareness and decoding skills and lesser gains in fluency and reading comprehension. The drawback of this approach is that we still cannot know with certainty that an increase in these skills caused an increase in reading achievement. However, as more complex predictions become confirmed, alternative explanations become less likely.

Another example is a study examining whether hypothesized treatment effects had an impact on the constructs it was supposed to affect and had little or no impact on constructs that are unrelated to outcome. The experimenter might hypothesize, for example, that treatments that affect reading skills would have minimal effects on mathematical computational skills. But if it were discovered that a reading treatment had comparable rather than distinctly different effects on reading and mathematical computational skills, then the causal mechanisms of the treatment effects would be called into question. This type of hypothesis testing is commonly referred to as testing for *discriminant validity*.

With all these techniques, it is useful to keep in mind that the goal is to minimize threats to validity that are introduced by the inability to randomly assign units to conditions. Yet, all else being equal, a randomized experimental design will always be a more powerful mechanism for causal explanation than a quasi-experimental design. Researchers are encouraged to employ randomized experimental designs whenever possible. It is often the case that the researcher may employ a quasi-experimental design because it is easier than trying to randomize units to treatments. We want to make it clear that this choice does come at the cost of a loss of causal information.

Propensity Scores

One statistical technique designed to address the selection bias that occurs with quasi-experiments is called *propensity score analysis* (Luellen, Shadish, & Clark, 2005; Rosenbaum & Rubin, 1983). Propensity score analysis models the likelihood of a subject belonging to either the treatment group or the control group. The theory behind it states that if you can completely model the selection process (how people were placed into groups), you would be able to statistically control·for any biases that result from the use of nonrandom assignment to condition. In random assignment, for example, the propensity score for each person is known. A randomized experiment with two groups would yield a 50% chance of being in the treatment or the control group for each person, or a propensity score of .50. Similarly, if a researcher could use information about the participants in a quasi-experimental study, he or she could model assignment of these individuals to the treatment or control group, and scores from this model could be used as a covariate (or blocking variable) in another model that is investigating treatment effects.

Propensity score analysis has grown in popularity over recent years (Luellen et al., 2005) as a way to reduce the impact of selection bias on the conclusions obtained from quasi-experimental designs. However, it should be noted that there are some strong assumptions with this approach, and there are still a number of basic research issues that need to be addressed. For example, there is an assumption that all the variables that went into the selection process have been measured and perfectly modeled. This will almost never be the case. Additionally, it is unknown how accurately the selection process needs to be modeled in order for propensity score analysis to prove useful and not misleading. Although this technique shows promise in reducing the effects of selection bias, more work needs to be done before its real value in causal inferencing is known.

STANDARDS OF QUALITY FOR EXPERIMENTAL
AND QUASI-EXPERIMENTAL DESIGNS

We propose that experiments and quasi-experiments can be evaluated on the basis of two related criteria: the adequacy of the hypothetical counterfactual and how well a design addresses the four types of validity we described earlier in this chapter (from Shadish et al., 2002). These criteria provide benchmarks by which standards of quality can be assessed.

Adequacy of the Hypothetical Counterfactual

As stated earlier in this chapter, treatment effects are evaluated against what the investigator thinks would have happened had the treatment not been given. In this regard, the adequacy of the hypothetical counterfactual is of paramount importance. Accordingly, the control group must be comparable to the treatment group in all respects except for the experimental treatment in order for posttreatment differences between the groups to have any meaning. It is also possible to construct a control group that would help control for peripheral effects of the treatment. That is, a good control group need not only be one where the experimenter passively observes what is happening to the group. Control groups can also be actively constructed so that effects from treatment can become less ambiguous. One example of this circumstance is a study in which a researcher was interested in assessing a particular small-group remedial program designed to increase reading ability. The researcher could design an experiment that identified children who might benefit from remedial reading and then randomly assign them to small groups that received either the remedial reading program (treatment) or extra help in math. The math group would serve as a control group that is specifically designed to assess the effects of receiving extra attention in small groups, which, in this example, is confounded in the experimental condition. One could then argue that any differences between these groups could be attributed to the effects of the content of the remedial reading program and not to the extra attention each student receives during small-group instruction, regardless of the nature of that instruction. Thus, inadequate control groups would be defined as contrast groups that are not comparable to the treatment groups on important pretreatment variables. Control groups that differ from the treatment group in uncontrolled ways can introduce other possible causes for the observed treatment effect. Unfortunately, this will always be true in the case of quasi-experimental designs, and statements about treatment effects will be less powerful when they emanate from quasi-experimental designs. This is because we are less confident that mechanisms that could affect treatments are accounted for in the quasi-experimental design. However, as we indicated earlier, these designs can still provide some useful information. The degree to which any such design can do so depends largely on its ability to account for plausible alternative explanations for the treatment effects and should be judged accordingly.

Threats to Validity

Quality studies that employ experimental and quasi-experimental designs must also be able to adequately address threats to validity. Studies using these designs can be evaluated in terms of how well they have addressed these threats. The experimenter's ability to account for threats to validity directly constrains his or her ability to draw causal inferences from a study employing a particular design. In the next section, we summarize two literacy studies—one experimental and one quasi-experimental—and attempt to evaluate them against the criteria presented previously. To protect the innocent, we have decided to evaluate two studies of our own (Foorman, Francis, Fletcher, Schatschneider, & Mehta, 1998; Vellutino & Scanlon, 1987).

EXPERIMENTAL DESIGN EXEMPLAR

A study that exemplifies several of the advantages and disadvantages of implementing an experimental design was conducted by one of us some years ago (Vellutino & Scanlon, 1987). A major objective of this study, among others, was to evaluate the relative merits of using a whole (sight) word meaning–based approach to teaching word identification compared with a code-based (phonics) approach singly or in combination. In accord with the view that children must have ready access to both the names and meanings of printed words as integrated wholes and the sounds associated with their component letters (or combinations of their letters) in order to learn to identify them, the investigators hypothesized that a treatment condition that facilitated the complementary use of both approaches would result in better performance on an experimental task that simulated beginning reading than would treatment conditions that facilitated the use of one without the other. Participants (units) in the study were poor and normally developing readers in second and sixth grades. Each was initially selected on the basis of performance on an oral reading test and, thereafter, on the basis of intellectual and exclusionary criteria typically used to distinguish between children with and without specific reading disability. Participants in each reader group at each grade level were also assessed on pretreatment measures of phoneme segmentation and letter–sound (pseudoword) decoding ability before being randomly assigned to one of five experimental conditions: three treatment and two control conditions. Thus, the fully crossed design was a 2 × 2 × 5 randomized block design (2 reader groups × 2 grade levels × 5 experimental conditions) with 20 possible cells (i.e., groups assigned to given conditions). Note that the poor readers at each grade level performed significantly below the normal readers on both of the pretreatment tests of phoneme segmentation and letter–sound decoding, which indicated that they had deficient phonological skills. This was of interest because one objective of the study was to evaluate differential response to treatments in the poor- and normal-reader groups.

One of the treatment conditions (phoneme segmentation training [PST]) was designed to foster an analytic disposition to search for letter–sound invariance in printed words, and it simulated the code-oriented approach to reading instruction. It consisted of an ordered series of training activities designed to foster phoneme segmentation of spoken and written words and pseudowords followed by activities designed to facilitate functional use of an alphabetic coding strategy to mediate word identification. The alphabetic coding activities initially entailed practice (15 trials) in learning to identify four printed trigraphs composed of novel alphabetic characters (*sij, suf, dij, duf*), using letter–sound strategies to do so. This task was followed by a transfer of learning task in which permuted forms of the initial training set (*jid, juf, sif, dus*) were presented to assess children's ability to generalize letter–sound knowledge acquired during initial learning (15–20 trials). The children were encouraged, on both tasks, to search for letter–sound invariance to aid word identification. The training activities for the PST condition were completed in 5 or 6 days, and after no more than a 2-day hiatus, the children were presented with a new set of printed trigraphs composed of novel alphabetic characters (*gov, goz, vab, zab*) and were given 20 paired-associates (whole-word) learning trials to assess their ability to use a code-oriented (analytic) strategy to learn to identify these trigraphs (code acquisition training). The next day, they were given reversed derivatives of these stimuli (*vog, zog, bav, baz*) to learn to identify (code acquisition transfer) using the same paired-associates format. Because the experimenters were interested in whether the children could independently implement the (hypothesized) disposition to search for letter–sound invariance the PST condition was designed to foster, they were not told of the alphabetic properties of the novel trigraphs on either the initial learning or the transfer learning tasks. The code acquisition training and transfer tasks were the primary outcome measures used to assess treatment effects in this study and were administered to participants exposed to the three treatment conditions and one of the two control conditions. Participants in the other control condition were presented only with the code acquisition transfer task (see later discussion).

The second treatment condition (response acquisition [RA]) was our analogue of the whole-word/meaning-based approach to word identification (often called "sight word" learning). The initial phase of the training implemented in this condition consisted of a phonological memory task designed to familiarize the children with the oral counterparts (names) of the trigraphs they would encounter on the initial learning task used as one of the outcome measures (code acquisition training). It involved 20 free-recall trials using an alternating presentation/test format. Thus, on a given trial, the experimenter presented all four nonsense syllables, then had the child recite digits backward, and after a 6-second hiatus asked the child to recall these stimuli in any order. After a short break, the child learned to associate these same stimuli with pictures of novel cartoon animals so as to imbue them with meaning. The intent of this training was to help ensure that the children in this condition would have ready access to the verbal response counterparts of the trigraphs they would encounter on the code acquisition training task and that they would be learning to read "words" that were meaningful to them. RA training was followed by presentation of the same code acquisition training and transfer tasks administered to the PST group no more than 2 days after training was completed.

Children in the third treatment condition (PSTRA) received both phoneme segmentation/alphabetic coding and RA training, followed by presentation of the same initial learning and transfer learning tasks administered to the PST and RA groups 1 or 2 days after training was completed. Of the two control conditions, one (C-1) entailed exposure to both the initial learning and transfer learning tasks, and the other (C-2) entailed exposure to only the transfer learning task. The C-1 condition allowed the investigators to evaluate the differential effects of the three types of training on the children's ability to learn to identify (read) printed words derived from an alphabet and, thereafter, capitalize on their alphabetic properties in learning new words. Because it controlled for generalization and intrusion (reversal) errors that might be caused by previous exposure to words presented on the initial learning task (e.g., calling *zog/zob/* or calling *bav/vab/*, analogous to calling *was/saw/*), the C-2 condition allowed the investigators to evaluate the effects of the three treatment and the C-1 control conditions on the children's tendency to make such errors. In all instances, assessments on pre- and posttreatment measures and implementation of experimental conditions took place in a quiet room outside the participants' classroom. Note also that, for all five experimental conditions, time spent with an examiner was equated through "filler" activities unrelated to the experimental tasks.

Finally, to further evaluate the differential effects of the treatment conditions, an alternate form of the phoneme segmentation test administered to all participants before they were exposed to given experimental conditions was administered to each participant approximately 2 weeks after administration of the paired-associates task used as the primary outcome measure (see Figure 9.1 for a summary of the design).

Space limitations preclude a detailed account of results from this study. It will suffice to point out that the data were consistent with the hypothesis that the whole-word/meaning-based and code-oriented approaches to word identification are both important components of reading instruction insofar as the children exposed to the treatment conditions that simulated these approaches (RA and PST, respectively) performed significantly better

Experimental conditions	Phonemic segmentation training	Response acquisition		Code acquisition	
		Free recall	Picture–syllable association	Symbol–syllable training	Symbol–syllable transfer
PST	X	N.A.	N.A.	X	X
RA	N.A.	X	X	X	X
PSTRA	X	X	X	X	X
CONTROL-1	N.A.	N.A.	N.A.	X	X
CONTROL-2	N.A.	N.A.	N.A.	N.A.	X

FIGURE 9.1. Order of tasks administered to subjects in each experimental condition of the study of the effects of phonemic segmentation training and response acquisition training on code acquisition. N.A., not administered (filler activities unrelated to the experiment were substituted in order to control for time spent with the examiner outside of the classroom); PST, phonemic segmentation training; RA, response acquisition; PSTRA, phonemic segmentation training and response acquisition; CONTROL-1, received both symbol–syllable training and symbol–syllable transfer tasks; CONTROL-2, received only symbol–syllable transfer task.

on the initial learning task (code acquisition training) used as the primary outcome measure than did the control children exposed to this task (C-1). Moreover, the children exposed to the condition that incorporated both approaches (PSTRA) performed significantly better on the code acquisition training task than did those exposed to the other three conditions. This pattern of results was observed in all reader groups at all grades levels, with the exception of the second-grade poor readers. The second-grade poor readers who were exposed to the PST condition performed as well as those in the group exposed to the PSTRA condition, and both of these groups performed better on the initial learning task than did the second-grade poor readers exposed to the RA and C-1 conditions. However, on the transfer learning task (code acquisition transfer), the children in all the reader groups exposed to conditions that facilitated the use of letter sounds to mediate word identification (PST and PSTRA) performed significantly better than did children in any of the other groups and made fewer generalization and intrusion errors (e.g., *was/saw* types of reversals) from the initial learning task than did children in all other groups, save for the C-2 control children who had not been exposed to the initial learning task. Finally, children in the PST and PSTRA groups performed better on the posttreatment phoneme segmentation test than did children in all other groups.

The study just described provides a reasonable illustration of the relative merits of randomized designs in general and randomized factorial designs in particular. In regard to the validity of causal inferences about given treatment effects, the fact that children in each reader group at each grade level were randomly assigned to each of the five experimental conditions, and that sample sizes were adequate for the contrasts of interest, minimized most of the various threats to internal validity discussed (e.g., selection bias, history, testing, instrumentation, regression to the mean), except for attrition and exposure to pretreatment testing. Attrition was not a problem in this study because the experimental itinerary was implemented very soon after participants were identified, which resulted in an attrition rate of zero. Pretreatment testing effects (e.g., test–retest) were minimized by the use of an alternate form, at posttest, of the phoneme segmentation test administered at pretest and by the fact that the primary outcome measures were experimental tasks that the participants had not previously encountered. Moreover, given that the experimental design incorporated different treatments tied directly to different predicted effects on different outcome measures, in addition to two control groups allowing evaluation of these predicted effects, there were several complementary sources of counterfactual inference provided by this design. Thus, by most standards, this study had a high degree of internal validity. This conclusion is buttressed by the finding that treatments effects were replicated across different groups of participants.

That statistical conclusion validity was reasonably high in this study is suggested by the finding that treatment effects were generally robust (p values typically < .001), implying adequate power, and that the pattern of results was replicated across participant groups using different outcome measures, implying adequate reliability of assessment instruments and experimental results. Similarly, the construct validity and external validity of the participants in this study seems ensured by (1) the fact that poor- and normal-reader groups were selected in accord with psychometric and exclusionary criteria typically used to distinguish these groups; (2) the finding that group differences were observed on independent measures that typically distinguish the groups (e.g., phoneme segmentation and pseudoword decoding) as well as on experimental measures that should (theoretically) distinguish between them; and (3) the fact that results can be generalized to both typical and diverse samples of participants (i.e., poor and normal readers in second and sixth grades). One can also have confidence in the construct validity of the treatment and outcome measures insofar as each was defined on the basis of theoretical analyses of word-recognition processes in developing readers grounded in a great deal of empirical research. Moreover, typical threats to construct validity of treatments, such as treatment diffusion, mono-operation bias, and mono-method bias, were minimized by the use of a factorial design, by the use of different outcome measures tied to different predicted outcomes, and by the finding that hypothesized outcomes on these measures were observed in different populations of participants. Little can be said of the construct validity of the settings in which the experiment was conducted, except that they constituted a random sampling of "quiet rooms outside the child's classroom" and, therefore, could be considered representative examples of such settings.

Perhaps the major problem with the Vellutino and Scanlon (1987) study is the external validity of the treatment effects observed in the study under the conditions in which these effects were observed. It will suffice to point out that because reading instruction is carried out in classrooms rather than in restricted laboratory-like settings, such as those used in the study, with instruction implemented with an entire class (or small groups) rather than with one child at a time, and because the different treatments were "capsule versions" of the different approaches to reading instruction that used novel materials to control for previous learning and were implemented over restricted periods of time, it was not clear at the time the study was conducted that obtained results would generalize to more natural settings. To be more specific, it must be acknowledged that children do not normally acquire new vocabulary words by associating them with cartoon characters, which was our method of imbuing the nonsense words used in certain of the experimental conditions with meaning. Moreover, many of the measures used on the simulated reading tasks involved reading of nonsense words, and nonsense words are not in children's listening vocabularies. Similarly, children do not normally acquire different reading strategies and learn to read new words over the 1- to 8-day time period that encompassed the different experimental conditions compared in this study. Thus, the simulated reading tasks presented to the children who participated in this study were clearly artificial, as were the experimental conditions under which they were presented, and the external validity of this study can justifiably be questioned. Yet, despite this weakness, recent intervention research has provided independent confirmation that both meaning-based and code-oriented approaches to instruction are important ingredients in facilitating the acquisition of functional literacy skills (e.g., Foorman et al., 1998; Hiebert & Taylor, 2000; Torgesen, 2000; Vellutino et al., 1996), thereby lending additional support for one of the central hypotheses the study was designed to evaluate. Indeed, the fact that this hypothesis has been cross-validated in classroom, small-group, and one-to-one tutoring studies, as well as in a randomized experiment designed to simulate beginning reading, is rather compelling and reinforces our assertion that conducting programmatic research and multiple experiments across many venues is a critically important ingredient in validating causal inferences in literacy research.

AN EXEMPLAR OF A QUASI-EXPERIMENTAL DESIGN

One example of a literacy research study that employed a quasi-experimental design was conducted by a group of literacy researchers, of which one of us was a member (Foorman et al., 1998). This year-long study was designed to compare the effects of three types of literacy instruction on a group of children receiving Title I services. Two hundred eighty-five first- and second-grade students received one of three types of classroom reading programs. The programs differed in the amount of direct instruction in alphabetic coding that the children in each classroom received. The *direct code* group received explicit instruction in letter–sound correspondences and practiced using them in decodable text. The *embedded code* group received less direct instruction but practiced with systematic sound–spelling patterns that were embedded in text. The *implicit code* group received implicit instruction in the alphabetic code within the context of text reading. A fourth group was identified in the study as a *control group* that received the school district's standard form of reading instruction, which was similar to the type of implicit instruction that the children in the implicit code group received, except that the teachers in the control group did not receive supplementary assistance in implementing the instruction (see discussion later).

Randomly selected children from each classroom were assessed five times a year to evaluate growth in reading and reading-related skills. To evaluate fidelity of treatments, reading instruction in experimental classrooms either was audiotaped or was monitored by trained observers to assess whether the teacher was adhering to the reading program. Teacher ratings of child performance and behavior were also obtained, along with school records of attendance. Achievement data from this study were analyzed using hierarchical linear modeling to assess growth in reading and end-of-year outcomes. The results of the study indicated that children who received direct code instruction improved significantly faster in the acquisition of word-identification skills than did children who received implicit code instruction, with the embedded code groups not differing significantly from either the direct code or implicit code groups. The impact of direct code instruction was moderated by initial level of phonological processing skills in that those children with the lowest levels of phonological processing skills benefited the most from direct code instruction.

Unfortunately, the experimental and control groups were constituted based on the willingness of teachers and other school officials to participate in the study and not via random assignment. This meant that other strategies had to be employed to ensure that treatment effects were due to the experimental treatments and not to extraneous or confounding variables. A combination of strategies was employed to achieve this objective. First, the study used two comparison groups. We wanted to know whether explicit instruction was better than implicit instruction in helping children from disadvantaged backgrounds to learn how to read. The school district in which the study was conducted had already been using implicit instruction in all its schools. In most cases, allowing classroom teachers to implement the type of reading instruction they would normally implement would provide a natural instance of a hypothetical counterfactual. However, in this case, we were concerned that the mere implementation of any new program might have an effect, which would be a concern for both experimental and quasi-experimental research designs. The teachers in the experimental conditions were slated to receive extensive training over the summer and support throughout the year to implement the new treatments. This presented the possibility that attending reading workshops (for any program) over the summer and receiving supplemental support might themselves cause reading scores to improve. So we constituted another group (the implicit code group) that received implicit instruction that was essentially the same as that implemented in control classrooms, but the teachers from these classrooms also received extensive training during the summer and support throughout the year, just like the direct code and embedded code groups. Thus, any differences between the two implicit code groups could be attributed to the differential training they received in providing implicit instruction.

Because random assignment was not possible in this study, serious threats to internal validity had to be addressed. Our first concern was that the groups would not be comparable at the beginning of the year on variables that we thought would impact reading. To address these concerns, we analyzed pretest data and found that the four groups did not significantly differ on word reading and phonological awareness. Although these groups were still vulnerable to a hidden unobserved bias, we tried to provide evidence that the groups were comparable on variables that were important to reading. We also examined variables that might have had an impact on children throughout the year. Specifically, there were no differences among the groups in rates of attrition or in school attendance. Moreover, teachers across all conditions were reported as implementing their respective reading programs with a high level of fidelity. Because we tested children five times throughout the year, practice effects were highly probable. With this type of design, the experimenter has no way of knowing how much of the growth during the year might be due to practice effects. However, it seemed reasonable to assume that practice effects would affect all groups equally, and that the impact of test practice on differences between group means would be minimal.

Statistical conclusion validity was addressed in a number of ways. First, we took into account the fact that these students were not statistically independent of each other because some of the children in the study came from the same classroom. One assumption common to all inferential statistical procedures is that each observation is independent of each other. This assumption, called the *independence assumption*, is one of the most important assumptions in statistics. Indeed, even small violations of independence can lead to a large increase in type I error rate (Scariano & Davenport, 1987; Stevens, 1992). In this study, we could not assume that children in the same classroom were independent of each other. That is, we had to account for the possibility that teachers influence the children in their classrooms in ways that might make them more similar to each other than students in other classrooms. This is why we employed hierarchical linear modeling (HLM) as our main statistical tool. HLM allows for the estimation of treatment effects while accounting for the fact that children may not be statistically independent of each other.

Other statistical techniques were employed to provide additional control over extraneous influences. We had originally planned to use initial levels of phonological awareness measured at pretest as a covariate in the analyses, but while examining the assumption of homogeneity of regression, we discovered that phonological awareness at pretest interacted with the treatment to produce differential results. We explored this interaction and found that the effects in the treatment groups were more pronounced for children who had lower initial levels of phonological awareness skill. So, in this instance, the effects of initial levels of phonological awareness were more adequately accounted for in the model, and we would have lost important information about causal relationships of interest in this study had we not evaluated the moderating effects of phonological awareness and simply used this measure as a pretest covariate.

We also tried to control for type I error by using the Bonferroni correction to adjust the alpha level for the groupwise mean comparisons. A more stringent approach would have been to also correct for the number of different dependent variables that were analyzed. When considering ways to limit type I error, there is a balance that must be struck between statistical power (the ability to detect an effect if it exists) and controlling type I error. All else being equal, the power of a particular test will decrease as the control for type I error increases (Maxwell & Delaney, 1990). We decided that we would lose too much statistical power to correct for the total number of comparisons being made. However, we did leave ourselves open to the criticism that type I error was not adequately controlled.

We also addressed concerns about construct validity and monomethod bias by making multiple assessments of the variables thought to be important in studying the impacts of the treatment. We assessed phonological awareness using seven different tests and reading using two tests of word identification and two tests of reading comprehension. Some constructs, however, were only measured by one test (such as IQ and vocabulary). When designing studies, it is difficult to balance the amount of assessment time with the number of constructs that the researcher would like to measure.

Finally, the evidence for the external validity of results from this study is less clear. Although the study was conducted in a school-based setting, there are some weaknesses to the design of the study that could mitigate generalizations to the target population. First, this was not a random sample from a population of all children receiving benefits from Title I funds. Thus, it is not possible to estimate how this sample might be different from the population of Title I students at large (e.g., those outside the geographic area where we conducted the study). In this sense, it was a sample of convenience. So it is difficult to say how these results would replicate in another Title I sample. Also, the teachers who implemented the experimental reading programs that were administered to the various classrooms received support and training throughout the school year. Thus, it is possible that these same effects may not be observed in another sample if the level of support provided were to change. This underscores the importance of multiple studies that employ different designs possessing different strengths and weaknesses to attempt to triangulate on the existence and strength of a particular effect. In fact, the results from this study are consistent with the findings from an increasingly large body of studies demonstrating that explicit training to facilitate functional use of the alphabetic principle does have positive effects (e.g., Ball & Blachman, 1991; Blachman, 1997; Bradley & Bryant, 1983; Torgesen, 2000; Vellutino et al., 1996).

SUMMARY

Because of significant methodological advances in the basic and applied sciences, especially during the 20th century, literacy researchers now have access to a multitude of methods for addressing important questions in research concerned with literacy development and how best to facilitate adequate literacy development. The method(s) employed in conducting any piece of research in this area of inquiry will, of course, depend on the nature of the questions addressed, but for purposes of establishing causal relationships that will generalize across units, treatments, outcome measures, and settings, the experimental method is the method of choice. In this chapter, we discussed the two most general and widely used experimental methods for establishing causal relationships: the experimental design and the quasi-experimental design. We discussed these designs within the context of a validity typology forwarded by Shadish and colleagues (2002) and pointed out their similarities. Both entail deliberate manipulation of treatments for the purpose of observing hypothesized effects; both ensure that hypothesized causes precede hypothesized effects; both are based on the principle of counterfactual inferencing, insofar as both incorporate procedures (e.g., control groups) that allow the experimenter to approximate effects on outcome measures under the hypothetical circumstance where treatments had and had not been administered to the same units; and both incorporate procedures that allow the experimenter to minimize and/or assess the influence of extraneous factors that could produce the effect(s) hypothesized to be attributed to the treatment(s). However, in experimental designs units are assigned to experimental conditions randomly, whereas in quasi-experimental designs units are assigned to treatments nonrandomly, typically for practical reasons.

In discussing the advantages and disadvantages of both designs, we pointed out that randomized experimental designs are better able to create adequate hypothetical counterfactuals than quasi-experimental designs because they create experimental groups that are, on average, similar to one another on relevant variables before treatments are administered; they decrease the plausibility of most threats to internal validity (save for attrition) by distributing them randomly across experimental conditions, thereby increasing the probability that systematic differences that occur between treatment and control groups are due to experimental treatments rather than to extraneous factors. In contrast, quasi-experimental designs must rely more heavily on additional design features (e.g., pretreatment assessment, additional control groups, coherent pattern matching) and statistical controls to identify and control plausible threats to internal validity and ensure adequacy of counterfactual inferencing.

Finally, to concretize the methodological issues we discussed concerning threats to validity and standards of quality in experimental design, we described, in some detail, two studies that have appeared in the literacy research literature in recent years, one exemplifying a randomized experimental design and the second exemplifying a quasi-experimental design. We underscored the strengths and weaknesses of each vis-à-vis the threats to validity and standards of quality we outlined earlier. In so doing, we hope that we have made it clear that no experimental design perfectly controls all threats to validity, and all have flaws and weaknesses that limit their contribution to the research community and to the knowledge base. Indeed, a causal relationship that is detected in a single experiment must be independently replicated in programmatic research and across variations in units, treatments, outcome measures, and settings before the research community can have any faith in that relationship. This is one reason why the knowledge base in a given area of inquiry tends to accumulate slowly. That said, each individual experiment, in its own way, contributes incrementally to programs of research that can eventually offer clear and reasonably coherent conclusions about literacy education.

ACKNOWLEDGMENTS

Much of the work discussed in this paper was supported by grants from the National Institute of Child Health and Human Development (NICHD). The data for the experimental study reported in Vellutino and Scanlon (1987) were collected under the auspices of NICHD Grant No. RO1 HD 09658, awarded to Vellutino. Other NICHD grants involving Vellutino contributed to the creation of this chapter, specifically Nos. RO1 HD34598 and RO1 HD42350. The data for the quasi-experimental study reported in Foorman et al. (1998) were supported by NICHD Grant Nos. HD 30995 and HD 28172, awarded to Barbara Foorman. Support for the revision of this chapter was provided by NICHD Grant No. P50 HD052120 awarded to Christopher Schatschneider (co–principal investigator).

REFERENCES

Abelson, R. P. (1995). *Statistics as principled argument*. Hillsdale, NJ: Erlbaum.

Backman, J. E., Mamen, M., & Ferguson, H. B. (1984). Reading level design: Conceptual and methodological issues in reading research. *Psychological Bulletin, 96*, 560–568.

Ball, E. W., & Blachman, B. A. (1991). Does phoneme awareness training in kindergarten make a difference in early word recognition and developmental spelling? *Reading Research Quarterly, 26*, 49–66.

Blachman, B. A. (1997). Early intervention and phonological awareness: A cautionary tale. In B. A. Blachman (Ed.), *Foundations of reading acquisition and dyslexia: Implications for early intervention* (pp. 409–430). Mahwah, NJ: Erlbaum.

Bradley, L., & Bryant, P. E. (1983). Categorizing sounds and learning to read—A causal connection. *Nature, 301*, 419–421.

Bryant, P., & Goswami, U. (1986). Strengths and weaknesses of the reading level design: A comment on Backman, Mamen, and Ferguson. *Psychological Bulletin, 100*, 101–103.

Campbell, D. T., & Stanley, J. C. (1963). *Experimental and quasi-experimental designs for research*. Chicago: Rand McNally.

Dawes, R. M. (1994). *House of cards: Psychology and psychotherapy built on myth*. New York: Free Press.

Drake, S. (1981). *Cause, experiment, and science*. Chicago: University of Chicago Press.

Fisher, R. A. (1925). *Statistical methods for research workers*. Edinburgh, Scotland: Oliver & Boyd.

Fisher, R. A. (1935). *The design of experiments*. Edinburgh, Scotland: Oliver & Boyd.

Foorman, B. R., Francis, D. J., Fletcher, J. M., Schatschneider, C., & Mehta, P. (1998). The role of instruction in learning to read: Preventing reading failure in at-risk children. *Journal of Educational Psychology, 90*, 37–55.

Hiebert, E. H., & Taylor, B. M. (2000). Beginning reading instruction: Research on early interventions. In M. L. Kamil, P. B. Mosenthal, P. D. Pearson, & R. Barr (Eds.), *Handbook of reading research* (Vol. III, pp. 455–482). Mahwah, NJ: Erlbaum.

Hume, D. (1999). *An enquiry concerning human understanding* (T. L. Beauchamp, Ed.). Oxford, UK: Oxford University Press. (Original work published 1748)

Kenny, D. A. (1975). A quasi-experimental approach to assessing treatment effects in the nonequivalent control group design. *Psychological Bulletin, 82*, 345–362.

Lewis, D. (1973). Causation. *Journal of Philosophy, 70*, 556–567.

Luellen, J. K., Shadish, W. R., & Clark, M. H. (2005). Propensity scores: An introduction and experimental test. *Evaluation Review, 29*, 530–558.

Maxwell, S. E., & Delaney, H. D. (1990). *Designing experiments and analyzing data: A model comparison approach*. Belmont, CA: Wadsworth.

Mill, J. S. (1987). A system of logic. In R. Ryan (Ed.), *Utilitarianism and other essays* (pp. 113–131). New York: Penguin. (Original work published 1843)

Rosenbaum, P. R., & Rubin, D. B. (1983). The central role of the propensity score in observational studies for causal effects. *Biometrika, 70*, 41–55.

Scariano, S. M., & Davenport, J. M. (1987). The effects of violations of the independence assumption in the one way ANOVA. *American Statistician, 41,* 123–129.

Shadish, W. R., Cook, T. D., & Campbell, D. T. (2002). *Experimental and quasi-experimental designs for general causal inference.* Boston: Houghton Mifflin.

Stevens, J. (1992). *Applied multivariate statistics for the social sciences* (2nd ed.). Hillsdale, NJ: Erlbaum.

Torgesen, J. K. (2000). Individual differences in response to early interventions in reading: The lingering problem of treatment resisters. *Learning Disabilities Research and Practice, 15*(1), 55–64.

Vellutino, F. R., & Scanlon, D. M. (1987). Phonological coding, phonological awareness, and reading ability: Evidence from a longitudinal and experimental study. *Merrill–Palmer Quarterly, 33,* 321–363.

Vellutino, F. R., & Scanlon, D. M. (1989). Some prerequisites for interpreting results from reading level matched designs. *Journal of Reading Behavior, 21*(4), 361–385.

Vellutino, F. R., Scanlon, D. M., Sipay, E., Small, S., Pratt, A., Chen, R., et al. (1996). Cognitive profiles of difficult-to-remediate and readily remediated poor readers: Early intervention as a vehicle for distinguishing between cognitive and experiential deficits as basic causes of specific reading disability. *Journal of Educational Psychology, 88,* 601–638.

Winship, C., & Morgan, S. L. (1999). The estimation of causal effects from observational data. *Annual Review of Sociology, 25,* 659–707.

CHAPTER 10

Revisiting the Connection between Research and Practice Using Formative and Design Experiments

Barbara A. Bradley
David Reinking

There has always been a great divide between education
research and practice.
—COLLINS (1999, p. 289)

Education is not in need of research to find out how it works.
It is in need of creative invention to make it work better.
—EBEL (1982, p. 18)

We welcome this opportunity to update a chapter that we wrote for the first edition of this book. An update is clearly justifiable because, as would be expected for a relatively new and evolving approach to research, there are important new developments to report. For example, much more has been published about what is now often referred to generically as design research or design-based research. Most notably, there are now two edited books about design research (Kelly, Lesh, & Baek, 2008; van den Akker, Gravemeijer, McKenney, & Nieveen, 2006) and another that explicates formative and design experiments in relation to language and literacy research (Reinking & Bradley, 2008). Furthermore, beyond the themed issue in *Educational Researcher* (Kelly, 2003) that we drew upon in our former chapter, two other respected research journals have devoted issues to this approach: *Educational Psychologist* (Sandoval & Bell, 2004) and the *Journal of the Learning Sciences* (Barab & Squire, 2004).

Paralleling this increased attention, more literacy researchers are conducting research guided by the principles and perspectives of design, and they are publishing their results in a variety of outlets (e.g., Baumann, Ware, & Edwards, 2007; Boling, 2008; Bradley & Reinking, in press; Fisher, Frey, & Lapp, 2009; Ivey & Broaddus, 2007; Massey, 2007; McKenney & Voogt, 2009; Taboada & Rutherford, in press). Furthermore, and significantly, the U.S. government has changed its views on educational research and is now calling for studies that involve more authentic collaborations among practitioners, researchers, and policymakers, which is more consistent with design research. Funding agencies, such as the Institute of Education Sciences, are emphasizing educational research that focuses on process, not simply outcomes (Viadero, 2009). For example, the rationale for goal 2 under many of the multi-goal-structured funding programs through the U.S. Department of Education, including literacy research, states, "To develop or improve education interventions requires an iterative process of designing, testing, revising, and testing to produce a product or system that functions in the way that the developer intends for it to function and that can be implemented in actual education delivery settings (e.g., schools)."

Despite these new developments, the central rationale and guiding questions that underlie formative and design experiments, as we first wrote about them, remain unchanged. That is, how can and how should literacy research inform instructional practice? How can the long-lamented gap between research and practice be closed? Furthermore, the primary reasons why educational researchers have gravitated toward this approach have remained unchanged. Specifically, educational researchers are often attracted to this approach because they are dissatisfied with more established and widely used experimental or naturalistic methodologies. The warrant for that dissatisfaction can be found in considering the long-standing gap between conventional research methodologies and instructional practice, which we highlighted in our original chapter.

For example, at the time we wrote this chapter for the first edition, the U.S. government was vigorously promoting the view that experimental methods should be the gold standard for implementing scientifically based reading instruction (National Reading Panel, 2000). Those who hold this view—and many researchers and policymakers still do—believe that practitioners should implement literacy instruction to be consistent with generalizations derived from carefully controlled experiments. They see the role of literacy research as a systematic winnowing to determine which among many alternative instructional interventions or approaches work best on average. What works best is typically defined narrowly as instruction that results in statistically superior student achievement based on quantifiable measures. Determining what works best on average to promote educational achievement is useful information, but it does not inherently provide guidance about what factors might be relevant to successful implementation in a particular context. Focusing on tournament-style research to see which instructional interventions are left standing after experimental comparisons also promotes misguided notions such as best practice, which is an unattainable goal in any absolute sense and likewise devalues professional judgment (Reinking, 2007).

Researchers who employ naturalistic methodologies, on the other hand, also generate useful information but of a different kind. Because such methodologies are suited to a deep examination of particular instructional contexts, they produce data that are perhaps more useful in helping practitioners understand the complexities and subtleties of instructional practice. When studying classroom instruction, these researchers often aim to reveal aspects of instructional practice that might otherwise go unnoticed by practitioners or that might help them better understand and reflect on their practice. Strong generalizations about practice or conclusions about best methods are not typically the goal of such studies, although they may be guided by and interpreted in light of pedagogical theories, educational philosophies, or ideologies designed to provide a broad frame for instruction. The topics investigated typically are not related to conventional measures of achievement but, instead, tend to focus on dimensions of literacy such as developing motivation to read, acquiring personal agency through texts, and promoting sociocultural awareness. However, studies using naturalistic methods rarely provide explicit guidance that directly informs practitioners.

For many researchers, the best of all worlds remains one in which these two broad methodological options would be complementary, perhaps creating a synergy that would guide teachers and improve instructional practice toward realizing a wide range of valued goals for literacy instruction. However, that has rarely happened, and researchers often remain inside their methodological silos with little dialogue or synthesis. We have seen no significant movement that brings these two research traditions closer together since we wrote our chapter for the previous edition. Neither have we seen any new evidence that experimental or naturalistic approaches have begun to influence directly and pervasively instructional practice. The conclusions drawn about the failures of education research to influence practice by writers we cited in our early version of this chapter still hold (e.g., Collins, 1999; Eisenhart & Borko, 1993; Labaree, 1998; Lagemann, 2000). In fact, to that list we could add work that has been published more recently such as Pressley, Graham, and Harris (2006) in the area of literacy and more general commentaries on education research, such as Barab and Squire (2004), Hoadley (2004), Hostetler (2005), Lewis, Perry, and Murata (2006), and Reeves (2006). And although we have become aware of some evidence that the academic reward structure at some institutions is shifting slightly toward acknowledging the value of making tangible improvements in practice, the following quote from Eisenhart and Borko (1993) still seems current: "Researchers see the significance of research in terms of its implications for understanding far-ranging repercussions, predicting and improving the future, information policy, or getting tenure, whereas teachers usually want research results to bear directly on their classroom practice" (p. 79). To graphically illustrate the disconnection between research and practice, consider the printed program for the annual meeting of the American Educational Research Association. Each year it is the size of the phone book for a major city. Yet it is unclear what specific advances the research reported has made each year toward directly informing practitioners about how they can improve education practice.

Thus, we continue to believe that the gap between research and practice remains wide and that literacy researchers still need to refocus their methodological emphases to address specifically how promising instructional interventions might be implemented in classrooms to achieve valued pedagogical goals (see Dillon, O'Brien, & Heilman, 2000). We continue to need methodologies that acknowledge the complexities of classroom teaching and that align with the day-to-day management of that complexity. We continue to need approaches that enlighten practitioners about research-based pedagogies to enhance literacy but also provide them with specific insights about how they might effectively implement instructional interventions. More than ever, we believe, design research has the potential to narrow the gap between research and practice and can contribute to synthesizing in action the work of researchers who hold diverse methodological perspectives (McCandliss, Kachman, & Bryant, 2003). In the remainder of this chapter, we revisit and update our earlier explication of formative and design experiments in light of new developments and our new personal understandings of this approach and its use in literacy research.

WHAT ARE FORMATIVE EXPERIMENTS AND DESIGN EXPERIMENTS?

Classroom life, in my judgment, is too complex an affair
to be viewed or talked about from any single perspective.
—JACKSON (1990, pp. xxi–xxii)

An Update on Terminology

In the earlier version of this chapter, we referred to studies using this approach as formative or design experiments. These terms can be traced to the earliest roots of this approach, as explained in a subsequent section of this chapter. These terms continue to be used. Literacy researchers, in particular, for reasons that are not clear, seem to prefer the term *formative experiment*. For example, to our earlier citations of literacy research using this terminology (Jiménez, 1997; Lenski, 2001; Reinking & Watkins, 2000; Neuman, 1999) we can add Baumann and colleagues (2007), Bradley and Reinking (in press), Fisher and colleagues (2009), Ivey and Broaddus (2007), Massey (2007), and Taboada and Ruhterford (in press). Researchers in other content areas such as mathematics education or instructional technology tend to prefer the term *design experiments* (e.g., Cobb, Confrey, diSessa, Lehrer, & Schauble, 2003), as do those invested in more conventional experimental approaches and in creating a science of design (e.g., see Kelly et al., 2008; van den Akker et al., 2006). However, perhaps because of uncertainty about distinctions among these different terms and because there have been somewhat different emphases around some core attributes of this approach, there is a trend toward using broader, more encompassing terms such as *design research* or *design-based research*. Thus, for the remainder of this chapter, we use the term *formative experiments* to refer to how this approach has been understood and used, particularly among literacy researchers, and the term *design research* as a generic, more encompassing term that refers to a variety of terms and emphases among a broader range of education research that all share a core of defining attributes (see later section on defining methodological characteristics).

What Design Research Does That Other Approaches Typically Do Not

The study of how educational interventions work can never be
far removed from the task of engineering them to work better.
        —NEWMAN, GRIFFIN, AND COLE (1989, p. 147)

Educational research often sits in the uneasy intersection
between science and engineering.
        —FEUER, TOWNE, AND SHAVELSON (2002, p. 28)

Design research in general and formative experiments in particular fill a neglected gap in research aimed at guiding instruction because they address more directly the questions and issues that practitioners face and that are not addressed as authentically or as directly by other research methodologies. That is, scientific experiments comparing the effectiveness of alternative instructional interventions may provide useful generalizations across diverse contexts. However, scientific experiments, of necessity, can focus only on relatively few variables, and they assume that other potentially influential variables have random effects. The wide range of variation that is inherent in classrooms and schools, which can often have important influences on the effectiveness of an intervention, cannot be studied in a single conventional experiment. Furthermore, for experimental research to be valid, an instructional intervention must be implemented in a standard fashion, not adapted to unique or changing conditions (see Reinking & Pickle, 1993, for an example of how this is problematic). As we have argued elsewhere (Reinking & Bradley, 2008), this requirement that interventions be implemented with fidelity is the antithesis of formative experiments and design research. Formative experiments and design research aim to identify and understand any salient factors that enhance or inhibit an intervention's effectiveness while it is being implemented and then to modify or adapt the intervention based on that analysis. Ignoring the panoply of variables that are continually fluctuating in classrooms, or assuming that they are random factors and failing to adapt instruction to those variables, is contrary to the essence of effective teaching. Naturalistic studies, on the other hand, may document the complexity and subtleties of implementing an intervention, but they do not typically address how that complexity might be managed by a practitioner working to accomplish specific pedagogical goals. Formative experiments and design research, unlike experimental or naturalistic studies of instructional interventions, thus, accommodate both the variation inherent in classrooms and the need to adapt interventions in response to relevant variation.

To simplify for the sake of comparison, a controlled experiment might ask: "Which intervention is better on average, X or Y?" (What is best?) A naturalistic study might ask: "When implementing intervention X (or Y), what happens?" (What is?) Design research, on the other hand, is better suited for the following type of question: "Given that intervention X (or pedagogical theory Y) shows promise to bring about a valued pedagogical goal, how can it be implemented to accomplish that goal?" (What could be?) Other key questions are important to understanding design research in general and formative experiments in particular: for example, What factors enhance or inhibit an intervention's effectiveness in moving toward the pedagogical goal? How might the intervention or its implementation be modified, in light of these factors, to be more effective? It is these latter two questions that make a formative experiment formative. That is, formative experiments, like design research in general, entail an iterative process of data collection to determine what is or is not working, followed by carefully reasoned modifications, as needed, to enhance the effectiveness of the intervention. In short, the primary focus is to achieve a pedagogical goal, which is accomplished by recognizing the complexity of the instructional environment and making adaptations or modification to the environment or the intervention, as needed.

Formative experiments, and design research in general, are also experiments but in a sense broader than the formal hypothesis testing that guides a conventional, rigorously controlled conventional experiment. Schön (1987), in his seminal book on reflective practice, argued that several forms of experimentation are useful and that three forms are used simultaneously by reflective practitioners: (1) *exploratory experimentation*, which is action just to see what happens; (2) *move-testing experimentation*, which is aimed at determining whether an action is affirmed or negated toward a desired end and noting any unintended consequences; and (3) *hypothesis testing*, which is formal experimentation to see whether alternative hypotheses are affirmed or negated. Design research employs all three types of experimentation, just as reflective teachers do, but also entails a more systematic record of this experimentation and typically includes collegial discussions and overt reflections based on careful data collection. Thus, design research, because it addresses questions clearly relevant to practitioners and employs forms of experimentation similar to what practitioners use, is more directly related to practice than are other forms of research and is, therefore, more likely to appeal to practitioners. A further advantage of formative experiments, and design research in general, when compared with more conventional research methodologies is that they draw on and acknowledge the importance of intuitive professional knowledge, incorporating that knowledge within a systematic framework for practice-oriented research.

Formative experiments and other approaches to design research may be particularly appealing to practitioners because they mimic the process of effective teaching, and they facilitate a collaborative relationship with researchers grounded in authentic practice. However, this collaboration does not necessarily mean that practitioners and researchers share equal roles and responsibilities for conducting the research and need not be collaborative research in the strictest sense. Rather, we believe that design research aligns well with what Cole and Knowles's (1993) described as a teacher development partnership. Specifically, they stated,

> True collaboration is more likely to result when the aim is *not* for *equal* involvement in all aspects of the research; but, rather, for *negotiated and mutually agreed upon* involvement where strengths and available time commitments to process are honored. (p. 486)

In addition to developing a professionally productive relationship with practitioners, researchers rely on a practitioners' knowledge and expertise to assist in the identification of factors that can enhance or inhibit an instructional intervention's effectiveness and the development of realistic adaptations that might be made to the intervention and the classroom environment.

Engineering is a useful analogy for conceptualizing this approach in relation to other education research methodologies, and here the term *design experiment* might be more apt. Engineers make use of theoretical and empirical research to design something of functional utility. Their work builds bridges (sometimes literally) between theory, research, and practical application. But workability in the real world is the essence of their work, where occasionally relevant variables only emerge in real-world applications that go beyond purely theoretical or laboratory-centered research. Wind tunnels are clearly useful in designing airplanes consistent with the principles of aerodynamics, but wind tunnels do not readily simulate the sustained wear some parts experience during thousands of hours of flying under extremely different conditions. Furthermore, the work of engineers in designing practical application can sometimes clarify or stimulate the need for more theoretical and laboratory investigations. In fact, Stokes (1997) has argued that often the most important theoretical concepts in science emerge when scientists focus their attention on achieving practical goals. He highlights Louis Pasteur's work aimed at seeking ways to preserve food, which led to the field of microbiology, as a classic example of how the distinction between basic and applied research can be an unfortunate dichotomy.

Likewise, knowledge of what has or has not worked under a variety of practical conditions allows engineers and mechanics to acquire useful intuitive knowledge that may lead them occasionally to work outside or beyond accepted theory and research. Duffy (1994) has acknowledged that such intuitive knowledge is necessary for teaching. He stated, "Viewing research findings as something to be handed down as technical information ignores the reality that teachers must make strategic decisions about when to apply findings, how to adapt them to certain situations and even when it might be appropriate to ignore the findings altogether" (p. 19). Thus, formative experiments and design research value and systematically identify how the intuitive knowledge of experienced practitioners might elucidate and refine, and perhaps occasionally negate, the findings generated by other research methodologies. In that sense, this approach focuses on what has been referred to as conditional knowledge (Paris, Lipson, & Wixson, 1983) and the knowledge that is necessary to be a successful practitioner in ill-structured domains such as teaching (Spiro, Feltovich, Jacobson, & Coulson, 1992).

Furthermore, Hargreaves and Stone-Johnson (2009) have suggested that the evidence useful to teachers must take into account the multilayered dimensions of teaching, including the technical, intellectual, experiential, emotional, moral, ethical, political, situated, and cultural aspects of their individual practice. Formative experiments, in particular, as they have been used in literacy research, do not overlook or underestimate practitioners' perspectives in these areas when implementing an intervention and in accounting for its success, or the lack thereof, in accomplishing a goal. Teachers' beliefs about teaching are one domain into which an intervention needs be integrated and sometimes negotiated and adapted. Similarly, Reigeluth, and Frick (1999) have pointed out that most research of instructional interventions has focused almost exclusively on effectiveness, most often in relation to measurable academic achievement. However, relatively few have focused on efficiency (e.g., whether an intervention is economically feasible and logistically practical) or on appeal (e.g., whether teachers and students find an instructional intervention engaging, and whether teachers will use it after the researcher leaves the classroom). Finally, as discussed further in subsequent sections of this chapter, formative experiments, as we have conducted them in our own work, are driven by a clearly articulated instructional goal that must be explicitly justified as worthy and important. Thus, this approach encourages researchers not only to address explicitly a specific pedagogical goal but also to position their work explicitly in terms of the goal's pedagogical value. In other approaches to classroom research, the pedagogical goal and its value are often assumed or implicit. For example, what are the short- and long-term goals of an intervention such as Readers' Theatre and, more importantly, why are those goals important?

Thus, design research is grounded in an engineering metaphor instead of the laboratory or the lens metaphors that ground conventional scientific experiments or naturalistic inquiry. More literally, Sloane and Gorard (2003) have raised the question of whether education research should be conceptualized primarily as an engineering science rather than a social science. Going further, Reeves (2006) has even suggested that such an orientation is the only socially responsible approach to education research. Ecology is another apt metaphor because in this approach classrooms are acknowledged to be complex environments with multiple layers of interacting variables and where changing one variable often affects many others. In fact, ecology is a metaphor that is employed in conventional scientific experiments, which are often judged on how well they balance an inherent tension between experimental and ecological validity. However, in design research that tension does not exist because data collection and analyses are driven by ecological validity. Another type of validity that is more central to this approach is consequential validity (Messick, 1992). By identifying specific goals and explicitly justifying their importance, researchers who conduct design research are clearly focused on the authentic pedagogical, not just the theoretical, consequences of their work.

ORIGINS AND HISTORICAL ROOTS

Ignorance is a better starting place than truth for assessing the usefulness of educational research . . . some research projects are of little use to researchers or practitioners even though they reflect our highest ideals of truthfulness in data collection and analysis.
—WAGNER (1993, p. 15)

Tracing the origin of design research is akin to identifying the headwaters of a river. There seems to be no single, clearly identifiable source for this approach. Instead, formative experiments have emerged from and been supported by the ideas of diverse researchers and writers in the late 1980s and early 1990s who shared a dissatisfaction with experimental methods as a means for informing instructional practice. On one hand, some researchers, such as Moll and Diaz (1987), who have a more sociocultural viewpoint and who gravitated toward qualitative methods, saw improving education as the critical goal of educational research, and they saw the limitations of conventional scientific experiments in reaching that goal. Others, such as Bruce and Rubin (1993), argued for what they called "situated evaluation," which emerged from their insight that teachers did not necessarily implement innovative instructional interventions—in this case a computer-based intervention to enhance purposeful reading and writing—in ways consistent with the intent of the developers. Other researchers invested in finding insights about learning using conventional experiments saw the limitations of trying to move their findings from the laboratory to classrooms. Most prominent of the researchers in that category is Ann Brown, highly regarded for her work related to metacognition and reading. In an often-cited article pointing to the origins of design research, Brown (1992) described her own turn as a classical theorist and laboratory-oriented researcher to *design experiments*, a term she attributed to Collins (1992). Brown stated, "As a design scientist in my field, I attempt to engineer innovative educational environments and simultaneously conduct experimental studies on those innovations" (p. 141).

Jacob (1992), who discussed what she called formative experiments in her chapter in the *Handbook of Qualitative Research in Education*, traced their roots to neo-Vygotskian scholars (e.g., Davydov, 1988) and to cognitive psychologists interested in the social construction of psychological tasks. Newman and colleagues (1989) articulated some of the tenets of this view, and subsequently Newman (1990) used the term *formative experiment* to describe his study of how computer technology might be used to enhance scientific thinking among middle school students. This study was important because it was the first to outline and illustrate a specific methodological framework for conducting a formative experiment.

Since the mid-1990s, literacy researchers have conducted studies that fall into the general category of design research. An indication that formative experiments have entered the mainstream of literacy research is that several of these studies have been published in *Reading Research Quarterly*, a highly regarded outlet for literacy research (Ivey & Broaddus, 2007; Jiménez, 1997; Neuman, 1999; Reinking & Watkins, 2000). Contemporary with our own research using this methodology, we have attempted to articulate the basis and need for formative experiments and, more important, how this approach might be translated into specific methods for conducting a formative experiment (Baumann, Dillon, Shockley, Alvermann, & Reinking, 1996; Reinking & Bradley, 2008; Reinking & Pickle, 1993; Reinking & Watkins, 2000). For example, a framework for conceptualizing, conducting, and reporting formative experiments initially used by Reinking and Watkins (2000) and detailed subsequently in this chapter has informed several other investigations in literacy (Bradley & Reinking, in press; Fisher et al., 2009; Ivey & Broaddus, 2007; Lenski, 2001; Massey, 2007; Taboada & Rutherford, in press). Nonetheless, there are several other frameworks for conducting design research that might guide researchers who take this approach (e.g., Bannan-Ritland, 2003; Clements, 2009; Gravemeijer & Cobb, 2006; Reigeluth & Frick, 1999).

There is no agreed-upon epistemological foundation for design research, and perhaps none is needed if it is viewed basically as a design or engineering science. However, we believe that formative experiments and design research fit naturally with the philosophical tenets of pragmatism, which has been associated with education and with education research since John Dewey and has been revived as a paradigm useful to education research in general (Cherryholmes, 1993) and to literacy research in particular (Dillon et al., 2000). Pragmatism seems especially well suited to the aims and methods of formative experiments. For example, it allows for more epistemological flexibility in method and analysis, focuses on useful ends, and encourages a democratic involvement of multiple stakeholders. Formative experiments and design research also naturally connect with mixed methods approaches to research, which have been linked epistemologically to pragmatism (Tashakkori & Teddlie, 1998, 2003).

DISTINGUISHING METHODOLOGICAL CHARACTERISTICS

Educational research is evolving; its designs and procedures
are not cast in stone. Conscientious researchers are
continually trying out new methods . . . to make their work
stronger, more compelling, and more useful.
—EISENHART AND BORKO (1993, p. 11)

Researchers who consider their research to fall under the umbrella of design research have taken somewhat different approaches, adopting different terminology and conducting their research following different models with different emphases and different approaches to data collection and analyses. Nonetheless, there is a core of defining characteristics that unite this relatively new approach to education research and that distinguish it from other approaches. Furthermore, the absence of any of these characteristics within a particular study raises questions about its conceptual authenticity as an example of design research. Adapting and extending the work of Cobb and colleagues (2003), we believe that the following general characteristics define that common core:

1. *Theoretical.* Theory plays a predominant role in design research, but, unlike other approaches to classroom research, it is grounded more specifically in efforts to design effective, workable, and appealing instruction. A focus on theory also distinguishes design research from related data collection methodologies such as formative evaluation (Flagg, 1990) and rapid prototyping (Tripp & Bichelmeyer, 1990), which are efforts focused entirely on developing an instructional artifact, typically uninformed by theory. As with other research methodologies, theory in design research is used to justify the importance of the inquiry, to provide a rationale for the intervention, to interpret findings, to contextualize conclusions, and so forth. However, as Cobb and colleagues (2003) stated, the purpose of design experiments is "to develop a class of theories about both the *process* of learning and the *means* that are designed to support learn-

ing." Furthermore, they stated that in developing theories "design experiments create conditions . . . [that] place these theories in harm's way" and that theory "must do real work" by being *accountable to the activity of design*" (p. 10). According to Cobb and colleagues, these theories are humble and grounded in the local, not grand explanatory theories such as a general theory of motivation and learning that might be applied generally to all learning contexts but that can be mitigated by other factors in particular contexts.

2. *Goal oriented*. Design research investigates how to improve education and learning in authentic instructional environments toward well-specified goals that are explicitly justified in relation to theory and practice. For example, researchers conducting formative experiments explicitly identify and justify a goal, which is accompanied by a scholarly explanation of why it is worthy of investigation. Furthermore, that goal becomes a reference point for collecting and analyzing data, for making modifications to the intervention and/or the instructional environment, and for determining the extent to which progress has been made.

3. *Intervention centered in authentic instructional contexts*. The central object of study in design research is an instructional intervention that is a mechanism for facilitating a pedagogical goal or sometimes to test a theory in the crucible of practice. The intervention may be innovative and aimed at addressing a problematic area of instruction, or it may be a well-known intervention that has been investigated extensively using other methodologies. It may be a well-defined instructional activity or a coherent set of activities, and it must be justified in terms of theory, any previous empirical work that exists, and its promise for improving instructional practice. The intervention must also be studied in an authentic instructional environment where variations are allowed to occur naturally and where instructional responses to those variations are not constrained by the researcher but rather studied within a framework that encourages adaptation, which leads to the next characteristic.

4. *Adaptive and iterative*. In design research, a researcher begins with an assumption that an instructional intervention implemented at the beginning of a study may be quite different from the one that emerges at the end of the investigation. That is, as the initial intervention is implemented within continuous cycles of data collection and analysis that aim to determine what contextual factors enhance or inhibit the intervention's effectiveness, the new data obtained are then used to modify the intervention and how it is implemented, as needed. Whether these cycles of implementation and revision are well defined or fluid, a researcher must provide evidence of rigorous data collection and analysis to guide modifications within this iterative process and to determine whether desired effects were achieved. Because a researcher engages in an ongoing determination of

progress toward a pedagogical goal, establishing a baseline of conditions and/or performance may be necessary. That design research is iterative and involves fine-tuning instructional interventions across many cycles of data collection and responses to those data also suggests that studies should be conducted across a reasonable amount of time, usually months.

5. *Transformational.* Although this characteristic may not always be explicitly acknowledged in a particular study, there is often an assumption that the intervention may transform teaching and learning or the educational environment in some way. That assumption is based on the fact that the intervention was most likely selected for its strong potential to further a worthy educational goal that has been difficult to attain. Thus, design researchers are often guided by the realization that the intervention and its implementation may produce important unintended consequences. Looking for unintended consequences is also an incubator for building theory and for generating ideas for further research.

6. *Methodologically inclusive and flexible.* Conceptualizing and conducting design research is not driven mainly by a particular method or approach to collecting and analyzing data. Any approach to data collection and analysis may be appropriate to design research if it informs the implementation of an intervention, enables a researcher to determine where participants are in relation to the pedagogical goal being sought, and/or provides understandings of key factors and processes that inform practice and the testing, refinement, or development of pedagogical theory. Consequently, too, approaches to data collection and analysis may be adapted formatively in response to developments during an investigation or to a realization that more useful data or approaches might be better suited to circumstances that only become clear during data collection. The data may be quantitative (e.g., establishing a baseline of performance, attitudes, and motivation using standardized instruments that is compared pre- and postexperiment). However, because formative experiments clearly fall into what Salomon (1991) has termed *systemic*, as opposed to *analytic*, research, collecting and analyzing qualitative data are essential to conducting a formative experiment. Published formative experiments in literacy typically have involved mixed methods with all the attendant concerns, advantages, and standards of rigor associated with that research methodology (see Chatterji, 2004; Johnson & Onwuegbuzie, 2004: Tashakkori & Teddlie, 1998).

7. *Pragmatic.* This characteristic, which we associate at least tacitly with design research, refers more broadly to the tenets of pragmatism as a philosophical position than to simply a focus on what works. For example, pragmatism values intuitive knowledge and promotes democratic ideals, including the involvement of practitioners and students in setting research agendas and modifying interventions. They invite more authentic collab-

orative relationships between researchers and teachers. Pragmatism also does not engage in arguing the ultimately unanswerable epistemological questions about knowledge and knowledge generation that often distracts researchers using other approaches (see Dillon et al., 2000). A pragmatic view also focuses more on processes than on establishing clear causal relationships.

Standards of Rigor

For design research, standards of rigor exist in two dimensions. First, there are the standards of rigor normally associated with conventional approaches to collecting and analyzing qualitative or mixed methods data as they are employed in a particular study. For example, using multiple sources of data, triangulation of findings, member checks, and other means of building the trustworthiness of conclusions seems particularly important for design research. The second dimension includes standards of rigor associated specifically with design research. Although there is not widespread agreement on such standards, we believe that there are several likely candidates, which we have discussed in detail (see Reinking & Bradley, 2008). For example, we believe that studies should exhibit conceptual rigor, which is primarily conceptualizing, conducting, and reporting research that is consistent with the defining characteristics outlined in the previous section. Studies that have all or most of these defining characteristics are more conceptually rigorous and true to the essence of this approach.

Rigorous studies also provide sufficient time to explore the effects of the intervention and any modifications made to it. Months of concentrated data collection are often demanded. In our own work using formative experiments, we plan projects that go through several phases throughout a school year starting with 4–6 weeks of gathering ethnographic data to characterize the environment, several more weeks to gather baseline data, at least 10–16 weeks of implementing and revising the intervention being studied, and then baseline assessments and postintervention interviews. Rigorous studies should also embrace interdisciplinary perspectives and multiple theories, which is ideally accomplished through interdisciplinary teams of researchers, although that ideal is often not feasible. Rigor can also be enhanced by purposeful and careful selection of an appropriate research site and explaining how and why it was selected. Usually, sites where the odds of either failure or success are almost guaranteed are not the best starting points for initial investigations. It is also particularly important that a report of a study using this approach not suggest that the researcher is an advocate for the intervention or is romanticizing its potential and effects.

Because design research is pragmatic and guided by the metaphors of engineering and ecology, researchers need to be skeptical, open to rejecting preferred aspects of the intervention or preferred theories when they are not working well, comfortable with highlighting failures and problems, and cautious about overselling the merits of an intervention as a pedagogical panacea.

AN EXEMPLAR OF A FORMATIVE EXPERIMENT

As we indicated early in the chapter, several formative experiments in the area of literacy research have been published since we wrote an earlier version of this chapter. Thus, we have selected a more recent study conducted by Ivey and Broaddus (2007) as an exemplar for this updated version. As in the original chapter, we choose their study because (1) it focuses on literacy, (2) it was rigorously peer reviewed and published in a highly regarded journal, (3) it involved extensive data collection and analysis for an entire school year, and (4) it illustrates many of the characteristics of design research discussed previously in this chapter. To contextualize their study, Ivey and Broaddus investigated how to engage seventh- and eighth-grade native Spanish speakers in reading and writing during a language arts class. They also employed a set of questions that characterize the framework first proposed by Reinking and Watkins (2000), which has also been used by other literacy researchers (Bradley & Reinking, in press; Fisher, Frey, & Lapp, 2009; Lenski, 2001). Thus, each of the questions that follow represents a framework that has been used in several literacy studies. However, it is important to note that it is only one of several frameworks and approaches that might be employed within design research. It is also important to note that we have not included the authors' citations supporting the work reported in their article. We encourage interested readers to read the original article for such detail.

What Is the Pedagogical Goal and What Theory Establishes Its Value?

The pedagogical goal of the Ivey and Broaddus (2007) study was to facilitate the engagement of reading and writing among seventh- and eight-grade native Spanish-speaking students who had recently immigrated to the United States and who were just beginning to read, write, and speak English. That goal was justified on the basis of theoretical and empirical research demonstrating the importance of engagement to learning, as opposed to compliance, and that time spent engaged in literacy activities is critical for reading achievement and vocabulary development. For example, they reported research suggesting that when students participate in classroom reading activities, they are more likely to read outside of school. Furthermore, when students are engaged in reading and writing outside of school, they are more likely to develop reading and writing competencies. Thus, engaging second-language learners who are just learning English in reading and writing activities in school is important for initiating learning inside and outside of school and for developing reading and writing competency.

What Classroom Intervention Has Potential to Achieve the Pedagogical Goal?

In conceptualizing the instructional intervention for their study, Ivey and Broaddus (2007) were informed by the existing literature comparing (1) first- and second-language literacy acquisition and (2) second-language literacy and adolescent literacy. Considering the points of disconnection and intersection across the literature, the researchers and teacher determined that the intervention should consist of two basic parts: self-selected readings and teacher-directed reading–writing activities. The decision to prioritize reading and writing above other literacy-related activities was based on evidence that engaged reading is associated with reading achievement and that it was the best context to meet the individual needs of students. To facilitate students' engagement during these activities, the researchers and teacher recognized the importance of providing a wide range of materials that varied in reading level, genre, and topic as well as culturally relevant materials. Furthermore, during self-selected reading, rather than model good reading habits, the teacher and researchers both coached and read to individual students. In addition, because these students were still developing reading skills and needed support, the adults focused on providing instructional support that encouraged student engagement, such as repeated reading, shared reading, and paired reading, rather than instruction that might interrupt student reading. Finally, teacher-directed reading–writing activities were initially conducted in whole-class or small-group settings and primarily focused on concepts likely to inspire students, such as topics that they may find personally or cultural relevant or topics considered to be appealing to young adolescents.

What Factors Enhance or Inhibit the Effectiveness of the Intervention in Achieving the Pedagogical Goal?

Guided by principles underlying mixed methods research, researchers conducting formative experiments often collect and analyze both qualitative and quantitative data for the purpose of determining progress toward a pedagogical goal and determining what factors enhance or inhibit progress. Toward that end, Ivey and Broaddus (2007) primarily collected and analyzed qualitative data. Specifically, data included classroom observations, student interviews, teacher–researcher debriefings, artifacts of students' reading and writing activities, reading logs, and researchers' notes and reflections, as well as frequency counts to document changes in the instructional environment. Using constant-comparative analysis, the researchers identified emerging hypotheses about factors that enhanced or inhibited progress toward the pedagogical goals, and they used that information to determine which practices needed to be discontinued, adapted, or transformed.

How Can the Intervention Be Modified to Achieve the Pedagogical Goal More Effectively?

A distinguishing characteristic of a formative experiment is that the intervention is modified, as needed, during the experiment toward more effectively or efficiently attaining the pedagogical goal that drives the investigation. Thus, on the basis of data collection and analysis, Ivey and Broaddus (2007) identified three categories of modification to improve the intervention aimed at increasing student engagement in reading and writing. First, despite providing a variety of materials for the students, the research team quickly realized that the materials were not meeting the individual needs of students during self-selected or teacher-directed activities. That is, to increase engagement, they needed a more deliberate approach to match students to text, and they needed to consider more carefully which materials were more effective for specific purposes. Over time they identified more appropriate materials that engaged students who were learning how to read, write, and speak English. Second, despite initially providing instructional supports, the researchers discovered that students needed additional teacher support to create meaning when using the texts. That is, choral and echo reading, which are helpful with younger literacy learners, were ineffective for many of the older second-language learners. Thus, two additional instructional practices to support students' ability to make meaning were added: (1) teacher read-aloud and book talk prior to students' self-selecting text and (2) teacher support to identify and explain unfamiliar concepts while students read. The last category of modification involved the scaffolding of writing experiences. That modification became necessary because the initial intervention that included the use of culturally relevant materials to inspire writing was, for many reasons, ineffective. Consequently, the teachers and researchers implemented the language experience approach, which had been shown to have potential for students of diverse background. Furthermore, because students were struggling with syntax and vocabulary, the teacher and researchers found that students became more engaged when they were provided a model for writing, particularly books that included familiar language or repetitive phrases. In sum, when data collection and analysis revealed that the initial instructional intervention, ground in theory and research, was "put to work," many of the intervention practices did not meet the individual needs of students, and it was necessary to draw on other theory and research to redesign the intervention.

What Unanticipated Positive or Negative Effects Does the Intervention Produce?

This question is consistent with the rationale for a formative experiment because it acknowledges that instructional interventions are never implemented in a vacuum and that complex interacting variables with multiple effects operate in any instructional context. Thus, upon reviewing the data, one unanticipated effect was the predominant role the researchers played in the intervention compared with the teacher and her assistants. This unanticipated effect occurred, in part, as the intervention evolved from a whole-class and small-group intervention to individual and paired work and as the adults become more proactive in regard to instruction students. That situation was compounded by the fact that the researchers gravitated toward the students who were the least engaged in reading and writing, and, thus, it become more imperative to modify the instructional intervention to meet their needs.

This situation highlights a potential challenge in conducting a formative experiment. That is, because this approach is a collaboration between researchers and teachers, the traditional roles assumed by researchers and teachers are often blurred. In this case, this shift led to the researchers assuming a stronger role in the implementation the intervention. Although this does not undermine issues illuminated by this study or the practices the researchers identified as effectively engaging second-language learners in reading and writing, it does underscore a defining characteristic of a formative experiment, which is to understand how an instructional intervention can be implemented effectively in an authentic instructional environment. As Ivey and Broaddus (2007) noted, they played a more prominent role in identifying and implementing modifications to the intervention. Thus, as they suggest, researchers may need to actively plan for opportunities to collaborate with teachers, and when researchers are involved with the implementation of intervention, they need to plan for gradual release of responsibility from the researchers to the teacher.

Has the Instructional Environment Changed as a Result of the Intervention?

This question is closely related to the previous one and is founded on the assumption that interventions most worthy of investigation are not only those that have potential to accomplish a pedagogical goal but often also those that have strong potential to transform positively the teaching and learning environment. Thus, the pedagogical goal of the Ivey and Broaddus (2007) study was to increase students' engagement in reading and writing; therefore, it would seem to have the potential to transform the class into a community of literacy learners. Yet data collection and analysis revealed little engagement in a whole-class or small-group teaching format because engagement differed from student to student. Thus, to meet the needs of the class and the pedagogical goal of the study, the instructional environment shifted from whole-class and small-group work to individual and paired work. Furthermore, rather than the intervention activities per se leading the change, the adults needed to be more proactive and deliberate in identifying effective materials and practices and providing intensive individual instruction. Thus, data collection and analysis revealed that the instructional environment was transformed from class-oriented instruction to instruction matched to the individual needs of students.

CHALLENGES, LIMITATIONS, AND FUTURE DIRECTIONS

Because the literature on design research and the number of published studies that have used this approach have more than doubled since we wrote the original version of this chapter, it is now clearer where it stands within the larger landscape of education research. It is also clearer what challenges and limitations must be addressed and what the future may hold. The steadily increasing attention to design research within the research community, reinforced by the generally positive reactions we typically receive when we introduce this approach to our colleagues, to students, and to teachers, suggests that it still holds the conceptual power and intuitive appeal that captured the hearts and imaginations of its earliest pioneers such as Ann Brown. Nonetheless, it is also still the case that researchers and students using this approach may encounter misunderstandings, if not resistance, from reviewers of their work, although we suspect less so than when we wrote the original chapter. We believe its legitimacy has been adequately sealed within the mainstream of education research.

The increased attention has also attracted serious critiques that have identified conceptual, methodological, and practical issues and limitations that must be acknowledged and addressed. Most prominently, design research continues to project an amorphous methodological identity, as reflected in its unsettled terminology. Furthermore, although we have begun to see some boundary crossing, different disciplines within education and researchers from different methodological orientations still tend to conceive and implement this approach in sometimes fundamentally different ways and with different conceptual emphases. That may not necessarily be a limitation, especially if there is a common core of defining characteristics and generally accepted standards for rigor, such as those we have outlined in previous sections of this chapter. In fact, methodological openness and flexibility are two of those defining characteristics.

Nonetheless, this ambiguity and separation are often not well received by those who are more accustomed to tighter conceptual and methodological definitions and standards. For example, Dede (2004), in his thoughtful critique of design research, characterized it as "a kind of 'Swiss Army

Knife' of research . . . [entailing methods that] do a little of everything, but do nothing particularly well" (p. 106). Design research has also been criticized for being underconceptualized theoretically because of its focus on workability (see diSessa & Cobb, 2004) and overmethodologized, producing copious and unwieldy data (e.g., Dede, 2004). Likewise, Kelly (2004) argued that design research must be "undergirded by a conceptual structure that forms the basis for the warrants for [its] claims," or it will "contribute only haphazardly to an aggressive science of learning" (p. 118).

Design research certainly does run against the grain of firmly entrenched concepts in education research, such as establishing causal relations or expecting valid findings to generalize from a sample to a larger population. But rethinking or expanding these ideas is perhaps one of the important contributions of this approach because it reveals the limitations of investing too heavily in those concepts if we are to acknowledge the inherent messiness of classrooms, teaching, and learning and if we are to close the gap between research and practice. For example, design research, we believe, has reintroduced the need for broader views of generalization such as those proposed by Firestone (1993). In his view, generalization is more than extending the findings of a sample to a population; it also includes theoretical generalization (e.g., can theory generalize to practice?) and case-to-case generalization (e.g., a specific case generalizes more validly to another case in a similar context than it does to all cases in general). These concepts of generalization are particularly compatible with design research and may help education research break away from the constraints and limitations associated with trying to be strictly a social science (see Lagemann, 2000).

In our own involvement with conducting formative experiments, we have faced troubling methodological issues and practical challenges. For example, when we work closely with teachers in classrooms, we often become a factor influencing the direction and success of the intervention, which muddies our findings (see also the exemplar in the previous section). However, it also forces us to consider longer term relationships with teachers and to create research agendas that include multiple iterations over years and that involve a fading of our direct involvement, perhaps followed by a formative experiment that investigates a teacher development model aimed at helping teachers to invest in and implement the intervention. We have also struggled with deferring to teachers' judgment, beliefs, routines, and so forth when their perspectives and practices differ from our own deeply held beliefs about pedagogy. These, however, are important struggles that inform and enrich our research and keep us grounded in the realities of day-to-day practice in education and respectful of teachers' professional prerogatives. Such useful struggles are also a positive contribution of design research.

We do not believe that these challenges and limitations exceed those associated with other methodological approaches, and we believe that some of them may be resolved as researchers gain more experience with design research and reach more consensus about its conceptual and methodological base and about standards of rigor. We are especially encouraged about the future because of funding agencies' increased acknowledgment of design research as a legitimate and desirable approach to research. Thus, we remain confidently optimistic about the future of design research and look forward to the directions this approach will take in the future and the extent to which it will be adopted by a new generation of researchers. We hope to have much more to report should this book eventually go into a third edition.

REFERENCES

Bannan-Ritland, B. (2003). The role of design in research: The integrative learning design framework. *Educational Researcher, 32*(1), 21–24.

Barab, S., & Squire, K. (2004a). Design-based research [Special issue]. *Journal of the Learning Sciences, 13*(1).

Barab, S., & Squire, K. (2004b). Design-based research: Putting a stake in the ground. *Journal of the Learning Sciences, 13*, 1–14.

Baumann, J. F., Dillon, D. R., Shockley, B., Alvermann, D. E., & Reinking, D. (1996). Perspectives for literacy research. In L. Baker, P. Afflerbach, & D. Reinking (Eds.), *Developing engaged readers in school and home communities* (pp. 247–270). Mahwah, NJ: Erlbaum.

Baumann, J. F., Ware, D., & Edwards, E. C. (2007). "Bumping into spicy, tasty words that catch your tongue": A formative experiment on vocabulary instruction. *The Reading Teacher, 61*(2), 108–122.

Boling, E. C. (2008). Learning from teachers' conceptions of technology integration: What do blogs, instant messages, and 3D chat rooms have to do with it? *Research in the Teaching of English, 43*(1), 74–100.

Bradley, B. A., & Reinking, D. (in press). A formative experiment to enhance teacher–child language interactions in a preschool classroom. *Journal of Early Childhood Literacy, 11*(3).

Brown, A. L. (1992). Design experiments: Theoretical and methodological challenges in creating complex interventions in classroom settings. *Journal of the Learning Sciences, 2*(2), 141–178.

Bruce, B. C., & Rubin, A. (1993). *Electronic quills: A situated evaluation of using computers for classroom writing.* Hillsdale, NJ: Erlbaum.

Chatterji, M. (2004). Evidence on "what works": An argument of extended-term mixed methods (EDMM) evaluation designs. *Educational Researcher, 33*(9), 3–13.

Cherryholmes, C. H. (1993). Reading research. *Journal of Curriculum Studies, 25*, 1–32.

Clements, D. H. (2009). Design experiments and curricular research. In A. E. Kelly, J. Y. Baek, & R. A. Lesh (Eds.), *Handbook of design research methods in education: Innovations in science, technology, engineering, and mathematics learning and teaching* (pp. 410–422). New York: Taylor & Francis.

Cobb, P., Confrey, J., diSessa, A., Lehrer, R., & Schauble, L. (2003). Design experiments in education research. *Educational Researcher, 32*(1), 9–13.

Cole, A. L., & Knowles, J. G. (1993). Teacher development partnership research: A focus on methods and issues. *American Educational Researcher Journal, 30*(3), 473–495.

Collins, A. (1992). Toward a design science of education. In E. Scanlon & T. O'Shea (Eds.), *New directions in educational technology* (pp. 83–103). New York: Springer-Verlag.

Collins, A. (1999). The changing infrastructure of education research. In E. C. Lagemann & L. B. Shulman (Eds.), *Issues in educational research: Problems and possibilities* (pp. 289–298). San Francisco: Jossey-Bass.

Davydov, V. V. (1988). Problems of developmental teaching: The experience of theoretical and experimental psychological research. Part 2. *Soviet Education, 30*(9), 3–83.

Dede, C. (2004). If design-based research is the answer, what the question? *Journal of the Learning Sciences, 13*(1), 105–114.

Dillon, D. R., O'Brien, D. G., & Heilman, E. E. (2000). Literacy research in the next millennium: From paradigms to pragmatism and practicality. *Reading Research Quarterly, 35*, 10–26.

diSessa, A. A., & Cobb, P. (2004). Ontological innovations and the role of theory in design experiments. *Journal of the Learning Sciences, 13*(1), 77–103.

Duffy, G. G. (1994). How teachers think of themselves: A key to mindfulness. In J. N. Mangieri & C. Collins (Eds.), *Creating powerful thinking in teachers and students: Diverse perspectives* (pp. 3–25). Fort Worth, TX: HarperCollins.

Ebel, R. (1982). The future of educational research. *Educational Researcher, 22*(7), 5–11.

Eisenhart, M., & Borko, H. (1993). *Designing classroom research: Themes, issues, and struggles.* Boston: Allyn & Bacon.

Feuer, M. J., Towne, L., & Shavelson, R. J. (2002). Reply to commentators on "Scientific culture and educational research." *Educational Researcher, 31*(8), 28–29.

Fisher, D., Frey, N., & Lapp, D. (2009). Meeting AYP in a high-need school: A formative experiment. *Journal of Adolescent and Adult Literacy, 52*(5), 386–396.

Firestone, W. A. (1993). Alternative arguments for generalizing from data as applied to qualitative research. *Educational Researcher, 22*(4), 16–23.

Flagg, G. N. (1990). *Formative evaluation for educational technologies.* Hillsdale, NJ: Erlbaum.

Gravemeijer, K., & Cobb, P. (2006). Design research from a learning design perspective. In J. van den Akker, K. Gravemeijer, S. McKenney, & N. Nieveen (Eds.), *Educational design research* (pp. 17–51). New York: Routledge.

Hargreaves, A., & Stone-Johnson, C. (2009). Evidence-informed change and the practice of teaching. In J. D. Bransford, D. J. Stipek, N. J. Vye, L. M. Gomez, & D. Lam (Eds.), *The role of research in educational improvement* (pp. 89–109). Cambridge, MA: Harvard Education Press.

Hoadley, C. M. (2004). Methodological alignment in design-based research. *Educational Psychologist, 39*, 203–212.

Hostetler, K. (2005). What is "good" education research? *Educational Researcher,* *34*(6), 16–21.

Ivey, G., & Broaddus, K. (2007). A formative experiment investigating literacy engagement among adolescent Latina/o students just beginning to read, write, and speak English. *Reading Research Quarterly, 42*(4), 512–545.

Jackson, P. W. (1990). *Life in classrooms.* New York: Teachers College Press.

Jacob, E. (1992). Culture, context, and cognition. In M. D. Lecompte, W. L. Millroy, & J. Preissle (Eds.), *The handbook of qualitative research in education* (pp. 293–335). San Diego, CA: Academic Press.

Jiménez, R.T. (1997). The strategic reading abilities and potential of five low-literacy Latina/o readers in middle school. *Reading Research Quarterly, 32,* 224–243.

Johnson, R. B., & Onwuegbuzie, A. J. (2004). Mixed methods research: A research paradigm whose time has come. *Educational Researcher, 33*(7), 14–36.

Kelly, A. E. (Ed.). (2003). The role of design in educational research [Special issue]. *Educational Researcher, 32*(1).

Kelly, A. E. (2004). Design research in education: Yes, but is it methodological? *Journal of the Learning Sciences, 13*(1), 115–128.

Kelly, A. E., Lesh, R. A., & Baek, J. Y. (Eds.). (2008). *Handbook of design research methods in education: Innovations in science, technology, engineering, and mathematics learning and teaching.* New York: Routledge.

Labaree, D. (1998). Educational researchers: Living with a lesser form of knowledge. *Educational Researcher, 27*(8), 4–12.

Lagemann, E. C. (2000). *An elusive science: The troubling history of education research.* Chicago: University of Chicago Press.

Lenski, S. D. (2001). Intertextual connections during discussion about literature. *Reading Psychology, 22,* 313–335.

Lewis, C., Perry, R., & Murata, A. (2006). How should research contribute to instructional improvement? The case of lesson study. *Educational Researcher, 35*(3), 3–14.

Massey, D. D. (2007). "The Discovery Channel said so" and other barriers to comprehension. *The Reading Teacher, 60*(7), 656–666.

McCandliss, B. D., Kachman, M., & Bryant, P. (2003). Design experiments and laboratory approaches to learning: Steps toward collaborative exchange. *Educational Researcher, 32*(1), 14–16.

McKenney, S., & Voogt, J. (2009). Designing technology for emergent literacy: The PictoPal initiative. *Computers and Education, 52,* 719–729.

Messick, S. (1992). The interplay of evidence and consequences in the validation of performance assessments. *Educational Researcher, 23*(2), 13–23.

Moll, L., & Diaz, S. (1987). Change as the goal of educational research. *Anthropology and Education Quarterly, 18,* 300–311.

National Reading Panel. (2000, April). *Report of the National Reading Panel: Teaching children to read.* Retrieved January 25, 2003, from *www.nichd.nih.gov/publications/nrp/smallbook.cfm.*

Neuman, S. B. (1999). Books make a difference: A study of access to literacy. *Reading Research Quarterly, 34,* 286–311.

Newman, D. (1990). Opportunities for research on the organizational impact of school computers. *Educational Researcher, 19,* 8–13.

Newman, D., Griffin, P., & Cole, M. (1989). *The construction zone: Working for cognitive change in school.* Cambridge, UK: Cambridge University Press.

Paris, S. G., Lipson, M. Y., & Wixson, K. K. (1983). Becoming a strategic reader. *Contemporary Educational Psychology, 8,* 293–316.

Pressley, M., Graham, S., & Harris, K. (2006). The state of educational intervention research as viewed through the lens of literacy intervention. *British Journal of Educational Psychology, 76,* 1–19.

Reeves, T. (2006). Design research from a technology perspective. In J. van den Akker, K. Gravemeijer, S. McKenney, & N. Nieveen (Eds.), *Educational design research* (pp. 52–66). New York: Routledge.

Reigeluth, C. M., & Frick, T. W. (1999). Formative research: A methodology for creating and improving design theories. In C. M. Reigeluth (Ed.), *Instructional-design theories and models: Volume II. A new paradigm of instructional theory* (pp. 633–651). Mahwah, NJ: Erlbaum.

Reinking, D. (2007). Toward a good or better understanding of best practice. *Journal of Curriculum and Instruction.* Accessed December 15, 2007, from *www.joci.ecu.edu/index.php/JoCI/article/view/59/5/.*

Reinking, D., & Bradley, B. A. (2008). *On formative and design experiments: Approaches to language and literacy research.* New York: Teachers College Press.

Reinking, D., & Pickle M. (1993). Using a formative experiment to study how computers affect reading and writing in classrooms. In D. J. Leu & C. K. Kinzer (Eds.), *Examining central issues in literacy research, theory, and practice* (pp. 263–270). Chicago: National Reading Conference.

Reinking, D., & Watkins, J. (2000). A formative experiment investigating the use of multimedia book reviews to increase elementary students independent reading. *Reading Research Quarterly, 35*(3), 384–419.

Salomon, G. (1991). Transcending the qualitative-quantitative debate: The analytic and systemic approaches to educational research. *Educational Researcher, 20*(6), 10–18.

Sandoval, W. A., & Bell, P. (Eds.). (2004). Design-based research methods for studying learning in context [Special issue]. *Educational Psychologist, 39*(4).

Schön, D. A. (1987). *Educating the reflective practitioner.* San Francisco: Jossey-Bass.

Sloane, F. C., & Gorard, S. (2003). Exploring modeling aspects of design experiments. *Educational Researcher, 32*(1), 29–31.

Spiro, R. J., Feltovich, P. J., Jacobson, M. J., & Coulson, R. L. (1992). Cognitive flexibility, constructivism, and hypertext: Random access instruction for advanced knowledge acquisition in ill-structured domains. In T. M. Duffy & D. H. Jonassen (Eds.), *Constructivism and technology of instruction: A conversation* (pp. 57–75). Hillsdale, NJ: Erlbaum.

Stokes, D. E. (1997). *Pasteur's quadrant: Basic science and technological innovation.* Washington, DC: Brookings Institution Press.

Taboada, A., & Ruhterford, V. (in press). Developing reading comprehension and academic vocabulary for English language learners through science content: A formative experiment. *Reading Psychology.*

Tashakkori, A., & Teddlie, C. (1998). *Mixed methodology: Combining qualitative and quantitative approaches.* Thousand Oaks, CA: Sage.

Tashakkori, A., & Teddlie, C. (Eds.). (2003). *Handbook of mixed methods in social and behavioral research*. Thousand Oaks, CA: Sage.

Tripp, S. D., & Bichelmeyer, B. (1990). Rapid prototyping: An alternative instructional design strategy. *Educational Technology Research and Development, 38*(1), 31–44.

van den Akker, J., Gravemeijer, K., McKenney, S., & Nieveen, N. (Eds.). (2006). *Educational design research*. New York: Routledge.

Viadero, D. (2009, December 2). New head of U.S. research agency aims for relevance. *Education Week*. Retrieved December 29, 2009, from *www.edweek.org/ew/articles/2009/12/02/13ies.h29.html?tkn=ZPWF3L3M AyZRicsjuIeFWk8IzEH+Gargt6Y9*.

Wagner, J. (1993). Ignorance in educational research: Or how can you not know that? *Educational Researcher, 22*(5), 15–23.

CHAPTER 11

Historical Research

Norman A. Stahl
Douglas K. Hartman

Everything has a history. Everything that exists in the present comes out of the past. Indeed, as Benjamin (2007) explains, "The house of the present is filled with windows into the past" (p. 2). The purpose of this chapter is to strengthen the way we look through these windows. For example, an individual who attended an elementary school in the United States or Canada is probably familiar with the basal readers used for formal reading instruction. These comprehensive, leveled anthologies of stories, skills, activities, and worksheets have been the prevailing instrument for teaching reading throughout North America. A publishing house carefully designs each new edition of these materials. Even though a youngster probably uses the newest basal series currently on the market, each series has a history that is several hundred years old, reaching back through the "Dick and Jane" readers of the mid-20th century to the *McGuffey* readers of the latter 19th century to Webster's "Blue-back Spellers," and even back to the *New England Primer* and beyond. The sight lines linking past basal readers to present ones never break.

Looking for historical signs in these readers is like being an archeologist or geologist. But instead of digging into the earth to uncover the past, the historical researcher digs into the visible, everyday elements of reading materials to find the historical roots from which they sprang. The features, layout, and content of the current basal readers are just the uppermost layer of history. From these readers we can make inferences about reading curriculum in the last few years, but what about the historical roots of the previous generations of readers? How far into the past can we see through the pages of current readers?

If we study the passage of time between *McGuffey's* rural farm dit-ties to Dick and Jane's suburban neighborhood happenings to today's tales from urban and global communities, we come to understand some of the cultural, political, demographic, technological, and economic movements that have shaped each successive generation of readers and the history of U.S. reading instruction. The more we understand the changes made in the readers, when they were made, who made them, and why, the better equipped we will be to see into the kind of future we as literacy profession-als may be heading.

To look through windows into the past requires that we also be able to look *at* the windows too. To do this requires a kind of double-double vision, where we look not only at the historical artifact (such as a text-book, journal, photo, or letter) but also at ourselves analyzing the artifact as well as the historical profession as it discusses its collective analyzing of artifacts. We can almost see the rough outlines of three concentric circles in this description, with the artifact in the inner circle, us in the middle circle, and the profession in the outer one. To acquire this vision, we begin by focusing on the outer circle, the profession. The questions and conversa-tions that occupy historians' lives have a history of their own. In our mind's eye, the windows in this house are the logical starting place for learning to look through any window into the past, whether it is reading instruction, basal readers, or the French Revolution. The fundamental questions for anyone embarking on historical work in any area are *What is history?* and *Why should we do it?*

WHAT IS HISTORY?

There is no single answer to the first question, What is history? But there are answers that mark the terrain better than others. Wood Gray (1991) suggests that three features are essential to any response: history as hap-pening, record, and field of study.

History Is Happening

First and foremost, *history is a happening*: Everything that has ever occurred or been thought about from the beginning of time right up to the last elapsed moment is history. To bring this concept directly back to us as readers, our very identity is as much or more historical as it is present or future oriented: Our having learned to read with a "Dick and Jane" reader or with an SRA kit is history. Our moment in the present is but fleeting, as it quickly becomes our contribution, meaningful or not, to history. It is only the future that is infinite and beyond the scope of history until it too becomes history—something that is assured to happen.

History Is the Record

Second, *history is the record* of things in the present that become the past. This is the record we studied as part of a fifth-grade social studies unit on the Civil War with Miss Jameson or in our foray into 10th-grade world history at Abraham Lincoln High School. The locations of these happenings for each of us are different, as are the times, but the experience was likely to have been much the same. We studied the record of important events and the thoughts and actions of those of great minds (i.e., the elite) as selected for us by the elders of our society. Yet for most of us history as a record of world literacy or reading instruction never received more than passing attention in our undergraduate or graduate training either.

Unlike history as a happening, history as a record has quite finite parameters. About 5,000 years ago, with the growing complexity of economic and political activity throughout ancient Mesopotamia and Egypt, writing was invented—and the record of history began (Diringer, 1962; Fischer, 2004b). It is the period since then that the great preponderance of the Western historical record is focused on. With the development of printing in the West, the documentary record was more likely to survive. Furthermore, with each new technology for capturing the present, there is less and less that cannot be preserved for the historical record if there is an archive, whether physical or digital, to preserve the documentary evidence.

In the field of literacy, we may propose that there are three areas of history as record: the history of reading instruction (e.g., Mathews, 1966; Smith, 2002), the history of literacy (e.g., Cavallo & Chartier, 2003; Fischer, 2004a; Manguel, 1996), and the history of the book or print culture (e.g., Darnton, 1990; Johns, 2000). Each area provides opportunity to learn of literacy history, but we must be careful not to confuse the study of history with the conduct of the historical method (Leedy & Ormrod, 2009).

History Is a Field of Study

Finally, *history is a field of study* where the practice of historical method—known as historiography—is undertaken by institutionally trained academics or self-trained amateurs. In its earliest practice, history was written in the form of chronicles that praised a monarch or glorified a city or state. It was with the coming of Herdotus and Thucydides that the writing of history began to seek the "truth" and examine relationships between cause and effect. With the arrival of the Middle Ages and the decline of classical civilization in the West, the historical method also slipped into the dark ages. Not until the philosophy of the rationalists evolved during the Enlightenment of the 18th century did a comprehensive study of history once again emerge. It was in Germany at the University of Berlin in the 1820s that Leopold von Ranke advocated the systematic approach to evaluating primary source documents and the practice of presenting the past "as it actually happened" (*wie es eigentlich gewesen ist*). As *historicism* spread through the academic community, the foundation for history as an academic discipline based on examination and evaluation of primary sources was set in place for the modern era.

Throughout the next two centuries, various theoretical constructs and, hence, research agendas, such as that of the positivists, the progressives, the social historians, the followers of the Annales School, the proponents of cliometrics, the Freudians, and the postmodernists among others, evolved so that historians interpret our past through different lenses (Brundage, 2007; Gilderhus, 2009).

These different theories motivate, animate, and position historical research and, hence, lead to different ways of knowing the past. History is not a single interpretation of events that is carved in stone for future generations. Political, economic, nationalistic, or pedagogical agendas (often one and the same) value one interpretation over another in a particular spatial and temporal context. Thus, history is a dynamic field of study, and it has (and likely will continue) to change through the development of new theories and the process of revisionism. Each generation and each group selects and integrates the data (facts) and the artifacts of the past with the current cultural, social, economic, and political interpretations of the world, the new tools and approaches to inquiry, and the newly discovered historical sources and data to re-create and understand the past. As such, history is more than the simple story of the chronological march of time. For a more in-depth discussion on historiography across time, see Gilderhus (2009) and Tosh (2006).

A WORKING DEFINITION FOR THE HISTORY OF LITERACY

With Gray's (1991) three features in mind—history as happening, record, and field of study—we propose a working definition of history, akin to that of Borg, Gall, and Gall (1993): History *is the interpretative reconstruction of the known past*. This definition highlights three elements of historical analysis.

1. History is an *interpretation* of the past. It involves the careful weighing and sorting of evidence into patterns, arguments, and narratives based on judgment. It is more than marshaling a chronology of acts. History is the production of meanings for an audience relative to a purpose.
2. History is *reconstruction* of the past. It is a refabricating of something that once was. It is not the same thing as the actual event or

episode. History is a "making again" of an account or explanation that re-presents that which already happened.

3. History is about the *known* past. There is much in the past that was and happened, but we can only know pieces and parts of it because of the evidence that remains. That which can be known, then, is that which has been saved or survived into the present for interpretation and reconstruction.

As a whole, we think this working definition offers considerable flexibility. The focus can be on an individual, a group, a movement, an institution, a place, or an era (Best & Kahn, 1989; Skager & Weinberg, 1971). In the literacy field, this activity might entail the investigation of the impact of educational policies, legislation, and laws (Right to Read, Goals 2000, No Child Left Behind, Race to the Top), curriculum models and movements (basal systems, whole-language philosophy, Initial Teaching Alphabet, Direct Instruction, Guided Reading), instructional methods and materials (KWL, phonics workbooks, Dolch word materials), or assessment practices (informal reading inventories, miscue analysis, standardized testing) across time or within defined eras. The focus could also be on the lives and contributions of distinguished literacy educators or researchers, such as Edmund Burke Huey, William S. Gray, Noah Webster, and Arthur I. Gates, or the literative lives of the nonelites, be they teachers, administrators, or former students.

The historical process might be used to study the development and influence of specific educational institutions either in higher education (e.g., the Center for the Study of Reading and the college reading programs in Georgia throughout the 1980s) or in the PreK–12 environment (e.g., the Benchmark School, the Calhoun Colored School, and University of Chicago Laboratory School). Finally, the literacy historian can delve into the roots of current literacy practices, techniques, or strategies to discover whether they were developed to meet instructional parameters that no longer exist today or to learn whether they have fallen victim to the "confusions of time" such that application and delivery no longer resemble the original constructs (Skager & Weinberg, 1971). Conversely, the literacy historian can identify instructional activities or movements that were lost to the times (Stahl, King, & Eilers, 1996) but would have practical application for the current educational scene.

As an interpretive and reconstructive process, historical topics are not considered in isolation. Each builds on, borrows from, and gives to the philosophies, thoughts, and movements of institutions within a particular era or an identified setting. In addition, the researcher must be cognizant of the historical events beyond the literacy field that might have influenced the issue or event. For instance, the growth of postsecondary reading programs in the early 1950s as well as the birth of both the Southwest Reading Conference (to become the National Reading Conference and now the Literacy Research Association [LRA]) and the College Reading Association (now the Association of Literacy Educators and Researchers [ALER]) would not likely have happened if the Congress had not passed the Serviceman's Readjustment Act of 1944 (i.e., the G.I. Bill of Rights) leading to enrollment of tens of thousands of returning service personnel in postsecondary education and in college reading courses.

A working definition of history, such as the one we have proposed, is rooted in two broad categories of historical research: (1) *document/artifact analysis*, which requires the researcher to examine document objects such as birth records, census data, photographs, correspondence (written and digital), contracts, commission reports, textbooks, trade books, workbooks, newspapers, periodicals, manuscripts, diaries and journals, videotapes, and speech transcripts (McDowell, 2002), and (2) *oral history analysis*, where individuals who lived through an event or era or knew individuals of importance to the research are interviewed. Oral history analysis, also known as oral biography, oral chronicles, and life history, produces the oral evidence that is preserved through the process of transcription (Baum, 1987; Caunce, 1994; Kyvig & Marty, 2000; Sitton, Mehaffy, & Davis, 1983; Thompson, 2000).

WHY UNDERTAKE HISTORICAL RESEARCH IN LITERACY?

The second question fundamental to those embarking on historical research in literacy is, Why do it? Not surprisingly, there are a number of related responses to this query (Cohen & Manion, 2007; Good, 1966; Stahl, 2002). One is that historical research in literacy forms the reading field into a professional community with a history that is known, valued, and disseminated to the current and future generations of literacy specialists. History provides us with a sense of honor as a profession, all the while focusing us on the unique onus we bear as reading educators and researchers.

The research also yields insights into pedagogical problems that could not be achieved by other means. It informs us about how our current curricular systems came into being and to how to build a sound basis for future directions. It permits us to use past practices to evaluate emerging and current practices. It allows us to identify and evaluate recurrent trends in literacy education. It assists us in understanding the relationship between politics and literacy education, school and society, local and central governments, and teachers and students. It provides a greater understanding about the dynamics of change in education. Finally, historical research in literacy informs that variations of even the most protracted problems of our day have been tackled in one manner or another by previous generations of literacy specialists.

THE RESEARCH PROCESSES FOR THE HISTORICAL ANALYSIS OF LITERATE PRACTICE

We now turn from the larger questions about historical methodology to the specific skills, strategies, and procedures that mark the path through historical inquiry in literacy. As with any research endeavor, there is a process that outlines the general flow of historical research, allowing for false starts, recursions, digressions, and revisions. The outline that follows suggests the general flow of historical inquiry but also acknowledges the vagaries inherent to the flow. We begin with the all-important first step: choosing a topic.

Choosing the Topic

When selecting a topic, Gray (1991) recommends that historical researchers consider the topic's (1) value, (2) originality, (3) practicality, and (4) unity of theme. Nailing down the topic enables us to focus on those things that will help us tell our story. Conversely, it helps us set aside things that are not useful to our storytelling. Experience shows us that the beginning researcher of literacy's history often proposes a topic that is too broad in nature. A topic's focus may be delimited chronologically, spatially, thematically, or by a combination of these three parameters. Hence, we may need to focus— and refocus—the investigation through a continuous narrowing process. Often this action includes the formulation of at least a tentative working hypothesis or a set of guiding questions. Yet, with a working hypothesis, it may be revised through new questions, new foci, or new goals after the collection, evaluation, and initial analysis of appropriate data.

Collecting Evidence

Unlike other forms of research, a historian does not create evidence. Rather, the historian uses that which is available. In collecting evidence, the researcher is likely to examine both primary sources and secondary sources. *Primary sources* are original documents, artifacts, remains, or relics associated with the topic under investigation. Documents and artifacts are records of eyewitnesses or direct outcomes of incidents. These items are intentionally or unintentionally left in order to provide a firsthand record of the event. As Ary, Jacobs, and Razavich (2002) note, "Only the mind of the observer intrudes between the original event and the investigator" (p. 450).

Examples of primary sources for literacy education include those works of (1) a personal nature (e.g., manuscripts, personal journals, memoirs, diaries, marginal notes, blogs, autobiographies, private and public letters, memos, and e-mails), (2) a public nature (e.g., written transcriptions and oral testimonies from participants and observers, photographs, films, and audio, video, or digital recordings), (3) a professional nature (e.g., community and school newspapers, magazines, journals, school bulletins, curriculum guides, courses of study/units, textbooks/workbooks, children's books, software, student work, portfolios, report cards, record books, and examinations), and (4) an official nature (e.g., official records, minutes and reports of legislatures, school boards, state and county offices of education, specific schools, postsecondary institutions, or special task forces; certificates, licenses, and credentials; evaluation and research data/reports to local, state, and federal agencies, and census reports, immigration records, and laws).

Remains or relics associated with a particular person, group, institution, or periods in time were not meant to transmit information across time as part of the record, but, nonetheless, they can shed light on a research question. In literacy education, these may include school buildings and specific rooms (e.g., reading clinics and resource rooms), classroom furniture (e.g., language centers), period technology (e.g., tachistoscopes, controlled readers, and language masters), tools (e.g., handwriting implements), teaching materials (e.g., basals and software), student work samples (e.g., completed handwriting manuals, spelling books, and portfolios), and so on.

Secondary sources do not have a direct relationship to the case under study. The individual writing or talking about the event was not present as the incident unfolded. This narrator obtained the description of the event or era from another source, which may or may not have been a primary source (e.g., Wyatt, 1992). Examples of secondary sources covering literacy history include textbooks (Anderson & Dearborn, 1952), history books (Balmuth, 2009), articles in an encyclopedia (Monaghan, Hartman, & Monaghan, 2002; Rose, 2002), reviews of research (Stahl & Henk, 1986), and reprints or reproductions of materials (Gorn, 1998; Robinson 2000) or prints of originals (Nolin, Swan, & West, 1991). The literacy historian may find an extensive list of secondary sources by consulting the books reviewed in the *History of Reading News* found on the History of Reading Special Interest Group webpage at *www.historyliteracy.org.* Another valuable source is the annotated bibliography *Historical Sources in U.S. Reading Education 1900–1970* (Robinson, 2000) as well as the International Reading Association's Web resource "History of Reading: Overview" with its bibliographies of (1) Resources and Selected Topics in the History of Reading and Writing and (2) Persons Who Influenced Reading Instruction in Colonial America and the United States (*www.reading.org/Resources/ResourcesByTopic/HistoryofReading/Overview.aspx*). Secondary source materials will be of interest because they present a particular vantage on primary sources and the topic itself, and secondary sources may also review previously unread bibliographic information that should be read on the topic of interest. Furthermore, the review of secondary sources will assist the researcher in focusing on or narrowing down a topic of interest and hence assist with the development of research questions.

Nevertheless, secondary sources are always imbued with a point of view or are subject to erroneous information as interpretations of primary sources are reconveyed from person to person or from text to text. In addition, such works inevitably include the prejudices and the assumptions of the authors. The final point to be made is that each secondary source should be used with great care, with accurate citation and appropriate critique of the perspectives and biases found within the work. The reality is that most historical work in literacy will use a combination of primary and secondary sources in developing the report.

With most historical investigations, the primary sources are available in the rare book rooms of public and academic libraries or in archives associated with learned societies, religious groups, museums, and other archival sites around the globe or on the Internet. Archives that include artifacts needed for research in the history of literacy can be difficult to locate so Sears, Hartman, and Monaghan (2010a, 2010b, 2010c) have authored an extensive e-book of archives with respective listings of holdings and URLs for direct contact.

More recently, the field of historiography has been able to draw on a greater number of sources that can be classified as reproductions of primary sources (e.g., *New England Primer Enlarged*, 1800/1975; Stickney, 1885/1985; Webster, 1866/n.d.). Monaghan and Hartman (2000) noted that printed copies reproduced with "scrupulous care" can be acceptable substitutes for actual primary sources if the reproduction of the material fits the purpose of the research.

As we move more fully into the digital age, many primary and secondary sources are being preserved via digital technologies such as CD-ROMs and Internet sites. Such practices make the use of primary sources accessible to all historians, but these technologies require that the literacy historian become knowledgeable about and competent with online catalogs, online networks, search engines, and CD-ROM-based systems (see Benjamin, 2007; Galgano, Arndt, & Hyser, 2008; Greenstein, 1994; Reiff, 1991). When such materials are used in the research process, it is imperative that citations note the actual source of the evidence. While printed or digitalized reproductions may be acceptable for research purposes, the review of a document over the Internet will never replace the sensual experience or the being at one with the author through the holding and perusing of the primary source itself.

Regardless of one's use of primary sources or secondary sources or originals or reproductions, the historian must understand from the onset of the study that one can only investigate those topics (whether about events or people) for which either public or private documents and artifacts were preserved by official action or by happenstance for posterity or those events or people for which there are available and cognizant witnesses willing to discuss them for the record. As such, a historian should strive to review conscientiously the available data and then within the report discuss the depth and the breadth of the existing pool of documents (and, as possible, the degree to which historical traces have been lost over the years). Unfortunately, many historical narratives published in the education journals fail to provide information about the location, selection, and evaluation of both primary and secondary sources. Willis (2002), in her work on the Calhoun Colored School, presents such information in the text of the article.

Evaluating Evidence

While there is a degree of thrill in the hunt for materials, the responsibility of the historian does not end there. Indeed, potential problems may arise with the documents that have survived for the historian's review. In his seminal work on educational historiography, Kaestle (1988) poses four evaluative questions that literacy historians should use when interpreting artifacts:

- How conscientiously were the data reported in the first place?
- What individuals and institutional biases may have affected the results?
- What are the contradictions between different sources that claim to measure the same variables in the same population?
- Since the artifact of interest is removed in time (and likely in space) from the present, could its fundamental purpose or definition have been interpreted differently in the previous era than it is today?

These concerns call for us to evaluate critically the information under review. Historical criticism is the underlying foundation of historiography. Every time a historian accepts a piece of evidence or rejects another source and then interprets data in a research report, the act of historical criticism, either external or internal, is taking place (Issac & Michael, 1995). Careful, ordered evaluation of evidence in historical research leads the process to be more demanding than experimental methods. The analysis is not a one-time procedure that is run to "crunch" data but rather an ongoing vigilance to the questioning of data across the life of the project. Kaestle's (1988) four questions serve as a kind of analytic mantra to be asked and answered of all data gathered in historical research.

When we say that evidence is evaluated critically, we mean that it is evaluated through a two-step process of external and internal criticism. The act of *external criticism* (sometimes referred to as lower criticism) asks the question: Is the evidence under consideration authentic and genuine? There is a focus on the textual integrity of the document or source rather than the message it carries. In other words, the historian asks four questions: Who wrote the work? Where was the work authored? When was the document developed? Under what conditions was the work authored?

All the while, the historian is looking for frauds, distortions, or ghost-written works. For documents this process may include several steps: (1) the authentication of authorship through signatures, script, handwriting, and spelling style by comparison to known signatures, script, handwriting, and spelling from a particular person and historical period; (2) the verification through physical and chemical tests that the document's paper, parchment, cloth content, or inks were available in the period the document was purported to have been written; and (3) the matching of writing style and the point of view as evidenced in the document with texts previously verified as written by the individual. For relics, external criticism might include chemical analysis of paints and inks or even carbon dating of relics and remains.

The act of *internal criticism* (sometimes referred to as higher criticism) asks the question: What is the accuracy and worth of the evidence that has been unearthed? This is the case for both document analysis and oral history interviews. The historian seeks to establish the credibility of the informant by asking whether the individual was a credible or reliable observer/recorder of the event. One also asks whether there were any motives that might have induced the informant to overstate, misconstrue, or overlook information. Indeed, the historian looks for bias that is both sympathetically and antagonistically constituted within the data. For instance, the literacy historian would ask what the bias or subjectivity of information is based on the social, cultural, economic, or educational values and backgrounds of the individual(s) who authored the documents or provided the testimonies of the events of interest. One must query whether the informant's participation in the event influenced the reporting of the event and whether there is agreement in the report with other descriptions and reports of the event. If there are quantitative data, the historian must question whether it seems to be reasonable.

Internal criticism also requires that the historian turn inward to assess the extent and position of an implicit or explicit personal perspective demonstrated through the selection of either documents/artifacts or quantitative data to support the hypothesis and thus shape the interpretation of the evidence in the report. With oral history the researcher must ask about the bias or subjectivity that emerges from the interaction between interviewee and interviewer. Authors of literacy-oriented histories do not tend to describe explicitly how they undertook either external criticism or internal criticism. Still, such information is often hinted at within the footnotes for each article or chapter of a book.

Some scholars think that the distinction between external criticism and internal criticism is somewhat artificial (Gray, 1991). Instead, Gray (1991) suggests a set of heuristic questions that deal with opportunity, objectivity, transmission, and meaning. Whether one engages in formal criticism or follows Gray's informal approach, his or her historical study should report the processes of criticism used as well as his or her evaluation of the adequacy of the data used in support of the hypothesis.

Working with Evidence

The activity of taking notes when reviewing a document is as individualistic as is each historian, and in some cases it depends on the era in which the individual was trained. A time-honored tradition is the development of a manual note card system for both bibliographic notes and content notes, whether paper or digital.

Bibliographic cards contain standard reference information, including the name of the library or archive, specific cataloguing information for the document, and information about the source, the author, or the site. It is important to include complete documentation because reference styles for different scholarly journals and book publishers require different degrees of completeness for a referenced source.

Content cards contain the working material or facts that are extracted from the particular piece of evidence. In taking notes, one should be generous in the use of cards because this action will promote ease with the organization of the research report. The page number for the information's bibliographic source should be written down, verbatim quotes must be so noted but used sparingly on cards and in the report, and summarization of ideas and data should be used rather than simple copying of words (to prevent plagiarism). Personal inferences or ideas about the documents must be recorded so that they will not be confused with facts from the document when both are reviewed at a later date. While photocopying or scanning of documents might be desired, many archives will not permit such activities as the process damages the primary sources.

There are, however, traditions and inventions other than note cards for record keeping. We have colleagues who prefer to take notes in a composition book or journal and then reorganize the notes at a later date on note cards or in a digital data file. Others recommend the use of an audio recorder to dictate notes for future transcription and organization. Still others choose to use a laptop computer or netbook so digital note cards are taken at the time the source is reviewed, and then each saved digital note card is organized in a file corresponding to each source in a database. Through the use of a find feature, recurring words and phrases permit the location of text that can be moved into appropriate files. Still others use digital cameras or speech-to-text translation software (e.g., Dragon NaturallySpeaking).

Regardless of the process or medium used, it is imperative that one always match the information recorded to the source and the actual placement of the information in the source. This is particularly important when the archive is not immediately available so that reviewing the primary sources would not be possible for a second time.

Analyzing and Interpreting Evidence

When analyzing data, the first task is to make sure the data are dependable and relevant to the topic. Then the evidence is synthesized into a pattern that tests the hypothesis or answers questions guiding the work. This synthesis first requires that one employ a systematic plan for the organization, storage, and retrieval of the data collected. When Leedy (1958) undertook his expansive history of postsecondary reading, he organized data by cross-filing the bibliographic and factual data (cards or files) in triplicate by three general categories: (1) chronological order, (2) author or informant, and (3) subject of theme. Through such a scheme he was able to cross-reference, or link, common subject data separated by the intervention of other events and the passage of time. More recently, he advocated (Leedy & Ormrod, 2009) the use of a fourth classification: geography of event. The preparation and use of multiple files is facilitated through the use of index cards color coded to the classification category.

The process of constructing history is shaped by three factors: the philosophical stance held by the writer, the evidence that was examined in the available primary and secondary sources, and the researcher's interpretation of the data. The facts that are gathered by the historian say little in and of themselves. It is the interpretation of those facts that leads to understanding the hypothesis that was posed and the answering of the questions driving the study. The process of inductively interpreting the facts individually or in sets depends on having both mastery of the data and an understanding of the significance of that material.

Best and Kahn (1989) point out that a work can fall short because of oversimplification and illogical analysis when there are multiple and complex causes of events. On the other hand, the presentation of overgeneralizations based on insufficient evidence or false analogies when there are only superficial similarities is an equally serious problem. Kaestle (1988) follows the same track as he cautions historians to be careful not to confuse correlation with causality. Just because two events occurred simultaneously does not mean that one event caused the other.

Although it is expected that one will build an interpretive stance based on one's philosophy, politics, or even pedagogy of literacy as well as prior knowledge of the historical era and practice of historiography, the interpretation must be the result of acceptable and ethical scholarship. Making a case based on the selection of facts that are in agreement with the hypothesis while ignoring data that are not in accordance with a preferred outcome is not acceptable. The context of quoted ideas and passages must be honored, people and ideas must be treated in a just and scholarly manner, and both criticism and admiration will be tempered through professional ethics. Best and Kahn (1989) offer sage advice when they state that impartiality, and not neutrality, is the aim of systematic research presentation in history.

Kaestle (1988) suggests that historians consider two potentially over-looked issues when interpreting the evidence. First, we must distinguish between the evidence of ideas about how people should behave as opposed to the evidence about how people actually behaved during an era. Most of us are quite familiar with often-quoted statement that regardless of the policies and curriculum adopted by a school district, when a teacher closes the classroom door, literacy instruction becomes that with which there is the greatest comfort. Simply put, people may be told that they need to act in a particular way, but the actual behavior either explicitly or covertly may be different.

Second, it is necessary to distinguish between intent and consequence because the consequences of an event or a movement do not provide evidence of the participants' intent in undertaking the action under study. Intent must be based on specific evidence and not an inference from the consequences of the event. A historian has a great advantage in having the power of hindsight (Fendler, 2008). However, the participant in an event in history did not have the clairvoyant powers to predict the future.

Writing the Article or Book

Finally, the research article, thesis, dissertation, or book should be written to present the information in an understandable and interesting manner. We should be careful not to be overly sentimental, didactic, or persuasive. Generally, the work is presented in a form of a narrative, with an underlying chronological discourse pattern. Yet, as presented earlier in this chapter, discourse patterns associated with the theoretical perspectives of historiography have evolved in many directions; thus, there are no hard and fast structures for reporting the study. Still, several recommendations for writing a report have been put forward by literacy historians over the years.

First, the argument that drives the hypothesis should be stated explicitly in the initial stages of the work. Then, as each concept underlying the argument is put forth, it should be followed by examples for support and explication. Equally important is the provision for general historical context in the report as literacy events and personalities are intertwined with the greater cultural and societal events of the times. For instance, the impact of the Emergency School Education Act on the nation's literacy instruction during the presidency of Lyndon Johnson cannot be examined without attention to the administration's War on Poverty or the civil rights movement.

Second, the meaning of key terms should be clear. Kaestle (1988) describes two potential problems with the use of key terms in a research report. There is *vagueness*, or the use of umbrella/overarching terms that do not carry the necessary degree of specificity when precision of language is essential. Many terms, such as *literacy* itself, have lost the precision and focus that were once associated with them. Furthermore, there is *presentism*, or the act of applying current-era terms that did not exist in the past or that have since evolved etymologically to carry different denotations or connotations to past events, movements, and so on. For instance, we would need to consider carefully our era-appropriate use of terms such as *work-type skills, work–study skills, study skills, study strategies,* and *learning strategies* as the underlying concept evolved across the 20th century.

Third, the unresolved issues of our research findings should not be glossed over or hidden. Points in our work that are still open to conjecture or yet to be validated should be treated openly. Footnotes or endnotes should explicate the issue and evenhandedly present the logic and evidence supporting each one.

Fourth, both the audience and the disciplinary medium that best fits our work should guide where the manuscript is disseminated in the filed of literacy. Historical works in literacy are welcomed in the literacy journals sponsored by the International Reading Association, the Literacy Research Association, the Association of Literacy Educators and Researchers, and the College Reading and Learning Association among others. Such works may also find homes in other education journals, in history journals, and as books or monographs put out by university and scholarly presses. We suggest that any new author to the field review Monaghan and Hartman (2000) and Sears, Hartman, and Monaghan (2010b) before selecting a potential vehicle for publication.

Finally, we wish to make a point that comes from our shared experiences in reviewing historical research reports for journals, book publishers, and yearbooks over several decades. A manuscript that has problems with the presentation of the findings can often be revised to find an academic home and make a contribution to the scholarship of the profession. But a historical manuscript that rests on insufficient, flawed, or shoddy analysis of the data will be doomed from the start if the investigator did not use appropriate and rigorous research historical methods. In other words, there is truth in the old adage that an ounce of prevention is worth a pound of cure.

ORAL HISTORY

Oral history projects use the most fragile and irreplaceable form of historical trace, human memory, to reconstruct the known past. Indeed, the fleeting nature of memory is best expressed in the old African adage that acknowledges whenever an elder member of a community dies, an entire library is lost (Zimmerman, 1982). Extending this acknowledgment, Stahl and King (2000) argue that the legacy of the literacy community must be preserved through gathering transcriptions of personal and professional recollections and life stories of our senior colleagues. Stahl, King, Dillon, and Walker (1994) suggest that the oral history projects of the ALER (Linek et al., 2010a, 2010b), the LRA, and the learning assistance program at

National Louis University (Casazza & Bauer, 2006) have allowed us to (1) learn about the impact of both educational events and individuals through the saving of participants' and observers' recollections, which are unlikely to be saved in documents or the public record; (2) gain a more holistic vantage of our entire reading community by studying the observations of pre-K–16 literacy teachers; and (3) know the lineage of each succeeding academic generation to understand the impact our professional ancestors have had on each of us. We believe that oral histories about literacy can take the same step that Brandt (2001) did when she interviewed community members about the their literacy experiences across their school years and lifespan. Hence, the primary responsibility of oral historians in literacy is to save the record of individuals' contributions to the profession as well as individuals' views on pedagogical movements or literacy experiences encountered across the professional lifespan. Furthermore, oral historians have the opportunity to identify and record the underlining reasons, motivations, policies, and experiences behind individuals' life actions and scholarly endeavors.

The groundwork for undertaking an oral history interview involves immersion in the era or context in which the interviewee observed or participated. Interviewers in any project should consult era-appropriate primary sources and a range of secondary sources before conducting an interview and then again in seeking clarification of points raised during an interview. These works may include those that influenced the interviewee or were authored by the individual. If the oral history project focuses on a nonelite member of a professional group, consider visiting a state or local historical society's archive for regional data, a school district's or state educational agency's repository for district records and curriculum materials, or a postsecondary institution, such as the University of Pittsburgh or Northern Illinois University, that has a textbook collection. Review of such documents should help in the development of a purpose statement and the preparation of the questions to appear in the interview guide. In addition, gaining local color is possible through initial interviews of community members or family members.

The first step in undertaking an oral history project is the selection of individuals to be interviewed. Interviewees in the ALER and the LRA projects were from the category of individuals who have left a legacy through presentations at reading conferences, publication of professional articles, chapters and books, or service activities for organizations. Numerous individuals participating in the National Louis University project were not as likely to leave a written legacy of their careers or experiences. It may be even more important to capture the perspectives of the nonelite on the role literacy played within their personal or professional lives. Brandt (2001) demonstrates with her exemplary study of literacy in the lives of typical Americans the importance of selecting participants from varied economic, geographical, and cultural communities.

Once a potential interviewee has agreed to be interviewed, that person must be informed of the project's focus and the nature of the questions to be asked. The greater the rapport between the interviewer and the interviewee, the more apt that cooperation will be achieved and the interview process will be completed, particularly if there is a need for multiple interviews. The interviewee must be comfortable with the interview process and the recording of recollections through either audio or video technology.

Three cautionary notes need to be considered at this point in our discussion. First, it is essential that any participant possess the physical and mental capabilities to participate in the oral history interview. Second, unlike with other historical investigations that do not focus on the personal element, the consent of the interviewee to participate in the study and to permit archiving and future research use of the transcription is standard procedure. (Policies pertaining to institutional review of research involving human subjects are not quite as clear for oral history work as for most other forms of human subjects research. Hence, each literacy historian should read Shopes's [n.d.] treatise on the topic and then check with the office of research compliance at one's institution to learn of local requirements.) Finally, it is imperative that the researcher is competent with the technology to be used during the interview.

An interview guide composed of open-ended questions should be used to informally direct the interview process. Although not every oral historian uses such a guide, these are helpful for the less experienced interviewer, and guides assist the interviewer in obtaining data for cross-case analysis. Participants in the LRA project were given an 11-stage lifespan guide with multiple subcategories for interviewing members of the literacy profession (Stahl & King, 2000). Brandt (2001) includes an excellent guide that should be consulted in designing a protocol for interviewing individuals from the general public. As important as an interview guide might be, Stahl and King (2000) note that an interviewer should not be a slave to the guide, instead using it as a starting point for the interview process.

The heart of the oral history process is the interview. To ensure an optimal interview, we recommend taking several preparatory steps before the interview begins. First, in laying the groundwork, the interviewer must visit the interview site to learn about possible distractions or background noises that could interfere with the interview. The interviewer must be sure that both interviewer and interviewee will be seated comfortably and that the recorder will not be in the direct view of the interviewee. The interviewer should keep the initial dialogue conversational to break the ice, all the while making sure the technology is functioning properly. The opening recorded statements should identify the participant's name, the date, the time, the location, and the subject matter. Finally, the interviewer should share with the respondent four or five statements about the topic of the interview to activate prior knowledge. Throughout the interview, the questions in the guide provide a basic street map of the process. We are influenced by the seminal work of Baum (1987) for interview guidelines and suggest that the reader review this source for a comprehensive set of recommendations for undertaking the actual interview.

Once each interview is complete, the same identifying information as noted previously (e.g., interviewee's name, date, time) should be read into the recording. Shortly after the session is over, an initial review of the recording should be made so that any problems with the recording can be identified and self-notes can be taken while information is still fresh in the interviewer's mind. A copy of the recording should be produced and stored in an alternative setting for safekeeping according to an institution's review board policies.

The transcription process should be undertaken within a short time of the interview session. Transcriptions are developed directly from the tape in a verbatim manner. The transcript must be an accurate accounting of the verbal dialogue between the interviewee and the interviewer. (See Yow, 2005, for additional information on transcribing issues and procedures.) At a later date, the interviewer would ask the respondent to review the transcript for accuracy as well as personal comfort with the information provided.

The dissemination stage of a project is composed of two parts: immediate dissemination and long-term archival and dissemination functions. Immediate dissemination often takes the form of a presentation at an annual conference, the publication of either a report of an individual oral history (e.g., Dillon, 1985) or a report of thematically categorized oral histories (e.g., Clegg, 2003; King, 1991). Long-term archival requires that the researcher find a depository for the transcripts and the tapes/digital files so that future generations of researchers can review these materials in the years ahead. In some cases, local or state historical societies or university libraries will undertake the archival responsibilities for a project, or an organization's historian or archivist will maintain the project's data.

OPPORTUNITIES FOR HISTORICAL RESEARCH

The opportunities for individuals to raise and then answer questions through the historical method are numerous and are certainly needed at the cross-national, national, regional, and local levels. Topics that have been studied in the past are also always open for revisionist interpretations based on new and overlooked evidence as well as different philosophical perspectives. Hence, rather than offering specific topics for potential research, we refer the reader to the broadly defined avenues for historical research as put forward by Stahl and Hartman (2004) for literacy education, Stahl and King (2009) for postsecondary reading, and Skager and Weinberg (1971) for the general field of education.

The selection of a research topic is a very personal decision based on interest, prior knowledge, questions, and personal commitment. The researcher's selection of a method—whether document analysis, oral history, or a mixed method—will rest on the questions driving the research. Certainly, an individual should have the degree of interest in the topic and the competence with the method(s) that will drive the research endeavors forward through a multitude of tasks and across what is often a lengthy period of time. Any research undertaking should also be guided by an understanding of the standards and the parameters described throughout this chapter.

An evolving mastery of the historical method should not stop an individual from undertaking historical research or from becoming a literacy historiographer. As Butchart (1986) counsels, "There is no need to be intimidated. You need not know all the methods or even most of them. The work of the historian has more in common with old craft traditions than with modern professions. Native intelligence, careful work, and a willingness to learn are the only prerequisites" (p. 9). Still, our experience suggests that a new literacy historian will find value in reading texts on historiography (Tosh, 2006), pedagogical historiography (Butchart, 1986; Goodson & Sikes, 2001; McCulloch & Richardson, 2000), and literacy historiography (Gilstad, 1981; Monaghan & Hartman, 2000; Moore, Monaghan, & Hartman, 1997).

Furthermore, the first steps of becoming a literacy historian need be taken in monastic solitude. The new historiographer will find support through membership in the International Reading Association's History of Reading Special Interest Group. The online site (*www.historyliteracy. org*) contains several e-books on resources for the conduct of literacy research. One of the works, *Connecting to Others Who Do Research on the History of Literacy* (Sears, Hartman, & Monaghan, 2010c), provides information on organizations supporting individuals who study the history of literacy.

AN EXEMPLAR OF HISTORICAL RESEARCH

We selected an exemplar study of historical research on literacy research by drafting a list of texts that demonstrated the essential criteria for good historiography outlined previously in this chapter. Although the list of texts was not as long as might be developed for same empirical methodologies, there were numerous works, both recent and older, that could serve the purpose of exemplifying very well-researched and well-written historical research on literacy. Through several conversations in trying to narrow down the options, we kept coming back to the body of work authored by E. Jennifer Monaghan. Indeed, we came to understand that there are really two definitions of the word *exemplar*. First, the word can focus on an individual who has been a torchbearer, a mentor, and a legacy for the profession. Second, it can be a particular professional work that serves as a model work for future researchers. For us, both E. Jennifer Monaghan and her work are the prime examples of both definitions.

Author

Monaghan, who has authored such seminal works as *A Common Heritage: Noah Webster's Blue-Back Speller* (1983) and *Learning to Read and Write in Colonial America* (2005), is one of the most important literacy researchers to publish in the field across the past three decades. From her exemplary body of research on literacy history and histiography, we have selected "Family Literacy in Early 18th Century Boston: Cotton Mather and His Children," which appeared in *Reading Research Quarterly* (1991), to serve as an exemplar of historical research in the field of literacy.

Introductory Matter

Monaghan begins our exemplar with a brief discussion of what was in 1991 the literacy field's evolving understanding of family literacy, emergent literacy, and out-of-school literacy practices. In a sense, this introductory section provides an advance organizer that assists with activating the reader's prior knowledge of the topics in the article that are removed in time (if not space). Although such might not be important in a scholarly venue for historians having a specialization in colonial America, it serves an important purpose for the typical readership of *Reading Research Quarterly*.

Following the same line of reasoning, Monaghan (1991) then discusses the shift in the research in educational history from in-school practices to influences external to the schoolhouse, such as the community, church, and home. Yet Monaghan (p. 344) points out, "Despite these similar changes of heart within the two separate disciplines of reading research and the history of education, scholars have yet to take a fresh look at a history of American reading instruction that has been informed by these insights." The published work on literacy education in colonial America as found in 1991 focused on textbooks or English spelling. Research also existed on the colonial family, as historians had been studying quantitative data from demographic sources to learn of the family structure and governance and also qualitative data found in diaries, letters, and religious materials/records to learn of the psychological aspects of family life. Yet the study of literacy within the family circle presented a pristine topic, and diaries and letters could serve as a window into the literacy life of the colonial family. A set of diaries authored by Cotton Mather, serving as primary sources, provided just such a window.

Cotton Mather and His Works

Cotton Mather (1663–1728) was an iconic figure in early New England as one of the ministers in Boston's North Church and as the author of numerous religious texts and tracts, including *Wonders of the Invisible World, Magnalia Christi Americana, Bonifacius,* and *Ratio Disciplinae.* Throughout his life, Mather kept a diary that he started each year on his birthday. Although not all of his diaries survive, 16 diaries can be found in the Massachusetts Historical Society archives, nine are in the archives of the American Antiquarian Society, one is housed with the Congregational Library Society, and another can be found at the University of Virginia. More importantly for the scope of this research, these works have been edited and published in three volumes, which served as the primary sources for Monaghan's work. As noted earlier, when based on proper historical criticism of the primary sources (as had been done with the diaries), such reproductions and collections can serve as de facto primary sources (while protecting fragile works). Still, one must understand that since the research is limited to the diaries that have been located and preserved, there are gaps in the corpus, which could suggest alternative theories if available. In order to gain a fuller picture of Mather's life and beliefs, Monaghan consulted his other works, including *Paterna,* his autobiography, and *The Life of the Very Reverend and Learned Cotton Mather, D.D. & F.R.S.,* the biography authored by his son Samuel Mather (1729).

Purpose for Research

As with any research endeavor, the researcher must formulate a guiding purpose for any historical study. Monaghan wished to learn of early colonial New England family literacy practices as evidenced within the entries found in the extant Mather diaries. More specifically, she was interested in determining how the Mather children surviving beyond infancy developed literacy, how these literate behaviors were employed at home, how the parents and other adults influenced their literacy activities, and what literacy experiences were engaged in by the household. Monaghan directed specific attention to variables of gender, class, and race. Yet she provided a caveat from the onset that, given Mather's highly literate background and his elite status in the community, the findings from the research should not be considered either typical or representative of the population.

Mather: The Man

In the first formal section of the article after the front matter, Monaghan (1991) provides the readership with fundamental knowledge of the man, the time, and the place. Initially, she covers the scholarship on Cotton Mather. Monaghan drew heavily on the work of respected scholars who focused on the colonial era. Through these secondary sources, we learn that Mather was at the very least a complex individual with interests in theology, medicine, science, community charity, and even the evils of witchcraft. His *Magnalia Christi Americana* is considered one of the early classics of American literature. Monaghan notes that while Mather's three biographers have examined his family life, other scholars have paid less attention to the topic. As for other scholars drawing upon the diaries to examine the family, there had been but a small degree of their use before this article was authored. In her background coverage of Mather, Monaghan employs secondary sources. Such is a rather normal way that scholars develop initial knowledge of an individual or an event before narrowing a research topic and then proceeding to delve into primary sources. Monaghan gives credit to Kenneth Silverman's 1984 biography, *The Life and Times of Cotton Mather*, for providing her with numerous references that assisted her in undertaking this work.

Monaghan (1991) next describes the literacy environment in Boston during the first 20 years of the 18th century. Without such background information, the reader would have difficulty understanding the primary source examples drawn from the diaries that follow later in the article. Again, the author uses respected secondary sources to demonstrate that Boston had grown into an urbanized center of commerce, social sophistication, and greater secularization. The educational environment included three writing (penmanship/bookkeeping) schools and two Latin schools preparing boys for college and the ministry. She also shows that Boston had a flourishing trade in both imported and indigenously prepared books, a growing printing capacity, and two newspapers. Literacy instruction in New England is portrayed by examining accounts in secondary sources as well as the author's extensive research on colonial literacy. After noting that our knowledge of teaching literacy in this environment contains holes, she discusses what is known about the period: The teaching of reading was followed by writing instruction, which was followed by mathematics instruction; initial instruction was provided by females and later instruction was delivered by males; and reading and writing in the colony served both important religious purposes and necessary secular purposes.

Monaghan (1991) then turns to examine Mather's literacy background. She contends that the education of Mather's children can only be understood in the context of his own education. Hence, she first details the literate lives of his grandfather, Richard Mather, and then his father, Increase Mather, and his mother, Maria Mather, all important figures in the development of the Bay Colony. As the narrative continues, the author draws from both Mather's autobiography as well as respected secondary sources to paint a picture of a young man gifted in communicative arts who taught himself to write before attending school, who read voraciously exhibiting skill with skimming, summarizing, and paraphrasing, who mastered Latin by age 11, who graduated from Harvard University at age 15, and who was ordained at 22 years of age. Throughout his life, he valued reading and writing (composition) to the degree that he attempted regularly to impart such values on others. By the time he passed on, he had authored at least 444 books or pamphlets, including a reading instructional text for youngsters entitled *Good Lessons for Children*.

The Diaries

As the author transfers attention to the diaries, she first informs the reader that Mather sought for the diaries to be a vehicle for spiritual improvement. While he does mention important personal events, he does not dwell on external events. There was no desire for the audience of the journals to be the greater public. Quite the contrary, he hoped they would provide guidance to his children as well as explanation for his fatherly actions. In addition, the diaries became sources as he worked on *Paterna*, his autobiography. Monaghan points out that such purposes must be kept in mind as one judges the value of the works as evidence.

Besides considering the purpose of the diaries, Monaghan felt that Mather's process of composing these works was also worthy of consideration. Throughout each of the natal years from 1681 to February 1711, Mather kept regular notes on the events of his life. Then at the end of each natal year, he transferred the most important transcriptions into a diary. Each year he also developed a list of "contrivances to do good," which were also integrated into the annual diary. Monaghan points out that these diaries were thus retrospective in nature as opposed to a regular record. Furthermore, we do not know what information Mather chose not to integrate into the annual diary and why certain notes might have been cast aside.

Then in 1711 through 1724, the content of Mather's diaries shifted from recollections of past actions to a focus on his plans for improvement, entitled "Good Devised." These entries took the form of questions pertaining to different groups in his life, including his family. A most positive happenstance for this study was that the GD for Mondays was "What is to be done in my family," which included Mather's literacy plans for his children. The diaries from this era tended to be longer in length, and entries were often more explicit in detailing his planned activities with his children, although we do not know the degree to which these plans were implemented. Still, Monaghan makes the assumption that Cotton was a man who did carry out his plans, and she points out that intent provides valuable insight to a person's value system.

Finally, Monaghan considers the diaries "veracity as a source" as a form of criticism. In other words, might Mather have distorted the entries for any reason? When one reads the entries pertaining to his troubled marriage to his third wife, such distortions or extreme prejudices might be interpreted. Yet Monaghan believes that his entries pertaining to his children's literacy were of fair treatment, showing both desired outcomes and less than desired outcomes equally. She felt that there was no reason to disbelieve the evidence that surfaced.

Diary Evidence

The heart and soul of this article for both the educational historian and the literacy professional is the second major section, which focuses on the primary source diary evidence. Monaghan parses the diary evidence such that the segments correspond roughly to each of his three marriages: Abigail from 1686 to 1702, with four of nine children living beyond infancy (Katharin, 1689; Abigail, 1694; Hannah, 1697; and Increase Jr., 1699); the widow Elizabeth Clark Hubbard from 1703 to 1714, with two of six children living beyond infancy (Elizabeth, 1704; Samuel, 1706); and Lydia George (1715 to 1728), producing no children but in time a fair degree of turmoil and stress for Mather.

Hence, as would be expected, Monaghan's narrative is presented in a chronological discourse pattern. Throughout the analysis of the diaries, Monaghan follows a macrostructure where she integrates a life event with a family literacy-oriented theme, which she then explicates upon by presenting specific events and quotations from the respective diary. Across the years (diaries) and the many entries, themes evolve and reappear again. The examples of family literacy practices woven throughout the diary entries include oral reading in various family settings, personal and educative writing activities, sharing of religious and other texts, summarization and interpretation of texts, reading and writing as 1700s versions of bibliotherapy, and formal and informal education practiced in the greater family circle as influenced by the pious and often stark realities of urban life in early colonial New England.

Integration of the Findings

It is in the final, discussion section of the article that Monaghan (1991) pulls together the various data points that have been mined from Mather's many diary entries across the years of his maturity. It is here that her work comes full circle, returning to the very purposes and questions that guided the initial work. Superordinate themes emerged from the study of the diaries and the associated primary sources. First, Monaghan draws conclusions about general literacy instruction of the period in that she confirms the earlier research findings on the sequence of literacy instruction, the importance of religion but with the growing secular nature of education, the gender of teachers at the various levels, and the content of instruction. Second, she addresses the role of gender, class, and race. The Mather home was patriarchal, and the males were the favored gender, with greater attention directed to their formal and informal educations. Yet, given the class distinctions in the New England early colonial society, his daughters, as members of the middle class, were expected to master the pen. Furthermore, Mather was interested in the literacy development of his slaves at least in the sense of learning to read for conversion. In fact, he opened a school for African Americans and Native Americans in 1717.

Another theme is presented through her discussion of literacy in the family setting. Monaghan proposes that literacy through "bed-book" reading, peer and intergenerational instruction, and Mather's literacy assignments for the children had an important but not overreaching role in promoting family interactions. Literacy was a communal family activity, particularly through oral reading of scripture and Mather's bible stories. Mather promoted family literacy in that he modeled literate behaviors, directed children to complete specific reading and writing assignments, taught them how to comprehend text through both examples and explanation, and demonstrated how "life, language, and literacy" are interrelated.

The last theme is, in a sense, an assessment of Mather's success as a literacy promoter and provider. Monaghan points out that none of the children rose to his level as an author, but given his prodigious production of texts such a goal would be unreachable for all but a limited number of gifted individuals. Still, she suggests that the members of the family, upon reaching adulthood, held the same views of the importance of literate behaviors as the family patriarch.

What, then, does this study demonstrate to the potential literacy historian? Clearly, it answers questions about how one family from early colonial New England used both reading and writing as part of and in promotion of a literate environment. And while the Mather family can hardly be called typical of colonial America or even colonial Boston, the work served as one of the cornerstones for what was to become Monaghan's defining tome on literacy in colonial America from north to south: *Learning to Read and Write in Colonial America* (2005).

But Monaghan's study does more than provide a historicized piece to the family literacy puzzle. As an exemplary study, it illustrates the two core strategies for doing sound methodological work with data from literacy's past: *questioning* and *connecting*. She questioned and connected at several levels in her study. At the *data level*, Monaghan *questioned* the data by interrogating the motives and purposes of the sources (and their authors), asking why some data are available—and not others—and framing queries that guided ongoing handling of the data. She *connected* the data by linking primary and secondary sources, sequencing the data temporally and thematically, and comparing differences and similarities. At the *interpretive level*, Monaghan *questioned* her interpretations of the data by cross-examining the durability of the connections she made between data to warrant her claims. She *connected* her interpretations of the data to her other interpretations, sorting and sifting interpretive themes into more encompassing themes. And at the *discourse level*, Monaghan questioned her interpretations of the data by pitting them against the interpretations of other scholars, asking how they would challenge the robustness of her themes. She connected her interpretations of the data by associating them with the interpretations of other scholars, acknowledging points where her interpretations imbricate, valvate, and separate from those of others.

We close this chapter where we began. Everything has a history, including literacy. Everything that exists in the present—textbooks, articles, correspondence, tests, methods, theories, diaries, software, this chapter, and the other chapters in this volume—comes out of literacy's past. There are rigorous methods for interpreting these artifacts from the past. The twin strategies for doing rigorous interpretive work on literacy's history are *questioning* and *connecting*. Through interrogation and linking, an interpretive reconstruction of our knowable past is made. Regrettably, there is relatively little known about literacy's past compared with other fields and professions. Fortunately, there are ample data and new interpretive tools available for making that past known. There has never been a better time and greater need for such research to be conducted.

REFERENCES

Anderson, I. H., & Dearborn, W. F. (1952). *The psychology of teaching reading.* New York: Roland Press.

Ary, D., Jacobs, L. C., & Razavich, A. (2002). *Introduction to research in education* (6th ed.) Belmont, CA: Wadsworth/Thompson Learning.

Balmuth, M. (2009). *The roots of phonics* (rev. ed.). Baltimore: Brookes.

Baum, W. K. (1987). *Oral history for the local historical society.* Nashville, TN: American Association for State and Local History.

Benjamin, J. R. (2007). *A student's guide to history* (10th ed.). New York: Bedford/ St. Martin's.

Best, J. W., & Kahn, J. V. (1989). *Research in education* (6th ed.). Englewood Cliffs, NJ: Prentice Hall.

Borg, W. R., Gall, J. P., & Gall, M. D. (1993). *Applying educational research: A practical guide* (3rd ed.). New York: Longman.

Brandt, D. (2001). *Literacy in American lives.* Cambridge, UK: Cambridge University Press.

Brundage, A. (2007). *Going to the sources: A guide to historical research and writing* (4th ed.). Wheeling, IL: Harlan Davidson.

Butchart, R. E. (1986). *Local schools: Exploring their history.* Nashville, TN: American Association for State and Local History.

Casazza, M. E., & Bauer, L. (2006). *Access, opportunity, and success: Keeping the promise of higher education.* Westport, CT: Greenwood Press.

Caunce, S. (1994). *Oral history and the local historian.* London: Longman.

Cavallo, G., & Chartier, R. (2003). *A history of reading in the west.* Amherst: University of Massachusetts Press.

Clegg, L. B. (2003). *The empty schoolhouse: Memories of one-room Texas schools.* College Station: Texas A&M University Press.

Cohen, L., & Manion, L. (2007). *Research methods in education* (6th ed.). London: Routledge.

Darnton, R. (1990). What is the history of the books? In R. Darnton (Ed.), *The kiss of Lamourette: Reflections in cultural history* (pp. 107–135). New York: Norton.

Dillon, D. (1985). Ira E. Aaron: A qualitative case study of a career history. *Georgia Journal of Reading, 11*(1), 18–25.

Diringer, D. (1962). *Writing.* New York: Praeger.

Fendler, L. (2008). The upside of presentism. *Paedagogica Historica, 44*(6), 667–690.

Fischer, S. R. (2004a). *A history of reading.* London: Reaktion Books.

Fischer, S. R. (2004b). *A history of writing.* London: Reaktion Books.

Galgano, M. J., Arndt, J. C., & Hyser, R. M. (2008). *Doing history: Research and writing in a digital age.* Belmont, CA: Wadsworth Cengage Learning.

Gilderhus, M. T. (2009). *History and historians: A historiographical introduction* (7th ed.). Englewood Cliffs, NJ: Prentice Hall.

Gilstad, J. R. (1981). Methodology of historical research of reading instruction: Principles and criteria. *Reading World, 20,* 185–196.

Good, C. V. (1966). *Essentials of educational research.* New York: Meredith.

Goodson, I., & Sikes, P. (2001). *Life history research in educational settings.* Buckingham, UK: Open University Press.

Gorn, E. J. (Ed.). (1998). *The McGuffey readers: Selections from the 1879 edition.* Boston: Bedford/St. Martin's.

Gray, W. (1991). *Historian's handbook: A key to the study and writing of history* (2nd ed. reissued). Prospect Heights, IL: Waveland Press.

Greenstein, D. I. (1994). *A historian's guide to computing.* New York: Oxford University Press.

Issac, S., & Michael, W. B. (1995). *Handbook in research and evaluation* (3rd ed.). San Diego, CA: EdITS.

Johns, A. (2000). *The nature of the book: Print and knowledge in the making.* Chicago: University of Chicago Press.

Kaestle, C. F. (1988). Recent methodological developments in the history of American education. In R. M. Jaeger (Ed.), *Complementary methods for research in education* (pp. 61–71). Washington, DC: American Educational Research Association.

King, J. R. (1991). Collaborative life history narratives: Heroes in reading teachers' tales. *Qualitative Studies in Education, 4*(1), 45–60.

Kyvig, D. E., & Marty, M. A. (2000). *Nearby history* (2nd ed.). Walnut Creek, CA: AltaMira Press.

Leedy, P. D. (1958). *A history of the origin and development of instruction in reading improvement at the college level.* Unpublished doctoral dissertation, New York University. (University Microfilms No. 59–01016)

Leedy, P. D., & Ormrod, J. E. (2009). *Practical research—Planning and design* (9th ed.). Upper Saddle River, NJ: Merrill Prentice Hall.

Linek, W. M., Massey, D. D., Sturtevant, E. G., Cochran, L., McClanahan, B., & Sampson, M. B. (2010a). *The College Reading Association legacy: A celebration of fifty years of literacy leadership, Volume I.* St. Cloud, MN: Association of Literacy Educators & Researchers.

Linek, W. M., Massey, D. D., Sturtevant, E. G., Cochran, L., McClanahan, B., & Sampson, M. B. (2010b). *The College Reading Association legacy: A celebration of fifty years of literacy leadership, Volume II.* St. Cloud, MN: Association of Literacy Educators & Researchers.

Manguel, A. (1996). *A history of reading.* New York: Viking-Penguin Books.

Mathews, M. (1966). *Teaching to read: Historically considered.* Chicago: University of Chicago Press.

McCulloch, G., & Richardson, W. (2000). *Historical research in educational settings.* Buckingham, UK: Open University Press.

McDowell, W. H. (2002). *Historical research: A guide for writers of dissertations, theses, articles and books.* New York: Longman.

Monaghan, E. J. (1983). *A common heritage: Noah Webster's blue-back speller.* Hamden, CT: Archon Books.

Monaghan, E. J. (1991). Family literacy in early 18th century Boston: Cotton Mather and his children. *Reading Research Quarterly, 26*(4), 342–370.

Monaghan, E. J. (2005). *Learning to read and write in colonial America.* Amherst: University of Massachusetts Press.

Monaghan, E. J., & Hartman, D. K. (2000). Undertaking historical research in literacy. In M. Kamil, P. Mosenthal, P. D. Pearson, & R. Barr (Eds.), *Handbook of reading research: Volume III* (pp. 109–121). Mahwah, NJ: Erlbaum.

Monaghan, E. J., Hartman, D. K., & Monaghan, C. (2002). History of reading instruction. In B. J. Guzzetti (Ed.), *Literacy in America: An encyclopedia of history, theory and practice* (Vol. 1, pp. 224–231). Santa Barbara, CA: ABC/CLIO.

Moore, D. W., Monaghan, E. J., & Hartman, D. K. (1997). Values of literacy history. *Reading Research Quarterly, 32*, 90–102.

New England Primer Enlarged. (1975). Highland Park, NJ: Drier Educational Systems. (Original work published 1800)

Nolin, L., Swan, H. A., & West, P. C. (1991). *Historical images of education: Prints from the Blackwell history of education research collection.* DeKalb: Northern Illinois University.

Reiff, J. L. (1991). *Structuring the past: The uses of computers in history.* Washington, DC: American Historical Association.

Robinson, R. D. (2000). *Historical sources in U. S. reading education 1900–1970: An annotated bibliography.* Newark, DE: International Reading Association.

Rose, J. (2002). History of the book. In B. J. Guzzetti (Ed.), *Literacy in America: An encyclopedia of history, theory and practice* (Vol. 1, pp. 231–233). Santa Barbara, CA: ABC/CLIO.

Sears, L. A., Hartman, D. K., & Monaghan, E. J. (2010a). Connecting to others who do research on the history of literacy. Retrieved from *www.historyliteracy.org/publications.html.*

Sears, L. A., Hartman, D. K., & Monaghan, E. J. (2010b). Disseminating research on the history of literacy. Retrieved from *www.historyliteracy.org/publications.html.*

Sears, L. A., Hartman, D. K., & Monaghan, E. J. (2010c). Locating data for research on the history of literacy. Retrieved from *www.historyliteracy.org/publications.html.*

Shopes, L. (n.d.). Oral history, human subjects, and institutional review boards.

Retrieved June 12, 2010, from *www.oralhistory.org/do-oral-history/oral-history-and-irb-review/*.

Silverman, K. (1984). *The life and times of Cotton Mather.* New York: Harper & Row.

Sitton, T., Mehaffy, G. L., & Davis, O. L. (1983). *Oral history: A guide for teachers (and others).* Austin: University of Texas Press.

Skager, R. W., & Weinberg, C. (1971). *Fundamentals of educational research: An introductory approach.* Glenview, IL: Scott Foresman.

Smith, N. B. (2002). *American reading instruction* (Special ed.). Newark, DE: International Reading Association.

Stahl, N. A. (2002). Epilogue. In N. B. Smith (Ed.), *American reading instruction* (Special ed., pp. 413–418). Newark, DE: International Reading Association.

Stahl, N. A., & Hartman, D. K. (2004). Doing historical research on literacy. In N. K. Duke & M. H. Mallette (Eds.), *Literacy research and methodologies* (pp. 170–196). New York: Guilford Press.

Stahl, N. A., & King, J. R. (2000). Preserving the heritage of a profession through California Reading Association oral history projects. *The California Reader, 34*(1), 14–19.

Stahl, N. A., & King, J. R. (2009). History. In R. F. Flippo & D. C. Caverly (Eds.), *Handbook of college reading and study strategy research* (2nd ed., pp. 3–25). New York: Routledge.

Stahl, N. A., King, J. R., Dillon, D., & Walker, J. (1994). The roots of reading: Preserving the heritage of a profession through oral history projects. In E. G. Sturtevant & W. Linek (Eds.), *Pathways for literacy: 16th Yearbook of the College Reading Association* (pp. 15–24). Commerce: East Texas State University.

Stahl, N. A., King, J. R., & Eilers, V. (1996). Postsecondary reading strategies: Rediscovered. *Journal of Adolescent and Adult Literacy, 39*(5), 368–379.

Stickney, J. (1985). *Classics for children: A primer.* Boston: Ginn & Co. (Original work published 1885)

Thompson, P. (2000). *The voice of the past: Oral history* (3rd ed.). Oxford, UK: Oxford University Press.

Tosh, J. (2006). *The pursuit of history* (4th ed.). New York: Longman.

Webster, N. (n.d.). *The elementary spelling book, being an improvement on the American spelling book.* New York: American Book Company. (Original work published 1866)

Willis, A. I. (2002). Literacy at Calhoun Colored School 1892–1945. *Reading Research Quarterly, 37,* 8–44.

Wyatt, M. (1992). The past, present, and future need for college reading courses in the U.S. *Journal of Reading, 36*(1), 10–20.

Yow, V. R. (2005). *Recording oral history: A guide for the humanities and social sciences.* Lanham, MD: AltaMira Press.

Zimmerman, W. Z. (1982). *Instant oral biographies.* New York: Guarionex.

CHAPTER 12

Developing Affective Instrumentation

William A. Henk
Michael C. McKenna
Kristin Conradi

The value of most literacy research depends on the integrity of the means used to assess the phenomena under study. Surely, the creation of valid and reliable *cognitive* measurements for reading, writing, and other language processes presents its share of noteworthy challenges (Gronlund, 1993). It is no small feat to generate higher level achievement items and to identify authentic literacy tasks that measure not only what they purport (i.e., validity) but that do so in a genuinely dependable manner (i.e., reliability). Even so, as complicated as cognitive assessments can be to produce for use in literacy contexts, the development of *affective* indices represents an even more formidable task. As Athey (1985) has suggested, the affective aspects of literacy tend to be ill-defined and involve "shadowy variables" that are difficult to conceptualize, measure, and address (p. 527).

Indeed, we believe that the special challenges inherent in the development of affective instruments make their consideration particularly instructive relative to the broader issues of instrument development in literacy research. Understanding the nature of these challenges and arriving at creative ways of meeting them can enhance one's understanding and appreciation of the issues entailed in cognitive instrument development.

In this chapter, we attempt to lay the groundwork for improving the current state of affective-related literacy measurement. To do so, we discuss the importance of rigorous affective instrument development, note the challenges inherent in creating such measures, and outline the attributes of desirable affective research tools. The heart of the chapter then describes specific procedures for developing these tools. We conclude by sharing our personal experiences with the instrument development process, highlighting the insights we have gained through our work on measuring reading and writing attitudes and self-perceptions.

Interestingly, a fair amount of literacy research involves the assessment of affective constructs of varying type and scope despite their elusive nature and attendant measurement obstacles. Measures can be self-report instruments. They can be used to guide observations or to note behavioral or physiological markers. They can be forced-choice or open-ended in nature and can occur in experimental, descriptive, qualitative, longitudinal, and even case study research. The measures can inform both large-scale and small-scale investigations. From a developmental standpoint, affective measures can be found in studies whose emphasis ranges from emergent through adult and even family literacies. Within these studies, topics might range from literacy instruction and assessment to cultural and linguistic diversity, digital technologies, urban education, task engagement, and pre-service and in-service teachers' professional growth, to name just a few (Henk, 1999).

The respective affective constructs might be broadly defined (e.g., motivation for reading) or quite narrowly designed for a very specific purpose within a particular study (e.g., confidence about decoding a specific list of unfamiliar words, attitude toward reading a certain type of poetry, and teacher beliefs about the need for precise spelling in a particular writing genre). In the case of broadly defined affective constructs, the development of the instrument itself is often the whole purpose of the research effort. By specifying the development process and reporting the instrument's psychometric properties, authors who are engaged in this kind of research harbor the expectation that the tool will be used widely (Henk & Melnick, 1995; McKenna, Kear, & Ellsworth, 1995).

Despite the importance of these kinds of efforts, affective measures are not overly plentiful in the professional literature, in all probability because they represent exhaustive undertakings and are overshadowed by pressures to demonstrate cognitive growth. More frequently, instrument development is done to target the narrower affective measurement goals of an investigation, and the creation of the tools may not need to be quite as intensive. In either case, for the research to truly be of value, it is critical that both broadly and narrowly defined instruments be held to very high standards. Unfortunately, regardless of the type and scope of this research and its diversity of topics, constructs, and developmental parameters, the affective measures in many literacy-oriented studies lack genuine psychometric integrity (Henk & Melnick, 1992). As a result, the findings cannot be regarded as altogether truthful or trustworthy, and the merit and usefulness of the work, which might otherwise be exemplary, can be called into question. In other words, literacy studies will only be as strong as their weakest links, and the measurement of affective elements seems to achieve this dubious distinction with considerable frequency.

Our twofold hope in presenting this information is to help literacy professionals of all types become more informed consumers of research involving affective measures and to provide a working knowledge of the instrument development process for individuals who may either want or need to fashion such tools. In the latter case, we recommend that readers seek knowledge and expertise beyond the scope of this chapter by consulting books devoted to instrument development (e.g., de Vaus, 2002; Dillman, Smyth, & Christian, 2009; Fowler, 2009; Gable & Wolf, 1993) and by collaborating with a measurement specialist.

Also, it should be noted that our treatment of affective instrument development in this chapter focuses on larger scale, broadly based measures. We believe this focus provides ample coverage of key concepts that can and should be applied to more narrow affective measures as well. That is, essentially the same procedures should be followed in the development of narrow, smaller scale measures, although to a somewhat lesser extent. Whether large-scale or small-scale measures are to be created, we maintain that it is important for readers to have a solid sense of the nature and scope of the process, particularly the rigor necessary to ensure quality. Likewise, we focus on forced-choice types of instruments rather than open-ended approaches to gathering affective data, such as interview protocols and questionnaires (see Baumann & Bason, Chapter 18, this volume, for a discussion of interview and survey research). At the same time, however, we believe that our sections on desirable attributes of affective items and on the steps of the instrument development process itself can be helpful to researchers interested in those types of measures as well.

WHY AFFECTIVE INSTRUMENT DEVELOPMENT IS IMPORTANT

Achievement and Affect

The importance of developing high-quality affective instrumentation derives from the critical link between achievement and affect in literacy learning (Purves & Beach, 1972; Walberg & Tsai, 1985). Clearly, the attitudes, values, expectations, and beliefs that individuals possess will play a vital role in shaping their engagement with reading, writing, and other literacy processes. We have long known, for instance, that children who believe they are competent readers outperform those who fail to hold such beliefs and that children who perceive reading as valuable and personally relevant will approach reading in a more deliberate and engaged way (Ames & Archer, 1988; Dweck & Elliott, 1983; Paris & Oka, 1986; Schunk, 1985). Likewise, we know that children who report positive associations with literacy will tend to read and write more often, for greater periods of time, and with heightened intensity. Accordingly, this deeper engagement translates to superior reading and writing ability (Anderson, Fielding, & Wilson, 1988; Foertsch, 1992). By the same token, we know that when children harbor negative feelings about literacy, their achievement tends to suffer (Spaulding, 1992). These disaffected children, and similarly afflicted adults for that matter, will either avoid literacy tasks at nearly every opportunity or read and write with little passion, commitment, or intensity.

In some ways, of course, a circular, chicken-and-egg causality exists between achievement and affect. Just as negative attitudes can curtail achievement, problems in learning to read can lead to negative attitudes, and so forth. A dismal downward spiral can result (McKenna, 2001), and research has documented a Matthew effect over time as the attitudes of the best and worst readers diverge (McKenna, Kear, et al., 1995). In his classic study of avid adult readers (whom he described as "ludic"), Nell (1988) could find only one characteristic that all of them shared: proficiency. Reading ability does not ensure positive attitudes, but it is almost certainly a prerequisite. The complex relationship between achievement and affect makes it imperative for teachers and researchers to monitor affective dimensions of reading growth and for instrument developers to provide them with the tools they need to do it.

Gaps in the Field

Not surprisingly, then, the affective domain remains an area of keen interest for both literacy educators and researchers (Cramer & Castle, 1994; Henk & Melnick, 1998; Mathewson, 1985; Turner & Paris, 1995). Regrettably, despite the significant role of affective variables in influencing literacy-related motivation (e.g., attitudes, self-perceptions, beliefs), there is a striking lack of valid and reliable instrumentation to tap these constructs. This dearth is particularly acute in terms of quantitative group surveys that can function as a natural complement to individually administered qualitative instruments (McKenna & Kear, 1990). Moreover, the scarcity serves as an ongoing obstacle to the assessment of the reading and writing profiles of individual children as well as to the more expansive goal of evaluating affective aspects of literacy interventions and programs. The lamentable result is that our instructional practices in literacy have not fully benefited from this potentially useful information.

The history of affective instrument development in literacy pales in comparison with the rich tradition enjoyed by cognitive measurements (Henk & Melnick, 1995). Because constructs in the affective domain are more difficult to operationalize and measure, researchers have been unwilling or unable to embrace the profound challenges that empirically sound literacy instrumentation demands. Put another way, high-quality affective instruments require adherence to an intense multistage validation process that many developers, intentionally or unintentionally, circumvent. As a result, most instruments exhibit weak psychological grounding, small and idiosyncratic samples, and psychometric inadequacies (McKenna, Kear, et al., 1995). These conditions compromise construct validity and internal scale reliabilities and surely threaten external generalizability. Such draw-backs are especially problematic in studies whose affective measures lack appropriate theoretical grounding or are so vaguely defined that they seem to be more a function of intuition than disciplined inquiry.

OUR WORK BRIEFLY NOTED

Despite the many barriers to developing high-caliber affective measure-ments, recent decades have witnessed some noteworthy progress in assess-ing these aspects of literacy. For instance, McKenna and Kear (1990) developed the Elementary Reading Attitude Survey (ERAS), a very popu-lar and useful instrument that taps elementary school children's attitudes toward both academic and recreational forms of reading. Another affec-tive instrument that has emerged, the Reader Self-Perception Scale (RSPS), measures how children in grades 4 through 6 feel about themselves as readers (Henk & Melnick, 1992, 1995), and somewhat more recently the Writer Self-Perception Scale (WSPS) has been used to assess how children at these upper elementary levels feel about themselves as writers (Bottomley, Henk, & Melnick, 1997). Still more recently, Kear, Coffman, McKenna, and Ambrosio (2000) introduced the Writing Attitude Survey (WAS), an instrument for use in grades K–12, and McKenna, Conradi, Lawrence, and Jang (2009) developed the Survey of Adolescent Reading Attitudes (SARA), designed for grades 6–12. All five of these self-report instruments have been validated systematically, and each gauges dimensions of affect that clearly influence literacy engagement. Most important, they allow for a richer appraisal to be made of an individual's literacy orientation and per-mit various approaches to reading and writing instruction to be compared along key affective lines.

Our work in developing these multifactor, forced-choice, self-report instruments served as true learning experiences for us. While the three of us were well versed in assessing the cognitive domain, the affective domain represented something of a stretch. None of us possessed a firm under-standing of the steps involved in the affective instrument development process, nor did we possess a priori direct experience with sophisticated statistical tools such as factor analysis that are used to evaluate affective scales. Among many lessons learned, we came to know that affective liter-acy constructs do indeed tend to defy operationalization and are otherwise resistant to capture.

In comparing our respective bodies of work in the affective domain, we also learned that our approaches, although quite similar, were not identical. For example, the ERAS built on a rather long history of moderately success-ful attempts to measure attitude toward reading, but its unique contribu-tions centered on differentiating between academic and recreational forms of reading and on invoking large-scale norming. The SARA, introduced two decades after the ERAS, not only complemented it by including the middle and secondary grades but added the notion of digital environments to the concepts of academic and recreational reading. The WAS expanded on earlier work by Knudson (1991, 1992, 1993), whose three scales covered grades K–12. The WAS represented a consolidated and expanded version of Knudson's item sets and, equally important, served to establish norms. The RSPS and WSPS broke new ground by adapting Bandura's (1977, 1982) theory of self-efficacy to reading and writing and by adhering to rigorous standards for factor analysis. For the purposes of illustration, we use the RSPS as our exemplar for large-scale affective instrument development in this chapter.

The Motivation to Read Profile (MRP; Gambrell, Palmer, Codling, & Mazzoni, 1996), another well-developed, larger scale affective literacy instrument, deals with self-concept and reading task value. It followed yet another development pathway centered on expert ratings of content validity and internal consistency estimates. Pitcher and colleagues (2007) later modified this instrument for use with adolescents and developed the Adolescent Motivation to Read Profile. Likewise, the Motivation for Reading Questionnaire by Wigfield and Guthrie (1997) took still another route. This latter instrument was predicated on an earlier study involving interviews and classroom observations, and its item writing corresponded to three major categories of motivation: self-efficacy, intrinsic and extrinsic motivation and learning goals, and social aspects of motivation. In turn, these categories were further divided into a total of 11 aspects of motivation, and these aspects were analyzed using internal consistency estimates, item-to-total correlations, interscale correlations, and factor analysis. We regard this work as one of the better examples of smaller scale affective instrumentation specifically developed for an explicit purpose within a single literacy study, although there may be some question about the factor-analytic procedures that were used. While we do not discuss the study at length here, we encourage readers who are interested in consuming or conducting this kind of research to consult the work and judge its value themselves.

Across all the aforementioned instruments, differences in the nature of the affective constructs themselves and their respective foundations allowed for varied yet equally defensible approaches to instrument development. This assertion drives our current thinking that there is simply no one lockstep method for creating sound affective literacy measurements. The model we describe later in this chapter, then, represents a flexible prototype that will lend itself to both large- and small-scale applications. The key point, however, is that meticulous affective instrument development—and meticulous development for instruments of any kind—leads to higher quality in the literacy studies that deploy them.

CONSIDERATIONS FOR AFFECTIVE LITERACY INSTRUMENTS

Appropriate Purposes and Uses of Affective Instruments

Affective literacy instruments can be used for a wide range of research purposes. In *experimental* research, these tools and their component scales can yield scores that function as primary or secondary dependent variables. Employed properly, they are particularly well suited to serving as final outcome measures in studies comparing the impact of different methods of reading and writing instruction (e.g., Bottomley, Truscott, Marinak, Henk, & Melnick, 1999; McKenna, Stratton, Grindler, & Jenkins, 1995). Some interesting situations could emerge from this type of research, especially when literacy achievement is considered together with affective factors. That is, it would be enlightening to note instances in which dramatic affective changes occur, yet literacy achievement remains equivalent between groups. In such cases, a method might still be defensible on its affective merits alone. Conversely, an intervention might enhance literacy achievement but fail to exert a significant affective impact or even have a negative impact. While growth in achievement would commend the approach, the likelihood of its promoting lifelong literacy learning would be debatable.

Scores from affective instruments can also be used as blocking (categorical) variables and covariates in experimental literacy research. In the former case, subjects can be grouped for investigation in terms of having high or low levels of a particular affective construct such as attitude toward writing. These differentiations would enable researchers to explore interactions between degrees of the affective construct and various instructional treatments. As covariates, however, affective measures taken at the outset of an experiment can be used to adjust both cognitive and affective posttest measures statistically. For example, if one group of subjects held an initial affective advantage of some kind, an analysis of covariance could be computed to adjust posttest measures accordingly. In turn, this adjustment would help to ensure the fairness and merit of the comparison. Using covariation as a statistical control is important when the researcher suspects a logical relationship, often causal, between the affective construct and posttreatment indices of the intervention's effectiveness.

In *descriptive* research, an affective instrument might serve the role of trait indicator or as a predictor or criterion variable in regression analyses. As a trait indicator, it would function much like a blocking variable. For instance, classroom observations might be made more meaningful when the findings are viewed in light of children having been classified as possessing high or low levels of an affective construct such as literacy self-esteem or perceived locus of control. When applied to regression analyses, the construct and its scale scores could be used, singularly or among a list of factors, to predict some outcome. Applied this way, they could possibly be correlated with various other affective or achievement measures or included among several predictor variables aimed at explaining some criterion. For that matter, the affective scores might also serve as the very criterion variables that the researcher is trying to predict. Regrettably, relatively few examples of appropriately developed affective instruments for descriptive literacy research exist.

Although the present volume focuses on literacy *research*, it bears mentioning that affective instruments are often used by educators to inform instructional *practice*. Data yielded by affective scales such as the ERAS, SARA, WAS, RSPS, WSPS, and the MRP's Reading Survey and Conversational Interview can be used for diagnostic purposes with individual children (McKenna & Dougherty Stahl, 2009). Often this information helps to explain why certain children fail to achieve their literacy potential. For example, a child with average or higher intelligence might not be performing as expected because her literacy attitudes, self-perceptions, or motivation might be below par. Likewise, a teacher can create a class profile using tools of this type to give strategic direction to enhancing the affective climate for literacy learning (see Bottomley et al., 1997, for an explanation). In this instance, the data would indicate whether the classroom environment contributes positively or negatively to various aspects of children's affective literacy perceptions.

Considerations in Developing Affective Literacy Instruments

Appropriate Wording of Items

If an instrument is to elicit responses that accurately reflect an individual's feelings, beliefs, or behaviors, the clarity of items is essential. Items that do not clearly communicate what the researcher wishes to know pose threats to reliability and validity alike. The following six guidelines may help refine an instrument prior to field testing by improving the clarity and precision of items. We base these guidelines loosely on questions posed by de Vaus (2002).

1. *Keep the language simple.* Be mindful of the age of the participants you intend to target. Avoid words and expressions they are unlikely to know. Aim for simple grammatical structures and shorten overall length of items where feasible. If you find it impossible to simplify an item to the point at which intended participants are likely to understand it, it may be better to eliminate the item than to risk its being misunderstood.

2. *Avoid items that ask two questions in one.* The question, "How often do you read to your children?," for example, assumes that the respondent has children. One technique for avoiding this pitfall is to use filter questions. In this instance, the respondent would first be asked, "Do you have young children?" Only if the answer is "yes" would the question about read-alouds be raised. Filter questions have long been used in print instruments but are also well suited to Web-based surveys.

3. *Avoid leading items.* The way an item is worded can bias responses in a particular direction. Consider: "Do you agree with the large body of scientific research proving that the method of repeated readings contributes to oral reading fluency?" Incorporating such biases may occasionally be deliberate (e.g., in political polling), but it can prevent a researcher from discovering participants' true perspectives. A better option is "Do you agree with research indicating that the method of repeated readings may contribute to oral reading fluency?"

4. *Avoid negatively worded items.* These can be difficult to understand, especially for children. Consider a statement such as this: "If I do not read my assignments, I may not graduate." In this case, the double negative may confuse students, who may assume that by agreeing to the statement they are somehow indicating that it is desirable not to read one's assignments. A related problem involves items that have an orientation that is the reverse of the others. In the ERAS, for example, a positive response to each item involves the broadly grinning Garfield at the far left. In developing the instrument, however, items such as the following were initially considered: "How would you feel if there were no books?" To respond to this item by circling the grinning Garfield would reflect a negative attitude, unlike all the other items. Researchers occasionally embed items such as this one with reverse directionality in order to detect a response set (i.e., a tendency to respond in like manner to every item without deliberation). But reversing the order of the response categories can be confusing, especially to young children, and some researchers deliberately avoid this practice (e.g., Ragheb & Beard, 1982). Besides, there is other evidence that a response set may be present, as when a child renders uniformly positive or negative responses.

5. *Use words that have similar meanings for everyone.* This is not always possible, of course, but you should attempt to anticipate how the terms you use are likely to be interpreted. In a survey of struggling secondary students (McKenna, 1986), participants were asked to rate various reading topics. They rated "science" low even though their ratings of several science-related topics were much higher. It appears likely that they associated the term *science* with a school subject and summarily dismissed it as boring. (Conducting cognitive interviews during survey development can help prevent these problems. See our later discussion on this topic.)

6. *Make sure the frame of reference is clear.* Respondents may find it difficult to answer unless certain parameters are clarified. Consider: "How many hours per week do you spend reading?" A student may well wonder if the questioner intends to include assigned reading or just leisure reading.

Ease of Responding

In open-ended instruments requiring written responses, the chief factor to consider is an appropriate amount of space in which to write. The amount provided must be adequate for the responses sought. It may also convey a subtle message about the extent of elaboration expected. In forced-choice instruments, requiring the respondent to select from among several options, the mechanics of responding should be as simple as possible (e.g., checking, circling, bubbling). Experienced examinees should have no problem with response columns, where the categories appear only once per page at the top of each column or in a legend at the beginning of the instrument. For young children, however, it is imperative to repeat the categories *for each item*, whether they are words, pictures, or numbers. Looking elsewhere for reference points and keeping one's bearings on the page while doing so are sophisticated skills that young children may lack.

Another consideration is whether the respondent is expected to read the items. When the target group comprises mature readers, this expectation is usually realistic. However, when the instrument targets young children or older struggling readers (often the case in reading-related assessments), the examiner must take into account possible decoding deficits of the target group. If these difficulties are likely to interfere with comprehension of items, then the items must be read aloud by the examiner while the children respond.

Clear Directions

Respondents must understand exactly what is requested of them. Mature individuals, with experience in responding to affective instruments, may need little else than a straightforward, directive sentence. In the case of children, however, more may be required. A sample item might be included so that the task is fully exemplified. The examiner might be instructed to make a transparency of the response categories and to explain them carefully. In the case of the ERAS, for example, pilot testing revealed that younger students tended to confuse the second and third pictures of Garfield, which differ only around the mouth. In one, Garfield is slightly smiling; in the other, he wears a slight frown. By pointing out this distinction, the ambiguity was eliminated. It is important to try to anticipate such problems or at least to address them during the piloting process.

Length and Order

Generally, the longer the instrument, the more reliable it is. This is why piloting typically begins with an overabundance of items and then pares them down to a manageable number that is still high enough for adequate reliability. A balance must be sought between too few items (resulting in low reliability) and too many (resulting in fatigue and distraction). Some authorities (e.g., de Vaus, 2002) recommend arranging the instrument so that it progresses from conceptually simpler items to those requiring more thought and striving for a logical "flow" from item to item. In designing the instrument, it is also important to consider potential context, or order, effects (see Tourangeau & Rasinski, 1988; Tourangeau, Rips, & Rasinski, 2000). Earlier questions can have a priming effect on how a respondent answers subsequent questions.

Steps for Validating Affective Literacy Instruments

Our recommended process for developing valid and reliable affective literacy instrumentation is adapted from Gable (1986) and employs ideas from Willis (2005). The process involves several related steps, all of which contribute to the caliber of the final affective instrument (see Table 12.1). In general, as adherence to the process increases, one can expect a higher standard of quality. We present a preferred order of steps, but the actual sequencing can be varied somewhat. Because the instruments can be scaled in different ways, it may make sense to diverge from the prescribed format.

Identify the Constructs and Conceptual Definitions

Every meaningful affective instrument, like any cognitive instrument, begins with an exhaustive review of the relevant literature. The literature review allows the developer to determine the specific constructs to study and to create conceptual and operational definitions of the constructs. This step ensures that the instrument receives appropriate theoretical grounding, and it reveals the full history of the construct's treatment in the field.

TABLE 12.1. Steps in the Affective Instrument Development Process

1. Identify the constructs and conceptual definitions.
2. Conduct focus groups and/or observations
3. Develop operational definitions and generate the potential item pool.
4. Select a scaling technique.
5. Conduct a judgmental review of items.
6. Identify a response format.
7. Develop directions for responding.
8. Prepare draft and final instruments.
9. Conduct cognitive interviews.
10. Gather and analyze pilot data from appropriate samples.
11. Revise the instrument.
12. Conduct a final pilot study.
13. Produce the final instrument.
14. Conduct additional validity and reliability analyses.
15. Consider social desirability.
16. Prepare documentation for the instrument.

The developer learns how the construct or related constructs have been conceived, how they have been defined, and how they have been measured. In turn, this knowledge assists the researcher in refining the construct and its measurement by pointing to the breaking of new ground. Basically, the review enables the developer to build on the sum total of previous work related to the literacy phenomena under study.

With regard to the RSPS, Henk and Melnick (1992) originally sought a theoretical framework that would undergird the instrument. A review of the literature suggested that Bandura's (1977, 1982) theory of self-efficacy held excellent promise as a model to apply to the construct of reader self-perceptions. These researchers noted Bandura's four major categories of self-efficacy (performance, observational comparison, social feedback, and physiological states) and began thinking seriously about how to define each of these concepts as a prelude to drafting the items themselves.

Conduct Focus Groups and/or Observations

Since theoretical constructs can be quite abstract, it behooves survey developers to conduct focus groups after reviewing the relevant literature (Fowler, 2009; Groves et al., 2009). These focus groups, conducted with the study population, give researchers an opportunity to consider the constructs and conceptual definitions they have developed in light of the perspectives and experiences of the participants. Findings from the focus group could occasion a return to the literature and the exploration of an additional construct. Also, these findings should help researchers not only refine and sensitize their questions but also frame them in a way more relevant to the audience.

Alternatively, because focus groups, particularly with young children, may be difficult to conduct, researchers may choose to conduct observations of their study population. These observations could yield relevant, insider information not found in the literature.

Develop Operational Definitions and Generate the Potential Item Pool

Once the literature has been properly reviewed and the conceptual definitions have been established, operational definitions must be developed. This notion of jumping the gap between the conceptual variable and the operational definition is extremely important. The operational definitions drive the writing of the items and result in the belief statements to be used in the instruments. Depending on the type of scaling, the developer might purposely create statements (or adjectives) that (1) collectively span favorable, neutral, and unfavorable aspects of the construct's continuum; (2) can be judged to be either favorable or unfavorable but not neutral; or (3) form the extremes of the favorable or unfavorable continuum. In any event, the items must be written with the greatest of care if the construct is to be assessed effectively.

Select a Scaling Technique

There are multiple techniques available to scale affective characteristics, including equal-appearing intervals (Thurstone, 1931), latent-trait analysis (Lazarsfeld & Henry, 1968), summated ratings (Likert, 1932), and the semantic differential (Osgood, Suci, & Tannenbaum, 1957). As Gable and Wolf (1993) suggest, all the techniques attempt to locate an individual's response on a bipolar evaluative dimension with respect to a given target object. Each scaling technique results in a single affective score derived on the basis of responses to a set of belief statements.

The most popular scaling technique is Likert's summated rating. A Likert scale allows for the summation and averaging of scaled responses—that is, attaching numbers to levels of meaning. Likert scales typically involve using statements that span the construct's continuum, but this is not always the case. With the RSPS, a Likert-type scale was used, but to some extent, with its focus on factor analysis, the interpretation resembled latent-trait analyses. That is, Likert response choices, which typically span a continuum (such as *strongly agree, somewhat agree, neither agree nor disagree, somewhat disagree,* and *strongly disagree*) were used, and the factor analysis used these response patterns to designate items as belonging to one of the principal RSPS scales.

Osgood's semantic differential, another type of scaling, involves the use of bipolar adjectives (e.g., valuable–worthless and excitable–calm). Respondents are asked to rate the object along the line between the two anchoring antonyms. The semantic differential centers on a person's subjective understanding of the connotative meanings of words' *evaluation, power,* and *activity.* These three measurable, underlying dimensions of attitude are used by individuals to evaluate everything in their social environment, regardless of language or culture. A discussion of differentiated intensity, which typically accompanies any description of the semantic differential (i.e., evaluative, potency, and activity dimensions), is beyond the scope of this chapter; however, suffice it to say that these types of scales typically comprise evaluative adjectives, with only a few adjectives from the potency and activity dimensions included as anchors to clarify the interpretation of a later factor analysis (Gable, 1986). The problem with the semantic differential is that it does not distinguish beyond a single evaluative continuum, with positive attitude at one end of the scale and negative attitude at the other end. That is, it does not actually identify any individual emotions.

Still another scaling technique is Thurstone's equal-appearing interval. Here, a large number of statements pertaining to the attitude topic are generated, and judges rate them in terms of whether they are positive, negative, or neutral. Items are then selected to create a scale that has several items for each gradation of attitude toward the topic, ranging from some very positive items, some less positive items, and so on. In responding to the final scale, subjects choose only those items that reflect their attitudes.

Conduct a Judgmental Review of Items

One of the most important steps in the affective instrument development process involves the rating of proposed statements or items by content experts (de Vaus, 2002). Again, this step will vary somewhat depending on the scaling technique, but in all cases the judges must review and evaluate the statements or adjectives in terms of how well they relate to the conceptual definitions of the affective construct. The review might also involve rating the assignment of items to scale categories as well as how favorable or unfavorable they are (as with equal-appearing intervals), how well they relate to the conceptual definitions and categories (latent traits), or their relative positivity or negativity and the extent to which the statements reflect the conceptual definition and categories (summated ratings).

With the RSPS, the developers asked content experts to rate items in terms of which categories the statements best represented and the strength of the association to the category. The original content validity rating scale appears in Figure 12.1. Note that the adult judges were asked to assign each of the proposed 49 items to one of Bandura's self-efficacy dimensions (or a default "other" category) and to rate how strongly they felt the statement fit the category. In effect, the judgmental review examines the degree of fit of items within categories. Beyond the actual rating of the items, the judgmental review provides insight into the clarity of the directions and the operational definitions of the categories. It is essential that these aspects of the task are clear so that the fit of the items is the only factor being measured. The developer hopes not only that the items are placed in the intended categories but also that the placements are robust ones.

Making subjective judgments about items is intended to help ensure that they, in fact, gauge the constructs we intend to measure. Put another way, such judgments can be effective in establishing the instrument's validity. It is important, however, to note that this attribute can never be absolutely established. It is rather a case to be made, and the greater the variety of evidence one can offer, the more persuasive that case becomes. To the expert judgment of items, for example, we might compare the scores on a newly developed instrument with those of an established measure, thus producing evidence of concurrent validity. We might demonstrate that scores on the new instrument correlate with future outcomes as evidence of predictive validity. We might document that scores are related to present circumstances in logical ways. Higher reading attitude scores should, in theory, be related to public library visits or the likelihood of having a library card—evidence of construct validity. The best affective instruments offer more than a single source of validation as the developers make their case to prospective users and to consumers of research employing those instruments.

Content Validity Rating Form
Self as Reader Scale

Instructions

1. Read the conceptual definitions for each category listed below. For each item stem, please fill in the category letter (A, B, C, D, E) that you believe each statement best fits. (Statements not fitting any category should be placed in Category E.)

2. Please indicate *how strongly you feel about your placement of the statement into the category* by filling in the appropriate rating number as follows:

     3—no question about it
     2—strongly
     1—not very sure

Categories	Conceptual Definitions
A. Performance	An individual's self-perception of ability based upon any of the following: —*past success or failure* with the task —the amount of *effort* necessary to be successful —the ease or *difficulty* of the task —task *persistence* —the *need for assistance* with the task —*patterns of progress* with the task —*seeking* or *avoiding* the task —belief in the *effectiveness of task-related instruction*
B. Observational Comparison	An individual's self-perception of ability based on observations of *how similar others (especially peers) perform the task*
C. Social Feedback	An individual's self-perception of ability based on *direct and indirect feedback from others*
D. Physiological States	An individual's self-perception of ability based on *bodily feedback* (such as comfort, calmness, trembling, and sweating) while engaged in the task
E. Other	Statement does not fit into any of the above categories

FIGURE 12.1. Original content validity rating form for the Reader Self-Perception Scale.

Identify a Response Format

The scaling technique selected will largely determine the response format. When using the latent-trait and Likert techniques, the format must allow the respondent to indicate relative degrees of agreeing, importance, or frequency, most often using a 5- or 6-point scale. The equal-appearing-intervals technique requires a format that enables respondents to select statements that describe the target being rated, whereas the semantic differential uses bipolar adjectives (antonyms) that appear at the ends of the response continuum.

Develop Directions for Responding

As noted previously, clear directions for responding to the instrument are critical, and precise wording becomes even more vital when young children represent the target group. Vague, incomplete, or overly complex directions can literally ruin the instrument. Just as the items should be written at an appropriate readability level for all respondents, the directions must be equally comprehensible. Respondents need to know exactly what they are supposed to do. To achieve this goal, it is useful to provide a supplementary oral script or set of guidelines for the administrator to follow. These instructions often go well beyond the written directions provided on the instrument. They might explain the purpose of the instrument, help put respondents at ease, elaborate on response options, elucidate sample items, encourage honesty and completeness, note any time limits, or describe what to do when problems occur during the task as well as when they have finished their work. As a cross-check, directions should be reviewed by colleagues and tested on members of the target group.

Prepare Draft and Final Instruments

Considerable care should be taken in formatting the instrument. The layout should make appropriate use of spacing and should be designed to be not only attractive but also fully functional. The size and color of the paper as well as the style and size of font can give the instrument a professional appearance. The arrangement of print on the page should lead the respondent effortlessly through the instrument. Directions should be clearly marked, and the scaling information should stand out visually and be stated in explicit terms. The focal point of any sample items should be completely familiar to the respondents, and an explanation linked to the response choices should be given. Again, a small number of colleagues should be consulted regarding the clarity of the directions, the readability of the items, and the ease of responding. A well-designed, easily read protocol signals to the respondent that the task is a serious one.

Conduct Cognitive Interviews

To determine whether the questions are being interpreted the way the developers intended, it is important to conduct cognitive interviews with sample population representatives (for an in-depth discussion, see Willis, 2005; Willis, Royston, & Bercini, 1991). There are two types of cognitive interview techniques: think-alouds and cognitive probing. In the first technique, participants are asked to think aloud (e.g., "Tell me what you are thinking") while answering survey questions. The researcher then takes note of how the participant not only interprets the question but also comes to a decision.

Results from think-alouds could indicate that a question is too confusing. For example, when a think-aloud was done with the SARA, a student stopped after reading the question, "How do you feel about getting a book or a magazine for a present?" He then said, "Well, is it a present I'm getting just because or is it a present that I get for my birthday? Because if it's just because then I'm happy, because I like it when people give me stuff. But if it's for my birthday, I'd rather get a video game. So I guess my answer is somewhere in the middle" (McKenna et al., 2009).

Because think-alouds encourage respondents to verbalize their thoughts while reading and responding to questions, they give the researcher insight into how answerable the question is. Unfortunately, the process can be both time consuming and awkward (Beatty & Willis, 2007). Instead, researchers can target respondents' interpretation of select questions by using cognitive probes. These probes are used by the researcher after a respondent has answered a question and shed insight into how the respondent interprets specific terms or phrases. There are six common cognitive probes: (1) comprehension/interpretation probes, (2) paraphrasing, (3) confidence judgments, (4) recall probes, (5) specific probes, and (6) general probes (Willis, 2005, p. 48).

We used cognitive probing techniques while developing the SARA (McKenna et al., 2009). One of our original questions had to do with how students feel about reading graphic novels. Almost all respondents had indicated very favorable attitudes toward reading them, and we soon found out why. Using a comprehension/interpretation probe, we asked respondents "What does the term *graphic novel* mean to you?" Although a few respondents answered "comic books," more than half said that graphic novels were books about sex. Although we were interested in measuring how students feel about the graphic novel format, we had to delete the question from our survey because it was not measuring what we thought it was measuring.

Gather and Analyze Pilot Data from Appropriate Samples

A major criticism of many existing affective measures is that they have not been tested with large enough samples to ensure stability. It is recommended that there be six to 10 times as many respondents as there are statements in the instrument in order to conduct a factor analysis (Gable, 1986). Although this number may seem large for a pilot study, these data represent crucial determinants of the validity, reliability, and scoring scheme of the instrument. The pivotal issue here, though, is not so much the size of the pilot sample but rather the variability and representativeness of its response patterns compared with the target population. When the response patterns do not match the larger population, both the factor structure and internal consistency of the scales will be compromised. A mismatch can occur if the heterogeneity of the target population is not adequately reflected in the sample. For example, an instrument designed to assess the reading attitudes of inner-city children at risk should not be piloted with a sample of affluent suburban children. Therefore, it is suggested that the sample vary with regard to ability, gender, curriculum track, school type, and the like. By the same token, once the results are finalized, they should not be generalized to other populations because the factor structure of the affective construct is likely to vary across different ages and grade levels. We suspect that the challenges of large-scale sampling represent a prevalent disincentive for developing high-quality affective measures, particularly for small-scale applications.

There are three key analyses associated with pilot data: item analysis, factor analysis, and reliability analysis. Item analyses involve response frequencies, percentages, measures of central tendency and variation, and correlations. Typically, items exhibiting unusually high or low means and small standard deviations warrant closer inspection and should be considered for elimination or revision. The items should also be significantly related to the scale score that represents all the valid items defining the scale. In turn, the categories or scales constituting the affective construct should probably be correlated with one another, but only moderately so. If the correlations are too high, it would indicate that the scales share so much variance as to be essentially measuring the same factor.

Factor analysis is a sophisticated statistical procedure that specifies which items are being responded to on a similar basis. The analysis presumes that there is a psychological reality to likenesses in response patterns that signal the presence of construct validity. Consequently, a factor analysis can tell the researcher which specific items belong to particular scales.

The output of a factor analysis resembles a matrix in which the columns equal the number of significant factors revealed by the procedure, and each item is represented by a unique row. For each item, a weight is calculated under each significant factor, and the researcher pays special attention to the largest positive coefficient in the row, assuming that the item is most related to, or loads on, this factor (see Table 12.2). Ideally, all the items presupposed to represent a particular scale will load most on that factor. In the case of the RSPS, the hope was that there would be four significant factors corresponding to Bandura's self-efficacy dimensions. For the ERAS, it was hoped that two significant factors would emerge corresponding to attitudes toward academic and recreational reading. Within each of these scales, the desired result was that all the items revealed by the judgmental review as being strongly associated with a particular scale or category would, in fact, show the highest factor loadings on the same factor. When the items cluster in this manner, the assumption is that the

TABLE 12.2. Factor Analysis of Reader Self-Perception Scale Items

Item	1	2	3	4
R10	**.706**	.103	.179	.152
R13	**.563**	.201	.205	.198
R15	**.705**	.131	.170	3-780E-02
R18	**.809**	8.943E-02	7.719E-02	.147
R19	**.706**	.109	.186	.196
R23	**.670**	.300	.194	−1.061E-02
R24	**.699**	.323	.189	.138
R27	**.657**	.308	.154	8.778E-02
R28	**.601**	.294	.239	6.449E-02
R4	.160	.211	**.695**	.290
R6	.230	2.594E-02	**.670**	7.633E-.02
R11	.265	5.502E-02	**.741**	.245
R14	.402	.129	**.497**	8.898E-02
R20	.300	.109	**.790**	.161
R22	.172	.380	**.663**	.229
R2	6.099E-02	.208	6.468E-02	**.780**
R3	.248	.123	.298	**.626**
R7	9.430E-02	.255	.301	**.568**
R9	.183	.220	.327	**.405**
R12	.368	9.111E-02	.225	**.597**
R17	.201	.177	.181	**.776**
R30	.141	.255	.303	**.527**
R31	.259	.198	.211	**.681**
R33	7.227E-02	.369	6.030E-02	**.605**
R5	3.554E-02	.284	.101	**.477**
R8	.246	**.581**	4.009E-02	.277
R16	.275	**.708**	6.126E-02	.309
R21	.177	**.682**	.211	1.412E-02
R25	.234	**.671**	.171	.124
R26	.262	**.754**	.119	.168
R29	.215	**.800**	9.396E-02	.205
R32	.176	**.768**	9.880E-02	.215

Note. Principal-component analysis with varimax rotation. **Boldface** indicates the highest factor loading for each item. Factor 1 = Progress; Factor 2 = Observational Comparison; Factor 3 = Social Feedback; Factor 4 = Physiological States.

instrument has psychometric integrity. Achieving a desirable factor structure is an extremely difficult task, and this fact, coupled with the numerous conceptual complexities associated with factor-analytic techniques (e.g., multivariate mathematical modeling, extraction methods, assumptions of models, rotational patterns), drives our recommendation to seek the services of an expert consultant when engaged in affective literacy instrument development.

Pilot data also need to be examined in terms of scale reliabilities. A reliability coefficient is calculated for each item cluster indicated by the factor analysis. The coefficient indicates the extent to which the items making up the scale are internally consistent. Cronbach's alpha is the statistic most commonly used for this computation (Cronbach, 1951). For affective measures, reliability coefficients of .70 or higher are considered to be acceptable (Gable, 1986), whereas coefficients of .90 are required for cognitive measures. Computer programs such as SPSS (Statistical Package for the Social Sciences) can indicate the alpha coefficient that would exist when a particular item is removed from the scale. As a general rule, the discarding of items with low item-to-scale correlations should increase the reliability for the remaining items, especially when the number of items per scale is limited.

Revise the Instrument

The analysis of the pilot data will point the developer to ways that the instrument could or should be modified. Usually this process involves deleting, adding, refocusing, or rewording items. These changes should improve the clarity of the items while increasing the validity and reliability of the instrument as a whole.

Conduct a Final Pilot Study

When the revisions to the instrument are extensive, it will be necessary to collect and analyze additional pilot data. Fortunately, careful attention to previous steps often precludes the need for a final pilot study. However, if any doubt remains, it is advisable to conduct the "extra" pilot because unstable factor structures and reliabilities will undermine the future usefulness of both large- and small-scale affective measures.

Produce the Final Instrument

Steps should again be taken to produce a fully functional, professional-looking final instrument. Most important, it should be reinspected for physical layout and ease of reading.

Conduct Additional Validity and Reliability Analyses

Once the factor structure appears to be stable and the items have been refined, the examination of validity should be extended by correlating the instrument with other known related measures and conducting additional factor analyses. For instance, the concurrent validity of the RSPS was established by correlating each of its subscales with the subscales of the ERAS. Moreover, various types of factor rotations can be undertaken to ensure that the factor structure will hold up in the future. Likewise, additional types of reliability evidence could be sought, such as stability/reliability, to check that the affective construct and its scales are constant over time. All this extended information contributes to a meaningful understanding of scores derived from the new affective instrument.

Consider Social Desirability

The term *social desirability* (SD) generally refers to the tendency to respond in a manner inconsistent with one's true feelings but, rather, consistent with what the respondent believes the examiner wishes. For example, an individual may harbor negative feelings toward reading but respond to the contrary on a written survey. SD poses a threat to the internal validity of affective instruments, and it behooves investigators to acknowledge the extent to which the tendency to produce SD responses may have influenced results. As an illustration of the SD tendency to portray one's feelings more positively than they truly are, consider the fourth item of the ERAS (McKenna & Kear, 1990, p. 630): "How do you feel about getting a book for a present?" Some students who know they would, in fact, be disappointed at this prospect may nevertheless respond affirmatively in order to please the teacher. Does this mean that ERAS scores are always inflated? Is the problem likely to occur more frequently at some grade levels? Most important, are there precautions an investigator can employ to mitigate the difficulty?

Screening for SD Bias. A quick way of screening for such bias is to identify children who have provided the most positive response to every item. Such a pattern does not, of course, confirm that they were dissembling (i.e., creating a false appearance), but it would be consistent with an SD tendency. Other evidence may support or refute the suspicion of false appearances, such as an individual child's classroom behavior with respect to reading.

From the standpoint of instrument development, it is important to consider first whether such a scale should be used at all. There is some evidence that the use of open-ended projective techniques, in which children respond to incomplete sentences, may reduce the effects of SD (Patnaik & Puhan, 1988). It may be more difficult for children to generate an SD response without the prompt that is available in a scale format. Projective instruments are more difficult to evaluate, however, and their results are not easy to aggregate for quantitative analysis. Moreover, because SD research has been mainly conducted in the field of clinical psychology with older, abnormal populations, it is difficult to infer much about the SD bias of instruments designed to measure literacy affect with normal children in classrooms.

Correlation with an SD Scale. An SD scale measures the tendency of an individual to produce socially desirable responses. If a literacy scale is being developed, one method of detecting an SD bias is to administer the new instrument together with an SD scale and to measure the degree to which the two are correlated. An investigator hopes for a zero correlation between the SD measure and the scale being developed.

In theory, the extent to which children may produce SD responses on a newly developed measure of literacy affect can be determined by simultaneously administering the new instrument with the Children's Social Desirability Questionnaire (CSDQ; Crandall, Crandall, & Katkovsky, 1965). If a significant Pearson product–moment correlation coefficient were obtained, then (1) the new instrument could be revised to reduce the correlation, (2) the coefficient could be reported as a limitation of subsequent investigations, or (3) a multiple regression analysis could be computed in order to remove the effects of SD. We suspect, however, that the SD bias among children tends to be overestimated by instruments like the CSDQ. Consider the following item: "Do you always enjoy yourself at a party?" The correct answer to this question is supposed to be "no." That is, the instrument developers assumed that to respond affirmatively means the child is dissembling. The reasoning is that no one has fun at every party one attends. Although this may be true for adults, whose more extensive experiences tend to include a boring party or two, the experiences of young children are likely to be quite different, so that it is clearly possible to provide an honest positive response. This unintended artifact may explain findings suggesting that SD bias tends to decline as children get older (Cruse, 1963; Walsh, Tomlinson-Keasey, & Klieger, 1974). The slight SD bias found in ERAS scores (McKenna, Stratton, & Grindler, 1992) can probably be safely discounted for this reason.

Prepare Documentation for the Instrument

If the affective instrument is intended for large-scale use, documentation for administration, scoring, and interpretation should be made available to colleagues through a test manual, website, or professional publication of some sort. The documentation should explain the pragmatic and theoretical rationale for the instrument, describe the instrument development process in sufficient detail to allow for replication, report validity and reliability data, and provide tables to enable score interpretation.

INSIGHTS AND LESSONS LEARNED

There is no question that we learned many valuable lessons as a result of our experiences developing affective literacy instruments. We realized very quickly, for instance, that when the wording of an item is not ideal, all manner of outcomes can occur and none of them are good. It has amazed us how a single less-than-perfect word choice can utterly compromise the measurement characteristics of an otherwise reasonable item. Without a doubt, the developer of an affective literacy measure must strive for explicitness because anything less will engender flawed response patterns. Beyond precision, the developer must carefully anticipate how items are going to be interpreted by respondents. The intent of an item must be absolutely straightforward because any lack of clarity, any potential ambiguity, any unexpected word connotation, or any deviation from the nature of the construct will invariably cause the item to perform poorly.

We also learned that one of the greatest challenges in affective instrument development involves getting the factor-analytic model to converge and the individual items to load properly. It is not uncommon for the factor structure to contain either fewer or more factors than the intended model, and there are often items that simply do not load on the expected scales. In the development of both the ERAS and the RSPS, the original factor structures did not manifest as originally hoped, and there were individual items whose factor loadings were undesirable. For instance, the ERAS factor structure initially indicated three factors, when the model called for two factors that represented attitudes toward academic and recreational reading, respectively.

The initial RSPS factor structure was even more problematic. Three factors came together as predicted (observational comparison, social feedback, and physiological states); however, the items identified in the judgmental review as belonging to the performance category failed to coalesce in anything even remotely close to a meaningful way. In this case, it was not a simple matter of some less-than-ideal word choices in the items. Something was fundamentally wrong with the category from a measurement standpoint. The developers struggled intensely with this psychometric dilemma, trying to find a solution that would galvanize the category. They came to realize that the problem stemmed from the multifaceted way that the performance dimension had been operationalized initially by Bandura (i.e., success, effort, ease, persistence, need for assistance, avoidance, progress, and instructional effectiveness) and later in the instrument's judgmental review. The items reflected dimensions that were simply too disparate to allow for the scale to converge. Clearly, a unifying concept was needed to align as many of those dimensions as possible. Fortunately, an insightful graduate student who assisted with the project, Sylvia Rosen, commented informally that most of the dimensions might fall under the single aspect of progress. That conclusion proved to be invaluable. The performance items were rewritten to force the progress dimension by contrasting past reading status with current reading status (e.g., "I can figure out words better than I could before" or "When I read, I don't have to try as hard as I used to"). Once these changes were made, a second piloting was conducted, and a new factor structure emerged. Four scales were indicated whose respective items clustered tightly within them, as hoped. This new structure occurred because the revamped progress scale finally converged.

Interestingly, using the concept of progress, as opposed to performance, made the development of the subsequent WSPS much easier (Henk, Bottomley, & Melnick, 1996; Henk et al., 1997). Likewise, the development of the new RSPS2 for students in grades 7 and above, which is nearing completion, also benefited from the progress versus performance differentiation (Melnick & Henk, 2005; Melnick, Henk, & Marinak, 2009). In the former instance, though, the factor structure took an unexpected turn; namely, two distinct dimensions of writing progress resulted: general progress (e.g., "My writing has improved") and specific progress (e.g., "The order of my sentences makes better sense now"). Without advance planning on the developers' part, a second scale whose characteristics were extremely desirable literally presented itself. The key point here is that it takes considerable time and energy, and sometimes good fortune, to achieve the desired factor structure and individual item factor loadings.

As we reflect on our experiences, we understand why it might be that high-quality affective literacy measures have tended to be in short supply. Certainly, the complexities of factor analysis techniques alone represent a deterrent; however, assuming that researchers are aware of the formal instrument development process, we believe that its intensity discourages interested researchers from embracing such a formidable challenge. Not only does faithfulness to the process require extensive labor, but it also requires an abundance of time. For researchers who want to use a specialized affective measure as only one narrow aspect of their work, the cost in time and energy might seem particularly exorbitant relative to the outcome. The seduction here would be to dilute the meticulous technical development of the measures in the interest of generating results in a more timely fashion. We believe that, in the interest of true disciplined inquiry, the additional quality assurances are more than worth the price; they are essential.

Our primary goal in writing this chapter has centered on advancing the field of literacy as it pertains to measuring affect. To that end, we have attempted to inform all readers about proper procedures for developing affective instruments. More specifically, we hope that at one important level our treatment of the topic here directly enhances the caliber of affective indicators literacy researchers will use in their work. At another level, we hope to sharpen the critiques of literacy professionals when they consume research literature involving affective measurement. At an intervening level, we hope to encourage the gatekeepers of the professional discourse on literacy to exercise the highest standards of evaluation when reviewing research whose findings have affective underpinnings and implications. Editors, reviewers, newsletter editors, Webmasters, and executive board members of professional organizations alike should insist that all affective claims are ultimately grounded in defensible measurement paradigms. In sum, by trying to raise the bar for affective measurement at all these levels, our fondest wish is that the field of literacy, and all its numerous stakeholders, will be better served.

REFERENCES

Ames, C., & Archer, J. (1988). Achievement goals in the classroom: Students' learning strategies and motivation processes. *Journal of Educational Psychology, 80*, 260–267.

Anderson, R. C., Fielding, L. G., & Wilson, P. T. (1988). Growth in reading and how children spend their time outside of school. *Reading Research Quarterly, 23*, 285–303.

Athey, I. (1985). Reading research in the affective domain. In H. Singer & R. B. Ruddell (Eds.), *Theoretical models and processes of reading* (3rd ed., pp. 527–557). Newark, DE: International Reading Association.

Bandura, A. (1977). Self-efficacy: Toward a unifying theory of behavioral change. *Psychological Review, 84*, 191–215.

Bandura, A. (1982). Self-efficacy mechanism and human agency. *American Psychologist, 37*, 122–147.

Beatty, P. C., & Willis, G. B. (2007). Research synthesis: The practice of cognitive interviewing. *Public Opinion Quarterly, 71*, 287–311.

Bottomley, D. M., Henk, W. A., & Melnick, S. A. (1997). Assessing children's views about themselves as writers using the Writer Self-Perception Scale. *The Reading Teacher, 51*, 286–296.

Bottomley, D. M., Truscott, D. M., Marinak, B. A., Henk, W. A., & Melnick, S. A. (1999). An affective comparison of whole language, literature-based, and basal literacy instruction. *Reading Research and Instruction, 38*(2), 115–129.

Cramer, E. H., & Castle, M. (Eds.). (1994). *Fostering the love of reading: The affective domain in reading education.* Newark, DE: International Reading Association.

Crandall, V. C., Crandall, V. J., & Katkovsky, W. (1965). A children's social desirability questionnaire. *Journal of Consulting Psychology, 29*, 27–36.

Cronbach, L. J. (1951). Coefficient alpha and the internal structure of tests. *Psychometrika, 16*, 297–334.

Cruse, D. B. (1963). Socially desirable responses in relation to grade level. *Child Development, 34*, 777–789.

de Vaus, D. A. (2002). *Surveys in social research* (5th ed.). New York: Routledge.

Dillman, D. A., Smyth, J. D., & Christian, L. M. (2009). *Internet, mail, and mixed-mode surveys: The tailored design method* (3rd ed.). Hoboken, NJ: Wiley.

Dweck, C., & Elliott, E. (1983). Achievement motivation. In P. Mussen & E. M. Hetherington (Eds.), *Handbook of child psychology: Vol. 4. Socialization, personality, and social development* (pp. 643–691). New York: Wiley.

Foertsch, M. A. (1992). *Reading in and out of school: Factors influencing the literacy achievement of American students in grades 4, 8, and 12 in 1988 and 1990* (Vol. 2). Washington, DC: National Center for Education Statistics.

Fowler, F. J. (2009). *Survey research methods* (4th ed.). Thousand Oaks, CA: Sage.

Gable, R. K. (1986). *Instrument development in the affective domain*. Boston: Kluwer-Nijhoff.

Gable, R. K., & Wolf, M. B. (1993). *Instrument development in the affective domain: Measuring attitudes and values in corporate and school settings* (2nd ed.). Boston: Kluwer-Nijhoff.

Gambrell, L. B., Palmer, B. M., Codling, R. M., & Mazzoni, S. A. (1996). Assessing motivation to read. *The Reading Teacher, 49*, 518–533.

Gronlund, N. (1993). *How to make achievement tests and assessments* (5th ed.). New York: Allyn & Bacon.

Groves, R. M., Fowler, F. J., Couper, M. P., Lepkowski, J. M., Singer, E., & Tourangeau, R. (2009). *Survey methodology* (2nd ed.). New York: Wiley.

Henk, W. A. (1999). *Exploring how kids feel about themselves as readers and writers*. Paper presented at the annual meeting of the Keystone State Reading Association, Hershey, PA.

Henk, W. A., Bottomley, D. M., & Melnick, S. A. (1996). Preliminary validation of the Writer Self-Perception Scale. In E. G. Sturtevant & W. M. Linek (Eds.), *Growing literacy: Eighteenth yearbook of the College Reading Association* (pp. 188–199). Harrisonburg, VA: College Reading Association.

Henk, W. A., Bottomley, D. M., Melnick, S. A., Truscott, D. M., Finke, J. A., Rickelman, R. G., et al. (1997). The Writer-Self Perception Scale: A cumulative validation update. In C. K. Kinzer, K. A. Hinchman, & D. J. Leu (Eds.), *Inquiries in literacy theory and practice: Forty-Sixth Yearbook of the National Reading Conference* (pp. 555–563). Chicago: National Reading Conference.

Henk, W. A., & Melnick, S. A. (1992). The initial development of a scale to measure "perception of self as reader." In C. Kinzer & D. Leu (Eds.), *Literacy research, theory, and practice: Views from many perspectives: Forty-First Yearbook of the National Reading Conference* (pp. 111–117). Chicago: National Reading Conference.

Henk, W. A., & Melnick, S. A. (1995). The Reader Self-Perception Scale (RSPS): A new tool for measuring how children feel about themselves as readers. *The Reading Teacher, 48*, 470–482.

Henk, W. A., & Melnick, S. A. (1998). Upper elementary-aged children's reported perceptions about good readers: A self-efficacy influenced update in transitional literacy contexts. *Reading Research and Instruction, 38*, 57–80.

Kear, D. J., Coffman, G. A., McKenna, M. C., & Ambrosio, A. L. (2000). Measuring attitude toward writing: A new tool for teachers. *The Reading Teacher, 54*, 10–23.

Knudson, R. E. (1991). Development and use of a writing attitude survey in grades 4 and 8. *Psychological Reports, 68*, 807–816.

Knudson, R. E. (1992). Development and application of a writing attitude survey for grades 1 to 3. *Psychological Reports, 70*, 711–720.

Knudson, R. E. (1993). Development of a writing attitude survey for grades 9 to 12: Effects of gender, grade, and ethnicity. *Psychological Reports, 73*, 587–594.

Lazarsfeld, P. F., & Henry, N. W. (1968). *Latent structure analysis*. Boston: Houghton Mifflin.

Likert, R. (1932). A technique for the measurement of attitudes. *Archives of Psychology, 140*, 152.

Mathewson, G. C. (1985). Toward a comprehensive model of affect in the reading process. In H. Singer & R. B. Ruddell (Eds.), *Theoretical models and pro-*

cesses of reading (3rd ed., pp. 841–856). Newark, DE: International Reading Association.

McKenna, M. C. (1986). Reading interests of remedial secondary school students. *Journal of Reading, 29,* 346–351.

McKenna, M. C. (2001). Development of reading attitudes. In L. Verhoeven & C. Snow (Eds.), *Literacy and motivation: Reading engagement in individuals and groups* (pp. 135–158). Mahwah, NJ: Erlbaum.

McKenna, M. C., Conradi, K., Lawrence, C., & Jang, B. G. (2009, December). *A national survey of adolescent attitudes toward reading.* Paper presented at the meeting of the National Reading Conference, Albuquerque, NM.

McKenna, M. C., & Dougherty Stahl, K. A. (2009). *Assessment for reading instruction* (2nd ed.). New York: Guilford Press.

McKenna, M. C., & Kear, D. J. (1990). Measuring attitude toward reading: A new tool for teachers. *The Reading Teacher, 43,* 626–639.

McKenna, M. C., Kear, D. J., & Ellsworth, R. E. (1995). Children's attitudes toward reading: A national survey. *Reading Research Quarterly, 30,* 934–956.

McKenna, M. C., Stratton, B. D., & Grindler, M. C. (1992, November). *Social desirability of children's responses to a reading attitude survey.* Paper presented at the annual meeting of the College Reading Association, St. Louis, MO.

McKenna, M. C., Stratton, B. D., Grindler, M. C., & Jenkins, S. (1995). Differential effects of whole language and traditional instruction on reading attitudes. *Journal of Reading Behavior, 27,* 19–44.

Melnick, S. A., & Henk, W. A. (2005, April). *Validation of a reading self-perception scale for use in secondary grades.* Paper presented at the annual conference of the American Educational Research Association, Montreal.

Melnick, S. A., Henk, W. A., & Marinak, B. A. (2009, October). *Validation of the Reader Self-Perception Scale 2 (RSPS2) for use in grades 7 and above.* Paper presented at the annual conference of the Northeastern Educational Research Association, Rocky Hill, CT.

Nell, V. (1988). *Lost in a book: The psychology of reading for pleasure.* New Haven, CT: Yale University Press.

Osgood, C. E., Suci, C. J., & Tannenbaum, P. H. (1957). *The measurement of meaning.* Urbana: University of Illinois Press.

Paris, S. G., & Oka, E. R. (1986). Children's reading strategies, metacognition, and motivation. *Developmental Review, 6,* 25–56.

Patnaik, S., & Puhan, B. N. (1988). Immunity of projective-inventories to social desirability. *Psychological Studies, 33*(2), 132–136.

Pitcher, S. M., Albright, L. K., DeLaney, C. J., Walker, N. T., Seunarinesingh, K., Mogge, S., et al. (2007). Assessing adolescents' motivation to read. *Journal of Adolescent and Adult Literacy, 50,* 378–396.

Purves, A. C., & Beach, R. (1972). *Literature and the reader: Research in response to literature, reading interests, and the teaching of literature.* Urbana, IL: National Council of Teachers of English.

Ragheb, M. G., & Beard, J. G. (1982). Measuring leisure attitude. *Journal of Leisure Research, 14,* 155–167.

Schunk, D. H. (1985). Self-efficacy and classroom learning. *Psychology in the Schools, 22,* 208–223.

Spaulding, V. (1992). The motivation to read and write. In J. W. Irwin & M. A.

Doyle (Eds.), *Reading/writing connections: Learning from research* (pp. 177–201). Newark, DE: International Reading Association.

Thurstone, L. L. (1931). The measurement of attitudes. *Journal of Abnormal and Social Psychology, 26,* 249–269.

Tourangeau, R., & Rasinski, K. A. (1988). Cognitive processes underlying context effects in attitude measurement. *Psychological Bulletin, 103,* 299–314.

Tourangeau, R., Rips, L. J., & Rasinski, K. A. (2000). *The psychology of survey response.* Cambridge, UK: Cambridge University Press.

Turner, J. C., & Paris, S. G. (1995). How literacy tasks influence children's motivation for literacy. *The Reading Teacher, 48,* 662–673.

Walberg, H. J., & Tsai, S. (1985). Correlates of reading achievement and attitude: A national assessment study. *Journal of Educational Research, 78,* 159–167.

Walsh, J. A., Tomlinson-Keasey, C., & Klieger, D. M. (1974). Acquisition of the social desirability response. *Genetic Psychology Monographs, 89,* 241–272.

Wigfield, A., & Guthrie, J. T. (1997). Relations of children's motivation for reading to the amount and breadth of their reading. *Journal of Educational Psychology, 89,* 430–432.

Willis, G. B. (2005). *Cognitive interviewing: A tool for improving questionnaire design.* Thousand Oaks, CA: Sage.

Willis, G. B., Royston, P., & Bercini, D. (1991). The use of verbal report methods in the development and testing of survey questionnaires. *Applied Cognitive Psychology, 5,* 251–267.

CHAPTER 13

Meta-Analysis

Adriana G. Bus
Marinus H. van IJzendoorn
Suzanne E. Mol

WHAT IS META-ANALYSIS?

Meta-analysis is the empirical analysis of empirical studies—that is, the quantitative analysis and synthesis of a set of related empirical studies in a well-defined domain. Similar to narrative reviews of extant literature on a specific hypothesis or theory, meta-analysis tests hypotheses and aims at uncovering trends and gaps in a field of inquiry. Different from narrative reviews, meta-analysis uses rigid, replicable analytic procedures. A common and defining characteristic of all meta-analytic approaches is the use of a specific set of statistical methods compared with the methods used in primary research. The reason is simple: In primary research the unit of analysis is the individual participant (or class or other group), whereas the unit of meta-analysis is the study result. Study results are usually based on different numbers of participants, and they are, therefore, point estimates with different precision and confidence boundaries (Mullen, 1989). It would be incorrect to give a significant correlation of .30 in a sample of 50 participants (confidence interval: [.02, .53]) the same weight as a correlation of .30 in a sample of 500 participants (confidence interval: [.22, .38]). Basically, however, meta-analytic research follows the same steps and standards as empirical research.

Meta-Analysis as a Step in a Research Program

Meta-analysis can be applied most fruitfully within research programs in which studies with similar designs or measures accumulate over the years.

270

In the spiral of research efforts, primary studies, secondary analyses, replications, and meta-analyses each play their crucial roles in promoting our understanding (see van IJzendoorn, 1994, for further details). In primary studies, data are collected to test a hypothesis derived from a well-articulated theory; the hypothesis often will be stated in the form: Variable X is associated with variable Y, or X is causally related to Y. In correlational or experimental designs, measures prototypical to assess X and Y are being used, and the results are, therefore, comparable across studies. If the results of the first empirical study on the association between X and Y are remarkable because of their effect size or direction, the next step in the spiral of research may be the secondary analysis of this first study. The secondary analysis uses the data as collected in the primary study, and through recoding with a different coding system and reanalyzing these data with different statistical methods, the original outcome is scrutinized.

The reanalysis may lead to falsification of the original outcome, as in Kamin's (1974) reanalysis of some of Burt's data on the heredity of intelligence in twins. In some cases, it may be difficult, however, to make the original data available for further study (Wolins, 1962). In any case, replication studies should then be performed to test the same hypothesis with new data that are collected in a different sample and with different designs or measures. If the number of replications increases, and if characteristics of replication studies vary, the meta-analytic approach is feasible to synthesize the literature and to test the effects of variations in study characteristics on the outcome of the studies. Because meta-analyses are based on numerous decisions about collecting, coding, and analyzing the pertinent studies, meta-analytic results, in their turn, need to be replicated as well (Lytton, 1994). Even if replications of meta-analyses yield the same results, they will never constitute the final argument in the spiral of scientific research. On the contrary, the most fruitful meta-analyses will lead to new hypotheses for further primary study (Eagly & Wood, 1994).

Figure 13.1 presents a process model of progress in research programs through different methodologies. Meta-analyses have not been positioned in a more crucial role than any other systematic form of inquiry. Meta-analyses are part of a series of connected steps in the description and explanation of human behavior that never reaches a final point (van IJzendoorn, 1994).

A BRIEF HISTORY OF META-ANALYSIS

A century ago Karl Pearson (1904) reported on one of the first meta-analytic combinations of the outcomes of a set of medical studies, and during the past few decades the approach became extremely popular in the so-called evidence-based medical science. It was the educational researcher Glass (1976) who coined the concept "meta-analysis" some 25 years ago

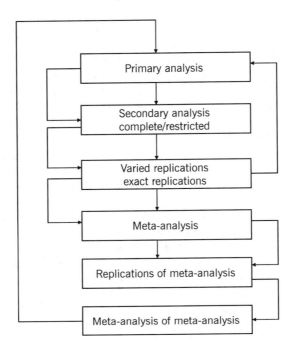

FIGURE 13.1. A process model of different types of replications. From van IJzendoorn (2002). Copyright 2002 by Bohn Stafleu Van Loghum. Adapted by permission.

and introduced it into the educational and behavioral science. He provided one of the most controversial examples of its application on psychotherapy studies, arguing that, in general, psychotherapy had considerable effect but that no specific treatment modality stood out (Smith & Glass, 1977).

To our knowledge, one of the first meta-analyses in reading was conducted by Kavale on correlates of reading: visual perceptual skills, auditory perceptual skills, and auditory–visual integration. He simply provided average correlations across studies between these predictors and success or failure in reading (Kavale, 1980, 1981, 1982; Kavale & Forness, 2000). During the past 15 years, meta-analysis has become widely used and hotly disputed in educational science. In fact, it seems that it has been applied on a much wider scale in education than in any other social or behavioral science. The reason may be that educational policy decisions (like medical decisions) are supposed to be based on a firm foundation of empirical data (Slavin, 2002). Every decade the number of scientific papers is doubling (Garfield, 1979), and it becomes impossible even for the specialists—let alone the policymakers and practitioners—to keep track of the literature in their own field. "What Works Clearinghouse" (WWC; see *ies.ed.gov/ncee/*

wwc) is set up to support educators and the U.S. Department of Education in making evidence-based recommendations about the effectiveness of programs, policies, and practices in a wide range of areas. More importantly, meta-analyses are increasingly being used to monitor new developments in any area of the social and behavioral sciences (Sutton & Higgins, 2008). In reading research more than 90 meta-analyses have been conducted, in particular on interventions to enhance the development of reading abilities in children (see Table 13.1).

In the past, narrative reviews were considered the royal road to the synthesis of literature, and some narrative reviews indeed were very powerful in shaping the future of a field of inquiry (e.g., Adams, 1990). In a narrative review of high standards, the author tries to make sense of the literature in a systematic and, at the same time, creative way. In formulating a hypothesis for review in a precise manner, and in collecting systematically the pertinent papers to address the issue, the narrative reviewer does not act much differently from the meta-analyst. It is in the stage of data analysis that the narrative and meta-analytic reviewer go separate ways. Narrative reviewers may have the focus of telling readers what the field has and has not investigated more than what has been found. Insofar as they focus on conceptual analysis of studies, these might not include numerical results at all—as in a review of ethnographies of home literacy practices in different communities. The meta-analysts, on the contrary, proceed in a statistically rigorous way, analyzing studies that include numerical results. Effect sizes, quantitative indexes of relations among variables, are used to compare and communicate the strength of the summarized research findings (Hedges, 2008).

Cooper and Rosenthal (1980) showed experimentally that narrative reviewers are more inclined to commit type II errors (i.e., they tend to not reject the null hypothesis although it should be rejected on statistical grounds). Cooper and Rosenthal asked 41 graduate students and senior researchers to review a set of seven studies on the association between sex and persistence in performing rather dull tasks. Half of the reviewers were randomly assigned to a course on meta-analysis. Seventy-three percent of the untrained narrative reviewers found no association; only 32% of the meta-analysts came to this conclusion. The correct outcome was that female participants are significantly more persistent in performing boring tasks than males. In particular, in cases in which studies show insignificant trends, the accumulated effect size across these studies tends to be underestimated. Besides, narrative reviews are also more vulnerable to psychological factors. Bushman and Wells (2001) had 280 undergraduate students review 20 fictional studies, of which the salience of the title and serial order were manipulated. Interestingly, salient titles for the positive results led to overestimates of the actual relation, whereas salient titles for the negative results led to an underestimation of the effect magnitude (Bushman & Wells, 2001). It should be noted that despite this potential bias, nar-

TABLE 13.1. Focal Questions in Meta-Analyses in the Domain of Reading

Book reading

- Is there a relation between parent–preschooler book reading and emergent and conventional reading? (Bus et al., 1995)
- Does book reading in schools affect oral language and reading skills? (Blok, 1999)
- Does dialogic reading intensify the effects of parent–child picture storybook sharing? (Mol, Bus, De Jong, & Smeets, 2008)
- Does trained interactive teacher behavior as a part of book reading improve young children's language and print-related skills? (Mol, Bus, & De Jong, 2009)
- Do shared-reading interventions impact young children's early literacy skills? (NELP, 2008, Chap. 4)

Phonemic awareness instruction

- Does phonemic awareness training affect learning-to-read processes in a positive and substantial way, and are programs combining phonemic awareness training with letters and words more effective? (Bus & van IJzendoorn, 1999)
- Is phonemic awareness instruction effective in helping children learn to read? If so, under what circumstances and for what children? (Ehri, Nunes, Willows, et al., 2001)

Preschool intervention

- Do preschool intervention programs cause a positive effect on reading achievement? (Goldring & Presbrey, 1986; NELP, 2008, Chap. 6)
- What are the effects of preschool programs on children's intellectual, socioemotional, and language abilities? (Leseman, Otter, Blok, & Deckers, 1998, 1999)

Beginning reading methods

- Are whole-language or language experience approaches more effective than basal readers? (Stahl & Miller, 1989)
- Is whole-language instruction effective compared with basal instruction for kindergarten to third-grade students with low socioeconomic status? (Jeynes & Littell, 2000)
- Does systematic phonics instruction help children learn to read more effectively than nonsystematic phonics instruction or instruction teaching no phonics (i.e., language activities)? (Camilli, Vargas, & Yurecko, 2003; Camilli, Wolfe, & Smith, 2006; Ehri, Nunes, Stahl, & Willows, 2001; Hammill & Swanson, 2006; Stuebing, Barth, Cirino, Francis, & Fletcher, 2008)

Reading comprehension instruction

- Does vocabulary instruction affect reading comprehension? (Stahl & Fairbanks, 1986)
- Does sentence-combining promote reading comprehension? (Fusaro, 1992)
- Does instruction in question asking affect reading comprehension? (Rosenshine, Meister, & Chapman, 1996)
- Which forms of comprehension instruction improve reading comprehension? (National Reading Panel, 2000)
- How effective is repeated reading on comprehension, and what are essential instructional components? (Therrien, 2004)
- Does enhancing students' reading engagement increase reading comprehension? (Guthrie, McRae, & Klauda, 2007)
- What is the role of classroom discussion on students' text comprehension? (Murphy, Wilkinson, Soter, Hennessey, & Alexander, 2009)

(cont.)

TABLE 13.1. *(cont.)*

Acquiring vocabulary through reading

- Does instruction in deriving meaning from context improve skills to derive meaning from context? (Fukkink & De Glopper, 1998)
- Do children incidentally derive new words from texts? (Swanborn & De Glopper, 1999)

Effects of multimedia

- Does the Lightspan program (computer games to improve school-based achievement) improve reading comprehension, reading vocabulary, sounds/letters, and word reading? (Blanchard & Stock, 1999)
- How effective are computer-assisted instruction programs in the phase of beginning reading? (Blok, Oostdam, Otter, & Overmaat, 2002)
- What is the effectiveness of information and communication technology on the teaching of spelling? (Torgerson & Elbourne, 2002)
- How effective is the use of technology (e.g., electronic books) in language education and language learning? (Zhao, 2003; Zucker, Moody, & McKenna, 2009)
- What is the effect of using glosses (e.g., level of instruction, text type) in multimedia learning environments for enhancing L2 reading comprehension? (Abraham, 2008; Taylor, 2006)
- What is the impact of digital tools on the reading performance of middle school students? (Moran, Ferdig, Pearson, Wardrop, & Blomeyer, 2008)

Other aspects of reading instruction

- Does some form of guided oral reading stimulate reading achievement? (National Reading Panel, 2000)
- What is the impact of summer school programs (i.e., remedial, acceleration) on students' reading skills? (Cooper, Charlton, Valentine, & Muhlenbruck, 2000)
- Do cognitive paradigms targeting domain-specific learning activities improve effectiveness of reading instruction? (Seidel & Shavelson, 2007)

Bilingual education

- Does learning to read in the native language promote reading achievement in the second language? (Greene, 1997; Rolstad, Mahoney, & Glass, 2005; Slavin & Cheung, 2005; Willig, 1985)

Instruction of children with reading disabilities

- What is the overall effectiveness of sight word teaching for individuals with moderate and severe disabilities? (Browder & Xin, 1998)
- Does direct instruction yield higher effect sizes than strategy instruction in groups with learning disabilities? (Swanson, 1999; Swanson & Hoskyn, 1998)
- Do studies using strategy instruction or direct instruction yield higher effect size estimates than studies using competing models? (Swanson & Sachse-Lee, 2000)
- Do instructional components predict positive outcomes for adolescents with learning disabilities on measures of higher order processing? (Swanson, 2001)
- How effective is the Reading Recovery program for low-performing first-grade students? (D'Agostino & Murphy, 2004)
- Does treatment to improve expressive or receptive phonology, syntax, or vocabulary affect children with primary developmental speech and language disorders? (Law, Garrett, & Nye, 2004)
- What is the supplemental effect of out-of-school programs on reading achievement of at-risk students from kindergarten to high school? (Lauer et al., 2006)

(cont.)

TABLE 13.1. *(cont.)*

- Do metacognitive strategies improve the reading comprehension levels of students with learning disabilities? (Sencibaugh, 2007)
- How do interventions targeting decoding, fluency, vocabulary, and comprehension influence comprehension outcomes for secondary students with reading difficulties? (Edmonds et al., 2009)

Effects of grouping and tutoring

- Does one-to-one tutoring on reading promote reading skills? (Elbaum, Vaughn, Hughes, & Moody, 2000)
- Is effect size of reading instruction related to grouping format (e.g., pairing, small groups)? (Elbaum et al., 1999; Elbaum, Vaughn, Hughes, Moody, et al., 2000)
- Is parental involvement related to children's academic achievement (i.e., reading)? (Fan & Chen, 2001; Jeynes, 2002, 2005; NELP, 2008, Chap. 5; Sénéchal & Young, 2009)
- Do volunteer tutoring programs in elementary and middle school improve reading skills? (Ritter, Barnett, Denny, & Albin, 2009; Torgerson, King, & Sowden, 2002)

Effects of school organization

- Do second graders who have received 2 years of instruction in smaller classes score significantly higher in reading than second graders in larger classes? (McGiverin, Gilman, & Tillitski, 1989)
- Does reading achievement decline over summer holiday? (Cooper, Nye, Charlton, & Lindsay, 1996)
- Does homework improve academic achievement (i.e., reading)? (Cooper, Robinson, & Patall, 2006)

Processes explaining reading (dis)abilities

- Are auditory perception skills related to reading? (Kavale, 1980, 1981)
- Is visual perception an important correlate of reading achievement? (Kavale, 1982)
- Which of six variables (language, sensory skills, behavioral-emotional, soft neurological, IQ, and teacher ratings) provide the best early prediction of later reading difficulties? (Horn & Packard, 1985)
- Do dyslexic readers and normal readers differ in terms of phonological skill despite equivalent word-recognition abilities? (Herrmann, Matyas, & Pratt, 2006; van IJzendoorn & Bus, 1994)
- Do measures that tax the processing as well as the storage resources of working memory predict reading comprehension better than measures that tax only the storage resources? (Daneman & Merikle, 1996)
- Is a regularity effect also present in a group with learning disabilities? (Metsala, Stanovich, & Brown, 1998)
- Do children with learning disabilities differ from normal-achieving children in immediate memory performance, and does this difference continue? (O'Shaughnessy & Swanson, 1998)
- Do underachieving students with and without a learning disabilities label differ in reading performance? (Fuchs, Fuchs, Mathes, & Lipsey, 2000)
- Do children with reading disabilities and low achievers share a common deficit in phonological processing, memory, and visual-spatial reasoning? (Hoskyn & Swanson, 2000)
- What is the relative importance of auditory and visual perception in predicting reading achievement? (Kavale & Forness, 2000)
- Is it valid to use IQ discrepancy for the classification of reading disabilities? (Steubing et al., 2002)

(cont.)

TABLE 13.1. *(cont.)*

- Which brain areas are consistently activated during aloud single word-reading tasks? (Turkeltaub, Eden, Jones, & Zeffiro, 2002)
- Are rapid naming and phonological awareness as strong predictors of word reading as related reading abilities? (Swanson, Trainin, Necoechea, & Hammill, 2003)
- What is the influence of school mobility in the United States on reading achievement in the elementary grades? (Mehana & Reynolds, 2004)
- Can the relative variability of psychophysical performance in dyslexic readers compared with normal readers be attributed to general nonsensory difficulties? (Roach, Edwards, & Hogben, 2004)
- Does sampling affect studies linking genes to complex phenotypes such as reading ability/disability and related componential processes? (Grigorenko, 2005)
- What are the patterns of convergence in neuroanatomical circuits underlying phonological processing in reading alphabetic words and logographic characters? (Tan, Laird, Li, & Fox, 2005)
- Are gender differences present in reading achievement, and do these change with age? (Lietz, 2006; Lynn & Mikk, 2009)
- What is the magnitude and consistency of balance difficulties in the dyslexia population, and which sampling or stimulus characteristics modulate this effect? (Rochelle & Talcott, 2006)
- Do children with and without specific language impairments show performance differences in nonword repetition? (Graf Estes, Evans, & Else-Quest, 2007)
- What are the links between school entry skills/school readiness and later school reading achievement? (Duncan et al., 2007; La Paro & Pianta, 2000)
- What is the role of working memory measures (e.g., task modality, the attentional control involved) in distinguishing between performance of poor and good reading comprehenders? (Carretti, Borella, Cornoldi, & De Beni, 2009)

rative reviews remain indispensable, in particular in those areas in which a restricted number of empirical studies have been conducted or in the absence of strong research programs that unify the empirical approaches and make them comparable for meta-analytic purposes. Researchers sometimes persist in conducting a meta-analysis even when the exhaustive literature search results in the inclusion of only two or three studies (e.g., Sénéchal & Young, 2008; Torgerson, Porthouse, & Brooks, 2003; Zucker, Moody, & McKenna, 2009).

STAGES AND QUALITY STANDARDS IN META-ANALYSIS

Meta-analysis and primary studies are structured in similar ways. In fact, meta-analysts should proceed through the same stages as the primary researchers (Cooper, 1982). The meta-analysis should start with the formulation of a specific, theoretically relevant conceptual framework. Its domain should be clearly defined, and the central meta-analytic question should be theoretically derived and meaningful ("precise and relevant hypothesis"). When a meta-analyst is not sensitive to such substantive issues, a meta-analysis can become a pointless, merely statistical exercise (Littell, Corcoran, & Pillai, 2008). For example, when synthesizing the effects of interventions on struggling readers' reading comprehension, the validity and/or practical use of the summary effects can be questioned when interventions with a focus on fluency, decoding, comprehension, and multiple components are heaped together (see Edmonds et al., 2009). That is, even though the dependent measure is comparable and the target groups are similar, it is difficult to disentangle the kind of intervention that might support the comprehension skills of children with reading disabilities, especially when the number of studies per subtype is less than four.

In the next stage, the meta-analyst should systematically collect the relevant published as well as unpublished literature from at least three different sources. The "snowball" method (using references lists from key papers in the field), the "invisible college" approach (using key figures in the field to collect recent or unpublished materials), and computer searches of subject indexes such as ERIC, PsycInfo, Medline, Proquest UMI Dissertations, and Google Scholar or citation indexes such as SSCI or SCI may be used in a multimethod combination.

In some meta-analytic approaches, selection of studies is based on the idea that only randomized experimental designs produce valid findings to be taken seriously. The WWC (2008), for example, uses eligibility screens in which randomization, level of attrition, and equivalence of treatment and control groups are taken into account to select studies that meet the evidence standards fully or with reservations. The National Reading Panel (NRP) also objects to inclusion of all studies regardless of design features. Restrictions of the type of papers to be included, however, may imply an untenable reduction of the available evidence. For instance, the NRP discards the many correlational investigations in the area of reading research (NRP, 2000; Williams, 2001), which means a loss of potentially important information. It should also be noted that in this respect the meta-analytic method is basically indifferent: The central hypothesis should decide about the feasibility of selection criteria, and when this hypothesis is not stated in strictly causal terms there is no reason to leave correlational studies aside. Furthermore, the impact of the quality of research on effect sizes can be examined by testing whether the overall effect is influenced by the presence of studies with other designs than randomized controlled trials (Rosenthal, 1995). In this respect, the exhaustive search for pertinent literature is preferred compared with the best evidence approach (Slavin, 1986), in which only the qualitatively sound studies would be allowed to enter a meta-analysis. Because of their emphasis on explanation of variability in effect sizes, in recent meta-analytic approaches it is preferred to test whether quality of research (which always is a matter of degree and a matter of different strengths and weaknesses) explains variation in study results in order to make the process of study selection and evaluation transparent and to maximize the power of the analyses. Mol, Bus, and De Jong (2009), for instance, created a scale to score whether the researchers checked the use of trained techniques in the experimental group, the quality of reading sessions within the control group, and the actual frequency of book reading in the experimental and the control groups. Experimental designs outperformed quasi-experiments on the scale, but intervention outcomes were not affected by the experiment fidelity score nor did quasi-experiments reveal higher effect sizes than true experiments for children's language and literacy measures.

The basic problem to be faced in this stage of the meta-analysis is the "file drawer" problem (Rosenthal, 1991). Primary researchers know that it is easier to get papers published in which they report significant results than to guide papers into print with null results regardless of the quality of the study (Begg, 1994). This publication bias may even lead to the unfortunate situation that the majority of papers remain in the file drawers of disappointed researchers, whereas only a minority of papers with significant results are published (Cohen, 1990). Average or combined effect sizes of published papers may, therefore, present an inflated picture of the real state of the art in a specific field. The number of unpublished papers with null findings that are needed to make the meta-analytic outcome insignificant can be estimated (the "fail-safe number"; Rosenthal, 1991). A publication bias can be visually inspected by a funnel plot, which is a scatter plot of the effect size against sample size that will be skewed and show asymmetry (i.e., due to a lack of small effect sizes) when a publication bias is present (Lipsey & Wilson, 2001). The file drawer problem may suggest that a priori selection of only published papers is not always warranted. Although published studies have been subjected to more or less thorough reviewing procedures and, therefore, seem to carry more quality weight than unpublished studies, the reasons for remaining unpublished may be unrelated to quality. In many cases, it is, therefore, better to collect all studies regardless of origin or status and to analyze post hoc whether publication status makes a difference in combining effect sizes ("unbiased and exhaustive set of papers"). To assess the likely impact of a publication bias, the "trim and fill" method can be used to estimate the unbiased effect size, by estimating the number of missing studies from an asymmetrical funnel plot and calculating an adjusted point estimate and variance (Duval & Tweedie, 2000a, 2000b).

Studies may report effects on several dependent measures for similar outcome measures. To avoid a situation in which studies with more results have a greater impact, the effect sizes should be aggregated within studies and domains. For example, when a study reports outcomes for one receptive and two expressive vocabulary measures, the expressive outcomes are aggregated in a first step (domain) and combined with the effect size of the single receptive measure in a second step in order to calculate a vocabulary composite per study. Separate meta-analyses can be conducted to examine differential treatment effects per outcome measure (e.g., Does dialogic reading affect expressive vocabulary more strongly than receptive vocabulary skills?; see Mol, Bus, De Jong, & Smeets, 2008) as long as each study contributes one effect size to each analysis. Creating a rather broad composite such as "academic achievement," in which a variety of reading, mathematical, and/or grade-related measures are aggregated, might limit the interpretation of specific treatment effects. Another complicating factor may be that experiments include two or more interventions but only one control group. Effect sizes are dependent if the same control group is used to calculate the effect sizes for each treatment (e.g., Ehri, Nunes, Willows, et al., 2001). Gleser and Olkin (1994) state that in multiple-treatment studies "the treatments may all be regarded as instances or aspects of a common treatment construct." Furthermore, they state that "there is strong reason a priori to believe that a composite effect size of treatment obtained by combining the end point effect sizes would adequately summarize the effect of treatment" (p. 351). Another, more pragmatic solution of the multiple-interventions problem is to divide the sample size of the control group in the same number of subgroups as there are interventions in order to avoid the situation in which control subjects count for more than one unit of analysis.

Studies may use a variety of outcome measures to test effects, which makes outcomes difficult to interpret. For instance, Stahl, McKenna, and Pagnucco (1994) noted that whole-language researchers increasingly preferred to use attitude toward reading rather than direct measures of performance assessment. Whole-language advocates assert that the key to learning language well rests in enjoying the learning process. They state that because whole language constitutes a more natural way of learning language, students will enjoy learning more and hence learn more. For instance, the study by Jeynes and Littell (2000) includes various attitude measures, and it is unclear what nonattitudinal effects are measured. The lower effect sizes for reading achievement measures indicates that measures such as attitude toward reading produce larger effect sizes than direct measures of performance.

The retrieved papers, dissertations, and unpublished documents are considered to be the raw data to which a coding system is applied to produce the variables to be used in the analysis. The application of the coding system should be tested for intercoder reliability. The coding system contains potential moderator variables that can be used to explain the variability of the effect sizes in the specific set of studies. The variables in the coding system should, therefore, be theoretically relevant and constitute pertinent moderator hypotheses. In view of the relatively small number of studies included in most meta-analyses, the coding system should not be too extended. If potential moderators exceed the number of studies, inflated meta-analytic outcomes may be the nonreplicable result ("reliable and concise coding system"). On the other hand, if the number of studies per moderator is too small, the power will be too low to detect meaningful differences in effects across subgroups (Hedges & Pigott, 2004). We suggest that a minimum of four (Bakermans-Kranenburg, van IJzendoorn, &

Juffer, 2003; Mol et al., 2008, 2009) or five (Seidel & Shavelson, 2007) studies per subgroup is needed to reliably interpret any contrast.

Data analysis often consists of three steps (Mullen, 1989). First, the central tendency of the study results is computed (i.e., the combined effect size). Because p values heavily depend on the number of observations, recent meta-analyses focus on the combined standardized differences between the means of the experimental and the control groups. The statistic used to assess the effectiveness of a treatment or other variable is the effect size (ES), d, which measures how much the mean of the treatment group exceeds the mean of the control group in standard deviation units. ES expresses how many standard deviation units treatment groups differ from control groups without treatment. An ES of 1.0 indicates that the treatment group mean is 1 standard deviation higher than the control group mean, whereas an ES of 0 indicates that treatment and control groups mean are identical. A mean effect, of which the precision is addressed by the 95% confidence interval (CI), is considered significant if the CI does not include zero. Differences between estimates can be interpreted as significant when the CIs do not overlap. According to Cohen (1988), an ES of $d = 0.20$ is considered small, an ES of $d = 0.50$ moderate, and an ES of $d = 0.80$ or above large ($r = .10$ is small, $r = .30$ is moderate, $r = .50$ is large). Translated into percentiles, $d = 0.20$ indicates that the treatment has moved the average child from the 50th to the 58th percentile; $d = 0.50$ indicates that the treatment has moved the child, on average, to the 69th percentile; $d = 0.80$ indicates that the treatment has moved the child, on average, to the 79th percentile. As an alternative, Rosenthal and Rubin (1982) suggested the binominal ES display (BESD), which indicates the change in predictive accuracy attributable to the relationship in question and is computed from the formula .50 ± ($r/2$). The BESD shows the extent to which prediction is enhanced (i.e., the percentage increase in prediction) with the use of intervention X to predict reading skill Y (for details, see later discussion).

A weighted ES is mostly used to adjust for the bias resulting from small sample sizes (i.e., the tendency of studies with small samples to overestimate effects). Unweighted ds are sometimes presented to provide information about the direction of biases related to sample size. The ES can be computed on the basis of the standard deviations of the control group (Glass, 1976), the pooled standard deviations (Rosenthal, 1991), or the pooled variance (Hedges & Olkin, 1985). Cohen's d, for instance, is calculated as the difference between control and experimental treatment posttest mean scores (partialed for the influence of pretest scores if information is available) divided by the pooled standard deviation. Alternatively, the test statistics (F, t, χ^2) can be transformed into an ES (Rosenthal, 1991). In practice, different strategies do not seem to make a substantial difference (Johnson, Mullen, & Salas, 1995).

Second, the variability of the results around this central tendency is assessed, and outliers as well as homogeneous subsets of studies are identified. To determine whether a set of ds shares a common ES, a homogeneity statistic—Q, which approximates chi-square distribution with k − 1 degrees of freedom, where k is the number of ESs—can be computed. Homogeneity analysis compares the amount of variance exhibited by a set of ESs with the amount of variance expected if only sampling error is operating. I-squared (I^2), another indicator of homogeneity, describes the impact of heterogeneity on a meta-analysis by measuring the degree of inconsistency between studies. Values that exceed 70% should invite caution about the homogeneity of the mean effect (Petticrew & Roberts, 2006). If sets of study results remain heterogeneous, combined ES computed on the basis of the fixed model may be biased estimates; that is, it cannot be concluded that they are a sample from the same population, and a random model should be preferred (Hedges, 1994). In the random-effects model, studies are also weighted by the inverse of its variance, but, in addition, it accounts for within-study error as well as between-study variation in true effects (Borenstein, Hedges, Higgins, & Rothstein, 2009). If a distribution of study results is extremely skewed and shows several outlying values, the average ES does not adequately represent the central tendency. Inflated meta-analytic findings may result from ignoring heterogeneity in study outcomes, and the (more conservative) random model may lead to lower estimates for the combined ES as well as larger confidence boundaries (Hedges, 1994).

Third, through a moderator analysis, the meta-analysts try to explain the variability on the basis of study characteristics. A significant chi-square indicates that the study features significantly moderate the magnitude of ESs. For example, intervention studies with randomized designs may, on average, yield smaller effects than those without randomization. Mostly the analyses do not include tests of interactions between moderator variables because the number of comparisons is insufficient in many cases. It should be noted that in meta-analytic as well as in primary studies every subject or sample should be counted independently from each other and only once. That is, if a study presents more than one ES for the same hypothesis, these ESs should be combined within the study before it is included in the overall meta-analysis ("independent and homogeneous ESs").

The interpretation of the size of the combined effects is a matter of much debate (McCartney & Rosenthal, 2000). In a meta-analysis, van IJzendoorn and Bus (1994) showed that a powerful explanation of dyslexia, the phonological deficit hypothesis, explains only 6% of the variance in dyslexia ($d = 0.48$), which is about a 0.5 standard deviation difference between the experimental and the control groups. Bus, van IJzendoorn, and Pellegrini (1995) showed that the association between preschool storybook sharing and later literacy was even stronger ($d = 0.59$), explaining about 8% of the variance in children's literacy skills. A correlation of .28 between book sharing and reading may seem a rather modest outcome. However, in terms of the BESD (Rosenthal, 1991), this effect is sizable.

The BESD is defined as the change in success ratio because of an intervention. The BESD shows the extent to which prediction is enhanced (i.e., the percentage increase in prediction) with the use of intervention X to predict reading skill Y. If we equal the combined ES $d = 0.59$ with an $r = .28$, the success ratio in the experimental group would be: $.50 + (.28/2) = .64$; the success ratio in the control group would be $.50 - (.28/2) = .36$. It should be noted, therefore, that it certainly can make a tremendous difference in the lives of young children whether or not they are read to by their parent. The difference between the experimental and the control groups would amount to a substantial difference if we translate this outcome to the millions of children who may profit from book reading (Rosenthal, 1991). Taking into account that experimental studies revealed outcomes similar to correlational/longitudinal/retrospective studies, this meta-analysis provides a clear and affirmative answer to the question of whether or not storybook reading is one of the most important activities for developing the knowledge required for eventual success in reading. Therefore, parental storybook reading should be recommended because in terms of BESD it makes a difference for many thousands of preschoolers ("BESD interpretation of ES"). In the same vein, phonological deficit is correctly considered as a main cause of dyslexia.

The basic stages and quality standards of a meta-analysis may be summarized as follows:

1. Hypothesis formulation
   - *Precise and relevant hypothesis*
2. Retrieval and coding of studies
   - *Unbiased and exhaustive set of papers*
   - *Reliable and concise coding system*
3. Analysis of study results and characteristics
   a. Central tendency
   b. Variability
   c. Moderators
   - *Independent and homogeneous ESs*
4. Interpretation of meta-analytic outcomes
   - *BESD interpretation of ES*

WHAT KINDS OF QUESTIONS ARE APPROPRIATE FOR META-ANALYSIS?

Review of Meta-Analyses in Reading Research

In his comprehensive book *Progress in Understanding Reading*, Keith Stanovich (2000) states that we make progress by accumulating evidence from a host of interlocking studies, each of which may be of fairly low diagnosticity but that, taken together, present a coherent picture and warrant firm conclusions. He concludes: "We are a science that is custom-made for meta-analysis" (p. 3). To find out to what extent the advice of one of the most influential reading researchers was followed, we listed the meta-analyses in the various domains of reading in Table 13.1 on pages 274–277. We used a computer search of PsycInfo and ISI, with the key words *literacy and meta-analysis* and *reading and meta-analysis* to trace the relevant meta-analyses. In 2003, when the first version of this chapter was written, about 40 studies were detected since 1982. Even after excluding book chapters and dissertations, an additional set of about 60 meta-analyses on reading resulted from a new search in 2009 (see Table 13.1 for a summary of the reviews we could trace). Assuming that since 1966 approximately 130,000 research studies on reading have been conducted, with perhaps another 15,000 appearing before that time (NRP, 2000), only a small part of all available studies is meta-analyzed. The 90 meta-analyses cover at most 5% of all available studies on reading.

Meta-analysis appears a useful tool to test theories of reading problems, as Metsala, Stanovich, and Brown (1998) showed. Their synthesis of research counters a prediction based on classic dual-route models of word recognition that children with reading disabilities show an absent or reduced regularity effect even though separate studies support this hypothesis. The regularity effect in reading has been defined as the observation of superior performance in recognition of regular versus exception words. It is assumed that if the phonological route is less available as a result of impairment, the advantage for regular words should be eliminated or reduced. Children with learning disabilities should prefer a direct visual route without phonological mediation above an indirect route through phonological processing that involves stored spelling–sound correspondences in order to circumvent phonological coding. The synthesis of a series of small-scale studies is not in line with the dual-route model. It shows that both individuals with reading disabilities and normally achieving readers show a regularity effect and that ESs indicating higher scores on regularly spelled words were not related to reading level. Regardless of the reading level, regularly spelled words are easier to read than irregularly spelled words. Metsala and colleagues reported heterogeneity in ESs that cannot be explained as an effect of reading level. Carrying out secondary analyses on this data set with Comprehensive Meta-Analysis (Statistical Solutions Limited), the ESs appear to be homogeneous within the groups of normally developing and children with learning disabilities.

Even though not all individual studies report a regularity effect for children with reading problems, the results combined across the studies revealed a regularity effect. This finding is similar to results from the van IJzendoorn and Bus (1994) and Herrmann, Matyas, and Pratt (2006) meta-analyses on the pseudoword deficit of individuals with reading problems. That is, even when individual studies did not report a significant pseudoword reading deficit for participants with reading disabilities relative to reading level–matched participants, overall the studies did show this pattern when the results were combined across studies. The synthesis of studies on the regularity effect does not harmonize with the available theoretical models, and thus new models and further research are required to understand reading problems. The finding that both groups are susceptible to the regularity effect is inconsistent with the dual-route models of word reading but consistent with emerging connectionist models and their empirical findings on reading disability.

Most meta-analyses on reading synthesize the results of intervention studies. In an attempt to settle an ongoing debate on the best method to teach beginning reading skills, studies contrast whole language with basals (Jeynes & Littell, 2000; Stahl & Miller, 1989), systematic phonics instruction with no or incidental instruction in phonics (Ehri, Nunes, Stahl, & Willows, 2001), or reading instruction in the first or second language for bilingual children (Greene, 1997; Rolstad, Mahoney, & Glass, 2005; Slavin & Cheung, 2005). Other studies synthesize effects of special measures: programs to instruct phonemic awareness (Bus & van IJzendoorn, 1999; Ehri, Nunes, Willows, et al., 2001), guided oral reading (NRP, 2000), book reading in groups (Blok, 1999; Mol et al., 2009), question generation (NRP, 2000), repeated reading (Therrien, 2004), reading engagement (Guthrie, McRae, & Klauda, 2007), classroom discussion (Murphy, Wilkinson, Soter, Hennessey, & Alexander, 2009), or learning to derive word meaning from context (Fukkink & De Glopper, 1998). Furthermore, it is evaluated how direct and strategy instructions support groups with learning disabilities (Edmonds et al., 2009; Sencibaugh, 2007; Swanson & Sachse-Lee, 2000) and whether one-to-one tutoring in reading (D'Agostino & Murphy, 2004; Elbaum, Vaughn, Hughes, & Moody, 2000; Ritter, Barnett, Denny, & Albin, 2009; Torgerson, King, & Sowden, 2002) or instruction in small groups especially stimulates these children's reading development (Elbaum, Vaughn, Hughes, & Moody, 1999; Elbaum, Vaughn, Hughes, Moody, & Schumm, 2000). Few studies test effects of school organization on reading achievement: class size (McGiverin, Gilman, & Tillitski, 1989) or summer holiday (Cooper, Nye, Charlton, & Lindsay, 1996). The effectiveness of children's learning experiences outside the classroom is examined by evaluating studies on parent involvement (National Early Literacy Panel [NELP], 2008; Sénéchal & Young, 2008) and out-of-school programs (Cooper, Charlton, Valentine, & Muhlenbruck, 2000; Lauer et al., 2006). Only a few studies focus on interventions in the preschool ages and test effects of book reading in the family (Bus et al., 1995; Mol et al., 2008; NELP, 2008) or preschool intervention programs (Goldring & Presbrey, 1986; Leseman, Otter, Blok, & Deckers, 1998, 1999; NELP, 2008). Recently, the increasing number of single studies that explore the opportunities of the computer for language instruction made some (preliminary) meta-analyses possible (Blok, Oostdam, Otter, & Overmaat, 2002; Moran, Ferdig, Pearson, Wardrop, & Blomeyer, 2008; Torgerson & Elbourne, 2002; Zucker et al., 2009).

Not all research domains are ready for meta-analysis despite numerous studies. The NRP did not succeed in finding sufficient studies to meta-analyze effects of all formal efforts to increase the amounts of independent or recreational reading that children engage in, including sustained silent reading programs, because of a lack of studies that meet NRP standards such as experimental or quasi-experimental designs, including a control group (NRP, 2000). They concluded that it would be difficult to interpret the small collection of studies that remained as representing clear evidence that encouraging students to read more actually improves reading achievement. Only three of the remaining studies reported any clear reading gains from encouraging students to read. However, one may wonder to what extent the selection criteria were responsible for this (counterintuitive) result. The selection of studies did not include a screening of studies in order to ensure that the participants needed what the treatment was designed to influence. The NRP routinely selected and analyzed studies that experimentally tested the efficacy of encouraging students to read more without ensuring that the participants in the selected studies indeed did not have the ability and opportunity outside of school to read independently (cf. Cunningham, 2001). Interestingly, the number of studies that correlated leisure-time reading activities to students' reading abilities is largely sufficient to synthesize quantitatively. Mol and Bus (in press) included 40 studies targeting children attending grades 1–12 and 30 studies targeting undergraduate and graduate students. Their meta-analysis showed that the correlation between leisure-time reading and students' reading comprehension and technical reading and spelling skills became stronger with age, which is in line with a model of reciprocal causation. More proficient readers are more likely to choose to read more frequently, which, in turn, will improve their reading abilities and their eagerness to read (Stanovich, 1986).

Meta-Analyses about Meta-Analyses

The set of meta-analyses reports effects of instruction on reading comprehension ($N = 19$) and on word recognition ($N = 11$). In 2003 we carried out a similar meta-analysis of meta-analyses. A striking result is that since then the number of meta-analyses targeting word recognition hardly increased ($N = 1$), whereas there was a substantial growth in number for reading comprehension ($N = 6$). From the stem-and-leaf display (Figure 13.2), it appears that both word recognition and reading comprehension are susceptible to specific forms of instruction. Insofar as several dependent measures were available, we selected tests with established (by the experimenter or someone else) construct validity and reliability (using multiple measures of reliability) above experimenter tests.

When a series of word-recognition outcomes were reported, we left out outcomes for selected words (e.g., pseudo- or only regularly spelled

Word Recognition		Reading Comprehension
	1.2	3
	1.1	8
	1.0	
	.9	15
2	.8	
5	.7	2
	.6	7
7554	.5	
10	.4	133
2	.3	01245666
70	.2	58
	.1	
	0	

FIGURE 13.2. Stem-and-leaf display of d indexes for effects of interventions on achievement test scores in word recognition and reading comprehension. Combine the stem (.1, .2, .3, etc.) with the leaves to the left and to the right to find d values. Stem combined with leaves to the right represents reading comprehension and stem combined with leaves to the left word recognition. For instance, in the range .2 to .3 one intervention caused an effect size (ES) of 0.28 on reading comprehension and another caused an ES of 0.27 on word recognition. Note that many ds for reading comprehension concentrate between 0.3 and 0.4 and ds for word recognition between 0.5 and 0.6.

words). For both word recognition and reading comprehension, outcomes are homogeneous according to an analysis on this data set with Comprehensive Meta-Analysis, even though the interventions cover a variety of instructions varying in form (group vs. one-to-one tutoring) and ranging from phonemic awareness to deriving meaning from context. Only a meta-analysis on the effects of reading comprehension interventions revealed outlying results (d = 1.23; Edmonds et al., 2009). As outlined previously, a rather diverse mix of intervention types might result in summary effects that are hard to interpret theoretically.

Another notable result is that ESs for word-recognition skills exceed those for reading comprehension. With word recognition as a dependent variable, the median ES of interventions is about 0.5 standard deviation. With reading comprehension as the dependent measure, it is about 0.33 standard deviation. These outcomes are similar whatever the focus of the study: improving word recognition, practicing comprehension skills, or one-to-one tutoring. In other words, word recognition is more susceptible to instruction than text comprehension. Reading comprehension is more strategic and based on higher level skills and may, therefore, be less trainable than decoding that is based on low-level skills. Interventions that include strategic and other higher level processes promise progress in comprehension (Pressley & Harris, 1994), but not to the same extent as a training of lower level skills warrants progress in word recognition. Because the interventions varied so much, we were unable to test characteristics of instruction. For instance, assuming that instruction on comprehension supports skills beyond those stimulated by word recognition, one may expect that the effect of comprehension instruction on comprehension is quite a bit higher than the effect of word-recognition instruction on comprehension, particularly after the early grades.

Quality of Meta-Analyses in Reading

Most syntheses of research satisfy the criterion that ESs across comparisons are independent (68%). Intercoder reliability for coding the set of studies on these methodological characteristics and hereafter discussed measures was satisfactory. Reliabilities of moderator variables are not always reported (36%), and neither do meta-analysts always make an estimate of a publishing bias (21%). To prevent independence of ESs various strategies may be used. Some adjust the sample size for significance tests so that a single subject's data did not count more than once. In other studies a combined effect is estimated, and subsequent contrasts between two or more kinds of interventions are not tested (Bus & van IJzendoorn, 1999). Some studies ignore the problem and use the same control group more than once (e.g., Ehri, Nunes, Willows, et al., 2001).

In most cases, Q statistics are reported (70%), but a majority of studies applied a fixed model even though the populations did not involve a common ES estimate, as indicated by the tests of homogeneity (e.g., Bus et al., 1995; Elbaum, Vaughn, Hughes, & Moody, 2000), or did not report which model was used at all (e.g., Sensibaugh, 2007; Therrien, 2004). Sometimes authors may draw strong conclusions and bold implications for practice from a combined ES even though the point estimate is not representative of the central tendency in the total set of studies. In that case, conclusions are at least premature. Large variation in ESs requires a random-effects model, which implies a broader confidence interval and a higher chance that the ES is not significantly different from zero. This scenario, however, not always holds, as can be illustrated for the book-reading study. We reanalyzed the data of the book-reading meta-analysis with a random-effects model because the overall point estimate of ES was not based on a homogeneous set of studies (Bus et al., 1995). Reanalyzing the combined effects for book-reading outcomes with a random-effects model, we found outcomes that were very similar to those resulting from a fixed model. A point estimate of $r = .27$ for the overall effect of book reading on emergent literacy, reading achievement in school age, and language skills remains significant, as indicated by a 95% CI ranging from .21 to .32. A meta-analytic update of parent–child book reading, covering studies between 1994 and 2008, showed almost identical random effect sizes: $r = .34$ (95% CI = [.26, .40]) for oral language and $r = .28$ (95% CI = [.22, .36]) for emergent literacy (Mol & Bus, in press).

META-ANALYTIC EXEMPLAR

Numerous studies relate phonemic awareness and reading achievement, but various questions remain unresolved because characteristics of replication studies vary. As the number of studies replicating the relationship between reading and phonemic awareness increases, quantitative synthesis of the research is warranted to test the effects of variations in study characteristics on the outcome of the studies (Bus & van IJzendoorn, 1999).

Precise and Relevant Hypotheses

First, we wondered whether phonemic awareness indeed is the single strongest predictor of reading development, as is often suggested (e.g., Elbro, 1996), and whether effects of alternative experiences as book reading are minor compared with a training of phonemic awareness. Another aim of this meta-analysis was to test whether children learn about the phonemic structure of words more easily when they learn to interpret spellings as maps for pronunciations. Therefore, we tested effects of characteristics of training programs, making a distinction between purely phonetic training, phonetic training embedded in letter practice, and phonetic training embedded in reading and writing practice.

A Homogeneous Set of Studies

Several meta-analyses have been subjected to thorough and sometimes harsh criticism because of the heterogeneity of independent variables across intervention studies and the heterogeneity of the interventions themselves (Dunst & Snyder, 1986; but see Casto & Mastropieri, 1986). Dunst and Snyder (1986), for example, conclude that the Casto and Mastropieri (1986) findings cannot be the basis for policy: It would be both dangerous and unwarranted to develop policy about early intervention based on their flawed meta-analyses. We circumvented this problem by carefully selecting studies that test effects of training phonological awareness. We put considerable effort into excluding reading instruction programs that focus on the instruction of reading skills.

Reliable and Concise Coding System

As we have shown earlier, the heterogeneity of the studies can be productively used to explain variation between study outcomes. The meta-analysts should pay systematic attention to the discrimination of relevant subsets of more homogeneous studies, using quantitative approaches based on expert ratings. In the synthesis of phonemic awareness research, we therefore coded characteristics of the training program (purely phonetic, embedded in a letter training, or embedded in reading and writing practice), setting (training with a group or individual), number of training sessions, and the person who implemented the training (teacher vs. examiner). Quality of study designs is never an easy all-or-nothing decision; in the meta-analysis of training phonological awareness, quality dimensions were tested by coding design characteristics (randomized, matched, or not) and kind of control group (no treatment, dummy treatment, or some related training). Two coders coded all relevant studies separately and succeeded in reaching agreement on these characteristics of the phonemic awareness interventions.

The synthesis of phonemic awareness training studies revealed that a purely phonemic training such as the thoroughly replicated Lundberg program is less effective than a program such as Sound Foundations that includes letter training in addition to phonological awareness. This meta-analytic finding is in line with Ehri's (1979) assumption that letters appear to function as an intermediary because they may facilitate the discrimination of phonemes. The results support a theory with important practical implications; that is, letters draw the child's attention to the sounds in spoken words, and a distinct visual symbol for each phoneme may anchor the phonemes perceptually (Adams, Treiman, & Pressley, 1998).

Independent and Homogeneous ESs

An important criticism concerns the dependence of ESs within a study, thus violating crucial assumptions of independence of observations. To prevent studies with more than one training group and only one control group from inflating the number of participants, we combined the ESs of the interventions within the study. This practice is now recommended in standard introductions to meta-analysis (Cooper & Hedges, 1994), and it would be important to replicate the contaminated meta-analyses following this guideline.

Diffuse comparisons of ESs within phonemic awareness training studies showed considerable heterogeneity of results, which led to a search for a more homogeneous subset of studies. The training experiments with randomized or matched groups of participants from the United States met this criterion, and we computed a point estimate of the ES for this subset of studies separately. In this homogeneous set of experimental studies with

more than 700 children, experimentally manipulated phonological awareness explains about 12% of the variance in word-identification skills. The
combined effect with controlled designs is $d = 0.70$, $r = .33$ ($p < .001$) for
reading.

New Insights and New Hypotheses to Be Tested

From a meta-analysis of 36 studies, we concluded that experimentally
manipulated phonological awareness is a substantial predictor of reading but not the single strongest predictor. Compared with the outcome for
phonemic awareness, early storybook reading leading to emergent literacy
skills predicts reading skills somewhat less strongly than experimentally
manipulated phonological awareness, but the difference is only marginal
(Bus et al., 1995). Interestingly, Mol and colleagues (2009) showed that
knowledge about reading skills in kindergartners gained about 7% ($d =
0.53$) from reading storybooks interactively, while adults in the experimen-
tal groups were not instructed to refer to letters or sounds in words. In
other words, it is not only direct training of phonemic awareness that supports emergent literacy and thus later literacy. Emergent literacy supported
by phonological awareness training as well as book reading appears to be
important in shaping the early reading process. Thus, these meta-analyses
may mark a new stage in the systematic study of reading development with
emphasis on both "outside-in" as well as "inside-out" factors that stimulate emergent literacy (cf. Whitehurst & Lonigan, 1998). Future research
should test the specific additive or interactive effects of formal and informal
experiences with aspects of written language and how they promote reading development.

CONCLUSION

Meta-analysis not only provides a summary of research but also produces
new insights and facts. Through meta-analysis we use the combined power
of the primary studies to address issues that otherwise would require hun-
dreds of participants and many different interventions within the same
study. Only a meta-analysis could show that the teacher expectancy effect
works better when the teachers do not know their pupils for more than a
few weeks (Raudenbush, 1984).

Combining the results of several meta-analyses, researchers are able
to construct models of associations between theoretically important variables that are not yet combined in any separate empirical study and to
show at what point the model still is incomplete. For instance, we combined
meta-analyses on the associations between book reading and literacy and
phonemic training and reading to show that not just formal training but
informal experiences are relevant to becoming literate. New meta-analytic

approaches for creating and testing causal and multilevel models have been proposed (Cook et al., 1992; van den Noortgate & Onghena, 2003) and will continue to develop in decades to come.

REFERENCES

Abraham, L. B. (2008). Computer-mediated glosses in second language reading comprehension and vocabulary learning: A meta-analysis. *Computer Assisted Language Learning, 21*, 199–226.

Adams, M. J. (1990). *Beginning to read. Thinking and learning about print.* Cambridge, MA: MIT Press.

Adams, M. J., Treiman, R., & Pressley, M. (1998). Reading, writing, and literacy. In I. E. Sigel & K. A. Renninger (Eds.), *Handbook of child psychology: Child psychology in practice* (Vol. 4, pp. 275–355). New York: Wiley.

Bakermans-Kranenburg, M. J., van IJzendoorn, M. H., & Juffer, F. (2003). Less is more: Meta-analyses of sensitivity and attachment interventions in early childhood. *Psychological Bulletin, 129*, 195–215.

Begg, C. B. (1994). Publication bias. In H. Cooper & L. V. Hedges (Eds.), *The handbook of research synthesis* (pp. 399–409). New York: Russell Sage Foundation.

Blanchard, J., & Stock, W. (1999). Meta-analysis of research on a multimedia elementary school curriculum using personal and video-game computers. *Perceptual and Motor Skills, 88*, 329–336.

Blok, H. (1999). Reading to young children in educational settings: A meta-analysis of recent research. *Language Learning, 49*, 343–371.

Blok, H., Oostdam, R., Otter, M. E., & Overmaat, M. (2002). Computer-assisted instruction in support of beginning reading instruction: A review. *Review of Educational Research, 72*, 101–130.

Borenstein, M., Hedges, L. V., Higgins, J. P. T., & Rothstein, H. R. (2009). *Introduction to meta-analysis.* West Sussex, UK: Wiley.

Browder, D. M., & Xin, Y. P. (1998). A meta-analysis and review of sight word research and its implications for teaching functional reading to individuals with moderate and severe disabilities. *Journal of Special Education, 32*, 130–153.

Bus, A. G., & van IJzendoorn, M. H. (1999). Phonological awareness and early reading: A meta-analysis of experimental training studies. *Journal of Educational Psychology, 91*, 403–414.

Bus, A. G., van IJzendoorn, M. H., & Pellegrini, A. D. (1995). Joint book reading makes for success in learning to read: A meta-analysis on intergenerational transmission of literacy. *Review of Educational Research, 65*, 1–21.

Bushman, B. J., & Wells, G. L. (2001). Narrative impressions of literature: The availability bias and the corrective properties of meta-analytic approaches. *Personality and Social Psychology Bulletin, 27*, 1123–1130.

Camilli, G., Vargas, S., & Yurecko, M. (2003). Teaching children to read: The fragile link between science & federal education policy. *Education Policy Analysis Archives, 11*. Retrieved November 11, 2009, from *epaa.asu.edu/epaa/v11n15/*.

Camilli, G., Wolfe, P. M., & Smith, M. L. (2006). Meta-analysis and reading policy: Perspectives on teaching children to read. *Elementary School Journal, 107,* 27–36.

Carretti, B., Borella, E., Cornoldi, C., & De Beni, R. (2009). Role of working memory in explaining the performance of individuals with specific reading comprehension difficulties: A meta-analysis. *Learning and Individual Differences, 19,* 246–251.

Casto, G., & Mastropieri, M. A. (1986). The efficacy of early intervention programs: A meta-analysis. *Exceptional Children, 52,* 417–424.

Cohen, J. (1988). *Statistical power analysis for the behavioral sciences.* Hillsdale, NJ: Erlbaum.

Cohen, J. (1990). Things I have learned (so far). *American Psychologist, 45,* 1304–1312.

Cook, T. D., Cooper, H., Cordray, D. F., Hartman, H., Hedges, L. V., Light, R., et al. (1992). *Meta-analysis for explanation: A casebook.* New York: Russell Sage.

Cooper, H., Charlton, K., Valentine, J. C., & Muhlenbruck, L. (2000). Making the most of summer school: A meta-analytic and narrative review. *Monographs of the Society for Research in Child Development, 65,* 1–127.

Cooper, H., & Hedges, L. V. (Eds.). (1994). *The handbook of research synthesis.* New York: Russell Sage.

Cooper, H., Nye, B., Charlton, K., & Lindsay, J. (1996). The effects of summer vacation on achievement test scores: A narrative and meta-analytic review. *Review of Educational Research, 66,* 227–268.

Cooper, H., Robinson, J. C., & Patall, E. A. (2006). Does homework improve academic achievement?: A synthesis of research, 1987–2003. *Review of Educational Research, 76,* 1–62.

Cooper, H. M. (1982). Scientific guidelines for conducting integrative research reviews. *Review of Educational Research, 52,* 291–302.

Cooper, H. M., & Rosenthal, R. (1980). Statistical versus traditional procedures for summarizing research findings. *Psychological Bulletin, 87,* 442–449.

Cunningham, J. W. (2001). The National Reading Panel report. *Reading Research Quarterly, 36,* 326–335.

D'Agostino, J. V., & Murphy, J. A. (2004). A meta-analysis of reading recovery in United States schools. *Educational Evaluation and Policy Analysis, 26,* 23–38.

Daneman, M., & Merikle, P. M. (1996). Working memory and language comprehension: A meta-analysis. *Psychonomic Bulletin and Review, 3,* 422–433.

Duncan, G. J., Claessens, A., Huston, A. C., Pagani, L. S., Engel, M., Sexton, H., et al. (2007). School readiness and later achievement. *Developmental Psychology, 43,* 1428–1446.

Dunst, C. J., & Snyder, S. W. (1986). A critique of the Utah State University early intervention meta-analysis research. *Exceptional Children, 53,* 269–276.

Duval, S., & Tweedie, R. (2000a). A nonparametric "trim and fill" method for accounting for publication bias in meta-analysis. *Journal of the American Statistical Association, 95,* 89–98.

Duval, S., & Tweedie, R. (2000b). Trim and fill: A simple funnel-plot-based method of testing and adjusting for publication bias in meta-analysis. *Biometrics, 56,* 455–463.

Eagly, A. H., & Wood, W. (1994). Tying research synthesis to substantive issues. In H. Cooper & L. V. Hedges (Eds.), *The handbook of research synthesis* (pp. 485–502). New York: Russell Sage.

Edmonds, M. S., Vaughn, S., Wexler, J., Reutebuch, C., Cable, A., Tackett, K. K., et al. (2009). A synthesis of reading interventions and effects on reading comprehension outcomes for older struggling readers. *Review of Educational Research, 79*, 262–300.

Ehri, L. C. (1979). Linguistic insight: Threshold of reading acquisition. In G. Waller & G. MacKinnon (Eds.), *Reading research: Advances in theory and practice* (Vol. 1, pp. 63–111). New York: Academic Press.

Ehri, L. C., Nunes, S. R., Stahl, S. A., & Willows, D. M. (2001). Systematic phonics instruction helps students learn to read: Evidence from the National Reading Panel's meta-analysis. *Review of Educational Research, 71*, 393–447.

Ehri, L. C., Nunes, S. R., Willows, D. M., Schuster, B. V., Yaghoub-Zadeh, Z., & Shanahan, T. (2001). Phonemic awareness instruction helps children learn to read: Evidence from the National Reading Panel's meta-analysis. *Reading Research Quarterly, 36*, 250–287.

Elbaum, B., Vaughn, S., Hughes, M. T., & Moody, S. W. (1999). Grouping practices and reading outcomes for students with disabilities. *Exceptional Children, 65*, 399–415.

Elbaum, B., Vaughn, S., Hughes, M. T., & Moody, S. W. (2000). How effective are one-to-one tutoring programs in reading for elementary students at risk for reading failure? A meta-analysis of the intervention research. *Journal of Educational Psychology, 92*, 605–619.

Elbaum, B., Vaughn, S., Hughes, M. T., Moody, S. W., & Schumm, J. S. (2000). How reading outcomes of students with disabilities are related to instructional grouping formats: A meta-analytic review. In R. M. Gersten & E. P. Schiller (Eds.), *Contemporary special education research: Syntheses of the knowledge base on critical instructional issues. The LEA series on special education and disability* (pp. 105–135). Mahwah, NJ: Erlbaum.

Elbro, C. (1996). Early linguistic abilities and reading development: A review and a hypothesis. *Reading and Writing, 8*, 453–485.

Fan, X., & Chen, M. (2001). Parental involvement and students' academic achievement: A meta-analysis. *Educational Psychology Review, 13*, 1–22.

Fuchs, D., Fuchs, L. S., Mathes, P. G., & Lipsey, M. W. (2000). Reading differences between low-achieving students with and without learning disabilities: A meta-analysis. In R. M. Gersten & E. P. Schiller (Eds.), *Contemporary special education research: Syntheses of the knowledge base on critical instructional issues* (pp. 81–104). Mahwah, NJ: Erlbaum.

Fukkink, R. G., & De Glopper, K. (1998). Effects of instruction in deriving word meaning from context: A meta-analysis. *Review of Educational Research, 68*, 450–469.

Fusaro, J. A. (1992). Meta-analysis of the effect of sentence-combining on reading comprehension when the criterion measure is the test of reading comprehension. *Perceptual and Motor Skills, 74*, 331–333.

Garfield, E. (1979). *Citation indexing. Its theory and application in science, technology, and humanities.* New York: Wiley.

Glass, G. V. (1976). Primary, secondary and meta-analysis of research. *Educational Research, 5*, 3–8.

Gleser, L. J., & Olkin, I. (1994). Stochastically dependent effect sizes. In H. Cooper & L. V. Hedges (Eds.), *The handbook of research synthesis* (pp. 339–355). New York: Russell Sage.

Goldring, E. B., & Presbrey, L. S. (1986). Evaluating preschool programs: A meta-analytic approach. *Educational Evaluation and Policy Analysis, 8*, 179–188.

Graf Estes, K., Evans, J. L., & Else-Quest, N. M. (2007). Differences in the nonword repetition performance of children with and without specific language impairment: A meta-analysis. *Journal of Speech, Language, and Hearing Research, 50*, 177–195.

Greene, J. P. (1997). A meta-analysis of the Rossell and Baker review of bilingual education research. *Bilingual Research Journal, 21*, 103–122.

Grigorenko, E. L. (2005). A conservative meta-analysis of linkage and linkage-association studies of developmental dyslexia. *Scientific Studies of Reading, 9*, 285–316.

Guthrie, J. T., McRae, A., & Klauda, S. L. (2007). Contributions of concept-oriented reading instruction to knowledge about interventions for motivations in reading. *Educational Psychologist, 42*, 237–250.

Hammill, D. D., & Swanson, H. L. (2006). The National Reading Panel's meta-analysis of phonics instruction: Another point of view. *Elementary School Journal, 107*, 17–26.

Hedges, L. V. (1994). Statistical considerations. In H. Cooper & L. V. Hedges (Eds.), *The handbook of research synthesis* (pp. 29–38). New York: Russell Sage.

Hedges, L. V. (2008). What are effect sizes and why do we need them? *Child Development Perspectives, 2*, 167–171.

Hedges, L. V., & Olkin, I. (1985). *Statistical methods for meta-analysis.* New York: Academic Press.

Hedges, L. V., & Pigott, T. D. (2004). The power of statistical tests for moderators in meta-analysis. *Psychological Methods, 9*, 426–445.

Herrmann, J. A., Matyas, T., & Pratt, C. (2006). Meta-analysis of the nonword reading deficit in specific reading disorder. *Dyslexia, 12*, 195–221.

Horn, W. F., & Packard, T. (1985). Early identification of learning problems: A meta-analysis. *Journal of Educational Psychology, 77*, 597–607.

Hoskyn, M., & Swanson, H. L. (2000). Cognitive processing of low achievers and children with reading disabilities: A selective meta-analytic review of the published literature. *School Psychology Review, 29*, 102–119.

Jeynes, W. H. (2002). A meta-analysis: The effects of parental involvement on minority children's academic achievement. *Education and Urban Society, 35*, 202–218.

Jeynes, W. H. (2005). A meta-analysis of the relation of parental involvement to urban elementary school student academic achievement. *Urban Education, 40*, 237–269.

Jeynes, W. H., & Littell, S. W. (2000). A meta-analysis of studies examining the effect of whole language instruction on the literacy of low-SES students. *Elementary School Journal, 101*, 21–33.

Johnson, B. T., Mullen, B., & Salas, E. (1995). Comparison of three meta-analytic approaches. *Journal of Applied Psychology, 80*, 94–106.

Kamin, L. J. (1974). *The science and politics of I.Q.* New York: Wiley.

Kavale, K. A. (1980). Auditory-visual integration and its relationship to reading achievement: A meta-analysis. *Perceptual and Motor Skills, 51*, 947–955.

Kavale, K. A. (1981). The relationship between auditory perceptual skills and reading ability: A meta-analysis. *Journal of Learning Disabilities, 14*, 539–546.

Kavale, K. A. (1982). Meta-analysis of the relationship between visual perceptual skills and reading achievement. *Journal of Learning Disabilities, 15*, 42–51.

Kavale, K. A., & Forness, S. R. (2000). Auditory and visual perception processes and reading ability: A quantitative reanalysis and historical reinterpretation. *Learning Disability Quarterly, 23*, 253–270.

La Paro, K. M., & Pianta, R. C. (2000). Predicting children's competence in the early school years: A meta-analytic review. *Review of Educational Research, 70*, 443–484.

Lauer, P. A., Akiba, M., Wilkerson, S. B., Apthorp, H. S., Snow, D., & Martin-Glenn, M. L. (2006). Out-of-school-time programs: A meta-analysis of effects for at-risk students. *Review of Educational Research, 76*, 275–313.

Law, J., Garrett, Z., & Nye, C. (2004). The efficacy of treatment for children with developmental speech and language delay/disorder: A meta-analysis. *Journal of Speech, Language, and Hearing Research, 47*, 924–943.

Leseman, P. P. M., Otter, M. E., Blok, H., & Dekkers, P. (1998). Effecten van voor- en vroegschoolse educatieve centrumprogramma's. Een meta-analyse van studies gepubliceerd tussen 1985 en 1996 [Effects of preschool intervention programs. A meta-analysis of studies published between 1985 and 1996]. *Nederlands Tijdschrift voor Opvoeding, Vorming en Onderwijs, 14*, 134–154.

Leseman, P. P. M., Otter, M. E., Blok, H., & Dekkers, P. (1999). Effecten van voorschoolse educatieve centrumprogramma's. Een aanvullende meta-analyse van studies gepubliceerd tussen 1985 en 1996 [Effects of preschool intervention programs. An additional meta-analysis of studies published between 1985 and 1996]. *Nederlands Tijdschrift voor Opvoeding, Vorming en Onderwijs, 15*, 28–37.

Lietz, P. (2006). A meta-analysis of gender differences in reading achievement at the secondary school level. *Studies in Educational Evaluation, 32*, 317–344.

Lipsey, M. W., & Wilson, D. B. (2001). *Practical meta-analysis.* Thousand Oaks, CA: Sage.

Littell, J. H., Corcoran, J., & Pillai, V. K. (2008). *Systematic reviews and meta-analysis.* New York: Oxford University Press.

Lynn, R., & Mikk, J. (2009). Sex differences in reading achievement. *TRAMES, 13*, 3–13.

Lytton, H. (1994). Replication and meta-analysis: The story of a meta-analysis of parents' socialization practices. In R. van der Veer, M. H. van IJzendoorn, & J. Valsiner (Eds.), *Reconstructing the mind: Replicability in research on human development* (pp. 117–150). Norwood, NJ: Ablex.

McCartney, K., & Rosenthal, R. (2000). Effect Size, practical importance, and social policy for children. *Child Development, 71*, 173–180.

McGiverin, J., Gilman, D., & Tillitski, C. (1989). A meta-analysis of the relation between class size and achievement. *Elementary School Journal, 90*, 47–56.

Mehana, M., & Reynolds, A. J. (2004). School mobility and achievement: A meta-analysis. *Children and Youth Services Review, 26*, 93–119.

Metsala, J. L., Stanovich, K. E., & Brown, G. D. A. (1998). Regularity effects and the phonological deficit model of reading disabilities: A meta-analytic review. *Journal of Educational Psychology, 90,* 279–293.

Mol, S. E., & Bus, A. G. (in press). To read or not to read: A meta-analysis of print exposure from infancy to early adulthood. *Psychological Bulletin.*

Mol, S. E., Bus, A. G., & De Jong, M. T. (2009). Interactive book reading in early education: A tool to stimulate print knowledge as well as oral language. *Review of Educational Research, 79,* 979–1007.

Mol, S. E., Bus, A. G., De Jong, M. T., & Smeets, D. J. H. (2008). Added value of dialogic parent–child book readings: A meta-analysis. *Early Education and Development, 19,* 7–26.

Moran, J., Ferdig, R. E., Pearson, P. D., Wardrop, J., & Blomeyer, R. L. (2008). Technology and reading performance in the middle-school grades: A meta-analysis with recommendations for policy and practice. *Journal of Literacy Research, 40,* 6–58.

Mullen, B. (1989). *Advanced basic meta-analysis.* Hillsdale, NJ: Erlbaum.

Murphy, P. K., Wilkinson, I. A. G., Soter, A. O., Hennessey, M. N., & Alexander, J. F. (2009). Examining the effects of classroom discussion on students' comprehension of text: A meta-analysis. *Journal of Educational Psychology, 101,* 740–764.

National Early Literacy Panel. (2008). *Developing early literacy: Report of the National Early Literacy Panel.* Washington, DC: National Institute for Literacy.

National Reading Panel. (2000). *Report of the National Reading Panel: Teaching children to read: An evidence-based assessment of the scientific research literature on reading and its implications for reading instruction: Reports of the subgroups.* Rockville, MD: NICHD Clearinghouse.

O'Shaughnessy, T. E., & Swanson, H. L. (1998). Do immediate memory deficits in students with learning disabilities in reading reflect a developmental lag or deficit?: A selective meta-analysis of the literature. *Learning Disability Quarterly, 21,* 123–148.

Pearson, K. (1904). Report on certain enteric fever inoculation statistics. *British Medical Journal, 3,* 1243–1246.

Petticrew, M., & Roberts, H. (2006). *Systematic reviews in the social sciences; A practical guide.* Oxford, UK: Blackwell.

Pressley, M., & Harris, K. R. (1994). Increasing the quality of educational intervention research. *Educational Psychology Review, 6,* 191–208.

Raudenbush, S. W. (1984). Magnitude of teacher expectancy effects on pupil IQ as a function of the credibility of expectancy induction: A synthesis of findings from 18 experiments. *Journal of Educational Psychology, 76,* 85–97.

Ritter, G. W., Barnett, J. H., Denny, G. S., & Albin, G. R. (2009). The effectiveness of volunteer tutoring programs for elementary and middle school students: A meta-analysis. *Review of Educational Research, 79,* 3–38.

Roach, N. W., Edwards, V. T., & Hogben, J. H. (2004). The tale is in the tail: An alternative hypothesis for psychophysical performance variability in dyslexia. *Perception, 33,* 817–830.

Rochelle, K. S. H., & Talcott, J. B. (2006). Impaired balance in developmental dyslexia?: A meta-analysis of the contending evidence. *Journal of Child Psychology and Psychiatry, 47,* 1159–1166.

Rolstad, K., Mahoney, K., & Glass, G. V. (2005). The big picture: A meta-analysis of program effectiveness research on English language learners. *Educational Policy, 19,* 572–594.

Rosenshine, B., Meister, C., & Chapman, S. (1996). Teaching students to generate questions: A review of the intervention studies. *Review of Educational Research, 66,* 181–221.

Rosenthal, R. (1991). *Meta-analytic procedures for social research* (rev. ed.). Newbury Park, CA: Sage.

Rosenthal, R. (1995). Writing meta-analytic reviews. *Psychological Bulletin, 118,* 183–192.

Rosenthal, R., & Rubin, D. B. (1982). Further meta-analytic procedures for assessing cognitive gender differences. *Journal of Educational Psychology, 74,* 708–712.

Seidel, T., & Shavelson, R. J. (2007). Teaching effectiveness research in the past decade: The role of theory and research design in disentangling meta-analysis results. *Review of Educational Research, 77,* 454–499.

Sencibaugh, J. M. (2007). Meta-analysis of reading comprehension interventions for students with learning disabilities: Strategies and implications. *Reading Improvement, 44,* 6–22.

Sénéchal, M., & Young, L. (2008). The effect of family literacy interventions on children's acquisition of reading from kindergarten to grade 3: A meta-analytic review. *Review of Educational Research, 78,* 880–907.

Slavin, R. E. (1986). Best-evidence synthesis: An alternative to meta-analytic and traditional reviews. *Educational Researcher, 15,* 5–11.

Slavin, R. E. (2002). Evidence-based education policies: Transforming educational practice and research. *Educational Researcher, 31,* 15–21.

Slavin, R. E., & Cheung, A. (2005). A synthesis of research on language of reading instruction for English language learners. *Review of Educational Research, 75,* 247–284.

Smith, M. L., & Glass, G. V. (1977). Meta-analysis of psychotherapy outcome studies. *American Psychologist, 32,* 752–760.

Stahl, S. A., & Fairbanks, M. M. (1986). The effects of vocabulary instruction: A model-based meta-analysis. *Review of Educational Research, 56,* 72–110.

Stahl, S. A., McKenna, M. C., & Pagnucco, J. R. (1994). The effects of whole-language instruction: An update and a reappraisal. *Educational Psychologist, 29,* 175–185.

Stahl, S. A., & Miller, P. D. (1989). Whole language and language experience approaches for beginning reading: A quantitative research synthesis. *Review of Educational Research, 59,* 87–116.

Stanovich, K. E. (1986). Matthew effects in reading: Some consequences of individual differences in the acquisition of literacy. *Reading Research Quarterly, 21,* 360–407.

Stanovich, K. E. (2000). *Progress in understanding reading; Scientific foundations and new frontiers.* New York: Guilford Press.

Stuebing, K. K., Barth, A. E., Cirino, P. T., Francis, D. J., & Fletcher, J. M. (2008). A response to recent reanalyses of the National Reading Report: Effects of systematic phonics instruction are practically significant. *Journal of Educational Psychology, 100,* 123–134.

Stuebing, K. K., Fletcher, J. M., Ledoux, J. M., Lyon, G. R., Shaywitz, S. E., &

Shaywitz, B. A. (2002). Validity of IQ-discrepancy classifications of reading disabilities: A meta-analysis. *American Educational Research Journal, 39,* 469–518.

Sutton, A. J., & Higgins, J. P. T. (2008). Recent developments in meta-analysis. *Statistics in Medicine, 27,* 625–650.

Swanborn, M. S. L., & De Glopper, K. (1999). Incidental word learning while reading: A meta-analysis. *Review of Educational Research, 69,* 261–285.

Swanson, H. L. (1999). Reading research for students with LD: A meta-analysis in intervention outcomes. *Journal of Learning Disabilities, 32,* 504–532.

Swanson, H. L. (2001). Research on interventions for adolescents with learning disabilities: A meta-analysis of outcomes related to higher-order processing. *Elementary School Journal, 101,* 331–348.

Swanson, H. L., & Hoskyn, M. (1998). Experimental intervention research on students with learning disabilities: A meta-analysis of treatment outcomes. *Review of Educational Research, 68,* 277–321.

Swanson, H. L., & Sachse-Lee, C. (2000). A meta-analysis of single-subject-design intervention research for students with LD. *Journal of Learning Disabilities, 33,* 114–136.

Swanson, H. L., Trainin, G., Necoechea, D. M., & Hammill, D. D. (2003). Rapid naming, phonological awareness, and reading: A meta-analysis of the correlation evidence. *Review of Educational Research, 73,* 407–440.

Tan, L. H., Laird, A. R., Li, K., & Fox, P. T. (2005). Neuroanatomical correlates of phonological processing of Chinese characters and alphabetic words: A meta-analysis. *Human Brain Mapping, 25,* 83–91.

Taylor, A. (2006). The effects of CALL versus traditional L1 glosses on L2 reading comprehension. *CALICO Journal, 23,* 309–318.

Therrien, W. J. (2004). Fluency and comprehension gains as a result of repeated reading: A meta-analysis. *Remedial and Special Education, 25,* 252–261.

Torgerson, C. J., & Elbourne, D. (2002). A systematic review and meta-analysis of the effectiveness of information and communication technology (ICT) on the teaching of spelling. *Journal of Research in Reading, 25,* 129–143.

Torgerson, C. J., King, S. E., & Sowden, A. J. (2002). Do volunteers in schools help children learn to read?: A systematic review of randomised controlled trials. *Educational Studies, 28,* 433–444.

Torgerson, C. J., Porthouse, J., & Brooks, G. (2003). A systematic review and meta-analysis of randomised controlled trials evaluating interventions in adult literacy and numeracy. *Journal of Research in Reading, 26,* 234–255.

Turkeltaub, P. E., Eden, G. F., Jones, K. M., & Zeffiro, T. A. (2002). Meta-analysis of the functional neuroanatomy of single-word reading: Method and validation. *NeuroImage, 16,* 765–780.

van den Noortgate, W., & Onghena, P. (2003). Multilevel meta-analysis: A comparison with traditional meta-analytical procedures. *Educational and Psychological Measurement, 63,* 765–790.

van IJzendoorn, M. H. (1994). Process model of replication studies: On the relations between different types of replication. In R. van der Veer, M. H. van IJzendoorn, & J. Valsiner (Eds.), *Reconstructing the mind: Replicability in research on human development* (pp. 57–70). Norwood, NJ: Ablex.

van IJzendoorn, M. H. (2002). Methodologie: Kennis door veranderen, de empirische benadering in de pedagogiek. In M. H. van IJzendoorn & H. de Frankrijker (Eds.), *Pedagogiek in beeld* [Education in pictures] (pp. 2–35). Houten, The Netherlands: Bohn Stafleu Van Loghum.

van IJzendoorn, M. H., & Bus, A. G. (1994). Meta-analytic confirmation of the nonword reading deficit in developmental dyslexia. *Reading Research Quarterly, 29,* 266–275.

What Works Clearinghouse. (2008, December). Procedures and standards handbook (version 2.0). Retrieved November 28, 2009, from *ies.ed.gov/ncee/wwc/pdf/wwc_procedures_v2_standards_handbook.pdf.*

Whitehurst, G. J., & Lonigan, C. J. (1998). Child development and emergent literacy. *Child Development, 69,* 848–872.

Williams, J. (2001). Commentary: Four meta-analyses and some general observations. *Elementary School Journal, 101,* 349–354.

Willig, A. C. (1985). A meta-analysis of selected studies on the effectiveness of bilingual education. *Review of Educational Research, 55,* 269–317.

Wolins, L. (1962). Responsibility for raw data. *American Psychologist, 17,* 657–658.

Zao, Y. (2003). Recent developments in technology and language learning: A literature review and meta-analysis. *CALICO Journal, 21,* 7–27.

Zucker, T. A., Moody, A. K., & McKenna, M. C. (2009). The effects of electronic books on pre-kindergarten-to-grade-5 students' literacy and language outcomes: A research synthesis. *Journal of Educational Computing Research, 40,* 47–87.

CHAPTER 14

Mixed Research Techniques in Literacy Research

Anthony J. Onwuegbuzie
Marla H. Mallette

In the concluding chapter of this volume, Duke and Mallette posit five messages they hope readers will consider regarding literacy research methodologies. Messages 4—Synergy across research methodologies is possible, powerful, and advisable—and 5—We must urgently and actively pursue synergy across research methodologies—apply not only across the contents of this volume but also within this single chapter on mixed research in literacy. Although we agree that synergy can be achieved by looking across studies that use an individual methodology (i.e., monomethodology), we contend that synergy can be achieved within a well-designed mixed research study as well.

WHAT IS THIS METHODOLOGY?

Quantitative Research

As can be seen from some of the previous chapters in this book, quantitative research represents a very useful set of techniques for addressing research questions in the field of literacy that necessitate the collection, analysis, and interpretation of numeric data. In particular, quantitative research is extremely useful for describing, explaining, and predicting human phenomena. Quantitative researchers often attempt to study phenomena under controlled conditions via experiments as a means of identifying cause-and-effect relationships. Under optimal conditions (e.g., large and random samples), findings from quantitative research studies can be generalized from the sample to the population from which the sample was drawn. For example, descriptive research could be used to determine the literacy rates in an underlying population. Correlational research could be utilized to examine the relationship between levels of literacy and academic performance among eighth-grade students. Experimental research could be used to determine the effect of a reading program on literacy rates. In any case, if designed in an optimal way, in which rigor is maximized, quantitative research can inform the field of literacy.

Qualitative Research

In contrast, qualitative research represents a very useful set of techniques for addressing research questions in the field of literacy that necessitate the collection, analysis, and interpretation of nonnumeric data (e.g., words, observations, drawings, pictures, images). Qualitative research is extremely useful for exploring, discovering, describing, and constructing human phenomena. More specifically, it generally is used to obtain insights into experiences and the meaning(s) attached to these experiences of selected individuals (e.g., biography, autobiography, case study, life history, oral history, auto-ethnography) and groups (e.g., ethnography, grounded theory, phenomenology, critical theory), which, under optimal conditions (e.g., data saturation, theoretical saturation, informational redundancy), can achieve *verstehen*, or understanding. For example, a case study could be used to study reading strategies of a particular student or group of students. An ethnographic study could be employed to describe and interpret the cultural behaviors, customs, and experiences of a group of Hispanic first-grade students who are learning to read. A phenomenological inquiry could be utilized to describe the meaning of the lived experiences for struggling readers in the fifth grade. Grounded theory research could be used to generate or expand a theory associated with new literacies. Whatever the research design or method used, qualitative research could inform theory and model development if it is conducted in a way that yields insights into psychological, social, and/or cultural processes and practices that exist within a specific setting, location, context, event, activity, incident, time, and/or experience.

Limitations of Quantitative and Qualitative Research

Unfortunately, although both quantitative research and qualitative research represent powerful approaches for addressing an array of research questions in the field of literacy, they each have important weaknesses. In particular, quantitative research studies typically yield data that do not explain the reasons underlying prevalence rates, relationships, or differences that have been observed by the literacy researcher. Simply put, quantitative research is not adequate for addressing "why" and "how" questions. Rather, it is better suited to "answering questions of who, where, how many, how much, and what is the relationship between specific variables" (Adler, 1996, p. 5). In contrast, as noted by Onwuegbuzie and Johnson (2008), "Qualitative research is typically based on small, nonrandom samples . . . which means that qualitative research findings are often not very generalizable beyond the local research participants" (p. 441). Instead, the strength of qualitative research lies in its ability to understand the emic, or insider's perspective; to capture the essence of a lived experience of one or more individuals; to identify the structure of a lived experience; to understand the meaning of psychological phenomenon and relationships among variables as they occur naturally; to understand the role that culture (e.g., ethnicity, gender, age) plays in the context of phenomena; and to understand psychological processes that are reflected in language, thoughts, and behaviors from the perspective of the participants themselves.

Because of the strengths and weaknesses inherent in monomethodological research, in recent years, an increasing number of researchers from various fields and disciplines have been advocating that research studies include *both* quantitative and qualitative research within the same inquiry, commonly termed *mixed methods research*—or what we and several other researchers (e.g., Johnson & Onwuegbuzie, 2004) prefer to call *mixed research* to reflect the fact that that this research paradigm involves much more than the mixing of methods. However, mixed research has not been utilized as much within the field of literacy. This inattention to mixed research might stem from the fact that, in general, the benefits of using mixed research have not been made clear enough to literacy researchers. We focus on this approach for the remainder of this chapter.

Mixed Research Defined

According to Johnson, Onwuegbuzie, and Turner (2007), broadly speaking, mixed research is:

> An intellectual and practical synthesis based on qualitative and quantitative research; it is the third methodological or research paradigm (along with qualitative and quantitative research). It recognizes the importance of traditional quantitative and qualitative research but also offers a powerful third paradigm choice that often will provide the most informative, complete, balanced, and useful research results. Mixed methods research is the research paradigm that (a) partners with the philosophy of pragmatism in one of its forms (left, right, middle); (b) follows the logic of mixed methods research (including the logic of the fundamental principle and any other useful logics imported from qualitative or quantitative research that are helpful for producing defensible and usable research findings); (c) relies on qualitative and quantitative viewpoints, data collection, analysis, and inference techniques combined according to the logic of mixed methods research to address one's research question(s); and (d) is cognizant, appreciative, and inclusive of local and broader sociopoliti-

cal realities, resources, and needs. Furthermore, the mixed methods research paradigm offers an important approach for *generating* important research questions *and* providing warranted answers to those questions. This type of research should be used when the nexus of contingencies in a situation, in relation to one's research question(s), suggests that mixed methods research is likely to provide superior research findings and outcomes. (p. 129)

HISTORY OF MIXED RESEARCH

Teddlie and Johnson (2009a, 2009b) identified five methodological stages that have occurred since the 19th century. Stage 1, the formal emergence of the social and behavioral sciences in the 19th and early 20th centuries, was characterized by the development of various disciplines (e.g., sociology) within the social and behavioral sciences, the emergence of classical and logical positivism and idealism, the birth of the hypotheticodeductive model, the emergence of psychology, and the development of basic statistical and anthropological methods. Stage 2, the traditional period (1900– World War II), was characterized by the discrediting of logical positivism, the continued development of qualitative research methods, and the uncontroversial but limited use of mixed research. Stage 3 was the postpositivist era (end of World War II–1970), characterized by further extensions to the hypotheticodeductive model; the promotion of postpositivism; the emergence of grounded theory, which "provided qualitative researchers with a more systematic procedure for inductively generating theories and analyzing narrative data" (Teddlie & Johnson, 2009b, p. 70); the emergence of multimethod designs; and the promotion of the use of quantitative and qualitative methods in social research. Stage 4, diversification of and advances in methodologies in the human sciences (1970–1990), reflected the advancement of all research paradigms, the emergence of the causal model of explanation in quantitative research, the emergence of newer paradigms such as constructivism that led to paradigm wars and the assertion that it was inappropriate to mix quantitative and qualitative methods because of fundamental differences (i.e., incompatibility thesis; cf. Howe, 1988), the promotion of pragmatism, the development and popularity of qualitative methods (cf. Lincoln & Guba, 1985), and the continued development of rationale for the use of mixed research (e.g., triangulation; cf. Greene, Caracelli, & Graham, 1989). Stage 5, the institutionalization of mixed methods as a distinct methodological orientation (1990–present), marked the beginning of conversations between quantitative and qualitative researchers, the publication of seminal works promoting mixed research as a separate research movement, the widespread publication of mixed research studies throughout the human sciences, and the conceptualization that "much if not most research is inherently mixed" (Teddlie & Johnson, 2009b, p. 79).

These five methodological stages that spanned the 19th and 20th centuries underwent three methodological waves: quantitative research, qualitative research, and mixed research. These three research paradigms prevailed in various forms. Thus, mixed research is not new. In fact, as contended by Tashakkori and Teddlie (2003), "Some of the most famous and influential research of the 20th century could be accurately referred to as mixed methods" (p. 697). However, these studies did not involve the use of mixed research in any formal manner. In particular, the authors did not refer to their studies as representing mixed research.

History of Mixed Research in the Literacy Field

Research in the field of literacy also has undergone these three methodological waves. Each of these three research communities has made important contributions to the literacy field. In fact, in the field of literacy, researchers informally have been mixing methods for decades, although these studies were not classified as mixed research. Thus, the emergence of (formal) mixed research as an explicit design in particular and as a methodology in general is still in its early stages (see, e.g., Calfee & Sperling, 2010).

In tracing the history of mixed research in literacy, we characterize its evolution in three phases. In the first phase, from the 1970s through the 1980s, mixed research studies, although limited in number, typically were quantitative, with qualitative data added to support the quantitative findings. The second phase, which began in the late 1980s and continued through the early 2000s, was characterized by studies that included both quantitative and qualitative research designs. The current phase, consisting of research published from the early 2000s to the present, includes studies in which authors explicitly state that their design represents mixed research and, as such, the methodology is more integrative. The following section provides examples of studies from each phase.

Phase 1

One of the earliest examples of mixed research that we located was published in 1971 by Fareed. In this study, Fareed investigated how skilled middle school students comprehended both historical and biological texts. As a Phase 1 study, this research was written with a predominantly quantitative focus. However, representative of this phase, qualitative data were included in the discussion under the heading of "Ancillary Findings" (p. 522). Perhaps even more interesting in considering the time of this study was the qualitative language the author used in characterizing these data as *emerging* findings. A second example, by Garner (1980), followed a similar structure. Garner investigated comprehension monitoring of good and poor middle school readers. Similar to that of Fareed (1971), Garner's

(1980) study was a quantitative research report. She also added the qualitative findings to the discussion to lend support to her statistical results.

Phase 2

In contrast to the Phase 1 studies, in Phase 2 research, both quantitative and qualitative methods were described in the Method section, and both the quantitative and qualitative findings were reported in the Results section. Typically, these studies could be best characterized as having separate quantitative and qualitative sections; yet the authors tended to weave the findings together in the discussion. O'Brien and Martin's (1988) study on the nature of figurative language in comprehension represents an early example of mixed research. Similar to the design of current mixed studies, their research comprised three types of analyses: (1) correlations, (2) regression analysis, and (3) logical analyses. As is characteristic of this phase of mixed research, O'Brien and Martin discuss the findings from each analysis separately and then integrate the findings in the discussion.

A second common feature of mixed research during this time period was the selection of a subsample from the larger sample for the qualitative phase. For example, Purcell-Gates and Dahl (1991) chose 12 "focal children" (p. 4) from their larger sample of 35 children in their study investigating how children of low socioeconomic status experienced a skills-based curriculum. Freppon (1991) chose 24 informants, six children from four classrooms, for the qualitative dimension in her study comparing skills-based classrooms with literature-based classrooms. Interestingly, and perhaps caught in the midst of the qualitative and quantitative paradigm wars, in both of these studies, the subsamples were randomly selected as opposed to purposefully selected, with the latter being more typical of qualitative research.

Toward the end of this time period, with qualitative research being embraced and legitimized in the field of literacy, researchers began providing stronger and more compelling rationales for the qualitative component of their mixed research. For example, Gaskins (1996) explored the effects of emotional involvement with text on reading comprehension. Although the primary analysis used in this study compared differences in responses among two experimental groups and a control group, Gaskins also interviewed the participants. What sets this study apart was the inclusion of qualitative data and the rationale Gaskins provided for its inclusion:

> *Data pertaining to the research questions.* In addition to providing support for key assumptions underlying the study, the subjects' comments provided a means for gaining further insights into the effect of issue-related emotional involvement on a subject's interpretation of a text pertaining to that issue. The subjects' comments are particularly important because they provide a vital manifestation of the effects the quantitative data support without voice.

The quantitative data analyses provided statistically significant support for the hypothesis that subjects' degree of emotional involvement with one of the teams in the passage would have an effect on the way in which the subjects interpreted that passage, but the subjects' comments elaborated on that finding and gave the data a more personal voice. (pp. 395–396)

Bloodgood (1999) examined the importance of name writing among young children. In her abstract, she identified the design as representing both quantitative and qualitative research. She stated: "Sixty-seven 3-, 4-, and 5-year-olds, their teachers, instructional aides, and six case-study parents participated in a yearlong qualitative and quantitative study" (p. 343). In the Method section, she further elaborated on the importance of mixing both qualitative and quantitative methodologies:

> Experimental and naturalistic strategies were used in this study to explore name's role in literacy acquisition. Quantitative measures provided a database that was analyzed for evidence of growth across the year and relationships among literacy tasks. Qualitative information from observations and interviews supplied the why and how behind the data through prolonged engagement, thick description, and analysis of emerging themes (Lancy, 1993; Patton, 1990). (p. 348)

Through her use of mixed methods, Bloodgood provided compelling evidence on the importance on name writing in early literacy learning. Although the quantitative data clearly demonstrated the importance of name writing as an indicator of early literacy knowledge, the qualitative data provided a more nuanced understanding of the various patterns that occur regarding how that knowledge develops.

Phase 3

In the current phase of mixed research studies in literacy research, many researchers label the design as mixed methods. In addition, and in contrast to the previous phase, rather than providing rationales for quantitative and qualitative methods, researchers tend to provide a theoretical rationale for the use of mixed research. One of the first examples of research in this time period that we located was Bauman and colleagues' (2002) study on the effectiveness of teaching morphemic analysis and context clues on reading vocabulary and comprehension. They described the design as follows:

> The overall design involved a mixed method of quantitative and descriptive design. Specifically, one of Tashakkori and Teddlie's (1998) "dominant-less dominant mixed method designs" was employed, "in which one paradigm and its methods are dominant, while a small component of the overall study is drawn from an alternative design" (p. 44). The dominant design was quantitative and involved a between-subjects, pretest-posttest, control-group, quasi-

experiment (Campbell & Stanley, 1966), with the student as the unit of analysis. The independent variable was group membership, which had four levels: morphemic-only instruction (MO), context-only instruction (CO), combined morphemic-context instruction (MC), and instructed control (IC). The less-dominant design involved descriptive data on students' vocabulary learning gathered through individual interviews with students selected from each treatment group. (p. 156)

In addition, they provided similar support in their explanation of data analysis: "Data from the dominant–less-dominant design were analyzed according to a sequential quantitative-qualitative data analysis process (Tashakkori & Teddlie, 1998, p. 127)" (p. 161). In the Results section, they separated the quantitative and qualitative findings; yet the discussion centered on the findings as a mixed research study, thereby providing a more complex understanding of their findings. Patterson, Henry, O'Quin, Ceprano, and Blue (2003) investigated the effectiveness of the Waterford Early Reading Program on young children in the state of New York. In their study, Patterson and colleagues not only integrated quantitative and qualitative research but also provided a strong rationale for the use of mixed research:

RATIONALE FOR CHOICE OF METHODOLOGY

Mixed methods. A review of the appropriateness of different paradigms and outcome measures for reading research led to the decision in the present study to adopt a mixed qualitative and quantitative design. We chose mixed methodology design to allow us to explore contextual factors that might affect literacy growth.

Miles and Huberman (1994), although focused primarily on qualitative analysis, discussed the benefits of linking qualitative and quantitative analysis. Our study aligns with what they saw as a first linkage between qualitative and quantitative methods, the "quantizing level, where information can be either counted directly or converted into ranks or scales" (p. 42). From our analysis of the qualitative data we discovered teacher variables that were subsequently used in quantitative analysis. (p. 184)

Prevalence of Mixed Research Studies in Literacy Research

Although, as noted previously, mixed research studies in the area of literacy have been published for several decades, and mixed research has become popular in many fields such as mathematics education (Hart, Smith, Swars, & Smith, 2009), literacy research has been dominated by monomethodological research approaches. Indeed, Reinking and Alvermann (2007) documented that of the 51 studies published in *Reading Research Quarterly* between 2003 and 2007 (i.e., Volumes 38–42) that represented one of the three research paradigms, only two (3.9%) were mixed research in orientation; of the remaining studies 25 were quantitative and 24 were qualitative. Furthermore, Mallette, Moffit, Onwuegbuzie, and Wheeler (2008), in their examination of 139 articles published in two leading journals—*Reading Research Quarterly* and *Journal of Literacy Research*—representing the field of literacy from 2003 to 2008, classified only 9% of the studies as representing mixed research, with the remaining studies representing monomethodology research (i.e., 47% quantitative, 44% qualitative). Thus, the goal of the remainder of this chapter is to facilitate understanding of mixed research in the literacy field.

STAGES OF THE MIXED RESEARCH PROCESS

According to Collins, Onwuegbuzie, and Sutton (2006), mixed research involves 13 steps, grouped within three stages.

> *Formulation stage*: (1) determining the mixed goal of the study, (2) formulating the mixed research objective(s), (3) determining the rationale of the study and the rationale(s) for mixing quantitative and qualitative approaches, (4) determining the purpose of the study and the purpose(s) for mixing quantitative and qualitative approaches, (5) determining the mixed research question(s).
>
> *Planning stage*: (6) selecting the mixed sampling design, (7) selecting the mixed research design.
>
> *Implementation stage*: (8) collecting quantitative and/or qualitative data, (9) analyzing the quantitative and/or qualitative data using quantitative and/or qualitative analysis techniques, (10) validating/legitimating the mixed research findings, (11) interpreting the mixed research findings, (12) writing the mixed research report, and (13) reformulating the mixed research question(s).

These 13 steps are both interactive and recursive. What most distinguishes the mixed research process from the monomethodology research processes is that the former necessitates that researchers make decisions about not only the individual quantitative research and qualitative research components but also how these components relate to each other.

Research Formulation Stage

Determining the goal (Step 1) involves making a decision about the overall long-term aim of the mixed research study. Here, researchers can use Newman, Ridenour, Newman, and DeMarco's (2003) framework as a guide. These authors have identified nine goals: The researcher can aim to predict;

add to the knowledge base; have a personal, social, institutional, and/or organizational impact; understand complex phenomena; measure change; test new ideas; generate new ideas; inform constituencies; or examine the past. The research goal leads directly to the research objective (Step 2). In this step, the researcher should determine which of the following five major standard research objectives are pertinent for both the quantitative and qualitative phases of the study: *exploration* (i.e., using primarily inductive techniques to explore a concept, phenomenon, or context in order to make tentative inferences; *description* (i.e., identifying and describing the antecedents and nature of phenomena); *explanation* (i.e., developing or expanding theory in an attempt to clarify the relationship among concepts, constructs, or phenomena and identify reasons for occurrences of events); *prediction* (i.e., using prior knowledge or extant theory to predict what will occur at a later point); and *influence* (i.e., manipulating one or more variables or conditions in an attempt to produce an expected or desired result) (Johnson & Christensen, 2008). Both the qualitative and quantitative phases of each mixed research study can be linked to one or more of these five research objectives.

The third step of the mixed research process is to determine the research mixing/rationale. This step not only involves determining the rationale of the study (i.e., why the study is needed) but also identifying the rationale for mixing quantitative and qualitative approaches. Collins and colleagues (2006) identified the following four major rationales for mixing quantitative and qualitative approaches (i.e., why mixing is needed): *participant enrichment* (i.e., mixing quantitative and qualitative techniques for the rationale of optimizing the sample, e.g., increasing the number of participants), *instrument fidelity* (i.e., maximizing the appropriateness and/or utility of all quantitative and qualitative instruments used in the study, e.g., via a pilot study), *treatment integrity* (i.e., mixing quantitative and qualitative procedures in order to assess the fidelity of interventions, treatments, or programs), and *significance enhancement* (i.e., mixing quantitative and qualitative techniques in order to optimize data interpretations). Alongside identifying the research/mixing rationale, researchers should determine the research/mixing purpose (Step 4). Collins and colleagues identified 65 purposes for mixing quantitative and qualitative approaches (i.e., how the mixing will occur), categorized under one of the four major rationales (i.e., participant enrichment, instrument fidelity, treatment integrity, significance enhancement). Also, in determining the purpose of mixing, we recommend that researchers use Greene and colleagues' (1989) framework, in which they identified five broad purposes of mixed methods studies: *triangulation* (i.e., seeking convergence and corroboration of findings from different methods that examine the same phenomenon); *complementarity* (i.e., seeking elaboration, enhancement, illustration, and clarification of the findings from one method with results from the other method); *initiation* (i.e., identifying paradoxes and contradictions that lead to the reframing of the research questions); *development* (i.e., using the findings from one method to help inform the other method); and *expansion* (i.e., seeking to expand the breadth and depth of the study by using different methods for different research components). Identifying the research purpose helps the researcher develop appropriate research questions (Step 5). For example, if the purpose of the research is triangulation, then both the quantitative and qualitative sets of research questions should most likely lead to an investigation of the same outcome or phenomenon. Conversely, if the purpose of the research is initiation or development, then the quantitative research question should be conditional on the qualitative research question or vice versa (cf. Onwuegbuzie & Leech, 2006).

Determining the research question(s), the fifth and final step of the research formulation stage, is central in the mixed research process. However, the development of research questions does not occur only at the fifth step of the mixed research process; these questions are reevaluated during data collection (Step 8), data analysis (Step 9), data legitimation (Step 10), and/or data interpretation (Step 11) and might be reframed at any of these phases. Furthermore, these research questions are reevaluated after the study has been completed, leading to modified and/or additional research questions (Step 13).

Onwuegbuzie and Leech (2006) introduced the concept of mixed research questions, defining them as

> Questions that embed both a quantitative research question and a qualitative research question within the same question. That is, mixed methods research questions combine or mix both the quantitative and qualitative research questions. Moreover, a mixed methods research question necessitates that both quantitative data and qualitative data be collected and analyzed either concurrently, sequentially, or iteratively before the question is addressed. (p. 483)

During the research conceptualization stage, the review of the literature plays a vital role. Leech and Onwuegbuzie (2010a, 2010b) suggest that the role of the literature review should be made explicit. As recommended by Onwuegbuzie, Collins, Leech, Dellinger, and Jiao (2010), literacy researchers should treat the information from articles extracted for their literature review as data that provide both qualitative and quantitative information and, therefore, can be analyzed using qualitative and quantitative approaches—what Sandelowski, Voils, and Barroso (2006) call mixed research syntheses—including creating meta-inferences (i.e., inferences from qualitative and quantitative information integrated into a whole). Studies involving meta-analyses (Glass, 1976), metasyntheses (Sandelowski & Barroso 2006), and metasummaries (Sandelowski & Barroso, 2003)—that involve analysis of a set of quantitative or qualitative studies on a given topic—play a vital role in mixed research syntheses whenever they are available. Furthermore, all literature should be examined and assessed for trustworthiness, credibility, dependability, legitimation, validity, plausibility, applicability, consistency, neutrality, reliability, objectivity, confirmability, and/or transferability (cf. Leech, Dellinger, Brannagan, & Tanaka, 2010).

Research Planning Stage

In Collins and colleagues' (2006) mixed research process framework, the research planning stage involves selecting the mixed sampling design (Step 6) and the mixed research design (Step 7). These steps are both interactive and iterative because choice of sampling design affects the selection of research design and vice versa. With regard to the sampling design, Onwuegbuzie and Collins (2007) provided a typology for classifying mixed sampling designs according to the time orientation of the components or phases and the relationship of the qualitative and quantitative samples: *identical* (i.e., exactly the same participants are involved in both the qualitative and quantitative phases of the study), *parallel* (i.e., the samples for the qualitative and quantitative components of the research are different but are drawn from the same population of interest), *nested* (i.e., the participants selected for one phase of the study represent a subset of those sample members selected for the other component of the research), or *multilevel* (i.e., the use of two or more sets of samples that are extracted from different levels of the population of interest, e.g., elementary school children vs. language arts teachers). The two criteria, time orientation (two levels) and sample relationship (four levels), yield eight different types of major sampling designs that mixed researchers have at their disposal. Another useful typology of sampling schemes is that developed by Teddlie and Yu (2007), who subdivided sampling schemes into the following four types: probability sampling, purposive sampling, convenience sampling, and mixed methods sampling.

For the research design step (i.e., Step 7), numerous useful typologies and frameworks have emerged. A particularly useful typology is that developed by Teddlie and Tashakkori (2006, 2009). These authors conceptualized what they termed the *methods-strands matrix* by crossing the number of methods used with the number of research components, or strands. The multistrand mixed methods cell in the matrix contains five families of mixed research designs: *parallel* (i.e., the quantitative and qualitative phases of the study occur in a parallel manner either at approximately the same time or with a time lag), *sequential* (i.e., the quantitative and qualitative phases of the study occur in chronological order), *conversion* (i.e., the mixing of quantitative and qualitative approaches occurs when one type of data [quantitative or qualitative] is transformed and then analyzed both quantitatively and qualitatively), *multilevel* (i.e., the quantitative data are collected at one level of analysis, e.g., child, and the qualitative data are collected at another level, e.g., parent, either concurrently or sequentially), and *fully integrated* (i.e., the mixing of quantitative and qualitative approaches occurs in an interactive, e.g., interdependent or iterative, manner at all stages of the study).

Teddlie and Tashakkori (2009) outlined seven criteria that authors use to create their mixed research design typologies: number of methodological approaches used, number of strands or phases, type of implementation process, stage of integration of approaches, priority of methodological approach, functions of the research study, and theoretical or ideological perspective. These authors also separate mixed research designs into mixed methods monostrand designs (i.e., comprising monostrand conversion designs, which "are used in single-strand studies in which research questions are answered through an analysis of transformed [quantitized and qualitized] data" [p. 149]) and mixed methods multistrand designs (i.e., containing at least two research strands that comprise the following five families: parallel mixed designs, sequential mixed designs, conversion mixed designs, multilevel mixed designs, and fully integrated mixed designs). Creswell and Plano Clark's (2007) "parsimonious and functional" (p. 59) typology of mixed research designs consists of four design types: triangulation, embedded, explanatory, and exploratory.

Leech and Onwuegbuzie's (2009) presented a three-dimensional typology, in which mixed designs can be represented as a function of three dimensions: *level of mixing* (i.e., fully mixed [mixing of quantitative and qualitative approaches within or across the data collection, analysis, and interpretation stages] vs. partially mixed [mixing only at the data interpretation stage]), *time orientation* (i.e., concurrent [quantitative and qualitative phases occur at approximately the same point in time] vs. sequential [phases occur one after the other]), and *emphasis of approaches* (i.e., equal status [quantitative and qualitative components have approximately equal emphasis] vs. dominant status [one component has higher priority than the other]). Leech and Onwuegbuzie's typology thus can be characterized by a 2 (fully mixed vs. partially mixed) × 2 (concurrent vs. sequential) × 3 (equal status vs. dominant status-quantitative vs. dominant status-qualitative), which yields 12 types of mixed research designs.

Johnson and colleagues (2007) provided a useful way of framing mixed research studies. Specifically, they conceptualized mixed research as being either quantitative dominant, qualitative dominant, or equal status. According to Johnson and colleagues,

> Qualitative dominant mixed methods research is the type of mixed research in which one relies on a qualitative, constructivist-poststructuralist-critical view of the research process, while concurrently recognizing that the addition of quantitative data and approaches are likely to benefit most research projects. (p. 124)

In contrast,

> Quantitative dominant mixed methods research is the type of mixed research in which one relies on a quantitative, postpositivist view of the research process, while concurrently recognizing that the addition of qualitative data and approaches are likely to benefit most research projects. (p. 124)

Finally, equal status designs involve the approximately equal use of quantitative and qualitative epistemologies, techniques, methods, approaches, concepts, or language within the same mixed research study.

The utility of this tripartite conceptualization of mixed research designs is that it allows mixed research to be conducted within both quantitative and qualitative research studies without the researchers having to be mixed researchers. In other words, researchers with a quantitative orientation can conduct mixed research and yet maintain quantitative assumptions and stances (e.g., postpositivism). Similarly, researchers with a qualitative orientation can conduct mixed research and yet maintain qualitative assumptions and stances (e.g., constructivism, critical theory). Thus, this tripartite conceptualization makes mixed research accessible not only for mixed researchers but also for both quantitative and qualitative researchers.

Research Implementation Stage

The research implementation stage comprises the following four interactive and cyclical steps: data collection (Step 8), data analysis (Step 9), data legitimation (Step 10), and data interpretation (Step 11). With respect to data collection, Johnson and Turner's (2003) typology contains six specific data collection strategies in mixed research: mixture of open- and closed-ended items on one or more questionnaires; mixture of depth and breadth interviewing; mixture of a priori and emergent/flowing focus group strategies; mixture of standardized open- and closed-ended predesigned tests; mixture of standardized/confirmatory and less structured/exploratory observation, alternating between participatory and nonparticipatory researcher roles; and mixture of nonnumeric and numeric documents, consisting of archived data based on open- and closed-ended items. Most recently, Teddlie and Tashakkori (2009) presented 30 between-strategies mixed data collection combinations (e.g., quantitative observations with qualitative-based focus group) and six within-strategies mixed methods data collection combinations (e.g., quantitative interview and qualitative interview).

Data collection is followed by data analysis (Step 9). Most recently, Onwuegbuzie and Combs (2010) conducted a comprehensive review of the literature, identifying virtually every known methodological work (e.g., article, editorial, book chapter, conference paper) in the area of mixed analyses and identified 13 criteria that authors have used to create their mixed analysis typologies. This led to them developing the following comprehensive and inclusive definition or summary of what is called mixed analysis:

Mixed analysis involves the use of both quantitative and qualitative analytical techniques within the same framework, which is guided either a priori, a posteriori, or iteratively (representing analytical decisions that occur both prior to the study and during the study). It might be based on one of the existing mixed methods research paradigms (e.g., pragmatism, transformative-emancipatory) such that it meets one or more of the following rationales/purposes: triangulation, complementarity, development, initiation, and expansion. Mixed analyses involve the analyses of one or both data types (i.e., quantitative data *or* qualitative data; or quantitative data *and* qualitative data) which occur either concurrently (i.e., in no chronological order), or sequentially in two phases (in which the qualitative analysis phase precedes the quantitative analysis phase or vice versa, and findings from the initial analysis phase informs the subsequent phase) or more than two phases (i.e., iteratively). The analysis strands might not interact until the data interpretation stage, yielding a basic parallel mixed analysis, although more complex forms of parallel mixed analysis can be used, in which interaction takes place in a limited way before the data interpretation phase. The mixed analysis can be design-based, wherein it is directly linked to the mixed methods design (e.g., sequential mixed analysis techniques used for sequential mixed methods designs). Alternatively, the mixed analysis can be phase-based, in which the mixed analysis takes place in one or more phases (e.g., data transformation). In mixed analyses, either the qualitative or quantitative analysis strands might be given priority or approximately equal priority as a result of a priori decisions (i.e., determined at the research conceptualization phase) or decisions that emerge during the course of the study (i.e., a posteriori or iterative decisions). The mixed analysis could represent case-oriented, variable-oriented, and/or process/experience oriented analyses. The mixed analysis is guided by an attempt to analyze data in a way that yields at least one of five types of generalizations (i.e., external statistical generalizations, internal statistical generalizations, analytical generalizations, case-to-case transfer, naturalistic generalization). At its most integrated form, the mixed analysis might involve some form of cross-over analysis, wherein one or more analysis types associated with one tradition (e.g., qualitative analysis) are used to analyze data associated with a different tradition (e.g., quantitative data). (pp. 425–426)

In Step 10, the legitimation of both the quantitative and the qualitative data is assessed. For the quantitative phase, literacy researchers should assess threats to internal validity and external validity (e.g., Campbell, 1957; Campbell & Stanley, 1963; Cook & Campbell, 1979; Huck & Sandler, 1979; McMillan, 2000; Onwuegbuzie, 2003; Smith & Glass, 1987) as well as measurement validity (Messick, 1989, 1995; Onwuegbuzie, Daniel, & Collins, 2009). With regard to the qualitative phase, literacy researchers should assess threats to trustworthiness, credibility, dependability, authenticity, verification, plausibility, applicability, confirmability, and/or transferability of data (e.g., Creswell, 2007; Guba & Lincoln, 1989; Lather, 1993; Lincoln, 1995; Lincoln & Guba, 1985; Maxwell, 1992, 1996, 2005; Miles & Huberman, 1994; Onwuegbuzie & Leech, 2007).

Onwuegbuzie and Johnson (2006) developed a typology for legitimation issues that are pertinent to the overall mixed research study. Specifically, this typology consists of nine legitimation types pertaining to the overall mixed research process: *sample integration* (i.e., extent to which the relationship between the quantitative and qualitative sampling designs yields quality meta-inferences); *inside–outside* (i.e., extent to which the researcher accurately presents and appropriately utilizes the insider's [emic] view and the observer's [etic] view for purposes such as description and explanation); *weakness minimization* (i.e., extent to which the weakness from one approach is compensated by the strengths from the other approach); *sequential* (i.e., extent to which the researcher has minimized the potential problem wherein the meta-inferences could be affected by reversing the sequence of the quantitative and qualitative phases); *conversion* (i.e., extent to which the quantitizing or qualitizing yields quality meta-inferences); *paradigmatic mixing* (i.e., extent to which the researcher's epistemological, ontological, axiological, methodological, and rhetorical assumptions and stances that underlie the quantitative and qualitative approaches are successfully combined or blended into a usable package); *commensurability* (i.e., extent to which the meta-inferences made reflect a mixed worldview based on the cognitive process of gestalt switching and integration); *multiple validities* (i.e., extent to which addressing legitimation of the quantitative and qualitative components of the mixed research study result from the use of quantitative, qualitative, *and* mixed validity types, yielding high quality meta-inferences); and *political* (i.e., extent to which the consumers of mixed research value the meta-inferences stemming from both the quantitative and the qualitative components of a study).

Once validated/legitimated, these data then are interpreted (Step 11). Leech and Onwuegbuzie (2004) identified four types of significance in social science research, which very much applies to literacy research: *statistical significance* (i.e., the probability that observed results from the sample could have occurred if the null hypothesis is true), *practical significance* (i.e., the educational value of the results, e.g., effect size, which represents a family of indices that measure the size of a relationship or difference), *clinical significance* (i.e., the extent that an intervention or treatment makes a real difference to the quality of life of the participants or to those with whom they interact or encounter), and *economic significance* (i.e., economic value of the finding, e.g., effect of the intervention).

With respect to the overall mixed research study, Teddlie and Tashakkori (2009) developed an interpretive framework for inference quality. This framework comprises the following 10 aspects of quality: *design suitability* (i.e., "Are the methods of study appropriate for answering the research questions?"; "Does the design match the research questions?"; "Does the mixed methods design match the stated purpose for conducting an integrated study?"; "Do the strands of the mixed methods study address the same research questions [or closely related aspects of the research question]?"); *design fidelity* (i.e., "Are the qualitative, quantitative, and mixed methods procedures or design components capturing the meanings, effects, or relationships?"); *within-design consistency* (i.e., "Do the components of the design fit together in a seamless manner?": "Do the strands of the mixed methods study follow each other (or are they linked) in a logical and seamless manner?"); *analytic adequacy* (i.e., "Are the data analysis procedures/strategies appropriate and adequate to provide possible answers to research questions?"; "Are the mixed methods strategies implemented effectively?"); *interpretive consistency* (i.e., "Do the inferences closely follow the relevant findings in terms of type, scope, and intensity?"; "Are multiple inferences made on the basis of the same findings consistent with each other?"); *theoretical consistency* (i.e., "Are the inferences consistent with theory and state of knowledge in the field?"); *interpretive agreement* (i.e., "Are other scholars likely to reach the same conclusions on the basis of the same results?"; "Do the inferences match participants' constructions?"); *interpretive distinctiveness* (i.e., "Is each inference distinctively more credible/plausible than other possible conclusions that might be made on the basis of the same results?"); *integrative efficacy* (i.e., "Do the meta-inferences adequately incorporate the inferences that are made in each strand of the study?"; "If there are credible inconsistencies between inferences made within/across strands, are the theoretical explanations for these inconsistencies explored and possible explanations offered?"); and *interpretive correspondence* (i.e., "Do the inferences correspond to the stated purpose/questions of the study?"; "Do the inferences made in each strand address the purposes of the study in that strand?"; "Do the meta-inferences meet the stated need for using a mixed methods design?").

Writing the research report (Step 12) is the penultimate step in the mixed research process. Several authors have provided guidelines for writing mixed research reports (e.g., Creswell & Plano Clark, 2007; Johnson & Onwuegbuzie, 2008; Leech & Onwuegbuzie, 2010a, 2010b; Leech, Onwuegbuzie, & Combs, in press; Tashakkori & Creswell, 2007a).

Once the research report has been written, the researcher reformulates the research questions (Step 13), which, in turn, might lead to a reformulation of the research goal (Step 1), research objective (Step 2), research/mixing rationale (Step 3), and/or research/mixing purpose (Step 4) in subsequent studies. Alternatively, the research goal, research objective, and research purpose may not be changed, and, instead, the reformulation of the research question directly leads to a reformulation of the mixed sampling design (Step 6) and research design (Step 7). Thus, in subsequent studies, Steps 6–11 are repeated until all research goals, objectives, purposes, and questions are adequately addressed and *verstehen* is reached.

APPROPRIATE RESEARCH QUESTIONS FOR MIXED RESEARCH

As noted earlier, research questions play a central role in mixed research. In the words of Johnson and Onwuegbuzie (2004), "What is most fundamental is the research question—research methods should *follow* research questions in a way that offers the best chance to obtain useful answers" (pp. 17–18). Tashakkori and Creswell (2007b) have conceptualized an excellent typology for classifying mixed research questions, which outlines three ways that research questions are constructed in mixed research. The first technique for constructing research questions in mixed research involves writing separate quantitative and qualitative questions followed by an explicit mixed research question. The second method involves writing an overarching mixed or integrated research question, subsequently broken down into separate quantitative and qualitative subquestions to address in each phase or component of the investigation. Tashakkori and Creswell (2007b) contend that this type of research question is more common in parallel studies (i.e., the findings of both the quantitative and the qualitative phases are interpreted and written up separately) and concurrent studies (findings stemming from one phase [e.g., quantitative phase] do not inform the qualitative phase [e.g., qualitative phase]) than in sequential studies (i.e., either the quantitative or qualitative phase is conducted first, which then informs the subsequent phase). Although this overarching question might be implicitly present, it might not be explicitly stated. In the third method, research questions for each phase are written as the study evolves. If the first phase is quantitative in nature, the question would be framed as a quantitative research question. If the second phase is qualitative, the question would be framed accordingly. As such, this method of constructing research questions is more relevant to sequential studies than to concurrent or parallel studies. Consistent with Onwuegbuzie and Leech (2006), Tashakkori and Creswell (2007b) recommended the development of a single mixed research question that addresses the nature of mixing and integration or a single mixed research question that transcends any subsequent quantitative and qualitative subquestions.

CLAIMS FOR MIXED RESEARCH

Mixed researchers make several common claims about mixed research. The ultimate common claim is that mixed research represents a distinctive methodology; that is, it is a methodology that is distinct from both quantitative and qualitative methodologies (cf. Greene, 2006, 2008). Stemming from this claim are many others about mixed research. In particular, a major premise of mixed research is that "many research questions and combinations of questions are best and most fully answered through mixed research solutions" (Johnson & Onwuegbuzie, 2004, p. 18). However, some of the claims differ as a function of the philosophical assumptions and stance of the mixed researcher. Interestingly, Onwuegbuzie, Collins, and Leech (in press) identified the following 12 mixed research stances: pragmatism-of-the-middle philosophy (Johnson & Onwuegbuzie, 2004), pragmatism-of-the-right philosophy (Putnam, 2002; Rescher, 2000), pragmatism-of-the-left philosophy (Maxcy, 2003; Rorty, 1991), anticonflationist philosophy (Bryman, 1992; Hammersley, 1992; Layder, 1993; Roberts, 2002), critical realist orientation (Christ, 2010; Houston, 2001; Maxwell, 2004; McEvoy & Richards, 2003, 2006), dialectical (Greene, 2008; Greene & Caracelli, 1997; Maxwell & Loomis, 2003), complementary strengths (Brewer & Hunter, 1989; Morse, 2003), transformative-emancipatory (Mertens, 2003), aparadigmatic (Patton, 2002; Reichardt & Cook, 1979), substantive theory (Chen, 2006), communities of practice (Denscombe, 2008), and, most recently, dialectical pragmatist (Johnson, 2009). For instance, whereas dialectical pragmatists believe that different epistemological perspectives can be incorporated or mixed (e.g., postpositivism and constructivism), mixed researchers who adopt the complementary strengths stance believe that, although the paradigms are not necessarily incompatible, they are substantively different, and thus methods used for different paradigms should be kept separate to preserve paradigmatic and methodological integrity (Greene, 2007).

STANDARDS OF QUALITY FOR MIXED METHODOLOGY RESEARCH

O'Cathain (2010) has provided the most comprehensive framework to date for assessing quality in mixed research. Her quality framework consists of the following eight domains of quality: planning quality, design quality, data quality, interpretive rigor, inference transferability, reporting quality, synthesizability, and utility.

Planning Quality

This domain refers to how well the underlying mixed research study has been planned and thus is relevant for mixed research proposals. It comprises the following four components: *foundational element* (i.e., the extent to which the review of the literature is sufficiently comprehensible and critical to situate the study and drive the research question and study design); *rationale transparency* (i.e., the extent to which a justification is provided for using mixed research approaches); *planning transparency* (i.e., the extent to which elements of the mixed research study [e.g., paradigm, planned design, data collection, analysis, reporting] are described in sufficient detail); and *feasibility* (i.e., the extent to which the design, and each component, can be undertaken given the available resources [e.g., time, money]).

Design Quality

This domain pertains to the adequacy of the design used in the mixed research study and comprises the following four elements: *design transparency* (i.e., the extent to which there is adequate description of the mixed research design type from an existing typology or an adequate description of the elements of design if the mixed research design used is new); *design suitability* (i.e., the extent to which the design is appropriate for addressing the overall research question, is consistent with or matches the rationale for combining approaches, and is appropriate for the stated paradigm); *design strength* (i.e., the extent to which the strengths and weaknesses of the methods are considered in order to minimize bias and optimize the breadth and depth of the mixed research study); and *design rigor* (i.e., the extent to which methods are implemented in a way that is consistent with the mixed research design).

Data Quality

This domain, which refers to the quality of data collection and data analysis, comprises the following five components: *data transparency* (i.e., the extent to which each method is described in sufficient detail, including its role within the study); *data rigor/design fidelity* (i.e., the extent to which each method is implemented with rigor); *sampling adequacy* (i.e., the extent to which the sampling scheme and sample size for each method are adequate for the underlying design); *analytic adequacy* (i.e., the extent to which the data analysis techniques are appropriate for the research question and are undertaken adequately); and *analytic integration rigor* (i.e., the extent to which any integration that occurs at the analysis stage of a mixed research study is robust [e.g., data transformations used are justified]).

Interpretive Rigor

According to O'Cathain (2010), this domain refers to the extent that the conclusions stem directly from the findings. It comprises the following eight components: *interpretive transparency* (i.e., the extent to which it is clear which findings have emerged from which methods); *interpretive consistency* (i.e., the extent to which the inferences are consistent with the findings on which they are based); *theoretical consistency* (i.e., the extent to which the inferences are consistent with current knowledge or theory); *interpretive agreement* (i.e., the extent to which other researchers are likely to arrive at the same interpretations and conclusions based on the findings presented); *interpretive distinctiveness* (i.e., the extent to which the conclusions drawn are more credible than any other conclusions); *interpretive efficacy* (i.e., the extent to which the meta-inferences from the whole study adequately reflect inferences that stem from both the qualitative and the quantitative findings and inferences); *interpretive bias reduction* (i.e., the extent to which the explanations are given for inconsistencies that emerge between the findings and inferences); and *interpretive correspondence* (i.e., the extent to which the inferences correspond to the purpose of the study and research questions).

Inference Transferability

This domain, which refers to the extent that the conclusions in a mixed research study can be applied or generalized to other entities or settings, comprises the following four elements: *ecological transferability* (i.e., the extent to which the meta-inferences and conclusions can be transferred to other contexts and settings); *population transferability* (i.e., the extent to which the meta-inferences and conclusions can be transferred to other individuals and groups); *temporal transferability* (i.e., the extent to which the meta-inferences and conclusions can be transferred to the future); and *theoretical transferability* (i.e., the extent to which the meta-inferences and conclusions can be transferred to other methods of measuring behavior).

Reporting Quality

This domain refers to the extent that the final report is of optimal quality. It comprises the following three elements: *report availability* (i.e., the extent to which the study is successfully completed within allocated resources [e.g., time, money]); *reporting transparency* (i.e., the extent to which the key aspects of the study are reported); and *yield* (i.e., the extent to which the whole is greater than the sum of its parts).

Synthesizability

This domain refers to the appraisal of whether a mixed research study is justified to include in an evidence synthesis and/or of the weight given to the mixed research study within the synthesis. O'Cathain (2010) recommends the use of Pluye, Gagnon, Griffiths, and Johnson-Lafleur's (2009) scoring system for appraising mixed research based on 15 quality criteria, six for the qualitative research components (i.e., qualitative objective or question; appropriate qualitative approach or design or method; description of the context; description of participants and justification of sampling; description of qualitative data collection and analysis; discussion of researchers' reflexivity); three for the quantitative experimental components (i.e., appropriate sequence generation and/or randomization; allocation concealment and/or blinding; complete outcome data and/or low withdrawal/dropout); three for the quantitative observational components (i.e., appropriate sampling and sample; justification of measurements [validity and standards];

control of confounding variables); and three for the mixed research components (i.e., justification of the mixed methods design; combination of qualitative and quantitative data collection analysis techniques or procedures; integration of qualitative and quantitative data or results).

Utility

This final domain in O'Cathain's (2010) set refers to the utility of a mixed research study and comprises utility quality (i.e., the extent to which the findings are used by consumers and policymakers).

AN EXEMPLAR OF MIXED RESEARCH

We selected "Doctoral Students' Perceptions of Barriers to Reading Empirical Literature: A Mixed Analysis" (Benge, Onwuegbuzie, Mallette, & Burgess, 2010) as our exemplar study because it adheres to all of the standards of quality in mixed research discussed previously (O'Cathain, 2010). The planning quality domain is evident in the section describing the study. In providing a rationale, the authors not only make a claim for the importance of the study but they also provide a compelling rationale for using a mixed design. The design quality domain suggests the importance of the research questions matching the design. In quality mixed studies, there can be qualitative questions and quantitative questions; yet most importantly there ought to be mixed research questions. In the Benge and colleagues (2010) research, the following questions guided the study:

Quantitative Research Questions
1. What is the level of reading comprehension among doctoral students?
2. What is the level of reading vocabulary among doctoral students?

Qualitative Research Question
3. What are the perceived barriers to reading empirical articles of doctoral students?

Mixed Research Questions
4. What is the prevalence of each of the perceived barriers to reading empirical articles of doctoral students?
5. How do these perceived barriers to reading empirical articles relate to one another?
6. What is the relationship between reading ability (i.e., reading com-

prehension, reading vocabulary) and perceived barriers to reading empirical articles of doctoral students?

7. Which perceived barriers predict the levels of perceived difficulty doctoral students experience in reading empirical research articles?

Clearly, there is a good balance of qualitative and quantitative questions, and the overarching questions are mixed.

The next several domains, data quality, interpretive rigor, and transferability, are necessary in all rigorous research. However, in mixed studies, it is imperative that the standards of quality are met for qualitative, quantitative, and mixed research. Benge and colleagues (2010) met these standards by beginning with a large sample size ($N = 205$), using multiple data sources (i.e., Nelson–Denny Reading Test and the Reading Interest Survey), and sophisticated data analysis techniques. The analytic scheme was a sequential mixed analysis (SMA; Onwuegbuzie & Teddlie, 2003; Tashakkori & Teddlie, 1998), which

> involved the use of both qualitative and quantitative data analysis procedures in a sequential manner—specifically, an iterative manner—commencing with quantitative analyses, followed by qualitative analyses that built upon the quantitative analyses, followed by quantitative analyses of the qualitative data. This sequence of analysis involved abductive reasoning that oscillated between inductive reasoning and deductive reasoning (Morgan, 2007). (p. 60)

The SMA included six analytic stages utilizing descriptive statistics, thematic analysis, principal-component analysis, correlations, canonical correlation analysis, and confirmatory analysis.

Perhaps, though, it is the reporting quality domain that truly makes this an exemplar study. That is, the written report of this study follows the format suggested in this chapter by detailing the 13 methodological steps. In fact, these steps are used as section headings, which aids in the understanding and importance of each step in the research process. This study exemplifies the standards of quality in mixed research and in doing so not only reports the findings but also builds the case for the importance of mixed research in literacy.

CONCLUSIONS

Approximately 40 years have passed since the publication of the first mixed research article in a first-tier journal representing the field of literacy. Although this time period has witnessed rapid growth in the number of mixed research studies published that represent other fields, the field of literacy has not kept pace. For example, the 3.9% prevalence rate documented by Reinking and Alvermann (2007) and the 9.4% rated observed by Mallette and colleagues (2008) were much lower than prevalence rate of 31% reported by Ross and Onwuegbuzie (2009) for articles published in two mathematics education journals over a 5-year period and the prevalence rate of 16% reported by Alise and Teddlie (2010) for articles published in 2005 in the top five journals (based on the impact factor) in two applied disciplines (i.e., nursing, education). Yet, as observed in the exemplar study discussed in this chapter, combining quantitative and qualitative research approaches has conceptual and methodological appeal, enabling literacy researchers "to be more flexible, integrative, and holistic in their investigative techniques, as they strive to address a range of complex research questions that arise" (Powell, Mihalas, Onwuegbuzie, Suldo, & Daley, 2008, p. 306).

Furthermore, mixed research techniques can be used for participant enrichment, instrument fidelity, treatment integrity, and significance enhancement (Collins et al., 2006) and for the purpose of triangulation, complementarity, initiation, development, and expansion (Greene et al., 1989). Thus, we recommend that more mixed research studies be conducted in literacy research when the research question warrants such investigations. When literacy researchers conduct mixed research, we recommend that they describe clearly and completely the methodological techniques used and delineate clearly their paradigmatic orientations, preferences, and philosophical assumptions and stances that drive their mixed research studies. The question should no longer be *whether* mixed research techniques should be used but *how*. After all, mixed research techniques are a natural extension of the mixed methods procedures that literacy practitioners use in their day-to-day activities.

REFERENCES

Adler, L. (1996). Qualitative research of legal issues. In D. Schimmel (Ed.), *Research that makes a difference: Complementary methods for examining legal issues in education* (NOLPE Monograph Series No. 56, pp. 3–31). Topeka, KS: National Organization on Legal Problems of Education.

Alise, M. A., & Teddlie, C. (2010). A continuation of the paradigm wars? Prevalence rates of methodological approaches across the social/behavioral sciences. *Journal of Mixed Methods Research, 4*, 103–126.

Bauman, J. F., Edwards, E. C., Font, G., Tereshinki, C. A., Kame'enui, E. J., & Olejnik, S. (2002). Teaching morphemic and contextual analysis to fifth-grade students. *Reading Research Quarterly, 37*, 150–176.

Benge, C., Onwuegbuzie, A. J., Mallette, M. H., & Burgess, M. L. (2010). Doctoral students' perceptions of barriers to reading empirical literature: A mixed analysis. *International Journal of Doctoral Studies, 5*, 55–77.

Bloodgood, J. W. (1999). What's in a name?: Children's name writing and literacy acquisition. *Reading Research Quarterly, 34,* 342–367.

Brewer, J., & Hunter, A. (1989). *Multimethod research.* Thousand Oaks, CA: Sage.

Bryman, A. (1992). Quantitative and qualitative research: Further reflections on their integration. In J. Brannen (Ed.), *Mixing methods: Qualitative and quantitative research* (pp. 89–111). Aldershot, UK: Avebury Press.

Calfee, R., & Sperling, M. (2010). *On mixed methods: Approaches to language and literacy research.* New York: Teachers College Press.

Campbell, D. T. (1957). Factors relevant to the validity of experiments in social settings. *Psychological Bulletin, 54,* 297–312.

Campbell, D. T., & Stanley, J. C. (1963). *Experimental and quasi-experimental designs for research.* Chicago: Rand McNally.

Chen, H. T. (2006). A theory-driven evaluation perspective on mixed methods research. *Research in the Schools, 13*(1), 75–83.

Christ, T. W. (2010, April). *Critical realism and pragmatism as a lens for mixed methods research.* Paper presented at the annual meeting of the American Educational Research Association, Denver, CO.

Collins, K. M. T., Onwuegbuzie, A. J., & Sutton, I. L. (2006). A model incorporating the rationale and purpose for conducting mixed methods research in special education and beyond. *Learning Disabilities: A Contemporary Journal, 4,* 67–100.

Cook, T. D., & Campbell, D. T. (1979). *Quasi-experimentation. Design and analysis issues for field settings.* Chicago: Rand McNally.

Creswell, J. W. (2007). *Qualitative inquiry and research design: Choosing among five approaches* (2nd ed.). Thousand Oaks, CA: Sage.

Creswell, J. W., & Plano Clark, V. L. (2007). *Designing and conducting mixed methods research.* Thousand Oaks, CA: Sage.

Denscombe, M. (2008). Communities of practice: A research paradigm for the mixed methods approach. *Journal of Mixed Methods Research, 2,* 270–283.

Fareed, A. H. (1971). Interpretive responses in reading history and biology: An exploratory study. *Reading Research Quarterly, 6,* 493–532.

Freppon, P. A. (1991). Children's concepts of the nature and purpose of reading in different instructional settings. *Journal of Reading Behavior, 23,* 139–163.

Garner, R. (1980). Monitoring of understanding: An investigation of good and poor readers' awareness of induced miscomprehension of text. *Journal of Reading Behavior, 12,* 55–63.

Gaskins, R. W. (1996). "That's just how it was": The effect of issue-related emotional involvement on reading comprehension. *Reading Research Quarterly, 31,* 386–405.

Glass, G. (1976). Primary, secondary, and meta-analysis of research. *Educational Researcher, 5*(10), 3–8.

Greene, J. C. (2006). Toward a methodology of mixed methods social inquiry. *Research in the Schools, 13*(1), 93–98.

Greene, J. C. (2007). *Mixed methods in social inquiry.* San Francisco: Jossey-Bass.

Greene, J. C. (2008). Is mixed methods social inquiry a distinctive methodology? *Journal of Mixed Methods Research, 2,* 7–22.

Greene, J. C., & Caracelli, V. J. (1997). Defining and describing the paradigm issue in mixed-method evaluation. In J. C. Greene & V. J. Caracelli (Eds.), *Advances in mixed-method evaluation: The challenges and benefits of integrating diverse paradigms* (New Directions for Evaluation, No. 74, pp. 5–17). San Francisco: Jossey-Bass.

Greene, J. C., Caracelli, V. J., & Graham, W. F. (1989). Toward a conceptual framework for mixed-method evaluation designs. *Educational Evaluation and Policy Analysis, 11*, 255–274.

Guba, E. G., & Lincoln, Y. S. (1989). *Fourth generation evaluation.* Newbury Park, CA: Sage.

Hammersley, M. (1992). Deconstructing the qualitative–quantitative divide. In J. Brannen (Ed.), *Mixing methods: Qualitative and quantitative research* (pp. 39–55). Aldershot, UK: Avebury Press.

Hart, L. C., Smith, S. Z., Swars, S. L., & Smith, M. E. (2009). An examination of research methods in mathematics education (1995–2005). *Journal of Mixed Methods Research, 3*, 26–41.

Houston, S. (2001). Beyond social constructionism: Critical realism and social work. *British Journal of Social Work, 31*, 845–861.

Howe, K. R. (1988). Against the quantitative-qualitative incompatability thesis, or, Dogmas die hard. *Educational Researcher, 17*(8), 10–16.

Huck, S. W., & Sandler, H. M. (1979). *Rival hypotheses: Alternative interpretations of data based conclusions.* New York: HarperCollins.

Johnson, R. B. (2009). Comment on Howe: Toward a more inclusive "Scientific research in education." *Educational Researcher, 38*, 449–457.

Johnson, R. B., & Christensen, L. (2008). *Educational research quantitative, qualitative, and mixed approaches* (3rd ed.). Thousand Oaks, CA: Sage.

Johnson, R. B., & Onwuegbuzie, A. J. (2004). Mixed methods research: A research paradigm whose time has come. *Educational Researcher, 33*(7), 14–26.

Johnson, R. B., & Onwuegbuzie, A. J. (2008). Mixed research. In R. B. Johnson & L. B. Christensen (Eds.), *Educational research: Quantitative, qualitative, and mixed approaches* (3rd ed., pp. 439–459). Thousand Oaks, CA: Sage.

Johnson, R. B., Onwuegbuzie, A. J., & Turner, L. A. (2007). Toward a definition of mixed methods research. *Journal of Mixed Methods Research, 1*, 112–133.

Johnson, R. B., & Turner, L. A. (2003). Data collection strategies in mixed methods research. In A. Tashakkori & C. Teddlie (Eds.), *Handbook of mixed methods in social and behavioral research* (pp. 297–319). Thousand Oaks, CA: Sage.

Lather, P. (1993). Fertile obsession: Validity after poststructuralism. *Sociological Quarterly, 34*, 673–693.

Layder, D. (1993). *New strategies in social research: An introduction and guide.* Cambridge, UK: Polity Press.

Leech, N. L., Dellinger, A., Brannagan, K. B., & Tanaka, H. (2010). Evaluating mixed research studies: A mixed methods approach. *Journal of Mixed Methods Research, 4*, 17–31.

Leech, N. L., & Onwuegbuzie, A. J. (2004). A proposed fourth measure of significance: The role of economic significance in educational research. *Evaluation and Research in Education, 18*, 179–198.

Leech, N. L., & Onwuegbuzie, A. J. (2009). A typology of mixed methods research designs. *Quality and Quantity: International Journal of Methodology, 43*, 265–275.

Leech, N. L., & Onwuegbuzie, A. J. (2010a). Guidelines for conducting and reporting mixed research in the field of counseling and beyond. *Journal of Counseling and Development, 88,* 61–69.

Leech, N. L., & Onwuegbuzie, A. J. (2010b). Guidelines for conducting and reporting mixed research in the field of stress and coping and beyond. In G. S. Gates, W. H. Gmelch, & M. Wolverton (Series Eds.) & K. M. T. Collins, A. J. Onwuegbuzie, & Q. G. Jiao (Eds.), The Research on Stress and Coping in Education Series: Vol. 5. *Toward a broader understanding of stress and coping: Mixed methods approaches* (pp. 77–104). Charlotte, NC: Information Age.

Leech, N. L., Onwuegbuzie, A. J., & Combs, J. C. (in press). Writing publishable mixed research articles: Guidelines for emerging scholars in the health sciences and beyond. *International Journal of Multiple Research Approaches.*

Lincoln, Y. S. (1995). Emerging criteria for quality in qualitative and interpretive research. *Qualitative Inquiry, 1,* 275–289.

Lincoln, Y. S., & Guba, E. G. (1985). *Naturalistic inquiry.* Beverly Hills, CA: Sage.

Mallette, M. H., Moffit, C., Onwuegbuzie, A. J., & Wheeler, K. (2008, December). *Early literacy research: Exploring trends and political influences.* Paper presented at the annual meeting of the National Reading Conference, Orlando, FL.

Maxcy, S. J. (2003). Pragmatic threads in mixed methods research in the social sciences: The search for multiple modes of inquiry and the end of the philosophy of formalism. In A. Tashakkori & C. Teddlie (Eds.), *Handbook of mixed methods in social and behavioral research* (pp. 51–89). Thousand Oaks, CA: Sage.

Maxwell, J. A. (1992). Understanding and validity in qualitative research. *Harvard Educational Review, 62,* 279–299.

Maxwell, J. A. (1996). *Qualitative research design.* Newbury Park, CA: Sage.

Maxwell, J. A. (2004, April). *Realism as a stance for mixed methods research.* Paper presented at the annual meeting of the American Educational Research Association, San Diego, CA.

Maxwell, J. A. (2005). *Qualitative research design: An interactive approach* (2nd ed.). Newbury Park, CA: Sage.

Maxwell, J. A., & Loomis, D. M. (2003). Mixed methods design: An alternative approach. In A. Tashakkori & C. Teddlie (Eds.), *Handbook of mixed methods in social and behavioral research* (pp. 241–272). Thousand Oaks, CA: Sage.

McEvoy, P., & Richards, D. (2003). Critical realism: A way forward for evaluation research in nursing? *Journal of Advanced Nursing, 43,* 411–420.

McEvoy, P., & Richards, D. (2006). A critical realist rationale for using a combination of quantitative and qualitative methods. *Journal of Research in Nursing, 11,* 66–78.

McMillan, J. H. (2000, April). *Examining categories of rival hypotheses for educational research.* Paper presented at the annual meeting of the American Educational Research Association, New Orleans, LA.

Mertens, D. (2003). Mixed methods and the politics of human research: The transformative-emancipatory perspective. In A. Tashakkori & C. Teddlie (Eds.), *Handbook of mixed methods in social and behavioral research* (pp. 135–164). Thousand Oaks, CA: Sage.

Messick, S. (1989). Validity. In R. L. Linn (Ed.), *Educational measurement* (3rd ed., pp. 13–103). Old Tappan, NJ: Macmillan.

Messick, S. (1995). Validity of psychological assessment: Validation of inferences from persons' responses and performances as scientific inquiry into score meaning. *American Psychologist, 50,* 741–749.

Miles, M., & Huberman, A. M. (1994). *Qualitative data analysis: An expanded sourcebook* (2nd ed.). Thousand Oaks, CA: Sage.

Morse, J. M. (2003). Principles of mixed methods and multimethod research design. In A. Tashakkori & C. Teddlie (Eds.), *Handbook of mixed methods in social and behavioral research* (pp. 189–208). Thousand Oaks, CA: Sage.

Newman, I., Ridenour, C. S., Newman, C., & DeMarco, G. M. P. (2003). A typology of research purposes and its relationship to mixed methods. In A. Tashakkori & C. Teddlie (Eds.), *Handbook of mixed methods in social and behavioral research* (pp. 167–188). Thousand Oaks, CA: Sage.

O'Brien, D. G., & Martin, M. A. (1988). Does figurative language present a unique comprehension problem? *Journal of Reading Behavior, 20,* 63–87.

O'Cathain, A. (2010). Assessing the quality of mixed methods research: Towards a comprehensive framework. In A. Tashakkori & C. Teddlie (Eds.), *Handbook of mixed methods in social and behavioral research* (2nd ed., pp. 531–558). Thousand Oaks, CA: Sage.

Onwuegbuzie, A. J. (2003). Expanding the framework of internal and external validity in quantitative research. *Research in the Schools, 10*(1), 71–90.

Onwuegbuzie, A. J., & Collins, K. M. T. (2007). A typology of mixed methods sampling designs in social science research. *Qualitative Report, 12,* 281–316. Retrieved from *www.nova.edu/ssss/QR/QR12-2/onwuegbuzie2.pdf.*

Onwuegbuzie, A. J., Collins, K. M. T., & Leech, N. L. (in press). *Mixed research: A step-by-step guide.* New York: Taylor & Francis.

Onwuegbuzie, A. J., & Combs, J. P. (2010). Emergent data analysis techniques in mixed methods research: A synthesis. In A. Tashakkori & C. Teddlie (Eds.), *Handbook of mixed methods in social and behavioral research* (2nd ed., 397–430). Thousand Oaks, CA: Sage.

Onwuegbuzie, A. J., Daniel, L. G., & Collins, K. M. T. (2009). A meta-validation model for assessing the score-validity of student teacher evaluations. *Quality and Quantity: International Journal of Methodology, 43,* 197–209.

Onwuegbuzie, A. J., & Johnson, R. B. (2006). The validity issue in mixed research. *Research in the Schools, 13*(1), 48–63.

Onwuegbuzie, A. J., & Leech, N. L. (2006). Linking research questions to mixed methods data analysis procedures. *Qualitative Report, 11,* 474–498. Retrieved from *www.nova.edu/ssss/QR/QR11-3/onwuegbuzie.pdf.*

Onwuegbuzie, A. J., & Leech, N. L. (2007). Validity and qualitative research: An oxymoron? *Quality and Quantity: International Journal of Methodology, 41,* 233–249.

Patterson, W. A., Henry, J. J., O'Quin, K., Ceprano, M. A., & Blue, E. V. (2003). Investigating the effectiveness of an integrated learning system on early emergent readers. *Reading Research Quarterly, 38,* 172–207.

Patton, M. Q. (2002). *Qualitative research and evaluation methods.* Thousand Oaks, CA: Sage.

Pluye, P., Gagnon, M., Griffiths, F., & Johnson-Lafleur, J. (2009). A scoring system for appraising mixed methods research, and concomitantly appraising qualitative, quantitative and mixed methods primary studies in mixed studies reviews. *International Journal of Nursing Studies, 46,* 529–546.

Powell, H., Mihalas, S., Onwuegbuzie, A. J., Suldo, S., & Daley, C. E. (2008). Mixed methods research in school psychology: A mixed methods investigation of trends in the literature. *Psychology in the Schools, 45,* 291–309.

Purcell-Gates, V., & Dahl, K. L. (1991). Low-SES children's success and failure at early literacy learning skills-based classroom. *Journal of Reading Behavior, 23,* 1–34.

Putnam, H. (2002). *The collapse of the fact/value dichotomy and other essays.* Cambridge, MA: Harvard University Press.

Reichardt, C. S., & Cook, T. D. (1979). Beyond qualitative versus quantitative methods. In T. D. Cook & C. S. Reichardt (Eds.), *Qualitative and quantitative methods in evaluation research* (pp. 7–32). Thousand Oaks, CA: Sage.

Reinking, D., & Alvermann, D. E. (2007). Editorial: Reflections of our editorship. *Reading Research Quarterly, 42,* 460–466.

Rescher, N. (2000). *Realistic pragmatism: An introduction to pragmatic philosophy.* Albany: State University of New York Press.

Roberts, A. (2002). A principled complementarity of method: In defence of methodological eclecticism and the qualitative–qualitative debate. *Qualitative Report, 7*(3). Retrieved from *www.nova.edu/ssss/QR/QR7-3/roberts.html.*

Rorty, R. (1991). *Objectivity, relativism, and truth: Philosophical papers (Vol. 1).* Cambridge, UK: Cambridge University Press.

Ross, A., & Onwuegbuzie, A. J. (2009, March). *Prevalence of mixed methods research in mathematics education.* Invited Outstanding Paper presented at the annual meeting of the American Educational Research Association, San Diego, CA.

Sandelowski, M., & Barroso, J. (2003). Creating metasummaries of qualitative findings. *Nursing Research, 52,* 226–233.

Sandelowski, M., & Barroso, J. (2006). *Handbook for synthesizing qualitative research.* New York: Springer.

Sandelowski, M., Voils, C. I., & Barroso, J. (2006). Defining and designing mixed research synthesis studies. *Research in the Schools, 13*(1), 29–40.

Smith, M. L., & Glass, G. V. (1987). *Research and evaluation in education and the social sciences.* Englewood Cliffs, NJ: Prentice Hall.

Tashakkori, A., & Creswell, J. W. (2007a). Developing publishable mixed methods manuscripts [Editorial]. *Journal of Mixed Methods Research, 1,* 107–111.

Tashakkori, A., & Creswell, J. W. (2007b). Editorial: Exploring the nature of research questions in mixed methods research. *Journal of Mixed Methods Research, 1,* 207–211.

Tashakkori, A., & Teddlie, C. (1998). *Mixed methodology: Combining qualitative and quantitative approaches* (Applied Social Research Methods Series, Vol. 46). Thousand Oaks, CA: Sage.

Tashakkori, A., & Teddlie, C. (2003). The past and future of mixed methods research: From data triangulation to mixed model designs. In A. Tashakkori & C. Teddlie (Eds.), *Handbook of mixed methods in social and behavioral research* (pp. 671–701). Thousand Oaks, CA: Sage.

Teddlie, C., & Johnson, R. B. (2009a). Methodological thought before the 20th century. In C. Teddlie & A. Tashakkori, *Foundations of mixed methods research: Integrating quantitative and qualitative techniques in the social and behavioral sciences* (pp. 40–61). Thousand Oaks, CA: Sage.

Teddlie, C., & Johnson, R. B. (2009b). Methodological thought since the 20th century. In C. Teddlie & A. Tashakkori, *Foundations of mixed methods research: Integrating quantitative and qualitative techniques in the social and behavioral sciences* (pp. 62–82). Thousand Oaks, CA: Sage.

Teddlie, C., & Tashakkori, A. (2006). A general typology of research designs featuring mixed methods. *Research in the Schools, 13*(1), 12–28.

Teddlie, C., & Tashakkori, A. (2009). *Foundations of mixed methods research: Integrating quantitative and qualitative approaches in the social and behavioral sciences.* Thousand Oaks, CA: Sage.

Teddlie, C., & Yu, F. (2007). Mixed methods sampling: A typology with examples. *Journal of Mixed Methods Research, 1,* 77–100.

CHAPTER 15

Narrative Approaches

EXPLORING THE PHENOMENON AND/OR METHOD

M. Kristiina Montero
Rachelle D. Washington

I believe one of the principal ways in which we acquire,
hold, and digest information is via narratives.
—TONI MORRISON (1993)

Fundamental to understanding narrative as a research method and/or phenomenon to be studied is that people live out their lives narratively. People relate their lived experiences as stories—actual, fictional, or hypothetical. Some write them down while others engage in their oral tellings or retellings. Lived experiences can be narrated in linguistic (e.g., prose, poetry, oral storytelling) or nonlinguistic (e.g., painting, photography, collage, music, film, dance, sculpture) ways or some combination of the two (Barone & Eisner, 2006; Eisner, 1997).

Narrative research is about understanding experience as lived and told stories that capture unquantifiable personal and human dimensions of life (Clandinin & Connelly, 2000). It is the systematic study of plots, "the narrative structure through which people understand and describe the relationship among the events and choices of their lives" (Polkinghorne, 1995, p. 7), as well as a form of inquiry in which the researcher studies the lives of individuals and asks one or more individuals to provide stories about their lives through living, telling, retelling, and/or reliving (Connelly & Clandinin, 2006). Narrative research, a collaborative effort between researcher and participants, is an effective way to see the world through the eyes of others by using the lived, told, retold, and/or relived experiences as theory, data, and method. The narratives become subjects of interpretation to be guided by the various epistemological stances that guide individual and collective research agendas.

Through narratives, researchers and writers use multiple lenses to access richly textured human experiences (Coles, 1989; Morrison, 1993; Polkinghorne, 1988). These experiences can be captured in audio and video recordings and in transcriptions, field notes, journals, cultural artifacts, and other types of texts and have traditionally been analyzed and represented as autobiography, biography, and memoir, autoethnography, personal narrative, life and oral history, and forms of literary journalism (Alvermann, 2000). The globalized and far more socially conscious world in which we live facilitates communication across sociocultural, geopolitical, and socioeconomic boundaries. With this comes the need for a multifaceted understanding of narrative.

Autobiography, biography, and memoir, for example, have evolved as more a Western narrative construction and may not exist as genres in non-Western cultures or may exist differently from temporally structured Western narratives (Pavlenko, 2002). Because the organizational plot of any given story is not universal in nature, but bound by myriad sociocultural rules of form and purpose, and narrative research involves the study of human experiences as expressed in narrative, researchers need to carefully consider their research subjectivities and knowledge of narrative structure when reading and/or conducting cross-cultural narrative research. For example, in Africanist traditions, oral storytelling is cyclical in nature, and storytelling structures have been expressed through ring circles, which, in addition to linguistic communication, offer dance as communicative, spiritual, and sacred. Dau (2007), a member of the Dinka tribe in Sudan, explained how storytelling took on an important educational role to his people:

> I never had formal schooling in Duk County. The only schools were Muslim ones for the Arabs in the north, or Christian ones in the biggest villages of the south. But I did have an informal education based on stories and riddles. Father and mother told them at home, and the children shared them as well. The youngest boys and girls took their goats and sat under a tree to swap stories. I sat with them often. (p. 30)

Narrated experiences are open to interpretation (Bakhtin, 1935/1981), and in narrative inquiry narrated experiences must be interpreted. A narrative researcher accommodates the story, the teller, the context, and the listener by melding data collected from various sources into a collective narrative (Creswell, 2007; Patton, 2002). As a result, narratives are the stories that are lived, reserved, stored, storied, told, collected, written, researched, and validated. When dealing with narrative research that crosses sociocultural boundaries, the crises of legitimation and representation (Alvermann, 2000) are further compounded.

KEY HISTORY OF NARRATIVE INQUIRY IN LITERACY RESEARCH

Narrative inquiry has its intellectual roots in *narratology*. Some researchers' initial foray into narratives began by "drawing on narratology and the practices of writers" (Coulter & Smith, 2009, p. 608). The theory and study of narrative structure and its effects on the way individuals perceive the world around them is rhizomatic. The study of narrative occurs across myriad disciplines: literary theory, history, anthropology, drama, art, film, theology, philosophy, psychology, linguistics, and education in general (Connelly & Clandinin, 1990, p. 2). Relatively speaking, narrative inquiry is a growing methodology in education and the social sciences (Connelly & Clandinin, 2006), but in literacy education it is only in its embryonic stages.

Connelly and Clandinin (2006), leading authorities in narrative inquiry research in educational contexts, noted that narrative inquiry was only included in the last iteration of the American Education Research Association's *Handbook of Complementary Methods for Research in Education* (Green, Camilli, & Elmore, 2006); it did not appear in its preceding edition (Jaeger, 1988). Similarly, narrative inquiry was not included among the literacy research methodologies highlighted in the first edition of this book (Duke & Mallette, 2004). This omission was not a negligent act; rather, we believe it was narrative inquiry's lack of presence among influential literacy-related research. Simply put, narrative approaches to literacy research were not on the radar screen of most literacy researchers.

A landmark exploration of narrative approaches in literacy research appeared in the *Handbook of Reading Research*, Volume 3 (Kamil, Mosenthal, Pearson, & Barr, 2000). In Chapter 9 of the handbook, Alvermann (2000) presented literacy researchers with issues that define narrative inquiry as a way of knowing and writing and the implications of these issues for research and practice in literacy. She also provided three examples of how literacy researchers used narrative approaches to understand their own literate lives and the lives of those whom they study. However, because of the nascent nature of narrative inquiry in literacy research, the examples did not explicitly explore narrative inquiry, either as a method or as a phenomenon; rather, the examples were based on Alvermann's accurate interpretation of narrative approaches (autobiography and genres of narrative representation: performance texts and confessionals) as used in literacy-related research. A rich tradition of narrative inquiry has developed in the field of teacher education over the past two decades; however, narrative inquiry and inquiry into narrative as explicitly stated research methods have emerged in literacy researchers' gold standard publishing outlets (*Journal of Literacy Research* and *Reading Research Quarterly*) since approximately 2004.

In the field of literacy research, narrative research seems to be attractive to those who define literacy broadly, a definition that considers the social, cultural, historical, and political dimensions of literacy, for example, a multiliteracies definition of literacy, which focuses on broader modes of representation—linguistic, visual, audio, spatial, and gestural (Cope & Kalantzis, 2000)—or a definition of literacy as a social process (Barton, 1994; Street, 1995). It is also interesting to scholars who approach their work from a critical theory and social justice perspective because narrative inquiry has the potential to address grassroots issues such as learning about the impact of authentic writing experiences for incarcerated youth (Gordon, McKibbin, Vasudevan, & Vinz, 2007) or gaining insight into early language and literacy development rooted in family, cultural, school, and community experiences and contexts (Lapadat, 2004).

NARRATIVE INQUIRY AS SOCIALLY JUST RESEARCH

Narrative inquiry has the potential to use forms of expression relevant to the examination and celebration of lives, like grandmothers or community members called *lanterns* (Edelman, 1999), Holocaust survivors, students of limited formal education, busing and/or segregation victims to name a few. Narrative researchers can offer contextually, temporally, and socially rich understandings about research topics, such as the cultural contexts of literacy, literacy practices and processes, and literacy learning and teaching.

Narrative inquiry explores questions that lead to the understanding of storied human experiences and their impact on past, present, and future experiences of participants and researchers. It is a mode of inquiry that lends itself nicely to exploring questions about the relationship between thought and action (Hankins, 2003). For example, Montero's doctoral student, Joanne O'Toole, studied the contribution of prior language-learning experiences to the personal practical knowledge general education teachers draw on when teaching English language learners (ELLs) by exploring teachers' language-learning experiences, how they made sense of these experiences, and how these experiences impacted their attitudes toward ELLs and their teaching practices (O'Toole, 2010). Clandinin's doctoral students examined the lives of children, teachers, parents, and administrators as composed and lived out on school knowledge landscapes. Specifically, they examined what it meant to teach children in ethnically responsive and responsible ways and how parents were positioned in relation to the landscape of schools (Clandinin, Pushor, & Orr, 2007).

Narrative inquiry affords researchers a space to get up close and personal with their research participants. A valued characteristic in narrative inquiry design is that researchers need to deliberately imagine themselves as integral participants of the inquiry without necessarily being autobiographically involved. (The personal nature of narrative research is also viewed as an area of contention for individuals who believe that proximity to research distances oneself from objectivity of that which is being studied.) As narrative researchers, we aimed to decrease the distance between researcher and participant and opened ourselves to a form that was more congruent for the telling of stories. For example, in Washington, Bauer, Edwards, and McMillon-Thompson (2008), stories recollected from the authors' past lives and through dialoguing about both the process and product provided rich and diverse narratives of ways Black communities "do" language and literacy development. For example, consider the following:

> Every Sunday evening we attended Baptist Training Union where we learned about church etiquette, how to present ourselves properly in public, how to sit, walk, and curtsy. Everyone was taught how to speak clearly, using great inflection. Oral language development was a major part of our training. In fact, we practiced repeatedly until everything was second nature. (pp. 222–223)

According to Washington and her colleagues (2008), topics such as uncovering new literacies in and out of classrooms, acknowledging the role of family as a key to academic and social successes, using literacy to teach for social justice, heightening awareness of ELLs' needs are brought into their classrooms via stories. Stories can provide insight into and significance of the larger society, protect children from the pain the authors felt, and promote the learning of the whole child. The authors' specific stories acknowledged the power of narratives and the opportunity to write new pages to a history that has silenced and marginalized their presence and insistence to "hear our [their] own hearts and voices" (Omolade, 1994, p. 9).

Within Africanist communities, church is among the many spaces that contribute to literacy development. Consider the insights made by Hankins (2003) about Randel, the first-grade preacher in her narrative inquiry. When studying Martin Luther King, Jr.'s birthday, a student announced to Hankins that he, too, knew how to preach. Hankins ignored the student at first. She admitted in her notes, her data, that she was tired and frustrated that morning and wanted to get through the day. The student's incessant hand waving and wriggling in his seat led Hankins to let him go to the front of the room.

> "Well Randel, if you were going to preach today, what would you say?" I fully expected him to shrug his shoulders or give me a one-sentence answer. Instead, he slowly rose to his feet, then stood behind his chair, looking down at his hands for a moment as they gripped the back of it.
> Then he squared his shoulders and raised his voice, hands and eyes in tandem saying, "Does anyone have a problem they'd like to *lift up* today?"
> The children came to attention, as I did, and he repeated the question, "I say! Does anyone have a problem they'd like to lift up today?" He had the intonation of every Black preacher I'd ever heard. Then he began to move, to

walk rhythmically a little to the right and a little to the left, issuing the call. We were all responding to it at varying levels. (pp. 35–36)

What unfurled was spectacular. Randel proceeded to engage his classmates and teacher in the prosody and performance demonstrated by Black preachers. Randel's call and response was well received by many of his peers, who were familiar with this cultural practice. Hankins's (2003) use of narrative as theory, data, and method revealed experiences that articulate common mis/understandings. Students' agency and literacy development through performance found its place inside her classroom *and* alongside other acceptable literacy practices by incorporating culturally congruent practices, such as performance, into her teaching practice. Through Randel, we learn how students' cultural contexts allow us to hear the voice of the unheard.

As we look at those who arrived at their voice, largely represented in published autobiographies, biographies, and memoirs, there exist unheard voices that are equally relevant to understanding human experiences. Narrative research creates a space to listen to the voices of the unheard and to learn from them in a representation of their voice. In oral history and life history research, for example, one of its purposes is "to offer a voice to the unheard and unseen" (Howarth, 1998, p. v). Examples of such purpose can be seen in the work of Clegg (1997), who recorded the experiences of students who attended one-room schoolhouses in Texas; of Santoli (1988), who traveled across the United States and recorded the experiences of immigrants to the United States; and of Terkel (1972/1990), who recorded the experiences of the blue-collar worker in his book *Working: People Talk About What They Do All Day and How They Feel About What They Do.* In each of these oral history exemplars, the oral historians worked with everyday people. Terkel poignantly stated that he purposefully left out the voices of the dentists, doctors, and clergy people of the world because they had other forums in which to express themselves.

Conversely, narratives that reconnoiter the disruption of *common misunderstandings* (Barone, 2009; Coulter & Smith, 2009; Riessman, 1993) of those who reside on the periphery of society can benefit from the integration of narrative works in general and in literacy research specifically. To that end, there has to be a place to celebrate participants' performance (Hankins, 2003), unparallel storytelling (Pavlenko, 2002); cultural habits and language practices (Delpit, 1995; Heath, 1983), or definition of story (Coulter & Smith, 2009; Morrison, 1993). The richness of voice, of embodied presence available in modes (e.g., auditory, gestural, visual) tend to lie flat in traditional modes. However, narratives with its supportive strategies and techniques (e.g., poetic inquiry, arts-based inquiry, performance) possess a potent power for the otherwise powerless to effect change beyond the old modes of support, which have served the underrepresented or oppressed in limited ways.

Analyzing narratives can be seen as a "flexible and responsive methodology" that allows the voices of the participants to shine (Johnson-Bailey, 2002, p. 235); therefore, when using identifiers to draw attention to details in stories and to answer questions (Alexander, 1988; Etter-Lewis, 1993), the use of indicators of salience, such as frequency, omission, uniqueness, primacy, hesitation, negation, error, incompletion, and isolation (Alexander, 1988) could be identified as necessary elements in examining inquiry into narrative. As such, readers of research relying on the stories of human experience as primary sources of data "hope for a description and analysis of its complexity that identify concepts not previously seen or fully appreciated" (Glesne, 2005, p. 153).

Other researchers have found that—from self-study (Bullough & Pinnegar, 2001), study at the margins to center (hooks, 1996), study of the marginalized (Hankins, 2003; Johnson-Bailey, 2002, 2003), and study honoring the marginalized (Etter-Lewis, 1993)—documenting the lives of historically oppressed people can be transformative and celebratory. Riessman (1993) argued that narrative researchers must attend to what is said, the relationship between speakers, and how points are connected as key points in recognizing *story* as the object of investigation.

INQUIRY INTO NARRATIVE AND NARRATIVE INQUIRY: WHAT'S THE DIFFERENCE?

Narrative inquiry can be considered a subfield of qualitative research, which has the potential to address limitless questions concerning the qualities of human experience. It is used to describe research that relies on human stories as data, narrative in data analysis, and/or narrative as data representation. The distinctions and tensions are described in the literature under inquiry into narrative and/or analysis of narrative and narrative inquiry and/or narrative analysis. Note that the latter terms are the most confusing because they seem to connote a method; however, as is described later in this chapter, narrative inquiry or narrative analysis is both method and data or, for some, theory (Hankins, 2003). Narrative analysis, as described herewith, does not imply a method to analyze the various sources of narrative data as the term is used by Riessman (2008), Labov (1997) and Labov and Waletzky (1967/1997) or in methods of cultural (Tillman, 2002) and poetic (Prendergast, Leggo, & Sameshima, 2009) analyses, methods of data analysis that may offer unique vantage points of the stories of human experience. This said, such methods are useful when working with narrated stories as found in oral history or life history interview data, for example.

In this chapter, we try to clarify the confusion many novice researchers have between *inquiry into narrative* and *narrative inquiry*, but because inquiry into narrative receives greater attention in literacy research, we focus a large part of our attention on narrative inquiry. Both types of narrative research rely on many of the same data collection tools (e.g., interviews, journals/diaries, collection of artifacts, observation, field notes, data memos) as conventional qualitative research traditions. These tools help to elicit and capture the narrative construction, through which people make sense of their lives and the lives of others. As with other forms of qualitative research, narrative approaches, generally, are small in scope and time consuming. It is nearly impossible for one narrative researcher to work with many participants and still remain true to the process. The sociocultural contexts of participants, however, can be large (e.g., students' experiences in a school setting, children's experiences in an after-school reading program). For example, in recent work with students of interrupted formal education, Montero worked with a team of five doctoral students to understand the storied lives of 16 students from Burundi, Liberia, Somalia, Sudan, and Nepal (Montero et al., 2009).

Narrative can be used as a way of making sense of the data as well, and this is what primarily sets *inquiry into narrative* apart from *narrative inquiry*. As such, narrative inquiry has a "rough sense of narrative as both phenomena under study and method of study" (Clandinin & Connelly, 2000, p. 4). The narratives gathered through interview, for example, are the phenomenon of which narrative inquirers try to make sense, and narrative is also the method of analysis and representation. Some narrative researchers argue that interview data generate stories, and the narratives are ways of "recounting, constituting, representing and constructing the story" (Gordon, McKibbin, Vasudevan, & Vinz, 2007, p. 327). Qualitative researchers can and do produce powerful narratives; however, not all qualitative researchers are narrative researchers. Narrative inquiry moves beyond just telling stories; it retells and relives stories through analysis (Clandinin & Connelly, 1998, 2000). As such, narrative inquiry will rarely be presented uniquely as a narrative: Through the analysis, researchers make sense of the narratives under study (Bell, 2002).

Hankins (2003) creatively described narrative inquiry in the following manner: "Narrative data hold the confusions. Narrative methodology dissects it." (p. 15). Dissecting the confusion involves placing the narrative in a meaningful context that encompasses narrative inquiry's three elements: (1) temporality (understanding an event, person, or object in light of the past, present, and future); (2) sociality (understanding the personal conditions, e.g., feeling, hopes, desires, and the social conditions, e.g., environment, surrounding factors and forces); and (3) place (understanding the geophysical space in which the inquiry takes place) (Connelly & Clandinin, 2006). To dissect the confusions in the data, we narrate, in linguistic and/ or nonlinguistic ways, in research diaries, field texts, data memos, audio recordings, and drawings and doodles, for example, thereby making narrative the method as well as the data.

Narrating provides a space to think through, analyze, and process the confusions in the data. This also affords a space to incorporate data that are not part of the observable research (e.g., interview transcripts, field notes, examined archival documents, photographs) such as the narratives that take place during events, interpretive narratives about events, and/or the narrative that drove the selection of the event to analyze (Hankins, 2003). St. Pierre (1997) also offers us different types of nontraditional data—emotional, dream, sensual, and response—to interrupt the linear nature of narrative knowledge production in traditional qualitative research practices.

What serves as narrative data in narrative inquiry? Narratives are not found—they are coconstructed texts between researcher and participant (Riessman, 2008). Connelly and Clandinin (2006) describe two ways of conducting narrative inquiry: telling and living. *Telling* narrative inquiry focuses on the stories of life as lived and told in the past, such as those found in autobiographical, biographical, memoirs, and oral and life histories. These stories are best captured through interviews that are audio recorded and transcribed. It is the stories in the transcribed text that telling narrative inquirers must tease out and then make sense of through thematic, structural, dialogic/performance, and visual methods of analysis (Riessman, 2008), for example.

We relate Clandinin and Connelly's telling narrative inquiry to Polkinghorne's (1995) analysis of narrative or what Clandinin and Connelly (1994) termed *inquiry into narrative*, which moves from stories to common elements by using told stories as the data to be analyzed with paradigmatic processes such as methods consistent with grounded theory (Glaser & Strauss, 1967; Strauss & Corbin, 1998). In inquiry into narrative, researchers' interests are on the stories told or the interpretations and meaning generated (Connelly & Clandinin, 2006) in an effort to answer how and why a particular outcome came about or to understand how an individual acted in the concrete social world (Polkinghorne, 1995). Over a decade later, Polkinghorne (Clandinin & Murphy, 2007) went on record saying that analysis of narrative is a more general form of qualitative research and is not true to narrative inquiry, "which understands lives as unfolding temporally, as particular events within a particular individual's life" (Clandinin & Murphy, 2007, p. 636). Because this distinction has been made, researchers must be careful not to equate the analysis of interview data with narrative inquiry simply because "stories" were analyzed or a narrative text has been generated as part of the research findings. Key to narrative inquiry, whether telling or living, are the common elements of narrative inquiry discussed earlier in the chapter. It might be useful to think of narrative inquiry as an ecological, grassroots, and comprehensive approach to studying human experiences.

At this point in the history of literacy research, it is *inquiry into narrative* that one will find in most peer-reviewed academic journals. We believe that inquiry into narrative offers the literacy research community insights that perhaps would not easily be made without analyzing the lived experiences of others. For example, Chandler-Olcott and Kluth's (2008) examination of parents' roles in supporting the literacy development of students with autism analyzed narrative using book-length autobiographies authored directly by individuals with autism. According to the norms of inductive data analysis method, these researchers developed a set of criteria by which to choose the texts and then began to analyze them inductively by first developing a coding scheme and then reading the identified texts and analyzing them according to the rules they devised. On the basis of their inquiry into narrative, Chandler-Olcott and Kluth provided the literacy research community with insights into the various roles parents played in supporting literacy development for their children with autism-spectrum labels and advance preliminary knowledge about literacy development for students with autism researched from the perspective of individuals living with the disorder. Certainly, this is an advantage of narrative research: insight into an issue of interest from the perspective of those directly impacted. In this example, narrative research offers voice to the traditionally unheard and, therefore, could be considered, as we suggest, a socially just research methodology.

Living narrative inquiry is what distinguishes narrative inquiry most drastically from other modes of qualitative research. We relate Clandinin and Connelly's (2007) *living* narrative inquiry to Polkinghorne's (1995) narrative analysis, which moves from elements to stories and where the focus is on the local and the individual in relation to larger social, cultural, historical, and political contexts. Narrative analysis is a collection of described events that are synthesized or configured by a plot into a story or into a multitude of stories (Polkinghorne, 1995).

The path to narrative inquiry is not direct; rather, it is full of twists and turns (Clandinin & Connelly, 2000; Pinnegar & Daynes, 2007). Researchers often turn from positivistic research conceptions to narrative inquiry when they question the use of numbers as the exclusive way of representing data about human experience and/or question the adequacy of quantifiable data (survey questions, test scores) to account for the experiences they represent (Pinnegar & Daynes, 2007). The path to narrative inquiry is quick for some authors, and slow—perhaps spiraling or retreating—for others. We argue that the research traditions of any specific field of study frames how different approaches to research are communicated in the early stages of entrée into the field.

Considering the positivistic research traditions in literacy research (e.g., one of the gold standard journals for the field, *Journal of Literacy Research*, was called *Journal of Reading Behavior* until 1995), it is not surprising that in 1999, when Fitzgerald and Noblit published their study of first-grade ELLs' emergent reading, narrative inquiry was not identified as a methodological framework. Rather, they seemed to have written up their research framed according to the norms of the paradigmatic cognition (Polkinghorne, 1995) but having pushed the boundaries to be "more narrative than envisioned by Glaser and Strauss" (p. 174). Consider Fitzgerald's (1999) reflections on analyzing the data in her study, with Noblit, on first-grade ELLs' emergent reading. Their work echoes the characteristics of *living* narrative inquiry, the study of life as it unfolds:

> During my year with the children, my appraisal of the children's development happened daily. I was not just immersed in it; I was part of it, and it was part of me. . . . I had been listening to some of the children's oral reading tapes, and the children's voices on the tapes had quite suddenly made me feel closer to them . . . we talked about how we wanted the writing to convey some feeling about the scenes and the children and their families—because these were all central to the children's reading growth. . . . The interpretation of the data would be conveyed in part not just by what we said, but also by how we said it. "As we do the analyses and writing," George said, "think scene. Think "how can I show this, not tell it." (pp. 174–175)

Following suit to their narrative goals, the authors thought "scene" and were guided by the narrative research mantra: "How can I show this, not tell it?" (p. 175). Although Fitzgerald and Noblit (1999) did not explicitly state that they had engaged in a *living* narrative inquiry, their methodological description of data collection, analysis, and representation take into consideration many of the eight key elements of designing, conducting, and representing narrative inquiries (Clandinin et al., 2007), as described in the next section.

NARRATING STANDARDS: FIXED AND FLUID

The field of narrative inquiry is currently in a state of "fluid inquiry" (according to Schwab, as cited in Connelly & Clandinin, 2006)—a time "when longstanding assumptions and norms of a field are reexamined" (p. 478). As such, the criteria to define exemplary work in narrative inquiry are shifting as narrative researchers continue to define and redefine the method and phenomenon of their own work. Although guidelines for what constitutes quality narrative inquiry exist, the field of literacy research will eventually need to define its own criteria in recognition that "issues of quality and credibility intersect with audience and intended research purpose" (Patton, 2002, p. 1189) and explore in what ways narrative inquiry will best serve the field. For now, we can borrow and learn from researchers who engage in narrative inquiry across a variety disciplines.

What makes for good narrative research? The answer to this question largely depends on whether one considers *inquiry into narrative* or *narrative inquiry* (Connelly & Clandinin, 1990, p. 2). Standards for inquiry into narrative are more readily found in the literature because, as noted earlier, inquiry into narrative aligns more closely with well-established qualitative research (e.g., ethnography, case study, grounded theory). These methods have been widely used across time and disciplines, rich discussions have occurred over what is considered to be standards for quality research, and such standards have been more or less defined around the issues of trust-worthiness and methodological rigor (see, e.g., Charmaz, 2005; Creswell, 2007; Lincoln & Guba, 1985; Miles & Huberman, 1994; Patton, 2002). Although the standards can be viewed as fixed in inductive types of research, they become more fluid in narrative inquiry research because the evaluation criteria are still under development (Connelly & Clandinin, 2006). Before beginning to delineate what defines "good" and "bad" narrative inquiry research, we would like to echo Smith and Hodkinson's (2005) thoughts that any list of criteria used to distinguish the "good" research from the "bad" can (and should) be challenged, changed, and/or modified according to the specific needs of the research under production.

When trying to explicitly lay out the standards of quality narrative inquiry, we found ourselves in a difficult position because those who engage in narrative inquiry generally believe that researchers should not get lost in policing the rigor of a field under development at the expense of developing the method (Mishler, 1999), that the criteria that will define quality narrative inquiry should develop naturally as narrative inquirers conduct and publish their research and generate a critical mass of studies from which more specific standards of quality can be amassed and put to the test of time. In the same way, exemplars will also be more readily identi-fied; for example, in ethnography, Heath's (1983) *Ways with Words*, which continues to be cited as an exemplar, has stood the test of time. However, this rationale is not particularly useful, especially for the novice narrative inquirer, who may need a zoomed-in roadmap.

Connelly and Clandinin (2006) and Clandinin and colleagues (2007) stated that "good" narrative inquiry must address the commonplaces of narrative inquiry that frame the dimensions of the inquiry space (tempo-rality, sociality, and place, as discussed earlier) and should be guided by eight key design elements. Next is a skeletal outline of the elements that should be considered when designing, conducting, and representing narra-tive inquiry research (for more detailed information on the key elements, we recommend you consult the previously cited texts):

1. Explicit details of the personal, practical, and social reasons to jus-tify the research.
2. Explicit explanation of the phenomenon being studied through a narrative lens.
3. Explicit description of research methods used to study the phenom-enon to figure out the kinds of field texts needed to research the phenomenon while being attentive to the three commonplaces.
4. Explicit description of the analysis and interpretation process while considering the importance of the contextual and relational.

5. Clear explanation of how the phenomenon under study is situated in relation to the existing literature both within and outside the epistemological and ontological assumptions of the research being undertaken.

6. Explicit explanation of how the distinctive lenses used to inquire into the respective phenomena.

7. Explicit understanding that the ethical responsibilities of narrative inquiry go far beyond the ethical requirements of a university's ethics review board.

8. The research process, from beginning to end, must be narrative.

Clandinin, Connelly, and colleagues offer a detailed roadmap for evaluating narrative inquiry research; however, although their voices are prominent, they are not the only ones in the conversation. Next, we present what some of the conversations about quality narrative inquiry sound like.

Narrative inquiry distinguishes itself from traditional research methods in matters of purpose. It does not strive to discover and verify knowledge about the real state of the world; rather, it strives to portray experience, to question common understandings, and to offer a degree of interpretive space (Coulter & Smith, 2009, p. 577). Narrative inquiry is about questioning rather than hypothesizing, listening rather than categorizing, and presenting ambiguities rather than certainties (Gordon et al., 2007). Because narrative inquiry differs from paradigmatic research methods, Connelly and Clandinin (1990) caution that researchers cannot force traditional quantitatively oriented language, such as validity, reliability, and generalizability, to evaluate narrative research. Qualitative researchers like Denzin and Lincoln (2003), Lincoln and Guba (1985), and Peshkin (1988) have been making this point for decades, and narrative inquirers insist to join the same conversation.

Researchers conducting narrative inquiry have begun to acknowledge certain characteristics of quality pieces of narrative inquiry. Clandinin and Connelly argue that Van Maanen's (1988) criteria have been put forth as a starting point: *apparency* (easy to see and understand), *verisimilitude* (the quality of appearing to be true or real), and *transferability* (makes connections between elements of the study and readers' own experiences). Blumenfeld-Jones (1995) suggested that "fidelity" be a criterion for practicing and evaluating narrative research. Key to understanding fidelity is contrasting it with truth. He noted that in narrative inquiry it is not important to confirm or disconfirm the told story of experience (as historiographers try to do); rather, what is valued is that the researcher be able to accurately represent what the experience meant to the teller of the tale. Hence, fidelity according to Blumenfeld-Jones is "an obligation to preserve the bonds between the teller and receivers by honoring the self-report of the teller and the obligation of the original teller to be as honest as possible in the telling" (p. 28).

Our aim is to list criteria that are more specific to narrative inquiry. A good starting point to understanding what is valued in narrative inquiry research is eliminating that which is unvaluable, in other words, identifying characteristics of a "bad" narrative inquiry. Connelly and Clandinin (1990) noted that good pieces of narrative inquiry avoid the following errors: writing up the narrative of inquiry with "the illusion of causality" (p.7) and writing numerous "I's" (researcher participant, teacher) with an uncomfortable fraternal intimacy. Narrative inquiry aims to explain the whole: Narratives should not be driven toward a model of cause and effect; rather, a narrative helps explain the big picture in such a way that the reader is always connected to the whole without getting lost in the minutiae.

A good narrative influences the thinking, inquiry, and writing of other researchers. Peshkin (cited in Connelly & Clandinin, 1990, p. 8) suggested that a test to this end is to have others read the narrative inquiry research text and respond to a question such as "What do you make of it for your situation?" The transferability of the narrated experience is personal in nature, and one can only confirm the effect of the research text's transferability by receiving feedback from those who have read it. For example, evidence that there was transferability of Hankins's work was demonstrated in Dwayne Wright's thoughts, as quoted by Allen (2003), after having read her book.

> Dr. Hankins' book affected me as a teacher, researcher, activist, and human being. . . . Although [much] educational research focuses on those who are on the periphery of society, their actual voices are not present in the research. Hankins' narratives provide the vehicle for the historic voiceless to take part in the construction of the classroom. (p. x)

Additionally, when writing across the different voices represented in narrative inquiry, the writer (researcher) must be careful to respect the role of researcher subjectivities (Peshkin, 1988). Should these subjectivities get muddled, the generated narratives become chaotic in nature and, therefore, have more inherent limitations than application.

Researchers need to confront candidly issues of quality in research and particularly to thwart challenges associated with qualitative designs (Patton, 2002). To that end, researchers' tasks involve consideration of power and positionality coupled with deliberate jottings and note takings related to the same (Hankins, 2003; Wolcott, 2009). For example, Hankins noted how eye-opening these practices could be as she struggled with her subjectivities, power, and position. In one narrative account of children, she wrote:

> There are common teacher gripes about children which I abhor, argue against, am sickened by. There are statements such as "He started behind." " . . . I know what to do; I just need better clients." I fight those words but accept

too easily the confirmation I see everywhere that education is not the promise for poor children of color that it is for "us" [White, middle-class teachers]. It is monstrous that I moved all kinds of boundaries in my thinking when Eric [White student] couldn't read and added extra support to the fences of acceptance that Tommy [Black student] couldn't read. (p. 90)

Reflexivity aids researchers and practitioners in the telling of their work. Hankins's willingness to open up her teaching and learning journals, to "bear the burden," allows readers to witness the power of reflexive practice.

Narrative inquiry may be challenging to grasp for some readers because the "answers" may not be explicitly provided in a "findings" section of a research report; rather, they are found in contextualized text obtained through interpreted narratives of lived experience. To evaluate narrative inquiry, one must be of a narrative mindset when asking questions such as: Is the narrative inquiry easy to understand? Does the narrative appear to be real or true? Does the text transact with the reader in meaningful ways? What does the reader make of the text? Note that some of these questions cannot be answered unless multiple readers engage in the evaluation process.

EXEMPLARS OF NARRATIVE INQUIRY

To date, the use of narrative inquiry in literacy research has been limited both in quantity and in types of experience examined. Literacy researchers have primarily examined autobiographical (oral or written) accounts of experiences (e.g., Bell, 1995; Chandler-Olcott & Kluth, 2008; Lapadat, 2004; Lazar, 2007; McKinney & Giorgis, 2009; Perry, 2007, 2008; Rogers, Marshall, & Tyson, 2006; Syed, 2008) conducted in the framework of *inquiry into narrative*. Because narrative inquiry research is text heavy, many article-length reports discuss the methodological issues, for the most part, and narrative inquiry research is more completely written up as monographs. In educational studies, most of the exemplars we found were in the field of teacher education (see, e.g., Clandinin & Huber, 2005; Craig, 2009; Johnson & Golombek, 2002), perhaps because narrative inquiry is a methodology that appeals to teachers and teacher educators (Clandinin et al., 2007). Finding exemplars of narrative inquiry that explicitly examined issues related to literacy proved challenging. Herewith, we discuss two scholarly pieces: "Writing Out of the Unexpected: Narrative Inquiry and the Weight of Small Moments" (Gordon et al., 2007) and *Teaching through the Storm: A Journal of Hope* (Hankins, 2003).

Hankins's (2003) book-length narrative inquiry offers an example of a *living* narrative inquiry that uses narrative as data and method, whereas Gordon and colleagues' (2007) article-length narrative inquiry addresses "one of the unexpected moments of the project" (p. 329) as a way to learn how to conduct narrative inquiry and to add to the knowledge base of how narrative inquiry can inform language and literacy education. The two examples are different but will, it is hoped, serve to illustrate the multiple layers of narrative inquiry.

Although it is outside the scope of this chapter to discuss all of the points that one could evaluate in a piece of narrative inquiry, we deemed it important to discuss briefly how the three commonplaces of narratives inquiry are simultaneously explored in narrative inquiry—the defining characteristics that set narrative inquiry apart from other forms of qualitative research that explores narrative structures. Therefore, a beginning place to identify "good" narrative research is to find work that addresses the commonplaces—temporality, sociality, and place—simultaneously.

What make makes these exemplars "good" narrative inquiry? Both exemplars, from the beginning, draw the reader into the work, much like an award-winning author seduces the nighttime reader to keep reading into the wee hours of the morning. The narratives are multidimensional, and in the analyses the authors explicitly identified how their work was constantly being reshaped as a result of new information and the reading and rereading of created narratives used as data and in analysis. As Hankins (2003) noted, "Narrative method requires me to contextualize each narrative within the history of the classroom, within my own knowledge of the participant's past, within narrative theory, and within pedagogical considerations" (p. 15).

Hankins demonstrated deep understandings of time, personal conditions, and place in which the inquiry takes place. Consider the following excerpt, in which Hankins places the reader within her research context and helps the reader understand all of the complexities of teaching literacy skills to first graders in a school that caters to children from families living at or near the poverty line:

> I remember that I reached out to touch her arm. "I promise I will not neglect him. I promise I will protect him and teach him where he is and take him as far as he can go with me. I also promise you that I will not refer him for any testing or special service. He is *your* child. Help me know what you want me to do; we will work together."
>
> I told her about my sister and the pain that I recognized as belonging also to my own life. She listened as I talked about Kathy's struggles as a child with brain damage from birth, the multiple learning problems and the accompanying emotional distress it caused for her and for our entire family. I talked briefly about the pain of the unfixable. I saw her silent acknowledgment of my mother's pain as the briefest hint of softness passed her face. She nodded and stood up.
>
> As we walked to the door together, I gave her my home number. She took it but did not put it in her purse, which she clutched less tightly now. She turned and said "OK, then . . . I'll call you next week." Her voice seemed

tired but there was no mistake in her message of watchfulness as she left. (pp. 3–4)

In this short excerpt, we gain a better understanding of a child's mother, who is angry toward the institution of school and is hypervigilant of her son's progress in the hands of the "system." Earlier in the narrative, Hankins provides the reader with information about the mother's past that influences her reactions in the present and how she will act in the future. Through the narrative, we are also privy to the personal conditions of both the mother's and the teacher's feelings—fears in particular. We are also privy to rich description about the physical environment in which the scene takes place. The narrative presents an ecology of the situation that is easy to understand, appears true, and has the potential to make connections between elements of the study and the reader's own experiences.

Gordon and colleagues (2007) worked as a research team to understand how authentic writing experiences could be used as a tool to engage incarcerated students in writing. The article they wrote was a way to work through the challenges of narrative inquiry, so in a sense they engaged in a narrative inquiry of their personal experience of putting thought to action. As they worked, they "constantly reviewed our fieldnotes, transcripts of our ongoing discussion, and the questions that interested each of us" (p. 328). They each decided to write about a particular situation that occurred during the project and shared these writings with each other, which methodologically is an interesting way to approach narrative inquiry done as a group project.

Learning about data representation and use of coconstructed stories occurred after one of the researchers wrote the following text and presented it to her research group:

> A couple of weeks later, Elaine stopped me in the hallway to tell me what great success she was having with the oral histories. The students were reading and having animated discussions, and she was just about to assign the first writing assignment. I jumped at the chance when she invited me to listen as the kids read and discussed pieces from *Killing the Sky*. What I wasn't prepared for was how it felt to watch these student-readers, strangers to the Rikers Island student-writers I had come to know, interpret the lives and "characters" of the writers. It occurred to me that here was the—or at least one—audience that Jermaine and the others had been writing for, the nameless, faceless readers to whom they told their stories and had the power to "read" them as they wished. While on Rikers Island with Jermaine we could only imagine our readers, here was a very real classroom whose reading of the student-inmates cast new light on issues of representation. (p. 344)

Resulting from the contextualized understanding of issues of representation in their work was an understanding that "collective narrative inquiry was less about the pursuit of consistency and more about the fuller understanding we can achieve through multiple perspectives" (Gordon et al., 2007, p. 348). What made this work interesting to us was that the article represented both the process and the product of their inquiry as highly contextualized. Narrative inquiry forges a space to show the process as part of the product.

CONCLUDING THOUGHTS

Realistically, we acknowledge that there will never be a paradigm shift to narrative inquiry in the field of literacy research (nor are we arguing that there should be), however, we believe there should be a place for researchers to examine the living, telling, retelling, and reliving of human experiences that flesh out the three commonplaces of human experience: temporality, sociality, and place (Connelly & Clandinin, 2006). By including more narrative inquiry in the literacy research repertoire, readers may become more intimately connected to others' experiences and may look at their own research and life experiences in different ways in order to exact change. The appropriateness of narrative research to study the storied human experiences is reiterated by Hankins:

> Recognizing and piecing together what we understand of our own narratives and then connecting them, with some understanding, to the lives of others is somewhat like finding small pieces of a jigsaw puzzle that fit together, however gradually, to create a more complete picture. (p. 109)

Whether narratives help us make sense of our world as researchers or practitioners, we can use the diversity of narrative research to frame, invite, or expose issues relative to social justice, equity, classroom hierarchy, language habits and practices, curriculum and instruction, and literacy development inside and outside of schools.

REFERENCES

Alexander, I. E. (1988). Personality, psychological assessment, and psychobiography. In D. P. Adams & R. L. Ochberg (Eds.), *Psychobiography and life narratives* (pp. 265–294). Durham, NC: Duke University Press.

Allen, J. (2003). Foreword. In K. H. Hankins (Ed.), *Teaching through the storm: A journal of hope* (pp. ix–x). New York: Teachers College Press.

Alvermann, D. E. (2000). Narrative approaches. In M. J. Kamil, P. B. Mosenthal, P. D. Pearson, & R. Barr (Eds.), *Handbook of reading research: Volume III* (pp. 123–140). Mahwah, NJ: Erlbaum.

Bakhtin, M. M. (1981). Discourse in the novel (C. Emerson & M. Holquist, Trans.). In M. Holquist (Ed.), *The dialogic imagination* (pp. 259–422). Austin: University of Texas Press.

Barone, D. (2009). Comments on Coulter and Smith: Narrative researchers as witnesses of injustice and agents of social change? *Educational Researcher, 38*(8), 591–597.

Barone, T., & Eisner, E. W. (2006). Arts-based educational research. In J. L. Green, G. Camilli, & P. B. Elmore (Eds.), *Handbook of complementary methods in education research* (pp. 95–110). Mahwah, NJ: Erlbaum.

Barton, D. (1994). *Literacy: An introduction to the ecology of written language.* Cambridge, MA: Blackwell.

Bell, J. S. (1995). The relationship between L1 and L2 literacy: Some complicating factors. *TESOL Quarterly, 29*(4), 687–704.

Bell, J. S. (2002). Narrative inquiry: More than just telling stories. *TESOL Quarterly, 36*(2), 207–213.

Blumenfeld-Jones, D. (1995). Fidelity as a criterion for practicing and evaluating narrative inquiry. *International Journal of Qualitative Studies in Education, 8*(1), 25–35.

Bullough, R., & Pinnegar, S. (2001). Guidelines for quality in autobiographical forms of self-study research. *Educational Researcher, 30*(3), 13–21.

Chandler-Olcott, K., & Kluth, P. M. (2008). "Mother's voice was the main source of learning": Parents' role in supporting the literacy development of students with autism. *Journal of Literacy Research, 40*(4), 461–492.

Charmaz, K. (2005). Grounded theory in the 21st century: Application in social justice In N. K. Denzin & Y. S. Lincoln (Eds.), *Handbook of qualitative research* (3rd ed., pp. 507–535). Thousand Oaks, CA: Sage.

Clandinin, D. J., & Connelly, F. M. (1994). Personal experience methods. In N. K. Denzin & Y. S. Lincoln (Eds.), *Handbook of qualitative research* (pp. 413–427). Thousand Oaks, CA: Sage.

Clandinin, D. J., & Connelly, F. M. (1998). Asking questions about telling stories. In C. Kridel (Ed.), *Writing educational biography: Explorations in qualitative research* (pp. 245–254). New York: Garland.

Clandinin, D. J., & Connelly, F. M. (2000). *Narrative inquiry: Experience and story in qualitative research.* San Francisco: Jossey-Bass.

Clandinin, D. J., & Connelly, F. M. (Eds.). (2007). *Handbook of narrative inquiry: Mapping a methodology.* Thousand Oaks, CA: Sage.

Clandinin, D. J., & Huber, M. (2005). Shifting stories to live by: Interweaving the personal and professional in teachers' lives. In D. Beijaard, P. C. Meijer, G. Morine-Dershimer, & H. Tillema (Eds.), *Teacher professional development in changing conditions* (pp. 43–59). Dortrecht, The Netherlands: Springer.

Clandinin, D. J., & Murphy, M. S. (2007). Looking ahead: Conversations with Elliot Mishler, Don Polkinghorne, and Amia Lieblich. In D. J. Clandinin (Ed.), *Handbook of narrative inquiry: Mapping a methodology* (pp. 632–650). Thousand Oaks, CA: Sage.

Clandinin, D. J., Pushor, D., & Orr, A. M. (2007). Navigating sites for narrative inquiry. *Journal of Teacher Education, 58*, 21–35.

Clegg, L. B. (1997). *The empty schoolhouse: Memories of one-room Texas schools.* College Station: Texas A&M University Press.

Coles, R. (1989). *The call of stories: Teaching and the moral imagination.* Boston: Houghton Mifflin.

Connelly, F. M., & Clandinin, D. J. (1990). Stories of experience and narrative inquiry. *Educational Researcher, 19*(5), 2–14.

Connelly, F. M., & Clandinin, D. J. (2006). Narrative inquiry. In J. L. Green, G. Camilli, & P. B. Elmore (Eds.), *Handbook of complementary methods in education research* (pp. 477–487). Mahwah, NJ: Erlbaum.

Cope, B., & Kalantzis, M. (Eds.). (2000). *Multiliteracies: Literacy learning and the design of social futures*. New York: Routledge.

Coulter, C. A., & Smith, M. L. (2009). The construction zone: Literary elements in narrative research. *Educational Researcher, 38*(8), 577–590.

Craig, C. J. (2009). Research in the midst of organized school reform: Versions of teacher community in tension. *American Educational Research Journal, 46*(2), 598–619.

Creswell, J. W. (2007). *Qualitative inquiry and research design: Choosing among five approaches* (2nd ed.). Thousand Oaks, CA: Sage.

Dau, J. B. (2007). *God grew tired of us: A memoir*. Washington, DC: National Geographic.

Delpit, L. (1995). *Other people's children: Cultural conflict in the classroom*. New York: New Press.

Denzin, N. K., & Lincoln, Y. S. (Eds.). (2003). *Handbook of qualitative research* (3rd ed.). Thousand Oaks, CA: Sage.

Duke, N. K., & Mallette, M. H. (Eds.). (2004). *Literacy research methodologies*. New York: Guilford Press.

Edelman, M. W. (1999). *Lanterns: A memoir of mentors*. Boston: Beacon Press.

Eisner, E. W. (1997). The promise and perils of alternative forms of data representation. *Educational Researcher, 26*(6), 4–10.

Etter-Lewis, G. (1993). *My soul is my own: Oral narratives of African American women in the professions*. New York: Routledge.

Fitzgerald, J., & Noblit, G. W. (1999). About hopes, aspirations, and uncertainty: First-grade English-language learners' emergent reading. *Journal of Literacy Research, 31*(2), 133–182.

Glaser, B. G., & Strauss, A. L. (1967). *The discovery of grounded theory: Strategies for qualitative research*. New York: Aldine de Gruyter.

Glesne, C. (2005). *Becoming qualitative researchers*. New York: Allyn & Bacon.

Gordon, E., McKibbin, K., Vasudevan, L., & Vinz, R. (2007). Writing out of the unexpected: Narrative inquiry and the weight of small moments. *English Education, 39*(4), 326–351.

Green, J. L., Camilli, G., & Elmore, P. B. (Eds.). (2006). *Handbook of complementary methods in education research*. Mahwah, NJ: Erlbaum.

Hankins, K. H. (2003). *Teaching through the storm: A journal of hope*. New York: Teachers College Press.

Heath, S. B. (1983). *Ways with words*. Cambridge, UK: Cambridge University Press.

hooks, b. (1996). *Bone black: Memories of girlhood*. New York: Holt.

Howarth, K. (1998). *Oral history: A handbook*. Phoenix Mill, UK: Sutton.

Jaeger, R. M. (Ed.). (1988). *Complementary methods for research in education*. Washington, DC: American Educational Research Association.

Johnson, K. E., & Golombek, P. R. (Eds.). (2002). *Teachers' narrative inquiry as professional development*. Cambridge, UK: Cambridge University Press.

Johnson-Bailey, J. (2002). Cathy, the wrong side of the tank. In S. Merriam (Ed.), *Qualitative research in practice: Examples for discussion and analysis* (pp. 314–326). San Francisco: Jossey-Bass.

Johnson-Bailey, J. (2003). Enjoining positionality and power in narrative work: Balancing contentious issues and modulating forces. In K. deMarrais & S. D. Lapin (Eds.), *Perspectives and approaches for research in education and the social sciences* (pp. 123–138). Mahwah, NJ: Erlbaum.

Kamil, M., Mosenthal, P., Pearson, P. D., & Barr, R. (Eds.). (2000). *Handbook of reading research: Volume III.* Mahwah, NJ: Erlbaum.

Labov, W. (1997). Some further steps in narrative analysis. *Journal of Narrative and Life History, 7*(1–4), 395–415.

Labov, W., & Waletzky, J. (1997). Narrative analysis: Oral versions of personal experience. *Journal of Narrative and Life History, 7,* 3–38. (Original work published 1967)

Lapadat, J. C. (2004). Autobiographical memories of early language and literacy development. *Narrative Inquiry, 14*(1), 113–140.

Lazar, A. M. (2007). It's not just about teaching kids to read: Helping preservice teachers acquire a mindset for teaching children in urban communities. *Journal of Literacy Research, 39*(4), 411–443.

Lincoln, Y. S., & Guba, E. G. (1985). *Naturalistic inquiry.* Newbury Park, CA: Sage.

McKinney, M., & Giorgis, C. (2009). Narrating and performing identity: Literacy specialists' writing identities. *Journal of Literacy Research, 41*(1), 104–149.

Miles, M. B., & Huberman, A. M. (1994). *Qualitative data analysis* (2nd ed.). Thousand Oaks, CA: Sage.

Mishler, E. G. (1999). *Storylines: Craftartists narratives of identity.* Cambridge, MA: Harvard University Press.

Montero, M. K., Crandall, B., Mwambari, D., O'Toole, J., Stahl, N. A., Stevens, E., et al. (2009, December). *Local literacies, global visions: Documenting SIFEs' learning histories using oral history methodology.* Paper presented at the 58th National Reading Conference, Albuquerque, NM.

Morrison, T. (1993). Nobel lecture. In S. Allén (Ed.), *Nobel Lectures, Literature 1991–1995* (pp. 47–56). Singapore: World Scientific Publishing.

Omolade, B. (1994). *The rising song of African American women.* New York: Routledge.

O'Toole, J. (2010). *Language-learning experiences as a source of personal practical knowledge for general classroom teachers of English language learners.* Doctoral dissertation, Syracuse University.

Patton, M. Q. (2002). *Qualitative research and evaluation methods* (3rd ed.). Thousand Oaks, CA: Sage.

Pavlenko, A. (2002). Narrative study: Whose story is it, anyway? *TESOL Quarterly, 36*(2), 213–218.

Perry, K. H. (2007). Sharing stories, linking lives: Literacy practices among Sudanese refugees. In V. Purcell-Gates (Ed.), *Cultural practices of literacy: Case studies of language, literacy, social practice, and power* (pp. 57–84). Mahwah, NJ: Erlbaum.

Perry, K. H. (2008). From storytelling to writing: Transforming literacy practices among Sudanese refugees. *Journal of Literacy Research, 40*(2), 317–358.

Peshkin, A. (1988). In search of subjectivity—one's own. *Educational Researcher, 17*(7), 17–21.

Pinnegar, S., & Daynes, J. G. (2007). Locating narrative inquiry historically. In D. J. Clandinin (Ed.), *Handbook of narrative inquiry: Mapping a methodology* (pp. 3–34). Thousand Oaks, CA: Sage.

Polkinghorne, D. E. (1988). *Narrative knowing and human sciences.* Albany: State University of New York Press.

Polkinghorne, D. E. (1995). Narrative configuration in qualitative analysis. *International Journal of Qualitative Studies in Education, 8*(1), 5–23.

Prendergast, M., Leggo, C., & Sameshima, P. (Eds.). (2009). *Poetic inquiry: Vibrant voices in the social sciences.* Boston: Sense.

Riessman, C. K. (1993). *Narrative analysis* (Vol. 30). Thousand Oaks, CA: Sage.

Riessman, C. K. (2008). *Narrative methods for the human sciences.* Thousand Oaks, CA: Sage.

Rogers, T., Marshall, E., & Tyson, C. A. (2006). Dialogic narratives of literacy, teaching, and schooling: Preparing literacy teachers for diverse settings. *Reading Research Quarterly, 41,* 202–224.

Santoli, A. (1988). *New Americans: An oral history.* New York: Ballantine Books.

Smith, J. K., & Hodkinson, P. (2005). Relativism, criteria, and politics. In N. K. Denzin & Y. S. Lincoln (Eds.), *Handbook of qualitative research* (3rd ed., pp. 915–932). Thousand Oaks, CA: Sage.

St. Pierre, E. A. (1997). Methodology in the fold and the irruption of transgressive data. *International Journal of Qualitative Studies in Education, 10*(2), 175–189.

Strauss, A., & Corbin, J. (1998). *Basics of qualitative research: Techniques and procedures for developing grounded theory.* Thousand Oaks, CA: Sage.

Street, B. (1995). *Social literacies.* New York: Longman.

Syed, K. T. (2008). Voicing teachers' perspectives on professional development in literacy education. *Alberta Journal of Educational Research, 54*(3), 383–292.

Terkel, S. (1990). *Working: People talk about what they do all day and how they feel about what they do.* New York: Ballantine Books. (Original work published 1972)

Tillman, L. (2002). Culturally sensitive research approaches: An African-American perspective. *Educational Researcher, 31*(9), 3–12.

Van Maanen, J. (1988). *Tales of the field: On writing ethnography.* Chicago: University of Chicago Press.

Vasudevan, L., & Vinz, R. (2007). Writing out of the unexpected: Narrative inquiry and the weight of small moments. *English Education, 39*(4), 326–351.

Washington, R. D., Bauer, E., Edwards, P., & McMillon-Thompson, G. (2008). *Self-portraits of Black women scholars' literacy and identity.* In Y. Kim, V. V. Risko, D. Compton, D. Dickinson, M. Hundley, R. Jiménez, et al. (Eds.), *57th Yearbook of the National Reading Conference* (pp. 221–236). Chicago: National Reading Conference.

Wolcott, H. F. (2009). *Writing up qualitative research* (3rd ed.). Thousand Oaks, CA: Sage.

CHAPTER 16

Neuroimaging

Jack M. Fletcher
David L. Molfese
Panagiotis G. Simos
Andrew C. Papanicolaou
Carolyn Denton

Neuroimaging studies involving reading continue to attract attention in scientific circles and from the media. Although many involve children and adults identified with reading difficulties, studies involving functional neuroimaging also examine children in the process of learning to read. Using a variety of structural and functional imaging modalities, these studies address fundamental questions about the neural mechanisms supporting reading development. In this chapter, we examine the application of neuroimaging technologies to the study of reading. We begin with a brief explanation of different methods for structural and functional neuroimaging, focusing especially on the latter as these methods are seeing more widespread application. We then examine results of studies applying these technologies to a variety of questions involving the neural correlates of reading, with a specific focus on evaluating changes in brain activation patterns during reading intervention. We conclude with a study from our group in which functional neuroimaging was conducted as part of an intervention study of first graders at risk for reading difficulties.

HISTORICAL FOUNDATIONS OF NEUROIMAGING

The goal of neuroimaging research is to directly measure the structure and/ or function of the brain. Structural neuroimaging captures high-resolution images of brain anatomy, allowing comparison of structures in both normal and abnormal brains. Functional neuroimaging measures changes in brain activity during a cognitive task, such as reading or listening to language. Functional neuroimaging depends on structural neuroimaging in order to know which areas of the brain participate when completing a particular task. One of the goals of functional neuroimaging is the localization of function to specific areas of the brain. As illustrated in this chapter, it is an oversimplification to view neuroimaging as an extrapolation of the "medical model" to social and behavioral research or to see the application of neuroimaging to reading as a technology looking for a home. As with any method or technology, the key issues involve the questions that lead to the application of the method, the theory behind the application, and the integration of the results of studies using these methods with the broader area under investigation, in this instance reading.

ORIGINS

Both structural and functional neuroimaging have their origins in the need for noninvasive methods for examining the brain in clinical populations characterized by some form of injury, disease, or disorder to the brain. Prior to the advent of cerebral computed tomography (CT) scanning in the 1970s, methods for identifying brain abnormalities in patient populations were often surgically invasive or based on attempts to trace radioactive isotopes in the vascular system of the brain (angiography) or the injection of air into the ventricular system (pneumoencephalography). For patients undergoing neurosurgery, functional mapping methods that involved selective anesthesia of one of the cerebral hemispheres to lateralize language or memory, known as the Wada technique (Wada & Rasmussen, 1960), are still used as part of neurosurgical planning, especially for epilepsy. Such methods are essential for ensuring that the surgical procedure does not further debilitate the patient by removing an area of the brain critical for cognitive or motor function. For similar purposes, direct electrical stimulation of the cortex to map function in patients undergoing surgical ablation for control of epilepsy dates back to the seminal studies of Penfield and Roberts (1959). Finally, neurophysiological methods, such as electroencephalography (EEG) and evoked potentials, have also been used as noninvasive methods for identifying abnormal brain function (Papanicolaou, 1998).

None of these methods has been entirely satisfactory because they are either imprecise as a result of poor resolution for visualizing brain anatomy or very invasive or both. Yet the results of studies of patient populations with brain injury have long been used to advance hypotheses about relations of brain and behavior. The limits of inferences from injury or disease are well known. Damage to the brain does not necessarily indicate that the area would mediate function in a non-brain-injured person and certainly does not indicate how the behavior was acquired (Benton, 1962; Fletcher

& Taylor, 1984). Thus, researchers interested how the brain mediates and acquires behavior have long desired methods for the noninvasive study of the brain in clinical populations and in typically developing individuals.

CURRENT METHODS

With the development of CT scanning in the 1970s, modern neuroimaging began to take advantage of the growing availability of computer technologies. CT, like all other contemporary neuroimaging methods, is a computer-enhanced technology. In a CT scan, X-ray technology is used to take successive pictures (slices) of the brain, which are then reconstructed by computer technologies to reveal brain anatomy with much greater resolution. However, although CT scans were a significant advance over older methods, the skull remained a significant source of artifacts, and better resolution with less invasive methods was desired.

The development of magnetic resonance imaging (MRI) in the mid-1980s has largely superseded CT scans, although the latter continues to have significant clinical application. For research, MRI is preferred because it is noninvasive. No radiation is used and children as young as 6 years are usually able to participate in a study. The primary limitation is that all neuroimaging methods require the participant to sit still to avoid artifact as a result of motion, so children have to be able to understand this requirement and cooperate.

MRI scanning is an application of physics (Krasuski, Horowitz, & Rumsey, 1996). A simplified explanation revolves around the spinning of protons and neutrons in atoms. The spin results in the generation of magnetic energy. In an MRI machine, this magnetic spin is greatly magnified by applying a strong pulsating magnetic field, so that small differences in the magnetic energy can be detected. By manipulating magnetic pulse sequences, the MRI scanner is able to assess the effects of these sequences on the magnetic energy generated by different brain tissues. It can, therefore, contrast the brain's gray matter, white matter, and cerebrospinal fluid and the skull, dura, and other components of the brain. With the use of special software, the origin of these magnetic signals can be calculated precisely, so that an actual image of the brain can be constructed in three dimensions. The results of an MRI scan can also be digitized into a computer and actually measured to assess the volume of selected brain regions. In addition, the image can be resliced in different planes depending on the question of interest (Krasuski et al., 1996; Papanicolaou, 1998).

Functional imaging methods include older techniques, such as regional cerebral blood flow, in which radioactive isotopes are introduced into the body. The decay of these isotopes in the brain's vascular system can be measured as an index of blood flow. When different areas of the brain are engaged in a mental operation, the shifts in blood flow can be measured as an indicator of what areas of the brain are involved in the cognitive processing.

Regional cerebral blood flow has been superseded by other methods, such as single-photon emission computed tomography (SPECT) and positron emission tomography (PET). Like regional cerebral blood flow, these methods involve attempts to image brain metabolism through assessments of glucose consumption or blood flow. They also involve the use of some type of radioisotope, typically assessing different properties of decay to reconstruct pictures representative of changes in brain function.

More recently, the development of methods for rapid acquisition of MRI slices in the 1990s has largely been proven to be more sensitive to brain function, with much better temporal resolution. These methods essentially use conventional MRI scanners with software that permits fast image acquisition to detect alterations in blood flow and volume. No radiation is involved and, like a structural MRI, there is no need for injection of any contrast material. Functional MRI (fMRI) has generally superior temporal and spatial resolution compared with PET, SPECT, and other such methods. These methods are probably less sensitive to changes in blood flow than PET and SPECT, and the assessment of neuronal activity is indirect (Krasuski et al., 1996; Papanicolaou, 1998).

Direct assessments of neural activity also take place with neurophysiological methods, such as EEG and evoked potentials, or magnetoencephalography (MEG), also known as magnetic source imaging (MSI). The latter is unique in that it assesses neural activity in real time (Papanicolaou, 1998). All the functional imaging methods are discussed in more detail later.

THE NEUROSCIENCE OF READING

There has been great historical interest in brain structure and function in children and adults with unexpected reading difficulties. The earliest observations of unexpected reading failure led to hypotheses about the neural underpinnings of these severe disabilities (Hinschelwood, 1902). These observations were fueled by studies of clinical populations who lost some aspect of reading ability and subsequently underwent postmortem examination. By identifying the areas of the brain that had been damaged and linking findings across patients, theories of language and reading evolved that usually found their way to children with reading difficulties and no brain injury (Benton, 1975). These theories led to the conviction that these reading difficulties were intrinsic to the child and not due to environmental causes (Critchley, 1970; Orton, 1927). However, despite the tenacity of these convictions, the hypotheses were not really testable until the advent of modern neuroimaging, which has moved research from simple questions such as "Is the brain related to reading disability?" or "What areas of the brain 'cause' reading disability?" to much more complex questions involving the interplay of experience, instruction, and the brain in learning to read.

STRUCTURAL NEUROIMAGING

The initial structural MRI studies were significantly influenced by post-mortem studies of a few adults with a history of reading difficulties. These studies involved a total of 10 brains that had been accumulated over several years. The reports indicated that individuals with reading disabilities are anatomically different from normative expectations, although no control brains were employed. The differences involved the size of specific brain structures, focusing on an area of the temporal lobes, the planum temporale, known from lesion studies to be important for mediating language. Specific microscopic neuroanatomical anomalies were also reported (Filipek, 1996; Galaburda, 1993; Shaywitz et al., 2000). Examinations of the cerebellum in a subset of these brains (Finch, Nicolson, & Fawcett, 2002) revealed larger mean cell sizes in the medial posterior cerebellum relative to normal expectations as well as unexpected distributions of cells in several parts of the cerebellum.

The postmortem studies have not been without controversy (Filipek, 1996; Shaywitz et al., 2000). People do not usually succumb to reading problems, so it is a small, unusual sample of brains. In addition to concerns about the nature and definition of reading difficulties after the fact, it is not possible to relate the findings of an autopsy study to actual reading performance. Thus, when structural MRI became available, it was almost immediately used to study brain structure in children and adults with reading difficulties.

Structural Neuroimaging Studies of Reading Disability

Structural imaging studies are usually based on some type of voxel-counting methods (voxel-based morphometry), with the voxels then converted to estimates of the size of different regions. Programs for this type of analysis have been rapidly advancing and now are semiautomated and incorporate thin slices across the entire brain. Other methods are based on acquisitions that permit the measurement of water molecule diffusion, or diffusion tensor imaging (DTI). These methods are especially sensitive to the cerebral white matter and the fiber pathways that connect different regions of the brain.

Voxel-Based Morphometry

The initial structural neuroimaging studies used CT scans and anatomical MRI. Because CT scans did not prove particularly useful, and were done largely on a few adults and children who required an examination for clinical purposes, these studies are not discussed here (reviewed by Hynd & Semrud-Clikeman, 1989). Many voxel-based morphometry studies of brain anatomy—comparisons of brain volumes in "regions of interest"—have now been completed with children and adults who experience reading difficulties. These studies implicate several structures and regions of the brain (Filipek, 1996; Fletcher, Lyon, Fuchs, & Barnes, 2007; Shaywitz et al., 2000). However, the results are inconsistent across studies and are not reviewed in detail. The findings most consistently identified involve the planum temorale, where some comparisons in children and adults who vary in reading proficiency do not find the expected asymmetry (Hynd, Semrud-Clikeman, Lorys, Novey, & Eliopulos, 1990; Larsen, Hoien, Lundberg, & Ödegaard, 1990). Others find reversals in the expected patterns of asymmetry so that the planum temporale is larger in the right hemisphere of individuals with reading disability (Hynd et al., 1990). A third set of studies fails to identify differences in the size or symmetry of the planum temporale in people with reading disabilities (Eckert et al., 2003; Rumsey et al., 1997; Schultz et al., 1994).

If the region of interest is restricted to temporoparietal areas of the left hemisphere known to mediate language, results are more consistent, tending to show that these areas are smaller in people with reading disabilities (Filipek, 1996; Shaywitz et al., 2000). However, results are still mixed, with some studies reporting differences (Duara et al., 1991; Hugdahl et al., 2003; Kushch et al., 1993) and others not finding differences (Eckert et al., 2003; Hynd et al., 1990; Jernigan, Hesselink, Sowell, & Tallal, 1991).

Studies of the corpus callosum, the great commissure connecting the two hemispheres of the brain, have been mixed. Some studies report differences in the size and/or shape (Duara et al., 1991; Hynd et al., 1995), whereas others have not found differences (Larsen et al., 1990; Schultz et al., 1994).

In the cerebellum, Eckert and colleagues (2003) found that a group with dyslexia differed from controls in the right anterior lobe of the cerebellum. Brambati and colleagues (2004) and Rae and colleagues (2002) found differences in cerebellum volumes but in different regions. Kibby, Francher, Markanen, Lewandowski, and Hynd (2005) found small differences in total cerebellum volumes between children with dyslexia and typically achieving children. Laycock and colleagues (2008) reported that white matter (WM) volumes were larger in adults with dyslexia.

Diffusion Tensor Imaging

DTI is a newer application of MRI technology that uses specific image acquisition methods to trace the direction of WM pathways (anisotropy) in the brain. The diffusion of water across cellular compartments is measured and an apparent diffusion coefficient (ADC) is calculated. The ratio of parallel to perpendicular ADC can then be computed (Beaulieu, 2002). The diffusion of water molecules along fiber pathways is reported as fractional anisotrophy (FA). Values of FA are greatest for thick WM pathways, with myelinated fibers limiting the diffusion of water in the perpendicular direction (Beaulieu, 2002).

Several studies have applied DTI to comparisons of good and poor readers. Klinkberg and colleagues (2000) compared adults with and without a history of reading difficulties, observing less development of WM in language areas of the left hemisphere in those with reading disability. In a small sample, Deutsch and colleagues (2005) reported that FA is correlated with behavioral measurements of reading, spelling, and rapid-naming performance. They observed decreased FA in the left superior longitudinal fasciculus/temporoparietal WM and diffuse cerebral WM anomalies (corona radiata, internal capsule) in poor readers. Group differences in corpus callosum FA are not correlated with reading. Dougherty and colleagues (2005) reported a negative correlation between FA and phonological awareness in fibers connecting the temporal lobe, suggesting that good readers have fewer but larger axons connecting the two hemispheres. Niogi and McCandlis (2006) found that FA in left centrum semiovale, left superior corona radiate, and bilateral anterior corona radiate is correlated with standardized reading scores in typically developing children. They also observed FA orientation differences in left temporoparietal WM of the perisylvian language network in children defined with dyslexia compared with normal readers. Carter and colleagues (2009) examined regional differences in FA in left temporoparietal regions and left inferior frontal gyrus in 14 poor readers and 17 control children. They reported decreased FA in the WM connections to the left inferior frontal gyrus, left insula, and right frontal region. The FA metric from the left inferior frontal gyrus correlated with word-reading fluency. They concluded that the atypical microstructure of the left inferior frontal gyrus was "abnormal" in "dyslexia." Ben-Shachar, Dougherty, and Wandell (2007) concluded in a review of the literature on DTI and reading that three major WM pathways showed evidence of microstructural associations with poor reading and the language areas of the brain: corona radiata, superior longitudinal fasciculus, and corpus callosum.

Conclusions

Many of the differences across structural neuroimaging studies reflect variations in participant characteristics and imaging methods. This is technically complicated and time-consuming research. Although acquiring the images is relatively simple, the machines vary in technical characteristics and resolution. Methods for acquiring images vary and evolve over time with improved technology. Quantitative measurement of MRI is a tedious and time-consuming process because someone must digitize (preprocess) the scans and often must manually outline or edit the regions of interest, although semi-automated methods are now widely available and require less from the operator. Thus, samples tend to be small and variable. Factors such as age, gender, and handedness influence the anatomical organization of the brain, and these effects are magnified in small samples (Schultz et al., 1994). Thus, larger samples that are more homogeneous and precisely defined that use newer semi-automated methods are needed.

FUNCTIONAL NEUROIMAGING

Reflecting in part the dissatisfaction with the inconsistent results of structural neuroimaging studies, more recent research has emphasized the assessment of brain function using PET, fMRI, and MSI. In these studies, changes in brain metabolism or neuronal signaling are assessed in relation to some type of challenge task. For example, a child might be asked to read words or sentences. While reading, changes in the rate of communication among brain cells in different regions occur, resulting in increased regional brain metabolism. As a result there are local increases in blood flow in order to supply the increased metabolic activity with oxygen and glucose.

In contrast to studies of brain structure, the results of research on brain function tend to converge across methods and laboratories in good and poor readers (Eden & Zeffiro, 1998; Shaywitz & Shaywitz, 2005), although there are inconsistencies among studies with respect to the engagement of a particular area (Poeppel, 1996; Price & McCrory, 2005).

By way of overview, these studies indicate that a network of brain areas mediates different word-recognition processes as well as other processes involved in language and reading. These networks, however, vary with proficiency, showing different patterns of activation in poor readers versus more skilled readers. The areas most consistently involved in these networks include the ventral temporo-occipital region in the base of the brain, the temporoparietal region (including the posterior portion of the superior temporal gyrus, the angular and supramarginal gyri), and inferior frontal regions, predominantly in the left hemisphere (Eden & Zeffiro, 1998; Papanicolaou, Pugh, Simos, & Mencl, 2004; Shaywitz & Shaywitz, 2005). In this section, we review methods of functional neuroimaging and then turn to results of studies of brain function related to a variety of aspects of reading.

Functional Neuroimaging Methods

The four primary functional brain-imaging methods used to study reading vary in how brain function is measured and the spatial and temporal resolution of the modality (Papanicolaou, 1998): (1) PET, (2) fMRI, (3) MEG/MSI, and (4) magnetic resonance spectroscopy (MRS). Electrophysiological methods, such as EEG and event-related potentials, are also used to measure brain function. We do not discuss these latter methods because their capability for imaging of brain anatomy is not as developed as that of these four primary modalities (see Dool, Stelmack, & Rourke, 1993, for a review of research on reading difficulties using electrophysiological methods).

The principles of functional neuroimaging are similar across methods (Shaywitz et al., 2000). When an individual performs a cognitive or motor task, the changes in glucose metabolism (PET), blood flow (PET and fMRI), electrical activity (EEG or evoked potentials), magnetic activity (MSI), or brain chemistry (MRS) are recorded. A structural MRI scan is usually obtained, and the patterns of brain activation are superimposed on this MRI to identify the areas of the brain where changes are taking place. Most of these methods are safe and noninvasive and do not involve radiation and, therefore, can be used with children. Methods involving PET, however, require the use of a radioactive isotope that is ingested in order to measure changes in brain function. The exposure to small amounts of radioactivity precludes participation of children, unless they can directly benefit from PET because of a neurological condition (Papanicolaou, 1998).

Despite these differences across methods, there are common methodological features on which all functional neuroimaging modalities can be compared (see Billingsley et al., 2003). One major consideration involves the selection of tasks. Good imaging studies carefully outline the rationale behind the task selection. Task selection must be analytic and guided by strong theory. If the purpose is to image some aspect of cognition, the underlying cognitive theory should be well established independently of applications to neuroimaging. Other desirable characteristics include the need for adequate spatial resolution when identifying brain areas activated by a particular task. Imaging modalities vary considerably in their spatial resolution, with PET much weaker than fMRI and MSI (in conjunction with structural MRI). The imaging modality should provide information on the temporal resolution of the task, but this is possible in real time only with neurophysiological procedures (e.g., MSI) because hemodynamic shifts take time to occur and are often "after the fact." The images should reasonably converge across modalities, externally validating the different methods. Finally, the method should be easy to apply, especially in studies of children.

In evaluating an imaging study, the consumer must understand these issues and the strengths and weaknesses of different modalities. Consider, for example, the spatial resolution and temporal sensitivity of the four modalities. The metabolic activity recorded by PET and fMRI takes place after the actual processing has occurred, so that the temporal resolution of these methods is weak. The chemical shifts measured by MRS occur in real time but require longer acquisitions to measure the shift (Hunter & Wang, 2001). The spatial resolution of PET and MRS are poor, so the maps are aligned with a structural MRI scan to allow precise localization of brain activity associated with performance of a particular task. MSI, on the other hand, affords measurement of neurophysiological activity in real time (down to the millisecond) and provides information on the actual time course of neuronal events. MSI scans, however, do not convey structural information for the brain being imaged, so MSI activation maps are also superimposed onto a structural MRI scan. fMRI partially overcomes the temporal limitations of MRI by rapidly collecting serial magnetic resonance images in order to measure the changes in blood flow associated with cognitive activity (Papanicolaou et al., 2004; Shaywitz et al., 2000). Thus, spatial resolution with fMRI is excellent despite weak temporal resolution as the changes in blood flow do not precisely co-occur with the event. In contrast to fMRI, MSI is weak in detecting subcortical brain activity and is largely sensitive to surface cortical activation. These strengths and weaknesses help the consumer evaluate the contribution of different imaging studies.

In the next section, we review studies involving reading, focusing on fMRI and MSI as the most frequently applied and least invasive paradigms. However, across modalities, the findings converge in suggesting that tasks involving different aspects of reading are associated with increased activation in ventral occipitotemporal (or basal) regions, the posterior portion of the superior and middle temporal gyri extending into inferior parietal areas (supramarginal and angular gyri), and the inferior frontal lobe areas, primarily in the left hemisphere (Eden & Zeffiro, 1998; Papanicolaou et al., 2004; Rumsey et al., 1997; Shaywitz et al., 2000). There are inconsistencies involving the involvement of a particular area (Poeppel, 1996; Price & McCrory, 2005), but it is apparent that a network of areas is common across methods, activated to a different degree depending on the modality and the reading task. The network is clearly apparent in Figure 16.1, which illustrates the regions of interest.

Functional Neuroimaging Studies of Reading

The reading studies that we focus on involve different tasks that manipulate components of word recognition. This is partly because the studies have been oriented toward adults and children who have word-recognition difficulties, by far the most common form of reading disability (Shaywitz, 2004). Word-recognition tasks lend themselves to functional neuroimaging methods. Such tasks can closely link stimulus presentation and response, which helps interpret the time course of the cognitive operation. Word-recognition tasks can be manipulated to address a variety of component processes that are common to both aural language function and reading, such as phonological and semantic analysis, and others that are specific to print (visual and orthographic processing). It is possible to image other, more complex aspects of reading, such as fluency and comprehension. This goal is far more difficult to achieve because fluency and comprehension

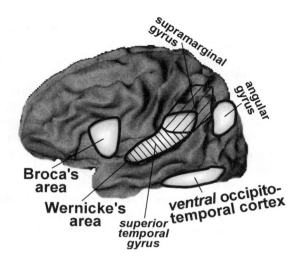

FIGURE 16.1. Model of a neural network for reading showing four major participating areas. Broca's area is responsible for phonological processing involving articulation mapping as in the pronunciation of words. Wernicke's area (which includes portions of the superior temporal and supramarginal gyri) is responsible for phonological processing involving letter–sound correspondence. The angular gyrus is a relay station that links information across modalities. The visual association cortex in the occipitotemporal region is responsible for graphemic analysis. Most of the empirical evidence that supports this model for the brain circuit that supports reading derives from the study of acquired reading difficulties secondary to brain damage (Damasio & Damasio, 1983; Henderson, 1986), although more recent studies of the effects of transient interference with normal function in certain areas, in the context of neurosurgical operations, generally corroborate earlier findings (e.g., Simos, Breier, Wheless, et al., 2000).

involve several component processes, the contribution of which to the overall pattern of brain activity must be isolated experimentally. This requires the use of a series of activation tasks, each placing differential demands upon one or more of the components of the reading function. Because the goal of functional neuroimaging is to relate components of a task to specific patterns of brain activation, tasks that permit this type of decomposition in relation to brain activation are highly desirable.

PET Studies

The earliest functional neuroimaging studies evaluated the activation patterns of adult good and poor readers using PET, an earlier emerging technology. They were done in adults because PET is invasive, involving injection of radioactive isotopes. The participant receives a preparation containing the isotope, which has known properties of decay. The rate of decay in different brain regions is measured as the person performs a task, thus providing evidence of the involvement of these regions.

Studies of adults with reading disabilities using PET have found reduced blood flow in the left temporoparietal area during performance of word and sentence reading and phonological processing tasks (Rumsey et al., 1992, 1997). Activation in the left inferior frontal areas was similar in good and poor readers (Rumsey et al., 1994). In addition, whereas good readers showed more activation of the left than right hemisphere in reading, poor readers did not show this asymmetry (Gross-Glenn et al., 1991). By examining relations among brain areas with respect to the relative degree of regional activity, Horwitz, Rumsey, and Donohue (1998) showed significant coactivation in good readers between the left angular gyrus and other brain areas during a phonological task. These measures of functional connectivity among reading areas in the left hemisphere were not as strong in poor readers.

fMRI Studies

The basis for fMRI involves changes in blood flow. If a cluster of neurons in the brain begins to participate in a particular cognitive operation, it increases the rate at which that group communicates with nearby neurons. Increased neurophysiological activity elevates the rate of metabolic processes that take place inside each neuron, which in turn causes increased consumption of oxygen. This results in a depletion of oxygenated blood (measured by the MRI as a change in the magnetic properties of oxygenated hemoglobin) in the region of these neurons. A change in oxygenated blood leads to a vascular reaction in which more blood is sent to this region, resulting in an oversupply of hemoglobin. The process takes as long as 10 to 14 seconds, and fMRI essentially detects these changes in oxygenation by measuring changes in the perturbation of the magnetic energy generated by changes in hemoglobin. To detect these changes, the distribution of hemoglobin is measured in resting states and then in response to activation and is depicted as color-coded maps overlaid upon the actual MRI images (Krasuski et al., 1996). As with PET, a careful approach to task construction is necessary to identify areas activated by different cognitive operations. The changes in hemoglobin distribution must be measured before, during, and after engagement in a cognitive task. To identify how different areas of the brain are engaged in a particular cognitive operation, metabolic changes related to overall brain function must be isolated so that the changes specific to a task can be identified. Different images can be compared and the specific components of activation identified by "subtracting" across images to remove aspects of the activation that are not specific to the operation of interest (Papanicolaou et al., 2004).

fMRI studies have proliferated to a point where meta-analytic syntheses have been performed that permit estimation of results across studies. Maisog, Einbinder, Flowers, Turkeltaub, and Eden (2008) completed a meta-analysis of fMRI and PET studies of adults defined with dyslexia and controls. Across studies, they reported reduced activation in left hemisphere regions involving ventral visual (occipitotemporal), temporoparietal (inferior parietal cortex, superior temporal gyrus), thalamus, and inferior frontal gyrus (see Figure 16.2). In the right hemisphere, reduced activation was apparent in fusiform, postcentral, and superior temporal gyri. Increased activation in poor readers was apparent in the right thalamus and anterior insula. There was no evidence across studies for differences in cerebellar activation or for increased activation of the inferior frontal region reported by Shaywitz and colleagues (2002). The most robust results occurred as reduced activation in the occipitotemporal regions of the left hemisphere, often interpreted as a visual "word form" region that in MEG studies reviewed later is activated early in the word-reading process but after primary sensory registration.

The second meta-analysis (Richlan, Kronbichler, & Wimmer, 2009) involved 17 fMRI or PET studies of reading or phonological processing in samples described as "dyslexic" versus "controls." No age restrictions were introduced. Reduced activation in the dyslexic groups was apparent in left hemisphere regions involving the temporoparietal (inferior parietal, supe-

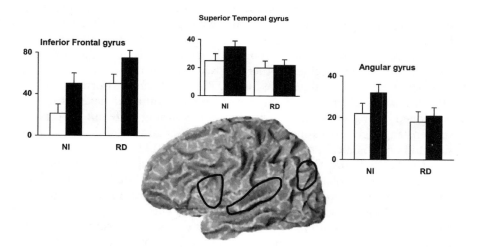

FIGURE 16.2. Relative degree of change in blood flow in response to an orthographic compared with a phonological task, using fMRI in nonimpaired readers (NI) and poor readers (RD). The number of activated image elements (pixels) within each area serves as the dependent variable. In posterior regions, such as the superior temporal and angular gyri, the change in activation is large in nonimpaired readers but small in poor readers. In contrast, anterior regions demonstrate increased activation in poor readers (inferior frontal gyrus) relative to nonimpaired readers (Shaywitz et al., 1998).

rior temporal, middle and inferior temporal regions) and occipito temporal regions. Underactivation of the inferior frontal gyrus and hyperactivity of the primary motor cortex and anterior insula were found.

Both these meta-analyses concurred in identifying areas outlined in Figure 16.2, as dysfunctional in poor readers. These areas include an occipitotemporal region that is often referred to as a visual "word form" region. This region is involved in the rapid processing of letter strings and orthographic patterns that links to higher order representations of words (Price & McCrory, 2005). In addition, there is underactivation of a temporoparietal system that is involved in assembling phonological representations of words in oral language processing and in reading. However, there is less evidence that the angular gyrus is part of this network (Richlan et al., 2009). Finally, there is evidence for underactivation of an inferior frontal region that mediates access to phonological and lexical representations of words and conflicting evidence for increased activity of motor regions often interpreted as a compensatory mechanism involving efforts to articulate unfamiliar words.

MSI Studies

Studies using MSI, or MEG (hereafter referred to as MSI), have also revealed reliable differences in activation patterns of children with reading disabilities and typically achieving children at group and individual levels. For these studies, activation maps are obtained while the children completed tasks involving listening to or reading real words or reading pseudowords and having to decide whether the pseudowords rhyme (Simos, Breier, Fletcher, Bergman, et al., 2000; Simos, Breier, Fletcher, Foorman, et al., 2000). Reading fluency and sentence comprehension tasks have also been developed, along with other experiments examining different aspects of spoken language processing, including word recognition and comprehension and phonological analysis (Billingsley et al., 2003).

Unlike PET and fMRI, MSI directly assesses neuronal signaling in real time (Papanicolaou, 1998; Papanicolaou et al., 2004). Neurons are constantly active, firing bursts of electrical signals in response to cognitive processes. MSI can identify where in the brain the discharges are occurring. Although the sources of these currents cannot be directly measured, these sources also produce small amounts of electromagnetic energy that emanate around the source and travel outside the head. These minute magnetic signals are not distorted by the passive electrical properties of brain tissue and can be captured by MSI in the form of a magnetic field (or magnetic flux) distributed along the head surface. Local, transient changes in magnetic flux are recorded by superconducting loops of wire (magnetometers) that are contained in a helmet-like device covering the head. On the basis of the recorded changes in the surface distribution of electromagnetic energy, researchers obtain precise location estimates for active neurons using simple statistical modeling techniques (Papanicolaou, 1998). Unlike PET and fMRI, MSI does not require subtraction methods. Like other neuroimaging techniques, it requires many trials and the results are averaged across trials, similar to evoked potential methods. However, the phenomena of interest occur in real time because the basis is neuronal signaling, not metabolism.

In a series of studies of adults and children who vary in reading proficiency, good and poor readers have not been found to differ in activation patterns when they *listened* to words, showing patterns predominantly in the left hemisphere that would be expected for such a task (Simos, Breier, Fletcher, Bergman, et al., 2000; Simos et al., in press). However, on *printed* word-recognition tasks, striking differences in the activation patterns of good and poor readers occur (see Figure 16.3). In the children who were good readers, there was a characteristic pattern in which the occipital areas of the brain that support primary visual processing were initially activated (not shown in Figure 16.3). Then the ventral visual association cortices in both hemispheres were activated, followed by simultaneous activation of three areas in the *left* temporoparietal region (essentially the angular, supramarginal, and superior temporal gyri, encompassing Wernicke's area). In the children with reading problems, the same pattern and time course were apparent, but the temporoparietal areas of the *right* hemisphere were

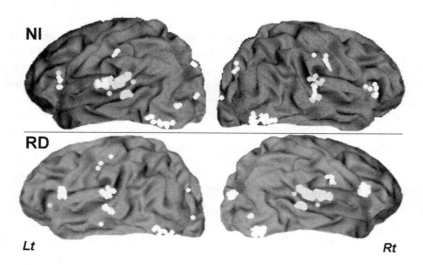

FIGURE 16.3. Three-dimensional renderings of MRI scans from a reader with impairment (lower set of images) and a nonimpaired reader (upper set of images) during a printed word-recognition task in an MSI study. Note the clear preponderance of activity sources in left (Lt) temporoparietal cortices in the proficient child and in homotopic right-hemisphere (Rt) areas in the poor reader. Data from Simos, Breier, Fletcher, Bergman, et al. (2000).

activated. On the whole, the findings are similar to those from the PET and fMRI studies, but the differences between good and poor readers are more strikingly lateralized, especially in areas associated with mapping of letters and sounds (see Figure 16.1).

In a more recent study using newer generation recording machines with more detectors and different analysis techniques, Simos and colleagues (in press) conducted continuous word-recognition tasks (auditory and visual) in children who experienced reading difficulties ($N = 44$) and typical readers ($N = 40$). Minimum norm estimates of regional neurophysiological activity were obtained from MSI recordings at 3-millisecond intervals. There were no differences in the auditory task. On the visual (reading) task, children with reading difficulties showed reduced activity in the superior and middle temporal gyri bilaterally during late phases of word reading. Increased activity in prefrontal, mesial temporal, and ventral occipitotemporal cortices, bilaterally, was apparent. The temporal profile of activity in the group with reading difficulties was markedly different from the nonimpaired group, showing simultaneous activity peaks in temporal, inferior parietal, and prefrontal regions.

Conclusions

Altogether, these functional neuroimaging studies suggest that in children with reading difficulties it is the functional connections among brain areas that account for differences in brain activation as opposed to specific or general dysfunction of any single brain area. A critical question is whether the patterns seen in the poor readers are compensatory or reflect the failure of instruction to impact the brain in a manner necessary to form the neural networks that support word recognition. Thus, the pattern may be similar to that seen in a young child who has not learned to read and may change by virtue of development, instruction, or even intervention. These studies may provide an example of how brain and environment interact in forming the neural networks supporting word recognition.

CHANGES IN BRAIN ACTIVATION IN RELATION TO INTERVENTION

The relation of neuronal activation changes and response to intervention has been evaluated on more than a dozen studies in this decade (Aylward et al., 2003; Eden et al., 2004; Odegard, Ring, Smith, Biggan, & Black, 2008; Meyler, Keller, Cherkassky, Gabrieli, & Jus, 2008; Richards et al., 2000, 2002, 2006; Shaywitz et al., 2004; Simos et al., 2002, 2005, 2007a, 2007b; Temple et al., 2003). These studies involve fMRI and MSI as well as one structural imaging study using DTI.

To illustrate, consider applications of fMRI to changes during reading intervention. Shaywitz and colleagues (2004) and Meyler and colleagues (2008) used fMRI to study children in elementary grades before and after year-long interventions. In Shaywitz and colleagues, the intervention results were reported in Blachman and colleagues (2004). Pre–post imaging comparisons showed that after the intervention students who received the experimental intervention showed greater activation of bilateral inferior frontal gyri, the left superior temporal sulcus, the occipitotemporal region, and the middle occipital gyrus as well as other regions. Shaywitz and colleagues interpreted these results as showing normalization of left occipitotemporal regions associated with efficiency in reading but noted compensatory changes involving the right frontal region. Meyler and colleagues performed fMRI after a year-long intervention of grade 5 poor readers. The participants were identified with a timed word task, so there is probably more heterogeneity compared with selection with an untimed task used in Shaywitz and colleagues. A sentence comprehension task was used to activate the brain. The primary finding was that the temporoparietal areas were underactivated bilaterally in poor readers at baseline but normalized with successful intervention. Unlike Shaywitz and colleagues, the occipitotemporal regions were not underactivated at baseline and did not show changes with intervention, most likely because of the differences in the activation task and selection criteria.

In one of the earliest studies, Simos and colleagues (2002) employed MSI before and after children with severe reading disability participated in an intense phonologically based intervention. The sample included eight children ranging in age from 7 to 17 years who had severe word-recognition difficulties. Six children read at the third percentile or below, and the other two read at the 13th and 18th percentiles, respectively. The children received intervention for 2 hours a day, 5 days a week, over an 8-week period, or about 80 hours of intensive phonologically based instruction per child. Before intervention, the eight children with dyslexia uniformly displayed the aberrant pattern of activation in the right hemisphere that has been reliably identified with MSI. After intervention, their word-reading accuracy scores improved into the average range. In addition, in each case, there was significant activation of neural circuits in the left hemisphere commonly associated with proficient word-reading ability. There was also a tendency for reduction in right-hemisphere activity. Figure 16.4 provides a representative example of the changes before and after intervention.

In a structural imaging study using DTI, Keller and Just (2009) compared FA in a subset of poor readers evaluated in Meyler and colleagues (2008) before and after a reading intervention. The intervention group showed a significant increase in FA along the left anterior centrum semiovale, which is involved in connectivity of language regions. No changes in FA were observed for the good readers or the poor readers who did

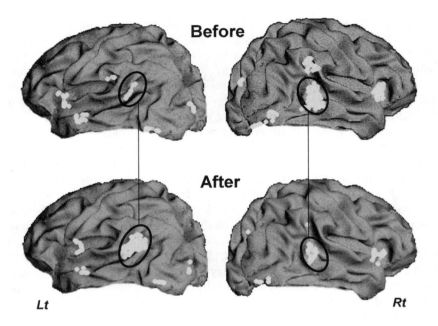

Before

After

Lt   *Rt*

FIGURE 16.4. Activation maps from a poor reader before and after intervention. Note the dramatic increase in left temporoparietal activation associated with the significant improvement in phonological decoding and word-recognition ability. Data adapted from Simos, Breier, Wheless, et al. (2002).

not receive intervention. The authors speculated that increased myelination along this WM pathway may be responsible for the increase in FA, although a mechanism by which myelination would increase has not been identified at present.

More recent studies have begun to examine inadequate responders to instruction. Simos and colleagues (2007a) found no changes in brain activity for three children who did not respond adequately to intervention. Odegard and colleagues (2008) conducted a postintervention comparison of adequate and inadequate responders and found differences predominantly in the left inferior parietal region. These results are consistent with the areas of increased activation involved in the temporoparietal regions in studies with pre–post comparisons of neural activity. It is likely that future studies will begin to focus more on children and adults who do not respond adequately to instruction.

These studies clearly show that the neural systems of poor readers are malleable and respond to instruction. In addition, although compensatory changes are apparent, most changes occur in the areas that typically subserve reading ability in typically developing children. The interventions tend to be intensive and do not address changes that might occur in the course of typical instruction, which is discussed in the next section.

AN EXEMPLAR OF FUNCTIONAL NEUROIMAGING

To illustrate the use of functional neuroimaging in the study of reading, we highlight a study that we completed using MSI (Simos et al., 2005). This study involved a group of children identified as at risk for reading difficulties at the end of kindergarten and a comparison group of children in the same classrooms who did not show risk characteristics. The at-risk children received different reading interventions in grade 1 designed to prevent reading difficulties in first grade. As part of this study, a subset of the at-risk and not-at-risk children received MSI scanning at the end of kindergarten and at the end of first grade.

Intervention Study

Procedures

The intervention study (Mathes et al., 2005) took place in six non–Title I schools in a large urban school district in Texas. Over each of 2 consecutive years, the risk status of all children in kindergarten in these schools was evaluated using the teacher-administered Texas Primary Reading Inventory (TPRI; Fletcher et al., 2002). Those children who were identified as at risk based on the screening section from the TPRI received additional assessments of word recognition and text reading to eliminate potential false-positive results because as the TPRI was designed to minimize the risk of missing children who might have reading problems, with the expected consequence of higher rates of false-positive results.

Those children who were identified as at risk were randomly assigned to one of three reading interventions. Two of these interventions involved small-group instruction using two different approaches. Both of these interventions took place in groups of three with a certified teacher supervised by the researchers. The instruction took place on a daily basis for about 40 minutes per day for 30 weeks. One intervention (proactive) was based on a direct instruction model that included explicit instruction in the alphabetic principle, fluency, and comprehension strategies. The other approach (responsive) explicitly taught the alphabetic principle, along with fluency and comprehension strategies, but in the context of reading and writing. The programs differed largely in that the proactive program had an explicit scope and sequence and used highly decodable text. In the responsive program, teachers are expected to respond to the needs of the children in the context of reading and writing, so there was no explicit scope and sequence.

Texts with high-frequency words were used. Both interventions were comprehensive, well-integrated approaches to reading instruction that included an explicit emphasis on teaching the alphabetic principle. In addition to the two groups of students who received a pull-out intervention, a third group of students remained in the classroom and did not receive a pull-out intervention unless it was provided by the school. As such, this group is not a traditional untreated control group but rather a comparison group addressing the value-added impact of small-group instruction on top of enhanced classroom instruction.

Results

Group averages across children who received the two pull-out interventions generally did not differ significantly across a wide range of assessments of word recognition, fluency, and comprehension (Mathes et al., 2005). There were some slight differences that would be expected on the basis of the program that was taught. For example, children in the proactive intervention had significantly higher word attack skills. Children who received either pull-out intervention performed at higher levels and showed greater growth than at-risk children who stayed in the classroom. At the end of the year, the number of children who were not reading in the average range was less than 1% for the proactive intervention, 8% for the responsive intervention, and 16% for children who stayed in the classroom.

Imaging Study

Procedures

Volunteers for the imaging study were recruited directly at the schools. The researchers attended different meetings of parents, including kindergarten graduation ceremonies, explaining the study and soliciting volunteers. When the children arrived at the laboratory, considerable time was taken to acclimate them to the procedure and help them become as comfortable as possible. The actual recording required about 10 minutes per task; the entire session lasted about 2 hours per child.

Scans were initially obtained at either the end of kindergarten or the beginning of first grade. The sample comprised 28 at-risk children (18 boys, 10 girls) and 17 not-at-risk children (10 boys, 7 girls). The average age was about 6½ years. At the end of first grade, we were able to reimage 33 of the 45 original participants. Seventeen were from the not-at-risk group, and 13 were students from the initial at-risk group who responded to systematic classroom instruction and/or pull-out intervention and read in the average range at the end of grade 1 (responders), and three were from the initial at-risk group who did not respond to the intervention and read below the 25th percentile (nonresponders).

During each of the two visits, children completed two activation tasks. One task required them to look at a letter of the alphabet and pronounce the most common sound associated with that letter. The second task required them to read aloud simple consonant–vowel–consonant pseudowords. To complete the tasks, the children were placed in a comfortable position lying down and looking at a screen projected on the ceiling. While the children completed each task, they were imaged with a whole-head neuromagnetometer array that consists of 148 magnetic sensors, housed in a magnetically shielded chamber. The results were obtained by averaging across the responses for each task.

Results

The specific methods used for signal processing, source localization, and coregistration with the anatomical MRI scan can be found in Papanicolaou and colleagues (2004). The results of the initial assessment before intervention were reported in Simos and colleagues (2002). Activity sources were consistently found in five regions of the brain: the posterior portion of the superior temporal gyrus, extending into the adjacent supramarginal gyrus (Wernicke's area); the angular gyrus; the bilateral inferior frontal gyrus (Broca's area); the ventral occipitotemporal (basal) region; and the lateral occipitotemporal region. Both occipitotemporal regions contain complex visual processing areas. Because MSI also provides information on cognitive processing in real time, two major components of the time course were identified. The early activity sources were largely in areas of the brain that are concerned with visual processing or print. The latest sources occurred largely after 150 milliseconds and involved the network of the brain regions listed previously.

The major differences between the groups are displayed in Figure 16.5, which illustrates the significant group × hemisphere × area interaction, which was mainly due to regional differences in the direction of quasilinear trends across groups. In posterior regions (angular gyrus and ventral occipitotemporal region bilaterally and Wernicke's area in the left hemisphere), there was greater activity for the not-at-risk group followed by the responders and least activity for the nonresponders. This trend was reversed in the right-hemisphere homologue of Wernicke's area and in the inferior frontal gyrus bilaterally. Hemispheric asymmetries in the degree of activity were found only in Wernicke's area but vary across groups: Not-at-risk children showed the expected left > right asymmetry, seen in older proficient children and adults, whereas responders displayed bilaterally symmetric activity. Nonresponders displayed a strikingly different pattern (right > left), which is typical of older children and adults with reading impairment. Group differences were also found with the respect to the relative timing of activity in certain areas, most prominent of which was the significant

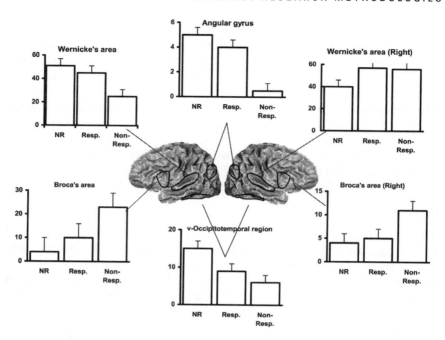

FIGURE 16.5. Group differences in the degree of brain activity in four major components of the reading circuit: temporoparietal cortex (posterior superior temporal and supramarginal gyrus, which includes Wernicke's area in the left hemisphere and the corresponding region in the right hemisphere), the angular gyrus, Broca's area (located in the inferior frontal gyrus), and ventral occipitotemporal cortex (located in the basal surface of the brain). Group differences were similar across tasks (letter–sound and pseudoword reading) in all areas with the exception of the inferior frontal gyrus, where group differences were more pronounced for the more demanding pseudoword reading task. Estimates of the degree of brain activity were obtained with MSI at the end of kindergarten. NR, children not at risk for developing reading difficulties ($N = 17$); Resp., children who were deemed to be at risk for developing reading difficulties in kindergarten, but responded to systematic classroom instruction and scored within the average range 1 year later ($N = 13$); Non-Resp., at-risk children who could be classified as reading disabled at the end of first grade ($N = 3$).

tendency for an early peak of activity in the left inferior frontal gyrus in the group of nonresponders compared with the two groups of children who displayed typical reading achievement outcomes at the end of grade 1.

There were significant developmental changes during the 1-year study period. Not-at-risk children and children in the responder group showed increased activation between kindergarten and grade 1 in the inferior frontal region and lateral occipitotemporal areas bilaterally and for both tasks.

Conversely, a significant reduction in degree of activity was found in the superior temporal gyrus in both hemispheres and tasks. There were no changes in the degree or latency of activity in these areas for the group of nonresponders.

These findings demonstrate that in the majority of beginning readers the general outline of the brain network that supports reading is already in place by the end of kindergarten. For a smaller proportion of children, this profile displays a less mature state, yet systematic classroom instruction is sufficient to help establish the "typical" network by the end of first grade. For a smaller proportion of at-risk children, however, classroom instruction alone is not sufficient to promote the developmental changes required for the establishment of an efficient brain network to support fluent reading. These children show distinct activation profiles during the initial stages of reading acquisition, resembling the profile found in older poor readers (Simos, Breier, Fletcher, Bergman, et al., 2000; Simos, Breier, Fletcher, Foorman, et al., 2000; Simos et al., 2002) even for tasks (letter–sound naming) that pose minimal demands for phonological decoding. Generally, changes in reading proficiency appear to parallel changes in neural activity, largely in the areas shown in Figure 16.2. For the majority of children, including those initially classified as at risk and who responded to classroom instruction, these changes represent an initial strengthening of the brain network that involves regions in the frontal lobes and in more posterior regions of the brain, especially the angular gyrus. This network is largely bilateral but in proficient readers is lateralized in the temporoparietal areas especially concerned with phonological analysis. There is less lateralization in the at-risk responder group. The nonresponder group showed much less change and little development of the left-hemisphere network.

RELEVANCE OF NEUROIMAGING TECHNOLOGIES TO READING RESEARCH

Reading researchers commonly ask why neuroimaging studies are relevant to reading research. It might be better to phrase the question in terms of why reading research is relevant to neuroimaging. In many of the studies that have been described, the key has been theory-driven applications of the technology to different research questions. The application of the imaging modality and the interpretation of the results have been heavily dependent on theory and research in the cognitive sciences. This research has helped focus the lens of the technology so that appropriate questions are asked and tasks are designed that are linked to those that have been used in the cognitive sciences.

In addition, questions that would be of interest to reading educators have been asked because individuals interested in intervention have participated in the neuroimaging studies. Thus, the early focus of the imaging studies on the results of intervention studies has been critical for the development and enhancement of neuroimaging technologies. By the same token, using neuroimaging in reading research, particularly in the intervention studies, has helped advance understanding of how children learn to read and why some struggle. In this regard, the results can be integrated into the larger body of knowledge regarding the critical role of phonological processing and word recognition as a key phase in learning to read and as an obstacle for many children who do not develop adequate word-recognition strategies. The fact that the neural systems can be shown to develop through interactions with the environment implies that they are not present at birth and that certain types of experiences are critical in developing these systems. Moreover, when children who are struggling to learn to read are examined, it becomes apparent that the systems are malleable and provide excellent examples of the plasticity and malleability of the brain for mediating different kinds of complex cognitive functions. The greatest relevance of neuroimaging studies is the clear indication that instructional approaches that are effective, whether they occur in the classroom or in a pull-out program, in children who are at risk or not at risk for reading difficulties, or in children and adults who either good or poor readers, can modify aspects of brain function that are known to be critical for the cognitive operations targeted by instruction. As demonstrated in this chapter, the research provides excellent examples of how teachers provide effective instruction that alters brain function and supports critical areas of learning. Ultimately, it is the teacher who has provided instruction that impacts the organization of the brain for reading.

As the studies reviewed in this chapter demonstrate, not only is reading research relevant to neuroimaging studies but neuroimaging studies are very relevant to reading research. In this chapter, we have attempted to show that the application of neuroimaging methods in reading is a significant accomplishment. It is more than a technology looking for a home. Rather, these applications are dependent on other areas of reading research that lead to the imaging study and are critical for the interpretation of results, in turn suggesting modifications of theories of reading development. The task is not to decide whether any body of knowledge in reading (or other areas of education and science) is good or bad. Rather, the task is to integrate results across the different domains of inquiry that pertain to reading. Neuroimaging studies cut across multiple research domains, including reading development, processing, and response to instruction for various age groups and levels of proficiency. This type of knowledge must be integrated into the broader knowledge of research on reading. At the most dramatic level, neuroimaging research shows that teaching affects the brain in positive, long-term ways that are essential for the development of the reader.

ACKNOWLEDGMENTS

Work reported on in this chapter was supported in part by grants from the National Science Foundation (No. 9979968: "Early Development of Reading Skills: A Cognitive Neuroscience Approach") and the Eunice Kennedy Shriver National Institute of Child Health and Human Development (No. HD38346: "Brain Activation Profiles in Dyslexia"; No. HD25802: "Center for Learning and Attention Disorders"; and No. P50 HD052117, Texas Center for Learning Disabilities). The content is solely the responsibility of the authors and does not necessarily represent the official views of the Eunice Kennedy Shriver National Institute of Child Health and Human Development, the National Institutes of Health, or the National Science Foundation.

REFERENCES

Aylward, E. H., Richards, T. L., Berninger, V. W., Nagy, W. E., Field, K. M., Grimme, A. C., et al. (2003). Instructional treatment associated with changes in brain activation in children with dyslexia. *Neurology, 22*, 212–219.

Beaulieu, C. (2002). The basis of anisotropic water diffusion in the nervous system—A technical review. *NMR in Biomedicine, 15*, 435–455.

Ben-Shachar, M., Dougherty, R. F., & Wandell, B. A. (2007). White matter pathways in reading. *Current Opinion in Neurobiology, 17*, 258–270.

Benton, A. L. (1962). Behavioral indices of brain injury in school children. *Child Development, 33*, 199–208.

Benton, A. L. (1975). Developmental dyslexia: Neurological aspects. In W. J. Friedlander (Ed.), *Advances in neurology* (pp. 1–47). New York: Raven.

Billingsley, R. L., Simos, P. G., Castillo, E. M., Maestú, F., Sarkari, S., Breier, J. I., et al. (2003). Functional brain imaging of language: Criteria for scientific merit and supporting data from magnetic source imaging. *Journal of Neurolinguistics, 16*, 255–275.

Blachman, B. A., Schatschneider, C., Fletcher, J. M., Francis, D. J., Clonan, S., Shaywitz, B., et al. (2004). Effects of intensive reading remediation for second and third graders. *Journal of Educational Psychology, 96*, 444–461.

Brambati, S. M., Termine, C., Ruffino, M., Stella, G., Fazio, F., Cappa, S. F., et al. (2004). Regional reductions of gray matter volume in familial dyslexia. *Neurology, 63*, 742–745.

Carter, J. C., Lanham, D. C., Cutting, L. E., Clements-Stephens, A. M., Chen, X., Hadzipasic, M., et al. (2009). A dual DTI approach to analyzing white matter in children with dyslexia. *Psychiatry Research: Neuroimaging, 172*, 215–219.

Critchley, M. (1970). *The dyslexic child*. Springfield, IL: Charles C Thomas.

Damasio, A. R., & Damasio, H. (1983). The anatomic basis of pure alexia. *Neurology, 33*, 1573–1583.

Dool, C. B., Stelmack, R. M., & Rourke, B. P. (1993). Event-related potentials in children with learning disabilities. *Journal of Clinical Child Psychology, 22*, 387–398.

Dougherty, R. F., Deutsch, G. K., Ben-Schachar, M., Potanina, P., Bammer, R., &

Wandell, B. (2005, November). *Callosal pathways associated with reading and phonological awareness in children.* Paper presented at the annual meeting of the Society for Neuroscience, Washington, DC.

Duara, R., Kushch, A., Gross-Glenn, K., Barker, W., Jallad, B., Pascal, S., et al. (1991). Neuroanatomic differences between dyslexic and normal readers on magnetic resonance imaging scans. *Archives of Neurology, 48,* 410–416.

Eckert, M. A., Leonard, C. M., Richards, T. L., Aylward, E. H., Thomson, J., & Berninger, V. W. (2003). Anatomical correlates of dyslexia: Frontal and cerebellar findings. *Brain, 126,* 482–494.

Eden, G. F., Jones, K. M., Cappell, K., Gareau, L., Wood, F. B., Zeffiro, T. A., et al. (2004). Neural changes following remediation in adult developmental dyslexia. *Neuron, 44,* 411–422.

Eden, G. F., & Zeffiro, T. A. (1998). Neural systems affected in developmental dyslexia revealed by functional neuroimaging. *Neuron, 21,* 279–282.

Filipek, P. (1996). Structural variations in measures in the developmental disorders. In R. Thatcher, G. Lyon, J. Rumsey, & N. Krasnegor (Eds.), *Developmental neuroimaging: Mapping the development of brain and behavior* (pp. 169–186). San Diego, CA: Academic Press.

Finch, A. J., Nicolson, R. I., & Fawcett, A. J. (2002). Evidence for a neuroanatomical difference within the olivo-cerebellar pathway of adults with dyslexia. *Cortex, 38,* 529–539.

Fletcher, J. M., Foorman, B. R., Boudousquie, A. B., Barnes, M. A., Schatschneider, C., & Francis, D. J. (2002). Assessment of reading and learning disabilities: A research-based, intervention-oriented approach. *Journal of School Psychology, 40,* 27–63.

Fletcher, J. M., Lyon, G. R., Fuchs, L. S., & Barnes, M. A. (2007). *Learning disabilities: From identification to intervention.* New York: Guilford Press.

Fletcher, J. M., & Taylor, H. G. (1984). Neuropsychological approaches to children: Towards a developmental neuropsychology. *Journal of Clinical Neuropsychology, 6,* 39–56.

Galaburda, A. M. (1993). The planum temporale. *Archives of Neurology, 50,* 457.

Gross-Glenn, K., Duara, R., Barker, W. W., Lowenstein, D., Chang, J.-Y., Yoshii, F., et al. (1991). Positron emission tomographic studies during serial word-reading by normal and dyslexic adults. *Journal of Clinical and Experimental Neuropsychology, 13,* 531–544.

Henderson, V. (1986). Anatomy of posterior pathways in reading: A reassessment. *Brain and Language, 29,* 119–133.

Hinschelwood, J. (1902). Congenital word blindness, with reports of 10 cases. *Ophthalmology Review, 21,* 91–99.

Horwitz, B., Rumsey, J. M., & Donohue, B. C. (1998). Functional connectivity of the angular gyrus in normal reading and dyslexia. *Proceedings of the National Academy of Sciences USA, 95,* 8939–8944.

Hugdahl, K., Heiervang, E., Ersland, L., Lundervold, A., Steinmetz, H., & Smievoll, A. I. (2003). Significant relation between MR measures of planum temporal area and dichotic processing of syllables in dyslexic children. *Neuropsychologia, 41,* 666–675.

Hunter, J. V., & Wang, Z. J. (2001). MR spectroscopy in pediatric neuroradiology. *MRI Clinics of North America, 9,* 165–189.

Hynd, G. W., Hall, J., Novey, E. S., Etiopulos, D., Black, K., Gonzales, J. J., et al. (1995). Dyslexia and corpus callosum morphology. *Archives of Neurology, 52,* 32–38.

Hynd, G. W., & Semrud-Clikeman, M. (1989). Dyslexia and brain morphology. *Psychological Bulletin, 106,* 447–482.

Hynd, G. W., Semrud-Clikeman, M., Lorys, A. R., Novey, E. S., & Eliopulos, D. (1990). Brain morphology in developmental dyslexia and attention deficit disorder/hyperactivity. *Archives of Neurology, 47,* 919–926.

Jernigan, T. L., Hesselink, J. R., Sowell, E., & Tallal, P. (1991). Cerebral structure on magnetic resonance imaging in language- and learning-impaired children. *Archives of Neurology, 48,* 539–545.

Keller, T. A., & Just, M. A. (2009). Altering cortical connectivity: Remediation-induced changes in the white matter of poor readers. *Neuron, 64,* 624–631.

Kibby, M. Y., Francher, J. B., Markanen, R., Lewandowski, A., & Hynd, G. W. (2005). A test of the cerebellar deficit hypothesis of dyslexia. *Journal of the International Neuropsychological Society, 9,* 219.

Klinkberg, T., Hedehus, M., Temple, E., Salz, T., Gabrieli, J., Moseley, M., et al. (2000). Microstructure of temporo-parietal white matter as a basis for reading ability: Evidence from diffusion tensor magnetic resonance imaging. *Neuron, 25,* 493–500.

Krasuski, J., Horowitz, B., & Rumsey, J. M. (1996). A survey of functional and anatomical neuroimaging techniques. In G. R. Lyon & J. M. Rumsey (Eds.), *Neuroimaging: A window to neurological foundations of learning and behavior in children* (pp. 25–55). Baltimore: Brookes.

Kushch, A., Gross-Glenn, K., Jallad, B., Lubs, H., Rabin, M., Feldman, E., et al. (1993). Temporal lobe surface area measurements on MRI in normal and dyslexic readers. *Neuropsychologia, 31,* 811–821.

Larsen, J. P., Hoien, T., Lundberg, I., & Ödegaard, H. (1990). MRI evaluation of the size and symmetry of the planum temporale in adolescents with developmental dyslexia. *Brain and Language, 39,* 289–301.

Laycock, S. K., Wilkinson, I. D., Wallis, L. I., Darwent, G., Wonders, S. H., Fawcett, A. J., et al. (2008). Cerebellar volume and cerebellar metabolic characteristics in adults with dyslexia. *Annals of New York Academy of Sciences, 1145,* 222–236.

Maisog, J. M., Einbinder, E. R., Flowers, D. L., Turkeltaub, P. E., & Eden, G. F. (2008). A meta-analysis of functional neuroimaging studies of dyslexia. *Annals of the New York Academy of Sciences, 1145,* 237–259.

Mathes, P. G., Denton, C. A., Fletcher, J. M., Anthony, J. L., Francis, D. J., & Schatschneider, C. (2005). An evaluation of two reading interventions derived from diverse models. *Reading Research Quarterly, 40,* 148–183.

Meyler, A., Keller, T. A., Cherkassky, V. L., Gabrieli, J. D. E., & Jus, M. A. (2008). Modifying the brain activation of poor readers during sentence comprehension with extended remedial instruction: A longitudinal study of neuroplasticity. *Neuropsychologia, 46,* 2580–2592.

Niogi, S. N., & McCandlis, B. D. (2006). Left lateralized white matter microstructure accounts for individual differences in reading ability and disability. *Neuropsychologia, 44,* 2178–2188.

Odegard, T. N., Ring, J., Smith, S., Biggan, J., & Black, J. (2008). Differentiating the neural response to intervention in children with developmental dyslexia. *Annals of Dyslexia, 58*(1), 1–14.

Orton, S. (1927). Specific reading disability—Strephosymbolia. *Journal of the American Medical Association, 90*, 1095–1099.

Papanicolaou, A. C. (1998). *Fundamentals of functional brain imaging*. Lisse, The Netherlands: Swets & Zetilinger.

Papanicolaou, A. C., Pugh, K., Simos, P. G., & Mencl, E. (2004). Functional brain imaging: An introduction to concepts and applications. In P. McCardle & V. Chabra (Eds.), *The voice of evidence: Bringing research to the classroom* (pp. 385–416). Baltimore: Brookes.

Penfield, W., & Roberts, L. (1959). *Speech and brain mechanisms*. Princeton, NJ: Princeton University Press.

Poeppel, D. (1996). A critical review of PET studies of phonological processing. *Brain and Language, 55*, 317–351.

Price, C. J., & McCrory, E. (2005). Functional brain imaging studies of skilled reading and developmental dyslexia. In M. J. Snowling & C. Hulme (Eds.), *The science of reading: A handbook* (pp. 473–496). Oxford, UK: Blackwell.

Rae, C., Harasty, J. A., Dzendrowskyj, T. E., Talcott, J. B., Simpson, J. M., Blarmire, A. M., et al. (2002). Cerebellar morphology in developmental dyslexia. *Neuropsychologia, 40*, 1285–1292.

Richards, T. L., Aylward, E. H., Berninger, V. W., Field, K. M., Grimme, A. C., Richards, A. L., et al. (2006). Individual fMRI activation in orthographic mapping and morpheme mapping after orthographic or morphological spelling treatment in child dyslexics. *Journal of Neurolinguistics, 19*, 56–86.

Richards, T. L., Berninger, V. W., Aylward, E. H., Richards, A. L., Thomson, J. B., Nagy, W. E., et al. (2002). Reproducibility of proton MR spectroscopic imaging (PEPSI): Comparison of dyslexic and normal-reading children and effects of treatment on brain lactate levels during language tasks. *American Journal of Neuroradiology, 23*(10), 1678–85.

Richards, T. L., Cornia, D., Serafini, S., Steury, K., Echelard, D. R., Dager, S. R., et al. (2000). The effects of a phonologically driven treatment for dyslexia on lactate levels as measures by proton MRSI. *American Journal of Neuroradiology, 21*, 916–922.

Richlan, F., Kronbichler, M., & Wimmer, H. (2009). Functional abnormalities in the dyslexic brain: A quantitative meta-analysis of neuroimaging studies. *Human Brain Mapping, 30*, 3299–3308.

Rumsey, J. M., Andreason, P., Zametkin, A. J., Aquino, T., King, A., Hamburger, S., et al. (1992). Failure to activate the left temporoparietal cortex in dyslexia. An oxygen 15 positron emission tomographic study. *Archives of Neurology, 49*, 527–534.

Rumsey, J. M., Nace, K., Donohue, B., Wise, D., Maisog, J. M., & Andreason, P. (1997). A positron emission tomographic study of impaired word recognition and phonological processing in dyslexic men. *Archives of Neurology, 54*, 562–573.

Rumsey, J. M., Zametkin, A. J., Andreason, P., Hanchan, A. P., Hamburger, S. D., Aquino, T., et al. (1994). Normal activation of frontotemporal language cortex in dyslexia, as measured with oxygen 15 positron emission tomography. *Archives of Neurology, 51*, 27–38.

Schultz, R. T., Cho, N. K., Staib, L. H., Kier, L. E., Fletcher, J. M., Shaywitz, S. E., et al. (1994). Brain morphology in normal and dyslexic children: The influence of sex and age. *Annals of Neurology, 35*, 732–742.

Shaywitz, B. A., Shaywitz, S. E., Blachman, B. A., Pugh, K. R., Fulbright, R. K., Skudlarski, P., et al. (2004). Development of left occipitotemporal systems for skilled reading children after a phonologically-based intervention. *Biological Psychiatry, 55*, 926–933.

Shaywitz, B. A., Shaywitz, S. E., Pugh, K. R., Mencl, W. E., Fulbright, R. K., Constable, R. T., et al. (2002). Disruption of the neural circuitry for reading in children with developmental dyslexia. *Biological Psychiatry, 52*, 101–110.

Shaywitz, S. E. (2004). *Overcoming dyslexia.* New York: Knopf.

Shaywitz, S. E., Pugh, K. R., Jenner, A. R., Fulbright, R. K., Fletcher, J. M., Gore, J. C., et al. (2000). The neurobiology of reading and reading disability (dyslexia). In M. L. Kamil, P. B. Mosenthal, P. D. Pearson, & R. Barr (Eds.), *Handbook of reading research: Volume III* (pp. 229–249). Mahwah, NJ: Erlbaum.

Shaywitz, S. E., & Shaywitz, B. A. (2005). Dyslexia (specific reading disability). *Biological Psychiatry, 57*, 1301–1309.

Shaywitz, S. E., Shaywitz, B. A., Pugh, K. R., Fulbright, R. K., Constable, R. T., Mencl, W. E., et al. (1998). Functional disruption in the organization of the brain for reading in dyslexia. *Proceedings of the National Academy of Sciences USA, 95*, 2636–2641.

Simos, P. G., Breier, J. I., Fletcher, J. M., Bergman, E., & Papanicolaou, A. C. (2000). Cerebral mechanisms involved in word reading in dyslexic children: A magnetic source imaging approach. *Cerebral Cortex, 10*, 809–816.

Simos, P. G., Breier, J. I., Fletcher, J. M., Foorman, B. R., Bergman, E., Fishbeck, K., et al. (2000). Brain activation profiles in dyslexic children during nonword reading: A magnetic source imaging study. *Neuroscience Reports, 290*, 61–65.

Simos, P. G., Breier, J. I., Wheless, J. W., Maggio, W. W., Fletcher, J. M., Castillo, E. M., et al. (2000). Brain mechanisms for reading: The role of the superior temporal gyrus in word and pseudoword naming. *NeuroReport, 11*, 2443–2447.

Simos, P. G., Fletcher, J. M., Bergman, E., Breier, J. I., Foorman, B. R., Castillo, E. M., et al. (2002). Dyslexia-specific brain activation profile becomes normal following successful remedial training. *Neurology, 58*, 1203–1213.

Simos, P. G., Fletcher, J. M., Sarkari, S., Billingsley, R. L., Francis, D. J., Castillo, E. M., et al. (2005). Early development of neurophysiological processes involved in normal reading and reading disability. *Neuropsychology, 19*, 787–798.

Simos, P. G., Fletcher, J. M., Sarkari, S., Billingsley-Marshall, R., Denton, C., & Papanicolaou, A. C. (2007a). Intensive instruction affects brain magnetic activity associated with reading fluency in children with persistent reading disabilities. *Journal of Learning Disabilities, 40*, 37–48.

Simos, P. G., Fletcher, J. M., Sarkari, S., Billingsley, R. L., Denton, C., & Papanicolaou, A. C. (2007b). Altering the brain circuits for reading through intervention: A magnetic source imaging study. *Neuropsychology, 21*, 485–496.

Simos, P. G., Rezaie, R., Fletcher, J. M., Juranek, J., Cirino, P. T., Li, Z., et al. (in press). Timing of regional brain activation associated with word recognition in children with reading difficulties. *Brain and Language.*

Temple, E., Deutsch, G. K., Poldrack, R. A., Miller, S. L., Tallal, P., Merzenich, M. M., et al. (2003). Neural deficits in children with dyslexia ameliorated by behavioral remediation: Evidence from functional MRI. *Proceedings of the National Academy of Sciences USA, 100,* 2860–2865.

Wada, J., & Rasmussen, T. (1960). Intracarotid injection of sodium amytal for the lateralization of cerebral speech dominance: Experimental and clinical observations. *Journal of Neurosurgery, 17,* 266–282.

CHAPTER 17

Single-Subject Experimental Design

Susan B. Neuman

Although studies of the individual have always had a place in educational and psychological research, investigations involving single subjects have become increasingly popular in recent years (Neuman & McCormick, 1995). Traditionally, single-subject experimental research has been useful in clinical applications where the focus has been on the therapeutic value of an intervention for the client. However, recent applications of single-subject research in areas such as literacy, language education, and cognitive psychology suggest that these designs provide a powerful way of examining interventions, particularly when reporting average differences for groups may have little meaning. Moreover, researchers (Cooper, Heron, & Heward, 2007) are increasingly turning to an analysis of single subjects in conjunction with other research techniques as a way of explicating findings, providing a more integrated and detailed analysis of the impact of interventions.

Why study the individual subject? For one, this approach allows researchers to examine the effects of an experimental treatment or treatments when it is difficult to obtain groups of subjects or when comparability among and between groups is difficult to establish. It can bypass an error often found in group-comparison studies—intersubject variability—because each individual serves as his or her own control. In addition, single-subject designs provide researchers with information on what may be important differences among individuals. For example, although a particular technique might work best for many students, for others an alternative technique may be superior. Furthermore, with replication, researchers can determine whether the intervention is effective for other individuals and in other settings, helping them build important theoretical links in establishing generalizability.

Single-subject experimental design, however, should not be confused with case study methods. Although both study the individual, in a single-subject experiment the investigator deliberately manipulates one or more independent variables. Single-subject experiments are designed to generate functional and causal statements, whereas case studies are designed to provide insight by describing phenomena.

This chapter describes the methodology, the most common procedures, and its uses and multiple applications in language and literacy research. Specifically, it addresses the unique questions that may be answered with the methodology and how these questions may be researched and analyzed. Furthermore, examples of literacy studies are woven throughout the descriptions to emphasize how these applications can address key questions, and the strengths and limitations, as well as the important considerations of validity and reliability are highlighted.

FEATURES OF SINGLE-SUBJECT EXPERIMENTAL RESEARCH

Beginning in the 1950s, single-subject experimental research designs came about largely in psychological studies to explore the aftermath of treatments with patients. These studies had to examine ongoing practice in contrast to waiting for extended posttest periods. Research designs were proposed that allowed researchers to measure changes in behavior for a particular person individually. Although case studies were used extensively at the time, therapists needed a design that could establish a causal relationship, as might be done with experimental research.

Single-subject experimental designs suited this purpose and today are considered to be one of the strongest designs against threats to internal validity that we have in our research arsenal (Kazdin, 2001). It works by having each participant serve as his or her own control. Basically, the participant is exposed to a nontreatment and a treatment phase and performance is measured during each phase.

Six common characteristics make this research design unique to other experimental designs (Alberto & Troutman, 2003). These characteristics, described next, form the fundamental features that set it apart from other approaches.

Baseline and Treatment Conditions

Each single-subject study involves at least one baseline and one treatment condition. The *baseline* refers to a period of time in which the target behavior (dependent variable) is observed and recorded as it occurs, without a special or new intervention. The baseline essentially provides the frame of reference against which all future behavior is compared. It is more than a single pretest. Because human behaviors can vary day to day, multiple opportunities must be given for the participant to exhibit a "typical" response; therefore, most researchers (Alberto & Troutman, 2003) recommend incorporating at least three to five data collection points during baseline.

For example, a researcher might be interested in examining the effects of an intervention designed to promote fluency. Prior to the intervention, the baseline period would be used to establish the typical fluency rate of the student by administering fluency assessments for several days beforehand. The baseline phase would continue until the researcher is able to achieve the stability of this target behavior—in this case fluency rate. The treatment condition is a period of time during which the experimental manipulation is introduced and the target behaviors continue to be observed and recorded.

Repeated Measurement

Another distinguishing feature of single-subject experimental research is the repeated and frequent measurement of responses throughout the intervention. This step is different from most experiments, in which the dependent variable is measured only once. Repeated measures are needed to discern a clear pattern of consistency in the behavior over time. They control for the normal variation of behaviors that is expected within short time interventions. This aspect of single-subject design is similar to time-series studies, which investigate groups rather than individuals. If researchers would find that, after a fluency intervention, fluency rates increase and stay at that rate after five or 10 additional trials, then they would have convincing evidence that the treatment was successful.

Single-Variable Rule

In a single-subject study, only one variable is manipulated at a time. This enables researchers to determine the impact of a specific variable on the observed outcomes. Suppose, for example, that a researcher was interested in examining the impact on a student's comprehension performance as a result of a technique called KWL (what do you Know; what do you Want to find out; what would you like to Learn more about) (Ogle, 1986). The researcher would probably establish baseline through multiple assessments of comprehension and then introduce the single treatment of KWL prior to reading the text. The researcher would then continue to assess comprehension in a similar manner as before the intervention began. If scores increased dramatically, the researcher could say with some degree of confidence that it was a result of KWL. In another example, following baseline, a teacher introduces a new basal reader. In the series, the comprehension exercises include previewing, summarizing, reciprocal teaching, and writing. Scores once again go up. However, in this case, the confounding of treatments means that it would be impossible to disentangle which of the treatments caused the effect. Consequently, in single-subject experimental research, only one independent variable usually can be examined at one time.

Internal Validity

Because subjects serve as their own controls in single-subject experimental research, there are fewer standard threats to the internal validity of an investigation than in some other research paradigms. Researchers also build into their studies procedures for assessing the integrity of the independent variable (McCormick, 1990). In some cases, observers are used to judge the integrity of the independent variable during the intervention period. The observer might use a fidelity checklist, noting the critical features of an intervention. This can allow the researcher to measure "drifts" from the planned procedures during the course of the experiment.

In literacy studies, the independent variable or treatment should be a discrete, behavioral treatment that can be conducted in a single session. Multidimensional interventions are not appropriate for single-subject designs. Topics such as examining the impact of "rereading" a text on comprehension or the effects of hearing a story read before reading the story on one's own may lend themselves especially well to single-subject designs. However, topics such as the effects of a new spelling program do not suit this research paradigm. This would likely include an extended intervention over several days with multiple expected outcomes. It would, therefore, be difficult to measure the integrity of the independent variable under such conditions.

Analysis of Data

In single-subject experimental design, conclusions about the effects of an intervention are based on the visual inspection of the data (Kazdin, 2010). At times visual analysis is joined with statistical analysis or combined with other research analyses. There are a number of reasons why the visual inspection of data is particularly compelling in this research design:

- Graphs with repeated measurement of student outcome allow for an ongoing analysis of student performance.
- Unlike traditional experimental research, there are no "objective" measures, such as levels of significance, that indicate the intervention's success. Rather, the researcher makes his or her own decisions about the educational benefits of the intervention based on a visual inspection of the data.
- Conclusions about an intervention's merits can be drawn relatively quickly. For example, if a fluency intervention yields large increases

in a student's fluency rate and there is evidence of maintenance, the researcher may decide to discontinue the study and implement the intervention in the instructional program immediately.

- Visual analysis presents a more conservative view of data analysis than other techniques. First, obviously, it is not influenced by sample size. Second, findings that might demonstrate statistical significance in group studies may not be educationally meaningful. Sometimes visual inspection of the data will demonstrate results that tests fail to find statistically. This is especially true with individuals who may not easily be identified in a group (e.g., those with learning disabilities).

To determine the effects of an independent variable, like fluency training, on the dependent variable, fluency rate, for example, the researcher would graph the data collected immediately following each session and visually inspect the differences between the baseline and treatment phases. If there was a clear distinction between baseline and treatment, the researcher would assume a functional relationship. Using a standard A-B-A withdrawal design (described later), for example, the researcher might reverse treatment—take away the intervention—to see whether the data return to baseline. If this occurs, then it is assumed that the intervention is the causal connection in improving the behavior.

External Validity

The most controversial aspect of single-subject experimental design relates to external validity, or the generalizability of the research. How do we know if the results found with one subject may apply to others?

In traditional experimental research, generality of effects is assumed with statistical significance. This term suggests that, given a different sample from the same population, the researcher would likely find the same results, according to certain probability levels ($p < .01$, for example). This statement assumes, therefore, that if the study were replicated, the results would be similar, give or take a margin of error.

The tactics taken by single-subject researchers are different than the traditional experimental paradigm. Some researchers, such as Axelrod and his colleagues, argue that "generalizability" is anathema to single-subject design (Axelrod, 1983). Given that the goal is to conduct a treatment for an individual, and individuals are different, there is no generalizability. "All we can do," Axelrod argues, "is to improve the life of an individual, one by one. If an autistic child no longer engages in self-inflicting activity like banging his head against a wall as a result of an intervention, then this is evidence that the treatment worked—for this child" (S. Axelrod, personal communication, December 14, 1994).

Other single-subject design researchers (Cooper et al., 2007), however, might argue for transferability rather than generalizability. Transferability implies an extension of the effects of the intervention to new populations. For example, a researcher may conduct the same experiment but with different subjects, who may have slightly different characteristics than the subject in the first study. This would provide an extension of their original study. Then they might carry out their intervention in a different context to further examine its transferability. Through repeated replications with different subjects, single-subject experimenters may make important theoretical linkages, establishing the credibility of their intervention to different subjects, different contexts, and different special populations.

EXPERIMENTAL LOGIC OF SINGLE-SUBJECT EXPERIMENTAL DESIGN

These six features of single-subject experimental design reflect an experimental logic basic to the research paradigm. The design is predicated on three major goals (McCormick, 1995): prediction, verification, and replication. By looking at Figure 17.1, we can see how they work.

Prediction is satisfied through repeated measurement of baseline data until stability is recorded. The logic works like this: If a student shows a consistent level of response throughout the baseline period, then the researcher can *predict* that his or her response will continue to fall within that particular level without additional intervention. Evidence of stability at baseline is foundational to the design. Although there are some variations in baseline 1 in Figure 17.1, it is evident that the measurement shows stability.

Verification is the second basic element in the experimental logic. Procedures for verification will be different across different single-subject designs, but essentially it refers to a requirement that the research must demonstrate that change in a particular score is functionally related to the intervention. For example, in a reversal design, the researcher would show verification by removing the independent variable and then collecting data on the dependent variable. If changes in scores were due to the independent variable, scores should return to baseline levels. This is what has occurred in baseline 2 in the figure. Scores increased as a result of the intervention and then returned to baseline after the independent variable was removed.

Replication serves as the basis for determining the reliability of the results. Repeating phases within experiments may confirm the results. It may also provide assurances that the intervention has consistent effects. In intervention 2 in Figure 17.1, scores return to their upward trend after the intervention is once again initiated.

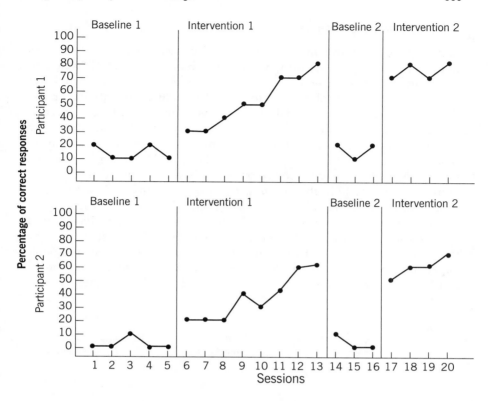

FIGURE 17.1. Example of a single-subject design study.

Requiring evidence of prediction, verification, and replication, therefore, demonstrates that there is a functional relationship between the intervention and the data that are collected. Consequently, the researcher can argue with full assurance for a causal relationship between the independent and dependent variables.

COMMON SINGLE-SUBJECT EXPERIMENTAL RESEARCH DESIGNS

There is no one particular single-subject design. Rather, there are three common types (Kazdin, 2001) and many, many variations within them. For current purposes, the following designs are discussed:

- A-B-A withdrawal designs.
- Multiple-baseline designs.
- Alternating-treatments designs.

A-B-A Withdrawal Designs

In the A-B-A withdrawal family of single-subject design strategies, "A" refers to the no-treatment, or control, phase of the experiment and "B" refers to the treatment phase. To conduct an A-B-A study, the first step would be to state the research problem in a manner that includes operational definitions of our experimental variables. This is very important because precise measurement is critical to examine both stability and variation. Consider a hypothetical example, illustrated in Figure 17.2. Suppose, for instance, that a teacher wanted to assess the impact of a shared book experience on a first-grade student's word-recognition skills. In this hypothetical example, graphed in Figure 17.2, the first baseline phase presents the percentage of target words the child recognized during participation in a reading program where there was regular sustained silent reading intermingled with skill and strategy instruction. This represents "business as usual." During the B phase, the teacher changed instruction to involve daily shared-book experiences, with tests that included the target words, and again recorded results from a word-recognition measure. To determine whether the stu-

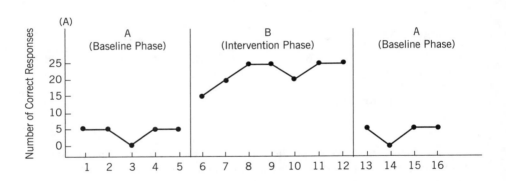

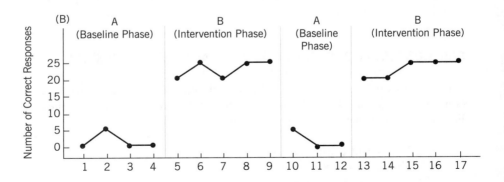

FIGURE 17.2. Example of a reversal design.

dent's increased proficiency in this phase was functionally related to the addition of the shared book experience to the program, the shared-book activity was dropped in a second baseline condition. In other words, in this third phase of the experiment, the teacher attempted to verify the prediction that the level of word recognition seen during the first baseline phase would continue if shared-book experiences were not added.

Given that other threats to internal validity are ruled out, the A-B-A design allows reasonable inferences about the effects of treatment. However, some would argue that it is educationally unfeasible to end with a baseline phase. Therefore, most studies would add an additional phase A-B-A-B to demonstrate once again the contribution of the intervention and its educational benefits for the child.

Multiple-Baseline Designs

In the multiple-baseline design, researchers typically vary one of three parameters (subject, behavior, or setting) while keeping the other two constant (Kucera & Axelrod, 1995). The approach takes repeated measures of baseline on two or more dependent variables. Once the baseline is stable, the researcher introduces the independent variable (such as an instructional method), applying it only to the first dependent variable, and continues to repeatedly measure the reader's performance on all the dependent variables. This means that data are collected on those dependent variables still in the baseline condition while at the same time only one independent variable is being manipulated at a time.

Let's take a hypothetical study on reading instruction using this design. Abigail, a fourth grader, has difficulty with reading comprehension, as evidenced by her inability to identify details as well as the main idea and inferencing in a story. The researcher is interested in examining the impact of a strategy designed to encourage Abigail to monitor her use of comprehension by thinking aloud and graphing the number of details she remembers each time she reads a story. Thinking aloud, in this case, is the independent variable. The dependent variables consist of details or literal comprehension, main idea, and inference. For each variable, a score of 0 to 4 was possible, with a total possible score of 12 (calculated by adding all the response skills together.)

Prior to the intervention, baseline data were collected on all three dependent variables, as shown in Figure 17.3. Starting in session 5, Abigail is taught to think aloud to find the literal details in the story. As indicated in the figure, Abigail increased her ability to identify details, moving from an average of 1.5 to 2.7 following this intervention. Meanwhile, the other baselines remained stable, indicating a lack of covariation between the dependent variables.

After some improvements in the first dependent variable were observed, beginning in session 9, Abigail is taught to use thinking aloud to focus on

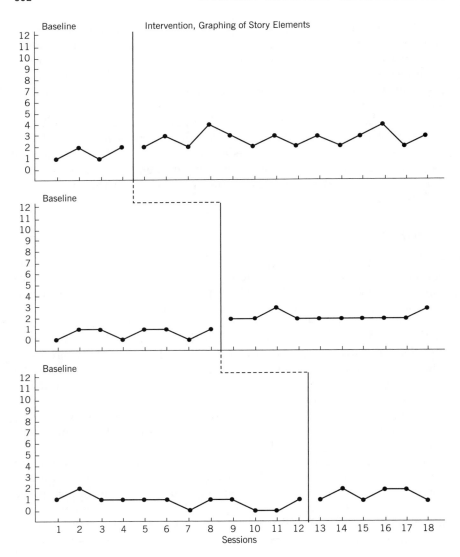

FIGURE 17.3. Example of a multiple-baseline approach.

the main ideas in the story. Then, following a favorable trend in the second dependent variable, the experimental variable is applied to the final condition (inferencing) in addition to the first two. Abigail's ability to identify details and main ideas increases in some sessions following the initiation of the intervention but not in others.

The multiple-baseline design demonstrated that the independent variable of thinking aloud used in this hypothetical study is responsible for some modest improvements in Abigail's ability to identify the main idea. The research design supports this conclusion because, in general, the improvements in Abigail's comprehension occurred only following each intervention, and similar improvements did not occur in the absence of intervention. However, there is considerable overlap in the data points between the baseline and intervention conditions, especially in conditions 1 and 3, in this case, the ability to use inferencing. Therefore, the results of this example indicate that although comprehension was helped somewhat by the use of thinking aloud, it did not appear to be particularly powerful. It is likely, then, that the researcher will turn to other interventions for helping Abigail improve her reading comprehension.

In this case, the multiple-baseline design is well suited for addressing many literacy questions. One caveat, however, should be considered prior to initiating a study with this type of design: Dependent variables need to be functionally independent of one another (so that baselines of still-untreated behaviors remain unaffected) and yet similar enough for each to respond to the same intervention (Kucera & Axelrod, 1995).

Alternating-Treatments Design

In this design, two or more distinct treatments are introduced, usually following a brief baseline phase. The treatments are then alternated randomly and continued until one treatment proves to be more effective than the other or until it is clear than no method is superior to another. During the entire experiment, the learner's performance for each treatment is plotted on a graph, and the effects of the treatment can be discerned easily by visual analysis. These procedures control for many possible threats to the internal validity of a study such as differential selection of subjects or history effects (Neuman, 1995).

Figure 17.4 provides an example of this design. Suppose a researcher was interested in examining the impact of a technique called previewing, an advanced organizer developed by Graves, Cooke, and LaBerge (1983) on students' comprehension performance compared with a prereading discussion or a no-discussion control condition. In this hypothetical example, assume that after each treatment three students read a passage and then were administered a 10-item comprehension measure. This order of the treatments was counterbalanced over a 10-day period, with each treatment applied in random order each day. In other words, each intervention had to "take turns" in terms of when it was applied. As noted in Figure 17.4, the data for each of the three learners, plotted separately for each intervention, clearly indicate that the previewing strategy in this case was more effective than the other treatment or control condition.

The alternating-treatments design has several important advantages for research and instruction. It can be used to compare different approaches relatively quickly, allowing for instructional decision making.

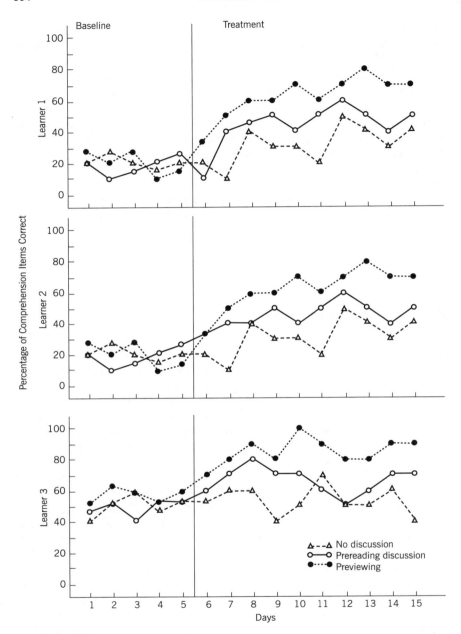

FIGURE 17.4. Example of an alternating-treatments approach.

The graphs are easy to interpret because the data points for each treatment are displayed simultaneously. Furthermore, this design can be used to examine applied questions within the context of instruction, with minimal interference to ongoing classroom activity. These advantages make the alternating-treatments design especially useful for teacher-researchers or action researchers in language and literacy.

STANDARDS OF QUALITY IN SINGLE-SUBJECT DESIGN

Single-subject design is a rigorous, scientific methodology if used appropriately. There are standards of quality. The following quality indicators should be considered when designing studies (Horner et al., 2005):

- Descriptions of participants and settings: Participants need to be described with sufficient detail to allow for others to replicate the experiment.
- Independent and dependent variables: Independent and dependent variables must be operationally defined. In the case of the independent variable, researchers need to identify a behavior that can be systematically manipulated and powerful enough to demonstrate immediate effects. In the case of the dependent variable, it is important to use a valid and reliable measure that generates a quantifiable index and can be measured repeatedly over time.
- Baseline: Baseline behaviors must be measured over a sufficient period of time to show stability prior to treatment. Baselines reveal a pattern of responding that are used to predict the pattern of future performance if the independent variable had not been introduced.
- Experimental control: The design must control for common threats to internal validity, such as testing effects, or multiple treatment interference. History sometimes poses a particular problem to the extent that these studies generally occur over time, rendering them more susceptible to intervening events.
- External validity: Experiments should be replicated across participants, settings, or materials.
- Social validity: Social validity is a term coined by single-subject design researchers to refer to the social importance and acceptability of treatment goals, procedures, and outcomes. It is somewhat akin to the notion of effect size, meaning that researchers examine whether the magnitude of change in the dependent variable has practical value and is generally important. Unlike other experiments, however, there is no ballpark definition of what constitutes social importance. Rather, it is determined on a case-by-case basis.

STRENGTHS AND LIMITATIONS

Taken together, single-subject designs can be particularly useful to answer a wide variety of literacy questions (Neuman & McCormick, 1995). These designs may be especially helpful when there is a wide disparity within groups. The personalized evaluation inherent in single-subject designs may present more accurate data on individual differences and may provide further insights on instructional improvements.

The design is ideal for applied settings and clinical practice: to address questions related to practice. It is also cost-effective. It can make causal statements that have traditionally required large sample sizes and extended periods of time. It can provide replications of the experiment across subjects or across settings that may extend its reliability.

However, the design is not without its limitations. Perhaps the greatest limitation for literacy researchers is related to carryover effects. Put simply, a skill once learned cannot be unlearned easily. Results from the previous phase may carry over into the next. This becomes a significant problem, for example, in A-B-A design since the strength of the design is to return to baseline.

Carryover also occurs in other designs, such as multiple-baseline or alternating treatments. In this case, it might look like multiple-treatment interference. Here there is a possibility that one treatment might influence or blend with another. This is a serious problem because it can muddy the waters, making it impossible to attribute the effects of a target behavior to a particular treatment. It may also limit the kinds of questions that can be asked and answered by the designs for literacy researchers.

In addition, treatments themselves must be potentially powerful enough to determine reasonably immediate effects. For example, it would not be wise to examine the effects of sustained silent reading versus strategic instruction on the percentage of time spent reading because it may take multiple sessions before the investigator observes real changes in the dependent variable. Related to this problem, treatments that are developed over a consecutive series of sessions cannot be measured in most of these designs. For example, if it typically takes a three-step procedure over a 3-day period for a phonics program to improve a student's performance in phonics, then it would be difficult to provide enough repeated measures to examine the effects. Finally, there may be the problem of order effects; that is, the ordering of the intervention or treatment is what accounts for the effect rather than the treatment alone.

Therefore, although these designs can be elegant and efficient for examining the effects of treatment, some constraints need to be considered when employing this design in language and literacy research. Being aware of the constraints, and organizing treatments and procedures accordingly, will enable investigators to use the design to their advantage, answering critical questions in educational research.

EXEMPLARS OF SINGLE-SUBJECT EXPERIMENTAL RESEARCH

I first became aware of this design through a study by Mudre and McCormick (1989) in *Reading Research Quarterly*. In this study, the authors used a multiple-baseline design to examine the effects of parent tutoring on children's comprehension skills. It was an elegant study and provided a clear rationale for why someone might choose to use the single-subject experimental design approach. First, although the children in the study were all underachievers, they exhibited very different reading difficulties. It would have been difficult to define them, given their age differences and reading difficulties, as a group. Second, the parents themselves had different skills; although they might be trained to use strategies to tutor their children, each would do this in a different way depending on their background characteristics and their child's needs. Third, it involved six parents and children. From a single-subject perspective, this would mean a potential of six replications; for a traditional study, it would be considered underpowered.

The authors chose the multiple-baseline approach because they wanted to examine how each strategy might influence readers' use of context, their self-corrections, and their literal comprehension skills. Following an extended baseline period, they began to introduce one tutoring strategy at a time and had parents' practice the strategy with the children. At each phase of the treatment, they could compare the strategy taught with the strategies not yet taught. In this way, they could determine whether the experimental variables were responsible for any of the changes seen. For example, during phase 1 of the intervention, parent cuing for self-correction was taught in a workshop, and all parent behaviors (self-correction cues, cues for context use, and praise) were measured for 5 days. A similar strategy was followed with the introduction to new strategies. Following the treatment period, they continued to follow the child's reading, looking first at whether the strategies taught were maintained and whether there might be transfer to a new reading task as a result.

They examined their data through graphic analyses, in combination with *t*-tests for correlated means. Specifically, they looked for indicators of low error rate in reading, use of context, and increases in self-corrections. They reported increases in the use of the desired strategies and continuous improvements for some children more than others.

What were benefits of using this design? The researchers were better able to determine which of the strategies was most effective; they could subsequently individualize instruction to meet the needs of the individual learners, and they could examine immediate effects through the graphing of data. It was ideal for a clinical setting. All of these factors are critically important when we work with children who have special strengths and needs.

On the basis of my readings of this article and others in special journals, I joined an informal group at the National Reading Conference, led by Sandy McCormick, to learn more about the methodology. Along with my graduate student, we thought that the single-subject design approach might be especially useful to examine parent–child interactions in the home setting. Specifically, our goal was to examine an intervention that might encourage teenage mothers to be more responsive to their child's interactions during literacy and play. Like Mudre and McCormick (1989), we were convinced that a study of individual subjects, given our work with individual differences among teen mothers, would better capture how they might respond to the intervention.

The first and most difficult step in our work (Neuman & Gallagher, 1994) was to operationalize our dependent variables. It made sense to break down our "interactional" goal into specific language interactions that could support children's receptive language. Three behaviors seemed to be critically related to children's language uses: mother's use of labeling (identifying objects); scaffolding (helping to refine the child's approximations to conventional uses); and contingent responsivity (responding to the child's queries with explanations and extensions). Piloting our work, we developed a set of definitions that could act as a codebook for parent–child interactions.

We designed the work as a multiple-baseline single-subject study, introducing each behavior one at a time while we continued to measure all three. First, we visited teen mothers in their homes, recording their language and interactions with their child. Following each visit, we coded and recorded each of the language activities and then plotted them on a graph for visual analysis. Once stability was reached, we introduced a literacy prop box in each home. Based on a theme of a post office, the prop box included a book and play objects related to theme. Every other week, we visited and emphasized one particular skill (e.g., labeling) and then in the subsequent week observed and coded mother–child interaction for that particular behavior as well as the others. Following the treatment, we then gave them a new set of materials and examined their behaviors, hoping that skills learned in one context would transfer to another. Finally, after 6 weeks, we once again observed to examine how these behaviors were maintained over time. Figure 17.5 gives an example from one of our mothers of how the data were graphed throughout the study.

What we found was that all six mother–child dyads clearly revealed changes in the frequency of cues from baseline to intervention. Although the changes differed in magnitude, the intervention produced distinct increases in mothers' uses of labeling, scaffolding, and contingent responsivity. Although scores declined with the transfer to new materials and maintenance, in almost all cases mothers continued to use these strategies to a greater extent than in baseline. Of the three interactional behaviors, cues for contingent responsivity seemed to remain more sustained throughout the study period, indicating mothers' increasing responsivity to their children's literacy initiatives.

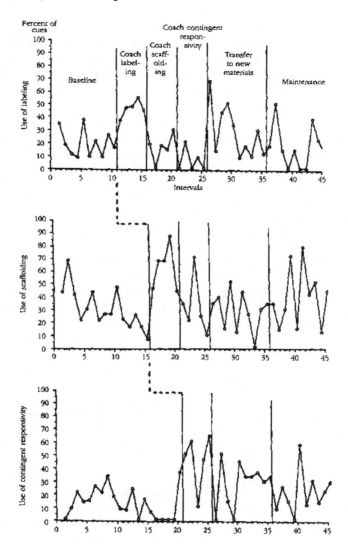

FIGURE 17.5. Example of a multiple-baseline design. From Neuman and Gallagher (1994). Copyright 1994 by the International Reading Association. Reprinted by permission.

We also examined the quality of parent–child interactions by transcribing the data. These data provided a good deal of information on the texture of the interactions that numbers or graphs could not adequately capture. Finally, we examined children's receptive language through the Peabody Picture Vocabulary Test and found dramatic and significant improvements as a result of the intervention (see Table 17.1).

Consequently, we believed that the multiple-baseline design was especially useful for examining our focus question: Does an intervention targeted to improving the quality of parent–child interaction work to enhance children's language development? It allowed us to argue that the intervention "caused" changes in children's language development. At the same time, it highlighted individual variation among our teen mothers. Traditionally, in many group designs, such variation is often not adequately recognized. It also provided a strong case for its effects, given that we had six overall replications.

Using the standards of quality described previously, both studies clearly exemplified these quality features. In both cases, in-depth descriptions of the participants were provided with highly detailed information on the criteria for their selection, their history, and the setting in which the experiment took place. For example, Mudre and McCormick based their work in the reading clinic at the university; Neuman and Gallagher worked in parents' homes.

Independent and dependent variables needed to be discrete, measurable, and clearly defined. In our case, identifying different types of language cues was complex, requiring us to carefully delineate and practice coding how these language cues might look across participants from different cultural perspectives. Since our work was conducted in the natural setting of the home, there was the potential for greater variation than for the cues used in the Mudre and McCormick study.

These studies also demonstrated the variance in baselines that is likely to occur in different studies. For example, Mudre and McCormick found stability rather quickly and, therefore, were able to move toward the manipulation of the independent variable, whereas our initial baselines indicated less stability, taking longer before we were able to establish a pattern of

TABLE 17.1. Pre- and Posttest Mean Percentile Scores, Standard Deviations, and Ranges on the Peabody Picture Vocabulary Test

Variable	N	M	SD	Range
Pretest	6	37.67	19.75	11–60
Posttest	6	74.17*	14.36	60–94

$*p < .01$.

response. Therefore, these studies clearly illustrate a central point about baselines: There is no set period of time for establishing baselines; different studies will need different time periods.

Both studies showed a fair amount of experimental control; however, in our study, clearly history might have been a factor in our results. For example, during the 3 months over the course of the study, some families experienced job losses, loss of shelter, and entanglements with law enforcement officials. We attempted to address these issues by carefully documenting these incidents in our participants' lives. Nevertheless, history was a threat to our internal validity.

Generalizability of data is always problematic in studies, regardless of methodology. However, for single-subject design, it has been particularly contentious given the limited sample size and the fact that participants in the research are seldom randomly selected. Extrapolation from the sample to a population constitutes the strongest argument for generalization (Palinscar & DeBruin-Parecki, 1995). The strength of the argument is, to a large extent, a function of the similarities between the participants in the research and those individuals to whom one wishes to generalize. In this case, Mudre and McCormick present an excellent example. Not only do they provide the standard demographic features of their sample, but they also report the sequence of steps they use in the selection process. Furthermore, in addition to the remediation children receive, they describe the nature and focus of all language and literacy instruction in which the children participated. By characterizing the emphases of instruction, the researchers allow the reader to consider how the intervention might be interacting with both the instructional histories and the instruction the children were receiving.

Finally, although both studies do not explicitly report their results in terms of social validity, their efforts to continue to systematically measure their dependent variables through maintenance and examine the transferability of behaviors beyond the interventions allowed for sound evidence for the benefits of the treatment on improving children's achievement.

CONCLUSION

In sum, single-subject design methods enable researchers to describe the variability predicted by current theory more precisely than is often possible with either group experiments or thick descriptions. This is important both to better inform practice and to help push our thinking and our theories about literacy development. We must also remember, however, that it is the question that drives the design parameters, not the methodology. Single-subject experimental research may be exquisitely tuned to answer some questions about literacy development and not to others. It may also work in combination with other methods, such as case studies and large-group experimental studies. Furthermore, it provides an efficient strategy for those interested in examining questions in clinical or classroom settings. At the same time, we must also remember that as our questions change, so does our understanding of the problems associated with using research methods for purposes other than those for which they have been traditionally employed.

Single-subject design provides an additional methodological tool to examine critical questions in literacy. In this respect, it provides new ways to inquire, expand theories, and stimulate further explorations in language and literacy development.

REFERENCES

Alberto, P., & Troutman, A. (2003). *Applied behavior analysis for teachers* (6th ed.). Upper Saddle River, NJ: Prentice Hall.

Axelrod, S. (1983). *Behavior modification for the classroom teacher.* New York: McGraw-Hill.

Cooper, J., Heron, T., & Heward, W. (2007). *Applied behavior analysis* (2nd ed.). Upper Saddle River, NJ: Prentice Hall.

Graves, M. F., Cooke, C. L., & LaBerge, M. J. (1983). Effects of previewing difficult short stories on low ability junior high school students' comprehension, recall, and attitudes. *Reading Research Quarterly, 18,* 262–276.

Horner, R., Carr, E., Halle, J., McGee, G., Odom, S., & Wolery, M. (2005). The use of single-subject research to identify evidence-based practice in special education. *Exceptional Children, 71,* 165–179.

Kazdin, A. (2010). *Single-case research designs: Methods for clinical and applied settings.* New York: Oxford University Press.

Kucera, J., & Axelrod, S. (1995). Multiple-baseline designs. In S. B. Neuman & S. McCormick (Eds.), *Single-subject experimental research applications for literacy* (pp. 47–63). Newark, DE: International Reading Association.

McCormick, S. (1990). A case for the use of single-subject methodology in reading research. *Journal of Reading Research, 13,* 69–81.

McCormick, S. (1995). What is single-subject experimental research. In S. B. Neuman & S. McCormick (Eds.), *Single-subject experimental research applications for literacy* (pp. 1–32). Newark, DE: International Reading Association.

Mudre, L. H., & McCormick, S. (1989). Effects of meaning-focused cues on underachieving readers' context use, self-corrections, and literal comprehension. *Reading Research Quarterly, 24,* 89–113.

Neuman, S. B. (1995). Alternating treatments designs. In S. B. Neuman & S. McCormick (Eds.), *Single-subject experimental research applications for literacy* (pp. 64–83). Newark, DE: International Reading Association.

Neuman, S. B., & Gallagher, P. (1994). Joining together in literacy learning: Teenage mothers and children. *Reading Research Quarterly, 29,* 382–401.

Neuman, S. B., & McCormick, S. (Eds.). (1995). *Single-subject experimental research: Applications for literacy.* Newark, DE: International Reading Association.

Ogle, D. (1986). KWL: A teaching model that develops active reading of expository text. *The Reading Teacher, 39,* 564–570.

Palinscar, A. M., & DeBruin-Parecki, A. (1995). Important issues related to single-subject experimental research. In S. B. Neuman & S. McCormick (Eds.), *Single-subject experimental research: Applications for literacy* (pp. 137–152). Newark, DE: International Reading Association.

CHAPTER 18

Survey Research

James F. Baumann
James J. Bason

What are elementary students' attitudes toward reading in school? What do middle school students choose to read in their free time outside school? How do high school teachers accommodate students who struggle to read and understand content textbooks? How do parents support at home the reading instruction their children receive at school? What content do university teacher educators cover in their elementary reading methods courses? What are the teaching experiences and knowledge base about reading of school district administrators? Answers to questions such as these can be addressed through survey research.

It is the purpose of this chapter to describe how surveys can be used by literacy researchers to address questions like the preceding about the characteristics of educational groups. We begin with a definition of survey research, followed by a brief history of literacy-related survey research. Next, we describe the types of surveys and address how survey researchers identify populations, draw samples, and make inferences from survey data. We then address the process in which researchers engage when implementing a survey inquiry, followed by a discussion of quality standards for survey research. We conclude by presenting two examples of survey research projects and a summary of the chapter.

WHAT IS SURVEY RESEARCH?

According to the American Statistical Association, the term *survey* "is used most often to describe a method of gathering information from a sample of individuals" (Scheuren, 2004, p. 9). *Survey research* involves a "study in which data are collected from part of a group, for the purpose of describing one or more characteristics of the whole group" (Jaeger, 1997, p. 450). These groups may be persons (e.g., seventh-grade teachers) or broader entities (e.g., a school district). A survey is different from a *census*, which attempts to gather information from an entire population.

Survey research requires systematic methods for collecting information (Groves et al., 2009) in order to generate quantitative descriptions (statistics) of a sample with the purpose of estimating aspects of the broader population (Fowler, 2009). Surveys are popular methods of collecting information from individuals and the preferred means to address a research question when it is most efficient to simply *ask* those who can inform the question. A survey typically involves the administration of a questionnaire or interview to a relevant group of individuals.

One way to describe surveys involves the degree of organization they entail. In this chapter, we focus on *structured surveys*, that is, research tools that have persons respond to a series of questions. These questions can be answered face to face or through written or electronic media. Structured surveys generate numerical data directly or data that can be categorized and tabulated such that the data can be explored quantitatively through descriptive or inferential statistics. In contrast, researchers can conduct *semistructured interviews* or *qualitative interviews*, in which the interviewer and interviewee engage in more of a conversation than a series of questions and answers. Structured and qualitative interviews address different research questions, and each has its place. Qualitative interviews generate very rich and in-depth data as opposed to structured interviews.

Groves and colleagues (2009) acknowledge that structured surveys are "rather blunt instruments for gathering information" but they argue that they also are very "powerful in producing statistical generalizations to large populations" (p. 406). We confine our discussion to structured interviews in this chapter and refer readers to other sources for information about semistructured or qualitative interviews (Gubrium & Holstein, 2002; Rubin & Rubin, 2005; Seidman, 1998).

Finally, it should be understood that surveys are not limited to humans. For example, a researcher might survey objects such as instructional materials or achievement records. Most educational survey research, however, involves questions about the attitudes, knowledge, experiences, and behaviors exhibited by *persons*: teachers, students, administrators, parents, policymakers, or others interested in education. Thus, we focus on survey research that has the potential to address research questions that describe human involvement in literacy education.

A BRIEF HISTORY OF SURVEY RESEARCH IN LITERACY

The beginnings of survey research can be traced to the late 19th century, with the modern era of sample surveys beginning in earnest in the early 20th century (Weisberg, Krosnick, & Bowen, 1996). The first survey research in literacy occurred in the early 1900s and was tied to what Venezky (1984) referred to as "school surveys," in which U.S. school districts evaluated their entire educational programs, including reading instruction. For example, Venezky described a survey in Cleveland as involving "analyses of the goals of reading instruction, the training of teachers, the methods and materials and time used, and the achievements of students in different components of reading" (p. 18).

Survey research in the social, behavioral, and educational sciences gained widespread acceptance in the 1950s, becoming one of the most popular and efficient methods of collecting information from individuals (Weisberg et al., 1996). In 1961 Austin, Bush, and Huebner described the Reading Survey as a "survey method for getting a complete perspective on the reading program" (p. 131), and several significant reading survey studies were conducted during this period. Austin and colleagues (1961) published *The Torch Lighters*, a mail survey of reading teacher education programs at 74 U.S. colleges and universities, which they replicated 13 years later (Morrison & Austin, 1977). In 2001, Hoffman and Roller reported a modified replication of *The Torch Lighters* with contemporary teacher educators.

As a follow-up to *The Torch Lighters*, Austin and Morrison asked in 1963 "What guidance do teachers receive *after* they complete their baccalaureate education?" (p. ix). They addressed this question in *The First R* (Austin & Morrison, 1963) by conducting a mail survey of administrators in 1,023 U.S. school districts about the content and conduct of reading instruction and by conducting follow-up on-site visits in 51 school districts. Barton and Wilder (1964) also reported an extensive study of reading that included face-to-face interviews with leading experts in reading education and mail surveys of university faculty, teachers and principals, and the general public. To provide a contemporary view of elementary reading instruction, Baumann, Hoffman, Duffy-Hester, and Ro (2000) conducted a modified replication of Austin and Morrison's *The First R*.

Survey research has flourished in the last dozen years. For example, researchers have conducted survey on topics as diverse as:

- Students' and teachers' reading habits, interests, attitudes, and motivations for reading (Gambrell & Hunter, 2000; Howard & Jin, 2004; Ivey & Broaddus, 2001; Kelley & Decker, 2009; Maynard,

MacKay, & Smyth, 2008; McKenna, Kear, & Ellsworth, 1995; Mellard, Patterson, & Prewett, 2007; Mokhtari, Reichard, & Gardner, 2009; Nathanson, Pruslow, & Levitt, 2008).

- Elementary teachers' literacy practices (Ford & Opitz, 2008; Fresch, 2003, 2007).
- Children's early literacy experiences (Al Otaiba, Lewis, Whalon, Dyrlund, & McKenzie, 2009; Hawken, Johnston, & McDonnell, 2005).
- Educators' views on assessments (Hoffman, Assaf, & Paris, 2001; Hoffman, Jenkins, & Dunlap, 2009).
- Teachers' concerns with vocabulary instruction (Berne & Blachowicz, 2008; Hedrick, Harmon, & Wood, 2008; Wood, Vintinner, Hill-Miller, Harmon, & Hedrick, 2009).
- Literacy educators' professional roles and development (Bean, Cassidy, Grumet, Shelton, & Wallis, 2002; Blamey, Meyer, & Walpole, 2008-2009; Commeyras & DeGroff, 1998; Hughes, Cash, Klingner, & Ahwee, 2001).
- Clinical programs (Cuevas, Schumm, Mits-Cash, & Pilonieta, 2006) and reading experts' opinions of trends in the field (Flippo, 1998).

Clearly, educators have used and continue to employ survey research methodology as a means to address a variety of questions about the nature of literacy programs and instruction.

TYPES OF SURVEYS

Surveys come in various forms and can be organized in different ways. The most common way to characterize surveys is by the method of data collection. Survey collection methods include face-to-face surveys, telephone surveys, mail surveys, technology-enhanced surveys, and mixed-mode surveys. The decision regarding which method to use is typically based on the nature and size of the population under study, the content of the information to be collected, the length of the survey, or the difficulty of the task respondents are asked to complete.

Face-to-Face Surveys

Face-to-face surveys, or structured personal interviews, are preferred by many survey researchers because they afford the most flexibility, allowing a researcher to control the dynamics of the interview process considerably. Although face-to-face surveys were once the most common type of survey method, today telephone, mail, and technology-based surveys are much more common because they can be conducted for a fraction of the cost (Brooker & Schaefer, 2006). However, several large national surveys still utilize face-to-face methods, among them the National Health Interview Survey (Centers for Disease Control and Preventions, n.d.) and the General Social Survey (National Opinion Research Center, n.d.).

Advantages of face-to-face surveys include the opportunity for the interviewer to ask for clarification, to ask follow-up or "branched" questions, and to observe and make note of surroundings. In addition, face-to-face surveys tend to produce high response rates. When depth of information and a flexible format are desired and feasible, a face-to-face survey may be the preferred method. When a researcher is interested in a rich, interactive description by a group of individuals on a specified topic, a focus group may be employed. Given the unique purposes and requirements of focus groups, however, we do not pursue them further in this chapter and refer interested readers to other sources (Greenbaum, 1998; Krueger & Casey, 2008; Stewart, Shamdasani, & Rook, 2006).

Telephone Surveys

When many interviews need to be conducted or the sample of prospective respondents is geographically dispersed, an alternative to face-to-face surveys is a *telephone survey*, which involves administering a questionnaire during a phone conversation. Telephone surveys retain some of the advantages of face-to-face surveys (e.g., the administrator can explain the purpose of a survey and ask follow-up or branched questions) while providing for a more economical way to gather information. In addition, a telephone survey researcher can inquire why an individual chooses to participate in a survey or not. Organizations such as the Harris Poll and the Gallup Poll conduct telephone interviews.

A common approach for identifying telephone numbers is to employ *random-digit dialing* (RDD), in which computers randomly generate telephone numbers such that every household in a given area (even those with unlisted numbers) has a known probability of being selected. This can result in highly accurate samples being drawn from specific populations.

The increasing proportion of persons who have replaced their landlines with cell phones (Blumberg & Luke, 2009), however, limits the ability of RDD procedures to produce a generalizable sample given that cell phone numbers are not routinely published. Cell phone–only households are disproportionately composed of single, young renters (Groves et al., 2009), so telephone samples can be skewed. Additionally, the use of caller ID technology, which can be used to screen calls, and a general increase in refusal rates among persons contacted for telephone surveys promote the likelihood of a *nonresponse bias* in telephone surveys, that is, the failure to adequately represent the views of those who choose not to participate (Groves, Dillman, Eltinge, & Little, 2002).

Major commercial survey companies have now developed sampling frames of cell phone–only households, and recent theoretical work (Lavrakas, 2007; Lepkowski et al., 2008) has indicated that conducting surveys with cell phone–household respondents is feasible, although cell phone interviews are more expensive than interviews conducted with landlines. One approach to correcting for bias among cell phone–only households is to include a subsample of cell phone–only respondents with a larger RDD survey (Link, Battaglia, Frankel, Osborn, & Mokdad, 2008). In spite of limitations of telephone surveys, it is generally agreed that they remain a viable and effective way to collect data from large samples of individuals.

Mail Surveys

An alternative to face-to-face and telephone surveys is a *mail survey*, which involves distributing a written questionnaire through the postal service. Advantages of mail surveys include relatively low cost, the ability to access a broad sample of potential respondents, and the possibility of obtaining a large number of responses. In addition, there is evidence that mail surveys tend to minimize *social desirability bias* (Tourangeau, Rips, & Rasinski, 2000)—that is, respondents answering in ways deemed to be socially acceptable or appropriate rather than reflecting their actual attitudes or behaviors—compared with other survey methods (Hochstim, 1967; Wiseman, 1972).

Mail surveys also have disadvantages. Although economical, they may not produce as a high a response rate as other types of surveys, one must rely on the respondent to interpret questions properly (i.e., no opportunity for clarification), a researcher has no control over the actual administration of the survey, and one cannot determine why persons in the sample chose to participate or not participate.

According to Scheuren (2004), "Mail surveys are a powerful, effective, and efficient alternative to their more expensive relatives—the telephone survey and the personal interview" (p. 51). Although mail surveys have limitations just like any type of survey, they have been and remain one of the most popular methods employed in literacy survey research (e.g., Austin & Morrison, 1961, 1963; Baumann, Hoffman, et al., 2000; Baumann, Ro, Duffy-Hester, & Hoffman, 2000; Commeyras & DeGroff, 1998; Hoffman et al., 2001; Hoffman & Roller, 2001; Hughes et al., 2001).

Technology-Enhanced Surveys

Technology provides survey researchers with a variety of data collection methods. Two we address here are Internet-based surveys and technology-enhanced telephone surveys. Internet surveys can be distinguished as either client-side surveys, which execute on a respondent's machine, or *server-side surveys*, which execute on a survey organization's Web server (Couper, 2008). Client-side surveys are typically called *e-mail surveys*, and they are not used today as widely as the more popular server-side surveys.

Web- and Internet-based surveys have the advantages of low cost and speed, but they are limited to special populations known to have high rates of Internet access. Thus, they may not represent broader populations. There currently is no known reliable means to access e-mail addresses, so it is difficult to obtain representative samples. These surveys are effective for known Internet users for whom e-mail addresses are readily accessible (e.g., literacy professors whose e-mail addresses are contained in university directories), but this requires the creation of specialized sample lists. With increasing Internet access in households and greater access to commercially available e-mail lists, however, it is likely that Web- and Internet-based survey use and credibility will increase in the future (Dillman, Smyth, & Christian, 2009).

Technology is also enhancing the application of more conventional survey procedures. *Computer-assisted telephone interviews* are becoming increasingly common, in which the interviewer reads questions from a computer screen and uses a keyboard to enter an interviewee's responses directly, enhancing the speed and reliability of telephone interview data. Similarly, one finds face-to-face surveys being administered by interviewees who use notebook computers to conduct *computer-assisted personal interviews* (Couper et al., 1998). Furthermore, to provide greater privacy to respondents in answering sensitive survey items and to assist respondents with poor reading skills, telephone audio-assisted and computer audio-assisted self-interviewing systems are increasingly common methods of data collection (Couper, 2008).

With the advent of computer programs that can recognize speech, telephone surveys can be administered through *interactive voice recognition*, in which a respondent calls a toll-free number and communicates directly by saying prescribed responses. Similarly, using *touch-tone data entry*, interviewees proceed through a prerecorded interview in which they are asked to enter responses through their telephone keypad. These approaches are most useful when factual information is required from the respondent or when respondent–interviewer interaction is not a necessary requirement for completing an interview (Couper et al., 1998).

Mixed-Mode Surveys

The *mode* of survey refers to the manner in which data are collected (Fowler, 2009). Traditionally, surveys involved a single mode, such as gathering data through a face-to-face survey, through the mail, or over the telephone. More recently, however, survey researchers have increasingly used more than one mode in a survey, or a *mixed-mode survey* (Dillman et al., 2009).

Researchers employ mixed-mode surveys for various reasons, such as to lower costs, to improve timeliness, to reduce coverage error, and to increase response rates (Dillman et al., 2009, Chap. 8). There are several different ways to mix modes. For example, one is to use a Web-based survey for an initial wave of data collection and then a telephone approach to reach nonrespondents to the Web-based method. Another way is to recruit participants using a telephone method and then employ a mail questionnaire to actually collect the data.

Although combining data collection approaches does generally increase response rates, there is a risk that respondents may answer survey items differently depending on the mode utilized (Fowler, 2009). In order to mitigate differential responses to mixed-mode surveys, Dillman (2000) suggests using *unimode construction* of survey items: "Unimode construction is writing and presenting of questions to respondents in such a way that assures receipt by respondents of a common mental stimulus, regardless of survey mode" (p. 232). For example, when conducting a telephone interview, interviewers typically do not read the "I don't know" option to respondents but only code it when it is offered. However, in self-administered modes, such as Web or mail, the "I don't know" option is listed so that respondents can choose it should it represent their knowledge or opinion on that item. Unimode construction seeks to prevent these types of differences from affecting survey response by ensuring that the questions in each mode are received in an identical way despite the mode being used.

TAILORED DESIGN

Most contemporary survey researchers employ some form of the *tailored design method*, which, according to Dillman and colleagues (2009), "involves using multiple motivational features in compatible and mutually supportive ways to encourage high quantity and quality of response to the surveyor's request" (p. 16). A goal of tailored design is to reduce survey errors in coverage, sampling, nonresponse, and measurement (Groves, 2004). A tailored design approach is based on a "social exchange perspective on human behavior . . . which suggests that respondent behavior is motivated by the return that behavior is expected to bring" (Dillman et al., 2009, p. 16). In other words, when a person trusts the group or individuals behind a survey and believes that the costs associated with responding (e.g., time) are outweighed by the potential benefits of the effort to respond, then there is a reasonable likelihood that the person will respond.

When employing a tailored-design method, most researchers use a mixed-mode survey. For example, consider a university researcher who is interested in surveying state language arts coordinators about their perceptions of a new federal elementary and secondary literacy initiative. A first step might be to use the Internet to search the department of education websites for all 50 states. This would elicit the names, e-mail addresses, and postal addresses of the language arts coordinators and language arts senior staff members.

Next, the researcher would send an official-looking e-mail (e.g., using a university logo and signature file) to all language arts coordinators and staff members identified. Within this e-mail, the researcher would explain the purpose of the national survey and indicate that each language arts staff member will receive shortly a survey in the mail. The mail survey—professionally looking and printed—would come with a cover letter written on the faculty member's university letterhead or that of the university's survey research center, if there is one. For surveys not returned within several weeks, the researcher would send a follow-up e-mail to nonrespondents, inviting them to complete the survey, which this time is attached to the e-mail. This tailored design method, which is intended to promote response rate and minimize survey error, can be used with surveys presented through other media or combinations of media, such as over the telephone or in face-to-face interviews.

POPULATIONS, SAMPLES, AND INFERENCES

When a researcher's question requires responses from a small number of persons, for example, learning about the content area reading practices of subject-matter teachers at a specific high school, then it makes sense to interview all individuals. This would involve a census of the entire *population*, or surveying all persons who fit a particular classification. A *population parameter* is a value that describes an entire population, for example, the *mean*, or average, number of years of teaching experience for the population of all full-time grade 10 English teachers in a specific public school district.

When the population under study is large, however, for instance, when Phi Delta Kappa annually polls Americans about their attitudes toward public schools (Bushaw & McNee, 2009), a census of the entire population is impractical, costly, or simply not possible. In this situation, other procedures are used to select a subset of the entire population. In fact, most surveys involve a subset of individuals from a population, or *sample*, and most survey researchers wish to gather data on a sample in order to generalize to a broader group, that is, to estimate a population parameter.

To be able to make generalizations from a sample to a population, a survey researcher must begin by specifying a *sampling frame*, which includes all the members of a given population. Frames, or populations, might be small or large. For example, large populations would include all full-time, public school kindergarten teachers in the United States or all school district superintendents in the 50 states. Examples of smaller populations would be all parents of K–5 students in a small, rural school district or all students who have completed an academic assistance course in reading within the past year at a small state university.

Once a sampling frame is specified, a researcher must determine how to select a *probability sample*, or a subset of the specified population to interview and from which one can make generalizations. Two common probability samples are a simple random sample and a stratified random sample. A *simple random sample* is one in which everyone in the sampling frame has an equal chance of being selected through some random process, such as computer random sampling. For example, randomly selecting 1,000 names from all full-time K–5 classroom teachers in the state of Georgia would be a simple random sample.

A *stratified random sample* involves selecting participants from certain subgroups, or *strata*, within a sample. For example, if there were smaller class sizes in the primary grades, there would be proportionally more teachers at those levels. In this situation, a researcher might identify each grade level as a stratum, or subgroup, and then randomly sample each grade level proportionate to its representation in the overall population. This would result in a sample that approximates the overall K–5 population better than a simple random sample.

When engaging in probability sampling research, any *sample statistic*, or value that describes the sample such as a sample mean, is not exact; there is some error associated with it. For instance, the average class size of a simple random sample of 1,000 full-time second-grade classroom teachers in Tennessee would be somewhat different from the actual population parameter should one be able to poll all teachers. If a researcher wishes to use sample statistics to estimate population parameters, the researcher needs to know and report the *sampling error*, or an estimate of the degree of error associated with a sample statistic. This estimate is commonly referred to as the margin of sampling error (American Association for Public Opinion Research, n.d.).

The *margin of sampling error* in a sample statistic is usually reported in plus or minus terms and at some degree of confidence. For example, Baumann, Hoffman, and colleagues (2000) reported that 1,207 responses to their teacher survey resulted in a 2.7% sampling error at the 95% confidence level. This means that any sample statistic they reported for the full sample of teachers would represent the "true" population parameter 95% of the time within ± 2.7% of the reported score.

The margin of sampling error is directly related to sample size. The larger the sample, the smaller the margin of error, the more the sample statistic approximates the population parameter, and the more confidence a consumer can have in the precision of survey results. For example, a simple random sample of 100 would result in a margin of error of approximately 10%, a sample of 500 about 4.5%, and a sample of 1,000 about 3% (Scheuren, 2004, p. 65). A larger sample size is always preferable, but from a cost and efficiency perspective, there often comes a point at which collecting additional cases is not worth the per-case cost. Once sample sizes reach about 1,000, the reduction in sampling error becomes smaller as more and more cases are added, which is why one often finds sample sizes of about 1,000 for public opinion polls.

One final point: The margin of sampling error as we have discussed it refers only to the sampling error. There are other possible errors in survey research, however. These *nonsampling errors* include poorly worded or confusing questions, nonresponse bias, and social desirability bias, to mention a few. Such nonsampling errors cannot be estimated mathematically, so a survey research consumer should be aware of these other sources of error (Fowler, 2009) and read an article critically in order to determine the degree to which the researcher has attempted to control for, or at least acknowledge, these additional sources of error.

SURVEY RESEARCH DESIGN PROCESS

Engaging in any scientific inquiry involves a careful, methodical process. Although there is no uniform, agreed-on number of steps in planning and conducting a survey research project, we present a six-step process that captures the essence of recommendations offered by other survey research methodologists (e.g., Jaeger, 1997).

1. *Formulate a research question.* If one accepts the notion that quality research begins not with methods but a carefully framed question (Shulman, 1997), then it follows that the selection of survey research as a method must depend on the formulation of a core research question that is amenable to being answered through a survey. Questions such as those we used to open this chapter are of the type that would be appropriate for a survey study. Theory should be used to guide the development of the research question, and a thorough literature review of past and current research should be conducted to craft specific research questions.

2. *Devise a measurement strategy.* In this step, a researcher must determine the type of survey and specific items that will best measure the features of the underlying psychological, behavioral, social, or educational topic or issue under consideration, or what is commonly referred to as *construct validity*. Special care also should be taken to ensure that measurement error is minimized. Although it is impossible to eliminate all measurement error, several sources of error can be reduced, including sampling, nonresponse, interviewer, and respondent error. Sampling error is probably the easiest source of error to control. If probability sampling procedures are used, the range of potential error is known by way of the sampling margin of error. Nonresponse error is more difficult to control. The lower the response rate in a survey, the greater the likelihood that nonresponders may be systematically different from responders. A researcher needs to

obtain additional information about nonrespondents in order to determine whether responders and nonresponders would have differed in the way they answered survey items. Interviewer error occurs when interviewers fail to follow standardized procedures, for example, not reading survey questions exactly as written. Training survey interviewers thoroughly minimizes interviewer errors. Finally, respondent errors occur when survey items are unclear; when respondents engage in *satisficing,* or selecting an answer considered to be reasonable to the researcher (see Krosnick, 1999); or when respondents provide answers to survey questions even when they may not actually have an opinion on the topic (Converse, 1964). A researcher has responsibility for constructing clearly worded items and for being aware of, minimizing, or at least acknowledging respondent error.

3. *Determine the sampling frame and data collection method.* The next step is to select the appropriate sampling frame, which will be determined, in large part, by the nature of the research question. If one wishes to seek information from teachers, for example, a researcher must determine which teachers to sample: their position, the grade levels they teach, their subject specialization, the type of schools in which they work (e.g., public vs. private), and the like. A researcher can make generalizations only from the limits of the sampling frame, so identifying the appropriate group to survey is essential. Once the relevant population has been specified, the researcher must determine which method will be used to collect survey data—that is, face-to-face, telephone, mail, technology-enhanced, or mixed-mode survey. Again, the research question, as well as pragmatics such as research budget and the availability of sampling sources (e.g., professional organization lists, U.S. Department of Education's Common Core of Data, marketing research lists), will generally guide a researcher in selecting the most suitable survey type.

4. *Establish sampling methodology and sample size.* The next step in the design process is to determine the method for sampling. If one is surveying a small population, it may be feasible to try to secure responses from all individuals in the population, that is, to conduct a census. If one is sampling a large population, which is typical in survey research, one must determine whether the sample will be a selective or a probability sample. If it is a *selective sample* (e.g., parents who are members of a local parent–teacher organization), one cannot make generalizations to a broader population of parents. There may be times when a selective sample is appropriate or when it is the only feasible option, but then a researcher must recognize that generalizing to a larger group is not possible. When using a *probability* (i.e., random) *sample*, which is the typical standard in survey research, the researcher should make a decision about sample size with the understanding of what the margin of error will be. When economically and pragmatically feasible, a sample should be sufficiently large in order to keep the margin of error reasonably low, so that statements about how a sample

may represent the population under study can be made within appropriate confidence limits. When smaller random sample sizes must be selected, a researcher must understand the limits this imposes on generalization and acknowledge those in the research report.

5. *Collect and analyze data.* Data collection should be systematic, thorough, and consistent with the accepted procedures for the type of survey employed (Groves et al., 2009, Chap. 5). For example, if a mail survey is used, the researcher should follow a series of phases in distributing, tracking, and monitoring the surveys to promote an acceptable response rate and minimize nonresponse bias (Dillman et al., 2009, Chap. 7). Likewise, data analysis procedures should be thoughtful, consistent with the research questions, and systematic. One must establish a data management and analyses plan prior to data collection, ideally when a study is conceived, so that analyses adequately test research questions. In some cases, simple descriptive statistics such as cross-tabulations will be sufficient and appropriate to answer research questions. In other cases, particularly when a probability sample is obtained, inferential statistics may be appropriate in order to make generalizations from the data. Procedures such as factor or path analyses are sometimes used in analyzing survey data. When inferential statistics are employed, attention should be paid in advance to sample size to ensure that adequate statistical power will be present for the analysis method to be used (Kraemer & Thiemann, 1987). In short, careful planning at the beginning of the survey process will ensure that analysis requirements are met satisfactorily.

6. *Report findings.* Survey researchers ought to have an intended audience in mind as a study is conceived and planned, and this same audience should be considered and addressed as a report is written. The information contained in the following section on quality standards for survey research and in Table 18.1 can also guide a survey researcher in preparing a research report. Although the form, style, voice, and level of detail may vary depending on one's audience and intended publication outlet (e.g., a research journal vs. a more applied serial), basic standards for reporting an inquiry should be followed. The sixth edition of the *Publication Manual of the American Psychological Association* (American Psychological Association, 2010) is a commonly used standard for writing for publication. Strunk and White's (2000) classic "little book," *The Elements of Style*, is always a useful tool for a writer who wishes to be concise and precise.

QUALITY STANDARDS FOR SURVEY RESEARCH

Consumers of survey research should be able to examine key components of a data collection effort to ensure that quality standards have been used, and it is the responsibility of survey researchers to ensure that they provide essential information to allow consumers to effectively evaluate a given survey effort. As a general rule, the methods and procedures reported in a survey should allow for replication of the study by other researchers. To accomplish this, the population under study should be clearly defined and the methods and procedures used to conduct the study stated explicitly. This includes how the sample was drawn, the exact questions used in the survey (the survey is often reproduced in an appendix to a report), the number of cases collected during the study, response rate information, the sampling margin of error, and data analysis procedures. Useful information about evaluating response rates, cooperation rates, and refusal rates for a study can be found through the American Association of Public Opinion Research (*www.aapor.org*) and the Council of American Survey Research Organizations (*www.casro.org*). Both of these professional associations provide valuable information on best practices for survey research (e.g., see *www.aapor.org/Best_Practices/1480.htm*), formulas to calculate response and refusal rates, and other helpful information to evaluate survey research quality.

As a further aide to evaluate survey research, we reproduce Jaeger's (1997) survey evaluation checklist in Table 18.1. Although Jaeger prepared this as a means to help research consumers evaluate published studies, it is also useful to survey researchers as they conceive of and implement their own studies.

EXAMPLARS OF LITERACY SURVEY RESEARCH

To illustrate the survey-research process in literacy, we have selected two example studies: Baumann, Hoffman, and colleagues' (2000) national survey of elementary reading instructional practices and Mesmer's (2006) national survey of primary teachers' uses of and beliefs about beginning reading materials. Table 18.2 contains a condensed version of Jaeger's (1997) survey evaluation criteria and presents a summary of how each literacy survey study compares with these standards.

A Survey of Elementary Reading Instruction Practices

Baumann, Hoffman, and colleagues (2000) conducted a modified replication of Austin and Morrison's 1963 *First R* study of U.S. public school elementary reading instruction. Noting that debate over the quality and status of elementary reading instruction preoccupied literacy professionals, policymakers, and the general populace in the late 1990s—just as it had in the early 1960s (Morrison, 1963)—the authors argued that a contemporary, empirical benchmark was needed to address the research question, "What is the nature of elementary reading instruction practices today?" (Baumann, Hoffman, et al., 2000, p. 342). Following a search for and

TABLE 18.1. A Short Checklist for Survey Evaluation

1. Does the report contain a list of specific research questions or issues the survey is intended to address?
2. Do the research questions posed by the investigators appropriately and adequately address the topic of the survey; e.g., in a survey on poverty in the United States, does the research include an examination of poverty as a function of race, level of education, and geographic location?
3. Are the research questions posed by the investigators well organized and well structured?
4. Does the report identify the target population to which generalization was desired?
5. Does the report describe available sampling frames?
6. Does the report indicate a close match between the target population and the operational population?
7. Does the report describe the sampling procedures used? Were probability sampling procedures used?
8. Are nonresponse rates reported for the entire survey and for individual questions?
9. Were nonresponse rates low enough to avoid substantial bias errors?
10. Are any analyses of potential sampling bias reported?
11. Are sample sizes sufficient to avoid substantial random errors? Are standard errors of estimate reported?
12. Is the primary mode of data collection (i.e., mailed questionnaires, telephone interviews, face-to-face interviews) consistent with the objectives, complexity, and operational population of the survey?
13. Are survey instruments provided in the report?
14. Are instructions for completing the survey clear and unambiguous?
15. Are questions on instruments clear and unambiguous?
16. Do questions on instruments encourage respondents' honesty in admitting lack of knowledge or uncertainty?
17. Are questions on instruments free from obvious bias, slanting, or "loading"?
18. Was the survey consistent with ethical research practice; e.g., was the anonymity and/or confidentiality of respondents protected?
19. Does the report contain a description of field procedures?
20. Are field procedures adequate and appropriate? Is it likely that major sources of bias error have been avoided?
21. Are data analyses clearly described?
22. Are data analyses appropriate to the purposes of the survey?
23. Did the survey provide answers to the research questions posed by the investigators?
24. Are the researchers' conclusions sound, or are alternative interpretations of findings equally plausible?
25. Does the survey report contain descriptions of deviations from plans for survey implementation and the likely consequences of such deviations?
26. Does the survey report contain an analysis of the quality of the survey?

Note. From Jaeger (1997, pp. 475–476). Copyright 1997 by the American Educational Research Association. Reproduced by permission.

TABLE 18.2. Evaluation Summary for the Survey Research Examples

Jaeger's (1997) criteria[a]	Studies critiqued	
	Baumann, Hoffman, et al. (2000)	Mesmer (2006)
Research questions (items 1–3)	• Theoretically and empirically based research question.	• Theoretically and empirically based research question.
Sampling and response rates (items 4–11)	• Probability sample of U.S. elementary teachers, with linked samples for administrators. • Overall survey response rates provided but not item-by-item rates. • Sample margin of error reasonable for primary survey but high for linked surveys.	• Probability sample for members of a professional organization of reading educators, so generalizations limited to this group. • Overall survey response rate provided but not item-by-item rates. • Reasonable sample margin of error reported.
Instrumentation (items 12–18)	• Teacher survey appended to article; administrator surveys available from authors. • Clear instructions for completing survey. • Detailed explanation of survey construction. • Clearly worded questions with no obvious bias in them. • No reliability or validity data provided.	• Survey appended to article. • Clear instructions for completing survey. • Survey construction described. • Clearly worded questions with no obvious bias in them. • No reliability or validity data provided.
Data-gathering procedures (items 19–20)	• Field and data-gathering procedures described in detail.	• Field and data-gathering procedures summarized.
Analyses and conclusions of report (items 21–26)	• Data analyses clearly described and appropriate for purpose of survey. • Descriptive statistics provided in detail and integrated into article narrative. • Thorough discussion of findings. • Limitations acknowledged. • Findings interpreted in relation to both relevant historic and contemporary work.	• Data analyses clearly described and appropriate for purpose of survey. • Descriptive and inferential statistics integrated into article narrative. • Detailed discussion of findings. • Limitations acknowledged. • Plausible interpretations of findings that are connected back to theoretical and research literature.

[a]Adapted from Jaeger's (1997) full survey evaluation checklist presented in Table 18.1.

reconstruction of original survey instruments, the researchers constructed three forms of a mail survey (classroom teacher, building administrator, and district administrator forms) that included multiple-choice, Likert, and open-ended response items that allowed for querying educators about contemporary issues and permitted cross-decade comparisons.

A probability sample of 3,199 elementary teachers was drawn from a national listing of more than 900,000 teachers. Modeling *First R* procedures, the building and district administrator samples were linked to the teacher sample, with teacher respondents identifying 623 building administrators, who, in turn, identified 91 district administrators for sampling. Mail surveys were distributed, collected, and analyzed by a university survey research facility. Response rates and sampling errors (at the 95% confidence level) were reported for the teacher (37.7% and 2.7%, respectively), building administrator (25.8% and 7.6%), and district administrator (52.7% and 14.1%) surveys.

Quantitative analyses involved the examination of descriptive statistics and selected cross-tabulations. A random subset of teacher open-ended response items and all administrator open-ended response items were analyzed qualitatively for themes and trends. Results, reported as percentages of respondents, were juxtaposed to *First R* data by categories, permitting a historic and contemporary look at elementary reading education practices.

Results revealed similarities between teachers of the 1960s and 1990s in that both tended to teach self-contained, heterogeneous classes of students; provided significant time for reading instruction; taught phonics explicitly; were generally not satisfied with their university training in reading instruction; administered required standardized tests; and were challenged by teaching underachieving readers. Differences were noted in the areas of instructional philosophy (a balanced, eclectic view in the 1990s vs. a skill orientation in the 1960s), instructional organization (more whole-class instruction in the 1990s vs. ability grouping in the 1960s), instructional materials (more use of trade books in the 1990s vs. primarily basal readers in the 1960s), early literacy instruction (the reading readiness perspective of the 1960s was supplanted by an emergent literacy orientation), and assessment (use of more nonstandardized, alternate assessments in the 1990s).

The authors noted that there were several parallel concerns expressed by teachers of the 1960s and 1990s—most significantly, an urgency to accommodate struggling readers—but they also commented that contemporary teachers and administrators were more likely to modify programs and explore alternate philosophical orientations than teachers and administrators of the past. They noted that reading instruction of the 1990s was "not some gussied-up version of the good old days," but instead they found "great energy," "a commitment to children, teaching, and learning," and "a sense of motivated urgency to adopt instructional principles, practices, and philosophies that will accommodate learners of today" (Baumann, Hoffman, et al., 2000, p. 361).

A Survey of Teachers' Opinions of Beginning Reading Materials

Mesmer (2006) also explored elementary reading instruction by investigating kindergarten through third-grade teachers' uses of and beliefs about beginning reading materials. She sought to answer three questions: (1) How do teachers select and use instructional materials? (2) What factors affect teachers' use of materials? (3) What are teachers' perceptions of newer basal reading materials that emphasize decodable texts (instructional selections that contain high proportions of words that can be pronounced through phonics skills that had been previously taught to children)?

Mesmer (2006) addressed these questions by conducting a mail survey that included 36 multiple-choice and Likert items and one open-ended response item. The sample consisted of 1,000 teachers randomly selected from a list of 5,000 members of the International Reading Association who identified themselves as K–3 teachers. Mesmer reported a 38% response rate, with a sampling error of 5.1% at the 95% confidence level. Quantitative analyses involved calculating descriptive statistics and conducting chi-square analyses to explore relationships between items. Constant comparative coding was conducted for responses to the open-ended response item.

Results revealed that teachers reported using children's literature and leveled texts almost daily; predictable, decodable, and vocabulary-controlled texts were used once or twice a week; and basals and workbooks were used infrequently. Contrary to the assertion that teachers were allowing decodable texts to supplant literature in beginning reading materials, Mesmer found that teachers used both types of materials as instructional needs dictated. For example, teachers reported using decodable texts most often when teaching phonics, literature when teaching comprehension, and leveled texts when teaching reading fluency.

Findings related to teachers' use of materials demonstrated that their grade-level assignment (K–3), teaching role (e.g., classroom teacher, reading teacher), and instructional approach (e.g., guided reading, 4/6 blocks, direct instruction) did not relate to their selection of instructional texts. Most teachers reported having complete or moderate choice in selecting materials, and they expressed having a balanced and eclectic perspective on reading instruction. Teachers sampled from Texas and California—states that required basal publishers to include decodable text in reading materials—reported using decodable texts more than teachers in other states. These same teachers, however, also reported using literature and leveled texts as frequently as teachers in other states, suggesting that state policies were not limiting them from using other instructional materials.

Mesmer (2006) stated that K–3 teachers were "doggedly pragmatic," discriminating consumers who selected and used a variety of materials on the basis of their instructional goals and that "educators need not worry about literature being pushed out of the curriculum" (p. 413). Consistent with findings from prior survey research (Baumann, Hoffman, Moon, & Duffy-Hester, 1998; Baumann, Hoffman, et al., 2000), Mesmer concluded that "teachers appeared to care most about resisting inappropriate uses of materials rather than resisting politically charged mandates, despite the debates in research circles" (p. 413).

SUMMARY

The purpose of this chapter was to provide an overview of survey research methods employed in literacy research. Survey research is a method for gathering information from a sample of individuals in order to describe characteristics of a larger group. Survey research has been employed in education and social sciences for the past 100 years, with increasing activity in the past decade. Commonly used methods involve collecting data through face-to-face, telephone, mail, technology-enhanced, and mixed-mode surveys. Most surveys involve probability samples from a specified population in order to make generalizations about the broader population. There is a generally accepted and implemented survey research design process that leads researchers from question-and-hypothesis formulation through sample description and data collection to data analyses and survey reporting. Quality standards can be applied to evaluate published surveys and to guide researchers in designing survey studies. The Baumann, Hoffman, and colleagues (2000) survey of elementary reading instruction practices and the Mesmer (2006) survey of primary teachers' use of beginning reading materials were presented as examples of literacy education survey research.

REFERENCES

Al Otaiba, S., Lewis, S., Whalon, K., Dyrlund, A., & McKenzie, A. R. (2009). Home literacy environments of young children with Down syndrome: Findings from a Web-based survey. *Remedial and Special Education, 31*(2), 96–107.

American Association for Public Opinion Research. (n.d.). Margin of sampling error. Deerfield, IL: Author. Retrieved from *www.aapor.org/Margin_of_Sampling_Error.htm.*

American Psychological Association. (2010). *Publication manual of the American Psychological Association* (6th ed.). Washington, DC: Author.

Austin, M. C., Bush, C. L., & Huebner, M. H. (1961). *Reading evaluation: Appraisal techniques for school and classroom.* New York: Ronald Press.

Austin, M. C., Morrison, C., Kenney, H. J., Morrison, M. B., Gutmann, A. R., & Nystrom, J. W. (1961). *The torch lighters: Tomorrow's teachers of reading.* Cambridge, MA: Harvard Graduate School of Education/Harvard University Press.

Austin, M. C., Morrison, C., Morrison, M. B., Sipay, E. R., Gutmann, A. R., Torrant, K. E., et al. (1963). *The first R: The Harvard report on reading in elementary schools.* New York: Macmillan.

Barton, A. H., & Wilder, D. E. (1964). Research and practice in the teaching of reading: A progress report. In M. B. Miles (Ed.), *Innovation in education* (pp. 361–398). New York: Teachers College, Columbia University.

Baumann, J. F., Hoffman, J. V., Duffy-Hester, A. M., & Ro, J. M. (2000). *The first R* yesterday and today: U.S. elementary reading instruction practices reported by teachers and administrators. *Reading Research Quarterly, 35,* 338–377.

Baumann, J. F., Hoffman, J. V., Moon, J., & Duffy-Hester, A. M. (1998). Where are teachers' voices in the phonics/whole language debate?: Results from a survey of U.S. elementary classroom teachers. *The Reading Teacher, 51,* 636–650.

Baumann, J. F., Ro, J. M., Duffy-Hester, A. M., & Hoffman, J. V. (2000). Then and now: Perspectives on the status of elementary reading instruction by prominent reading educators. *Reading Research and Instruction, 39,* 236–264.

Bean, R., Cassidy, J., Grumet, J. E., Shelton, D. S., & Wallis, S. R. (2002). What do reading specialists do?: Results from a national survey. *The Reading Teacher, 55,* 736–744.

Berne, J. I., & Blachowicz, C. L. Z. (2008). What reading teachers say about vocabulary instruction: Voices from the classroom. *The Reading Teacher, 62,* 314–323.

Blamey, K. L., Meyer, C. K., & Walpole, S. (2008–2009). Middle and high school literacy coaches: A national survey. *Journal of Adolescent and Adult Literacy, 52,* 310–323.

Blumberg, S. J., & Luke, J. V. (2009). Wireless substitution: Early release of estimates from the National Health Interview Survey, January–June 2008. Retrieved from National Center for Health Statistics website: *www.cdc.gov/nchs/data/nhis/earlyrelease/wireless200812.htm.*

Brooker, R., & Schaefer, T. (2006). *Public opinion in the 21st century: Let the people speak?* Boston: Houghton Mifflin.

Bushaw, B. J., & McNee, J. A. (2009). Americans speak out: Are educators and policy makers listening?: The 41st annual Phi Delta Kappa/Gallup Poll of the publics' attitudes toward the public schools. *Kappan, 91*(1), 9–23.

Centers for Disease Control and Prevention. (n.d.). About the National Health Interview Survey. Atlanta, GA: Author. Retrieved from *www.cdc.gov/nchs/nhis/about_nhis.htm#sample_design.*

Commeyras, M., & DeGroff, L. (1998). Literacy professionals' perspectives on professional development and pedagogy: A United States survey. *Reading Research Quarterly, 33,* 434–472.

Converse, P. E. (1964). The nature of belief systems in mass publics. In D. E. Apter (Ed.), *Ideology and discontent* (pp. 207–261). New York: Free Press.

Couper, M. P. (2008). *Designing effective Web surveys.* Cambridge, MA: Cambridge University Press.

Couper, M. P., Baker, R. P., Bethlehem, J., Clark, C. Z. F., Martin, J., Nicholls, W. L., et al. (1998). *Computer assisted survey information collection.* New York: Wiley.

Cuevas, P., Schumm, J. S., Mits-Cash, M., & Pilonieta, P. (2006). Reading clinics in the U.S.: A national survey of present practice. *Journal of Reading Education, 31*(2), 5–12.

Dillman, D. A. (2000). *Mail and Internet surveys: The tailored design method* (2nd ed.). New York: Wiley.

Dillman, D. A., Smyth, J. D., & Christian, L. M. (2009). *Internet, mail, and mixed-mode surveys: The tailored design method* (3rd ed.). Hoboken, NJ: Wiley.

Flippo, R. F. (1998). Points of agreement: A display of professional unity in our field. *The Reading Teacher, 52*, 30–40.

Ford, M. P., & Opitz, M. F. (2008). A national survey of guided reading practices: What we can learn from primary teachers. *Literacy Research and Instruction, 47*, 309–311.

Fowler, F. J. (2009). *Survey research methods* (4th ed.). Thousand Oaks, CA: Sage.

Fresch, M. J. (2003). A national survey of spelling instruction: Investigating teachers' beliefs and practice. *Journal of Literacy Research, 35*, 819–848.

Fresch, M. J. (2007). Teachers' concerns about spelling instruction: A national survey. *Reading Psychology, 28*, 301–330.

Gambrell, T., & Hunter, D. (2000). Surveying gender differences in Canadian school literacy. *Journal of Curriculum Studies, 32*(5), 689–719.

Greenbaum, T. L. (1998). *The handbook of focus group research.* Thousand Oaks, CA: Sage.

Groves, R. M. (2004). *Survey errors and survey costs.* New York: Wiley.

Groves, R. M., Dillman, D. A., Eltinge, J. L., & Little, R. J. A. (Eds.). (2002). *Survey nonresponse.* New York: Wiley.

Groves, R. M., Floyd, J. F., Couper, M. P., Lepkowski, J. M., Singer, E., & Tourangeau, R. (2009). *Survey methodology* (2nd ed.). Hoboken, NJ: Wiley.

Gubrium, J. F., & Holstein, J. A. (Eds.). (2002). *Handbook of interview research: Context and method.* Thousand Oaks, CA: Sage.

Hawken, L. S., Johnston, S. S., & McDonnell, A. P. (2005). Emerging literacy views and practices: Results from a national survey of Head Start preschool teachers. *Topics in Early Childhood Education, 25*, 232–242.

Hedrick, W. B., Harmon, J. M., & Wood, K. (2008). Prominent content vocabulary strategies and what secondary preservice teachers think about them. *Reading Psychology, 29*(5), 443–470.

Hochstim, J. R. (1967). A critical comparison of three strategies of collecting data from households. *Journal of the American Statistical Association, 62*, 976–989.

Hoffman, A. R., Jenkins, J. E., & Dunlap, S. K. (2009). Using DIBELS: A survey of purposes and practices. *Reading Psychology, 30*, 1–6.

Hoffman, J. V., Assaf, L. C., & Paris, S. G. (2001). High-stakes testing in reading: Today in Texas, tomorrow? *The Reading Teacher, 54*, 482–492.

Hoffman, J. V., & Roller, C. M. (2001). The IRA Excellence in Reading Teacher Preparation Commission's report: Current practices in reading teacher education at the undergraduate level in the United States. In C. M. Roller (Ed.), *Learning to teach reading: Setting the research agenda* (pp. 32–79). Newark, DE: International Reading Association.

Howard, V., & Jin, S. (2004). What are they reading?: A survey of the reading habits and library usage patterns of teens in Nova Scotia. *Canadian Journal of Information and Library Science, 28*(4), 25–44.

Hughes, M. T., Cash, M. M., Klingner, J., & Ahwee, S. (2001). Professional development programs in reading: A national survey of district directors. In J. V. Hoffman, D. L. Schallert, C. M. Fairbanks, J. Worthy, & B. Maloch (Eds.), *50th Yearbook of the National Reading Conference* (pp. 275–286). Chicago: National Reading Conference.

Ivey, G., & Broaddus, K. (2001). "Just plain reading": A survey of what makes students want to read in middle school classrooms. *Reading Research Quarterly, 36*, 350–377.

Jaeger, R. M. (1997). Survey research methods in education. In R. M. Jaeger (Ed.), *Complementary methods for research in education* (2nd ed., pp. 449–476). Washington, DC: American Educational Research Association.

Kelley, M. J., & Decker, E. O. (2009). The current state of motivation to read among middle school students. *Reading Psychology, 30*, 466–485.

Kraemer, H. C., & Thiemann, S. (1987). *How many subjects?: Statistical power analysis in research*. Thousand Oaks, CA: Sage.

Krosnick, J. A. (1999). Survey research. *Annual Review of Psychology, 50*, 537–567.

Krueger, R. A., & Casey, M. A. (2008). *Focus groups: A practical guide for applied research* (4th ed.). Thousand Oaks, CA: Sage.

Lavrakas, P. J. (Ed.). (2007). Cell phone numbers and telephone surveying in the U.S. [Special issue]. *Public Opinion Quarterly, 71*(5).

Lepkowski, J. M., Tucker, C., Brick, J. M., de Leeuw, E., Japec, L., Lavrakas, P. J., et al. (2008). *Advances in telephone survey methodology*. Hoboken, NJ: Wiley.

Link, M. W., Battaglia, M. P., Frankel, M. R., Osborn, L., & Mokdad, A. H. (2008). Comparison of address-based sampling (ABS) versus random-digit dialing (RDD) for general population surveys. *Public Opinion Quarterly, 72*(1), 6–27.

Maynard, S., MacKay, S., & Smyth, F. (2008). A survey of young people's reading in England: Borrowing and choosing books. *Journal of Librarianship and Information Science, 40*, 239–253.

McKenna, M. C., Kear, D. J., & Ellsworth, R. A. (1995). Children's attitudes toward reading: A national survey. *Reading Research Quarterly, 30*, 934–956.

Mellard, D., Patterson, M. B., & Prewett, S. (2007). Reading practices among adult education participants. *Reading Research Quarterly, 42*, 188–213.

Mesmer, H. A. E. (2006). Beginning reading materials: A national survey of primary teachers' reported uses and beliefs. *Journal of Literacy Research, 38*, 389–425.

Mokhtari, K., Reichard, C. A., & Gardner, A. (2009). The impact of Internet and television use on the reading habits and practices of college students. *Journal of Adolescent and Adult Literacy, 52*, 609–619.

Morrison, C. (1963). *A critical analysis of reported and recommended reading practices in the elementary schools*. Unpublished doctoral dissertation, Harvard Graduate School of Education, Cambridge, MA.

Morrison, C., & Austin, M. C. (1977). *The torch lighters revisited*. Newark, DE: International Reading Association.

Nathanson, S., Pruslow, J., & Levitt, R. (2008). The reading habits and literacy attitudes of inservice and prospective teachers: Results of a questionnaire study. *Journal of Teacher Education, 59*, 313–321.

National Opinion Research Center. (n.d.). General Social Survey. Chicago: Author. Retrieved from *www.norc.org/projects/general+social+survey.htm?wbcmod e=presentationunpublished.*

Rubin, H. J., & Rubin, I. S. (2005). *Qualitative interviewing: The art of hearing data* (2nd ed.). Thousand Oaks, CA: Sage.

Scheuren, F. (2004). What is a survey? Retrieved from *www.whatisasurvey.info.*

Seidman, I. (1998). *Interviewing as qualitative research: A guide for researchers in education and the social sciences* (2nd ed.). New York: Teachers College Press.

Shulman, L. S. (1997). Disciplines of inquiry in education: A new overview. In R. M. Jaeger (Ed.), *Complementary methods for research in education* (2nd ed., pp. 3–29). Washington, DC: American Educational Research Association.

Stewart, D. W., Shamdasani, P. M., & Rook, D. W. (2006). *Focus groups: Theory and practice* (2nd ed.). Thousand Oaks, CA: Sage

Strunk, W., & White, E. B. (2000). *The elements of style* (4th ed.). Boston: Allyn & Bacon.

Tourangeau, R., Rips, L. J., & Rasinski, K. (2000). *The psychology of survey response.* Cambridge, UK: Cambridge University Press.

Venezky, R. L. (1984). The history of reading research. In P. D. Pearson, R. Barr, M. L. Kamil, & P. Mosenthal (Eds.), *Handbook of reading research: Volume I* (pp. 3–38). New York: Longman.

Weisberg, H. F., Krosnick, J. A., & Bowen, B. D. (1996). *An introduction to survey research, polling, and data analysis.* Thousand Oaks, CA: Sage.

Wiseman, F. (1972). Methodological bias in public opinion surveys. *Public Opinion Quarterly, 36,* 105–108.

Wood, K., Vintinner, J., Hill-Miller, P., Harmon, J. M., & Hedrick, W. (2009). An investigation of teachers' concerns about vocabulary and the representation of these concerns in content literacy methodology textbooks. *Reading Psychology, 30,* 319–339.

CHAPTER 19

Verbal Protocols of Reading

Katherine Hilden
Michael Pressley

For more than a century, researchers have been listening to people think aloud in formal studies (e.g., Marbe, 1901/1964). Before that Aristotle and Plato urged others to talk about what was on their mind, and William James (1890) reported what people had to say about their thinking in the first comprehensive textbook detailing psychological theory. Although the most attention has been given to think-aloud studies of problem solving (see, e.g., Ericsson & Simon, 1984/1993), a growing body of research has implemented verbal protocol methodology to study adult reading processes. Fewer studies have used verbal protocols to examine the developing nature of reading in emerging readers. As it turns out, people are actually quite good at reporting the contents of their working memory (i.e., what they are currently consciously thinking about). That was much of the point of Ericsson and Simon's (1984/1993) book-length conceptual treatment of verbal protocols of thinking. One reason that is true is that working memory cannot contain much at any one moment. (Recall the 7 ± 2 formula that George Miller put forth in his 1956 article.) Thus, it is possible in a comment or two to get out what is in one's mind.

This chapter, originally by Pressley and Hilden, has been revised by Katherine Hilden for the second edition.

WHAT HAS VERBAL PROTOCOL METHODOLOGY TAUGHT US ABOUT READING?

With more than 40 reasonably independent verbal protocol analyses in the literature, Pressley and Afflerbach (1995) reasoned that there was a good chance that all important conscious processes of reading would have been captured in at least one of them. Thus, Pressley and Afflerbach catalogued all the processes reported in the various verbal protocols of adult reading available in the early 1990s, using grounded theory analysis (Strauss & Corbin, 1998), resulting in a theory of expert reading. The major claim of this theory is that the nature of constructively responsive reading is that good readers are constantly shifting their processing in response to text. To borrow Keene and Zimmermann's (1997) description, readers' minds resemble mosaics of thinking. The following consists of an extremely brief introduction to Pressley and Afflerbach's findings. Table 19.1 summarizes the processes detectable when readers think aloud as they read.

From Pressley and Afflerbach's (1995) summative work and the studies they reviewed, we now know that expert comprehenders actively make sense of a text before, during, and after reading. We have learned from verbal protocols that expert readers often preview a text before reading. Previewing can include skimming headers and illustrations to decide whether a text informs their reading goals. An initial preview can also activate prior knowledge related to topics covered in the text, which later aids in comprehension. Expert readers also use a repertoire of comprehension strategies while reading. Although readers normally read text from beginning to end, they often change their reading speed or skip around a text, depending on their interest in specific points covered in the text and the difficulty of the text. Also, expert readers often attempt to identify main ideas. They consciously make inferences by filling in gaps or make guesses about the author's intentions. As reading proceeds, active readers integrate ideas across the text (e.g., reflecting on the actions of a story in relation to the setting). Skilled readers also interpret texts and ideas in them: They summarize, generate visual images, and empathize (or not) with the ideas expressed by the author.

Finally, and most critically, expert readers monitor whether their strategies and text processings are producing the understanding they want. If expert readers feel they are not understanding a text, they may reread confusing parts, skip problematic sections, or look ahead for clarification. Because expert readers do not know the definition of every word in the texts they read, they look for content clues pertaining to the meaning of unfamiliar words or look up unknown words in a dictionary.

In short, when Pressley and Afflerbach (1995) reviewed existing verbal protocols of reading, they found that expert readers are massively active as they read. They are also massively aware, with their awareness affecting their processing of text. Such awareness is not cold cognition, with expert

TABLE 19.1. Conscious Processes of Reading Reflected in Verbal Protocols of Reading

Before reading

Constructing a goal for reading

Overviewing (skimming text)

Deciding to read/focus on only particular sections of text

Deciding to not read the text

Activating prior knowledge and related knowledge

Summarizing what was gained from previewing

Generating an initial hypothesis about content of the text

During initial reading of text

Generally beginning-to-end reading of text

Reading only sections believed to contain critical information

Skimming

If text is easy, read with automatic processes and few conscious strategies

Reading aloud

Repeating/restating text to hold in working memory

Repeating/restating a thought that occurred during reading

Making notes

Pausing to reflect on text

Paraphrasing part of text

Explicitly looking for related words, concepts, or ideas in text and using them to construct main idea, gist, or summary

Looking for patterns in the text

Predicting/substantiating predictions about content of text

Resetting reading/learning goals at a different level of understanding because text suggests more appropriate goal

Identifying important information in text (e.g., looking for what is "news" in text and looking for keywords, topic sentences, topic paragraphs)

Conscious inference making (e.g., inferring referents of pronouns, filling in gaps, inferring the meanings of unfamiliar vocabulary words, making inferences about the author, and deducing implied conclusions)

Integrating different parts of text (e.g., by holding representations of different parts of text in working memory, looking back and forth in text to pull meanings together, rereading text to increase connections, and making notes to assist integrative understanding)

Interpreting the text

Monitoring characteristics of text and the processing of the text (especially problems in processing text)

Reacting when problems during reading are detected (e.g., rereading for clarification, deciding to slow down and read more carefully, and deciding to just keep reading in hope that the meaning will become clearer later in the reading)

Evaluating (e.g., accepting and being skeptical—about both style and content of text)

(cont.)

TABLE 19.1 *(continued)*

After reading

Monitoring that the text is understood and deciding not to process text additionally or monitoring that more processing is required to get the meaning of the text

Rereading after the first reading

Recitation of text to increase memory of it

Listing pieces of information in text

Constructing cohesive summaries of text

Self-questioning, self-testing over content of text

Imagining how hypothetical situations might be viewed in light of information in text

Reflecting on information in text, with possibility of shift in interpretations as reflection proceeds

Rereading parts of text following reflection in order to rethink text based on insights gained during reflection

Continually evaluating and possibly reconstructing an understanding of the text

Changing one's response to a text as the understanding is reconstructed

Reflecting on/mentally recoding text in anticipation of using it later

readers often evaluating the style of the text (e.g., deciding whether it was poorly or well written) and its content (e.g., whether or not points made are valid). Sometimes readers' reactions are so charged that they literally stand up and cheer during reading or, alternatively, throw a text down in disgust.

AN EXEMPLAR STUDY: WYATT ET AL. (1993)

Wyatt and colleagues (1993) conducted a verbal protocol study that made clear the complex nature of conscious reading processes. Those researchers wanted to discover how skilled social scientists read in their areas of expertise. They had 15 professors in the social sciences read aloud an article of their choosing. Why 15 participants? The investigators' goal was to describe all the strategies used by social scientists as they read. Thus, the researchers listened to professors read until no new reading processes were identified. By the 10th reader, little new was being heard or observed. By the 15th reader, nothing new seemed to be entering the conclusions.

Why did Wyatt and colleagues decide to allow professors to read an article of their choosing instead of holding the article constant? This allowed each professor to select a piece that matched his or her very particular expertise and interest and therefore more closely mirrored how social scientists actually read. The professors had no difficulty talking aloud as they read the article. On the basis of direct observations of the reading (i.e., the researchers watched, listened, took notes, and reviewed audiotapes), the researchers coded the data, inventing the coding categories as needed. In other words, the authors used a grounded theory approach (Strauss & Corbin, 1990) to drive the data analysis. The coding scheme was constructed based on the reports of the readers, with the researchers revisiting the data until they were confident that every single process reported by readers was captured by coding categories. Three overarching categories were identified: text processing and comprehension strategies, monitoring of reading, and evaluation of the reading.

Compared with most other verbal protocols of reading, Wyatt and colleagues (1993) captured a greater diversity of reading processes. In particular, previously reported verbal protocols of reading conducted by information processing-oriented psychologists tended to report that readers used strategies and monitored. In contrast, verbal protocol studies carried out by rhetoricians reported reader evaluations more. Wyatt et al. succeeded in capturing in one study a fuller range of responses because of their general methodological tactics, particularly their use of grounded theory to construct categories rather than coming to the study with preformed categories (which was the universal approach to coding of data in previous research).

The careful reader might notice that the individual strategies that composed the general categories in the Wyatt and colleagues (1993) study closely resemble those summarized in Table 19.1, based on the analyses of more than 40 verbal protocol studies by Pressley and Afflerbach (1995). We believe this congruence reflects that in both studies data were imputed to a point when no new categories of verbal self-report were emerging. In addition, our reading of verbal protocol studies produced since 1995 (e.g., Crain-Thoreson, Lippman, & McClendon-Magnuson, 1997; Shearer, Lundeberg, & Coballes-Vega, 1997) is that they contain no processes not included in Pressley and Afflerbach (1995). Our confidence is high that Table 19.1 captures just about all the conscious processes during reading, at least those that can be verbalized.

QUESTIONS ABOUT CONDUCTING VERBAL PROTOCOLS IN READING

As with any methodology used to study reading, collecting verbal protocols has its advantages and disadvantages. This methodology can enlighten our understanding of such factors as reader characteristics—processes and strategies used by readers, readers' motivation and affect, the interaction of readers' motivation and affect with their cognitive responses—and the examination of contextual variables: text task, setting, and readability. By examining these factors as they relate to reading comprehension processes, verbal protocols research can be used to refine existing theory and break ground for new theory (Afflerbach, 2000). However, many questions remain related to collection, analysis, and interpretation of verbal protocols of reading.

Should Verbal Protocols Occur Retrospectively or Concurrently with Reading?

Frankly, the procedures and directions in verbal protocol studies have varied greatly from study to study. Sometimes readers are urged to report what they are thinking as they read, and sometimes reports are collected retrospectively. Ericsson and Simon (1984/1993) claimed that verbal protocols should be concurrent because verbal protocols are intended to reflect the contents of short-term memory—that is, what is currently in consciousness. From that perspective, only concurrent reports make sense, asking participants to report the thoughts in their head while they are having them. So what can be made of retrospective reports, for example, when readers are cued to stop after so much reading and report what they have been doing since last they were stopped by the researcher? In that case, whatever is being reported is stored in long-term memory rather than a report of current consciousness. Does that mean that retrospective reports are necessarily less accurate or complete? The answer is that we do not know with respect to protocols of reading, although Ericsson and Simon (1984/1993), largely on the basis of data from verbal protocol studies of problem solving, believed that retrospective reports were likely less complete and accurate than concurrent reports. There is a need for research to determine whether the conclusions about reading are different if protocols are collected concurrently versus retrospectively.

That said, we are going to take a stance on concurrent versus retrospective reports. Often, retrospective reporting involves a reader reporting recent processing on cue (e.g., when a blue dot occurs in the text; Olshavsky, 1976–1977). Crain-Thoreson and colleagues (1997) reported the only true experimental evaluation of the effects of prompted versus unprompted reports. They found that requiring readers to stop and report, rather than letting them report as they read and when they wished, affected the reports obtained from lower ability college readers but not higher ability college readers. Specifically, the low-ability readers were more likely to report that they were confused when they were reading passages that required them to stop at intervals and report processing. With high-ability readers, the requirement to stop did not have this effect. Thus, based on available evidence, at this point, a recommendation to collect concurrent or retrospective reports must be conditionalized: If the readers are capable and reading text that should cause few problems, concurrent reports probably are better. If the readers are less capable and reading texts that might be challenging to them, more valid reports might be obtained by signaling them to provide reports of their processing (i.e., with blue dots or some other place markers).

Should Verbal Protocols Be Interpretations of Processes or Direct Reports of Thinking?

Ericsson and Simon (1984/1993) recommended think-alouds as exact reports of what the thinker is thinking rather than reader interpretations of their processing. From their perspective, a report such as, "I can see a really frightened Scrooge!" would be more acceptable than a report such as, "I'm making mental images of what is in the story." Both types of reports, however, have been collected in studies. We know of no analyses that are revealing about how conclusions about reading processes are affected by whether readers report what they are thinking or report their thinking processes by name. After reading and reflecting on the verbal protocols of reading covered by Pressley and Afflerbach (1995) and some that have appeared since then, we do not have a firm stand on this issue, except that we believe readers should be allowed to speak their own minds. Thus, we advise researchers to instruct readers to report what they are thinking as they read without attempting to shape their reports further. Researchers should record the readers' verbal reports and then make sense of them.

Verbal Protocol Limitation: Cuing Reader to Researchers' Expectations

Perhaps the most objectionable situation occurs when a researcher telegraphs to the reader in advance of collecting the verbal protocol just which processes he or she is interested in. Pressley and Afflerbach (1995) reported examples of researchers letting readers know that they should be focusing on main ideas or summarizing or report what they are looking for as they go through text. In contrast are studies such as that of Wyatt and colleagues (1993), in which researchers were very careful not to cue readers to use particular processes. Our position is that this is the most defensible tactic if the goal is to understand readers' natural reading processes.

Thus, with respect to directions to participants, after thinking about many, many verbal protocols of reading, we recommend keeping instructions to participants general (e.g., "Please think aloud as you read. . . . Tell me what you are thinking as you read the text"). Definitely do not prompt particular processes.

Can Verbal Protocols Be Collected with Young Children as Developing Readers?

Although quite a few studies exist in which children and adolescents have provided verbal protocols, there seems to be an enduring question of whether less able readers and young children are capable of providing useful verbal protocols (Afflerbach & Johnston, 1984). Afflerbach and Johnston (1984) reasoned that because verbal ability is confounded with reading ability, younger and less verbal participants may produce poor think-alouds. They reasoned that young readers may not provide accurate think-alouds because they may not have sufficient metacognitive awareness of what they are thinking while reading. However, there is a small but growing body of research that suggests the viability of using this methodology with readers as young as second graders. For example, Brown, Pressley, van Meter, and Schuder (1996) studied the verbal protocols of second graders over the course of a year as a measure of improved reading comprehension. Alvermann (1984) used verbal protocols to investigate strategies that second graders used to comprehend narratives in basal readers. She concluded that the second graders in her study "seemed relatively at ease with the task" of thinking aloud (p. 186). Hilden (2006) found that second graders who read at or above grade level could verbally report their thoughts and feelings while reading narrative picture books aloud. Among other findings, Hilden discovered that, unlike their adult counterparts, only a minority of these younger readers actively constructed meaning before or after reading. The vast majority of their comments occurred while reading.

We suggest that when conducting verbal protocols of reading with younger students, researchers should have students read text within their reading level. If the students are asked to read overly difficult texts, their cognitive resources may be so taxed by reading that they cannot accurately verbalize their thoughts. However, this becomes an issue when developing students can only independently read simplistic text where there is little substance to comprehend. In order to deal with this issue, Hilden (2008, 2009) had second-grade students think aloud as an informational text was read to them. This research resulted in an inventory of 23 processes and six distinct profiles of comprehension of informational texts.

At the very least, we need more research about how early elementary school children are able to verbalize their thoughts while reading. This work is important because it has potential to inform developmental theories of reading. We look forward to learning much about how students' reading comprehension processes shift during development, expecting think-aloud data to prove very useful in illuminating developmental reading processes.

DETAILED REPORTING OF VERBAL PROTOCOL STUDIES

Although educational researchers have collected verbal protocols for a century, this is not a standardized methodology yet, making it daunting to compare findings across studies. Moreover, we do not think it makes sense for verbal protocol analyses to become standardized based on what is now known.

Indeed, the hallmark of this methodology is its open-ended nature, with a great strength being that verbal protocol studies can be flexibly fitted to the questions posed by the researcher rather than the questions needing to be adjusted to research methodology.

We do agree with Afflerbach (2000), however, that researchers should provide substantial detail about how they conducted their study and why they made the decisions they did with respect to text, participants, directions provided to participants, and analyses, including transcription, raters, how raters categorized participant responses, and reliability of ratings. We consider briefly each of these aspects of research design next.

Text Factors

When designing a verbal protocol study in reading, the researcher must decide what type of texts will be read. In the Wyatt and colleagues (1993) study, the goal was to investigate, as naturalistically as possible, how social scientists read for professional purposes. Therefore, each professor read an article of his or her choosing within his or her area of professional interest. In the Brown and colleagues (1996) study, the goal was to compare reading comprehension among students who had experienced strategy instruction and those who had not. Therefore, all participants read the same passage, a fairly easy but definitely grade 2–level story. The researchers wanted the readers to be able to read the story fluently, so that some of their cognitive capacity would be available for sense making rather than consumed by word-recognition demands (LaBerge & Samuels, 1974). In addition, if a researcher decided to have students read texts that were at a higher reading level than their own, verbal protocols might include more word-level strategies. Because there would probably be more miscomprehension than with texts that can be read fluently, there might also be more reports of fix-up strategies. In short, because the strategies reported might vary as a function of text features, at a minimum, the report of a study must include information about the text being read in relation to the reader. Wyatt and colleagues did that, as did Brown and colleagues.

Participants

It is always good to be clear about who is being studied before studying them. With respect to reading, the need is especially urgent. Thus, if it is a study of adult reading, much needs to be known about the participants besides the fact that they are adults: What is their educational level and previous reading achievement?

Are cultural, vocational, or avocational backgrounds relevant to the texts read in the study? With the exception of the vocational question, all the same issues pertain to child readers. Given the variety of educational approaches to reading, and the possibility that comprehension processing varies as a function of the reading program a child has experienced, often it will make sense to be clear about the type of reading instruction that participants experienced.

Given the intense, current interest in readers with learning disabilities, we are anticipating think-aloud studies involving readers who have difficulty reading. Researchers should be exceptionally clear about the nature of the reading difficulties of such participants, being as specific as possible.

Directions

Because of the potential for directions to bias the processing of participants in think-aloud studies, the researcher should be very clear about what is said to participants. Our advice earlier in this chapter boils down to directing participants' processing as little as possible. Simply ask participants to think aloud while they read, reporting what they are doing and thinking as they go through a text. Mention of specific reading or thinking processes has the potential to prompt participants to use those processes. Similarly, explaining thinking aloud by modeling with a short text can send the message to "do as I do."

That said, often more is going to have to be said for participants to know what is meant by "thinking aloud." In particular, it has been known since Piaget's early research that the younger the children, the greater the difficulty in getting them to think about thinking. On the basis of the experience in the Brown and colleagues (1996) study, we know that it takes awhile for some second graders to warm up to talking about what they are thinking as they read, at least in ways that obviously map to reading processes. Whatever is required to inform participants about their task in a study should be reported in detail so that consumers of the study can appraise whether the directions may have biased the results in one direction or another. Of course, the only way to know whether directions bias is to conduct experiments varying the degree of explicitness of directions given to participants, a direction we think should be pursued in the near future.

Tasks

An issue that has arisen repeatedly in the verbal protocols of reading literature is whether readers should be cued when to report their processing. Should participants be asked to stop reading at particular points to report on their processing or allowed to make reports of processing when they choose to do so? Certainly, the latter results in more natural reading, while the former provides greater research control, and with it the possibility of more easily comparing the processing of two readers because, at least, they will have provided reports of processing at the same points in text.

If a decision is made to cue, it is necessary to decide when to cue. For example, some studies cue at the sentence or individual line level (e.g.,

McGuire & Yewchuk, 1996; Meyers, Lytle, Palladino, Devenpeck, & Green, 1990; Wade, 1990), whereas others cue at the paragraph or section level (e.g., Loxterman, Beck, & McKeown, 1994). Also, the researcher must decide whether to show readers the whole passage at once or have them read the passage a line at a time (using note cards or by clicking through succeeding computer screens). Again, presenting the whole passage is more naturalistic than providing the passage a line at a time. Reading a line at a time interrupts the natural flow of reading, prevents readers from previewing texts by skimming, and prevents them from going back and rereading important parts of texts. On the other hand, the latter situation allows the researcher to know better just what the participant is reacting to at the moment.

Analysis Plan

What do researchers do with the verbal reports? At one level, the answer is obvious: They categorize them in order to characterize the readers' processing. But are these categories that were decided in advance (e.g., if researchers are interested in self-questioning during reading, they may have come to the study with various categories of self-questions that might occur), or are they decided in light of the data (e.g., if the readers never self-question while reading the focal text, there would be no self-questioning category in the results)?

If researchers are really interested in capturing the "mosaic" quality of the processing (Keene & Zimmermann, 1997), they might want to focus on strings of processes, for example, seeing how often a reader's thinking or strategies shifted during reading of a sentence, in a minute of reading, or while reading the caption of an illustration. The researchers often will have to make decisions about whether the data can be quantified. Often this will be challenging, with Wyatt and colleagues (1993) a case in point: They decided that processes could be classified as never occurring, observed once, observed a few times (i.e., two to four times), or observed a lot (i.e., five or more times). Any more fine-grained classification resulted in unreliable quantification. Whatever analysis decisions are made, researchers must specify them clearly and explain the rationale for the decisions. Often it is going to take some effort to come up with a reliable, credible analysis plan, one that can convince other scientists.

FUTURE DIRECTIONS

Verbal protocols of reading have provided valuable insights about the nature of constructively responsive reading. We know of no other method that reveals quite as much about active, strategic processes during reading.

Although not a completely clear window on how the mind processes text, it is a window that admits a great deal of light.

Nonetheless, we look forward to the day when there are many more verbal protocols of reading studies. For example, conducting additional verbal protocol studies of reading with different age groups could affect developmental theories of reading. In addition to focusing on younger readers, we also need more information on how various reader, text, and methodological factors influence readers' comprehension processes as measured by verbal protocols. Reader factors that require further study employing this method include motivation, purpose for reading, and ability level. One such innovative study in this area is Jiménez, Garcia, and Pearson's (1996) verbal protocol study of English language learners reading in English. They examined the reading strategies employed by Latina/o students who were identified as successful English readers.

Verbal protocol methodology also has the potential to enlighten our understanding of how various text characteristics impact the meaning-making process. Such text factors include examining different genres and text structures. Studies of reading comprehension of hypertext are also needed. Zhang and Duke's (2008) research on expert Internet readers represents a promising new direction in verbal protocol methodology. Norman (2010) has employed verbal protocol methodology in a novel way. She conducted focused think-alouds of second graders as they comprehended the graphics in informational texts.

We realize that we have focused exclusively on verbal protocols of reading. This is because we know of little research that uses verbal protocols to study writing processes. However, we believe that many of the factors involved in reading would also be important in writing. We look forward to research in this area as well.

REFERENCES

Afflerbach, P. (2000). Verbal reports and protocol analysis. In M. L. Kamil, P. B. Mosenthal, P. D. Pearson, & R. Barr (Eds.), *Handbook of reading research: Volume III* (pp. 163–179). Mahwah, NJ: Erlbaum.

Afflerbach, P., & Johnston, P. (1984). Research methodology: On the use of verbal reports in reading research. *Journal of Reading Behavior, 22,* 307–322.

Alvermann, D. E. (1984). Second graders' strategic preferences while reading basal stories. *Journal of Educational Research, 77,* 184–189.

Brown, R., Pressley, M., van Meter, P., & Schuder, T. (1996). A quasi-experimental validation of Transactional Strategy Instruction with low achieving second-grade readers. *Journal of Educational Psychology, 88,* 18–37.

Crain-Thoreson, C., Lippman, M. Z., & McClendon-Magnuson, D. (1997). Windows on comprehension: Reading comprehension processes as revealed by two think-aloud procedures. *Journal of Educational Psychology, 89,* 579–591.

Ericsson, K. A., & Simon, H. A. (1993). *Protocol analysis: Verbal reports as data.* Cambridge MA: MIT Press. (Original work published 1984)

Hilden, K. (2006, December). *Verbal protocols: A window into second graders' reading comprehension of narrative texts.* Paper presented at the annual meeting of the National Reading Conference, Los Angeles.

Hilden, K. (2008, December). *Connections between SpongeBob SquarePants and Zooplankton: The informational reading comprehension processes of second graders.* Paper presented at the annual meeting of the National Reading Conference, Orlando, FL.

Hilden, K. (2009, December). *Profiles of informational text comprehension in second grade.* Paper presented at the annual meeting of the National Reading Conference, Albuquerque, NM.

James, W. (1890). *The principles of psychology.* New York: Holt.

Jiménez, R. T., Garcia, G. E., & Pearson, P. D. (1996). The reading strategies of bilingual Latina/o students who are successful English readers: Opportunities and obstacles. *Reading Research Quarterly, 31,* 90–112.

Keene, E., & Zimmermann, S. (1997). *Mosaic of thought: Teaching comprehension in a reader's workshop.* Portsmouth, NH: Heinemann.

LaBerge, D., & Samuels, S. J. (1974). Toward a theory of automatic information processing in reading. *Cognitive Psychology, 6,* 293–323.

Loxterman, J. A., Beck, I. L., & McKeown, M. G. (1994). The effects of thinking aloud during reading on students' comprehension of more or less coherent texts. *Reading Research Quarterly, 29,* 352–365.

Marbe, K. (1964). Experimentell-psychologische: Untersuchungen uber das Urteil [Experimental psychology: Investigations about judging]. In J. Mandler & G. Mandler (Eds. & Trans.), *Thinking: From association to gestalt* (pp. 143–148). New York: Wiley. (Original work published 1901)

McGuire, K. L., & Yewchuk, C. R. (1996). Use of metacognitive reading strategies by gifted learning disabled students: An exploratory study. *Journal of Education of the Gifted, 19,* 293–314.

Meyers, J., Lytle, S., Palladino, D., Devenpeck, G., & Green, M. (1990). Think-aloud protocol analysis: An investigation of reading comprehension strategies in fourth- and fifth-grade students. *Journal of Psychoeducational Assessment, 8,* 112–127.

Miller, G. A. (1956). The magical number seven, plus-or-minus two: Some limits on our capacity for processing information. *Psychological Review, 63,* 81–97.

Norman, R. R. (2010). Picture this: Processes prompted by graphics in informational text. *Literacy Teaching and Learning, 14*(1–2), 1–39.

Olshavsky, J. L. (1976–1977). Reading as problem solving: An investigation of strategies. *Reading Research Quarterly, 4,* 655–675.

Pressley, M., & Afflerbach, P. (1995). *Verbal protocols of reading: The nature of constructively responsive reading.* Hillsdale, NJ: Erlbaum.

Shearer, B. A., Lundeberg, M. A., & Coballes-Vega, C. (1997). Making the connection between research and reality: Strategies teachers use to read and evaluate journal articles. *Journal of Educational Psychology, 89,* 592–598.

Strauss, A., & Corbin, J. (1990). *Basics of qualitative research: Grounded theory procedures and techniques.* Newbury Park, CA: Sage.

Strauss, A., & Corbin, J. (1998). *Basics of qualitative research: Grounded theory procedures and techniques* (2nd ed.). Newbury Park, CA: Sage.

Wade, S. E. (1990). Using think-alouds to assess comprehension. *The Reading Teacher, 43*, 442–451.

Wyatt, D., Pressley, M., El-Dinary, P. B., Stein, S., Evans, P., & Brown, R. (1993). Comprehension strategies, worth and credibility monitoring, and evaluations: Cold and hot cognition when experts read professional articles that are important to them. *Learning and Individual Differences, 5*, 49–72.

Zhang, S., & Duke, N. K. (2008). Strategies for Internet reading with different reading purposes: A descriptive study of twelve good Internet readers. *Journal of Literacy Research, 40*, 128–162.

CHAPTER 20

Toward a Pragmatics of Epistemology, Methodology, and Social Theory

Mark Dressman
Sarah J. McCarthey

This chapter represents our best attempt, as literacy researchers first and predominantly qualitative researchers and theorists second, to outline a pragmatic approach toward the development of literacy research practices that makes conscious use of both epistemological concerns and theory across a broad range of methodologies, or ways of doing, literacy research. Our view of pragmatism derives from the school of philosophy commonly known as American Pragmatism, a school founded in the latter half of the 19th and early 20th centuries by Charles Sanders Peirce, William James, and John Dewey. Its principles include the following:

> A metaphysics that emphasizes processes and relations; a naturalistic and evolutionary understanding of human existence; an analysis of intellectual activity as problem-oriented and as benefiting from historically developed methods; and an emphasis upon the democratic reconstruction of society through educational and other institutions. (Campbell, 1995, p. 14)

In addition, American Pragmatism avoids "ultimate" questions about the nature of reality, such as whether objective truth exists, and instead focuses on what the consequences of acting from a position of positive objectivity or taking a more tentative stance toward an observed phenomenon might be for individuals within a given situation.

By arguing for a *pragmatics* of literacy research, then, we mean that we intend to examine the relations among epistemology, theory, and methodology from a stance that is grounded in as full a view as possible of the actual conditions in which research is likely to be conducted rather than

in hypothetical conditions removed from the logistical, cultural, historical, and sociopolitical realities of actual schools, homes, and even laboratory settings. Moreover, a pragmatics of literacy research would focus on a
broad consideration of the ways in which a research project's epistemological assumptions, methods, and grounding in prior research and/or theory
transactionally (Dewey & Bentley, 1949) influence each other as well as
others' likely interpretations and uses of the knowledge generated from the
activity of the research.

In this chapter we also take into consideration the uses of theory, or
"theoretical frames," in literacy research. We acknowledge at the outset
that the terms *theory* and *theoretical* have many possible meanings among
literacy researchers and have traditionally referred to explanations of specific phenomena, such as phonemic awareness and its relationship to learning to decode text fluently or schema theory and its implications for comprehension, that are grounded in the empirical evidence of research into the
specific phenomena. When we use these terms in our discussion, however,
they specifically refer to the more recent practice on the part of qualitative
researchers to apply contemporary social theory—that is, theories originat-
ing external to the phenomenon on which the researcher is focusing, such
as Vygotsky's (1978) theory of the zone of proximal development, Foucaul-
dian theories of language and power (Rabinow, 1984), or feminist theories of discourse (e.g., Walkerdine, 1990). Although the use of theoretical
frames in literacy research is becoming an increasingly frequent feature of
literacy research and has considerable implications for many epistemological and methodological approaches to research, it has received little direct
attention or systematic scrutiny as an investigative practice. In this chapter, we consider how the use of such external grand narratives may have
pragmatic consequences for the ways that knowledge about literacy is both
conceptualized and produced (Dressman, 2007, 2008).

Our plan for discussing the issues we have outlined proceeds in three
sections. In the first, we consider the epistemological implications of four
methods of investigating an enduring and important research issue: the
effect of class size on teaching and learning. In the second section, we consider the current and possible roles of theoretical frames as methodological
tools. In our third and concluding section, we summarize our arguments
and suggest some broad pragmatic principles for the improvement of literacy research as an epistemological, methodological, and theory-building
enterprise.

EPISTEMOLOGY AND METHODOLOGY:
CONSIDERING FOUR APPROACHES

To illustrate the relationship between epistemology and methodology, we
explore one topic—class size and literacy teaching and learning—using

methods described in four chapters of this book. We became interested in using this issue to frame our discussion after reading the report of the National Research Council (2002), *Scientific Research in Education*, in which the debate about class size within the research literature is used to illustrate one of its six principles for conducting educational research: "using methods that permit direct investigation of the question" (p. 62). The authors of the report phrased the research question regarding class size and educational outcome in these terms: "Does reducing class size improve students' achievement?" (pp. 64–65).

From our perspective as former teachers, we found it puzzling that none of these studies or the report itself ever asked how a reduction or expansion in class size might positively, negatively, or neutrally affect not only student achievement but also the *nature of instruction* offered by teachers of smaller classes. Our conversations about the strengths and limitations of their review of the research on class size and its effects suggested to us that here was an issue that could provide a consistent context across which four research approaches and their implied epistemological perspectives might be considered. In this section, then, we consider four *hypothetical* studies based on the underlying assumptions of each research method. We do not consider issues such as cost or site selection but focus only on the methods and the underlying epistemologies implicit in their designs. Through our discussion, we hope to illustrate the epistemological strengths and weaknesses of each method and to demonstrate the importance of using all kinds of methods to understand literacy teaching and learning.

Experimental and Quasi-Experimental Designs

The primary concern in any experimental study is to control the procedures of investigation and a number of relevant variables in such a way that, in the end, any effects of the experimental condition can be logically attributed to the variable or variables under investigation. Experimental studies of human behavior rely on a number of key elements or principles in their design in order to ensure procedural control of possible external influences on outcomes. Among these are (1) the randomized selection and assignment of subjects; (2) the comparative use of at least two, and frequently more, groups, one of which is used as the control and one of which is identical to the control in all ways except in its addition of the "independent" variable under investigation; (3) contextual uniformity and procedural regularity across experimental groups, including clear operational definitions of all variables; and (4) measurement procedures that work to exclude or compensate for any human error or bias, and that are nearly always quantitative in nature.

An experimental study of the relations among class size, instructional practice, and student achievement would, at minimum, require the comparison of two groups in which the factor of instructional practice was varied and two groups in which the factor of class size was varied. Let us suppose that the instructional context of the study was 11th-grade American literature, that a large class was defined as having 30 students and a small class 15 students, that the two instructional practices to be compared were lecture/discussion and small-group literature study circles, and that the effects of the experiment were to be measured by a final 50-item multiple-choice test covering factual, interpretive, and critical comprehension of the novel. In an experimental study, the population would be defined as 11th-grade students of approximately the same age within that particular high school. Sixty students would be randomly selected and randomly assigned to four treatment groups (large-class lecture/discussion; small-class lecture/discussion; large-class study circles; small-class study circles) so that distribution of characteristics such as gender, ethnicity, social class, IQ, grade point average, and any other variable that might be confounded with the effects of class size and instructional practice on achievement would be distributed equally across the four groups. All four groups would need to read the same novel over the same period in identical physical conditions, using highly standardized instructional procedures for both the lecture/discussion and literature study format. Descriptive statistics of test scores for each group would be computed, and statistical procedures would be used to determine whether the differences between mean scores were significant. However, because the cell size for the small-group condition is relatively small, the experiment would probably need to be performed multiple times and the numbers and scores from identical groups would need to be combined before any parametric analyses could be validly performed.

The logistical problems inherent in conducting such an experiment within the context of a comprehensive high school, however, should be fairly obvious, necessitating the likelihood that the experiment would have to be conducted across multiple settings. For instance, in typical high school settings students are not randomly assigned to classes, teachers are likely to be less than enthusiastic about following an experimenter's scripted procedures, and administrative regulations and scheduling seldom allow for the regularity required by an experiment that is several weeks long. As a result, experimental literacy research of the type described previously may take two approaches. One approach is likely to be quasi-experimental, in which as many intervening variables as possible are controlled for but the selection and/or assignment of subjects is not randomized, instructional procedures may not be completely identical, and less powerful, sometimes nonparametric, statistical procedures are needed. In the other approach, the unit of analysis is considered not to be individual students but individual classrooms, which are, in turn, randomly selected and assigned to either the experimental or the control condition. Despite these challenges, some studies such as the Tennessee studies (Ritter & Boruch, 1999) have been conducted and shed light on the relationship between class size and student achievement.

The epistemological perspective embedded in this example enacts a view of human behavior that assumes that students and readers, like all other physical objects in a universe of discreet but classifiable physical objects, are above all else physical entities subject to dynamic laws of behavior. At the level of complex human behavior, these laws may not be the same as those that govern the physical universe; but because variables of human behavior are typically assumed to be normally distributed in the population, there is also assumed to be a regularity, or at least a normative pattern of distribution to them, that would allow the detection of predictable patterns among them. Patterned predictability in human behavior is the knowledge that experimentalists in literacy research seek, for when a prediction that is planned for comes true more times than chance will allow, then a true pattern—one that may not consider history or culture or individual experience—has been found and certainty has been obtained, at least for the population as it has been defined. Such knowledge, like knowledge about the laws of planetary movements or genetic heritability, remains true in all circumstances and is free of the emotional or cultural distortions that characterized belief about the heavens in Ptolemy's time or bloodlines in the middle ages. Thus, a fully randomized and procedurally controlled experiment testing the effects of two different class sizes and two different instructional practices on an objective measure of student achievement should yield reliable information—information that can be used to produce higher student performance in future 11th-grade American literature classrooms and that may be extended, with further experimentation, to other grade levels, student populations, and literary content.

The principal strengths of this epistemological perspective are its emphasis on the rationality of knowledge, the clarity of its argument that predictable patterns of human behavior can be known, and the trustworthiness and utilitarian value of knowledge that is considered to have essentially been *discovered* through its methods. If the previously described experiment yielded findings, for example, of higher performance in smaller classes but no effect for instructional practice, then school systems interested in improving student performance in literature classes would rationally be expected to reduce class size without concern for other changes that would be necessary to take instructional advantage of having fewer students in classes. Decision making based on what is generalizable beyond its immediate context is clearly the most powerful kind of knowledge from this perspective.

However, the enactment of such an epistemological perspective also has significant pragmatic limitations. As already mentioned, the need for full control of the experimental context may be practically impossible or, where possible, may produce a condition so significantly different from the actual school contexts that the experimental context itself becomes a threat to validity. Under quasi-experimental conditions, every compromise in control becomes a possible source of bias, which must be investigated and compensated for through statistical techniques and multiple experiments. Another limitation of the method involves the generalizability of findings. Suppose in the previous example that the student body of the high school or high schools in which the study was conducted was largely suburban, middle to upper middle class, and European American with a small minority of Latino but few African American students. Would findings from the study be generalizable to suburban African American populations? To rural European American populations? To bilingual urban populations? In the past 20 years, a significant body of research has demonstrated that variables such as ethnicity and linguistic background may interact significantly with variables such as class size and instructional practice. Today an awareness of the effect of these and other variables on educational outcomes would have to be controlled for, necessitating experiments with multiple student populations across multiple settings, before the evidence could be supported and generalized. But when the First Grade Studies of the 1960s were conducted, their effects were unknown and so were not considered in the studies' design, yet their findings were generalized to all students in the United States (Willis & Harris, 1997). This raises the question of what other as yet unforeseen variables may inadvertently bias findings whose epistemological foundations and practices provide a rational "guarantee" of their general effectiveness across any and all populations.

Finally, the need to operationally define a variable may produce an artificial rigidity in the practical application of a variable under experimental conditions and in the generalizability of findings. In other words, beyond the boundaries of its experimental definition, what constitutes a "large" class versus a "small" class? Is it 30 versus 15 students, as in the present example, or would a difference of 25 versus 20 or 40 versus 10 or 29 versus 17 students produce the same results? What constitutes instructional practice? Is it the size of small groups? The nature of the questions the teacher asks during whole-class discussion? The amount of interaction allowed during lectures? Or is it the teacher's enthusiasm for one practice over the other—and if so, how does one go about objectively measuring, much less controlling for, "enthusiasm"? Experimentalists might agree that generalizing the effects of a variable as defined beyond its boundaries should not be done, but in practice and policy these types of generalizations occur regularly.

In short, one pragmatic consequence of the epistemological perspective embedded within experimentalism is that it can encourage a false confidence about the ecological validity and the generalizability of findings beyond the experimental context in which they occurred. Moreover, the need for control within approaches that enact such an epistemology ultimately requires much manipulation of contexts and comparative replication across contexts to ensure the generalizability of findings within actual contexts. The defense of truth claims from such studies can become such an overriding preoccupation that experimentalists may attempt to account for more and more variability in their results and design ever more controlled conditions that are increasingly remote from the actual conditions of classrooms and instructional practice. Despite these limitations, controlled experiments continue to be used and provide useful information about aspects of literacy learning and teaching. Like other research methods, experimental designs address certain questions well, while being less effective at illuminating other important issues, particularly with respect to the social and organizational complexity of implementing new pedagogical practices.

Formative Experiments

In Chapter 10 of this volume, Bradley and Reinking provide seven characteristics of formative experiments: (1) theoretical—"theory . . . is used to justify the importance of the inquiry, to provide a rationale for the intervention, to interpret findings, to contextualize conclusions" (p. 198); (2) interventionist and (3) goal oriented—there is a planned intervention with the promise of improving education and a justification of the goal; (4) iterative—"the initial intervention is implemented within continuous cycles of data collection and analysis that aim to determine what contextual factors enhance or inhibit the intervention's effectiveness" (p. 199); (5) transformational—"intervention may transform . . . the educational environment in some way" (p. 200), including unintended consequences; (6) methodologically inclusive and flexible—it is likely that both quantitative and qualitative data will be collected and data collection may be adapted to the setting; and (7) pragmatic—pragmatism "values intuitive knowledge and promotes democratic ideals" (p. 200), with the likelihood of involving practitioners as well as researchers (see also Reinking & Bradley, 2007). It is, therefore, potentially a very powerful response to some of the problems of experimental research in that it attempts to account for the complexity of "real-life" situations and yet retains elements of control that would support claims of replicability and the objectivity of findings.

If we were to design a formative experiment to evaluate the effects of class size and instructional practice on students' achievement, we might begin by inviting four teachers within, for example, an upper elementary setting to collaborate with us. Through an agreement with the school administration, the size of two teachers' classes during the period that reading was taught would be reduced to approximately half—15 students—their usual size, with 30 students per class in the other two teachers' rooms. With the teachers, we would select a number of texts to be used in all four classrooms over the experimental period. The instructional intervention that we would be testing, literature study circles (e.g., Day, Spiegel, McLellan, & Brown, 2002; McMahon & Raphael, 1997), is grounded in both reader response theory (Rosenblatt, 1968) and theories of small-group interaction derived from the work of Vygotsky (1978) and other social constructivists. To collect baseline data, prior to the intervention we would observe the teaching of reading in each teacher's classroom, interview each teacher about his or her practices and philosophy, and collect test scores and survey data from the students about their attitudes toward reading in general and in class. We would share this theoretical rationale and the principles of literature study circles with the teachers and together design a plan for teaching one novel. During the instructional period, we would keep field notes of how each teacher actually arranged his or her class and students' interactions and collect any written responses to the reading or other artifacts that were produced. We would also collect quantitative information, such as tests of comprehension and vocabulary development given as summative assessments of the novel, and, if feasible, collect standardized reading test information. This information would be provided to teachers as feedback; a new plan for reading that addressed concerns and issues raised by the teachers, students, and researchers would be formulated for the reading of a second novel; and the process of reading and data collection would be repeated, and so on, through several trials.

As Bradley and Reinking note in Chapter 10 of this volume, the epistemological origins of formative experiments are multiple, ranging from design experiments in engineering to neo-Vygotskian research. But perhaps the best articulated perspective of those they name is that of American Pragmatist John Dewey (Dewey & Bentley, 1949). For Dewey, the world is not made up of discrete objects "bumping into" each other with causal effect; rather, what appear to be discrete objects are actually only temporary assemblages in transactional relation, entities whose encounters with other entities result in changes to both. One may describe and be able to predict the interaction of one entity with another when examined in isolation; but the full effects of any interaction are unforeseeable. Thus, the earth beneath us appears solid but is actually a shifting mass of continental plates whose collision, in turn, affects climate patterns, ocean currents, and biological evolution; a surge in one species' population reduces others and sows the seeds of its own extinction; one nation colonizes another but then must adapt itself to the mores and practices of its colony; and a single shift in a school's curriculum might produce not only an intended consequence but many others, both positive and negative, as well. Moreover, objective knowledge of phenomena such as plate tectonics, evolution, political science, or instructional theory may or may not allow one to predict the future shape of continents, how or which organisms will evolve, how two cultures will affect each other, or what the full outcome of an educational innovation might be. From a Pragmatist view, broad, general theoretical knowledge may have its function, but it is to inform, not direct, the development of understanding about a particular situation. What matters most is what Bradley and Reinking term *conditional knowledge*, that is, knowledge/information gained from a situation that can be used in future instances of that situation to produce a beneficial outcome locally and, with further modification and development, in other similar situations.

It is from an evaluation of the strengths and the limitations of an epistemology strongly influenced by the tenets of American Pragmatism that its consequences for formative experiments as knowledge-producing activities may best be observed. We begin by noting that philosophers have not named the school founded by Dewey, Charles Sanders Peirce, and William James *American* Pragmatism out of historical or nationalist impulse but rather as a way of describing it as something quintessentially and culturally *American*. That is why, to us as Americans ourselves and, we suspect, to other American readers, formative experiments, with their focus on problem solving and practicality, their mention of theory but focus on local situations, and the inclusion of a broad range of shareholders as well as a broad range of measurements, seem to make so much common sense. What makes common sense seem common, however, is often not a sharing of meanings or ideas but rather meanings and ideas that are so adaptable and open to interpretation that they can appeal to many different points of view without upsetting the sensibilities of a broad range of constituents. For example, in its heyday, whole language represented such a commonsense approach to literacy (see Dressman, McCarty, & Benson, 1998, for a discussion of its multiple meanings and implied practices), but its commonsense rationale may also explain why as a practice it was so hard to pin down and so hard to determine exactly what about its practices were effective and ineffective. So, too, in the foregoing example, practices such as literature study circles and reader response may be difficult, with so many stakeholders involved, to describe accurately. Not only may such "fuzziness" have an epistemological benefit, but it may also have a rhetorical and political benefit in that it keeps different groups with different interests and different ways of exercising power—that is, teachers, administrators, and researchers— seemingly collaborative and communicative, even though each may not be aware of the other's actual practices or reasoning. Differences in interpretation of what constitutes a literature circle or even an effective small-group activity as well as the practices these common terms name may vary widely across the four teachers and classrooms, and so any generalization about the effect of class size on reading achievement within each condition would be difficult to arrive at. Yet the common use of the same terms by all parties and the political need to appear "collaborative" in the research process may mask these underlying difficulties in the generalizability of findings.

A second, related attribute of the epistemology enacted by formative and design experiments that seems very American and also double-edged is the tension—some would say balance—between attention to theoretical (constitutional, federal) issues and local (historical, regional, state) circumstances. This tension, or balance, can be read from the wording of Bradley and Reinking's description of their first principle of formative and design experiments, when they note that theory "is used . . . to provide a rationale for the intervention, to interpret findings, to contextualize conclusions, and so forth" (Chapter 10, p. 198), but also quote Cobb, Comfrey, diSessa, Lehrer, and Schauble (2003) to note that "theory 'must do real work' by being *accountable to the activity of design*'" (p. 199). Thus, an epistemologically pragmatic compromise is arrived at whereby the status and existence of theory as an external form of knowledge is acknowledged but the organic integrity of local conditions is practically allowed to prevail. We would also point out that, in this case, keeping theory and practice separate in ways that limit the interaction of one with the other is distinctly out of character with American Pragmatism, but its consequence—the development of a rationalized insularity that acts to resist the insights of external criticism that theory can provide—may still be a distinctly *American* flaw. In other words, and as we discuss in greater detail in the conclusion of this chapter, the very fluid application of theoretical frameworks within formative experimental research may result in the legitimization of analyses and conclusions that a more critical and rigorous stance toward one's theory might avoid. In the present example, the cultural attraction of the concept of "literature study circles" may lead researchers and teachers to take an uncritical stance in their analysis of data and interpretation of findings—to assume in advance that literature circles are an effective approach to reading instruction and to discount the possibility that the practice itself rather than differences in class size might also contribute to outcomes in reading achievement across the four classrooms.

Case Studies

In Chapter 2 of this volume, Barone describes case studies as investigations of bounded systems such as an individual child or teacher (and all of his or her topic-related relations) or a particular setting, such as a classroom. Barone also cites Merriam (1998), who characterized case studies as having four additional characteristics. They are (1) particularistic (i.e., "the study is centered on a particular situation, program, event, phenomenon, or person," p. 8); (2) descriptive (i.e., "the researcher gathers rich description of the object of study," p. 8); (3) heuristic (i.e., they enrich a reader's understanding); and (4) inductive (i.e., "the data drive the understandings that emerge from the study," p. 8). The primary characteristic of a case study report is a strong narrative whose credibility is established through collecting multiple sources of data over time, creating a chain of evidence and analysis and considering ethical issues that often include the likely biases/frame of reference of the researcher.

Case study research has its origins in multiple disciplines, including anthropology (which, in turn, derived its methods from natural history), sociology (largely from a school of research developed at the University of Chicago in the 1930s), and clinical psychology and medicine, in which the case histories of individuals with striking psychological or medical problems are recorded, either as illustrative (teaching) examples of a phenomena or, for example, in Freudian psychoanalysis, as the grounds for theory building. Barone (Chapter 2, this volume) also cites Dyson's (1995) argument that case studies "do not offer information about causality regarding teaching practices" (p. 7) because the focus is on understanding a particular setting or individual within that setting (see also Dyson & Genishi, 2005). If the terms *causality* and *generalizability* imply a set of rules or laws that can be applied in circumstances that will produce a predictable outcome, as in genetics or physics, we would agree that case studies are not about causality or generalizability. However, we also would argue that there are other traditions and ways of understanding causality and generalizability, such as the study of evolutionary biology or the geophysics of plate tectonics, that, although not highly predictive, may be more powerful in their capacity for reconceptualizing the dynamics of a system and for generating hypotheses about a generalized phenomenon than the positivistic traditions of experimentalism or the commonsense pragmatism of formative experiments. Our task in this section, then, is to suggest how case studies allow us to understand certain phenomenon, to reconceptualize some dynamics such as student–teacher interactions, and to contribute to supporting or challenging theories. Additionally, through an outline of the epistemological assumptions that operate within the conceptualization, the data collection and analysis, and the "writing up" of case study research, we highlight some of the limitations of this method.

As a hypothetical case study, let us consider a situation in which a middle school teacher and two classes are observed and interviewed as they read the novel *Roll of Thunder, Hear My Cry* (Taylor, 1976). One class has 27 students, but the other is considerably smaller, with 17 students. The teacher organizes instruction in the smaller class using a literature-study-groups approach and uses more of a lecture/discussion method with the larger class. The focus is to understand how students in each of the classes experience instruction. Unlike formative experiments, the role of the researcher in this case study is not to participate in instructional decision making. Rather, she collects data naturalistically, through field notes and videotapes of both classes and interviews that are as nondirective as possible. In addition, four students from the smaller class and seven from the larger class are interviewed about their reading preferences and histories, artifacts such as their writing in response to the novel are collected, and test data and information from parent interviews and other classmates are gathered. Demographic characteristics, such as the race, gender, linguistic background, ethnicity, and social class of the class in general and of the focal students in particular, are also noted. During the analytical phase of the research, connections among the teacher's comments about his instructional practice and observations about the students, student behavior, and student comments; artifacts such as the student writing; transcripts of small-group and whole-class discussions; and demographic data are noted. In writing up the study, the researcher weaves these connections and their supporting data together to produce a clear and consistent account of events in both classrooms and draws conclusions about the experience of the teacher and students within literature study groups versus lecture/discussion formats with both small- and large-size classes. The narrative may be partly diachronic—focused on sequentiality over the course of the novel—but it is more likely to be more synchronic, or focused on broader dynamic principles observed in both classes and their likely influences on the reading of the focal students in both classes. Rather than compare outcomes in both classes in terms of student achievement, the researcher focuses on a comparative discussion of qualitative differences in participation level and the nature of students' responses to the novel, with specific reference to the focal students in each class.

The epistemology enacted through a case study such as the foregoing depends on three assumptions about how the human social world is organized, about how knowledge of that world is validated, and about the nature of knowledge about social experience in general. First, in the social world of human experience, people are not conceived of as free-standing individuals but as members of many different normative groups or categories that share a specific history of social, cultural, economic, political, religious, gendered, cognitive, or physical (to name the most prevalent types) experience. This shared experience is also assumed to have created structural conditions that produce behaviors, attitudes, and beliefs that the members themselves and/or outsiders identify as characteristic of that group. To identify an individual in a case study as a member of that group—to identify the teacher in the foregoing example as an active participant in the state affiliate of the National Council of Teachers of English (NCTE), for example, or to describe the setting of the school as suburban, or one focal student as Latino and another as a "struggling" reader—is to invoke, either implicitly or explicitly, powerful norms about the active members of NCTE, social class, race, language, and students with reading disabilities that can have a powerful influence on the sense a researcher gives, and the sense a reader takes, from a case study. Consequently, a second epistemological assumption is that individuals of a particular group stand in metonymic relation to the group(s) of which they are a part: Thus, to name a student as Latino is implicitly to generalize one's observations about that individual to Latino students in general, or to name a student as female or male is to suggest that all females or males may share some, if not all, of that student's gendered behavior. Thus, although the author of a case study may overtly claim that his or her findings cannot be generalized, the implicit message to readers might be that if an instructional practice worked in one setting or with one group of middle school students, it will work in a broad range of settings and with most groups of middle schoolers. This is even more powerfully so in cases in which little or no attention is paid by the researcher to the group characteristics of individuals or settings, and thus readers are left to assume that the findings of the study are applicable across a broader range of circumstances or conditions than is warranted. For example, although, as Barone (Chapter 2, this volume) notes, Bissex's (1980) study of her son's literacy development has been used to argue for emergent literacy practices across a broad range of sociocultural settings, the social and cultural capital that Bissex and her husband, two PhD students at Harvard University at the time of the study, brought to their son's education would not be a set of conditions that many other parents or schools might be able to reproduce.

When these two powerful epistemological assumptions are combined with the readability of case study narratives, not only may they encourage the overgeneralization of instructional approaches such as literature study groups in all settings and with all populations, but they may also have the negative practical consequence of reifying stereotypes about the assumed strengths or weaknesses of particular student groups or school settings. This may be the most problematic epistemological aspect of case study research. Yet this is not necessarily the case, particularly in studies in which the researcher is careful to make the multiplicity of groups that make up the identity of an individual or setting as a bounded system and their interaction (or transaction) a focus of the analysis and reporting.

A third epistemological assumption of more recent case studies, and in particular of those that take a poststructural perspective (see, e.g., Dressman, Wilder, & Connor, 2005; Foley, 1990; McCarthey, 1998, 2001), is that the behavior of individuals or groups within particular settings cannot usually be explained as either the additive or integrative result of all the groups to which they belong (e.g., gender, race, religion, linguistic background, and social class together) but rather as the practices and beliefs of these groups as they interact with *and contradict* one another in ways that challenge rather than uphold stereotypical views. Thus, in the aforementioned study, although the Latino focal student in the case study is bilingual and has only been in the United States for 2 years, he has been very successful in this context. Analyses of the data demonstrate that prior to coming to the United States, he was a highly proficient reader and writer of Spanish and has been encouraged to maintain his Spanish language proficiency in his home; moreover, transcripts of interviews with the researcher and of his interaction with peers in class show that he has found unexpected connections between his family's experiences in rural Mexico and the experiences of the Logans in the rural Great Depression setting of *Roll of Thunder, Hear My Cry* (Taylor, 1976). One of the greatest epistemological strengths of case study research, then, is its capacity to interrupt stereotypical assumptions about groups of students and settings, thus refining the normative findings of experimental and formative research (and accounting for the many exceptional cases that are often not reported in such studies) as well as suggesting new relationships among important social factors.

These epistemological features of case studies have another pragmatic element in common: the ways that case studies are often used to develop theories (in the sense of "grand narratives") about learning and, subsequently, to challenge or support them. Piaget's (1969) work, of course, is a compelling example of the development of theory from case studies; his theory of the development of cognitive structures is derived from his observations of his own three children. Case studies of individual children have also led to the development of theories (in the sense that they are grounded in the empirical evidence) about the ways in which children learn to read and write (e.g., Baghban, 1984; Bissex, 1980; Calkins, 1983). These case studies offer the opportunities to generalize to theory. In addition, some researchers (e.g., Lensmire, 2000; McCarthey, 1994, 2004, 2009) have begun with "grand narratives" such as Bakhtin's (1981) theory of dialogism and used case studies to support or challenge aspects of those theories. Case study research lends itself to both the development and challenge of theories because of the potential to examine the particular within the general and vice versa. However, like other methods, the case study approach is effective for examining some questions and not as appropriate for addressing others.

Discourse Analysis: Conversation

Conversational discourse analysis focuses on conversation as it is acquired, as it works in everyday life, as it evidences particular cultural norms, as it is constituent of activities, and as it reflects and reflexively sustains particular social order and relations (Florio-Ruane & Morrell, Chapter 6, this volume). Its methodology is rooted in the fields of anthropology, linguistics, sociology, and cultural studies, among others, and involves processes not so much of design or data collection as of analysis and interpretation. As Florio-Ruane and Morrell also note, discourse analysis has a long developmental history in the field of literacy studies, a history that complicates attempts to identify its epistemological assumptions. What began in the 1960s and early 1970s as a study of patterns of conversational exchange between teachers and students became, by the late 1970s and 1980s, a study of the role of culture as a mediator of communication and has since developed to include a study of discourse(s) as exercises in power relations. With each shift in focus has come a new, increasingly broad definition of what discourse is, and with it a concurrent broadening of the scope of its epistemological assumptions.

A study of class size and its relation to instructional approach that relied largely on discourse analysis would focus primarily on qualitative differences in conversations between a teacher and students and among students in two classes of different sizes. Suppose, as in the example presented of case studies, a teacher were reading *Roll of Thunder, Hear My Cry* (Taylor, 1976) with two middle school classes of different sizes. As a way of evaluating not the outcomes of student learning as measured by test scores but the quality of the discussions generated by lecture/discussion versus literature study groups, a researcher arranged to videotape all novel-related conversations in both settings and keep field notes from direct observation of most, if not all, relevant classes. In the preanalytical stage, each video-tape would be transcribed. In addition, the researcher might watch each videotape and annotate the written transcript to record visual information (i.e., how students were sitting, the position of the teacher relative to the students, and gestures) alongside the written transcript. In the second phase of analysis, the transcripts would be "coded" in some way to record salient features of the conversations between/among the teacher and students; pre-liminary hypotheses about the underlying issues, such as the dominance of one gender of speaker or the direction of the conversation and its relation to individuals in each tape, might be formed. In the third phase of analysis, repetitions of specific patterns might be identified, along with their relation to the broader context of the classroom. The researcher might "test" his or her hypotheses by allowing colleagues to view the tapes and comparing their observations/interpretations of exchanges with his or her own. These hypotheses might be compared with findings from other similar studies or with critical theoretical descriptions of discourse patterns as a way of establishing the generality of this "type" of conversation within classroom contexts. After the researcher was satisfied that he or she had identified a *pattern* of conversational exchange, the researcher would begin to write up the study, most likely framing its findings in a combined review of previous research and a review of theories of discourse that supported the broader point that he or she believed the analysis aligned with or challenged.

The epistemological axis on which assumptions about knowledge and knowing hinge in discourse analysis is, obviously, language. In early studies of conversation, language was frequently conceived of as the medium, or bearer, of meanings and, therefore, of knowing, a useful but inert tool of human invention that was separate from the world and from thinking about the world. In later conceptualizations, language and thought remained separate, but language was seen to operate as a constructive agent in its own right, through its syntactic logic and morphological, semantic roots of history, culture, and perception for its users. Following the precepts of Ferdinand de Saussure (1916/1966), linguists distinguished between two aspects of language—*la langue*, or the formal study of languages as sys-tems, and *la parole*, or the study of language in everyday use—a distinction that also parallels the epistemological distinction between having formal, articulated knowledge *about* a phenomenon and having a more informal, practical competence that comes from *being of* a phenomenon. Although some analysts of discourse focus on the competencies of *la parole*, those who focus on the ways in which language use constitutes power relations among its users also emphasize the systemic, structural (and structuring) aspects of language as a practice. For these latter analysts (e.g., Fairclough,

1989; Gee, 1999; Rabinow, 1984), people's use of language structures not only how they make sense of the world but whether their understandings will be valorized within their societies; thus, language not only structures ways of knowing but also affects the power that individuals are able to exercise in their political and economic lives.

How a discourse analyst conceives of the role of language in coming to know about the world is likely to influence the focus of his or her research. In the foregoing example, for instance, a researcher with a view of language as a tool of thought would likely focus on identifying typical patterns of interaction such as IRE (teacher Initiates; student Responds; teacher Evaluates; Mehan, 1979), students' participation, and the types of exchanges among individuals in classes of two different sizes. A researcher with a more "constructivist" view of thought and language might examine patterns of interaction but focus as well on the semantic and syntactic quality of the exchanges (i.e., how thoughts or ideas embodied in the utterances of a teacher or student or in the text of the novel were repeated or altered in the utterances of other students either in conversation or in writing). Finally, a discourse analyst who saw language as structuring power relations would also examine patterns of interaction and the ways in which words and phrases as well as larger structures such as plot and character circulated among classroom participants, but the focus in this case might be how the knowledge (i.e., written or verbal comments) displayed by some students was valorized while others' knowledge was not acknowledged by the teacher and by peers, or perhaps how power relations as described within the novel itself (e.g., the Logans' status as African American landowners; Cassie's run-in with a European American child) were responded to by the teacher, individual students, and the class as a whole.

A pragmatic strength of an epistemological view of research anchored in language is the power it gives a researcher to pinpoint precisely and concretely where learning occurs or breaks down within an instructional event. Experimentalist and formative experimentalists may produce causal explanations for the outcomes of instructional events, but their capacity to pinpoint exactly where and how related factors operate within an instructional event remains limited. Similarly, case study approaches may allow a researcher to identify the causal factors within a bounded system after the fact, but they do not necessarily provide the insight into the dynamics of an instructional event needed to influence future outcomes. Discourse analysis offers insight into how patterns of interaction within a classroom might be redesigned or reengineered to produce more equitable and/or more productive learning for students. However—and as discourse theorists from Derrida (1976) to Rabinow (1984) to Bourdieu (1977) to Gee (1999) to Fairclough (1989) would likely agree—because knowledge *about* a phenomenon is distinct from and not usually easily translated into the practical knowledge, or competence, that accrues from *being of* a phenomenon, knowing *about* patterns of discourse or the structures of discourse that also structure inequitable educational outcomes may not lead to changes in the actual practices of teachers or students within classroom settings.

Through the use of four illustrative studies, we have demonstrated the epistemological strengths and weaknesses of particular research methods. Each method can be powerful in illuminating some aspects of literacy teaching and learning but limited in its ability to inform us in other ways. For example, experimental designs, despite their limitations to generalize to all populations and their lack of consideration of culture and the individual, can still be used to produce predictable patterns about class size, instructional practices, and student achievement. Formative experiments, because of their pragmatic features, adaptability, and political benefits, can help address questions of what literacy practices work in what settings. Although case studies might be used to overgeneralize to theory or to reify stereotypes, they have the potential to provide rich data for understanding how individuals and groups experience different types of instructional practices. Likewise, discourse analysis can help us not only to understand differences in conversational exchanges in large and small classes but also to show how those patterns are mediated by power relationships. Yet the patterns in the classrooms studied may differ substantially from patterns in other classrooms and prevent us from using the information in ways that lead to changing inequitable practices. Underlying each of these methods is a view of knowledge that influences the development of research questions, the data sources, the data collection procedures, and types of analyses. By examining the underlying epistemologies of their methods, researchers can improve the formulation of their questions, procedures, and analyses.

SOCIAL THEORIES AS EPISTEMOLOGICAL RESOURCES

Beyond the epistemological assumptions enacted through the methodologies that literacy researchers use in their investigations, another source of assumptions about how the world is known and what constitutes knowledge has become quite commonplace in the last 20 years, particularly within qualitative methodologies. Unlike traditional reviews of literature, which focus on previous empirical studies related to a research topic, theoretical frames typically make reference to theories and theorists whose perspectives are related to but removed from the immediate context of the research setting. For example, while a study of class size and instructional practice might traditionally rely on previous studies of class size and findings from studies of instructional practices related to lecture/discussion and/or literature study groups, its theoretical frame might consist of a review of related concepts from the work of Russian literary theorist Mikhail Bakhtin (1981) as a way of framing an analysis of students' observed appropriation of language and ideas in their discourse about the novel they read, the work of social constructivists such as Vygotsky (1978) to characterize the analysis of small-group interactions, or the work of feminists and of Gee (1999) and Fairclough (1989) to support their analysis of power relations among participants.

We take the position that where they are employed with rigor and thoroughness, theoretical frames represent an important transmethodological innovation in the field of literacy research because they provide additional epistemological resources that can strengthen the truth claims of research findings derived through a broad range of methodological approaches in at least three interrelated ways. First, theoretical frames can help to expand the significance and implications of a research project beyond its immediate practical boundaries so that the project is comprehensive within, and more relevant to, the context of broader theoretical, social scientific issues. A study of class size considered within the structuralist perspective of Pierre Bourdieu's *Outline of a Theory of Practice* (1977), for example, becomes a study of the ways that space, time, and cultural logic interact within specific material, historical conditions. Similarly, the analysis of instructional practices in the teaching of *Roll of Thunder, Hear My Cry* (Taylor, 1976), when framed by a consideration of critical race theory and/or the discourse theories of Gee (1999) and Fairclough (1989), becomes a study in the ways that issues of power and racism are mediated by discourse conventions. A second related benefit is the external source of comparison and contrast for the analysis of data that theoretical frames can provide. Feminist theories of discourse, for example, might be used to account for gender differences in the ways that students participate in discussions conducted in whole-class versus small-group settings, but they may also provide an occasion for exploring contradictions, when findings do not align with what theory would predict. Moreover, where findings align with a particular theoretical frame or do not align, or where a theoretical frame is used for the first time to account for a particular phenomenon, not only the findings of the study but the theory used is itself expanded or refined or revised. Thus, a third benefit of the use of theoretical frames in literacy research is the opportunity for literacy researchers to contribute to the building of "grand" theories of human social behavior.

However, we would also argue that the realization of the epistemological benefits of using social theories in literacy research depends not merely on the use, or mention, of theory in the report of a study but more importantly on the quality, or nature, of that use. In a study of the uses of theoretical frames in literacy research conducted by one of us (Dressman, 2007), 69 studies published in major literacy research journals that made use of theoretical frames were studied to identify the types, extent, and functions of theory use. Four patterns of use and function were found for the studies. Fourteen of the 69 articles used theoretical frames as a "foundational platform," in which the discussion of the frame appeared in the introduction or early sections of the article and was not referred to again.

In these instances, the larger significance of a study to the broad theoretical principles of its frame was alluded to but never fully developed. Eleven of the remaining 55 articles used theoretical frames as a "focal apparatus," in which the theoretical frame was developed in the introduction of the article and referred to in the concluding discussion but did not figure into the report of the study's design or methods, its analysis, or its report of findings. In these instances, readers were reminded of the significance of the study to larger theoretical issues, but again the theoretical frame was not well integrated into the analysis of data.

Thirty-five of the remaining 44 studies used or made mention of a theoretical frame as a "discursive scaffold." In these articles, the theoretical frame was identifiable, either implicitly or explicitly, throughout most, if not all, sections of a research article, including the introduction, methods, analysis, discussion, and concluding parts of the published study. In these cases, the larger social scientific implications of the study were usually clearly apparent and the use of theory as a comparative structure—that is, as a way of "making sense" of the data and providing interpretive insight that might otherwise not be perceived—was evident. Yet it would be difficult in many of these cases to argue that this use of theory contributed much to the building or refinement of social theory itself. In fact, in a few (but not all) instances, a case could be made that the conclusions of the report were grounded more in the theoretical frame than in an analysis of the data—in other words, that the data and its analysis supported the theory rather than that the theory illuminated or supported the data.

Of the 69 studies, then, only nine made use of a theoretical frame as a "dialectical scaffold," in which theory was both compared, or aligned with findings, and contrasted—that is, in which theory was used analytically to both interrogate, and be interrogated by, the study's data. In these studies, the epistemological use of assumptions about how the world is known and the nature of knowledge itself not only foregrounded the broader social scientific implications of the study through the full use of the frame in most, if not all, sections of the published study but also provided an important "other" point of view against which to compare and contrast findings from the data and, in the process, contribute to the expansion, refinement, or revision of the theoretical frame itself.

CONCLUSION: PROCEED WITH CAUTION

In our pragmatic consideration of epistemology and theory in research methods, we have emphasized the ways in which research is actually conducted within schools and attempted to uncover the assumptions behind conducting various types of research. By analyzing the epistemological strengths and weaknesses of each of four research methods, we have noted that different methods are based on different epistemological assumptions, and that is one reason why they have different strengths and weaknesses from one another. We have also implied that within the epistemological strengths of a particular method lie some of its weaknesses. For example, on closer examination of the generalizability of experimental and quasi-experimental methods, we see that, in fact, it is nearly impossible to generalize the findings of a study to all groups; furthermore, the predictive nature and rationality of knowledge that is assumed using these methods may call for artificial conditions that are almost impossible to create in actual schools, resulting in knowledge that is limited in its utility to classrooms. The problem-solving focus within local settings available through the formative experiments addresses many of the issues created by experimental designs. Yet the collaborative, adaptable nature of the design makes the findings difficult to replicate but can also hide the underlying tensions between theory and practice or mask unintended consequences. Although case studies are intended to be particularistic and descriptive using narrative as the vehicle for communication, they may have the unintended consequence of encouraging unwarranted generalization. Potential gains in insight by focusing on language and equity issues through discourse analysis could be lost if those same insights do not lead to changes or to the establishment of more equitable relationships within classrooms.

We argue that, despite the limitations of each, every method has something valuable to contribute to literacy research, yet no one method can cover the range of issues that researchers need to address in literacy teaching and learning research. Differences in epistemological assumptions among the methods can be viewed as a strength rather than a liability because they produce different types of knowledge. Experimental studies can provide some generalizable information with the possibilities of predicting outcomes in a wide range of settings. Formative methods have the capability of solving curricular problems within local settings as information is produced in collaborative relationships. Case studies provide detailed narratives about particular individuals within a social setting with the power to generate hypotheses. Discourse analysis provides insight about where and how learning occurs within particular settings while embracing diversity and the power of language.

Our investigation of epistemological assumptions among research methods and the use of theory by literacy researchers has three implications for the improvement of research across methodologies. First, we argue for a rigorous skepticism and humility in any approach to conducting research in literacy. Researchers need to be aware of the assumptions underlying the methods they choose and consider the benefits and unintended consequences of their methods, not only from a practical point of view but also from an epistemological perspective. Researchers ought to ask: What are the bases for the claims made? When we focus on these aspects of human interaction, what are we leaving out? What can we learn from this design? What are the limitations of what we can learn? Realizing that each method has a range of strengths and weaknesses, we hope that researchers will question their own assumptions as well as those of the designs they choose to employ.

Second, although it may be tempting to suggest that a "mixed methods" approach to studying a phenomenon will ensure that a given topic is well covered, the simplicity of this proposal leaves us wary. The ways in which researchers consider the nature of knowledge may conflict with one another; therefore, simply combining methods together may not produce the types of useful data we need to make classrooms better places for our students but may result in a hodgepodge of information without theoretical grounding. The purposes of the research and the research questions frame the types of data to be collected and analyzed; the results of those analyses need to be represented in different forms such as tables, models, narratives, or themes that are consistent with the epistemological assumptions and research designs. Research questions, sources of data, and types of analyses and interpretations should be aligned with one another and rest on clear, but carefully examined, epistemological assumptions. Although we caution against mixing methods, we do recommend "triangulation" (a metaphor from qualitative methods; Stake, 1995) of research methods to improve educational policy and practices. For example, triangulation of research methods would include using multiple methods to study the same general topic, but the actual research questions and designs would differ from one another in scope, type of data collected, and forms of analyses and representations. Triangulation also involves using alternative means of confirming interpretations; therefore, researchers using different tools would check their findings on the same topic with one another. For example, experimentalists could look at what discourse analysts have found in specific classroom settings and vice versa. An additional aspect of triangulation is the idea of involving researchers in an examination of other researchers' raw data and interpretations. Why not have researchers who are designing formative experiments read the classroom narratives that case study researchers have written?

Our third implication relates to the use of theory in research methods. Although theoretical alignment can contribute to the readability of a research report, it does not substitute for validity. The benefits of theoretical frames in research reports include expanding the significance and implications of reports, providing opportunities for comparisons and contrasts of data, and building grand theories of social interaction, yet they need to be employed with greater caution than we have done previously. Just as we are suggesting that researchers need to consider and question the epistemologies of their methods, they also need to interrogate the theories they use to make their arguments. Literacy researchers need to not only build on the work of others from a variety of perspectives and methods but also continually engage in dialogue about the assumptions, interpretations, and consequences of their methods.

REFERENCES

Baghban, M. (1984). *Our daughter learns to read and write: A case study from birth to three.* Newark, DE: International Reading Association.

Bakhtin, M. M. (1981). *The dialogic imagination.* Austin: University of Texas Press.

Bissex, G. (1980). *Gnyx at wrk.* Cambridge, MA: Harvard University Press.

Bourdieu, P. (1977). *Outline of a theory of practice.* Cambridge, UK: Cambridge University Press.

Calkins, L. (1983). *Lessons from a child: On the teaching and learning of writing.* Exeter, NH: Heinemann.

Campbell, J. (1995). *Understanding John Dewey: Nature and cooperative intelligence.* Chicago: Open Court.

Cobb, P., Confrey, J., diSessa, A., Lehrer, R., & Schauble, L. (2003). Design experiments in education research. *Educational Researcher, 32*(1), 9–13.

Day, J. P., Spiegel, D. L., McLellan, J., & Brown, V. B. (2002). *Moving forward with literature circles.* New York: Scholastic.

de Saussure, F. (1966). *Course in general linguistics* (W. Baskin, Trans.). New York: McGraw-Hill. (Original work published 1916)

Derrida, J. (1976). *Of grammatology.* Baltimore: Johns Hopkins University Press.

Dewey, J., & Bentley, A. E. (1949). *Knowing and the known.* Boston: Beacon Press.

Dressman, M. (2007). Theoretically framed: Argument and desire in the production of general knowledge about literacy. *Reading Research Quarterly, 42,* 332–363.

Dressman, M. (2008). *Using social theory in educational research: A practical guide.* London: Routledge.

Dressman, M., McCarty, L., & Benson, J. (1998). "Whole language" as signifier: Considering the semantic field of school literacy. *Journal of Literacy Research, 30,* 9–52.

Dressman, M., Wilder, P., & Connor, J. C. (2005). Theories of failure and the failure of theories: A cognitive/sociocultural/macrostructural study of eight struggling students. *Research in the Teaching of English, 40,* 8–61.

Dyson, A. H. (1995). Children out of bounds: The power of case studies in expanding visions of literacy development. In K. Hinchman, D. Leu, & C. Kinzer (Eds.), *Perspectives on literacy research and practice* (pp. 39–53). Chicago: National Reading Conference.

Dyson, A. H., & Genishi, C. (2005). *On the case: Approaches to language and literacy research.* New York: Teachers College Press.

Fairclough, N. (1989). *Language and power.* London: Longman.

Foley, D. (1990). *Learning capitalist culture: Deep in the heart of Tejas.* Philadelphia: University of Pennsylvania Press.

Gee, J. P. (1999). *An introduction to discourse analysis: Theory and method.* New York: Routledge.

Lensmire, T. (2000). *Powerful writing, responsible teaching.* New York: Teachers College Press.

McCarthey, S. J. (1994). Authors, text, and talk: The internalization of dialogue from social interaction during writing. *Reading Research Quarterly, 29*(3), 201–231.

McCarthey, S. J. (1998). Constructing multiple subjectivities in classroom learning contexts. *Research in the Teaching of English, 32*, 126–160.

McCarthey, S. J. (2001). Identity construction in elementary readers and writers. *Reading Research Quarterly, 36*, 122–151.

McCarthey, S. J. (2004). Bakhtin's dialogism in a preschooler's talk. *Literacy Teaching and Learning, 8*(2), 27–62.

McCarthey, S. J. (2009). Understanding English language learners' identities from three perspectives. In G. Li (Ed.), *Multicultural families, home literacies, and mainstream schooling* (pp. 221–244). Charlotte, NC: Information Age.

McMahon, S. I., & Raphael, T. E. (Eds.). (1997). *The book club connection.* New York: Teachers College Press.

Mehan, H. (1979). *Learning lessons.* Cambridge, MA: Harvard University Press.

Merriam, S. (1998). *Case study research in education: A qualitative approach.* San Francisco: Jossey-Bass.

National Research Council. (2002). *Scientific research in education.* Washington, DC: National Academy Press.

Piaget, J. (1969). *Psychology of intelligence.* Paterson, NJ: Littlefield, Adams.

Rabinow, P. (Ed.). (1984). *The Foucault reader.* New York: Pantheon.

Reinking, D., & Bradley, B. A. (2007). *On formative and design experiments: Approaches to language and literacy research.* New York: Teachers College Press.

Ritter, G. W., & Boruch, R. F. (1999). The political and institutional origins of a randomized controlled trial on elementary school class size: Tennessee's Project STAR. *Educational Evaluation and Policy Analysis, 21*(2), 111–125.

Rosenblatt, L. (1968). *The reader, the text, and the poem.* Carbondale: Southern Illinois University Press.

Stake, R. E. (1995). *The art of case study research.* Thousand Oaks, CA: Sage.

Taylor, M. D. (1976). *Roll of thunder, hear my cry.* New York: Dial Books.

Vygotsky, L. (1978). *Mind in society: The development of higher psychological processes* (M. Cole, V. John-Steiner, S. Scribner, & E. Souberman, Eds. & Trans.). Cambridge, MA: Harvard University Press. (Original work published 1934)

Walkerdine, V. (1990). *Schoolgirl fictions.* New York: Verso.

Willis, A. I., & Harris, V. J. (1997). Expanding the boundaries: A reaction to the First-Grade Studies. *Reading Research Quarterly, 32*, 439–445.

CHAPTER 21

Conclusion

Nell K. Duke
Marla H. Mallette

What do we hope you take away from this book? Many things, of course, but there are five overarching messages that we believe are especially important:

• *Message 1: Many different research methodologies, in fact each research methodology discussed in this book and others, have valuable contributions to make to the study of literacy.* We believe that each chapter of this book helps to make this point. Each methodology featured includes references to studies that it is hard to deny are important—that have provided new insights, confirmed or disconfirmed previous thinking, moved research forward, and/or influenced classroom practice. Our field would be a lesser place were that type of research unavailable. What we would understand about literacy and literacy learning would be diminished.

Chapters in this book are not, of course, the only source of evidence for the value of many different research methodologies in our understanding of literacy. Perusal of seminal volumes in literacy, such as the *Handbook of Reading Research: Volume III* (Kamil, Mosenthal, Pearson, & Barr, 2000), the *Routledge International Handbook of English, Language and Literacy Teaching* (Wyse, Andrews, & Hoffman, 2010), and Approaches to Language and Literacy Research: An NCRLL Research in Language and Literacy Series (Alvermann & Allen, 2005–2010), demonstrates that many different types of research have influenced our understanding across the field. Studies widely cited within literacy include a vast array of different methodologies. Awards bestowed in the field, such as the International Reading Association Outstanding Dissertation Award, Dina Feitel-son Award, and Albert J. Harris Award, have been given to studies of a wide range of research methods. And many well-respected literacy schol-ars are on record espousing the value of many different types of research (e.g., Pearson, 2002; Pressley, Duke, & Boling, 2004; Purcell-Gates, 2001; Readence & Barone, 1996; Reinking & Alvermann, 2007; Wilkinson & Bloome, 2008).

The contribution of a variety of research methodologies to under-standing literacy is not simply an "in-house" phenomenon. Studies that have reached beyond the literacy research community to influence class-room practices in real schools with real children also include a range of methodologies. Take, for example, Shanahan and Neuman's (1997) list of the 13 studies that they believe have had the greatest influence on classroom practice:

Atwell, N. (1987). *In the middle.* Portsmouth, NH: Boynton/Cook, Heine-mann.

Bond, G. L., & Dykstra, R. (1967). The cooperative research program in first-grade reading instruction. *Reading Research Quarterly, 2,* 5–142.

Children's Television Workshop. (1969). *Sesame Street.* New York: Public Broadcasting System.

Clay, M. M. (1985). *The early detection of reading difficulties.* Auckland, New Zealand: Heinemann. (Original work published 1979)

Durkin, D. (1966). *Children who read early.* New York: Teachers College Press.

Durkin, D. (1978–1979). What classroom observations reveal about reading comprehension instruction. *Reading Research Quarterly, 14,* 481–533.

Freire, P. (1970). *Pedagogy of the oppressed* (M. B. Ramos, Trans.). New York: Herder & Herder.

Goodman, K. S. (1965). A linguistic study of cues and miscues in reading. *Elementary English, 42,* 639–643.

Graves, D. H. (1981). *A case study observing the development of primary children's composing, spelling, and motor behaviors during the writing process. Final report* (NIE Grant No. G-78-0174). Durham: University of New Hampshire. (ERIC Document Reproduction Service No. 218 653)

Pichert, J. W., & Anderson, R. C. (1977). Taking different perspectives on a story. *Journal of Educational Psychology, 69,* 309–315.

Read, C. (1971). Preschool children's knowledge of English phonology. *Har-vard Educational Review, 41,* 1–34.

Stein, N. L., & Glenn, C. G. (1977). An analysis of story comprehension in ele-mentary school children. In R. Freedle (Ed.), *New directions in discourse processing: Vol. 2. Advances in discourse processing* (pp. 53–120). Nor-wood, NJ: Ablex.

Sticht, T. G., Gaylor, J. S., Kern, R. P., & Fox, L. C. (1972). Project REAL-ISTIC: Determination of adult functional literacy skill levels. *Reading Research Quarterly, 7,* 424–465.

Methodologies used in these studies include oral miscue analysis, correlation, case study, experiment and quasi-experiment, design or formative experiment, ethnography, content analysis, instrument development, and discourse analysis. Even if one does not agree with all the articles on Shanahan and Neuman's list, or with the list of methodologies we have identified as represented in their list, this exercise certainly suggests that no one research methodology has a monopoly on high-impact research in literacy.

   • *Message 2: Different types of research are for different types of questions and claims. The match of research methodology to research questions and resulting claims is essential.* This message, too, should be evident in chapter after chapter of this book. Chapter authors discuss the types of questions to which their methodology is well suited and the types of claims that can be made on the basis of that methodology. If you want to understand what goes on in literature circle discussions, you surely will not turn to neuroimaging techniques. If you want to know whether and how neural activity differs for good and poor readers, discourse analysis is not the best choice. If you want to know when and how a reader brings prior knowledge to bear in his or her reading, verbal protocol analysis leaps out as a methodology to use. If your interest is in whether one method of spelling instruction results in better spelling performance than another, experimental research is likely the appropriate methodology. This may seem obvious, yet we routinely read studies in which the question asked and/or the claims made do not, in fact, match well the research methodology used. And we encounter rhetoric suggesting that some research methodologies are inherently best rather than best *for what*. As a field, we must demand that qualifier in discussions of research methodology.

   • *Message 3: There are standards of quality for every type of research. There is better and poorer quality research of every methodology.* A danger of arguing for the value of many different kinds of research and research perspectives is to imply that anything goes. We hope this book has resoundingly countered that implication. For each methodology chapter, authors were asked to identify standards of quality for research using that methodology. Each has done so, and without balking at the task. In the minds of these authors, well known and well respected for their use of their assigned methodology, there are indeed hallmarks of quality research. Anything does not go.

   We may, in fact, be more discerning of the quality and contribution of a given study when we seriously value many different research methodologies. Suppose, for example, that one is writing a review of literature on emergent literacy development. Assuming that there are limitations of space and reader attention, if one restricts the review primarily or exclusively to case study and ethnographic research, more attention to studies of those methodologies can be given than if the review includes as well findings from experimental and correlational studies. One might have to be more selective, then, about the studies of each methodology included. Of course, as we suggested in Message 2, one's question should be a driving force in determining what studies are afforded attention. But the quality of the work and its contribution can also be discriminating factors. Even in our everyday reading as scholars, the sheer number and range of different types of research that cross our desks means that we cannot attend to all studies; considerations of quality should help us decide which to attend to more closely.

• *Message 4: Synergy across research methodologies is possible, powerful, and advisable.* What if, starting tomorrow, we conducted nothing but high-quality, exemplary work within each of the research methodologies in this book? What if the standards of quality identified by authors in this volume were instantiated in each and every study? That would be fantastic, but it would not be enough. We need to work not only within but *across* these methods—what we call synergy of research methods.

Among the audience likely to read this book, at least, it seems a platitude to say this, but no number of experiments, in the absence of other types of research, will help us learn what we need to learn about literacy. Similarly, no number of case studies can, in themselves, help us understand everything we want to understand. Our richest and most productive knowledge base will come when different studies involving different research methodologies inform one another—when the whole of what we know in an area is built of many different kinds of parts, each doing what they do best, and together being much more than their sum.

Of course, synergy of research methodologies has occurred. In literacy we have many examples in which different studies conducted with different methodologies have informed one another and led to greater insight than could have come with one or the other. In the following paragraphs, we present two such examples. The examples are presented only briefly and undoubtedly incompletely. Our intent is not so much to focus on the historical particulars or particulars in content but rather simply to illustrate that this happens and should happen more often.

One insight made possible, we believe, by research of a variety of methodologies is the insight that teaching children that the speech stream is composed of phonemes can improve their word reading. *Research using technologies* designed to examine the speech stream revealed that phonemes in speech are not separate and distinct, as implied to our written orthography, but rather influence one another. Thus, it may be challenging for children to learn to tease out individual phonemes in words associated with particular letters (e.g., Liberman, Cooper, Shankweiler, & Studdert-Kennedy, 1967). *Research examining children's written text*, in particular their spellings, indicated that indeed part of what children are building when developing literacy is an understanding of relationship between the speech stream and orthography (e.g., Chomsky, 1970; Read, 1971). *Correlational studies* revealed relationships between the degree to which children were aware of the speech stream and their achievement and growth in literacy (e.g., Ehri, 1979; Share, Jorm, Maclean, & Matthews, 1984). *Experimental studies* indicated that if one engages children in activities to become more aware of phonemes in the speech stream, their reading and writing are improved (e.g., Ball & Blachman, 1991; Williams, 1980).

Another insight made possible by studies of a variety of methodologies is that teaching children about text structure improves their comprehension. *Verbal protocols* demonstrated that good readers attend to text structure when they read (see Pressley & Afflerbach, 1995, for a review). *Research comparing good and poor comprehenders* (in a sense a form of correlational research) found that good comprehenders attend more readily to text structure than poor comprehenders (e.g., Meyer, Brandt, & Bluth, 1980). *Experimental studies* revealed that teaching children to attend to text structure leads to better comprehension (Armbruster, Anderson, & Ostertag, 1987; Taylor & Beach, 1984). As with the phonemic awareness insight, it is not that each of these studies led independently to the insight but that they informed and built on one another. The researchers cited research of other methodologies and were clearly influenced by that work. Neither the richness nor the rapidity of identifying the insight could likely have occurred without the synergy of these different research methodologies.

We want to be clear that although we see the usefulness of mixed research, we are not talking here about mixing methodologies within a study but about different studies, of different methodologies, informing one another and larger insights. Of course, in some cases, mixed methodologies within a study are quite appropriate to a research question or set of questions and have important contributions to make (e.g., Tashakkori & Teddlie, 2003). However, we concur with Dressman and McCarthey's (Chapter 20, this volume) caution in mixing methods. That is, considering the standards of quality, intricacies of design, and need for thoughtful planning of mixed research as described by Onwuegbuzie and Mallette (Chapter 14, this volume), it would not serve the field well to simply mix methodologies if theoretical consistency and methodological rigor are not met throughout the study.

• *Message 5: We must urgently and actively pursue synergy across research methodologies.* In our commentary in *Journal of Literacy Research* discussed at the outset of this book, we argued that the field of literacy is in danger of increasing fragmentation (Duke & Mallette, 2001). For example, we cited Trika Smith-Burke's concern about the "splintering off" of the National Reading Conference into subgroups such as the American Reading Forum and the Society for the Scientific Study of Reading. We pointed out how Stanovich referred to the field of literacy as being "fractious." This trend toward fragmentation is of particular concern to us when research methodology is confounded with particular areas of study. For example, one finds few experimental studies of critical literacy and few case studies in the area of phonemic awareness, yet we believe it is possible to conduct high-quality research in both and see potential contributions to the field in both. For example, we might ask how comprehension achievement differs for children taught with and without critical literacy approaches (our hypothesis being that one would see higher comprehension achievement among students whose teachers taught with an emphasis on critical literacy). Or we might ask how a child with very strong or very weak phonemic awareness experiences phonemic awareness instruction in school (our interest in understanding whether a child whose phonemic awareness is extremely different from most of his or her peers experiences phonemic awareness instruction differently than intended). Of course, we are not advocating conducting research of every particular kind in every particular area just for the sake of doing it, but argue that particular research methodologies should not be dismissed out of hand as possible contributors to research in a particular area and, rather, that we should actively seek a variety of questions, and thus methodologies, that could contribute to work in a particular area. We believe this is an important step in reversing the trend of fragmentation in the field.

To close, we want to thank again the contributors of this book, whose work individually and collectively has powerfully supported the five messages we have offered here:

- Message 1: Many different research methodologies, in fact each research methodology discussed in this book and others, have valuable contributions to make to the study of literacy.
- Message 2: Different types of research are for different types of questions and claims. The match of research methodology to research questions and resulting claims is essential.
- Message 3: There are standards of quality for every type of research. There is better and poorer quality research of every methodology.
- Message 4: Synergy across research methodologies is possible, powerful, and advisable.
- Message 5: We must urgently and actively pursue synergy across research methodologies.

We hope that our work, and yours, will do justice to the high bar that our contributors have set.

REFERENCES

Alvermann, D. E., & Allen, J. (Eds.). (2005–2010). *Approaches to language and literacy research: An NCRLL research in language and literacy series.* New York: Teachers College Press.

Armbruster, B. B., Anderson, T. H., & Ostertag, J. (1987). Does text structure/summarization instruction facilitate learning from expository text? *Reading Research Quarterly, 22*, 331–346.

Ball, E. W., & Blachman, B. A. (1991). Does phoneme awareness training in kindergarten make a difference in early word recognition and developmental spelling? *Reading Research Quarterly, 26*, 49–66.

Chomsky, C. (1970). Reading, writing and phonology. *Harvard Educational Review, 40*, 287–309.

Duke, N. K., & Mallette, M. H. (2001). Critical issues: Preparation for new literacy researchers in multi-epistemological, multi-methodological times. *Journal of Literacy Research, 33*, 345–360.

Ehri, L. (1979). *Orthography and the amalgamation of word identities in beginning readers: Final report.* Davis: University of California. (ERIC Document Reproduction Service No. ED 188145)

Kamil, M. L., Mosenthal, P. M., Pearson, P. D., & Barr, R. (2000). *Handbook of reading research: Volume III.* Mahwah, NJ: Erlbaum.

Liberman, A. M., Cooper, F., Shankweiler, D., & Studdert-Kennedy, M. (1967). Perception of the speech code. *Psychological Review, 74*, 431–461.

Meyer, B. J. F., Brandt, D. M., & Bluth, G. J. (1980). Use of top-level structure in text: Key for reading comprehension of ninth-grade students. *Reading Research Quarterly, 16*, 72–103.

Pearson, P. D. (2002, May). *Up the down staircase: The role of research in policy and practice.* Paper presented at the annual convention of the International Reading Association, San Francisco.

Pressley, M., & Afflerbach, P. (1995). *Verbal protocols of reading: The nature of constructively responsive reading.* Hillsdale, NJ: Erlbaum.

Pressley, M., Duke, N. K., & Boling, E. C. (2004). The educational science and scientifically-based instruction we need: Lessons from reading research and policy making. *Harvard Educational Review, 74*(1), 30–61.

Purcell-Gates, V. (2001). The role of qualitative and ethnographic research. *Reading Online.* Retrieved from *www.readingonline.org/articles/Purcell-gates.*

Read, C. (1971). Preschool children's knowledge of English phonology. *Harvard Educational Review, 41*, 1–34.

Readence, J., & Barone, D. (1996). Expectations and directions for *Reading Research Quarterly*: Broadening the lens. *Reading Research Quarterly, 31*, 8–10.

Reinking, D., & Alvermann, D. E. (2007). Reflections on our editorship. *Reading Research Quarterly, 42*, 460–466.

Shanahan, T., & Neuman, S. (1997). Literacy research that makes a difference. *Reading Research Quarterly, 32*(2), 202–210.

Share, D. L., Jorm, A. F., Maclean, R., & Matthews, R. (1984). Sources of individual differences in reading acquisition. *Journal of Educational Psychology, 76*, 1309–1324.

Tashakkori, A., & Teddlie, C (2003). *Handbook of mixed methods in social and behavioral research*. Thousand Oaks, CA: Sage.

Taylor, B. M., & Beach, R. W. (1984). The effects of text structure instruction on middle-grade students' comprehension and production of expository text. *Reading Research Quarterly, 19*, 134–146.

Wilkinson, I. A. G., & Bloome, D. (2008). Research as principled, pluralistic argument. *Reading Research Quarterly, 43*, 6–8.

Williams, J. P. (1980). Teaching decoding with a special emphasis on phoneme analysis and phoneme blending. *Journal of Educational Psychology, 72*, 1–15.

Wyse, D., Andrews, R., & Hoffman, J. (Eds.). (2010). *The Routledge international handbook of English, language and literacy teaching*. London: Routledge.

APPENDIX

Alphabetical Listing of the Exemplars

Baumann, J. F., Hoffman, J. V., Duffy-Hester, A. M., & Ro, J. M. (2000). *The First R* yesterday and today: U.S. elementary reading instruction practices reported by teachers and administrators. *Reading Research Quarterly, 35,* 338–377. (**Survey**)

Beach, R., Enciso, P., Harste, J., Jenkins, C., Raina, S. A., Rogers, R., et al. (2009). Exploring the "critical" in critical content analysis of children's literature. In R. T. Jiménez, M. K. Hundley, V. J. Risko, & D. W. Rowe (Eds.), *58th Yearbook of the National Reading Conference* (pp. 129–143). Oak Creek, WI: National Reading Conference. (**Content Analysis**)

Benge, C., Onwuegbuzie, A. J., Mallette, M. H., & Burgess, M. L. (2010). Doctoral students' perceptions of barriers to reading empirical literature: A mixed analysis. *International Journal of Doctoral Studies, 5,* 55–77. (**Mixed Methods**)

Bus, A. G., & van IJzendoorn, M. H. (1999). Phonological awareness and early reading: A meta-analysis of experimental training studies. *Journal of Educational Psychology, 91,* 403–414. (**Meta-Analysis**)

Compton-Lilly, C. (2009). The complexities of reading capital in two Puerto Rican families. *Reading Research Quarterly, 42,* 72–98. (**Case Study**)

Cunningham, A. E., & Stanovich, K. E. (1997). Early reading acquisition and its relation to reading experience and ability ten years later. *Developmental Psychology, 33,* 934–945. (**Correlational**)

Dyson, A. H. (1999). Coach Bombay's kids learn to write: Children's appropriation of media material for school literacy. *Research in the Teaching of English, 33,* 367–402. (**Ethnography**)

Dyson, A. H. (2003). *The brothers and sisters learn to write: Popular literacies in childhood and school cultures.* New York: Teachers College Press. (**Ethnography**)

Foorman, B. R., Francis, D. J., Fletcher, J. M., Schatschneider, C., & Mehta, P. (1998). The role of instruction in learning to read: Preventing reading failure in at-risk children. *Journal of Educational Psychology, 90,* 37–55. (**Experimental and Quasi-Experimental**)

Gillen, J. (2009). Literacy practices in Schome Park: A virtual literacy ethnography. *Journal of Research in Reading, 32*(1), 57–74. (**Digital Contexts**)

Gordon, E., McKibbin, K., Vasudevan, L., & Vinz, R. (2007). Writing out of the unexpected: Narrative inquiry and the weight of small moments. *English Education, 39*(4), 326–351. (**Narrative Approaches**)

Hankins, K. H. (2003). *Teaching through the storm: A journal of hope.* New York: Teachers College Press. (**Narrative Approaches**)

Heath, S. B. (1982). What no bedtime story means: Narrative skills at home and school. *Language in Society, 11,* 49–76. (**Ethnography**)

Heath, S. B. (1983). *Ways with words: Language, life, and work in communities and classrooms.* Cambridge, UK: Cambridge University Press. (**Ethnography**)

Henk, W. A., & Melnick, S. A. (1995). The Reader Self-Perception Scale (RSPS): A new tool for measuring how children feel about themselves as readers. *The Reading Teacher, 48,* 470–482. (**Instrumentation**)

Hoffman, J. V., Sailors, M., Duffy, G. G., & Beretvas, N. (2004). The effective elementary classroom literacy environment: Examining the validity of the TEX-IN3 observation system. *Journal of Literacy Research, 36,* 303–334. (**Content Analysis**)

Ivey, G., & Broaddus, K. (2007). A formative experiment investigating literacy engagement among adolescent Latina/o students just beginning to read, write, and speak English. *Reading Research Quarterly, 42,* 512–545. (**Formative and Design Experiments**)

Marshall, E. (2004). Stripping for the wolf: Rethinking representations of gender in children's literature. *Reading Research Quarterly, 39,* 256–270. (**Content Analysis**)

Mesmer, H. A. E. (2006). Beginning reading materials: A national survey of primary teachers' reported uses and beliefs. *Journal of Literacy Research, 38,* 389–425. (**Survey**)

Michaels, S. (1981). "Sharing time": Children's narrative styles and differential access to literacy. *Language in Society, 10,* 423–443. (**Discourse Analysis: Conversation**)

Monaghan, E. J. (1991). Family literacy in early 18th century Boston: Cotton Mather and his children. *Reading Research Quarterly, 26,* 342–370. (**Historical**)

Morrell, E. (2008). *Critical literacy and urban youth: Pedagogies of access, dissent, and liberation.* New York: Routledge. (**Discourse Analysis: Conversation**)

Moss, B. (2008). The information text gap: The mismatch between non-narrative text types in basal readers and 2009 NAEP recommended guidelines. *Journal of Literacy Research, 40*(2), 201–219. (**Content Analysis**)

Mudre, L. H., & McCormick, S. (1989). Effects of meaning-focused cues on under-achieving readers' context use, self-corrections, and literal comprehension. *Reading Research Quarterly, 24,* 89–113. (**Single Subject**)

Neuman, S. B., & Gallagher, P. (1994). Joining together in literacy learning: Teenage mothers and children. *Reading Research Quarterly, 29,* 382–401. (**Single Subject**)

Purcell-Gates, V. (1993). I ain't never read my *own* words before. *Journal of Reading, 37,* 210–219. (**Ethnography**)

Simos, P. G., Fletcher, J. M., Sarkari, S., Billingsley, R. L., Francis, D. J., Castillo, E. M., et al. (2005). Early development of neurophysiological processes involved in normal reading and reading disability. *Neuropsychology, 19,* 787–798. (**Neuroimaging**)

Steinkuehler, C. (2006). Massively multiplayer online video gaming as participation in a discourse. *Mind, Culture and Activity, 13*(1), 38–52. (**Digital Contexts**)

Steinkuehler, C. (2007). Massively multiplayer online gaming as a constellation of literacy practices. *E-learning, 4*(3), 297–318. (**Digital Contexts**)

Vellutino, F. R., & Scanlon, D. M. (1987). Phonological coding, phonological awareness, and reading ability: Evidence from a longitudinal and experimental study. *Merrill-Palmer Quarterly, 33,* 321–363. (**Experimental and Quasi-Experimental**)

Wolfe, M. B., & Goldman, S. R. (2005). Relationships between adolescents' text processing and reasoning. *Cognition and Instruction, 23*(4), 467–502. (**Discourse Analysis: Written Text**)

Wyatt, D., Pressley, M., El-Dinary, P. B., Stein, S., Evans, P., & Brown, R. (1993). Comprehension strategies, worth and credibility monitoring, and evaluations: Cold and hot cognition when experts read professional articles that are important to them. *Learning and Individual Differences, 5,* 49–72. (**Verbal Protocols**)

Index